THE
ENERGY DESIGN
HANDBOOK

EDITED BY DONALD WATSON, FAIA

THE AMERICAN INSTITUTE OF ARCHITECTS PRESS

WASHINGTON, D.C.

The American Institute of Architects Press
1735 New York Avenue, N.W.
Washington, DC 20006

ISBN 1-55835-094-2

Cover design by Grafik Communications, Ltd., Alexandria, Va.

Contents

CHAPTER 10: ENERGY ANALYSIS

CHAPTER 11: ECONOMIC ANALYSIS

Tennessee Valley Authority Headquarters, Chattanooga, Tenn.
Architect: Architects Collaborative and Caudill Rowlett in joint venture
Consultants: Van der Ryn/Calthorpe Partners, William Lam
Photograph: Donald Watson

Introduction

1A. BASE CASE ENERGY PROFILE

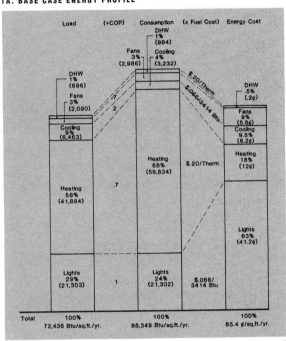

1B. SOLAR DESIGN ENERGY PROFILE

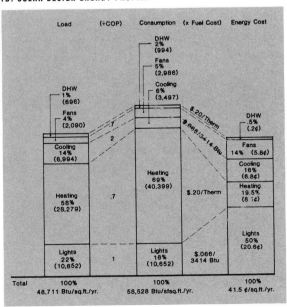

ARCHITECTURE: BORN OF CLIMATE, ENERGY, AND ENVIRONMENT

The anonymous beginnings of indigenous building and the great architectural traditions of the world have both demonstrated an understanding of climate-responsive design. This attitude on the part of builders from earliest history has contributed to the development of the familiar elements of many regional architectural styles.

Swiss and Himalayan builders, a hemisphere apart, had to respond to similar ecological conditions. The traditional Swiss farmhouse was typically oriented to the winter sun, with interior zones that could be closed off for winter heat conservation and roof lines angled to gain insulative value from snow buildup. The Himalayan builders of Tibet, Nepal, and Bhutan in their cold mountain climates developed remarkably similar design techniques.

The Islamic and Moorish architectural tradition developed out of the hot, dry climate conditions of the desert. For these cultures, the courtyard, shaded and often graced with plants and cooling water fountains, became the architectural version of "paradise on earth." The garden courtyards of the fourteenth century Palace of the Alhambra in Granada, Spain, exemplify this tradition. The hot, humid climate of the colonial southern United States led to designs such as the humble "dogtrot" house and the "high-style" plantation house, both of which made use of shaded porticoes, cross-ventilation, and ventilated roofs to combat the weather.

The Roman Forum Baths (circa 250 AD) at Ostia, near Rome, combined south-facing openings for direct solar heating and underfloor heat sources (oven flues placed under the

The Energy Design Process Illustrated (in images 1-5): Johnson Controls Office Building, Salt Lake City, Utah; Johnson Controls: Douglas Drake and John Schade; Energy Design Team: Donald Watson, FAIA; Fred Dubin; William Lam

1A-B. Setting Energy Design Goals – Comparison of prior Johnson Controls Office Building (base case) with proposed (solar) design

floors), perhaps the first example in the western world of radiant heating. Similar designs ultimately evolved in Scandinavia, Russia, Japan, and Korea. From the earliest time, buildings were oriented to benefit from the winter sun, if only through small doors and windows.

Beginning with the development of manufactured glass, effective methods of trapping the sun's heat were developed to warm buildings directly through large windows, skylights, and glass conservatories facing the sun. Early in the nineteenth century, greenhouse designers in Great Britain demonstrated that it was possible to "change the climate" through glass-enclosed conservatories when they created springtime conditions for plant propagation in their cool northern winters. Beginning around 1820, J. C. Loudon created a remarkable series of greenhouse designs that combined sunlight, thermal storage, sunshading, and underground radiant heating—the identical elements promulgated as "passive solar heating" 150 years later.

From these early experiments and the nascent disciplines of agricultural science and forestry grew the modern science of building climatology. Practitioners in this field produced the term "microclimate" to define the boundary layer near the ground where temperature and humidity are significantly affected by specific vegetation, soil, and land contours and in turn by what we build.

Beginning in the early 1930s, Chicago architects Fred and William Keck began a decade-long investigation of the combination of south-facing windows and exposed interior masonry for thermal storage. They developed the first residential designs in the United States to be called "solar houses." In the late 1930s, two renowned masters of modern architecture, Walter Gropius and Marcel Breuer, analyzed local climate and sun angles as determinants in the designs of their own homes in Lincoln, Massachusetts. The results of their analysis are evidenced by the generous south-facing, properly shaded windows in their residences. In his 1930s Usonian houses in Wisconsin and at Taliesin West in Arizona, Frank Lloyd Wright integrated and expressed the qualities of local climate and indigenous materials and landscaping. These structures give ample testimony to the idea that an understanding of local and regional climate and environment underlies a mastery of architecture, regardless of style.

In the 1950s climatic design was promoted in a series of articles published in *House Beautiful* and the *Bulletin of the American Institute of Architects* (1949-52) under the editorial direction of James Marston Fitch and Paul Siple. These articles featured both well-known and lesser known ways of utilizing climate design techniques, such as white reflective roofs for warm climates and earth-sheltering and solar orientation for cool climates. However, by the late 1950s, at the very point when climate-responsive design was widely promulgated in professional and popular housing journals, technological advances were made that allowed architects to ignore the local climate. With heat-resistant glass and compact mechanical heating and air conditioning, architects could design as they pleased, if at the cost of "thermodynamic elegance" or energy efficiency. The "era of air conditioning" had begun.

The Equitable Savings and Loan Building in Portland, Oregon, built in 1948, was the first fully sealed and air-conditioned modern office building in the United States. The Lever House, built in 1952, was among the first modern skyscrapers in New York City to use the newly developed heat-absorbing tinted glass as a means of reducing undesired solar gain. Shortly thereafter, the same glass technology was specified for the east- and west-facing curtain-wall windows of the United Nations Building in place of the exterior sunshades that architectural consultants Le Corbusier and Oscar Niemeyer had proposed. These buildings, rather than the earlier work of Wright, Gropius, and Breuer, helped to establish the modern style as one of glass curtain-wall construction, which dominated contemporary architecture in the ensuing decades. Sleek and modern-looking, they were copied throughout the globe, regardless of climate and orientation and far from the ideal of climate-responsive design. Their costs in comfort, energy efficiency, and environmental quality only later became fully evident.

In 1973 the OPEC embargo curtailed imported oil shipments to the United States and abruptly brought issues of oil dependence and energy cost to public awareness. Energy conservation in buildings was made part of national

2. PARAMETRIC ANALYSIS

B Series	% HEAT improvement	% COOL improvement	% TOTAL improvement	solar fraction	Btu/SF/DD SF=14,884 DD=6280
00 BASE CASE 68-75F setpoints	0	0	0	5	7.7
01 BASE CASE 68-80F setpoints	1	53	8	9	
02 BASE CASE 00 w/ 50% south glass	1	-3	1	9	
03 CASE 02 SOUTH GLASS w/ sunshading	1	3	1	8	
04 CASE 02 SOUTH GLASS w/ night-shades	2	3	2	8	
05 BASE CASE 00 w/ clerestory	5	-9	3	15	
06 CASE 05 CLERESTORY w/ sunshading	5	-7	4	14	
07 CASE 06 CLERESTORY w/ night-shades	6	-7	5	14	
08 BASE CASE 00 w/ earth-berms	3	10	4	8	
09 BASE CASE 00 w/ R 15.8 walls	3	13	5	8	
10 BASE CASE 00 w/ R 28 roof	3	29	26	11	
C Series					
C1 PROPOSED DESIGN 68-75F setpoints	51	-15	37	21	5.6
C2 PROPOSED DESIGN w/ lighting 1.5W/SF	48	-8	37	21	5.6
C3 PROPOSED DESIGN w/ night-shades	53	-15	39	21	5.5

2. Analysis of Design Options — Computer-based simulation of base case with various design options, indicating 39 percent overall improvement as target

energy policies throughout the industrialized world. One response to oil shortages in the United States was widespread interest in solar heating for houses, revitalizing the earlier work of the Keck brothers and other pioneers. At the time of the oil embargo in 1972-73, fewer than a dozen houses in the United States were heated with solar energy. A decade later passive and active solar heating was widely recognized, and many examples demonstrated that solar heating was a simple, straightforward approach that could reduce fossil fuel use and heating costs without changing accepted architectural styles and building practices.

The integration of design, climate, and human comfort— "the bioclimatic approach to architectural regionalism"—was first proposed in the mid-1950s by Victor and Aladar Olgyay. Their intention was to highlight the belief that architectural design should begin with understanding the physiological needs of human comfort and take advantage of local climatic elements to optimize these requirements naturally and efficiently. In the mid-1970s, the terms "passive solar design" and "energy-conscious design" were used to describe this attitude. Applied as a balanced approach to designing for all seasons, climatic design is now the accepted basis of environmentally responsive architecture.

Following the development of residential-scale solar applications in the 1970s, architects and engineers turned their attention to the design of energy-efficient approaches for larger buildings. One practical application of solar energy studied in that decade was daylighting, which has many instructive precedents in nineteenth-century factory and office buildings.

Climate-responsive and energy-efficient architecture and engineering are presented in this book as "energy design," which combines energy conservation, passive heating and cooling, daylighting, and the creation of beneficial microclimates in and around buildings. Energy design begins with an analysis of the "end use" comfort and energy requirements of a project: the temperature, humidity, air flow, and lighting levels required for human comfort. Energy efficiency is accomplished by matching the requirements for comfort to ambient energy sources, such as air and ground temperature, wind, sun, and daylight. Architectural elements that can be effective in energy design include the sun-facing side of the building as a site for direct winter solar heating; light wells or atriums within the building for natural lighting, solar heating, ventilation, and garden space; the roof area for skylights and solar collectors; and the basement or below-grade portions of a building for heat storage or ice-making for cooling. The building design itself is conceived as a natural energy system that restores environmental quality to its site. Through energy design the dynamic climatic effects on a building and site are explored as beneficial elements to creating comfortable, healthy, and inspirational settings, part of a supportive and productive environment that ultimately can contribute to sustaining the regional and global environment.

THE CHALLENGE OF ENERGY DESIGN

The Energy Design Handbook presents design concepts and methods architects and engineers can use to create climate responsive, energy-efficient architecture. Including reference material from the AIA Energy Practice Monograph Series and Continuing Education Program, the handbook brings together introductory explanations, guidelines, examples, and references of energy design strategies appropriate to particular climates and applications. Each chapter is written as a separate lesson module or "monograph" to facilitate self-study or classroom instruction. Together, they present a compendium of energy design concepts that architects should consider as part of any building design project. Whether for new construction or renovation, these concepts can help architects reduce the energy and environmental costs of building operation and ownership.

By employing energy design, architects can design buildings with energy costs and negative environmental effects 50 to 90 percent lower than those of conventional buildings. Buildings that have accomplished such reductions are well documented. It is a simple matter for architects and engineers to learn from and improve upon these examples. They can apply the energy design principles and practices described in the handbook without increasing construction

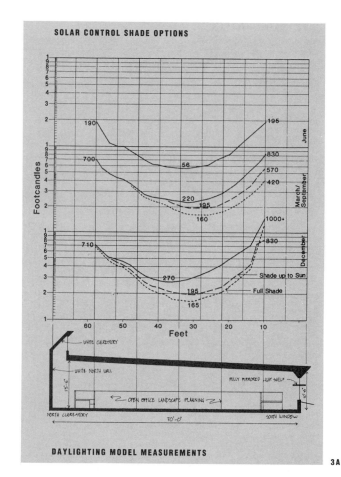

3A

3B

3C

costs, and the resulting life-cycle energy-cost savings will reduce the total cost of owning and operating the buildings they design.

Energy and environmental costs are most easily minimized by decisions made early in the design process. Energy features added after the design is complete are cumbersome and expensive. The best opportunities for energy design appear before major design decisions such as massing, orientation, and facade details are finalized. If these decisions are conceived and informed by energy design principles, the task of engineering design, lighting, and comfort controls is made far easier and less costly.

Energy design therefore challenges architects and their colleagues on the building design team to think about climate, orientation, daylighting, and the qualities of environment as part of the initial design conception. It also requires the architectural and engineering disciplines to work as a team early in the design phase and to conceptualize the

3A-C. Daylighting Analysis — The chart opposite shows daylight model testing and measurement at various times and seasons. The photograph on the left shows a light model test for December sun. Above is the completed design in place, with a light shelf light reflector along the south wall.

building as a system. This approach to energy design—designing a building to be part of its environment and undertaking the early design concept with an interdisciplinary team—has been proved to result in better buildings and lower costs. Most important to building owners and occupants, the design team's focus on climate, energy, comfort, and inspirational space from the very beginning of the design best assures successful performance and high quality.

THE ENERGY DESIGN PROCESS

The energy design concepts described in this book can be incorporated into the design of any project, beginning with the initial goal statement, site analysis, and schematic design and continuing through design development, lighting, mechanical systems engineering, construction, and use.

Project goal statement: If the cost of the salaries, productivity, motivation, and well-being of building occupants is included, the cost of energy is but a small portion of the total cost of building use and operation. However, from the same standpoint of human comfort and productivity, there is a high cost to design defects that result in poor building performance, poor lighting, or uncomfortable heating and cooling operation. It is thus instructive to mention in any program statement that improved environmental quality is the specific goal of the design. Such an improvement can be achieved by integrating the design disciplines of architecture, engineering, construction, lighting, mechanical systems, and environmental controls. Before design begins, it is important to consider human comfort and lighting, energy conservation, and creation of wholesome microclimates in and around the building. Goals should be developed both in qualitative and quantitative terms, with enough specificity to guide all members of the design team.

Site design: Site design includes analyzing the local climate to determine opportunities for passive heating and cooling, daylighting, and microclimate design. Chapter 1 describes techniques that can be used to document regional climate characteristics and microclimatic conditions at the site and to match them to the building energy demand profile. A beginning step is to analyze the local climate and to brainstorm various design concepts of massing, orientation, and/or envelope that might be appropriate. Chapter 1 provides an outline and sources of climatic design information detailing the characteristics and design options for all United States climates and locations.

A step in the site analysis is to check the local utility-rate structure to determine if the particular building type is a candidate for receipt of cost savings given for reducing energy use at peak hours. If peak hour demand charges do apply, this may provide financial incentive for using time-lag and thermal and "coolth" storage techniques to delay energy use from day to night or to off-peak hours. A further step suggested by the Chapter 1 site analysis method is to indicate graphically on a site plan or model all climatic data that affect the site, especially the solar orientation matched to the building's use. This data will suggest the foremost opportunities and liabilities for daylighting, winter heating, and/or seasonal shading requirements.

Schematic design: In the schematic design phase, the initial configuration of the building is proposed, including massing, orientation, and fenestration design. These features establish the basic thermodynamic and climate-responsive nature of the building from the point of view of its solar impact, daylighting, and insulation characteristics. The Chapter 2 discussion of the thermal envelope presents the basic options that ought to inform building massing and orientation. Passive heating and cooling concepts are detailed in Chapter 3, principally for residential and small-scale buildings but with some application to larger buildings. Chapter 4 describes sunshading strategies to be considered at the schematic design level and includes an overview of choices to be finalized during design development and construction detailing.

Directly related to solar impact, sunshading, and fenestration are the opportunities for daylighting, described in Chapter 5. The natural light available during average daytime conditions is typically more than fifty times the amount of light required for visual comfort. To use daylighting effectively requires light reflection and diffusion to reduce glare and

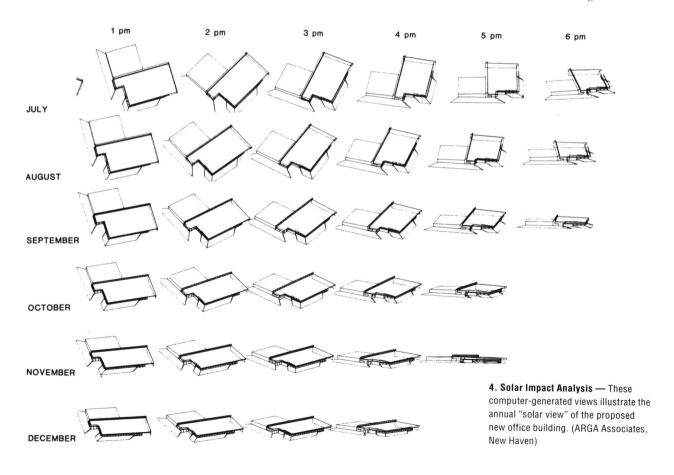

4. Solar Impact Analysis — These computer-generated views illustrate the annual "solar view" of the proposed new office building. (ARGA Associates, New Haven)

5. Post-occupancy Evaluation — The energy design strategies employed in this Johnson Controls project combined a well-insulated, earth-bermed envelope; passive solar gain; sunshading and daylighting with a clerestory skylight and light shelves; indirect halogen lighting with photocell light-level controls; evaporative cooling; and a computer-controlled energy management system. The building's energy consumption has averaged 37,000 Btu/yr., a full 30 percent less than the original target (ascribed to conservative assumptions used in the original analysis and later improvements in design). The total energy cost has averaged 50 cents/SF/year, substantially less than the $1.25 to $2.50/SF cost of conventional office buildings. Based on independent postoccupancy evaluation (Burt Hill Kosar Rittelmann Kantrowitz, 1987), employees rate the facility very high in aesthetic appeal and comfort. The energy design features added four percent to the construction cost of the building. Based on energy cost savings, this additional cost was repaid within the first four years of operation.

contrast and to spread and direct daylight into the building interior. Designing for natural lighting is much like designing a lighting fixture, in which the object is to make the light attractive and usable. The architect's task, however, is far more challenging because the light source (the sun), viewed from the building's position, appears to trace a different position throughout the day and year. As evidenced by notable masterworks of architecture throughout the globe, it is possible to come up with unique solutions to daylighting and sunshading that evolve from understanding the sun's apparent motion.

From an energy design standpoint, the percentage and size of window and skylight fenestration determines how much insulation the building envelope provides. Therefore, fenestration should vary according to building type, climatic characteristics, and orientation. Buildings in cool climates may have fewer windows, and buildings in warm climates will require sunshading or other solar controls. The average sky conditions, whether bright and sunny or predominantly cloudy, should determine the approach to window orientation and solar control. In northern hemisphere locations, windows facing directly south are ideal because they gain most winter sun and are easiest to shade. East- and west-facing windows gain little useful heat in winter and present the greatest challenge for summer shading. Daylighting options can be developed after the basic window configuration has been optimized for heating and cooling. If windows are placed strategically, daylighting can be effective even with relatively small window areas.

A basic concept of energy design—the view that a building is a climate-responsive environmental system—is thus reflected in the schematic design phase. At this stage the building's response to the sun and climate—its opportunities to gain winter heat, provide summer shading, and open the building to natural light throughout the year—are determined.

Design development and detailing: Chapter 6 provides an overview of heating, ventilation, and cooling (HVAC) systems from the standpoint of energy efficiency. In design development, all of the building subsystems—mechanical system layout and controls, lighting, acoustics, and interiors—should be designed as an integrated set. Just as with daylighting and electric light, the mechanical air systems of a building work best when they are conceived in conjunction with the interior spaces that are part of the natural air flow pattern. An example is interior atriums or light wells used both for natural light and air flow and supported by electric lighting and mechanical heating and cooling systems that complement the natural environmental qualities of heat, cooling, and light created by the architectural design.

The energy design process extends to architectural details, which might include fine-tuning the design of a sunshade to the specific profile of the local climate or detailing a wall section for a given thermal time-lag or insulation level. The handbook includes calculation methods for these details that allow an architect to design a building that is custom-tailored to its particular climate, site, and orientation.

Two remaining chapters of the first part of the handbook—Chapter 7, Active Solar Systems, and Chapter 8, Photovoltaics—describe the technologies for solar heating, cooling, and electricity. While a subject of research for dozens of years, both active solar systems and photovoltaics are still relatively new to conventional or widespread building practice. Both of these emerging technologies, which use the sun's energy to produce heating, cooling, and lighting, are of great interest from the standpoint of energy design. Some applications of active solar heating and photovoltaics are practical now, such as the use of active solar heating for hot water, pool, and process heating and the use of photovoltaics for independent electric generation for small scale or direct uses (for example to power fans for interior air circulation of passive solar heat gain). As conventional energy costs and liabilities increase, these renewable energy technologies will become increasingly important and economically competitive. Architects who become familiar with their design criteria will be able to incorporate them economically as integrated components of building design and as supplements or replacement of conventional energy sources.

The three additional chapters that compose the second part of the handbook provide calculation methods useful for preliminary design analysis, for example, in evaluating various schematic design options. The calculations are longhand procedures and, as such, have the educational advantage of demonstrating the physics of energy transfer between a building and the ambient environment. When the interactive nature of building-related variables is seen and understood by the architect, the importance of the many design assumptions and variables becomes all the more clear, for example, increasing insulation may allow reduced HVAC sizes, depending upon infiltration and air-change assumptions and other factors. A building is a complex thermodynamic system, a fact which these calculation methods begins to make clear. While there is an increasing number of computer-based calculation programs for simulation of building energy performance, familiarity with the hand-calculation methods provides a necessary introduction to understanding the importance of the assumptions made in computer simulations. Chapter 11, Economic Analysis, provides an introduction to life-cycle costing to help architects and engineers make design decisions that reduce the total operating costs of a building, which ultimately demonstrate to the building owner the value of the energy design principles and practices that are described in this handbook.

In sum, these energy design concepts and methods provide a simple, straightforward way to ensure that all buildings are optimally designed as climate-responsive, energy-efficient structures with integrated architectural, mechanical engineering, and lighting systems that improve the total quality of the building, its interior, and the surrounding landscape and environment. These approaches have been well researched and applied to numerous locations and building types throughout the United States and internationally. Recognizing that approximately 35 percent of energy use in the United States is consumed in heating, cooling, and lighting buildings, it is evident that architects and engineers who incorporate energy design concepts and methods into every design project can play a significant role in reducing energy consumption and environmental pollution.

Concern for the environment, and the emerging view that all human activity and enterprise ultimately affects the quality of biological and ecological health on earth, has resulted in an increased interest on the part of the architectural and building design professions in addressing not only the health, safety, and welfare of building occupants but also the health of the environmental and ecological systems affected by building design and construction. These concepts can be said to have evolved from the long-established Vitruvian "conditions for building well"—*utilitas, firmitas et venustas*, or commodity, firmness, and delight—an enduring definition that becomes richer as our conception of architecture becomes more responsible and profound.

PART ONE: DESIGN

CLIMATE AND SITE

Introduction

Because few areas of the world offer comfortable climate conditions year-round, architectural design has traditionally attempted to offer protection from the elements. In recent years it has become increasingly important to do so in an energy-conscious manner.

Energy-conscious design requires an understanding of climate and the factors that produce it. The first section of this monograph discusses the regional climatic categories used in making early design decisions and the more specific data on temperature, humidity, wind and insolation needed for subsequent design stages. It also discusses the availability and most useful formats of such data.

The second section discusses the climate-conscious selection and analysis of a specific site. It then describes how site elements—topography, water, and built forms—can be used or manipulated to achieve climate control before the building is designed. The section ends with a discussion of rules of thumb for site design.

University of Minnesota Bookstore
Bloomington, Minnesota
Architects: Myers and Bennett/BRW.

Regional Climatic Types

The purpose of categorizing geographical areas by climate is to develop a manageable number of guidelines for energy-conscious design. These regional guidelines are especially helpful in the programming and schematic phases of design, where basic energy-conserving strategies are selected. At the design development level, however, they must be coupled with analysis of the specific site, where topography, vegetation, proximity to water and other factors can sometimes radically alter the regional guidelines.

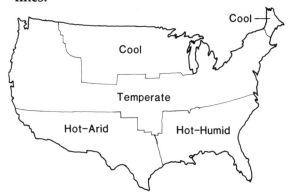

Major Climatic Regions of the United States

☐ Perhaps the most well-known categorization of climates in the United States is the four-climate scheme given in Victor Olgyay's *Design with Climate*: cool, temperate, hot-arid and hot-humid. This classification was based on W. Koppen's study of the relationship between climate and vegetation types.

☐ As early as 1949, The American Institute of Architects began developing the *House Beautiful* Climate Control Project, which divides the continental United States into 15 regions, and presents narrative and graphic formats for the following urban areas, with adjustment factors for their surrounding areas:
—Columbus, Ohio
—New York City
—Miami, Florida
—Arizona
—St. Louis, Missouri
—New Orleans, Louisiana
—Chicago, Illinois
—Washington, D.C.
—Boston, Massachusetts
—St. Paul, Minnesota
—Pittsburgh, Pennsylvania
—Charleston, North Carolina
—Portland, Oregon
—Albany, New York
—Denver, Colorado

☐ The *House Beautiful* data for these cities offer comprehensive climatic information tailored to the needs of the design process.

☐ More recently, the AIA Research Corporation has developed *Regional Guidelines For Energy-Conserving Homes*. This document divides the United States into 13 general climatic regions, based on heating and cooling needs, solar availability when temperatures are in the range of 50 to 65 degrees (F.) and the effects of diurnal temperature swings and humidity.

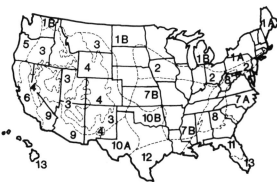

Macroclimatic Regions	
1A. Hartford, Conn:	7B. Little Rock, Ark.
1B. Madison, Wis.	8. Knoxville, Tenn.
2. Indianapolis, Ind.	9. Phoenix, Ariz.
3. Salt Lake City, Utah	10A. Midland, Tex.
4. Ely, Nev.	10B. Fort Worth, Tex.
5. Medford, Ore.	11. New Orleans, La.
6. Fresno, Calif.	12. Houston, Tex.
7A. Charleston, S.C.	13. Miami, Fla.

☐ These guidelines provide information on how to categorize the climate of a given site, and on the most effective strategies for each climatic type.

☐ Most guidelines, like the AIA/RC's *Regional Guidelines* focus on indigenous residential designs used before the invention of energy-intensive space-conditioning techniques after World War II. They highlight residential design because houses have high surface-area-to-volume ratio and, hence, greater sensitivity to climate. Nevertheless, such regional guidelines can give clues to the designer of energy-conscious commercial and industrial structures as well.

☐ The ongoing design guidelines being developed by the Tennessee Valley Authority further refine climatic types by dividing the Tennessee Valley region into four climatic zones.

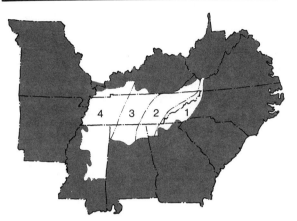

Tennessee Valley Climatic Zones

1. *Blue Ridge Region (Appalachian Mountains)*
2. *Great Valley*
3. *Cumberland Plateau*
4. *Mississippi Embayment (including Highland Rim and Central Basin)*

These guidelines present data for nine major urban areas, determined by temperature range, relative humidity, solar radiation, and wind speed and direction.

□ The various graphic formats developed by TVA are especially well suited to the needs of the design process. Data presented in raw tabular form can often be usefully translated by the designer into format provided by the TVA.

□ These contemporary homes reflect the climatic character of the regions for which they were designed. Like their pre-industrial counterparts—the New England salt box, the Midwestern ranch house, the Southern plantation and the pueblo of the Southwest—their forms, orientation and construction materials are a direct response to sun, wind, temperature and humidity.

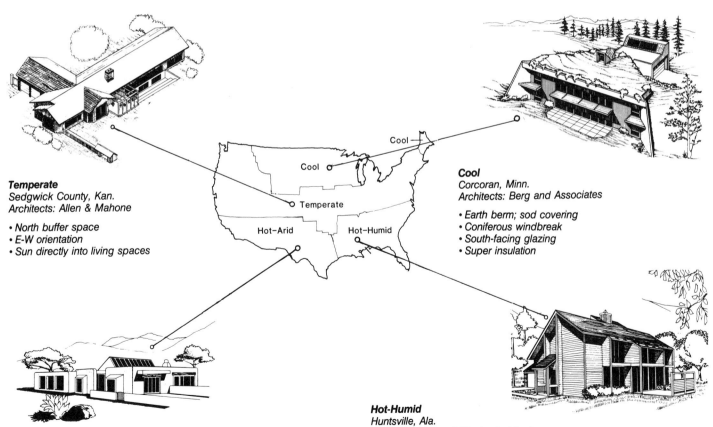

Temperate
Sedgwick County, Kan.
Architects: Allen & Mahone

• North buffer space
• E-W orientation
• Sun directly into living spaces

Cool
Corcoran, Minn.
Architects: Berg and Associates

• Earth berm; sod covering
• Coniferous windbreak
• South-facing glazing
• Super insulation

Hot-Arid
Santa Fe, N.M.
Architects: Stanley Associates

• Adobe construction
• Thermal mass and floors
• Cross ventilation

Hot-Humid
Huntsville, Ala.
Architects: Jones & Herrin, Architects
Solar Designer: Architectural Design Branch, TVA

• High ceilings
• Atrium space
• Deciduous trees to south
• Buffer space to north
• Cross ventilation, cupola

Climatic Data and Analysis

Pertinent climatic data for design analysis include temperature, solar insolation, wind, humidity and weather patterns. Although there are many sources of specific climatic data, two of the most common are the *Climatic Atlas of the United States* and "Local Climatological Data" summaries, both available from the National Oceanic and Atmospheric Administration (NOAA).

□ This *Climatic Atlas* presents annual and monthly weather data in tables and maps so the user can interpolate data for areas between those shown on the maps.

□ The "Local Climatological Data" summaries are available for about 300 locations across the country. They provide monthly summaries for a current year (preferably the Test Reference Year (TRY)); normal, mean and extreme averages for a 30-year period for many of the station locations as well as three-hourly observations of temperature, wind and humidity conditions and other data necessary for more detailed analysis.

"Climatic Atlas" Presents Annual and Monthly Weather Data

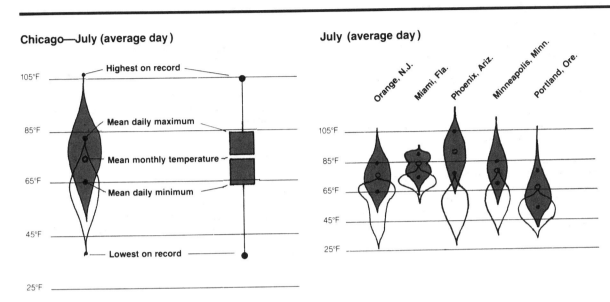

Chicago—July (average day)

July (average day)

Orange, N.J. Miami, Fla. Phoenix, Ariz. Minneapolis, Minn. Portland, Ore.

Temperature Data

Two images can be used to graph temperatures (chart at top). The tear drops, used for the AIA "House Beautiful" project in 1949 indicates by their width the duration of a temperature on an average day of a given month. The greater the overlap of wet and dry bulb drops, the higher the humidity, as comparison of Phoenix (dry) and Miami in July indicates above. The greater a region's diurnal temperature swing (left), the better thermal massing will ease temperature extremes.

Data	Source
Temperature	
—Means and extremes	—NOAA's "Local Climatological Data summaries" (LCDs)
—Design temperatures	—ASHRAE's "Fundamentals" handbook
—Diurnal Swings	—Calculated from NOAA's LCDs
—Degree days	—LCDs
Humidity	
—Wet-bulb temperatures	—LCDs
—Relative humidity	—LCDs
Sun	
—Insolation	—ASHRAE's "Applications" handbook
—Clear and cloudy days	—LCDs
—Percent possible sunshine	—LCDs
—Sun paths	—AIA's *Architectural Graphic Standards*
Wind Data	
—Mean speed and direction	—LCDs
Precipitation and Weather Data	—LCDs

Sources of Climatic Data

Climate of States

The two-volume Climate of States *contains chapters for every state. Each chapter includes the local climatological data summary for all NOAA stations in the state and a narrative summary of the climatological features of the state as a whole.*

Air Force Data

The U.S. Air Force publishes tables of weather data collected for each Air Force base.

Climatic Design

This reference text on climatic design principles and practices includes data for 30 representative U.S. cities and climates tabulated for psychrometric chart analysis. (See reference: Donald Watson and Kenneth Labs, Climatic Design, *McGraw-Hill, 1983 and 1993.)*

Climate Consultant

This software diskette for IBM-compatible personal computers plots typical meteorological year (TMY) data, including temperature, wind, percent of sunshine, psychrometric chart analysis, and sun charts. The program is cross-referenced to Climatic Design (see above). (Available from Prof. Murray Milne, UCLA Graduate School of Architecture and Urban Planning, Los Angeles, CA 90024.)

Typical Meteorological Year (TMY) Data for Microcomputers

SOLMET data is used to define a "typical" year of weather, termed the "typical meteorological year." Diskettes are available for most U.S. locations (250 weather stations); these cover solar radiation, temperature, humidity, wind speed, and cloud cover. (Available from Raymond J. Bahm, 2513 Kimberly Court, NW, Albuquerque, NM 87120.)

ATHENS, GEORGIA — MUNICIPAL AIRPORT — EASTERN — 33° 57' N — 83° 19' W — 802 FT. — 1977

Temperature Data: Record high and low; degree days.

Humidity Data: Wet and dry bulb; relative humidity every sixth hour.

Wind: Mean speed and prevailing direction.

Insolation: Sky cover.

Annual Summary Sheet:
The above chart of Normal Means and Extremes data can be used to graph charts for temperature, degree days, relative humidity and wind speeds.

Normals, Means and Extremes

Temperature

Dry-bulb temperature is the most basic indicator of the comfort needs of a site. The most basic climatic analysis relies on:
—temperature means and extremes
—design temperatures
—diurnal temperature swings
—degree days or degree hours.

☐ NOAA's "Local Climatological Data" summaries (LCDs) provide annual and monthly means, that is, average or normal, and extreme temperatures over a 30-year period. Daily maximum and minimum temperatures provide the mean low and high temperatures for each month. The monthly mean temperatures gives the average temperature for the entire month. *Climatic Atlas* also provides this data.

☐ Designing for the record high and low temperatures, especially when using natural conservation strategies, is not usually an optimal economic solution. It is better to design for the high summer and low winter temperatures that occur 95- or 97.5-percent of the time. The *Fundamentals* handbook prepared by the American Society of Heating, Refrigerating and Air-conditioning Engineers (ASHRAE) lists high summer temperatures as 1 percent, 2.5 percent and 5 percent, and low winter temperatures for 95 percent and 97.5 percent for almost 800 locations across the United States.

☐ Diurnal temperature swings can be plotted from LCDs for each month. The summary sheet for each month contains a "summary by hours" chart on the first page, presenting average monthly temperatures at three-hour intervals. These data can be graphed on a chart similar to the TVA format. A diurnal swing of 20 degrees (F.) or higher indicates that thermal mass storage or night ventilation could be an effective strategy.

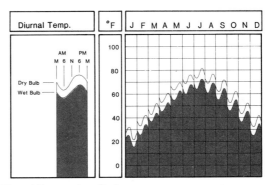

Diurnal Temperature Cycle

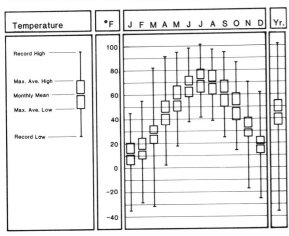

Temperature Range

☐ Many passive energy-conserving strategies, such as thermal mass storage and night ventilation, depend on the temperature swing that occurs on a 24-hour cycle. Diurnal temperature swings can be as great as 40 degrees (F.) in some areas of the country, allowing summer heat accumulated in the daytime to be released during the cool night.

State	City	Design Temperature				
		Winter		Summer		
		D.B. 99%	D.B. 97.5%	D.B. and Mean Coincident W.B.		
				1%	2.5%	5%
Al.	Birmingham	17	21	96/74	94/75	92/74
	Huntsville	11	16	95/75	93/74	91/74
Alaska	Anchorage	−23	−18	71/59	68/58	66/55
Ariz.	Flagstaff	−2	4	84/55	82/55	80/54
	Phoenix	31	34	109/71	107/71	105/71
	Tuscon	28	32	104/66	102/66	100/66
Ark.	Little Rock	15	20	99/66	96/77	94/77
Calif.	Bakersfield	30	32	104/70	101/69	98/68
	Fresno	28	30	102/70	100/69	97/68
	Los Angeles	41	43	83/68	80/68	77/67
	Palm Springs	33	35	112/71	110/70	108/70
	Sacramento	30	32	101/70	98/70	94/69
	San Francisco	35	38	82/64	77/63	73/62
Colo.	Boulder	−6	0	93/59	91/59	89/59
	Denver	−5	1	93/59	91/59	89/59
Conn.	Hartford	6	9	86/73	84/71	81/70
Del.	Wilmington	10	14	92/74	89/74	87/73
D.C.	Washington	14	17	93/75	91/74	89/74
Fla.	Gainsville	28	31	95/77	93/77	92/77
	Miami	44	47	91/77	90/77	89/77
	Orlando	35	38	94/76	93/76	91/76
	St. Petersburg	31	35	92/78	89/78	87/78
	Tampa	36	40	92/77	91/77	90/76
Ga.	Atlanta	17	22	94/74	92/74	90/73
	Augusta	20	23	97/77	95/76	93/76
	Macon	21	25	98/77	93/76	91/75
Hawaii	Honolulu	62	63	87/73	86/73	85/72
Idaho	Boise	3	10	96/65	94/64	91/64
	Pocatello	−8	−1	94/61	91/60	89/59
Ill.	Champaign	−3	2	95/75	92/74	90/73
	Chicago	−8	−4	91/74	89/74	86/72
Ind.	Fort Wayne	−4	1	92/73	89/72	87/72
	Indianapolis	−2	2	92/74	90/74	87/73
	Terra Haute	−2	4	95/75	92/74	89/73
Iowa	Des Moines	−10	−5	94/75	91/74	88/73
	Sioux City	−11	−7	95/74	92/74	89/73
Kan.	Dodge City	0	5	100/69	97/69	95/69
	Topeka	0	4	99/75	96/75	93/74
	Witchita	3	7	101/72	98/73	96/73
Ky.	Lexington	3	8	93/73	91/73	88/72
	Louisville	5	10	95/74	93/74	90/74
La.	Baton Rouge	25	29	95/77	93/77	92/77
	New Orleans	29	33	93/78	92/78	90/77
Me.	Augusta	−7	−3	88/73	85/70	82/68
	Bangor	−11	−6	86/70	83/68	80/67
Md.	Baltimore	10	13	94/75	91/75	89/74
Mass.	Boston	6	9	91/73	88/71	85/70
	Springfield	−5	0	90/72	87/71	84/69
Mich.	Detroit	3	6	91/73	88/72	86/71
	Grand Rapids	1	5	91/72	88/72	85/70
Minn.	Int'l. Falls	−29	−25	85/68	83/68	80/66
	Minneapolis	−16	−12	92/75	84/72	85/70
Miss.	Biloxi	28	31	94/79	92/79	90/78
	Jackson	21	25	97/76	95/76	93/76
Mo.	Jefferson City	2	7	98/75	95/74	92/74
	Kansas City	2	6	99/75	96/74	93/74
	St. Louis	2	6	97/75	94/75	91/74

State	City	Design Temperature				
		Winter		Summer		
		D.B. 99%	D.B. 97.5%	D.B. and Mean Coincident W.B.		
				1%	2.5%	5%
Mont.	Billings	−15	−10	94/64	91/64	88/63
	Helena	−21	−16	91/60	88/60	85/69
Neb.	Omaha	−8	−3	94/76	91/75	88/74
Nev.	Las Vegas	25	28	108/66	106/65	104/65
	Reno	5	10	95/61	92/60	90/59
N.H.	Concord	−8	−3	90/72	87/70	84/69
	Manchester	−8	−3	91/72	88/71	85/70
N.J.	Atlantic City	10	13	92/74	89/74	86/72
	Newark	10	14	94/74	91/73	88/72
	Trenton	11	14	91/75	88/74	85/73
N.M.	Albuquerque	12	16	96/61	94/61	92/61
	Santa Fe	6	10	90/61	88/61	86/61
N.Y.	Albany	−6	−1	91/73	88/72	85/70
	Buffalo	2	6	88/71	85/70	83/69
	New York	11	15	92/74	89/73	87/72
N.C.	Ashville	10	14	89/73	87/72	85/71
	Raleigh	16	20	94/75	92/75	90/75
	Winston-Salem	16	20	94/74	91/73	89/73
N.D.	Bismark	−23	−19	95/68	91/68	88/67
	Grand Forks	−26	−22	91/70	87/70	84/68
Ohio	Akron	1	6	89/72	86/71	84/70
	Cleveland	1	5	91/73	88/72	86/71
	Columbus	0	5	92/73	90/73	87/72
	Toledo	0	5	92/73	90/73	87/72
Okla.	Oklahoma City	9	13	100/74	97/74	95/73
	Tulsa	8	13	101/74	98/75	95/75
Ore.	Eugene	17	22	92/67	89/66	86/65
	Portland	17	23	89/68	85/67	81/65
Pa.	Harrisburg	7	11	94/75	91/74	88/73
	Philadelphia	10	14	93/75	90/74	87/72
	Pittsburgh	1	5	89/72	86/71	84/70
R.I.	Providence	5	9	89/73	86/72	83/70
S.C.	Charleston	24	27	93/78	91/78	89/77
S.D.	Pierre	−15	−10	99/71	95/71	92/69
	Rapid City	−11	−7	95/66	92/65	89/65
Tenn.	Chattanooga	13	18	96/75	93/74	91/74
	Memphis	13	18	98/77	95/76	93/76
	Nashville	9	14	97/75	94/74	91/74
Tex.	Austin	24	28	100/74	98/74	97/74
	Dallas	18	22	102/75	100/75	97/75
	El Paso	20	24	100/64	98/64	96/64
Utah	Salt Lake City	3	8	97/62	95/62	92/61
Vt.	Burlington	−12	−7	88/72	85/70	82/69
Va.	Charlottesville	14	18	94/74	91/74	88/73
	Norfolk	20	22	93/77	91/76	89/76
	Richmond	14	17	95/76	92/76	90/75
Wash.	Olympia	16	22	87/66	83/65	79/64
	Seattle	21	26	84/68	81/66	77/65
W. Va.	Charleston	7	11	92/74	90/73	87/72
Wis.	Green Bay	−13	−9	88/74	85/72	83/71
	Madison	−11	−7	91/74	88/73	85/71
	Milwaukee	−8	−4	90/74	87/73	84/71
Wyo.	Cheyenne	−9	−1	89/58	86/58	84/57
	Laramie	−14	−6	84/56	81/56	79/55

Design Temperatures

☐ "Degree days" are based on a selected indoor design temperature, usually 65 degrees (F.), and measure the amount of heating or cooling needed in an area. Heating degree days are determined by multiplying the number of degrees difference between the average outdoor temperature and the specified indoor temperature times the number of days that the outdoor temperature occurs. Cooling degree days are calculated by the same procedure.

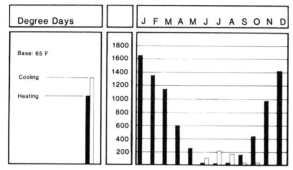

Heating and Cooling Degrees Days-Base 65 degrees (F.)

STATE	CITY	Average Monthly Heating Degree Days									
		SEPT	OCT	NOV	DEC	JAN	FEB	MAR	APR	MAY	TOTAL
Al.	Birmingham	6	93	363	555	592	462	363	108	9	2551
	Mobile	0	22	213	357	415	300	211	42	0	1560
Alaska	Fairbanks	642	1203	1833	2254	2359	1901	1739	1068	555	14,279
	Juneau	483	725	921	1135	1237	1070	1073	810	601	9075
Ariz.	Flagstaff	201	558	867	1073	1169	991	911	651	437	7152
	Tucson	0	25	231	406	471	344	242	75	6	1800
Ark.	Little Rock	9	127	465	716	756	577	434	126	9	3219
Calif.	Bakersfield	0	37	282	502	546	364	267	105	19	2122
	Sacramento	0	62	312	533	561	392	310	173	76	2419
	San Diego	21	43	135	236	298	253	214	135	90	1458
	San Francisco	102	118	231	388	443	336	319	279	239	3001
Colo.	Alamosa	279	639	1065	1420	1476	1162	1020	696	440	8529
	Denver	117	428	819	1035	1132	938	887	558	288	6283
Conn.	Hartford	117	394	714	1101	1190	1042	908	519	205	6235
Del.	Wilmington	51	270	588	927	980	874	735	387	112	4930
D.C.	Washington	33	217	519	834	871	762	626	288	74	4224
Fla.	Miami	0	0	0	65	74	56	19	0	0	214
	Tallahassee	0	28	198	360	375	286	202	36	0	1485
Ga.	Atlanta	18	124	417	648	636	518	428	147	25	2961
	Savannah	0	47	246	437	437	353	254	45	0	1819
Hawaii	Honolulu	0	0	0	0	0	0	0	0	0	0
Idaho	Boise	132	415	792	1017	1113	854	722	438	245	5809
Ill.	Chicago	117	381	807	1166	1265	1086	939	534	260	6639
	Springfield	72	291	696	1023	1135	935	769	354	136	5429
Ind.	Indianapolis	90	316	723	1051	1113	949	809	432	177	5699
Iowa	Des Moines	96	363	828	1225	1370	1187	915	438	180	6588
Kan.	Goodland	81	381	810	1073	1166	955	884	507	236	6141
	Topeka	57	270	672	980	1122	893	722	330	124	5182

STATE	CITY	Average Monthly Heating Degree Days									
		SEPT	OCT	NOV	DEC	JAN	FEB	MAR	APR	MAY	TOTAL
Ken.	Lexington	54	239	609	902	946	818	685	325	105	4683
La.	New Orleans	0	12	165	291	344	241	177	24	0	1254
	Shreveport	0	47	297	477	552	426	304	81	0	2184
Maine	Portland	195	508	807	1215	1339	1182	1042	675	372	7511
Md.	Baltimore	48	264	585	905	936	820	679	327	90	4654
Mass.	Boston	60	316	603	983	1088	972	846	513	208	5634
Mich.	Detroit	87	360	738	1088	1181	1058	936	522	220	6232
	Escanaba	243	539	924	1293	1445	1296	1203	777	456	8481
Minn.	Duluth	330	632	1131	1581	1745	1518	1355	840	490	10,000
	Minneapolis	189	505	1014	1454	1631	1380	1166	621	288	8322
Miss.	Jackson	0	65	315	502	546	414	310	87	0	2239
Mo.	Columbia	54	251	651	967	1076	875	716	324	121	5046
Mont.	Billings	186	487	897	1135	1296	1100	970	570	285	7049
	Missoula	303	651	1035	1287	1420	1120	970	621	391	8125
Neb.	North Platte	123	440	885	1166	1271	1039	930	519	248	6684
	Omaha	105	357	828	1175	1355	1126	939	465	208	6612
Nev.	Las Vegas	0	78	387	617	688	487	335	111	6	2709
	Reno	204	490	801	1026	1073	823	729	510	357	6332
N.H.	Concord	177	505	822	1240	1358	1184	1032	636	298	7383
N.J.	Trenton	57	264	576	924	989	885	753	399	121	4980
N.M.	Albuquerque	12	229	642	868	930	703	595	288	81	4348
N.Y.	Buffalo	141	440	777	1156	1256	1145	1039	645	329	7062
	New York	30	233	540	902	986	885	760	408	118	4871
N.C.	Charlotte	6	124	438	691	691	582	481	156	22	3191
	Wilmington	0	74	291	521	546	462	357	96	0	2347
N.D.	Bismarck	222	577	1088	1463	1708	1442	1203	645	329	8851
Ohio	Cleveland	105	384	738	1088	1159	1047	918	552	260	6351
	Columbus	84	347	714	1039	1088	949	809	426	171	5660
Okla.	Oklahoma City	15	164	498	766	868	664	527	189	34	3725
	Tulsa	18	158	522	787	893	683	539	213	47	3860
Ore.	Salem	111	338	594	729	822	647	611	417	273	4754
Pa.	Pittsburgh	105	375	726	1063	1119	1002	874	480	195	5987
	Williamsport	111	375	717	1073	1122	1002	856	468	177	5934
R.I.	Providence	96	372	660	1023	1110	988	868	534	236	5954
S.C.	Columbia	0	84	345	577	570	470	357	81	0	2484
S.D.	Rapid City	165	481	897	1172	1333	1145	1051	615	326	7345
Tenn.	Nashville	30	158	495	732	778	644	512	189	40	3578
Tex.	Brownsville	0	0	66	149	205	106	74	0	0	600
	Dallas	0	62	321	524	601	440	319	90	6	2363
	El Paso	0	84	414	648	685	445	319	105	0	2700
	Houston	0	6	183	307	384	288	192	36	0	1396
Utah	Salt Lake City	81	419	849	1082	1172	910	763	459	233	6052
Ver.	Burlington	207	539	891	1349	1513	1333	1187	714	353	8269
Va.	Lynchburg	51	223	540	822	849	731	605	267	78	4166
Wash.	Seattle	129	329	543	657	738	599	577	396	242	4424
W. Va.	Charleston	63	254	591	865	880	770	648	300	96	4476
Wis.	Green Bay	174	484	924	1333	1494	1313	1141	654	305	8029
Wyo.	Casper	192	524	942	1169	1290	1084	1020	651	381	7410

Heating Degree Days

13

Humidity

The simplest measure of humidity is the wet-bulb temperature, available from LCDs. The more closely the wet-bulb temperature matches the dry-bulb temperature the more humid the air. Wet-bulb temperatures are often mapped on a curve in tandem with dry bulb temperatures to get a rough idea of humidity.

☐ For design purposes, perhaps the easiest measurement of humidity is "relative humidity"—the percentage of water in the air compared to the maximum it can hold at a given temperature. At 100 percent relative humidity, the air cannot hold any more moisture; precipitation will occur should the temperature drop. Relative humidity data, available from LCDs, can be graphed in the same format as wet bulb temperatures.

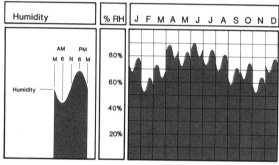

Relative Humidity

☐ The comfortable range of relative humidity depends on the dry bulb temperature, and can range from 20 to 60 percent.

☐ Excess humidity is a problem only during the cooling season. Most energy-conserving design options do not deal with humidity directly but rather increase natural ventilation and dessicant cooling to make a humid environment more comfortable; conversely, pools and fountains added to a dry site can make it feel cooler.

Government Service Insurance System Bldg.
Manila, Philippines
Architect: Jorge Y. Ramos & Associates
The Architects Collaborative

Architect Jorge Y. Ramos, with advice from The Architects Collaborative, will use natural wind ventilation to cool and dehumidify the Government Services Insurance System building located in hot, humid Manila, Philippines.

Covering the 1.35 million-sq. ft. of ground above spectacular Manila Bay, the V-shaped structure has its narrowest sides on the east and west, thus minimizing exposure to heat gain from the rising and setting sun. The large mass of the building will be broken into pods, which will act as wind scoops to catch and channel the cooling afternoon sea breezes throughout the building. Although the building will be fully air-conditioned, offices will have operable windows for additional natural ventilation.

The GSIS building's pods will also allow maximum penetration of natural light into the work areas. Overhangs will shade the southern facade from unwanted sun. Angular stepped-back slopes on the north side and the use of planters evoke the country's terraced rice fields. The building's annual energy budget is predicted to be half that of a similar building in Manila.

The building is composed of two parallel blocks, a one-story unit for heavy equipment and a two-stepping to three-story unit on the north. The two masses are linked by a 28-foot-wide central "interior street" that serves as a circulation spine as well as a buffer for noise and machine vibration.

The elevated roof on the north block is angled at 53 degrees (F.) to support the upper bank of collectors, and encloses most of the air-handling equipment. Monitors are interspersed between the fan rooms to provide clerestory lighting and dramatic vertical spaces in the interior street. The solar system also consists of some free standing collectors supported by space frames, spanning 84 feet.

Heat pumps are used to redistribute internally generated heat, and the system is expected to provide 80 percent of the building's heating requirements.

Government Service Insurance System Bldg.
Manila, Philippines
Architect: Jorge Y. Ramos & Associates
The Architects Collaborative

Photo: Sam Sweezy

Government Service Insurance System Bldg.
Manila, Philippines
Architect: Jorge Y. Ramos & Associates
The Architects Collaborative

Photo: Sam Sweezy

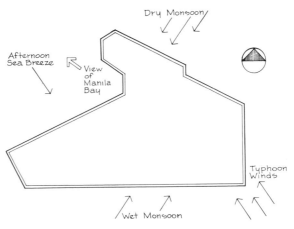

Dry Monsoon

Afternoon Sea Breeze

View of Manila Bay

Typhoon Winds

Wet Monsoon

Government Service Insurance System Bldg.
Manila, Philippines
Architect: Jorge Y. Ramos & Associates
The Architects Collaborative

Insolation

The sun is the deciding factor for many energy-conserving strategies. Once the designer of a residential or small commercial building has determined the basic climatic conditions of temperature and humidity, it becomes clear when the sun would be an asset for active or passive solar heating and when it should be blocked. For larger commercial buildings, on the other hand, detailed analysis of the availability of sunlight during different times of the year and during the day is often delayed until the schematic design phase, when building orientations, load profiles and materials are defined.

☐ The total amount of sunlight—direct, diffuse and reflected—that hits a horizontal surface is called "incident solar radiation" or insolation. It is heat energy measured in terms of BTU/sq.ft./hr. (or month or day) or Langleys/hr. This number does not appear in NOAA's LCDs, but is available in ASHRAE's *Applications* handbook and the *Climatic Atlas*, as well as in many solar handbooks such as Mazria's *Passive Solar Energy Book*.

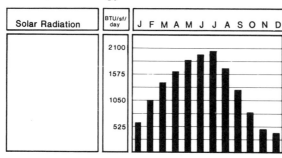

Solar Radiation

☐ The LCDs provide data on the number of hours the sun is up every day and, based on historical measurements, the "percent (of) possible sunshine" likely to be actually available. Percent possible sunshine in LCDs is averaged over each month. This percentage, multiplied by the solar radiation figure, will yield a monthly average of available insolation.

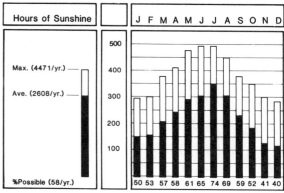

Hours of Sunshine

☐ For daylighting analyses, the distribution of sun from day to day can be seen from a plotting of data on clear and cloudy days, also available from LCDs.

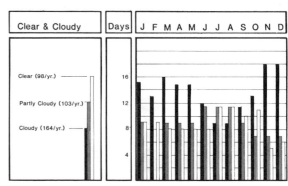

Clear and Cloudy Days

☐ The sun's position relative to the site is defined by the "altitude", which is the angle of the sun above the horizon, and "azimuth", which is the angle between the sun's position and true south. Once altitude and azimuth angles are known, the sun can be located at any time of day; and its path for any day can be drawn by connecting these points of location.

See Chapter 4, Shading and Sun Control: Solar Angles, p. 148.

Community College of Denver North Campus
Denver, Colorado
Architects: John D. Anderson Associates
Engineers: Bridgers and Paxton

John D. Anderson Associates, teamed with the mechnical engineering firm of Bridgers and Paxton, used 35,000 square feet of flat-plate liquid collector panels in a college building to take advantage of Denver's sunlight. Designed in 1973 at the advent of the "solar age," the solar system came in at 8.5 percent over the original building budget, but was estimated to have an 11-year payback period, considering projected escalations for natural gas.

The building is composed of two parallel blocks, a one-story unit for heavy equipment and a two-stepping to three-story unit on the north. The two masses are linked by a 28-foot-wide central "interior street" that serves as a circulation spine as well as a buffer for noise and machine vibration.

The elevated roof on the north block is angled at 53 degrees (F.) to support the upper bank of collectors, and encloses most of the air-handling equipment. Monitors are interspersed between the fan rooms to provide clerestory lighting and dramatic vertical spaces in the interior street. The solar system also consists of some free standing collectors supported by space frames, spanning 84 feet.

Heat pumps are used to redistribute internally generated heat, and the system is expected to provide 80 percent of the building's heating requirements.

Community College of Denver, North Campus
Denver, Colorado
Architects: John D. Anderson Associates
Engineers: Bridgers and Paxton

Photo: Andrew Kramer, AIA

Community College of Denver, North Campus
Denver, Colorado
Architects: John D. Anderson Associates
Engineers: Bridgers and Paxton

Photo: Andrew Kramer, AIA

Wind

NOAA's LCDs present wind data in terms of monthly average speed and prevailing direction. They also present the fastest speed recorded and its direction, which can help in wind load calculations. For more accurate calculations, the LCDs present three-hourly summaries for wind speed and directional data for each day of the month.

☐ "Wind roses" are a common graphic method for presenting wind data. The rose indicates frequency of occurrence, in percent of different wind speeds, for 16 directions. The size of the middle circle indicates the percent of time the wind is calm.

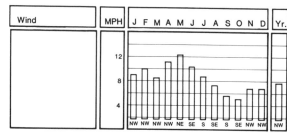

Wind Speed and Direction

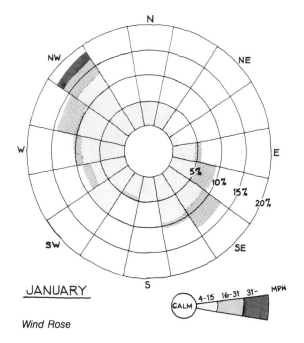

JANUARY

Wind Rose

Description	Wind ft/sec	Effects
Calm	0–2	Calm
Light air	5–7	No noticeable wind; direction shown by smoke.
Light breeze	9–12	Wind felt on face; newspaper reading becomes difficult.
Gentle breeze	14–17	Wind extends light flag; hair is disturbed; clothing flaps.
Moderate breeze	19–23	Dust, dry soil, and paper raised; rain and sleet driven; hair disarranged.
Fresh breeze	26–31	Force of wind felt on body; drifting snow becomes airborne; limit of agreeable wind on land.
Strong breeze	33–38	Umbrellas hard to use; difficulty walking and standing; wind noise in ears unpleasant; wind borne snow above head height (blizzard).
Near gale	40–48	Strong inconvenience felt when walking.
Gale	50–57	Generally impedes progress; great difficulty with balance in gusts.
Strong gale	59–66	People blown over by gusts; slight structural damage occurs; slate blown from roofs.
Storm	66 –	Seldom experienced on land; trees broken or uprooted; considerable structural damage occurs.

Wind Effects

Monticello
Charlottesville, Virginia
Architect: Thomas Jefferson

Thomas Jefferson's Monticello, near Charlottesville, Virginia, exemplifies excellent use of natural ventilation techniques. Through careful siting, Jefferson's design took advantage of natural features to achieve thermal comfort in Virginia's hot, humid summers. Contrary to the tradition of his day, Jefferson located Monticello on a hilltop rather than along a river's edge, to take full advantage of cooling breezes. He designed a floor plan to allow maximum cross ventilation throughout the house by means of strategically placed large windows. Covered arcades and porticoes contribute to the cooling effect by allowing air of lower-than-ambient temperatures into the building.

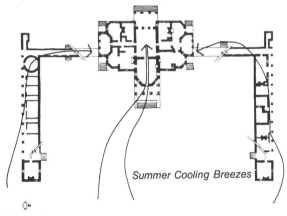

Summer Cooling Breezes

Monticello
Charlottesville, Virginia
Architect: Thomas Jefferson

Jefferson also induced natural ventilation by building Monticello's outbuildings with connecting underground passageways. Cool air from these subterranean passageways moves past wine cellars and food storage areas into the main portion of the house to replace warm air leaving it by convection. The operable skylights above Monticello's narrow interior stairways may have functioned as thermal chimneys for cooling the upper floors of the house.

Jefferson used massive brick construction at Monticello to reduce the direct gain of heat during the daytime hours and to delay transmission of the heat to the building's interior until late evening or night. These excellent cooling techniques make Monticello a cool, dry retreat even during the worst heat of August.

Monticello
Charlottesville, Virginia
Architect: Thomas Jefferson

Museum of Science and Industry
Tampa, Florida
Architect: Rowe Holmes Associates,
Architects

A modern day counterpart to Monticello that uses the wind for natural ventilation is the Museum of Science and Industry in Tampa, Fla. Designed by Rowe Holmes, the building not only houses exhibits of the area's heritage but is itself a learning tool to educate the public about energy and the environment.

The large space-frame roof, which connects the two rhomboidal masses of the building, is designed to capture prevailing east and northeast winds and channel them through the exhibit space by convection. Vents where the building planes intersect further channel the wind, and the system as a whole keeps the temperature 20 degrees (F.) cooler than the outdoors.

Museum of Science and Industry
Tampa, Florida
Architect: Rowe Holmes Associates, Architects

The roof also collects rain water (used for water energy technology exhibits) and will house a photovoltaic cell array in the near future.

Again responding to Tampa's climate, the museum rejects the traditional enclosed envelope in favor of a space two-thirds open. The envelope itself is built of insulating concrete block to further conserve energy. The two building masses are articulated by a break in the space frame caused by a linear skylight, which brings energy-saving daylight into the building's atrium. Light monitors bring natural light farther into the building.

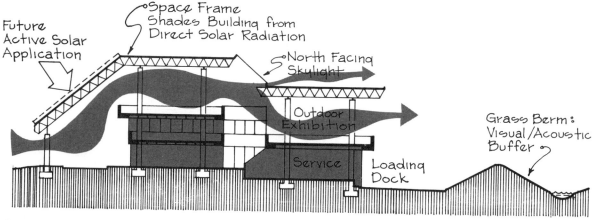

Museum of Science and Industry
Tampa, Florida
Architect: Rowe Holmes Associates, Architects

Museum of Science and Industry
Tampa, Florida
Architect: Rowe Holmes Associates, Architects

Precipitation and Weather Anomalies

Precipitation and weather anomalies, depending on the region, may also influence site selection and design strategies. Dense ground fog off the coast of San Francisco, for example, could influence building and solar collector orientation.

☐ The NOAA LCDs, which were originally developed for agricultural purposes, include precipitation data on monthly averages and extremes for rain and snow. For design purposes, the Tennessee Valley Authority has developed a graphic format for precipitation data.

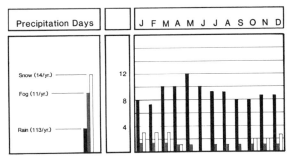

Precipitation Days

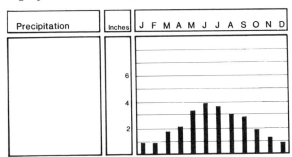

Precipitation

☐ Weather patterns and anomalies are most often found in narrative descriptions, such as those in the LCDs, the Gale Research Company's *Climate of the States* and various other climate-related publications.

☐ Only recently have these weather events been placed in graphic format, such as the data on summer warm-fronts prepared by TVA for its region.

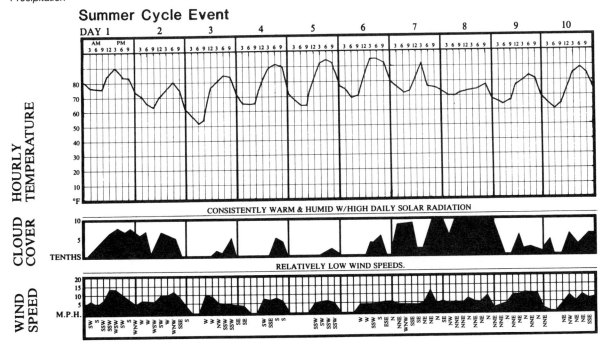

Weather Event (Graphic)

□ Narratives, as well as graphs, describe typical weather patterns that affect energy-conscious design. The following example is excerpted from "New State Office Building, Eighth and P Streets, Sacramento, California" by the Office of the California State Architect (1977).

□ Disastrous results can occur if the designer ignores clues presented by weather anomalies data. The accompanying photo shows devastation caused by flooding.

These are the last 5 days of a 9 day period in which fog blanketed the central valley below the 1000 to 1200 foot level. Often in the absence of a procession of winter storms across the valley at short intervals, a stable air mass forms in the central valley and lies stagnant. Extensive radiation cooling of the valley floor in still air causes the formation of dense ground or "tule" fog.

If the valley air mass is stable enough, the fog will persist for days, rising to form cloud cover during the warmer day and falling to ground level at night. The high humidity and lack of sunlight make this weather patterns distinctly uncomfortable, even though temperatures are in the low to mid 40's. The end of this pattern is dependent on other strong weather events, such as rainstorms or "northers".

In the event plotted the fog cycle was finally ended by a "norther". This event is the end of a longer than average series, but its conditions are entirely consistent with shorter events. Successions of 4 or more foggy days are common in Sacramento and an entire week of fog will occur once or twice each winter.

Weather Event (Narrative)

Flood Damage

Correlations

As with many facets of architectural design, the sum of the parts of climatic factors is different from the whole. Temperature, humidity, wind and sun data are pertinent to different design strategies, but must be considered simultaneously to gain a true picture of a site's climate. Correlations can most easily be made to temperature data, which is the base condition for judging comfort. A temperature of 77 degrees (F.), for example, can be comfortable on some days but too warm if accompanied by high humidity or intense sun.

☐ A psychrometric chart describes the relation between dry-bulb temperature, wet-bulb temperature and relative humidity. Plotting any two of these numbers will yield the third one. If the plot of actual data falls within the "comfort zone," the outside conditions on the site will be comfortable. By the accompanying method, the designer can construct a "climate envelope" that will describe annual external conditions.

☐ The overlay of the climate envelope on the psychometric chart will indicate the passive design strategies to alleviate conditions that would otherwise require mechanical heating and air-conditioning.

☐ Wind/Temperature correlations also help define the true nature of a climate. This effect is well-known as the wind-chill factor, which is expressed in terms of equivalent temperature. Wind/temperature correlations are especially important in colder climates.

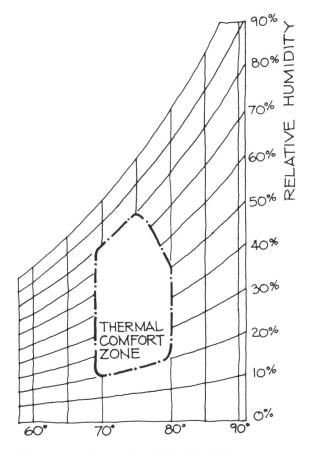

Comfort Zone

Wind Speed (m.p.h.)	Local Temperature (°F)										
	32	23	14	5	−4	−13	−22	−31	−40	−49	−58
	Equivalent Temperature (°F)										
CALM	32	23	14	5	−4	−13	−22	−31	−40	−49	−58
5	29	20	10	1	−9	−18	−28	−37	−47	−56	−65
10	18	7	−4	−15	−26	−37	−48	−59	−70	−81	−92
15	13	−1	−13	−25	−37	−49	−61	−73	−85	−97	−109
20	7	−6	−19	−32	−44	−57	−70	−83	−90	−109	−121
25	3	−10	−24	−37	−50	−64	−77	−90	−104	−117	−130
30	1	−13	−27	−41	−54	−68	−82	−97	−109	−123	−137
35	−1	−15	−20	−43	−57	−71	−85	−99	−113	−127	−142
40	−3	−17	−31	−45	−59	−74	−87	−102	−116	−131	−145
45	−3	−18	−32	−46	−61	−75	−89	−104	−118	−132	−147
50	−4	−18	−33	−47	−62	−76	−91	−105	−120	−134	−148
	Little Danger For Properly Clothed Persons			Considerable Danger			Very Great Danger				

Wind/Temperature Correlations

□ Computer generated "solar mountains," developed by Raymond Bahm, match solar radiation with mean daily temperatures. The elevations of the "mountains" document percent of simultaneous occurrence. Elevations to the left of the 65 degree (F.) line show a potential for solar heating. Elevations below 30 to 40 percent indicate low potential for significant solar contribution. Elevations in the upper right quadrant are the solar design optimum.

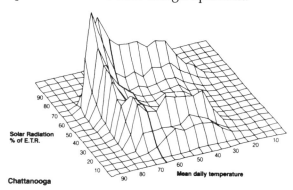

Solar Radiation % of E.T.R.

Mean daily temperature

Chattanooga

Albuquerque   Santa Maria, Ca.

Sun/Temperature Correlations

Chattanooga's "solar mountain" shows numerous cloudy days (low percentages of extraterrestrial radiation) as well as sunny days—a difficult solar location. Albuquerque (left) gets consistently higher insolation across the temperature range—an ideal solar location. Santa Maria's moderate winters and sunny conditions present an excellent opportunity for passive design solutions.

An Annual Climate Envelope, superimposed on a psychrometric chart, can give the designer indications of appropriate design strategies based on climate.

1. From the "Monthly Summary Sheets" of NOAA's *Local Climatological Data*, collect temperature and humidity data. Take the average monthly temperature (and its corresponding humidity) at 3 P.M.; and the average monthly temperature (and its corresponding humidity) at 3 A.M.

Example: (Minneapolis, June 1970)

	°F 3 A.M.	% RH		°F 3 P.M.	% RH
J					
F					
M					
A					
M					
J	64	79		79	51
J					
A					
S					
O					
N					
D					

2. Record monthly record high and low temperatures from NOAA's Annual Summary Sheet.

Example:

	Record High	Record Low
J		
F		
M		
A		
M		
J	99	37
J		
A		
S		
O		
N		
D		

Record High and Low Temperatures

3. On the psychrometric chart, plot a line for each month including:
— Average temperature and relative humidity at 3 A.M.; average temperature and relative humidity at 3 P.M. Connect the two points (a).
— Extend the line to record high and record low temperatures for each month (b).
— Determine the midpoints between both sets (a) and (b) points for each month. These midpoints will be connected to form the annual climate envelope(c).
— Where the climate envelope coincides with design strategies on the psychrometric chart, the strategies should be considered for externally dominated buildings.

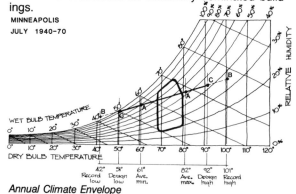

MINNEAPOLIS
JULY 1940-70

WET BULB TEMPERATURE

RELATIVE HUMIDITY

DRY BULB TEMPERATURE

| 42° | 51° | 61° | | 82° | 92° | 101° |
| Record low | Design low | Ave. min. | | Ave. max. | Design high | Record high |

Annual Climate Envelope

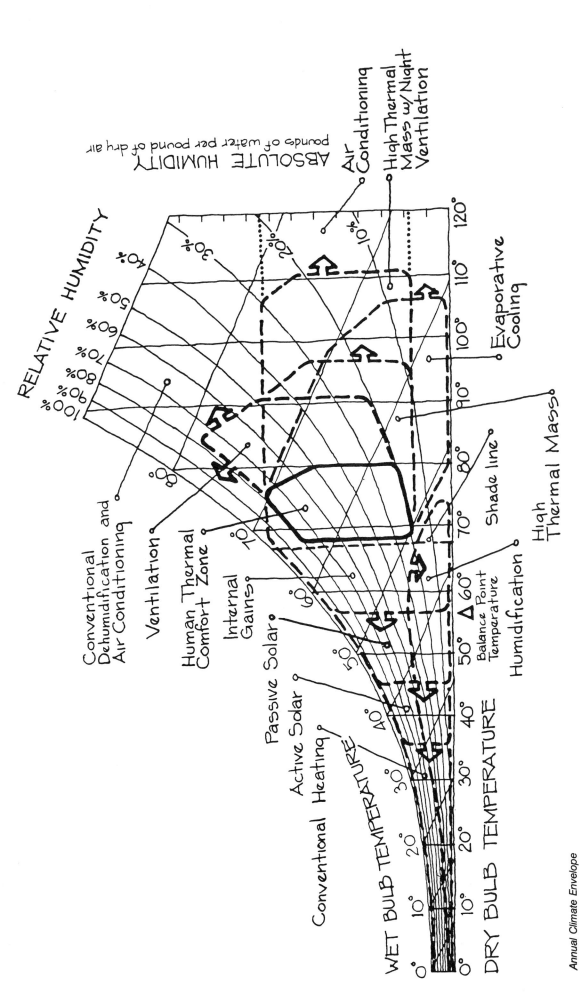

Annual Climate Envelope

Source: Givoni, Baruch and Milne, Murray, ©1981. Reprinted by permission of authors.

Site Analysis and Data

When faced with unfavorable climatic conditions, the designer will often find that optimal siting and site design can be more effective and less costly than mechanical means of making interiors comfortable.

☐ Once climatic data have been collected for a site, the general climatic picture presented must be coupled with analysis of particular site elements—topography, vegetation, water conditions on site, and built forms—all of which can affect the site's microclimate.

☐ The basic information needed for the site analysis includes:

Site Element	Source

Topography
   —Elevation
   —Hills and valleys
   —Slopes
   —Surface conditions
      (including reflections)
	Aerial photographs, contour maps, geological surveys, soil surveys.

Vegetation
   —Height
   —Mass
   —Silhouette
   —Texture (penetrability)
   —Location
   —Growth patterns
	Site analysis by investigation; knowledge of native and introduced vegetation; age, condition and utility of each existing plant type.

Water
   —Location
   —Ground water temperature
   —Existing aquifers
      and drainage patterns
	Aerial photographs, site surveys, local utility companies.

Built Forms
   —Location
   —Height
   —Surface conditions
   —Development plans
      on adjacent sites
	Sanborn maps, aerial photographs, local zoning ordinances and building codes, jurisdictional development plans.

☐ The designer may want to map individual site elements on overlays to get a composite view of their effects. Energy-conscious site analysis uses basically the same tools and methods used in traditional site analysis—it is only the interpretation and emphasis that are changed. The climatic and site analysis presented here determine only the *external* factors affecting building design. Only when the building's form and envelope are conceived, and its *internal* factors accounted for, can the concept of thermal balance be applied.

These preliminary site analyses were done by Johnson, Johnson & Roy for Newport West, a low-density townhouse development on a 60-acre site northeast of Ann Arbor, Mich. The major goals of the study were to provide a buffer strip to the east of the site, protect the natural habitat of a bordering hardwood forest, and take advantage of solar energy. The plan, which used cluster development, permitted 75 percent of the units to be favorably oriented toward the sun.

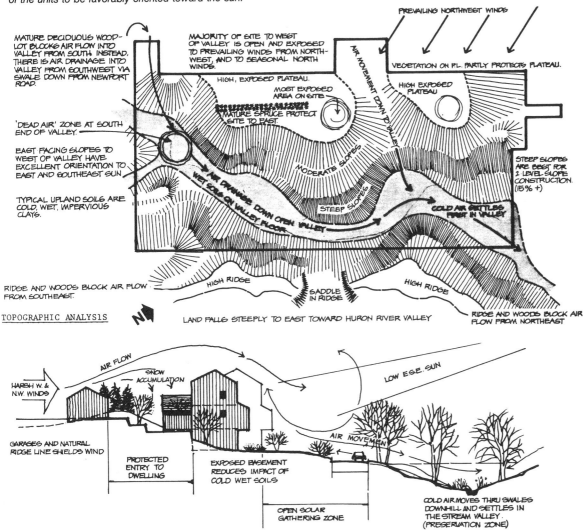

PREVAILING NORTHWEST WINDS

MATURE DECIDUOUS WOOD-LOT BLOCKS AIR FLOW INTO VALLEY FROM SOUTH. INSTEAD, THERE IS AIR DRAINAGE INTO VALLEY FROM SOUTHWEST VIA SWALE DOWN FROM NEWPORT ROAD.

MAJORITY OF SITE TO WEST OF VALLEY IS OPEN AND EXPOSED TO PREVAILING WINDS FROM NORTH-WEST, AND TO SEASONAL NORTH WINDS.

VEGETATION ON PL. PARTLY PROTECTS PLATEAU.

HIGH, EXPOSED PLATEAU.

MOST EXPOSED AREA ON SITE

HIGH EXPOSED PLATEAU

AIR MOVEMENT DOWN P. VALLEY

MATURE SPRUCE PROTECT SITE TO EAST.

'DEAD AIR' ZONE AT SOUTH END OF VALLEY.

EAST FACING SLOPES TO WEST OF VALLEY HAVE EXCELLENT ORIENTATION TO EAST AND SOUTHEAST SUN

TYPICAL UPLAND SOILS ARE COLD, WET, IMPERVIOUS CLAYS.

MODERATE SLOPES

AIR DRAINAGE DOWN OPEN VALLEY WET SOILS ON VALLEY FLOOR

STEEP SLOPES

STEEP SLOPES ARE BEST FOR 2 LEVEL SLOPE CONSTRUCTION. (15% +)

COLD AIR SETTLES FIRST IN VALLEY

RIDGE AND WOODS BLOCK AIR FLOW FROM SOUTHEAST.

HIGH RIDGE

SADDLE IN RIDGE

HIGH RIDGE

RIDGE AND WOODS BLOCK AIR FLOW FROM NORTHEAST

TOPOGRAPHIC ANALYSIS

N

LAND FALLS STEEPLY TO EAST TOWARD HURON RIVER VALLEY

AIR FLOW

SNOW ACCUMULATION

HARSH W. & N.W. WINDS

LOW E.S.E. SUN

AIR MOVEMENT

GARAGES AND NATURAL RIDGE LINE SHIELDS WIND

PROTECTED ENTRY TO DWELLING

EXPOSED BASEMENT REDUCES IMPACT OF COLD WET SOILS

OPEN SOLAR GATHERING ZONE

COLD AIR MOVES THRU SWALES DOWNHILL AND SETTLES IN THE STREAM VALLEY. (PRESERVATION ZONE)

Newport West
Ann Arbor, Michigan
Architect: Johnson, Johnson & Roy

Vegetation: Sun Control

The effects of vegetation on a site's microclimate can be considerable: trees can reduce both sunlight and windspeeds by 90 percent, and temperatures by 15 degrees (F.). In addition, vegetation can usually be manipulated more easily than topography or adjacent buildings.

☐ Deciduous trees are nature's answer to passive shading control because they shed their leaves in the winter when solar insolation is most welcome. Branches will still block a portion of the sun, as demonstrated by the accompanying graph.

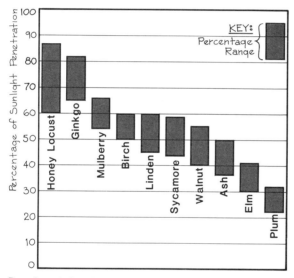

Bare Branch Sun Penetration for Various Tree Species

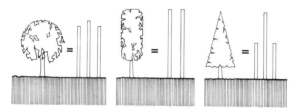

Set of Poles Represent Various Tree Crown Types

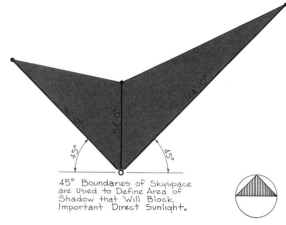

45° Boundaries of Skyspace are Used to Define Area of Shadow that Will Block Important Direct Sunlight.

Shadow Pattern of a Pole (Dec. 21 at 40° N Latitude on 10°/ SE. Slope)

☐ Aerial photographs indicate the shadows thrown by vegetation onto the site. Flag pole diagrams are another simple method of calculating shadows. The example presented calculates shadows for winter (worst-shadow condition) during the hours of usable sunlight (approximately 8 A.M. to 4 P.M.). If more detailed calculations are desirable, the values can be calculated for other times of the year or day. A pole is used because it is the simplest ground-anchored object that can cast a shadow. More complex objects such as trees or buildings can be represented by a composite of poles to calculate their shadow patterns.

☐ These adjoining tables give the shadow length on December 21st of a one-foot pole for varying latitudes and directions and degrees of slopes. The A.M. and P.M. values correspond to 45 degrees azimuths that are used to define the day's period of usable solar radiation. The figures are rounded off, and there may be some errors in shadow length for steeper slopes or taller buildings at 45 degrees and 48 degrees north latitude where the rounding off error may be multiplied extensively.

Latitude 25°

SLOPE	N AM	N NOON	N PM	NE AM	NE NOON	NE PM	E AM	E NOON	E PM	SE AM	SE NOON	SE PM	S AM	S NOON	S PM	SW AM	SW NOON	SW PM	W AM	W NOON	W PM	NW AM	NW NOON	NW PM
0%	2.1	1.1	2.1	2.1	1.1	2.1	2.1	1.1	2.1	2.1	1.1	2.1	2.1	1.1	2.1	2.1	1.1	2.1	2.1	1.1	2.1	2.1	1.1	2.1
5%	2.3	1.2	2.3	2.1	1.2	2.4	2.0	1.1	2.3	1.9	1.1	2.1	2.0	1.1	2.0	2.1	1.1	1.9	2.3	1.1	2.0	2.4	1.2	2.1
10%	2.5	1.3	2.5	2.1	1.2	2.7	1.8	1.1	2.5	1.7	1.0	2.1	1.7	1.0	1.8	2.1	1.0	1.7	2.5	1.1	1.8	2.7	1.2	2.1
15%	2.7	1.4	2.7	2.1	1.3	3.1	1.7	1.1	2.7	1.6	1.0	2.1	1.7	1.0	1.7	2.1	1.0	1.6	2.7	1.1	1.7	3.1	1.3	2.1
20%	3.0	1.5	3.0	2.1	1.4	3.6	1.6	1.2	3.0	1.5	1.0	2.1	1.6	0.9	1.6	2.1	1.0	1.5	3.0	1.2	1.6	3.6	1.4	2.1

Latitude 30°

SLOPE	N AM	N NOON	N PM	NE AM	NE NOON	NE PM	E AM	E NOON	E PM	SE AM	SE NOON	SE PM	S AM	S NOON	S PM	SW AM	SW NOON	SW PM	W AM	W NOON	W PM	NW AM	NW NOON	NW PM
0%	2.7	1.3	2.7	2.7	1.3	2.7	2.7	1.3	2.7	2.7	1.3	2.7	2.7	1.3	2.7	2.7	1.3	2.7	2.7	1.3	2.7	2.7	1.3	2.7
5%	2.9	1.4	2.9	2.7	1.4	3.1	2.4	1.4	2.9	2.4	1.3	2.7	2.4	1.3	2.4	2.7	1.3	2.4	2.9	1.4	2.4	3.1	1.4	2.7
10%	3.3	1.6	3.3	2.7	1.5	3.6	2.2	1.4	3.3	2.1	1.2	2.7	2.2	1.2	2.2	2.7	1.2	2.1	3.3	1.4	2.2	3.6	1.5	2.7
15%	3.7	1.7	3.7	2.7	1.6	4.4	2.1	1.4	3.7	1.9	1.2	2.7	2.1	1.1	2.1	2.7	1.2	1.9	3.7	1.4	2.1	4.4	1.6	2.7
20%	4.3	1.9	4.3	2.7	1.7	5.7	1.9	1.4	4.3	1.7	1.2	2.7	1.9	1.1	1.9	2.7	1.2	1.7	4.3	1.4	1.9	5.7	1.7	2.7

Latitude 35°

SLOPE	N AM	N NOON	N PM	NE AM	NE NOON	NE PM	E AM	E NOON	E PM	SE AM	SE NOON	SE PM	S AM	S NOON	S PM	SW AM	SW NOON	SW PM	W AM	W NOON	W PM	NW AM	NW NOON	NW PM
0%	3.5	1.6	3.5	3.5	1.6	3.5	3.5	1.6	3.5	3.5	1.6	3.5	3.5	1.6	3.5	3.5	1.6	3.5	3.5	1.6	3.5	3.5	1.6	3.5
5%	4.0	1.8	4.0	3.5	1.7	4.2	3.1	1.6	4.0	3.0	1.5	3.5	3.1	1.5	3.1	3.5	1.5	3.0	4.0	1.6	3.1	4.2	1.7	3.5
10%	4.6	2.0	4.6	3.5	1.8	5.3	2.8	1.6	4.6	2.6	1.5	3.5	2.8	1.4	2.8	3.5	1.5	2.6	4.6	1.6	2.8	5.3	1.8	3.5
15%	5.5	2.2	5.5	3.5	2.0	7.2	2.5	1.6	5.5	2.3	1.4	3.5	2.5	1.3	2.5	3.5	1.4	2.3	5.5	1.6	2.5	7.2	2.0	3.5
20%	6.8	2.5	6.8	3.5	2.2	11.4	2.3	1.7	6.8	2.0	1.3	3.5	2.3	1.3	2.3	3.5	1.3	2.0	6.8	1.7	2.3	11.4	2.2	3.5

Latitude 40°

SLOPE	N AM	N NOON	N PM	NE AM	NE NOON	NE PM	E AM	E NOON	E PM	SE AM	SE NOON	SE PM	S AM	S NOON	S PM	SW AM	SW NOON	SW PM	W AM	W NOON	W PM	NW AM	NW NOON	NW PM
0%	4.8	2.0	4.8	4.8	2.0	4.8	4.8	2.0	4.8	4.8	2.0	4.8	4.8	2.0	4.8	4.8	2.0	4.8	4.8	2.0	4.8	4.8	2.0	4.8
5%	5.7	2.2	5.7	4.8	2.2	6.2	4.1	2.0	5.7	3.8	1.9	4.8	4.1	1.8	4.1	4.8	1.9	3.8	5.7	2.0	4.1	6.2	2.2	4.8
10%	7.2	2.5	7.2	4.8	2.3	9.1	3.6	2.0	7.2	3.2	1.8	4.8	3.6	1.7	3.6	4.8	1.8	3.2	7.2	2.0	3.6	9.1	2.3	4.8
15%	9.6	2.9	9.6	4.8	2.6	16.6	3.2	2.0	9.1	2.8	1.7	4.8	3.2	1.6	3.2	4.8	1.7	2.8	9.6	2.0	3.2	16.6	2.6	4.8
20%	14.5	3.4	14.5	4.8	2.8	97.5	2.8	2.0	14.5	2.4	1.6	4.8	2.8	1.5	2.8	4.8	1.6	2.4	14.5	2.0	2.8	97.5	2.8	4.8

Latitude 45°

SLOPE	N AM	N NOON	N PM	NE AM	NE NOON	NE PM	E AM	E NOON	E PM	SE AM	SE NOON	SE PM	S AM	S NOON	S PM	SW AM	SW NOON	SW PM	W AM	W NOON	W PM	NW AM	NW NOON	NW PM
0%	7.2	2.5	7.2	7.2	2.5	7.2	7.2	2.5	7.2	7.2	2.5	7.2	7.2	2.5	7.2	7.2	2.5	7.2	7.2	2.5	7.2	7.2	2.5	7.2
5%	9.6	2.9	9.6	7.2	2.8	11.2	5.7	2.5	9.6	5.3	2.3	7.2	5.7	2.2	5.7	7.2	2.3	5.3	9.6	2.5	5.7	11.2	2.8	7.2
10%	14.6	3.4	14.6	7.2	3.1	25.6	4.8	2.5	14.6	4.2	2.2	7.2	4.8	2.0	4.8	7.2	2.2	4.2	14.6	2.5	4.8	25.6	3.1	7.2
15%	30.3	4.1	30.3	7.2	3.5	—	4.1	2.6	30.3	3.5	2.0	7.2	4.1	1.9	4.1	7.2	2.0	3.5	30.3	2.6	4.1	—	3.5	7.2
20%	—	5.2	—	7.2	4.0	—	3.6	2.6	—	2.9	1.9	7.2	3.6	1.7	3.6	7.2	1.9	2.9	—	2.6	3.6	—	4.0	7.2

Latitude 48°

SLOPE	N AM	N NOON	N PM	NE AM	NE NOON	NE PM	E AM	E NOON	E PM	SE AM	SE NOON	SE PM	S AM	S NOON	S PM	SW AM	SW NOON	SW PM	W AM	W NOON	W PM	NW AM	NW NOON	NW PM
0%	10.1	3.0	10.1	10.1	3.3	10.1	10.1	3.0	10.1	10.1	3.0	10.1	10.1	3.0	10.1	10.1	3.0	10.1	10.1	3.0	10.1	10.1	3.0	10.1
5%	15.8	3.5	15.8	10.1	3.3	20.5	7.5	3.0	15.8	6.7	2.7	10.1	7.5	2.6	7.5	10.1	2.7	6.7	15.8	3.0	7.5	20.5	3.3	10.1
10%	35.7	4.3	35.7	10.1	3.8	—	5.9	3.0	35.7	5.0	2.5	10.1	5.9	2.3	5.9	10.1	2.5	5.0	35.7	3.0	5.9	—	3.8	10.1
15%	—	5.4	—	10.1	4.4	—	4.9	3.0	—	4.0	2.3	10.1	4.9	2.1	4.9	10.1	2.3	4.0	—	3.0	4.9	—	4.4	10.1
20%	—	7.5	—	10.1	5.2	—	4.2	3.0	—	3.3	2.1	10.1	4.2	1.9	4.2	10.1	2.1	3.3	—	3.0	4.2	—	5.2	10.1

Shadow Length Tables

Calculating the Shadow Pattern of a Pole:
—pole is 30' high
—latitude of location is 40 degrees (F.)
—pole is on land that slopes to the southeast at a
 10 percent grade.

Step 1
In the accompanying Shadow Length Tables, go to
the appropriate latitude (in this case 40 degrees
(F.)) and read from the intersection of the "10
percent" and "S.F." columns.

Step 2
The values given in the table are for a 1 foot pole,
so they must be multiplied by the height of the
pole, in this case 30 feet.
A.M. Value times Pole Height equals A.M. Shadow
Length
$$(3.2 \times 30' = 96')$$
Noon Value times Pole Height equals Noon Length
$$(1.8 \times 30' = 54')$$
P.M. Value times Pole Height equals P.M. Length
$$(4.8 \times 30' = 144')$$

Step 3
Scale the shadow lengths out on paper as viewed
from overhead and connect the end points.

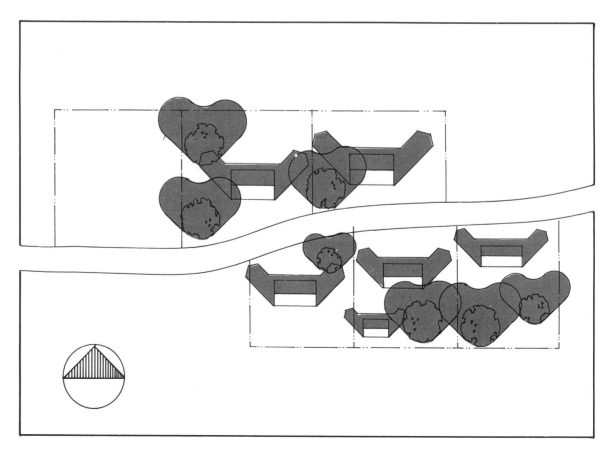

Shadow Patterns

Vegetation: Wind Control

Vegetation can have a considerable effect on the wind patterns of a site. Plants control the wind by obstructing, deflecting or guiding its flow, depending on the position and physical characteristics of the plant.

☐ Cooler winds flow downhill at night. Dense evergreen plants placed on a slope trap and hold cold wind flow upwind, thus creating cool spaces. Loose, deciduous plants create cool spaces on the downwind side by filtering the air.

COMMON NAME	Shape			Rate of Growth			Hardiness Zones									
	Columnar	Conical	Spreading	Slow	Medium	Fast	1	2	3	4	5	6	7	8	9	10
White fir		•				•				•						
Blue atlas cedar		•	•	•								•				
Deodar cedar		•		•									•			
Lawson false cypress	•	•		•							•					
Sawara false cypress	•	•		•					•							
Common China fir			•	•									•			
Italian pyramidal cypress	•			•									•			
Chinese juniper		•		•	•	•				•						
Western red cedar	•			•							•					
Eastern red cedar	•	•		•				•								
California incense cedar	•	•		•								•				
Dawn redwood		•				•					•					
Spruce																
Pine																
Yew podocarpus	•			•									•			
Golden larch		•	•	•								•				
Douglas fir		•	•	•	•						•					
Umbrella pine	•	•		•								•				
English yew		•	•	•								•				
Irish yew	•			•								•				
American arborvitae	•	•		•					•							
Giant arborvitae	•	•		•								•				

Physical Characteristics of Trees

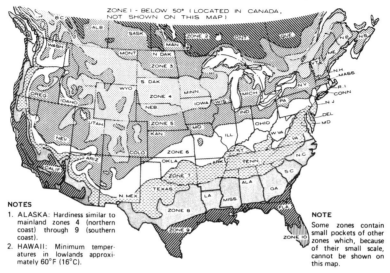

ZONE I - BELOW 50° (LOCATED IN CANADA, NOT SHOWN ON THIS MAP)

NOTE

The zone map shows in moderate detail the expected minimum temperature of most of the horticulturally important areas of the United States. Plants are listed in the coldest zone where they will grow normally, but they can be expected to grow in warmer areas.

APPROXIMATE RANGE OF AVERAGE ANNUAL MINIMUM TEMPERATURES FOR EACH ZONE

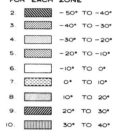

2.		−50° TO −40°
3.		−40° TO −30°
4.		−30° TO −20°
5.		−20° TO −10°
6.		−10° TO 0°
7.		0° TO 10°
8.		10° TO 20°
9.		20° TO 30°
10.		30° TO 40°

NOTES

1. ALASKA: Hardiness similar to mainland zones 4 (northern coast) through 9 (southern coast).
2. HAWAII: Minimum temperatures in lowlands approximately 60°F (16°C).

NOTE

Some zones contain small pockets of other zones which, because of their small scale, cannot be shown on this map.

Zones of Plant Hardiness

Source: The American Institute of Architects, *Architectural Graphic Standards Seventh Edition*, ©1981. Reprinted by permission of John Wiley & Sons, New York, New York.

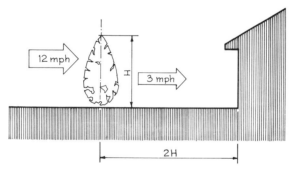

Wind Reduction

(A 20 foot Austrian Pine will reduce 12 m.p.h. winds to 3 m.p.h. for 40 feet on its leeward side.)

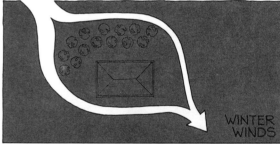

WINTER WINDS

SUMMER WINDS

Use of Windbreaks

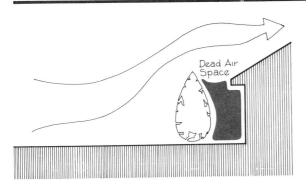

Dead Air Space Effect

☐ Hemlock, spruce, or other dense evergreens planted close together to form a solid wall along a building will create an area of dead air, much like a dead air space in the wall of a house. The temperature gradient between the inside of the building and the dead air space will be reduced and held relatively constant, thus preventing the escape of heat from the building.

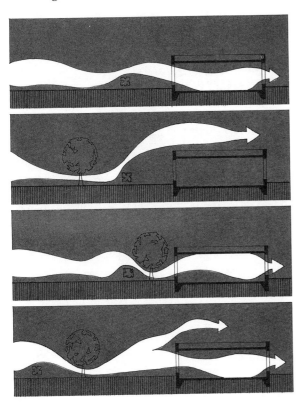

Wind Flow Effects

☐ Shelterbelts and windbreaks are most effective when placed perpendicular to prevailing winds. Wind velocity can be reduced by 50 percent for a distance of from 10 to 20 times the tree height downwind of a shelterbelt, with the degree of protection and wind reduction depending on the height, wind, length and penetrability of the plants used.

☐ Wind speed is also affected within or on the windward side of a windbreak. The wind speed is reduced for a distance of 300 feet on the windward or front side of a 30 foot high shelterbelt, for example, and is reduced for a distance of 900 feet downwind or behind the shelterbelt.

☐ The zone of wind reduction on the leeward and windward side of a barrier depends largely on the height of the barrier. The taller the trees, the more rows of trees are required for protection, because taller trees create more open shelterbelts. Instead of reducing the wind, avenues of trees open at the trunks can be used to increase wind speed, as the air stream is forced beneath the tree canopy.

☐ Trees can reduce wind velocity for an area extending 30 to 40 times the height of the trees leeward of the windbreak; the sharpest reduction in wind velocity extends from 10 to 15 times the height of the trees. Maximum shelter from the wind occurs at 3 to 5 times the tree height on the leeward side. The deeper the windbreak, the less penetrable it is. Depth has a negligible influence on reducing wind velocity at its leeward edge, but causes notable variation in the microclimate within the sheltered area. In a forest, for example, wind velocity is most reduced within the forest itself. The accompanying diagram, which shows the flow of wind over a forest block and a narrow shelterbelt, illustrates the influence the depth of a windbreak has on reducing flow.

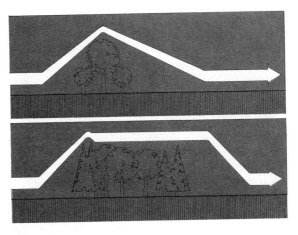

Diagram of Wind Flow

☐ An irregular windbreak that looks like the top of a picket fence is more effective than a uniform one in breaking up the airstream deflected over it. A mixture of plant species and sizes gives the windbreak a rough upper surface more effective in controlling wind.

☐ The most efficient ratio of height to length for windbreaks is 1:11.5. This ratio produces the greatest possible shelter effect, at least near the center of the shelterbelt. Air current sweeping around shelterbelts increases wind velocity, creating speeds at both ends of windbreaks that are higher than found in an open field.

☐ Frequent gaps in a shelterbelt can greatly increase wind velocity within the gap, but this draft does not extend laterally or affect wind abatement at a distance from the gap.

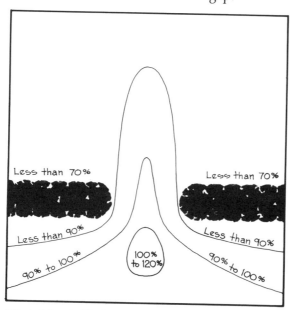

Effect of Gap in Windbreak on Percentage of Wind Velocity

☐ The more penetrable the windbreak, the longer the protected distance behind the windbreak. According to laboratory testing, when a windbreak is completely impenetrable, practically the entire wind force is deflected upward, over the barrier. Pressure behind the barrier is low because the wind does not pass through the barrier, causing a suction effect and forcing the air currents above the windbreaks downward. Shelterbelts with a cross section resembling a pitched roof are less effective in blocking winds than are those with vertical edges.

☐ Although a dense shelterbelt can provide a greater degree of shelter from the wind on the leeward, it provides a restricted zone of effective shelter downwind. A penetrable shelterbelt does not greatly reduce wind near the screen; but its overall effects extend a greater distance beyond. A penetrable shelterbelt has less suction than a dense one and it more gradually accelerates wind back to its original force. The optimum density for a shelterbelt is about 50 to 60 percent. This means that the leaves, branches, twigs and trunks should cover 60 percent of the frontal area of the belt. With this density, shallow belts will afford as much shelter as deeper belts of the same overall penetrability.

☐ Trees reduce windspeed by increasing resistance to air flow. In general, coniferous evergreens that branch to the ground are the most effective plants for year-round wind control. Deciduous trees are most effective for summer wind control. Wind velocity directly leeward of a dense spruce planting will be reduced 15 to 25 percent, and a loose barrier of Lombardy poplar will reduce velocity by 40 percent. Twelve m.p.h. winds will be reduced to three m.p.h. for a distance of 40 feet leeward of a 20 foot Austrian Pine. In landscaping a building to enhance wind control, the architect should consider the shape, growth rate and hardiness of the trees selected.

☐ Prevailing winds may change direction seasonally; therefore, plants should be of the type best suited for controlling winds from all directions. A dense coniferous windbreak on the northwest side of a structure, for instance, can protect it from harsh winter winds, and direct summer breezes around it. Wind can be slowed down or deflected to preserve warmth. It can also be accelerated and channeled through windbreak openings. The angle of the planting will control wind direction in reducing both interior heating and cooling.

Topography and Soil Conditions

Topography can greatly modify prevailing climatic conditions. The accompanying chart gives general modification effects of:
—elevation
—hills and valleys
—slopes
—aspects
—surface conditions, including reflectances.

☐ Elevation is a prime example of climate modifier. Temperature in the atmosphere decreases with altitude. In mountainous areas the temperature drops about 1 degree (F.) for every 330 foot rise in summer and for every 400 foot rise in winter.

☐ Mean wind speeds tend to increase with height. In mountainous areas at high altitudes where vegetation becomes very sparse, incoming short-wave radiation is not intercepted as it is at sea level by vegetation and physical features, and so tends to be greater. Averaged over a year, radiation at high elevations on cloudy days can be as much as 30 to 35 percent greater because diffuse radiation is intensified by the comparatively thin layer of cloud. Total precipitation also increases with height, and a greater percentage falls as snow rather than rain.

☐ Small differences in terrain can create remarkably large modifications in the microclimate. Cool air is heavier than warm air, and at night the outgoing radiation causes a cold-air layer to form near the ground surface. The cold air behaves like any liquid, flowing toward the lowest points. This flood of cold air causes islands of cold air. Accordingly, elevations that impede the flow of air affect the distribution of the nocturnal temperatures by dam action, and concave terrain formations become cold air lakes at night. The same phenomenon is enhanced when a large volume of cold air is involved, as in valleys.

☐ As an example, the valley walls and bottom surface cool off at night. Air flow occurs toward the valley floor. On the valley slopes, a series of smaller circulations mix with the neighboring warm air, causing intermediate temperature conditions. Accordingly, the temperatures at the plateau will be cold, and the valley floor will be *very* cold, but the higher sides of the slopes will remain warm. This latter area is referred to as the warm slope (thermal belt). In temperate zones, the thermal belt may be 10 degrees (F.) or more warmer than the valley, and therefore can be the most advantageous place for a building. However, if this location is exposed to crest winds that may offset higher temperatures, a more desirable place would be approximately halfway up the slope.

☐ Slopes influence wind speeds and directions and, indirectly, temperatures. Upslope and downslope winds can influence temperatures, either upward or downward, and inversions (warm air aloft) can cause cooler temperatures in valleys or at the base of slopes. Cold air drainage down slopes, especially at night and in cooler times of year, creates pockets of cold air and frost hollows. The angle of the slope determines the insolation of the surface.

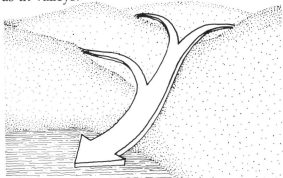

Cold Air Behaves Like a Liquid, Flowing Toward the Lowest Points

☐ The direction of the exposure of a slope, or "aspect" has an especially important effect on the amount of solar insolation received on a site. The accompanying figure shows the relationship between slope and aspect for three different times of the year, with the variations caused in the amount of insolation received.

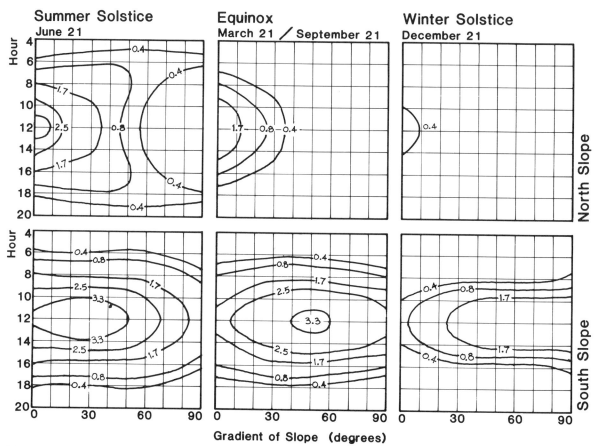

Influence of Aspect on Insolation

	Temperature			Humidity	Insolation		Wind	Precipitation	
	Minimum Temperature	Maximum Temperature	Heating Degree-Days	Humidity	Insolation	Cloud Cover	Wind Speed and Direction	Rainfall	Snowfall & Snow Cover
Elevation	Inverse relationship.	Inverse relationship.	Increase with height.	Fog moisture available to plants at greater heights.	Increases with height. Outgoing rad. remains same.	Increases with elevation. Fog also increases with height.	Increase speed with heights.	Rain increases with height. Proportion of rain of total precipitation decreases	Snowfall increases with height. Wetness of snow decreases with height.
Hills and Valleys	Frost follows & lower minimums Thermal band on slopes above valley inversion.	Max. temp. above valley on slope in winter. Max. temp. on valley floor rest of year.	Higher in valley than on slopes except at great heights.	Can trap moist air in valleys.	Can exclude early morning late afternoon radiation.	Cause increased cloudiness due to long-wave rad. decreased temp.	Passive effects greater as wind speed increases. Less wind in valleys except storms funnelled by valleys. Ventilation factor.	Windward and leeward slopes wet and dry respectively.	Snowfall increased on upper slopes except where swept by winds.
Slope	Cold air drainage can be directed. Direct relationship with speed of cold air drainage	Max. temp. highest at bottom of slope in summer. Variable location in winter.	Higher in valley than in thermal belt on above slope.	No direct influence.	Increases or decreases radiation, depending on slope angle.	Increased with slope angle.	Angle influences the speed of movement of cold air at night.	Windward and leeward slopes will be wet and dry (rain shadows) respectively.	Windward and leeward effects on snowfall.
Aspect	Aspect less important at night as temperature controlled by flow of cold air.	West slopes higher than east slopes. South slopes higher than north slopes. Valleys running N-S & south-facing slopes have highest max.	North-facing aspect will have higher HDD than south-facing aspect.	Absolute humidity not affected. Relative humidity is affected.	Will be most on south-facing & least on north-facing.	Extremely variable, depending upon time of year, air mass, etc.	Will depend on direction slope is facing and wind direction, e.g. windward or leeward.	Windward or leeward— either increase or decrease in rainfall.	Windard or leeward— either increase or decrease in snowfall. Snow cover greatest in NE slopes.
Nature of Surface	Higher with grass than with bare soil. Lowest with bare rock.	Lower with bare soil. Highest with bare rock.	Compaction of soil or surface can influence heating degree days.	Short grass evaporation greatest after rain. Water surface evaporation greatest on bright days and on days of drought.	High albedos reflect much radiation. Low albedos absorb shortwave and emit long-wave.	Low albedos can create convective clouds.	Roughness coefficient determines eddies and local currents.	No influence on rainfall but considerable on evaporation, percolation, run-off, etc.	No influence on snowfall but considerable influence on snow cover distribution.
Reflection	Can increase or decrease min. temperature considerably.	Can increase or decrease max. temperature considerably.	Can increase or decrease HDD.	Can increase or decrease evaporation & influence humidity.	Influences percentage of radiation absorbed.	Convective clouds predominate in the after- Layer clouds predominate after sunrise.	Can create pockets of ascending & descending air.	No direct influence.	Can influence snow cover e.g. localized melting.

Effects of Topography

☐ Ground surfaces such as asphalt, concrete or grass absorb, reflect and emit radiation in different ways, thus affecting its temperature, rainfall, and snow cover.

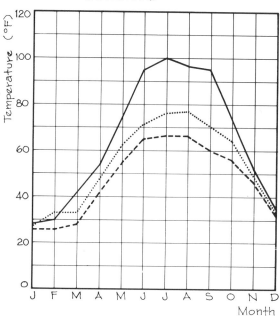

SURFACE
1. Black Asphalt ——————
2. Long Grass – – – – – – – –
   Outdoor Air ·····························

Monthly Surface Temperatures

Material	Surface Temp.	Dev. from Air
Dark Asphalt	124	+40
Light Asphalt (dirty)	112	+28
Concrete	108	+24
Short grass (1–2 inches)	104	+20
Bare ground	100	+16
Tall grass (36 inches)	96	+12

Surface Temperatures for Various Materials

☐ Soil type has a significance for underground buildings and basements. Tight clay soils, such as those that are highly impervious, require expensive water removal and waterproofing systems. The ideal type of soil for building is one which is highly permeable, permitting water to drain away rapidly. Soil temperature is also important, especially for underground structures.

☐ The relationships among wind speed, air temperatures and soil indicate that:

—wind speed increases with height above the ground
—in daytime the air temperature is highest just above the ground
—in summer, soil temperatures decrease with depth
—soil temperatures are highest in a very thin layer at the surface, often being well above the simultaneous air temperature.

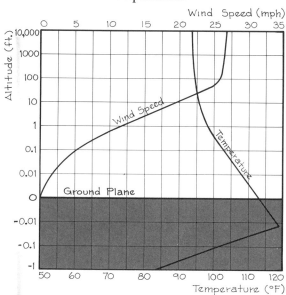

Relationship of Windspeed, Air Temperature and Soil Temperature

☐ Reflectance, or albedo, is a special characteristic of ground surfaces, important not only to thermal calculations, but also to daylighting strategies. Color, material and texture are all significant. Fresh snowfall, for example, creates a brilliant white surface that reflects more than 75 percent of the incoming solar radiation.

Surface	Reflectance %
Fresh snow cover	75–95
Dense cloud cover	60–90
Old snow cover	40–70
Clean firm snow	50–65
Light sand dunes, surf	30–60
Clean glacier ice	30–46
Dirty firm snow	20–50
Dirty glacier ice	20–30
Sandy soil	15–40
Meadows and fields	12–30
Densely built-up areas	15–25
Woods	5–20
Dark cultivated soil	7–10
Water surfaces, sea	3–10

Reflectances of Various Surfaces

Water

Site proximity to bodies of water also affects the microclimate. Because water has a higher specific heat than land, it is normally warmer in winter and cooler in summer, and usually cooler during the day and warmer at night, than the terrain. Accordingly, the proximity of bodies of water moderates extreme temperature variations, raising the temperature lows in winter and lowering the temperature highs in summer. At the largest scale, oceans and ocean currents have great impact on the temperature of coastal areas, where the water temperatures may be 30 degrees (F.) warmer than adjacent surfaces.

☐ Smaller bodies of water affect site conditions as well. For example, in the Great Lakes region, this effect raises the average January temperatures about 5 degrees (F.), the absolute minimum temperature about 10 degrees (F.), and the annual minimum about 15 degrees (F.). Average July temperature is decreased about 3 degrees (F.), with the annual absolute maximum decreased about 5 degrees (F.).

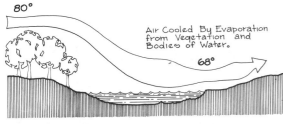

Cooling Effects of Water

☐ Water bodies also affect day-to-night temperature swings. In the diurnal temperature variations, when the land is warmer than the water, low cool air moves over the land to replace the updraft. During the day, such offshore breezes may have a cooling effect of 10 degrees (F.). At night the direction is reversed. The effects depend on the size of the body of water and are more strongly felt along the lee side.

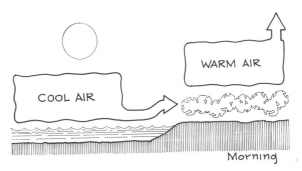

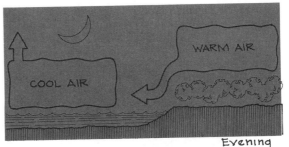

Diurnal Temperature Effects of Water

☐ The energy-conscious designer also needs to consider the ground water temperature. High ground water temperatures may indicate potential savings through effective use of solar hot water and heat pump systems. Water table levels can also influence the use of underground construction.

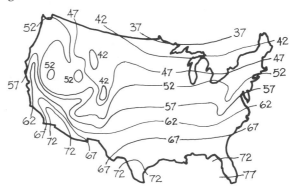

Ground Water Temperatures

Fallingwater
Bear Run, Pennsylvania
Architect: Frank Lloyd Wright

Frank Lloyd Wright's design of Fallingwater, located in Bear Run, Pa., cantilevers over the small stream called Bear Run, and offers a unique example of the use of water on a site.

Fallingwater
Bear Run, Pennsylvania
Architect: Frank Lloyd Wright

Built Forms

Existing or future built forms on a site will affect a building in much the same way as their natural counterparts. Buildings, walls and fences can be used like trees for windbreaks and deflectors. The surface qualities of built surfaces such as concrete must be considered for reflectivity and permeability like natural ground covers.

☐ Built forms can be classified in terms of horizontal and vertical surfaces. Vertical surfaces can be sized and defined for shading purposes in the same manner as trees, and for windscreening according to dimensions and penetrability.

☐ Horizontal surfaces include surface covers, such as paving and artificial turf, and architectural extensions, such as decks and canopies.

☐ The legal status of solar access has been controversial in recent years. It is generally agreed that owners have full right to sunlight falling "vertically" on their property. However, the right to sunlight that might be blocked by future build forms on an adjacent site is not universally acknowledged. In terms of future growth and solar access problems, the designer should consider possible conflicts with the jurisdiction's development policies, concerning:
—hillside/topography
—tree preservation
—tall buildings and high density
—exclusionary zoning.

☐ Further experience with such public policies and with recently developed solar access regulations, as well as with private agreements—covenants and easements—may be required to answer the questions raised by this issue.

☐ The accompanying sun charts provide a method by which the shading effect of built forms can be calculated.

1. Using a compass or transit, determine which direction is south; remember to correct for true south.

2. Aiming the hand level or transit true south, determine the altitude (angle above the horizon) of the skyline. Plot this point on the sun chart above the azimuth angle 0 degrees (true south).

3. Similarly, determine and record the altitude angle of the skyline for each 15 degrees (azimuth angle) along the horizon, both to the east and west of south, to at least 120 degrees. This is a total of 17 altitude readings. Plot these readings above their respective azimuth angles on the sun chart and connect them with a line.

4. For isolated tall objects that block the sun during the winter, such as land forms or buildings, find both the azimuth and altitude angles for each object and plot them on the chart.

5. Finally, plot the deciduous trees in the skyline with a dotted line. These are of special nature, because by losing their leaves in the winter they let most of the sun pass through as long as they are not densely spaced.

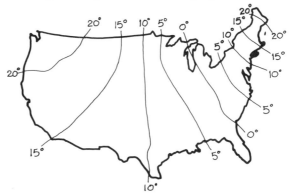

Compass Corrections for True South

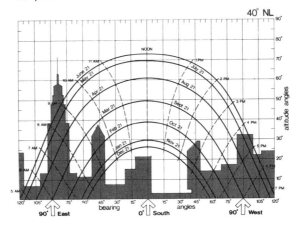

Plotting the Skyline

Source: Mazria, Edward, *The Passive Solar Energy Book*, ©1979. Reprinted by permission of author.

This completes the skyline. The open areas on the sun chart are the times when the sun will reach that point on the site.

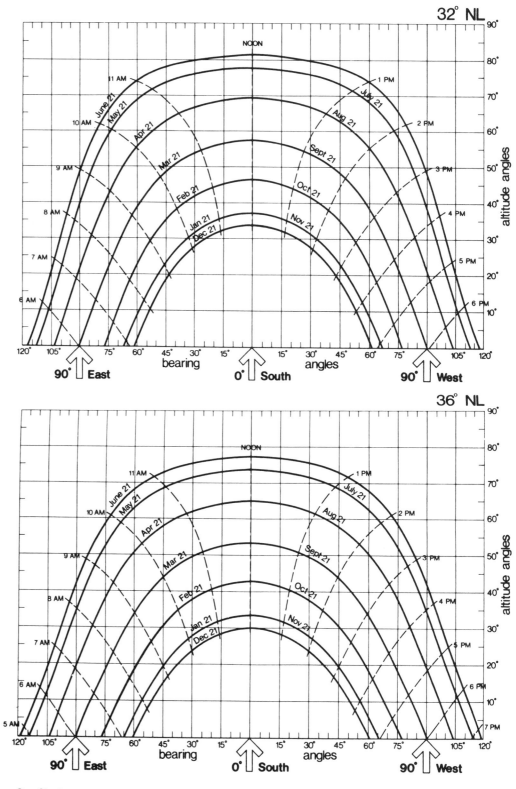

Sun Charts

Source: Mazria, Edward, *The Passive Solar Energy Book*, ©1979. Reprinted by permission of author.

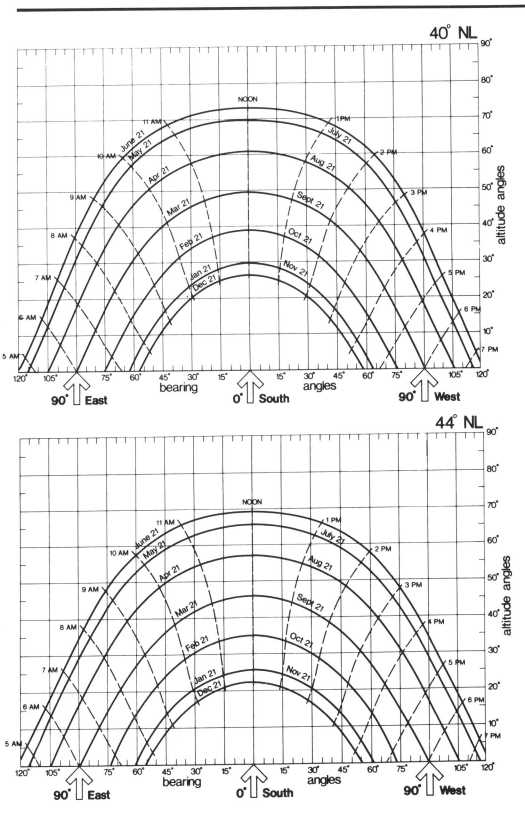

Sun Charts

Source: Mazria, Edward, *The Passive Solar Energy Book*, ©1979. Reprinted by permission of author.

Site Design

Knowledge of the site elements can be used not only to take advantage of existing site elements but also to improve the site's microclimate. At the preliminary schematic design phase, three general questions about a site's climatic conditions are pertinent.

—Is the site too warm or too cool?
—Too windy or not windy enough?
—Too humid or too dry?

☐ Some basic rules of thumb for manipulating site elements are as follows.

☐ If the site is too warm:
—use extensive turf and ground cover on the site
—use extensive coarse-textured, deciduous or coniferous shade trees and vines, especially on the south side
—plant to divert breezes to the building
—use trellises, arbors and canopies
—remove windbreaks
—locate buildings on leeward side of water
—provide fountains, pools, etc.
—use raised decks for pavings.

☐ If the site is too cool:
—locate to windward side of water
—maximize solar radiation by removing shade trees
—increase paved areas
—use fences and screens as windbreaks to deflect cold winds
—use light, lacy deciduous trees for shade
—use vegetational canopies to reduce night heat loss
—avoid pools and fountains on site

☐ If the site is too windy:
—screen north and west sides
—avoid valleys and hillside slopes
—depress outdoor areas below ground level if possible
—use heavy coniferous windbreaks

☐ If the site is not windy enough:
—remove undergrowth
—locate on a hilltop or narrow valley slope
—create diverters with vegetation, earth forms or built forms

☐ If the site is too humid:
—maximize solar exposure
—maximize air flow
—pave ground surfaces
—locate high on the site and provide extensive drainage system
—reduce vegetation, including canopy trees
—use vegetation with needle-like leaves to capture fog before it reaches the building.

☐ If the site is too dry:
—provide low windbreaks
—use irrigated turf or ground cover
—avoid large expanses of paving
—encourage overhead planting.

☐ Retrofitting a building to accommodate a solar collector may require extensive and costly changes. Retrofitting a site to accommodate a solar collector or to improve its functioning, however, may not be as substantial or costly.

☐ The first step of the retrofit design process is similar to site analysis, and involves recording:
—amount of solar radiation on the site
—time of day the sun hits the site
—impediments blocking the sun
—prevailing wind patterns
—impediments to wind movement
—areas where snow piles up
—damp or moist areas

☐ The existing site can be modified by adding, subtracting, thinning or moving objects on the site. Some things easily done to retrofit for energy conservation include:
—remove, thin or replace large deciduous trees on the south side to permit solar collection
—create outdoor sun pockets on the south or southwest
—provide solid wind screens to block winter winds
—replace turf with paving for a heat sink, if the site is too cool
—regrade earth to form berms around the building
—use louvered fence panels to allow for summer ventilation while deflecting cold winter winds

Oakland Community College Southfield Campus
Southfield, Michigan
Architects: Straub, Van Dine, Dzuirman Architects

The Oakland Community College, designed by Straub, Van Dine, Dzuirman/Architects, for the Southfield Campus, Southfield, Mich., deals with the special problem of energy-conscious site design in an urban context.

The following discussion is excerpted from the architect's own analysis of the site:

Subsurface Characteristics

The firm of Soils & Materials Testing, Inc., was retained to make 6 sample borings at representative locations within the site and to conduct tests on the samples to determine the general characteristics of the soil. This firm had done all of the soils investigation for the surrounding structures, and is knowledgeable in the local area. Three borings were done in September 1977 for a preliminary report and three borings were done in June 1978 for a final report.

Recommendations are that the building be supported on spread footings or a structural mat bearing at as high an elevation as is feasible, in the depth range of 8 to 12 feet below existing grade. The earth mound around the building must be allowed to settle independently of the building. If the soil from the mound hangs up on the side of the building, downdrag of the building could occur. To minimize this downdrag, a 2 foot layer of a pea gravel should be placed between the outside building wall and the mound. The building should be completely waterproofed and an underfloor drainage system installed. The seasonal perched water table makes this a necessity.

Surface Characteristics

The *Grade* of the site is essentially horizontal, however, with some mounds of fill deposited in both the north and south sections. Additionally there is a shallow ditch running across the site at about its midpoint. These surface variations are insignificant and do little to alter the site's basic *Flatness*.

Vegetation covers the site, mostly in the form of brush and scrub trees. A grove of 30 to 40 foot high trees in the south, through a visual relief, is not significant, being mostly a variety of Poplar—fast growing, soft wooded and short-lived.

Views from the site are of widely spaced high rise structures to the north and south, and low

rise apartments to the east. It is *Quiet*. Although it is immediately accessible to both Nine Mile and John Lodge, the site is essentially one block removed from the distractions of each.

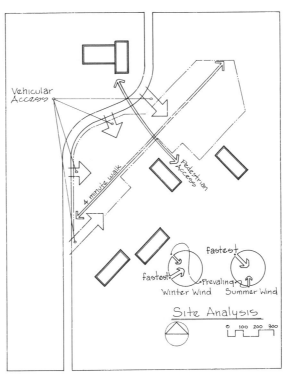

Oakland Community College
Southfield, Michigan
Architects: Straub, Van Dine, Dzuirman/Architects

Solar Considerations

Solar considerations are very important because their effect on energy use and energy conservation. The *Sun Angle Chart* shown for this latitude allows the computation on the sun angle meeting the site or building at any time of the day or any time of year. Extensive use of this chart will be made to study and compare exterior building designs.

In the solar study drawing solar angles are shown in general graphic terms for summer and winter. Also, shadows from adjacent buildings are projected for December 22 at 10:00 A.M., Noon and 2:00 P.M. These shadows are the maximum length for these times at any time of the year.

Wind

Cold *Winter Winds* are primarily from the *northwest* and *west*. The building should be protected on these sides with as few openings as possible.

Prevailing *Summer Winds* are from the *South*. Building openings and outdoor spaces should be oriented toward the south to catch the cooling effect of the summer winds.

Views

Views from the site to its surroundings are *not particularly inspiring* (typical suburban office and apartment towers surrounded by parking lots with little green space for relief). It would be best to *create pleasant views* for the building's occupants either within the building or within the site.

Downward Views onto the site from adjacent buildings are an important design consideration from all sides of the site. The resulting building is a structure buried by 18 inches of dirt and sod, which has 50 percent of the energy cost of a comparable size conventional structure, which admits natural light and summer breezes into its southeast exposure. The offset second floor also fosters admission of daylight. The grass and vegetation cover provides for further shading.

Oakland Community College Site Plan
Southfield, Michigan
Architects: Straub, Van Dine, Dzuirman/Architects

Oakland Community College
Southfield, Michigan
Architects: Straub, Van Dine, Dzuirman/Architects

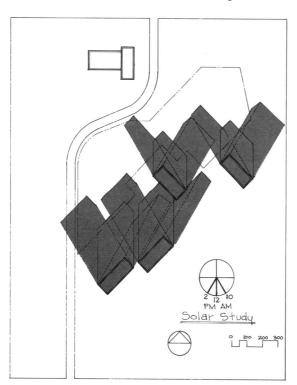

Oakland Community College
Southfield, Michigan
Architects: Straub, Van Dine, Dzuirman/Architects

THE BUILDING ENVELOPE

Introduction

The building envelope determines in large part the effects of external and internal forces on building spaces. It serves as a filter for light, air and heat flow in and out of the building. The various components of the envelope—wall, roof, slab and foundations—can serve as structural support for the building or, in the case of curtain wall panels, as a protective skin.

In this monograph, the envelope will be considered primarily in its role as a mediator of both external and internal thermal forces. Its effects on daylighting and ventilation are covered elsewhere in this handbook.

The three major factors determining heat flow in and out of a building are temperature differential, area of the building exposed to the elements and heat transmission value of the exposed area.

—The temperature differential is the difference between the outside and inside temperatures or between different temperatures in adjacent spaces.

—Exposed area, the number of square feet of surface exposed to the temperature differential, is determined by the form of the building.

—The transmission value of the envelope is the extent to which the envelope transmits heat into or out of a building. Manipulating the transmission value of the envelope's components is the topic of the sections titled "Dynamic Response of the Envelope," "Heavy Mass Construction," "Lightweight Construction," "Roof Construction," "Foundation and Underground Construction," "Fenestration," and "Insulation."

The transmission value of the envelope depends greatly on its materials. The "Envelope Materials" section discusses the hidden energy costs encountered when the life cycle of building materials is considered.

"Innovations in Envelope Design," the final section, discusses recent and forthcoming advances in envelope design, materials and design tools.

Photo: Norman McGrath

Niagara Falls Winter Garden
Niagara Falls, New York
Architect: Cesar Pelli & Associates

Heavy Mass Construction

Current design calculations for the building envelope, which are based on steady-state models, assume that only the U-values of opaque walls and the amount of glass in walls and roofs affect heating and cooling loads. Some dynamic thermal analysis has shown, however, that loads can be less with heavy walls than with light walls, even when U-values are equal.

☐ However at the present time, there is a lack of enough data available for a definitive statement on the effect of wall weight on building energy consumption.

☐ Energy analysts now generally agree on the superiority of dynamic energy models that take into account the ability of thermal mass to modify and delay heating and cooling loads.

The designer should, however, be aware that other factors also affect the performance of envelope components. These include:
—building orientation and aspect ratio
—color and texture of exterior surfaces
—wind velocities
—infiltration rates
—shading
—presence of moisture in the wall
—thermal bridges.

Masonry Construction

☐ The accompanying chart of time lags for common types of brick construction can be used to estimate when outside heat traveling through the wall will be delivered to the interior. The chart also gives heat gains in BTU/hr./sq. ft. for average and west (usually the worst case) orientation, which can be used in energy analysis calculations.

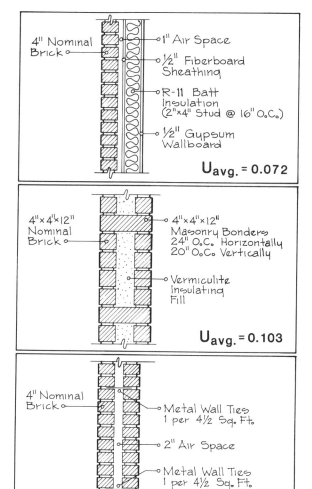

4" Nominal Brick
1" Air Space
½" Fiberboard Sheathing
R-11 Batt Insulation (2"x4" Stud @ 16" O.C.)
½" Gypsum Wallboard
$U_{avg.} = 0.072$

4"x4"x12" Nominal Brick
4"x4"x12" Masonry Bonders 24" O.C. Horizontally 20" O.C. Vertically
Vermiculite Insulating Fill
$U_{avg.} = 0.103$

4" Nominal Brick
Metal Wall Ties 1 per 4½ Sq. Ft.
2" Air Space
Metal Wall Ties 1 per 4½ Sq. Ft.
$U_{avg.} = 0.377$

U-Values of Masonry Walls

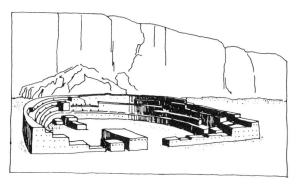

*The Pueblo Bonito
New Mexico*

Wall Section	Wall Description	Weight Pounds Per Sq. Ft.	U-Value (Winter)	Solar Heat Gain BTU/Hr/Sq.Ft. (Dark Color) Orientation		Time Lag (Hours)	Amplitude Decrement Factor
				Average	West		
	10″ Brick and brick cavity wall with 2″ polyurethane insulation board in cavity	79.0	0.058	1.17	1.06	8	0.14
	10″ Brick and brick cavity wall	78.5	0.370	7.73	8.29	8	0.08
	10″ Brick and lightweight concrete (100-pound density) block cavity wall with 2″ polystyrene insulation board in cavity	62.0	0.071	1.72	1.35	6	0.32
	10″ Brick and lightweight (100-pound density) block cavity wall	61.0	0.273	6.09	6.09	6	0.13
	8″ Brick and lightweight concrete (100-pound density) block, 2″ polystyrene insulation board, ½″ gypsumboard	64.0	0.073	2.06	1.75	4	0.40
	8″ Brick and lightweight concrete (100-pound density) block, 1 × 2 furring, ½″ gypsumboard	65.0	0.263	8.51	7.98	4	0.48
	4″ Brick curtain wall (partially reinforced or with highbond mortar), 2″ polystyrene insulation board ½″ gypsumboard	42.0	0.082	2.77	2.84	3	0.51
	4″ Brick veneer, ½″ insulation board sheathing, wood studs, full batt (R–11) insulation, ½″ gypsumboard	43.0	0.077	2.18	1.95	4	0.62

Thermal Characteristics of Mansonry Wall Construction

Wall Section	Wall Description	Weight Pounds Per Sq. Ft.	U-Value (Winter)	Solar Heat Gain BTU/Hr/Sq.Ft. (Dark Color) Orientation		Time Lag (Hours)	Amplitude Decrement Factor
				Average	West		
	8″ Brick wall (hollow units), 2″ polystyrene insulation board, ½″ gypsumboard	56.0	0.076	1.73	1.39	6	0.25
	8″ Brick wall (hollow units), 1 × 2 furring, ½″ gypsumboard	56.0	0.316	7.37	5.90	6	0.25
	8″ Brick wall (solid units), 1 × 2 furring, ½″ gypsumboard	82.0	0.343	8.45	6.62	6	0.32
	6″ Brick wall (hollow units), 2″ polystyrene insulation board, ½″ gypsumboard	46.5	0.078	2.29	1.94	4	0.45
	6″ Brick wall (hollow units), 1 × 2 furring, ½″ gypsumboard	47.5	0.325	9.95	8.44	4	0.45
	6″ Brick wall (solid units), 2″ polystyrene board, ½″ gypsumboard	63.5	0.080	2.25	1.91	4	0.40
	6″ Brick wall (solid units), 1 × 2 furring, ½″ gypsumboard	64.5	0.369	10.59	9.00	4	0.40
	6″ Precast concrete (140-pound density) sandwich panel, 2″ polyurethane core	47.5	0.065	1.82	1.55	4	0.40

Thermal Characteristics of Masonry Wall Construction

Concrete Construction

☐ The accompanying tables indicate the thermal resistance of concrete slabs and concrete masonry. Poured-in-place and precast concrete walls are fairly airtight and need special treatment only at the joints to decrease infiltration. Where the concrete wall abuts concrete columns, the joints should be sealed with caulking. The open joint between the wall and a spandrel beam above must be caulked or, alternatively, closed with a flexible membrane cemented and mechanically fastened to the beam and wall.

Concrete Type	Unit Weight (pcf)	Thickness of Concrete (in.)				
		1	2	4	6	8
Insulating— lightweight	20	1.43	2.86	5.72	8.58	11.44
	30	1.00	2.00	4.00	6.00	8.00
	40	.83	1.66	3.32	4.98	6.64
	50	.67	1.34	2.68	4.02	5.36
	60	.52	1.04	2.08	3.12	4.16
	70	.45	.90	1.80	2.70	3.60
	80	.37	.74	1.48	2.22	2.96
Structural— lightweight	90	.30	.60	1.20	1.80	2.40
	100	.24	.48	.96	1.44	1.92
	110	.19	.38	.76	1.13	1.51
	120	.14	.28	.57	.86	1.14
Structural— normal Weight	130	.11	.22	.43	.65	.87
	140	.083	.16	.33	.50	.67
	145	.075	.15	.30	.45	.60
	150	.065	.13	.26	.39	.52

Resistance Values for Concrete Slabs

Unit Weight (pcf)	Thickness With and Without Core Insulation									
	4 in.		6 in.		8 in.		10 in.		12 in.	
	Filled	Open	Filled	Open	Filled	Open	Filled	Open	Filled	Open
60	3.36	2.07	5.59	2.25	7.46	2.30	9.35	3.0	10.98	3.29
80	2.79	1.68	4.59	1.83	6.06	2.12	7.46	2.40	8.70	2.62
100	2.33	1.40	3.72	1.53	4.85	1.75	5.92	1.97	6.80	2.14
120	1.92	1.17	2.95	1.29	3.79	1.46	4.59	1.63	5.18	1.81
140	1.14	0.77	1.59	0.86	1.98	0.98	2.35	1.08	2.59	1.16

Resistance Values for Concrete Masonry

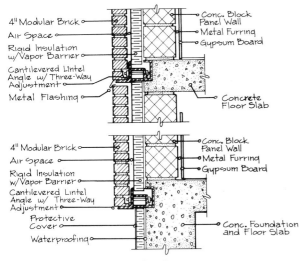

Concrete Block Construction Details

Heat Storage Capacity of Various Wall Types

Retrofitting Masonry Structures

□ The energy performance of most existing masonry buildings cannot be improved easily. One particular problem is that a wall constructed of relatively porous brick or stone with lime mortar allows free migration of water, especially in the form of vapor, through the wall in either direction. If this free vapor transfer is inhibited, as by vapor-proof sheet insulation applied directly to the inside of old masonry walls, a buildup of moisture in the core of the wall can cause breakdown of mortar and decay of the masonry.

□ Filling a cavity formed by furring with impermeable sheet or expandable foam will cause the same problem. If a solid masonry wall has plaster applied directly to the interior face, no improvement to the insulation should be attempted.

□ If the wall is furred, the cavity can be filled with granular cellular insulation of the bead type, poured in from the upper level or roof space. Alternatively, non-vapor-proof expandable insulation can be used. Regardless of insulation type, the open ends of furred spaces will confine convection currents and make the air space a more effective insulation.

□ If possible, insulation can be applied to the interior, as long as there is an air space of at least a half-inch between the masonry and the insulation. If loss of space is not a critical problem, internal stud furring with batts and additional vapor barriers can be used, as long as the air space is maintained.

□ If the original exterior face need not be retained, external insulation can be used to make the mass serve as heat storage. Again, an air space must be maintained. Sheet insulation can be applied over furring then covered with metal cladding or a similar material.

Hotsy Corporation Headquarters
Englewood, Colorado
Architects: Crowther Architects Group

The 29,000-sq. ft. Hotsy Corporation building uses heavy mass construction to store solar heat gain during the heating season. The precast concrete floor and wall panels are supplemented with cast-in-place concrete and steel for curvilinear sections. Heat (and, in the summertime, interior coolness), delayed by the thermal lag properties of the heavy concrete mass, is further delayed by stuccoed exterior insulation. This heavy mass is carefully placed to serve as the storage component for the building's direct-gain passive solar system.

Outer insulation wraps the thermal mass of the building. Careful construction largely eliminates thermal bridging, infiltration and exfiltration. The exterior building surface is textured to preserve a thin surface film of air. The building is oriented due south. Its dark south-face color favorably increases winter solar gains. Irregular exterior walls further increase the surface area of the south face for even greater energy gain. North and west exterior wall areas are minimized to consume less energy. The east exterior wall deflects cold winter winds and recessed windows reduce energy losses. The principal entries are weather-protected.

Additional energy measures include earth berming, deciduous planting, solar collectors on the roof and an economizer-cycle, variable-air-volume mechanical system that captures waste heat from people and lights.

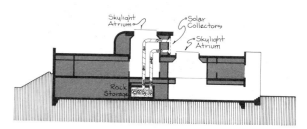

Hotsy Corporation Headquarters
Englewood, Colorado
Architects: Crowther Architects Group

Hotsy Corporation Headquarters
Englewood, Colorado
Architects: Crowther Architects Group

Hotsy Corporation Headquarters
Englewood, Colorado
Architects: Crowther Architects Group

Lightweight Construction

Lightweight construction includes glass and metal curtain walls, wood framing, and lightweight concrete. The two principal ways to reduce heat gain or loss in lightweight wall construction are thermal insulation and infiltration control.

Insulation

☐ Lightweight construction lacks heavy mass construction's inherent insulative ability. Thermal insulation (discussed in detail later in this monograph) is usually applied to lightweight walls to overcome this deficiency.

☐ Glazed areas of the envelope can be insulated through double or triple glazing and tinted/reflective glazing systems (see the "Sun Control and Shading" monograph of this handbook).

☐ The core material of a curtain wall panel, including its insulation, determines to a large extent its thermal resistance. The accompanying charts show typical insulating panel construction and properties of core materials.

☐ The joints between glass and metal curtain wall sections and the structure should incorporate thermal breaks to minimize heat loss from the interior to the exposed panels.

☐ Manufactured skin assemblies complete with exterior and interior finishes and an insulation core allow greater material economies; the sandwich panel design can improve both energy and structural efficiency by minimizing redundancy in design and optimizing the use of exterior materials such as aluminum, steel, concrete and masonry. The design integration of skin components with structural and other building systems is also becoming more refined.

☐ Condensation can be a problem in curtain walls. Metal and glass encourage condensation because they are impermeable to moisture and have low heat-retention capacity. A vapor barrier on or near the room-side wall face can keep water vapor from wall components. Insulating impervious surfaces within the wall reduces condensation by keeping them warmer than the dew point of the air contacting them. The walls should be detailed so that water vapor can escape to the outside and any condensation occurring within it will drain away via weeps.

☐ In wood-frame construction, insulating materials are usually batts, insulating boards, or loose fill. Vapor barriers between the insulation and the inside wall face are needed because condensation will both rot the framing and moisten the insulation, thereby negating its insulating property.

☐ Frame buildings also offer opportunities for retrofit applications, especially for cavity walls. Some vapor-proof expanding foams can be injected into the wall cavity between studs and between horizontal members such as girts and plates or diagonal braces, but many of these lose their effectiveness by not completely filling the cavity, by shrinking or by not adhering to studs. Such materials are generally superior to non-vapor-proof loose fill insulations, which often promote timber decay by getting soggy with condensation. Furthermore, blown-in insulation or poured insulation often packs down over the years, leaving a void near ceilings.

☐ When replacing interior wall surfaces, conventional glass or mineral fiber batt with integral vapor barrier, supplemented as needed by a plastic film vapor barrier, is the most effective. When the interior wall surfaces are of good quality or trim cannot be disturbed, the work can be done from the outside, particularly if the exterior has to be replaced. In this event, friction-fit batts can be placed between wall members and the outside reconstructed, including insulating board undersheathing, asphalt building paper, strapping and cladding. The vapor barrier in this case cannot be absolute; the permeable outer layers will allow vapor to escape, avoiding condensation.

☐ Masonry veneers over wood frame can be dealt with the same as ordinary frame buildings. Filling the cavity between the veneer and the undersheathing, however, usually destroys the weather screen effect of the veneer and in extreme cases can dislocate the veneer. Furthermore, the amount of insulation that can be placed in the cavity may not be enough to be of much benefit.

☐ Structural lightweight concrete offers less weight and several times the insulating power of standard concrete. Nominal reductions in the weight of concrete are generally brought about through the use of manufactured lightweight structural aggregates. Concretes produced with such materials are broadly classified as structural lightweight concretes, and they usually fall in the range of 90 to 120 pounds per cubic foot, wet-weight, or 80 to 110 pounds per cubic foot, oven-dry. The increased insulation is provided by the air trapped between the solid particles.

☐ Thermal conductivity of cellular concrete is proportional to density—the lighter the ma-

Wall Section	Wall Description	Weight Pounds Per Sq. Ft.	U-Value (Winter)	Heat Gain BTU/Hr/Sq.Ft. (Dark Color) Orientation		Time Lag (Hours)	Amplitude Decrement Factor
				Average	West		
	Metal panel curtain wall 2-layers 18-gauge steel, 2″ polyurethane insulation (between steel layers)	4.5	0.066	3.17	5.73	1	0.99
	Metal panel curtain wall 2-layers 18-gauge aluminum, 2″ polyurethane insulation (between aluminum layers)	2.0	0.066	3.20	5.78	1	0.99
	½″ Plywood siding, ½″ insulation board sheathing, wood studs, full batt (R–11) insulation, ½″ gypsumboard	5.0	0.076	3.05	4.60	2	0.75

Thermal Properties of Lightweight Walls

Typical Facing Materials

1. Aluminum or Stainless Steel Sheet, Textured or Smooth
2. Porcelain Enameled Metal
3. Glass Reinforced Plastic Sheet
4. Stone Chips in Plastic Matrix
5. Galvanized Bonderized Steel Sheet
6. Aluminum Sheet
7. Cement-Asbestos Board
8. Tempered Hardboard
9. Ceramic Tile in Plastic Matrix
10. Opaque Colored Glass

Insulated Curtain Walls
Typical Core and Facing Materials

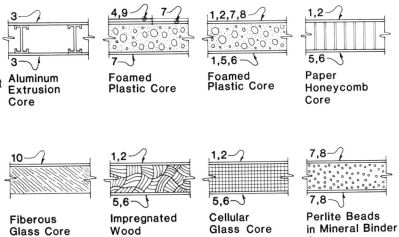

Insulating Curtain Wall Panels

Roof and Floor Conditions

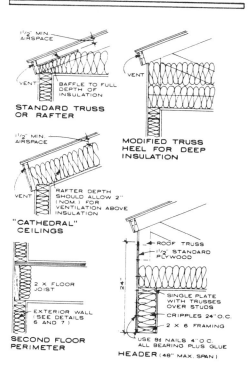

STANDARD TRUSS OR RAFTER

1½" MIN. AIRSPACE

VENT

BAFFLE TO FULL DEPTH OF INSULATION

MODIFIED TRUSS HEEL FOR DEEP INSULATION

VENT

"CATHEDRAL" CEILINGS

1½" MIN. AIRSPACE

VENT

RAFTER DEPTH SHOULD ALLOW 2" (NOM.) FOR VENTILATION ABOVE INSULATION

SECOND FLOOR PERIMETER

2 X FLOOR JOIST

EXTERIOR WALL (SEE DETAILS 6 AND 7)

HEADER (48" MAX. SPAN)

ROOF TRUSS

1½" STANDARD PLYWOOD

SINGLE PLATE WITH TRUSSES OVER STUDS

CRIPPLES 24" O.C.

2 X 6 FRAMING

USE 8d NAILS 4" O.C. ALL BEARING PLUS GLUE

Wall Conditions

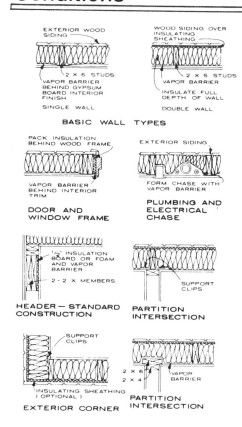

EXTERIOR WOOD SIDING

2 X 6 STUDS

VAPOR BARRIER BEHIND GYPSUM BOARD INTERIOR FINISH

SINGLE WALL

WOOD SIDING OVER INSULATING SHEATHING

2 X 6 STUDS

VAPOR BARRIER

INSULATE FULL DEPTH OF WALL

DOUBLE WALL

BASIC WALL TYPES

PACK INSULATION BEHIND WOOD FRAME

VAPOR BARRIER BEHIND INTERIOR TRIM

DOOR AND WINDOW FRAME

EXTERIOR SIDING

FORM CHASE WITH VAPOR BARRIER

PLUMBING AND ELECTRICAL CHASE

½" INSULATION BOARD OR FOAM AND VAPOR BARRIER

2 - 2 X MEMBERS

HEADER — STANDARD CONSTRUCTION

SUPPORT CLIPS

PARTITION INTERSECTION

SUPPORT CLIPS

INSULATING SHEATHING (OPTIONAL)

EXTERIOR CORNER

2 X 6

2 X 4

VAPOR BARRIER

PARTITION INTERSECTION

Foundation Conditions

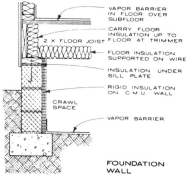

VAPOR BARRIER IN FLOOR OVER SUBFLOOR

CARRY FLOOR INSULATION UP TO FLOOR AT TRIMMER

2 X FLOOR JOIST

FLOOR INSULATION SUPPORTED ON WIRE

INSULATION UNDER SILL PLATE

RIGID INSULATION ON C M U WALL

CRAWL SPACE

VAPOR BARRIER

FOUNDATION WALL

Frame Construction: Insulation Placement

2 X 6 FRAMING (2 X 4 FRAMING REQUIRES FLASHING OVER INSULATION)

1½" NONABSORBENT RIGID INSULATION WITH PROTECTIVE FACE

CONTINUE INSULATION 12" TO 24" BELOW GRADE

GRADE BEAM

VAPOR BARRIER UNDER SLAB

2 X 6 FRAMING (2 X 4 FRAMING LEAVES INSULATION TO BE COVERED BY FLOORING)

INSULATION UNDER SILL PLATE

2" NONABSORBENT RIGID INSULATION

STEM WALL

Source: The American Institute of Architects, *Architectural Graphic Standards*, Seventh Edition, © 1981. Reprinted by permission of John Wiley & Son, Inc., New York, New York.

terial the better the insulation it provides. K-factors range from 0.51 for 20 pounds per cubic foot concrete to 2.3 for a 90 pounds per cubic foot mix. This means that a 10-inch wall of 40 pounds per cubic foot cellular concrete will have the same insulating value as a brick wall three times as thick or a standard concrete wall eight times as thick.

Infiltration Control

☐ Infiltration control requires a tightly sealed skin that has a vapor barrier and carefully sealed joints. Infiltration can account for 30 percent of the load in externally dominated buildings. In internally dominated buildings it may be a useful strategy for increasing fresh air as well as heat loss.

☐ In curtain-wall construction it is almost impossible to make water- and airtight joints to a steel frame. Weathertightness can be maximized by setting steel frames inside the "structural" wall with properly detailed movement joints in front of each column and spandrel.

☐ Expansion and contraction of wall materials caused by temperature changes is a major concern with curtain walls. Thermal expansion and contraction is much greater in metals and more rapid than in wood or masonry, and solar heat gain can raise the temperature of darker-colored metals on buildings to 170 degrees (F). in many parts of the country.

☐ Winds also contribute to the movement of the wall, affecting joint seals and wall anchorage. Positive or negative wind pressure can cause stress reversal on framing members and glass, and will cause water to travel in any direction (including upward) across the face of the wall — a potentially major cause of water infiltration.

☐ The ultraviolet spectrum of sunlight can cause breakdown of organic materials such as color pigments, plastic and sealants. Fading and failure of these materials can cause serious problems with weathertightness of the curtain wall.

☐ Metal and glass curtain walls thus require more careful design and skilled erection than other walls because of the need for joints that are flexible but minimize air and water infiltration.

IBM Regional Office
Southfield, Michigan
Architects: Gunnar Birkirts and Associates

The key element to energy conservation in Gunnar Birkirt's 14-story regional office for IBM is the copyrighted skin design. The 2-feet-high horizontal ribbons of glass make up only 20 percent of the total wall area. The glass is sloped inward to shield it from the sun for most of the working day yet still allow a view out and daylight penetration. In addition, curved reflector surfaces, extending 24 inches into the interior, direct and diffuse the daylight into the office spaces.

Panel treatment on the facades also helps conserve energy. The bright aluminum southern and western elevations reflect unwanted heat. By contrast, the charcoal grey north and east elevations absorb it. The designers expect a 40 percent savings in peak solar load, which will pay back in eight years the cost of square footage "lost" because of the 24-inch reflectors.

IBM Regional Office
Southfield, Michigan
Architects: Gunnar Birkirts and Associates

Roof Construction

Roofs can be important components of energy-efficient design. A building with a south-facing, sloped roof, for example, will experience intense solar radiation, and can be pitched to optimally accomodate active solar or photovoltaic arrays. Conversely, a flat roof in colder climates can be designed to take advantage of insulation provided by snow cover.

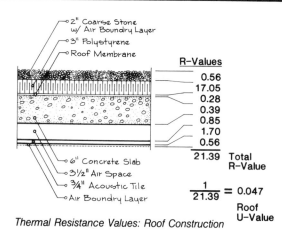

Thermal Resistance Values: Roof Construction

Thermal Resistance and Insulation

☐ The overall roof U-value must be calculated as part of the envelope analysis. In order to meet the cooling criteria of ASHRAE Standard 90A-80, the overall roof U-value must be less than or equal to 8.5 BTU/hr sq.ft./°F. The insulating properties of a roof can be enhanced in a variety of ways, including:
—increased thermal capacity
—roof ponds
—rooftop equipment rooms
—double skin with ventilation space between
—wind deflection devices
—light colors to reduce solar gain
—parapets for shading
—rough textures to increase the value of the roof's air film coefficient.

☐ For flat roofs, an inverted roof membrane assembly provides good insulation at the exterior limits of the enclosure system's concrete and steel construction. It is also useful for improving roof insulation on retrofit projects. For joist construction, batt insulation is satisfactory if adequate ventilation is provided to avoid condensation and deterioration of wood structural members.

Attics and Roof Spaces

☐ In woodframe construction, an unheated attic space provides a buffer between inside and out, and permits the use of inexpensive glass fiber batt and granular fill insulation. A minor heat sink effect is created as the attic space heats up during the day and reradiates the energy at night. In concrete and steel construction, unheated attic and roof spaces are difficult to design without creating thermal bridges that allow heat to escape. To avoid this, it is generally advisable to keep the insulation outside the structure, placing it as near the perimeter as possible.

☐ The accompanying figure indicates typical concrete roof construction and its overall U-value.

☐ For retrofit applications, the following situations require special attention:
—For quarter- or half-story roofs with sloping ceilings attached directly to the rafters, rigid insulation of the vaporproof type can be slipped down from the roof space formed by collar ties. Alternatively, the sloped section can be furred down and insulated, leaving the rafter space for air circulation.
—Flat or low sloping roofs with wood joist construction must have ventilation over the insulation and between the insulation and impervious roofing material. Additional venting to an existing system may be necessary.
—When insulation is combined with roofing, care must be taken to maintain the integrity of the roofing membrane as a waterproof skin. Insulation with a weatherproof surface is often applied over the roof membrane to deter cracking caused by shrinkage or thermal movements of the insulation.

Vapor Barriers

☐ In roof construction, as with foundations, vapor barriers are important between warm spaces and insulated areas. A continuous sheet, such as polyethylene film, can be used if the entire sheet (even where it rises over a joist) is covered with insulation. If not, the exposed film will promote condensation and joist decay. An alternative solution is to use friction-fit batts, with the vapor barriers set downward to the warm side.

Roof Openings and Skylights

☐ Solar gain through skylights can provide supplemental heat; excess heat buildup can be avoided by many of the means used for windows, such as heat reflecting glass and exterior and interior blinds (see "Shading and Sun Control" monograph in this handbook).

☐ Nighttime heat losses from skylights can be severe due to higher temperatures at the ceiling level and the greater pressure differ-

entials and wind velocities associated with roofs. Some possible solutions include:
—double or triple glazing
—glazing the bottom of the skylight opening
—insulated shutters.

☐ Skylights oriented toward the south and placed toward the rear (north) of the building, with the north wall a passive storage element, can be particularly effective.

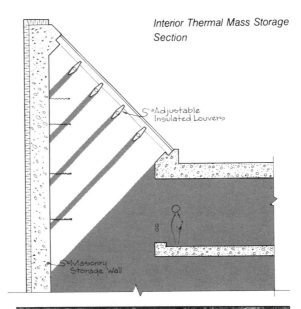

Interior Thermal Mass Storage Section

Adjustable Insulated Louvers

Masonry Storage Wall

Underground House
New Canaan, Connecticut
Architect and Builder: Donald Watson, FAIA

This earth-sheltered residence in a south-facing slope, built in 1985, offers high insulation for effective solar heating in winter and earth cooling in summer. The roof supports a garden and solar collectors used for a photovoltaic electricity supply and hot water heating. The chimney is insulated on the outside and capped with an adjustable damper to retain heat. A south-facing skylight sheds light into the two-story, top-lit atrium below.

Foundations and Underground Construction

Foundations and floor construction require much of the same treatment as walls, i.e., insulation and vapor barriers, to be energy-conserving.

The perimeter of unheated slabs on grade should be insulated in areas with 2500 or more degree days. The accompanying chart and diagram show appropriate R-values for slabs on grade in relation to heating degree days and alternative placements of insulation for slab on grade. Exterior waterproof insulation is generally used to avoid a thermal bridge created by discontinuity of the insulation.

Floors require insulation when they separate spaces with different temperatures, including floors separating occupied spaces from unoccupied spaces or parking spaces.

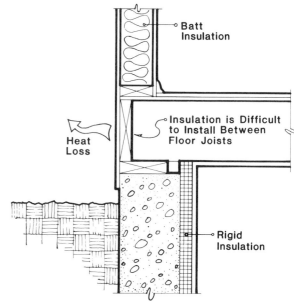

Thermal Bridge Caused Discontinuity of Insulation

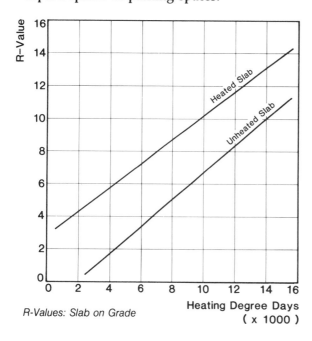

R-Values: Slab on Grade

Basements

☐ Concrete basements usually are not insulated unless they contain occupied spaces. If unheated, the floor assembly above it needs insulation. If the basement is heated, insulation is required on the underside of the floor 24 inches below grade as well as on the basement wall. A thermal bridge caused by discontinuity of insulation at the basement ceiling must be avoided. If there is a possibility of water in the basement, insulation should be stopped 2 inches above the floor.

Underground Construction

☐ Below the frostline, underground temperature remains stable at approximately 56 degrees (F.). The mass of the earth takes so long to heat up and cool down that it approximates this average temperature year-round, with only slight increases at the end of summer and slight decreases at the end of winter. In climates with severe winter or summer temperatures, underground construction provides a temperate outside design temperature, as well as reduced infiltration.

Underground space can be comfortable if:
—heated sources are evenly placed in the walls
—thermostats are located and used properly
—humidity is controlled
—ventilation is adequate.

Design Temperatures

☐ Daily temperature fluctuations at the ground surface approximate those of the air, but at approximately 2 feet down, daily fluctuations effectively disappear. Annual fluctuations of a few degrees occur in depths of 16–23 feet, depending on soil conditions. In most parts of the United States, ground temperatures below 20 feet are regarded as stable.

State	City	Mean Temperatures (tm)
Ala.	Auburn	64
Alaska	Anchorage	32
Ariz.	Phoenix	66
Calif.	San Francisco	57
Colo.	Denver	50
Conn.	Hartford	50
Del.	Wilmington	54
Fla.	Miami	75
Ga.	Atlanta	62
Idaho	Boise	51
Ill.	Chicago	50
Ind.	Indianapolis	53
Iowa	Des Moines	50
Kan.	Wichita	57
Ky.	Lexington	55
La.	New Orleans	69
Me.	Portland	46
Md.	Baltimore	55
Mass.	Boston	50
Mich.	Detroit	48
Minn.	Minneapolis	45
Miss.	Jackson	66
Mo.	St. Louis	56
Mont.	Great Falls	45
Neb.	Omaha	51
Nev.	Las Vegas	66
N.H.	Concord	46
N.J.	Trenton	54
N.M.	Albuquerque	56
N.Y.	New York	54
N.C.	Raleigh	60
N.D.	Fargo	40
Ohio	Cleveland	50
Okla.	Oklahoma City	61
Ore.	Portland	52
Pa.	Philadelphia	55
R.I.	Providence	50
S.C.	Charleston	66
S.D.	Sioux Falls	46
Tenn.	Memphis	62
Texas	Dallas	66
Utah	Salt Lake City	52
Vt.	Burlington	45
Va.	Norfolk	60
Wash.	Seattle	51
W. Va.	Charleston	57
Wisc.	Milwaukee	47
Wyo.	Cheyenne	45

Mean Temperatures (tm)

☐ In most parts of the country, stable ground temperatures are higher than the average annual air temperature by 2–3 degrees (F.). In areas with continuous heavy snow cover, the ground temperature can be more than 5 degrees (F.) above the average annual air temperature, making underground construction particularly attractive.

☐ Temperature in the soil lags behind the surface temperature in linear relation to depth. This lag amounts to about one week per foot in most soils. For example, if it is December at the surface, it is "September" at a depth of 12 feet. Therefore, the two maximum loads for heating and cooling (determined by ground and air temperature, respectively) are separated in time. This reduces overall peaks in both heating and cooling.

☐ A more accurate calculation for underground spaces uses mean ground surface temperature (Tgs) in place of the temperature differential (Δt) in the formula where Heat Loss = Δt UA. Tgs is calculated as follows:

$$Tgs = t_i - (t_m - Ap)$$
where:
  Tgs = mean ground surface temperature
  t_i = indoor temperature
  t_m = mean ground temperature
  Ap = amplitude, degree (F.)

☐ The annual variation in surface temperature, or amplitude (Ap) is designated on the accompanying chart. It is the average number of degrees (F.) that the ground temperature (about 4 inches below the surface) rises above and drops below the mean ground temperature.

☐ The mean ground temperature (t_m) is nearly the same as the mean air temperature, and this latter value, readily available from weather data, can be used in these calculations.

Heat Transmission

☐ It should be noted that most heat loss from shallow underground walls travels diagonally toward the surface rather than horizontally to the subsoil.

☐ The calculation of heat transmission through walls below grade, as with components above grade, begins with the determination of R-values. For each successive foot of wall below grade there exists a longer path to the ground surface and therefore a different R. Thus, if the wall supports 10 feet of earth, 10 separate R-values can be determined, one for

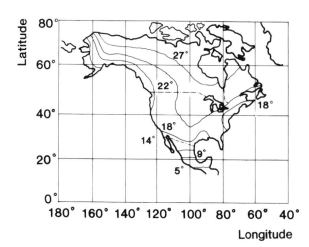

Ground Temperature Amplitudes (° F)

Example: A typical calculation of R and U for 1 square foot of wall begins with a determination of the heat loss path length. For example, the accompanying table indicates that a path length through the earth at the 6-foot level is 8.65 feet. The total R for 1 square foot of wall at that level is determined as follows:

Section	R
Outside surface	0.17
Earth—8.65 × 1.25	10.87
Wall, 8 inch concrete (145 pcf)	0.60
Inside surface	0.68
Total	12.26
$U = \dfrac{1}{12.26} = 0.082$	

each foot below grade, to arrive at an overall average value.

☐ When more accurate values are needed, the accompanying table, containing precalculated R and U-values per square foot of wall up to 12 feet below grade for the earth, can be used.

☐ It should be noted that the benefits of underground construction can also be achieved through berming. The R-value of the earth used for berming can be added to the overall R-value of the wall construction.

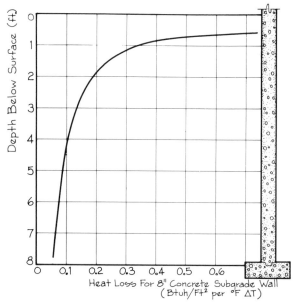

Heat Loss Through Underground Wall

Feet below grade	Earth path length (ft)	R* of earth	Block (135 pcf)		Block (95 pcf)		Concrete (145 pcf)		Concrete (110 pcf)	
			R	U	R	U	R	U	R	U
1	.68	.85	2.80	.357	3.55	.282	2.30	.435	3.21	.312
2	2.27	2.84	4.79	.209	5.54	.181	4.29	.233	5.20	.192
3	3.88	4.85	6.80	.147	7.55	.132	6.30	.159	7.21	.139
4	5.52	6.90	8.85	.113	9.60	.104	8.35	.120	9.26	.108
5	7.05	8.91	10.86	.092	11.61	.086	10.36	.097	11.27	.089
6	8.65	10.81	12.76	.078	13.51	.074	12.26	.082	13.17	.076
7	10.21	12.76	14.71	.068	15.46	.065	14.21	.070	15.12	.066
8	11.78	14.72	16.67	.060	17.42	.057	16.17	.062	17.08	.058
9	13.35	16.69	18.63	.054	19.39	.052	18.14	.055	18.05	.055
10	14.92	18.65	20.60	.049	21.35	.047	20.10	.050	21.01	.048
11	16.49	20.61	22.56	.044	23.31	.043	22.06	.045	22.97	.044
12	18.06	22.58	24.53	.041	25.28	.040	24.03	.042	24.94	.040

Based on 8-in.-thick walls. For each 2-in. added thickness, increase R values as follows:
.11 for 135-pcf block; .20 for 95 pcf block; .15 for 145-pcf concrete; .37 for 110-pcf concrete
*Based on R = 1.25/ft for earth. R and U values include R for earth.

R and U-Values of Walls Below Grade (per square foot of wall)

**New Canaan Nature Center Solar Greenhouse
New Canaan, Connecticut
Architects: Donald Watson, FAIA, and
Buchanan Associates**

The earth berm along three sides of this solar greenhouse, built in 1983, saves the cost of a deep foundation, adds insulation to retain heat in winter and cool air in summer, and supports an outdoor wildflower garden.

Mutual/United of Omaha Headquarters Addition
Omaha, Nebraska
Architect: Leo A. Daly

Mutual/United of Omaha Headquarters Addition
Omaha, Nebraska
Architects: Leo A. Daly

Several reasons contributed to the decision by Mutual/United of Omaha to build an underground addition to their international headquarters in Omaha, Nebraska. Primarily, a new building on grade would have had to be located in front of the present fourteen story structure, diminishing the prominence of the headquarters building and obstructing the view from inside the building. Secondly, the program called for replacement of the dining area, a facility which could most conveniently be located on the same level as the existing kitchen, one floor below grade. Thirdly, the other programmed spaces included several types of spaces such as record storage and

meeting rooms which could suitably be located below grade.

These factors, together with Mutual's ongoing interest in energy conservation made an underground structure feasible. The architectural solution places the 1,000 seat cafeteria, the visitors center and the library on the first level below grade, immediately below a 90′ diameter glass dome. This solar dome, the largest of its type in North America consists of an outside layer of tempered bronze-tinted glass and an inside layer of tempered clear glass, separated by a half-inch evacuated space. The second and third levels below grade include an automated record storage and retrieval system, which incorporates file areas previously distributed throughout the main building, making expansion space available on each tower floor. The

Mutual/United of Omaha Headquarters Addition
Omaha, Nebraska
Architect: Leo A. Daly

underground structure adds 184,000 square feet to Mutual's Headquarters.

The existing central energy plant had sufficient capacity to accommodate the low non-fluctuating heating and cooling load imposed by the underground building, a load further reduced by a waste heat recovery system. Preliminary reports of the first full year cycle indicate an energy reduction of 65 to 70 percent below that required for a comparable building above grade.

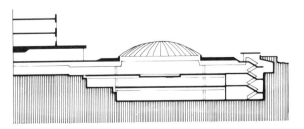

Mutual/United of Omaha Headquarters Addition
Omaha, Nebraska
Architect: Leo A. Daly

Insulation

Most buildings erected in the last 50 years have been of lightweight construction, which lacks the thermal storage properties of heavy mass construction. Low-density insulating materials have been developed to compensate for this reduced mass in structure. Insulation for lightweight construction can be selected on the basis of:

—physical structure
—moisture transmission
—fire resistance
—installation
—available sizes.

Summarized below are some of the major types of building insulation.

Aluminum Foil

—Aluminum foil insulation is single or multiple parallel layers of foil and kraft paper combinations with an airspace. Being a metal, aluminum foil is a good reflector but a poor absorber of radiation. It reflects 95 percent of the heat, absorbing only 5 percent.

—Aluminum foil is almost impervious, with a vapor barrier rating 0–0.02 perm.

—Aluminum is fire-resistant, but kraft paper laminate is not.

—It is easily installed.

—It comes 25" wide for rafters, joists or studs on 24" centers; 33" wide for 16" centers; and 36" wide for 16" centers where insulation is to be recessed.

Urethane

—Urethane is cellular plastic foam formed by the reaction of isocyanates and polyols. As it foams and expands, it entraps fluorocarbon vapor, which has extremely low heat conductance.

—Vapor transmission is 2–3 perms. A separate vapor barrier is needed.

—Urethane is combustible, and must be protected from fire by finish surface materials. It should not be used where temperatures exceed 200° (F.).

—Foam application requires special machines and skills. (Urethane board, another form of this substance, is light and easily worked.)

—Foam expands to fit any shape or size space. Tapered roofing sections are usually 2' × 4' or 3' × 4' boards, tapered 1/16", 1/8" or 1/4".

Expanded Polystyrene

—Expanded polystyrene is a polymer impregnated with a foaming agent that, when exposed to heat, creates a uniform, closed-cell structure highly resistant to heat flow and moisture penetration.

—It is combustible and must be protected by finish materials.

—It is easily cut for installation.

—It comes in lengths of 4', 6', and 8'; widths of 12", 16", 24", and 48"; thicknesses of 1/2" to 19"; and tapered roof insulation.

Extruded Polystyrene

—Extruded polystyrene is like expanded polystyrene except the extrusion process compresses the cells, leaving no voids, for better moisture protection.

—It is inherently resistant to all forms of moisture.

—It contains a flame retardant but is still considered combustible and must be protected.

—It is installed with mastic or self-tapping screws into metal studs.

—It comes in boards 8' long; 34" wide; 3/4", 1" and 2" thick. Tongue and groove sheathing is 8' long; 16" or 24" wide; 3/4", 1", and 2" thick. Roofing boards are 24" × 48"; 1", 1½" and 3" thick.

Cellular Glass

—Cellular glass is a lightweight, rigid insulation composed of millions of completely sealed glass cells per board.

—It is completely impervious to moisture.

—It is totally inorganic and noncombustible.

—Adhesive is used to hold glass board to wall surfaces.

—It comes in 24" × 48" boards in 1½" - 4" thicknesses; 12" × 18" × 24" flat blocks in thicknesses from 1½" - 4"; and tapered roof blocks 18" × 24" with tapers of 1/16", 1/8" or 1/4".

Fiberglass

—Fiberglass is made of fine wool-like compressible fibers spun from glass. It can be in loose form, in batts, or faced on one or both sides with paper or foil.

—Moisture transmission of foil-faced fiberglass is 0.5 perm; kraft-faced, 1.0 perm. Unfaced fiberglass should be protected with vapor barrier.

—Fiberglass is noncombustible, but its backing is not.

—The loose type is blown in. Most typical are batts stapled to framing or held in by friction fit.

☐ If the designer has determined the U-values necessary for different envelope components, the R-values of the structural components of the section are known, the correct thickness for the insulation can be determined on the basis of the appropriate R-value needed to yield an overall resistance for the compo-

Zone	Ceiling	Wall	Floor
1	19	11	11
2	26	13	11
3	26	19	13
4	30	19	19
5	33	19	22
6	38	19	22

NOTE: The minimum insulation R values recommended for various parts of the United States as delineated in the zone map.
Recommended Minimal Thermal Resistances (R) of Insulation

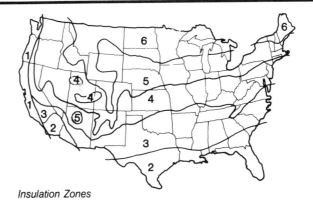

Insulation Zones

nent.

☐ The accompanying chart gives thermal resistance values for various types of insulation.

Location of Insulation

☐ Insulation can be effectively placed outside the wall, between wall components, or inside the wall. The accompanying chart compares the relative merits of inside and outside insulation (with a rain screen). The following rules of thumb apply for proper location and installation of insulation.

—Vapor barriers must fully cover all areas of the wall section. Edges should be sealed and joints overlapped.

—Attachment by gluing instead of stapling ensures secure vapor barriers.

—Low-density fibrous and loose fill insulations should not be compacted.

—Low-density fibrous and loose fill insulations should completely fill the space between studs of rafters to prevent infiltration.

—Fibrous batts installed vertically should *not* have air spaces on both sides.

Design	Exterior insulation: Supporting structure invisible	Interior insulation: Supporting structure visible
Thermal Characteristics	All requirements easily met. No problems in assessment of heat and sound protection. Vented airspace closely follows outside air pressure. All parts of structure exposed to similar temperature with only slight variation throughout year. Thermal problems associated with connections of interior and exterior structural elements eliminated. Window frame attached to warm side of wall, edge cooling effect minimized. Internal mass of building structures provides thermal 'flywheel' for heat storage.	Heat bridges pose problems at connections of interior and exterior structural elements, floor slabs and walls etc. Exterior structural mass possible modifier of interior temperature. Window frame and sill on cold side of wall, substantial edge cooling effect. Likelihood of cracks in back-up and cladding due to theramally induced expansion and contraction. Air leakages from this cause will result in condensation and degradation of wall materials. All materials outside insulation will fall below freezing.
Construction	No special requirements. Raw construction and completion simple to realize technically in traditional ways. Complex building geometrics require expensive construction for heat protection. Outside work requires scaffolding.	Special requirements re: heat bridges. During raw construction insulating slabs must be built in these areas: danger of damage to insulating slabs.

Characteristics of Insulation

—It is crucial to seal window frames, wall plates at foundations, and electrical outlets along the perimeter.

—The perimeter of the floor joist system in frame construction should be detailed to allow space for application of insulation along its length.

—To eliminate the problem of an air space behind outside insulation boards (which can reduce insulation value by 40 percent), insulation should be attached with a full coat of mastic.

—In heavy mass construction, insulation placement can have a great effect on the time lag of a composite wall. Insulation placed on the inside surface of a concrete wall can cause a time lag of 8 hours; in the middle, 10 hours; and on the outside, 13 hours.

Condensation and Vapor Barriers

☐ Vapor condenses on a surface when the temperature of that surface drops below the dew point of the surrounding air. If this vapor should condense on the insulation in a building envelope, the R-value of the insulation will drop considerably. To prevent this occurrence, it is necessary to use a vapor barrier on the *warm side* of the building envelope. In addition to condensation protection, a vapor barrier will prevent latent heat from escaping from the building during the winter. Conversely, outside latent heat will be prevented from entering a cool building during the summer. The accompanying diagram shows possible air movements through a wall and correct positioning of vapor barriers to avoid loss of insulation values and degradation of materials.

Air Spaces and Cavity Construction

☐ Heat flows from surface to surface across a cavity by convection, radiation and, if a thermal bridge is present, by conduction. The most critical aspects of cavity space design are dimension and enclosing surfaces.

Dimension

☐ The accompanying chart shows the variation of thermal resistance with the width of the air space. If the air space dimension is greater than approximately ¾ inch, the resistance value is lowered by convection currents. In a horizontal cavity, when the heat flow is from below, convection currents tend to be vertical; when heat flow is from above, they will be virtually eliminated, because the warm air will be at the top layer.

Building Insulations	Density (LB/CU FT)	Resistance (R) (HR/SQ FT °F BTU PER 1 IN. THICKNESS)
Fiberglass	0.6–1.0	3.16
Rock or slag wool	1.5–2.5	3.2–3.7
Cellulose	2.2–3.0	3.2–3.7
Molded polystyrene	0.8–2.0	3.8–4.4
Extruded polystyrene	0.8–2.0	3.8–4.4
Polyurethane	2.0	5.8–6.2
Polyisocyanurate	2.0	5.8–6.2
UREA Formaldehyde	0.6–0.9	4.2
Perlite (loose fill)	2–11	2.5–3.7
Vermiculite (loose fill)	4–10	2.4–3.0

Resistance Values for Types of Insulation

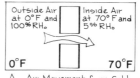

A. Air Movement from Cold to Warm. Condensation is Not Possible.

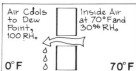

B. Air Movement from Warm to Cold. Condensation is Possible.

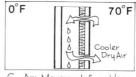

C. Air Movement from Warm to Cooler - Condensation may Occur.

D. Air Space on Both Sides of Insulation. Condensation may Occur.

E. Air Barrier on Cold Side - Danger of Condensation.

F. Air Barrier on Warm Side - No Danger of Condensation.

Air Movement Effects

Enclosing Surfaces

☐ Aluminum foil used in a single unventilated cavity reduces radiant heat transfer considerably. Foil also can be used to divide an unventilated vertical cavity into two parts, nearly doubling the insulation value, if both cavities are less than ¾ inch wide and there is a foil surface on one side.

☐ Aluminum foil can also be used in a horizontal cavity, ¾ inch or more wide, when the heat flow is downward, such as in a roof space.

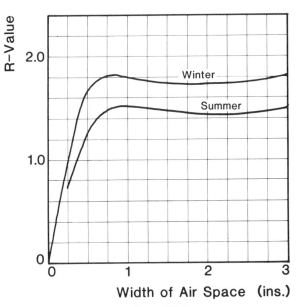

U-Values Varying with Air Space Width

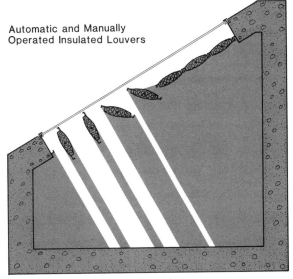

Automatic and Manually Operated Insulated Louvers

"Skylids"

In this particular situation, radiant heat transfer is the primary concern, because convection is virtually nonexistent.

Movable Insulation

☐ The use of movable insulation for window coverings is covered in detail in the "Shading and Sun Control" monograph in this handbook. In addition to movable insulation for window control, a variety of innovative insulating systems are available. Two examples illustrated here are "Skylids," developed by Zomeworks, Inc., and the "Skytherm Process," developed by Harold Hay. Zomeworks, Inc., for example, has developed a patented skylight which allows penetration of light and heat when desired and which automatically closes when conditions suggest it; canisters of freon gas are used to provide the control.

☐ Another approach has been patented by Harold Hay of Sky Therm Process and Engineering, Los Angeles. A flat roof structure supports black plastic bags, each of which is 8" deep and contains noncirculating water. During the day, the bags are exposed to the sun and act as both storage devices and radiators to the space below. At night, insulated shutters on the roof side are closed to keep heat from escaping to the night air. In warm weather, these shutters remain closed during the day and are opened at night. Hay's 36' × 52' case uses 7,000 gallons of water, providing the heat storage capacity of 16" of concrete at a dead weight equivalent to only 4" of concrete.

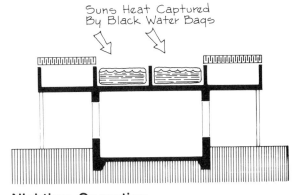

Nightime Operation

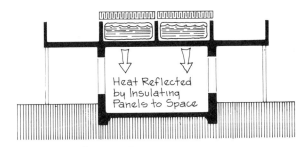

Daytime Operation

Sky Therm Roof

71

Fenestration

It is difficult to isolate the thermal transmission properties of windows and doors as components of the building envelope without taking into account the effects of daylighting, solar gain, and the need for shading control. A more complete discussion of these factors appears in this handbook's "Climate and Site," "Shading and Sun control" and "Daylighting" monographs.

Various types of glazing can be used to manipulate light transmittance and heat flow through glazing:
—heat absorbing glass
—heat reflecting glass
—glare control glass
—photochromatic glass
—surface films
—multiple glazing.

For purposes of this monograph the important points for consideration of fenestration in an energy efficient manner are:
—ratio of glass area to opaque area·
—frame construction
—infiltration and condensation.

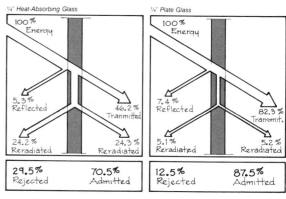

Solar Energy Transmission through Heat-Absorbing Single Glazing vs. Clear Glass

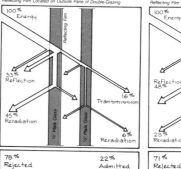

Effect of Reflecting Film Location on Heat Transmission Through Double Glazing

Glass Area to Opaque Area Ratio

☐ The accompanying chart and example demonstrate selection of glass/wall ratios for estimating purposes. These charts are only for making estimates in the initial design phase of a project. More thorough analyses of glass areas take into account factors such as framing, window tilt and orientation.

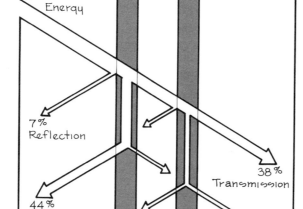

Solar Energy Transmission through Heat-Absorbing Double Glazing

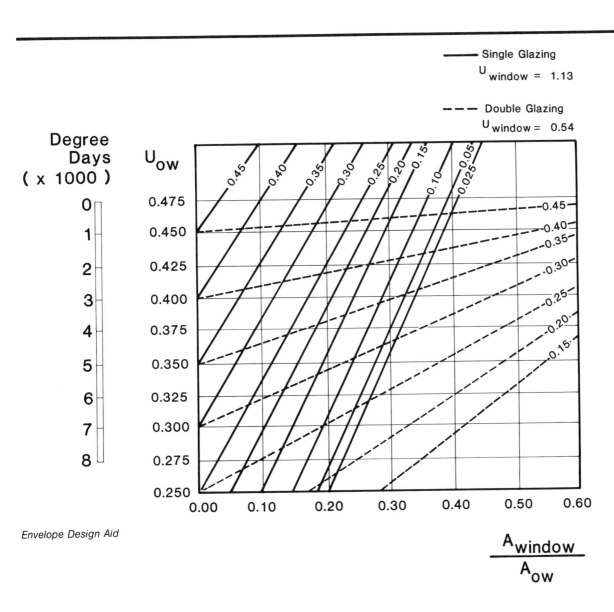

Degree Days (x 1000)

Single Glazing
$U_{window} = 1.13$

Double Glazing
$U_{window} = 0.54$

U_{ow}

0.45 0.40 0.35 0.30 0.25 0.20 0.15 0.10 0.025

0.45
0.40
0.35
0.30
0.25
0.20
0.15

0.475
0.450
0.425
0.400
0.375
0.350
0.325
0.300
0.275
0.250

0   1   2   3   4   5   6   7   8

0.00   0.10   0.20   0.30   0.40   0.50   0.60

$$\frac{A_{window}}{A_{ow}}$$

Envelope Design Aid

73

Example:
The designer can estimate quickly the consequences of varying the percentage glass type (single pane or double pane) in the gross exterior wall.

The problem can be phrased as follows: given the location, gross exterior wall area and construction, and using single glass, what is the maximum percent window area which will give a value of U_{ow} less than the maximum allowable?

Step 1. Compute $U_{opaque\ wall} = 0.195$

Step 2. Draw a horizontal line at 3,080 degree-days, or $U_{ow} = 0.4$, as illustrated.

Step 3. Where this horizontal line intersects the solid diagonal line (single glass) representing $U_{opaque\ wall} = 0.195$, project a vertical line down as shown. This line intersects the A_{window}/A_{ow} scale at 0.21, indicating that 21% window area (0.21 × 180,000 ft²) or 37,800 ft², represents the maximum permissible window area.

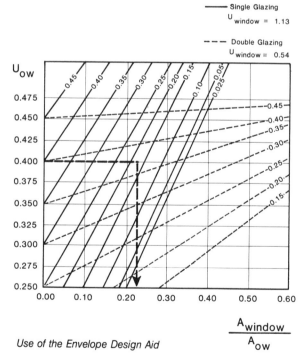

Use of the Envelope Design Aid

Condensation

☐ Condensation occurs on the inside surface of glass in the winter and on the outside in the summer. The accompanying graph can be used to predict the glazing U-value necessary to prevent condensation. To use the graph:

1. Find the point where the inside temperature and the design outdoor temperature coincide. Carry this line across horizontally to the right side of the chart.

2. Find the relative humidity percentage and draw a vertical line to meet the temperature line. The point where the two lines intersect indicates the minimum U-value of glazing necessary to avoid condensation.

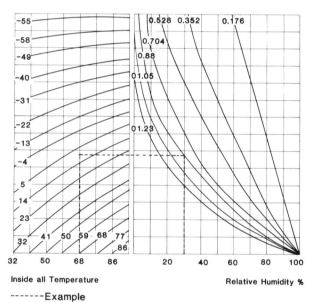

Inside all Temperature   Relative Humidity %

------Example

Condensation Prediction Curves

Infiltration

☐ Infiltration is the other major problem facing window designers. Heating loads due to infiltration of unconditioned air can exceed those due to transmission losses. In fact, it can account for one-third of the load in externally dominated buildings.

☐ Infiltration is caused by wind pressure and by stack effect. With air infiltration caused by wind pressure, air enters the building on the windward side, travels across the building, and exits on the leeward side, where air pressure is negative because of wind deflection over and around the building.

☐ With air infiltration caused by stack effect, warm air rises in the building and exfiltrates in the upper half of the building, drawing air into the lower half. This phenomenon causes air to move vertically through the building.

☐ Making a small building relatively airtight involves weatherstripping windows and doors and providing "air lock" entryways. Larger highrise buildings are more difficult, but respond reasonably well to proper sealing of joints and the use of revolving doors and vestibules on entranceways. Air curtains can be used effectively in low buildings, but they lose efficiency in cold climates.

☐ The accompanying chart can be used to determine infiltration rates.

Frames and Seals

☐ The window frame, if selected carefully, can add to the thermal resistance of the window assembly. The frame also determines the possibility of the addition of wind and sun shading devices. The color and reflectivity of window mullions can affect the heat gain of the window assembly. The accompanying chart indicates the thermal performance of some common window assemblies.

☐ Weatherstripping around the perimeter joints of an operable sash also effectively reduce air infiltration. The accompanying chart indicates infiltration reductions due to weatherstripping.

☐ Providing a thermal break in the path of heat flow through metal window frames can also reduce heat transmission. Aluminum conducts heat 1,770 times better than wood, offering little resistance to the flow of heat. This inherent disadvantage of metal window frames can be alleviated by thermally separating the inside of the frame from the outside of the frame. Two prevalent methods of providing a thermal separation are:

—Pouring polyurethane into a slot in the metal frame; then, after it has bonded and set, sawing away the metal bridging the slot.

—providing two separate frames linked together with a rigid vinyl insert.

Infill Material	Frame Material		
	Wood Wood/PVC	Steel/Aluminum with interrupted cold bridges	Steel/Aluminum
Insulated glazing (¼ in.)	.58	.62	—
Insulated glazing (½ in.)	.51	.58	.62
Triple glazing	.33	.37	.41
Double glazing (¾-1½ in.)	.45	.48	.51
Double glazing (1½-2¾ in.)	.41	.45	.48
Double glazing (+2¾ in.)	.45	—	—

U-Values of Frame-sash-infill Assemblies

Types	Wind Speed (mph)				
Wood Double Hung (average fit)					
Non-weatherstripped	7	21	39	59	80
Weatherstripped	4	13	24	36	49
Average reduction	38 percent reduction due to weatherstripping				
Wood Double Hung (poor fit)					
Non-weatherstripped	27	69	111	154	199
Weatherstripped	6	19	34	51	71
Average reduction	70 percent reduction due to weatherstripping				
Metal Double hung (unlocked)					
Non-weatherstripped	20	47	74	104	137
Weatherstripped	6	19	32	46	60
Average reduction	60 percent reduction due to weatherstripping				

Cubic Feet of Air Infiltration Per Foot of Crack, Per Hour

Specification	Material	Type or Class	Air Leakage
ANSI A134.1	Aluminum	A-B1 (Awning)	0.75 cfm/ft crack
		A-A2 (Awning)	0.50 cfm/ft crack
		C-B1 (Casement)	0.50 cfm/ft crack
		C-A2 (Casement)	0.50 cfm/ft crack
		C-A3 (Casement)	0.50 cfm/ft crack
		DH-B1 (Hung)	0.75 cfm/ft crack
		DH-A2 (Hung)	0.50 cfm/ft crack
		DH-A3 (Hung)	0.50 cfm/ft crack
		DH-A4 (Hung)	0.50 cfm/ft crack
		HS-B1 (Sliding)	0.75 cfm/ft crack
		HS-B2 (Sliding)	0.75 cfm/ft crack
		HS-A2 (Sliding)	0.75 cfm/ft crack
		HS-A3 (Sliding)	0.50 cfm/ft crack
		J-B1 (Jalousie)	1.50 cfm/ft^2
		JA-B1 (Jal-Awning)	0.75 cfm/ft crack
		P-B1 (Protected)	0.50 cfm/ft crack
		P-A2 (Protected)	0.50 cfm/ft crack
		P-A2.50 (Projected)	0.375 cfm/ft crack
		P-A3 (Projected)	0.50 cfm/ft crack
		TH-A2 (Inswinging)	0.375 cfm/ft crack
		TH-A3 (Inswinging)	0.50 cfm/ft crack
		VP-A2 (Pivoted)	0.375 cfm/ft crack
		VP-A3 (Pivoted)	0.50 cfm/ft crack
		VS-B1 (Vert. Sliding)	0.75 cfm/ft crack
ANSI A134.2	Aluminum	SGD-B1 (Sliding Glass Door)	1.0 cfm/ft^2
		SGD-B2 (Sliding Glass Door)	0.50 cfm/ft^2
		SGD-A2	0.50 cfm/ft^2
		SGD-A3 (Sliding Glass Door)	0.50 cfm/ft^2
ANSI A200.1	Wood	All Types Windows Class A	
		Class B	0.50 cfm/linear ft
			0.50 cfm/linear ft
ANSI A200.2	Wood	All Types Sliding Glass Doors	0.50 cfm/ft^2
Fed. MHC & SS 280.403	All	Windows (All Types) Sliding Glass Doors	0.50 cfm/ft^2
Fed. MHC & SS 280.405	All	Vertical Entrance	1.20 cfm/ft^2 (1976)
			1.0 cfm/ft^2 (1977)

Window and Door Air Leakage

☐ The effectiveness of the thermal break depends on the insulating value and thickness of the material used. An aluminum frame with a good thermal break has a U-value similar to that of insulating glass (U = 0.58) and performs substantially better than an aluminum frame with no thermal break, as shown for a 2 inch thick frame.

Types	Frame U-Value
Aluminum frame no break	U = 1.18
Aluminum frame with break	U = 0.60

☐ The benefit of providing a thermal break in the frame is proportional to the amount of frame area. The frame area can be as high as 20 percent of the total window area. In such a case, if the window is glazed with insulating glass, it is important that the frame not provide a "short circuit" for the heat flow.

☐ An analysis was performed on a hypothetical five bedroom bungalow with 998 square feet of floor area, 12 windows with a combined area of 221 square feet, two doors with a combined area of 37 square feet, and 4 inches of insulation in the walls and ceiling. The windows were average fitted and had rib-type metal weatherstripping. The interior temperature was to be maintained at 70° (F.). The following table summarizes the calculated reduction in winter heating costs due to weather stripping the windows of the hypothetical bungalow located in various cities. The costs have been calculated for natural gas at $0.21 per 100 cubic feet, 1000 BTU/cubic foot, and a furnace efficiency of 80 percent.

City	Degree Days	Fuel Cost due to Infiltration		Savings	Total Fuel Cost	
		Non-W.S.	W.S.		Non-W.S.	W.S.
Washington, D.C.	4,561	55.23	19.40	35.83	149.72	113.89
New York City	5,280	63.93	22.47	41.46	173.30	131.85
Chicago, Ill.	6,282	76.06	26.72	49.34	206.20	156.86
Minneapolis, Minn.	7,966	96.46	33.89	62.57	261.50	198.92
Grand Forks, N.D.	9,871	119.53	41.99	77.54	324.03	246.49

W.S. = Weatherstripped

Reduction in Winter Heating Costs (Hypothetical Bungalow)

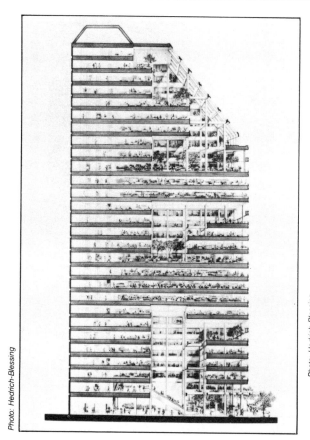

33 W. Monroe Office Building
Chicago, Illinois
Architects: Skidmore, Owings & Merrill

33 W. Monroe Office Building
Chicago, Illinois
Architects: Skidmore, Owings & Merrill

33 W. Monroe Office Building
Chicago, Illinois
Architects: Skidmore, Owings & Merrill

The 33 W. Monroe Office Building designed by SOM is comprised of three atriums. Stacked vertically within the building, each atrium is formed by overhanging office floors rising seven to 12 stories. The atriums serve as lobbies for the floors that rise above, creating the sense of three small buildings contained within one building envelope. Glass-enclosed office floors overlook the atrium, illuminated by natural light from the exterior window wall. Each atrium provides a year-round climate controlled space enhanced by foliage and fountains. The top atrium creates an atelier atmosphere with sloping glass. The atrium concept provides greater perimeter glass for each floor, a stronger leasing concept and a tremendous mechanical advantage.

An energy efficient exterior envelope was created utilizing only 38% glass. The total exterior glass surface as a ratio of floor area is about one-half that of a typical high-rise office building. The exterior glass is dual glazed, semi-reflective to reduce solar heat gain, minimize heat loss and afford a comfortable work environment.

The design approach maximizes energy conservation throughout this buidling. The low broad structure (optimum surface of volume ratio) lessens heat gain and loss through the surface which in itself minimizes energy waste with its low composition of dual glass (38%).

An innovative arrangement of three interior atriums provides maximum window exposure while necessitating minimum exterior window wall. The atrium concept accommodates a naturally illuminated and controlled interior environment.

78

Photo: Hedrich-Blessing

33 W. Monroe Office Building
Chicago, Illinois
Architects: Skidmore, Owings & Merrill

Envelope Materials

Building materials are important to energy conservation not only because their manufacture often involves the use of nonrenewable fuels but also because their raw materials in some cases are becoming scarce.

☐ Building experts estimate that 6.5 percent of the GNP of the United States each year is used to build, alter and maintain buildings. Some designers now consider the life cycle cost of buildings in terms of not only first and operating costs but also the energy needed to produce various building materials.

☐ The energy used to produce the materials for brick on woodframe envelope, for example, is four times that for a woodframe envelope (see accompanying figure). In typical residential construction this difference equals three to five years' operating energy. Such "embodied" energy, as indicated by the accompanying table, ranges from 630,000 BTUs per square foot for two to four family residential units to 2.07 million BTUs per square foot for laboratories.

☐ Research by the Advisory Council on Historic Preservation indicates that renovating existing buildings instead of building new ones can save considerable energy, both by using existing materials and by not demolishing existing buildings. (The latter can require up to 15,000 BTUs per square foot.)

☐ An awareness of the energy embodied in all steps of materials use can enable designers to make significant reductions in the energy consumed by the built environment.

☐ The energy embodied in the materials and equipment needed to construct a community

Construction	R Value		Embodied Energy (BTU/Sq. Ft.) in Bldg Section
1. Outside surface (15 mph wind)	.17		—
2. Wood shingles (½″ × 8″ lapped)	87		7,315
3. Bldg. paper (asphalt)	.15		—
4. Plywood (½″)	.62		7,705
5. 4″ airspace	.97		—
6. 2″ × 4″ @ 16″ O.C.	—	4.35	3,486
7. Gypsum wallboard (½″)	.45		6,920
8. Inside surface (still air)	.68		—
Total	3.91	4.35	25,426

Construction	R value		Embodied Energy (BTU/Sq. Ft.) in Bldg Section
1. Outside surface (15 mph wind)	.17		—
2. Brick & masonry (4″)	.44		105,004
3. 1″ airspace	.97		—
4. Building paper (asphalt)	.15		—
5. Plywood (⅜″)	.47		5,779
6. 4″ airspace	.97		—
7. 2″ × 4″ @ 16 O.C.	—	4.35	3,486
8. Gypsum wallboard (⅜″)	.32		5,297
9. Inside surface	.68		—
Total	3.98	4.35	119,566

Addition of Insulation	R Value	Embodied Energy (BTU/Sq. Ft.) in Bldg Section
Add 3½″ batt insulation	11.00	Add 6,860
Deduct R value of air space	.97	
	10.03	
Add to above R value	3.91	
Total	13.79	32,286

Addition of Insulation	R Value	Embodied Energy (BTU/Sq. Ft.) in Bldg Section
Add 3½″ batt insulation	11.00	Add 6,860
Deduct R value of air space	.97	
	10.03	
Add to above R value	3.98	
Total	14.01	126,426

Wood-Frame Wall

Brick on Wood-Frame Wall

Types	MBTU/Sq. Ft.
Residential—1 Family	700
Residential—2-4 Family	630
Residential—Garden Apt	650
Residential—High Rise	740
Hotel/Motel	1130
Dormitories	1430
Industrial Buildings	970
Office Buildings	1640
Warehouses	560
Garages/Service Stations	770
Stores/Restaurants	940
Religious Buildings	1260
Educational	1390
Hospital Buildings	1720
Other Nonfarm Buildings	1450
a. Amusement, Social & Rec	1380
b. Mis. Nonresidential Bldg	1100
c. Laboratories	2070
d. Libraries, Museums, etc.	1740

Embodied Energy of Materials and Construction per Building Type

Material	Unit	Embodied Energy Per Material Unit
Wood Products		
Lumber	bd. ft.	7,600-9,700
Flooring	bd. ft.	10,300
Window Units	ea.	1,127,000-1,830,000
Doors	ea.	
Plywood	sq. ft.	8,300-17,000
Prefab Members	bd. ft.	16,500
Glass Products		
Sheet Glass	sq. ft.	13,700-20,000
Plate Float	sq. ft.	34,600-54,700
Laminated	sq. ft.	113,500-212,500
Stone/Clay Products		
Portland Cement	bbl.	1,582,000
Brick	brk.	14,300-25,600
Clay Tile	brk.	27,700-33,400
Concrete Block	blk.	31,800
Steel Products		
Sheets	lb.	27,800
Shapes	lb.	18,700-26,900
Nonferrous Products		
Aluminum	lb.	96,000-116,000

Embodied Energy of Materials

college in Chicago, Illinois was recently analyzed. The three-story, 432,000 square foot building is a steel structure enclosed by steel and glass curtain walls. Note that the steel used represents 6.8 percent of the weight but 69.5 percent of the total energy.

Material	BTU/Unit Fabrication Energy	% of Total Weight	% of Total Energy
Aluminum	41,000/lb.	0.08	1.6
Ceiling Materials	1,500/lb.	0.5	0.3
Concrete	413/lb.	58.7	12.4
Concrete Block (8 × 8 × 16)	15,200/block	27.0	1.9
Copper	40,000/lb.	0.2	4.3
Dry Wall	2,160/lb.	4.2	0.7
Glass	12,600/lb.	0.2	1.2
Insulation		0.04	4.9
Duct-1 inch 3 lb.	51,400 sq. ft.		
Pipe-2 inch	7,700		
Building-Board	2,040		
Paint	4,134/lb.	0.04	0.1
Plumbing Fixtures		0.2	2.0
Roofing	6,945/sq. ft.	2.0	0.5
Steel	13,800/lb.	6.8	69.5
Vinyl Tile	8,000/lb.	0.04	0.6

Embodied Energy Analysis for Community College

Grand Central Arcade Restoration
Seattle, Washington

The Grand Central Arcade, an old hotel in the Pioneer Square Historic District of Seattle, was renovated to provide 80,000 square feet of commercial and office space. The embodied energy of materials and construction needed for this rehabilitation was 16,900 billion BTUs, compared to an estimated 108,800 billion BTUs for comparable new construction — an 84 percent reduction.

The rehabilitated building is estimated to consume about 6 percent more operating energy than the equivalent new building. This energy loss is so much smaller than the embodied energy savings that the energy investments required of the two alternatives will not be equivalent for more than 250 years.

Material	Energy/Unit	Quantity	Energy (MMBtu)
Wood studs	7,611/b.f.	14,300 b.f.	108.8
Wood doors	346,502/ea.	90 count	31.2
Plywood	5,779/s.f.	59,584 s.f.	344.3
Sheet glass	15,430/s.f.	9,090 s.f.	140.3
Float glass	54,672/s.f.	81 s.f.	4.4
Ceramic tile	68,660/s.f.	200 s.f.	13.7
Concrete block	31,821/ea.	615 count	19.6
Brick	4,985/ea.	2,663 count	13.3
Concrete	2,594,338/ c.y.	43 c.y.	111.6
⅝" gypsum board	5,297/s.f.	72,482 s.f.	383.9
6" batt insulation	8,345/s.f.	16,662 s.f.	139.0
Nails	34,016/lb.	1,376 lb.	46.8
Rebars	15,664/lb.	1,923 lb.	30.1
Angle iron	26,910/lb.	15,334 lb.	412.6
Steel strip	120,825/lb.	7,818 lb.	944.6
Steel beam	22,707/lb.	17,792 lb.	404.0
Steel bolts	26,625/lb.	120 lb.	3.2
Interior ap. paint	437,025/gal.	340 gal.	148.6
			3,300 MMBtu

Note: 70% of materials accounted for

Rehabilitation Materials Inventory for Grand Central Arcade Restoration

Grand Central Arcade Restoration
Seattle, Washington

Dynamic Response of the Envelope

Because both external and internal thermal forces change hourly, daily and seasonally, building envelopes should have the ability to react to these changes in much the same way that mechanical systems adjust their operation.

☐ Basically, the envelope can be responsive to the changing environmental forces in two ways: fixed response and dynamic response. Fixed response of the envelope relies on the fairly predictable nature of forces that affect the thermal load on a building. A typical example of a fixed response is the use of the envelope form to shade the building from unwanted sun. The designer can predict accurately the location and angles of the sun, designing overhangs or fins to shade exactly the area desired (see "Shading and Sun Control" monograph). This type of envelope response can be seasonal (shade during certain times of the year) or daily (shade during certain hours of the day).

☐ Another fixed response to changing environmental conditions is heavy mass envelope construction. Thermal inertia of the mass allows it to absorb heat from the sun during the day and release it to indoor spaces during later hours when it is needed. The effectiveness of thermal mass depends on a fairly predictable dynamic occurrence, the diurnal insolation of a given location.

☐ Dynamic responses can be more complex and tend to be used to respond to environmental changes that are difficult to predict, requiring monitoring to enable effective adjustment of the envelope. Some dynamic responses involve simple manual adjustment on the part of occupants, such as opening windows for natural ventilation or closing thermal shutters to the cold.

☐ As energy conserving techniques have become more sophisticated, envelope components have been developed to respond dynamically to changing environmental conditions. Often controlled by photocells or temperature sensors, these envelope components change the skin of the building to temper the effect of environmental forces, before use of the HVAC system is necessary.

☐ Some examples of dynamically responsive envelope components include:

—motorized shading controls for walls and windows, such as venetian blinds

—air doors that act as thermal barriers, with or without heaters depending on conditions

—movable shutters or insulation (manual or automated)

—mirror systems that adjust to optimize daylighting systems according to outdoor sky conditions.

☐ The responsiveness of the building envelope to dynamic building conditions can often be greatly enhanced by the use of an automated central control system that coordinates building systems to optimize their combined performance. A centralized control system can:

—monitor operating conditions of all building systems and adjust controls as needed

—monitor and record selected data to determine the effectiveness of the energy management system

—limit electrical demand peaks by shedding nonessential services according to predetermined priorities

—provide centralized information on age of all system components in use, spare parts and necessary tools and labor for maintenance.

☐ In general, rules of thumb for determining cost-effective candidates for central control include:

—buildings in excess of 20,000 square feet

—buildings with centralized rather than localized heating and cooling systems

—buildings with existing suitable telephone lines (wiring and communication costs are a major expense in central management systems).

Cary Arboretum: Plant Science Building
Millbrook, New York
Architect: Malcolm Wells

Cary Aboretum: Plant Science Building
Millbrook, New York
Architect: Malcolm Wells

The Plant Science Building of the Cary Aboretum complex located in Millbrook, New York, is an example of building design that responds dynamically to changing internal and external conditions. Architect Malcolm Wells and engineer Fred Dubin created a design that allows the building to respond to both seasonal and diurnal changes. It was carefully sited in order to take full advantage of a dense hemlock forest and hills to the north, which shelters it from cold winter winds. Two-thirds of the structure is buried underground, and the north, east and west sides of the building are earth-bermed. The foot-thick masonry walls and thick coating of outer insulation on the exposed walls and roof allow the building to collect and store heat during the day and release it to the interior spaces at night, thus taking advantage of the thermal inertia of mass construction.

Active solar collectors provide all of the domestic hot water heating and most of the space heating for the building. On the south walls of the building, large glazed areas admit direct solar heating and diffuse daylight. These windows respond dynamically to seasonal changes through the use of sun fins and overhangs to block out unwanted summer sun yet admit lower level winter sun. North oriented skylights allow natural light into the space. All glazed areas except the entrance vestibules are equipped with manually operated insulating shutters, used to respond to changing thermal needs.

During the summer, the building responds to cooling needs with roof overhangs on the south side of the building, thick insulation, and the cooling effect of the earth against the exterior walls. The building's windows are operable, to provide natural ventilation and take advantage of cooling breezes. Cold well water is routed directly to radiators in the system's air handling units to chill air when additional cooling is necessary.

The lighting system responds dynamically to the diurnal and seasonal variations in available natural light with skylights directly over work areas, task lighting, and the configuration of work spaces and space dividers.

A computerized control system selects combinations from twelve different modes of operation, always basing mode selection on the minimum energy consumption possible for existing conditions.

Cary Arboretum: Plant Science Building
Millbrook, New York
Architect: Malcolm Wells

Innovations in Envelope Design

Concerns about energy as well as impending shortages of materials have prompted the design and testing of new envelope materials and components. For example, materials research at the National Aeronautics and Space Agency (NASA) has yielded promising building technologies for the future. NASA researchers pioneered selective surfaces that control the emission or re-radiation of heat from absorber surfaces, reflective mirror films for glazing, flat conductor cable that permits elimination of ducts, cellulose insulation made by chemically treating shredded newspapers, new lightweight fire-resistant materials, photovoltaics and other solar applications.

☐ Research sponsored by the U.S. Department of Energy includes an attempt to develop a thermal storage wall in which the cavities of standard concrete blocks are filled with pouches of phase-changing materials. This would increase the storage capacity of each block more than eightfold.

☐ More dynamic building skins are also appearing. In the mid-1970's, Sean Wellesley-Miller and Day Charoudi, then at the Massachusetts Institute of Technology, explored the concept of a "cloud gel" membrane that responds to changing solar conditions by changing its degree of transparency. Such research continues today.

☐ "Double envelope" structures are both innovative and controversial. The occupied space is surrounded on four of its six sides (north and south walls, roof and floor) by an air space. The air space is, in turn, enclosed by an outer shell consisting of the roof, north and south walls, and exposed earth underneath the floor. The east and west walls are single walls.

☐ The double envelope concept is that the structure is heated by a convective loop of air that circles in the air space between the two shells. Air heated in a sunspace on the south rises through the inner space and falls down between the two north walls and under the house, where it gives up its remaining heat to the earth. The earth then stores the heat for nighttime use.

☐ The energy performance of double envelope structures has met their proponent's expectations, though there is doubt as to whether this is due primarily to the convective loop's heating or the insulating value of the wall/air/wall double envelope.

☐ Curtain wall technology has also experienced advances in terms of energy conscious design. Some aluminum sandwich panel manufacturers are looking to respond to passive solar design criteria and to take greater advantage of daylighting opportunities. Research and development is proceeding on thermal breaks, integrating glass areas as passive solar systems within the panels, the energy implications of air spaces within the panel, and upgrading quality criteria for long-term savings.

☐ Of perhaps equal importance to these design and materials innovations are the continuing improvements in the tools used in the design process itself. Research in the public and private sectors to determine the actual heat flow through building components has resulted in new tools and techniques that enable the designer to make more accurate energy flow predictions earlier in the design process.

☐ Progress in energy analysis, together with a wider availability of microcomputers, has led to the development of a variety of computer programs that analyze heat flow through the building envelope in terms of more realistic dynamic, as opposed to steady state, models. More detailed information appears in the "Energy Analysis" monograph in this handbook.

New Canaan Nature Center Solar Greenhouse
New Canaan, Connecticut
Architects: Donald Watson, FAIA, and
Buchanan Associates

This winter garden was designed to be a
visitors' education center and a working
greenhouse. The design combines features
for passive solar heating, daylighting and
energy conservation, and organic horticulture.

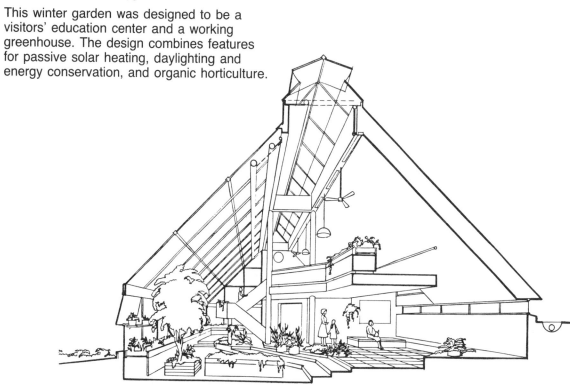

PASSIVE HEATING AND COOLING

Introduction

A passive heating or cooling system is one in which heating or cooling effect is obtained and distributed through a building by natural means, enabling the system to function with little or no external power. In the largest sense, a passive solar "system" is nothing more than the building itself, with many of its components serving a dual function—providing, for example, enclosure and structural stability as well as collecting, storing, and distributing thermal energy. Passive heating and cooling, therefore, is intrinsic to the building, affecting its site, landscaping, orientation, floor plan, circulation patterns, window placement, and building materials.

The most fundamental task facing the passive solar designer is to achieve a good understanding of both the static and dynamic energy needs of the building. This analysis enables the designer to choose appropriate design solutions. For example, the various available passive strategies differ in the time delay between the collection of energy and delivery of that energy to the load. The choice of direct gain versus indirect gain depends, among other things, on whether heating is needed during the day, evening, night, or at all. Another example is the trade-off between thermal mass and insulation. In the extreme case one can design either a very massive building that receives and stores solar heat or a well insulated "thermos bottle" with a few avenues for solar penetration. The economics of a project generally lead the designer to combine partial use of both strategies in the same building rather than going to either extreme. This allows a wide latitude for accommodating different building programs. A way to simplify the choice between the two is obtained by comparing the comfort conditions in the building to the daily and annual variations in the microclimate of the site and to the building's internal heat generation. If the resulting indoor climate is substantially within or close to the comfort zone, a high-mass building might smooth short-term temperature variations at the site and use less fossil energy. If the site conditions are substantially outside the comfort zone, then perhaps a tighter and more insulated building would use less energy.

When addressing passive solar design it is important to distinguish between two building load types:
—skin-load-dominated: loads determined by energy losses and gains through the building envelope (especially glass areas)
—internal-load-dominated: loads primarily generated internally by artificial lights, people and heat generating equipment.

Most current passive design tools and rules of thumb have been developed for residential and small commercial buildings. Their applicability to larger commercial buildings is limited and the weight of proper analysis and design must fall on the designer's judgment and expertise rather than on specified calculation procedures and methods. Most of the rules of thumb and data described in this monograph are appropriate to the design of smaller passive solar buildings for which the load requirement is determined primarily by energy losses and gains through the exterior surfaces of the building, with only a small contribution from sources of heat inside the building such as people, artificial lights, and equipment. The procedures are suitable for residences and small commercial buildings since internal sources of heat within these structures represent a small fraction of the total requirement, especially in colder climates.

This is not to say that passive heat cannot be used effectively in other buildings. But a large building (or even a small building with substantial heat-generating equipment) presents a heating situation entirely different from a small building's. Much or all of the heat required is internally generated, and cooling becomes the dominant design consideration for all but the coldest climates. Such structures require special consideration by designers in the application of passive solar gains, because improper design can create major overheating problems.

Design tools for direct gain thermal storage wall and sunspace approaches to passive are at the most advanced stage of development, and the designer of larger buildings can use these techniques with more confidence. The greatest number of experiments and analyses have been done for these types, and their performance is now very well characterized. Short of complex simulation and computer analysis techniques it is very difficult to model large commercial buildings and provide general rules for the design. However a few rules of thumb have been developed:

—Zone the building perimeter and treat this area as the passive portion. Design rules suitable for residences can then be applied within this space.

—If internal gains are low, passive heating should be considered; if internal gains are high, passive heating should probably not be used.

—Shading on east/west orientations avoids late/early gains, overheating and peak cooling load problems.

—Building can frequently be opened up to the north since cooling load problems will usually not occur.

—Atriums should be vented.

—Locate mass carefully; insulate where heat gain is undesirable or size to re-emit heat at proper time.

Passive Heating

Passive systems demand a skillful and total integration of all of the architectural elements within each space—glazing, walls, floor, roof and, in some cases, even interior surface colors, as well as the auxiliary heating system. At present, passive heating techniques are for the most part limited to smaller-scale applications because larger buildings usually need very little extra heat. Care should be taken to avoid overheating from solar gain in larger commercial buildings. The ways in which the glazing and thermal mass are designed generally determine the efficiency and level of thermal comfort provided by the system.

☐ Two concepts are critical to understanding the thermal performance of passive heated spaces:
—south-facing glass (or transparent plastic) for solar collection
—thermal mass for heat absorption, storage and distribution.

☐ A passive heating system can be divided into five elements: collector, absorber, storage, distribution and heat regulation.

—*Collector*: The solar collector is an area of transparent or translucent glazing located on the south-facing side of the building. The collector surface can be positioned vertically, as in windows, or sloped, as in a skylight on the roof, and should be oriented to solar south, plus or minus 30 degrees.

—*Absorber*: The absorber is the surface that is exposed (either directly or by reflection) to winter sunlight entering through the collector. The absorber converts the solar radiation into heat, which is then radiated or conducted away or transferred to air.

—*Storage*: The storage medium is a dense material that holds heat transferred to it from the absorber. The storage medium should be of an adequate, but not oversized volume and depth to hold the amount of solar heat collected, and is usually located in or adjacent to the rooms it is intended to heat. The absorber surface and storage medium frequently are one and the same, as in a brick floor or masonry wall.

—*Distribution*: The distribution element of a passive system is the method by which heat is delivered to the building. Distribution can be totally by natural means, such as reradiation and natural convection, or can be assisted by small fans or pumps to blow heat from the collector area to rooms or into remote storage. Caution should be exercised so that all ducts, plenums and insulation materials satisfy fire safety concerns.

—*Heat Regulation*: The heat regulation device, often termed the "control," can be an insulating medium to reduce heat loss through the collector during winter nights or cloudy periods or a shading or venting device to reduce heat gain during the summer.

☐ These elements interact as follows:
—The *collector* admits solar radiation onto the absorber.
—The *absorber* converts radiation to heat.
—The *storage* medium holds heat not immediately used.
—The *distribution method* transfers heat between the storage and the building as it is needed.
—The *controls* reduce heat loss through the collector or, during the summer, shade the collector or ventilate the building.

☐ The size and placement of the collector and storage are primarily responsible for overall thermal performance, since the system is driven by sunlight through the collector, and kept working during the night and cloudy periods by storage. The relationship of collection, storage and other elements to the conditioned spaces defines the three generic system types used to heat a building: direct gain, indirect gain, and isolated gain.

—*Direct Gain*: Sunlight enters the heated space, is converted to heat at absorbing surfaces, and is dispersed throughout the space and to the various enclosing surfaces and room contents. Different from residential buildings, glare from direct gain systems can be a large problem in commercial buildings if it's not properly controlled.

—*Indirect Gain*: Sunlight is absorbed and stored by a mass interposed between the glazing and the conditioned space. The conditioned space is partially enclosed and bounded by the thermal storage mass so that a direct thermal transfer is achieved between the mass and the space. Examples of the indirect approach are the thermal storage wall, thermal storage roof, and rooms adjacent to attached sunspaces.

—*Isolated Gain*: This is an indirect system except that there is a distinct physical and thermal separation between the thermal storage and the heated space. The convective loop is in this category. Thermal storage walls, thermal storage roofs and attached sunspaces can also be made into isolated systems by insulating between thermal storage and the heated space.

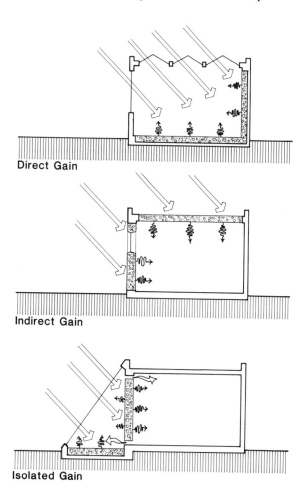

Basic Passive Heating Systems

The Campus Information Center
Rensselaer Polytechnic Institute
Troy, New York
Designers: Center for Architectural Research (RPI)

The Campus Information Center (CIC) at Rensselaer Polytechnic Institute, Troy, New York, integrates environmental controls, energy conservation measures, and passive solar design.

The building's large south elevation accommodates a sunspace that buffers the interior spaces. Infrequently used spaces, which do not have critical thermal requirements, are located along the northern perimeters. The corridor separating the northern spaces from the interior spaces contains a direct gain skylight (with reflectors) to warm and illuminate the buffer area and hallway. The effect is a cocooned central zone of thermally sensitive offices.

The mechanical system includes a variable air-volume system with an ethalpy-controlled economizer. If a particular space requires heat, the control system first searches the sunspace for air 10 degrees (F.) above the required temperature. If the system draws warm air from the sunspace, it then draws replacement air from the lobby, through a damper in the fireplace, to the sunspace. In this way, the biomass-fueled fireplace can serve the opposite end of the building.

If the sunspace cannot fill the demand, the system checks the temperature of the return air from the hallway and other spaces. Heat in the hallway, other offices, or the fireplace can thus be supplied throughout the building. If no heat can be obtained after 15 minutes of return-air sensing, then and only then does the duct electric heater provide heat to the space calling for heat. This multiple path system works in both the winter daytime and the nighttime modes, at 65 and 55 degrees (F.), respectively.

For cooling, the sunspace has a thermo-siphoning vent tower through which any trapped warm air can be expelled. A fan in the tower can augment this ventilation. If external conditions are satisfactory for cooling, the mechanical system circulates cool outside air to the offices. The cooler buffer spaces can also provide return air to lower the temperature in the cocooned spaces. Furthermore, nighttime flush cooling is possible. A backup refrigeration cooling system is actuated only when no other means are available.

Automatic thermal shades control the amount of solar energy within the sunspace in both the summer and winter. Manually operated movable insulation and reflectors at the hallway skylight function as both winter and summer energy flow controls. When a shade or movable insulation covers the windows, alternate glazing areas provide continued daylighting.

The Campus Information Center
Rensselaer Polytechnic Institute
Troy, New York
Designers: Center for Architectural Research (RPI)

Solar Collection

Every building collects some portion of the sunlight striking it, with building materials and color, orientation to the sun, and perimeter plan layouts determining how much. A well-designed building can take full advantage of this collection process and supplement it with heat storage, natural ventilation, and summer cooling capabilities.

☐ As has been discussed, there are two basic elements in a passive heating system: south-facing glass (or transparent plastic) for solar collection, and thermal mass for heat absorption, storage and distribution. It is a popular belief that a passive building must incorporate large quantities of these elements. However, while there must generally be some thermal mass and glazing, they need not be excessive.

Solar Collection Area

☐ A rule of thumb for collector sizing: a solar collection area of (R1) to (R2) percent of the floor area can be expected to reduce the annual heating load of a building in (location) by (S1) to (S2) percent, or, if R9 night insulation is used, by (S3) to S4) percent.

☐ The values of R1, R2, S1, S2, S3, and S4 appear in the accompanying table for the location of interest. It is recommended that the larger of the two glazing area values given not be exceeded, or building overheating can be anticipated on clear winter days.

City	R1	R2	S1	S2	S3	S4
Alabama, Birmingham	.09	.18	22	37	34	58
Alabama, Mobile	.06	.12	26	44	34	60
Alabama, Montgomery	.07	.15	24	41	34	59
Arizona, Phoenix	.06	.12	37	60	48	75
Arizona, Tucson	.06	.12	35	57	45	73
Arizona, Winslow	.12	.24	30	47	48	74
Arkansas, Fort Smith	.10	.20	24	39	38	64
Arkansas, Little Rock	.10	.19	23	38	37	62
California, Bakersfield	.08	.15	31	50	42	67
California, Fresno	.09	.17	29	46	42	67
California, Los Angeles	.05	.09	36	58	44	72
California, Oakland	.07	.15	35	55	46	72
California, Sacramento	.09	.18	29	47	41	66
California, San Diego	.04	.09	37	61	46	74
California, San Francisco	.06	.13	34	54	45	71
Colorado, Denver	.12	.23	27	43	47	74
Connecticut, Hartford	.17	.35	14	19	40	64
Delaware, Wilmington	.15	.29	19	30	39	63
DC, Washington,	.12	.23	18	28	37	61
Florida, Jacksonville	.05	.09	27	47	35	62
Florida, Miami	.01	.02	27	48	31	54
Florida, Orlando	.03	.06	30	52	37	63
Florida, Tallahassee	.05	.11	26	45	35	60
Florida, Tampa	.03	.06	30	52	36	63
Georgia, Atlanta	.08	.17	22	36	34	58
Idaho, Boise	.14	.28	27	38	48	71
Illinois, Chicago	.17	.35	17	23	43	67
Illinois, Springfield	.15	.30	19	28	42	67
Indiana, Fort Wayne	.16	.33	13	17	37	60
Indiana, Indianapolis	.14	.28	15	21	37	60
Iowa, Des Moines	.21	.43	19	25	50	75
Iowa, Sioux City	.23	.46	20	24	53	76
Kansas, Dodge City	.12	.23	27	42	46	73
Kansas, Topeka	.14	.28	24	35	45	71
Kansas, Wichita	.14	.28	26	41	45	72
Kentucky, Lexington	.13	.27	17	26	35	58

Solar Collection Area Values

City	R1	R2	S1	S2	S3	S4
Kentucky, Louisville	.13	.27	18	27	35	59
Louisiana, Baton Rouge	.06	.12	26	43	34	59
Louisiana, New Orleans	.05	.11	27	46	35	61
Louisiana, Shreveport	.08	.15	26	43	36	61
Maine, Portland	.17	.34	14	17	45	69
Maryland, Baltimore	.14	.27	19	30	38	62
Massachusetts, Boston	.15	.29	17	25	40	64
Michigan, Detroit	.17	.34	13	17	39	61
Michigan, Flint	.15	.31	11	12	40	62
Michigan, Grand Rapids	.19	.38	12	13	39	61
Minnesota, Duluth	.25	.50	-N	R-	50	70
Minnesota, Minneapolis-St. Paul	.25	.50	-N	R-	55	76
Mississippi, Jackson	.08	.15	24	40	34	59
Missouri, Kansas City	.14	.29	22	32	44	70
Missouri, Saint Louis	.15	.29	21	33	41	65
Montana, Billings	.16	.32	24	31	53	76
Montana, Helena	.20	.39	21	25	55	77
Nebraska, Omaha	.20	.40	21	29	51	76
Nevada, Las Vegas	.09	.18	35	56	48	75
Nevada, Reno	.11	.22	31	48	49	76
New Hampshire, Concord	.17	.34	13	15	45	68
New Jersey, Newark	.13	.25	19	29	39	64
New Mexico, Albuquerque	.11	.22	29	47	46	73
New Mexico, Roswell	.10	.19	30	49	45	73
New York, Albany	.21	.41	13	15	43	66
New York, Buffalo	.19	.37	-N	R-	36	57
New York, New York	.15	.30	16	25	36	59
New York, Syracuse	.19	.38	-N	R-	37	59
North Carolina, Charlotte	.08	.17	23	38	36	60
North Carolina, Greensboro	.10	.20	23	37	37	63
North Carolina, Raleigh-Durham	.09	.19	22	37	36	61
North Dakota, Bismarck	.25	.50	-N	R-	56	77
Ohio, Cincinnati	.12	.24	15	23	35	57
Ohio, Cleveland	.15	.31	11	14	34	55
Ohio, Columbus	.14	.28	13	18	35	57
Ohio, Toledo	.17	.34	13	17	38	61
Oklahoma, Oklahoma City	.11	.22	25	41	41	67
Oklahoma, Tulsa	.11	.22	24	38	40	65
Oregon, Portland	.13	.26	21	31	38	60
Oregon, Salem	.12	.24	21	32	37	59
Pennsylvania, Philadelphia	.15	.29	19	29	38	62
Pennsylvania, Pittsburgh	.14	.28	12	16	33	55
Rhode Island, Providence	.15	.30	17	24	40	64
South Carolina, Charleston	.07	.14	25	41	34	59
South Carolina, Columbia	.08	.17	25	41	36	61
South Dakota, Rapid City	.15	.30	23	32	51	76
South Dakota, Sioux Falls	.22	.45	18	19	57	79
Tennessee, Knoxville	.09	.18	20	33	33	56
Tennessee, Memphis	.09	.19	22	36	36	60
Tennessee, Nashville	.10	.21	19	30	33	55
Texas, Amarillo	.11	.22	29	46	45	72
Texas, Austin	.06	.13	27	46	37	63
Texas, Dallas	.08	.17	27	44	38	64
Texas, El Paso	.09	.17	32	53	45	72
Texas, Houston	.06	.11	25	43	34	59
Texas, San Antonio	.06	.12	28	48	38	64
Utah, Salt Lake City	.13	.26	27	39	48	72
Vermont, Burlington	.22	.43	-N	R-	46	68
Virginia, Norfolk	.09	.19	23	38	37	62
Virginia, Richmond	.11	.22	21	34	37	61
Washington, Seattle-Tacoma	.11	.22	21	30	39	59
Washington, Spokane	.20	.39	20	24	48	68
West Virginia, Charleston	.13	.25	16	24	32	54
Wisconsin, Madison	.20	.40	15	17	51	74
Wisconsin, Milwaukee	.18	.35	15	18	48	71
Wyoming, Casper	.13	.26	27	39	53	78
Wyoming, Cheyenne	.11	.21	25	39	47	74

In Dodge City a solar collection area of 12 to 23 percent of the floor area can be expected to reduce the fuel consumption of a building by 27 to 42 percent, or, if R9 night insulation is used, by 46 to 73 percent. A Dodge City building is to have a floor area of roughly 1,600 square feet. Thus the glazed area indicated by the rule of thumb will be in the range of 192 to 368 square feet. Within these rough bounds, one can begin schematic design.

The energy savings realized in this example would be approximately as follows:

Glazed Area (Sq. ft.)	Savings	
	With night insulation	Without night insulation
192	27 percent	46 percent
368	42 percent	73 percent

Orientation

☐ For Trombe walls and water walls the orientation of the solar glazing should lie between 20 degrees east and 32 degrees west of true south. Some designers prefer to use direct gain glazing oriented slightly east of true south to provide heat gain and daylight in the building early in the morning. This is especially important if the primary heating requirements are during the daytime hours.

☐ If one adheres to this rule of thumb the decrease in performance, compared to an optimal orientation, will nearly always be less than 10 percent and, more typically, will be less than 6 percent. The optimal orientation for five sites (Albuquerque, Madison, Medford, Boston, and Nashville) varies from 7 degrees east of true south to 15 degrees west of true south. The average optimum for these cities is 6 degrees west of south, with the following decreases in solar savings associated with variations from a true-south orientation:

—5 percent decrease at 18 degrees east or 30 degrees west

—10 percent decrease at 28 degrees east or 40 degrees west

—20 percent decrease at 42 degrees east or 54 degrees west.

☐ Note that this rule of thumb is based on sensitivity calculations done for Trombe walls and water walls. Another important consideration in selecting orientation is summer performance. Summer solar gains are very sensitive to orientation; large glass areas facing east or west orientations should be avoided as much to prevent summer overheating as to maximize winter performance.

☐ A local shading situation may warrant departure from this rule of thumb. For example, if the site has strong morning shade, a westerly orientation would be favored, and vice versa.

Vertical tilt (90 degrees) is far from the best, while a tilt of approximately 55 degrees is near the optimum. The reason for the optimum is much the same as it is for solar collectors in active systems; there is more sun received per unit of glazing area during the winter heating season on a tilted surface (as discussed in the "Shading and Sun Control" monograph in this handbook). The choice of vertical glazing by most designers is made in consideration of the inconvenience and lost space associated with a tilted surface, especially when it is serving a dual function as the south wall of the building. For clerestory windows and sunspaces, however, these considerations don't particularly apply, and tilted surfaces are often used.

Time	Heat Loss (BTU/Sq.Ft.)		
	Single Glazing	Double Glazing	Single Glazing (w/shutters [R-10] at night)
Daytime (9 hours)	368	211	368
Nighttime (15 hours)	679	390	51
Total heat loss	1,047	601	419

Effect of Insulating Shutters on Conduction Losses (Boston)

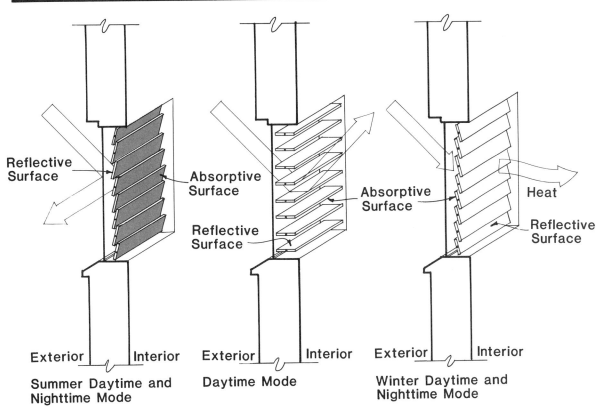

Reflective Surface
Absorptive Surface

Summer Daytime and Nighttime Mode

Absorptive Surface
Reflective Surface

Daytime Mode

Heat
Reflective Surface

Winter Daytime and Nighttime Mode

Reflective Insulating Blinds

Movable Insulation

☐ Although glass and clear or translucent plastics have the potential to admit large amounts of solar radiation and natural light into a space during the daytime, their poor insulating properties allow a large percentage of this energy to be lost back out through the glazing. In a well-insulated building, glazed openings (windows, skylights and clerestories) can be one of the largest sources of building heat loss. Approximately two-thirds of this heat loss occurs at night and can be greatly reduced by the use of movable insulation.

☐ Movable insulation can be divided into three categories: hand operated, thermally sensitive and motor driven.

☐ Hand-operated devices include sliding panels, hinged shutters and drapes. The initial cost is generally low, and the materials usually pay for themselves in energy savings within a few years.

☐ Thermally sensitive devices are activated by heat converted to mechanical movement. They function automatically and can be placed in areas difficult to reach, like skylights and high clerestory windows. These mechanisms use no electricity and are usually more expensive than hand-operated devices.

☐ Motor-driven applications can be activated manually or by automatic timers, thermostats or light-sensitive devices.

Reflectors

☐ A large amount of collector area (south-facing glass) may not be feasible or desirable in many building situations. In a number of situations, such as partial shading by nearby buildings or vegetation, esthetic considerations, or the limited availability of south wall for solar collection, large south-facing glass areas may not be possible. In addition, since glass is a poor insulator, it can be useful to minimize the area of glazing needed to heat a space. By using exterior reflectors, the amount of solar radiation transmitted through each square foot of glass can be dramatically increased.

☐ For vertical glazing a horizontal reflector roughly equal in width to the glazing and one to two times its height in length can be used. For south-sloping skylights the reflector should be located above the skylight at a tilt angle of approximately 100 degrees. The reflector should be approximately equal to the length and width of the skylight.

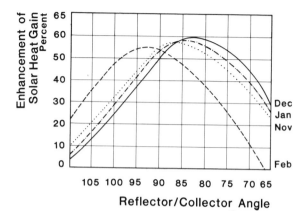

Heat Gain with Different Reflector Angles

Skylight Slope	North Latitude			
	36°	42°	48°	54°
horizontal	80°	76°	71°	66°
30°	100°	97°	93°	90°
40°	107°	103°	100°	97°
50°	113°	110°	107°	103°

Reflector Tilt Angles for South-Facing Skylights

Surface	Percentage of Specular Reflectance
Electroplated silver, new	0.96
High-purity aluminum, new, clean	0.91
Sputtered aluminum optical reflector	0.89
Back-silvered water white plate glass, new, clean	0.88
Aluminum, silicon-oxygen coating, clean	0.87
Aluminum foil	0.86
Aluminized Type C Mylar (from Mylar side)	0.76

Solar Reflections of Various Surfaces

Albuquerque Animal Control Center
Albuquerque, New Mexico
Architects: The Burns/Peters Group

The Albuquerque Animal Control Center provides small, functional office space for the center's staff, and comfortable kennels for the more than 200 dogs confined to the center. Although the site is restricted by several existing structures and an area designated for a future building, the center maximizes its southern exposure by being located on an east-west axis of the site. None of the trees on the site shade the building.

The design is a long, narrow, rectangular building. A 2,200-square-foot office area is heated primarily by a sophisticated active solar system that also supplies the building's domestic hot water. The system consists of 48 roof-top parabolic active solar concentrating collectors and a 1,500-gallon water tank. An additional 15 to 20 percent of the office's heat is provided by passive solar heat gain through the dark masonry exterior walls. To allow for time-lag heating at the office areas, only the north walls have been insulated; south walls are purely for thermal storage. A 4,300-square-foot kennel and support area (mechanical, food storage, dog and cat wards) is

passively heated by direct gain through a large, 6-foot-high clerestory window with an insulated, adjustable reflector panel. Hot water from the active solar system can be circulated through a radiant piping system in the kennel floor for backup heat and for taking the chill off the floor.

The dominant architectural feature is the shed roofline and clerestory window bank above the animal runs. The 48 solar collectors and steel supports dominate the office roof. The concrete block exterior walls are stained to match existing buildings on the site. A stuccoed fascia forms an overhang to shade windows from the summer sun. Appropriate portions of the roof are stained with a reflective color.

The passive system's primary feature is the clerestory window bank above the animal runs. During the day, direct and reflected sunlight enters through the single-glazed clerestory window. When open, an insulated panel reflects this energy down onto the concrete floor, which is stained dark brown to increase solar absorption, and onto heat-absorptive partitions. The mass of the floor and walls retains and reradiates heat throughout the day and most of the night. The adjustable panel closes to prevent heat loss or to

Albuquerque Animal Control Center
Albuquerque, New Mexico
Architects: The Burns/Peters Group

reduce the amount of sun penetration as needed.

The panel is controlled by a light sensor connected to a standard greenhouse-type vent controller. A thermostatically controlled ventilation fan is activated when the room temperature exceeds 65 degrees (F.). If the fan cannot bring the temperature down, the panel closes when the temperature reaches 70 degrees (F.). Both settings can be adjusted for maximum comfort.

The clerestory size and the mass volume have been optimized to achieve the required levels of performance. The clerestory includes 425 square feet of glass area, achieving a glass-area-to-floor-area ratio of 0.28. Approximately 1.1 cubic feet of concrete in the floor and partitions are provided for each square foot of glass area. This translates to 30 BTU/cu.ft./deg. (F.) of energy storage capacity, which is the minimum storage value recommended by the Los Alamos Scientific Laboratory.

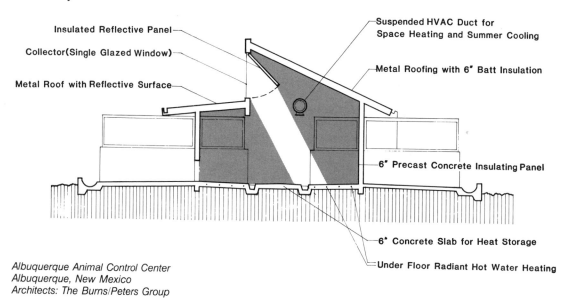

Insulated Reflective Panel

Collector(Single Glazed Window)

Metal Roof with Reflective Surface

Suspended HVAC Duct for Space Heating and Summer Cooling

Metal Roofing with 6" Batt Insulation

6" Precast Concrete Insulating Panel

6" Concrete Slab for Heat Storage

Under Floor Radiant Hot Water Heating

Albuquerque Animal Control Center
Albuquerque, New Mexico
Architects: The Burns/Peters Group

Solar Storage

Solar energy is an intermittent energy source. The availability of solar energy is affected by the daily day-night cycle and by the seasons, as well as by the changes in weather caused by clouds, rain or snow. The use of solar energy as an effective energy source for heating purposes is further complicated by the fact that the energy demand for many heating applications is out of phase with the availability of solar energy. In residential applications, for example, the bulk of the annual heating load occurs during the winter months, and the greater part of the daily heating load exists in the evenings. At both these times, the supply of solar energy is, on the other hand, the minimum.

☐ The effectiveness of solar energy as an energy source thus usually requires thermal storage within the solar heating system. Small heat storage capacities can help neutralize the fluctuations introduced by minor interruptions in weather, e.g., by the appearance of clouds. Larger storage capacities, on the other hand, can store enough heat while the sun is shining to meet the energy demands for daily or even seasonal periods. The optimal size of storage depends on the application, and is an interrelated function of weather, building heat load and heat losses, and collector area and efficiency.

☐ Storage is helpful under the following conditions:
—when heat is required at a time when it is not otherwise available
—when heat gains must be delayed. Mass can be used, for example, on a west wall of an office building to shift peak afternoon solar gains into unoccupied periods.
—when economic conditions, such as off-peak electric rates, make it better to use the energy stored in the mass at a time other than when it arrives in the building.

☐ Two critical problems that have occurred in past passive commercial building designs are:
—designers extending the concepts of residential use of mass, e.g., Trombe walls, to commercial buildings without accounting for differences in occupancy schedules
—designers not recognizing that, in internal-load-dominated buildings, the goal is to get rid of heat—a massive structure may in fact tend to retain that heat and keep it in the building at the wrong times.

☐ To effectively design passive buildings, designers must know what the energy require-ments are and when energy sources are available. Based on this information, which includes the major effects of occupancy patterns and climate, designers can determine whether storage and time delay of energy sources are desired to reduce peak loads and annual energy consumption.

Selecting Storage Systems
☐ At low temperatures, solar heat is stored in essentially two ways:
—as sensible heat in solids, e.g., masonry, rocks, or liquids such as water. The heat storage medium experiences an increase in temperature.

One Day Cycle

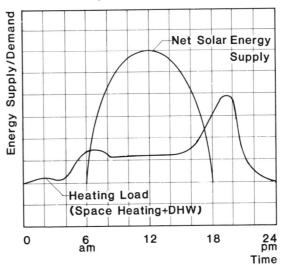

Annual Load

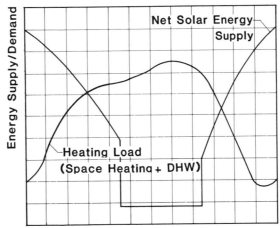

Daily and Annual Variation of Solar Energy and Energy Demands

—as latent heat of fusion in suitable chemical compounds, such as paraffin waxes and inorganic salt hydrates. The heat storage medium absorbs the heat as it undergoes a phase transition from the solid to the liquid state. For pure substances, the heat storage takes place at a constant temperature that corresponds to the melting point of the substance. However, a variety of problems exists for phase-change materials and they are not yet ready for widespread application.

☐ The choice of a thermal storage system must be based on the following criteria, with trade-offs made as necessary:

—storage capacity per unit mass and volume
—suitable properties in the operating temperature range
—uniform temperature
—capability to charge and discharge with the largest heat input/output rates but without large temperature gradients
—small self-discharging rate, i.e., small heat losses to the surroundings
—long reliable life
—inexpensive.

☐ Thermal storage determines the magnitude of temperature swings that will be experienced in a passive solar building. A building's *average* temperature can be in the comfort range but, if there is inadequate thermal storage, the temperature swing will be large, resulting in the building's being uncomfortably warm in the afternoon and uncomfortably cold at night. As shown in the accompanying graph, the difference between the average inside termperature and the average outside temperature is affected primarily by the building load and solar collector ratio, while the magnitude of the temperature swings is governed principally by the amount and the effectiveness of thermal storage.

☐ The volume of heat storage is usually limited as much by building area and construction costs, water availability and container sizes (for water storage systems) as by solar design factors. However, depending on the weather and building use characteristics, it can be desirable to limit the size of storage to only one day carry-over or to attempt a longer-term carryover by increased storage volume.

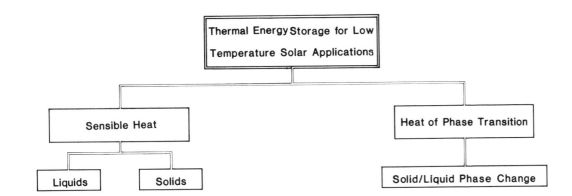

Thermal Energy Storage Techniques

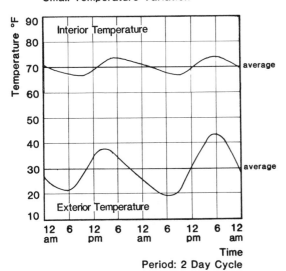

High Thermal Mass Wall :
Small Temperature Variation

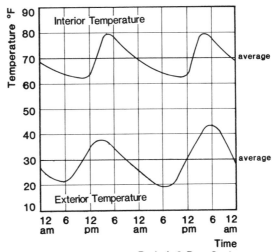

Low Thermal Mass Wall:
Large Temperature Variation

Average Temperature and Temperature Swing

Milford Reservation Environmental Center
Milford, Pennsylvania
Architects: Kelbaugh & Lee, Architects

In the Milford Reservation Environmental Center, in Milford, Pennsylvania, passive solar features provide 75 percent of the building's environmental conditioning. The center is a full-time home for 117 people in an area where the temperature frequently drops to 0 degrees (F.) or lower during the winter.

South-facing Trombe walls are located across the front of the lobby and the dining hall. The first is equipped with a hinged insulating reflector, which intensifies solar gain when open but inhibits heat loss when closed. The larger dining hall Trombe wall is supplied with pulldown shades inside the building. These are hidden from view in the walk-through space between the south wall and a ramp for the handicapped, which is covered with ventilating wood slats on the side facing into the room.

The middle of the building receives direct solar gain at all three levels. At the lowest, the classroom level, a water wall of large, portable water drums immediately behind low windows underneath work tables soaks up enough heat during the day to warm the rooms at night. At the middle, the dormitory level, light and solar radiation pass through clear windows into the main corridor, and then through glass-block walls into the bedrooms. The hall floors are dark for heat absorption, as are those of the upper-level bedrooms, which receive direct gain through their dormer windows.

Throughout the building, the internal structure, floors, walls, and some partitions are concrete to create mass for storing solar energy. At the north side, the building is partially buried, and this earth contact, plus a night fan venting system, eliminates the need for mechanical airconditioning. The thermal shutters, curtains, shades, blankets, drapes and vents that make the whole system work throughout the year are operated by the youth who use the building as part of the educational program.

Milford Reservation Environmental Center
Milford, Pennsylvania
Architects: Kelbaugh & Lee, Architects

104

Direct Gain Systems

The direct gain system is the most widely used passive solar building solution. With direct gain, the occupants are in direct contact with all five elements of the passive solar system-collector, absorber, storage, distribution and controls.

☐ Direct gain systems are characterized by daily indoor temperature fluctuations, which may range from 5 to 30 degrees (F.), depending on the location and size of solar windows, thermal mass and the color of interior surfaces. To prevent overheating, shading devices are used to reduce solar gain, or excess heat is ducted to rock bed storage or vented by opening windows or activating an exhaust fan.

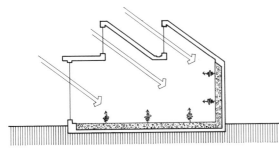

Direct Gain System

☐ The basic characteristics of the direct gain building are: a south-facing collector area, with the conditioned spaces exposed directly behind, and absorber/storage floors and walls.

☐ Typically, double-glazed windows, clerestories or skylights are used for collection. The floors, walls, ceiling or freestanding masonry elements or containers of water absorb heat at their surfaces and store it within their mass. Heat distribution from the storage is by reradiation and natural convection, regulated mainly by location of the storage medium with respect to the conditioned spaces. Heat loss to the outside is controlled by insulating the glazing at night or on sunless winter days.

☐ Physically the situation in direct gain is complex, especially the apportioning of the solar heat between lightweight, non-storage elements and massive heat-storing elements of the internal building environment. Solar gain through south-facing glass is easily calculated; however, predicting the amount of heat stored in the masonry or the daily temperature fluctuations in a space is presently beyond the capability of most building designers. Up to a point, the use of direct gain is fairly straightforward. If the heat from direct gain can be used in the building immediately, then there

is no need for storage. Thus direct gain can be used to supply up to 30 or 40 percent of the building requirements without special concern for thermal storage. As the glazing area is increased, it is essential to consider how the heat will be stored in the building materials and what temperature swings will result. If very large glazed areas are required, then the designer must use thermal storage very carefully or overheating will occur.

☐ The advantages of direct-gain systems are:
—flexibility of architectural design
—standard construction materials can be used
—ease of operation
—collection glass area provides light to occupied space and allows for additional view.

☐ The disadvantages are:
—building orientation is dictated by sun position, except for roof monitors
—glare and overheating are possible without well-designed controls
—ultraviolet degradation and fading of fabrics occurs without controls
—solar collection temperatures are limited by occupant comfort needs.

Collector

☐ In a direct gain system the most important factor in collecting the sun's energy is the size and placement of glazing. Glazing that faces south and opens directly into a space is an effective solar collector. Virtually all incoming sunlight is absorbed by the walls, floor, ceiling and other objects in the space and converted into heat. Openings that are designed primarily to admit useful solar energy into a space are sometimes referred to as "solar windows." The efficiency of solar windows as a collector depends on the climate. In very cold climates most or all of the heat collected will be lost back out the window unless night insulation is used.

Clerestory

☐ A clerestory is a vertical or near-vertical opening projecting up from the roof plane. It is a particularly effective way to direct sunlight entering a space so that it strikes an interior thermal storage wall. A clerestory should be located at a distance in front of the wall that ensures that direct sunlight will strike near the base of the wall during the winter. This distance will vary with latitude and ceiling height, but is roughly 1 to 1½ times the height of the wall.

☐ "Sawtooth" glazing is a series of clerestories, one directly behind the other. The saw-

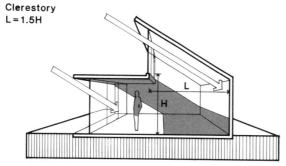

Clerestory
L = 1.5H

December 21

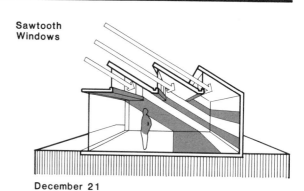

Sawtooth
Windows

December 21

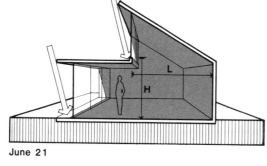

June 21

Clerestory Windows

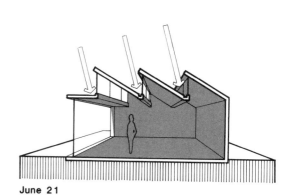

June 21

Sawtooth Windows

tooth configuration can effectively distribute sunlight over an entire space. As a rough guide, the angle of each clerestory roof (as measured from horizontal) should be equal to, or less than, the altitude of the sun at noon, on December 21, the winter solstice. This ensures that the clerestories will not shade each other during the winter hours of maximum solar radiation. If a steeper angle is used, then clerestories should be spaced apart accordingly.

Skylights

☐ Horizontal skylights are usually more effective when used with reflectors to increase solar gain in winter. They should also be shaded in summer to prevent excessive solar gain.

☐ Collecting sunlight through south-facing clerestories and skylights has several advantages. Sunlight admitted through the roof can be distributed to any part of a space or building. This allows for maximum freedom when locating an interior thermal storage mass. When properly designed, toplighting eliminates glare, because light entering the space from above reduces the contrast between interior surfaces and windows. Because clerestories and skylights are located high in a space, they also

reduce the chance of solar blockage by off-site obstructions and allow for large openings in crowded building situations where privacy is desirable.

☐ The accompanying table indicates the amount of south-facing glazing that will admit enough sunlight to keep the space at an average temperature of 65 to 70 degrees (F.) on sunny winter days.

Average Winter (clear-day) Outdoor Temperature	Glazing/Floor Area			
	36°NL	40°NL	44°NL	48°NL
Cold Climates				
20°F	.24	.25	.29	.31
25°F	.22	.23	.25	.28
30°F	.19	.20	.22	.24
Temperate Climates				
35°F	.16	.17	.19	.21
40°F	.13	.14	.16	.17
45°F	.10	.11	.12	.13

Sizing South-Facing Glazing

106

Multiple Glazing and Night Insulation

☐ The appropriate number of glazings and the use of night insulation over glazing in a direct gain building depends strongly on climatic conditions.

In mild climates, multiple glazings degrade daytime performance of night-insulated systems by reducing the daytime heat gain more than the glazing reduces nighttime heat losses. Therefore, only one glazing layer should be used in combination with night insulation. If no night insulation is used, the performance of double-glazed systems is significantly better than the performance of those with a single layer. However, there is very little to be gained by adding a third glazing layer to south-facing solar windows and almost no advantage to using a fourth.

☐ In harsh winter climates, on the other hand, night insulation is almost a necessity unless multiple glazings (three or more) are used or the direct gain component is a small part of a mixed system and is intended only as a quick source of solar heat for daytime use. Solar savings greater than 10 percent are not obtainable in double-glazed buildings without night insulation. Further, in harsh climates multiple glazings reduce daytime heat losses enough to improve the performance of night-insulated windows. Double glazing is significantly better than single, and triple glazing is slightly better than double when night insulation is used. The accompanying table shows glazing levels recommended for direct gain buildings.

Winter Climate	Number of Glazings	
	No Night Insulation	R9 Night Insulation
Santa Maria (mild)	2	1
Albuquerque (moderate)	2-3	1 or 2
Madison (severe)	3-5	2

Glazing Levels for Direct Gain Buildings

Absorber and Storage

☐ In some direct gain systems, excess heat is ducted from the direct gain space to other spaces and/or to remote rock bed or water storage for later use. More commonly, the heat is stored in thermal mass in the direct gain space. In this case, the absorber and storage are essentially the same. The absorption and storage of heat in a space are the primary challenge to the designer of a direct gain system. If a major reliance is to be placed on direct gain for space heating, roughly 65 percent of the solar energy admitted into a space must be stored in the walls and/or floor and/or ceiling for use during the night.

☐ The most effective heat storage within a space is in mass materials, whether masonry or water, that form the enclosing surfaces of the direct gain space or are within the direct gain space. Materials which are in direct sunlight are slightly more effective than other surfaces, but all are effective as long as they are in the direct gain space. Lightweight, dark colored materials in the sun can store little heat and thus become quite hot, transferring the absorbed solar radiation away relatively quickly to the room air by convection or by radiation to other surfaces. If most of the solar energy heats air instead of the storage mass wall or floor, there will be large rapid temperature increases in the space and, when the sun is clouded or goes down, large rapid temperature drops. Of equal importance, the storage mass will receive heat only from the warmed air, so the amount of heat the mass receives will be considerably less, and will be available after the sun is gone for a period considerably shorter than if the solar insulation had struck it directly. In other words, if the mass is not irradiated by direct or reflected sunlight, the ability of the mass to moderate temperature swings and its ability to provide heat when the sun is gone are reduced.

☐ Heat absorbed by the surface of the thermal mass wall or floor travels through the mass gradually by conduction. As the sun goes down, the heat in the deepest level of the mass gradually returns to the surface conductively. If the mass is too thick, the heat will not return to the surface until possibly 24 hours later, when the heat is unneeded because the wall or floor is again receiving solar radiation. If the mass is even thicker, the deeper portions do not receive any solar heat because they are insulated from it by the surface layers.

☐ The accompanying graph shows the diurnal heat capacity of walls and floors made of various thermal mass materials. The diurnal heat capacity of a material surface is the daily amount of heat per unit of surface area that is stored and then given back at night, per degree of temperature difference between day and night. The mass is assumed to be insulated on the side away from the room. Using this curve, it is possible to assess, for example, the increased value of a 6-inch concrete mass over a 5-inch concrete mass. The extra inch is only 35 percent as effective as the inch at the surface and so the designer might consider placing that extra inch somewhere else. Note that the effectiveness of concrete mass beyond an 8-inch thickness becomes negative because of the time-phasing discussed above. Brick and adobe mass walls and floors peak at about 5 inches.

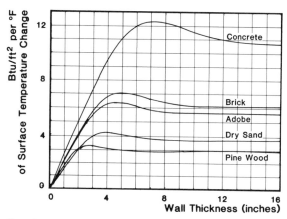

Heat Storage Capacity of Various Materials

☐ The most important parameter in direct gain design is the area of mass surface. A minimum of three times the glazing area is essential and six to nine times is recommended to control temperature swings.

☐ Direct sunlight can be diffused over the surface area of the thermal mass in a space by using a translucent glazing material, by placing a number of small windows so that they admit sunlight in patches, or by reflecting direct sunlight off a light-colored interior surface first, thus diffusing it throughout the space. The accompanying table gives recommended thermal storage mass of water or masonry for each square foot of south glazing, given the percentage of a building's heating load to be satisfied by a direct gain system. This assumes that the mass is in the direct sun all day as, for example, in a water wall. In direct gain situations this is adequate thermal storage, provided the mass is within the direct gain space or encloses the direct gain space, the mass is not insulated from the space, and the mass has an exposed surface area equal to at least three times the glazed area.

Expected Solar Savings	Recommended Effective Thermal Storage per sq ft of solar collection area	
	Pounds of Water	Pounds of Masonry
10%	6	30
20%	12	60
30%	18	90
40%	24	120
50%	30	150
60%	36	180
70%	42	210
80%	48	240
90%	54	270

Sizing Masonry and Water Storage

Color

☐ The lighter the color of a mass surface, the greater the number of multiple reflections within the interior of the conditioned space before transmitted solar radiation is absorbed within the zone. These multiple reflections tend to distribute heat more uniformly throughout the interior than would otherwise occur; unfortunately, however, they also increase the opportunity for solar radiation to escape back through the glazing or to heat the air higher than is needed.

☐ The accompanying table indicates typical solar absorptance values for various surfaces—although texture, tone, overcoats, binders, etc., can cause variations. As a rule of thumb, the overall absorptance of a space should be at least 0.5 but need not exceed 0.8 for effective absorption of solar radiation.

Element	α
Optical flat black paint	.98
Flat black paint	.95
Black lacquer	.92
Black concrete	.91
Dark brown paint	.88
Brown concrete	.85
Medium light brown paint	.80
Light gray oil paint	.75
Red brick	.70
Uncolored concrete	.65
Moderately light buff bricks	.60
Medium blue paint	.51
Light green paint	.47
White semi-gloss paint	.30
White gloss paint	.25
Silver paint	.25
White lacquer	.21
Polished aluminum reflector sheet	.12
Aluminized mylar film	.10

Solar Absorptance of Various Materials

☐ Consider, for example, a south-facing direct gain building with clerestory windows that illuminate a massive north wall and standard glazed areas on the south wall that illuminate a massive floor. The floor space is 1500 square feet, and the massive north wall is 60 feet long by 10 feet high for an area of 600 square feet, giving a total collector area of 2,100 square feet. All sections of the floor and north wall are exposed to sunlight. The north wall is painted a light color to direct most of the solar radiation down to the floor, which is a dark color. (The design rationale is that if most of the radiation is distributed over and absorbed fairly uniformly in the floor, a very comfortable environment will be created because the heat is kept low in the space offsetting the tendency for heat to stratify at the top.) The north wall is covered with white semi-gloss paint and a red brick is chosen for the floor. The absorptance table indicates a solar absorptance of 0.3 for white semi-gloss paint and 0.7 for red brick.

The area weighted average absorptance is thus 0.6, which is well within the recommended limit, even for this somewhat extreme example:

$$\frac{600}{2100} \times 0.3 + \frac{1500}{2100} \times 0.7 = 0.6$$

☐ Generally, however, designers should consider replacing massive components on which they desire a light color with nonmassive and possibly less expensive substitutes. Otherwise, the extra investment in the mass may not be cost-effective, because the mass is less able to serve its absorber function during both heating and cooling seasons. If, on the other hand, an excess of thermal storage mass is an inherent part of the building structure, and is economically competitive with lightweight alternatives, the question of surface color becomes less critical.

Location

☐ Recent studies indicate that the performance of direct gain buildings is relatively insensitive to the distribution of thermal storage mass within a space. The optimal location is on the floor directly behind the glazed area, although buildings with an identical amount of thermal storage mass in the walls will perform within a few percent of the optimal system. If one or more layers of the glazing are diffuse, the significance of mass distribution is further reduced because of the more uniform distribution of transmitted solar radiation about the enclosure. Since thermal storage mass located on east, west, or north walls is almost as effective as that located on the floor, it is generally desirable to distribute mass about the direct gain area as uniformly as possible. This is because a uniform distribution of thermal storage mass is conducive to a thermally uniform occupied space.

Friendship Federal Savings and Loan Association
Butler, Pennsylvania
Architects: Burt Hill Kosar Rittlemann Associates

In 1976 and 1977 the Pittsburgh-based Friendship Federal Savings and Loan Association built two branch offices (in Greensburg and Ingomar, Pennsylvania) using active solar systems—that is, systems which, although solar, use pumps, fans and mechanical equipment to move the collected solar energy around the buildings.

The newest branch office, located in Butler, Pennsylvania, was designed by the same architects—Burt Hill Kosar Rittlemann Associates—to use passive solar systems to supply a major portion of the building heating requirements. In this branch, the orientation, building materials and design of the structure allow it to make use of heat from sunlight passively without the need for electrically driven active solar collection and distribution equipment.

The architect's selection of the particular solar systems used in the Butler branch was based on the region's climate. Like most of Pennsylvania, the Butler area is characterized by mild summers that place only a small requirement on energy loads, and relatively harsh winters, with heating degree days averaging well over 5,000 annually. Under these conditions, the predominant building load and energy user is heating. All of the major passive features selected for the building are, therefore, designed primarily to provide maximum heating levels. Their ability to lower summer cooling loads as well is a welcome side benefit.

The building uses two passive solar approaches, a concrete masonry Trombe wall and a direct gain system. The Trombe wall concept is based on orienting a passive heat-absorbing wall to face the southern sun. The mass-covered wall absorbs large amounts of solar heat from the winter sun and either releases it immediately or stores it until needed. The direct gain system is similar in nature to the Trombe wall, but here sunlight passing through skylights or greenhouses strikes concrete or masonry walls and floors, which absorb its heat.

Friendship Federal Savings and Loan Association
Butler, Pennsylvania
Architects: Burt Hill Kosar Rittleman Associates

The direct gain heating takes advantage of the heat-retaining capacity of high-mass materials. In this case, the solar energy passes through a 150-square-foot skylight above the lobby and is absorbed as heat by the concrete floor, which is covered by heat absorptive dark grey slate, and a concrete block wall. To provide the necessary degree of control, the skylight is equipped with automatic movable shutters.

Together, the Trombe walls and the direct gain systems provide 50 percent of the annual requirements for heat in the building.

As with most passive systems it is difficult to separate the cost of the systems from the building costs, because the systems are an intrinsic part of the building structure.

☐ Friendship Federal estimates, however, that about $15,000 can be attributed to the passive solar installation. The entire construction budget for the building was $320,000.

☐ By comparison, Friendship Federal's costs for installing an active solar system on their first solar branch added some $20,000 to the construction cost. The second branch, built after a moratorium on new natural gas hookups, with an electric heat pump as a backup heat source, included $27,000 for its active solar system.

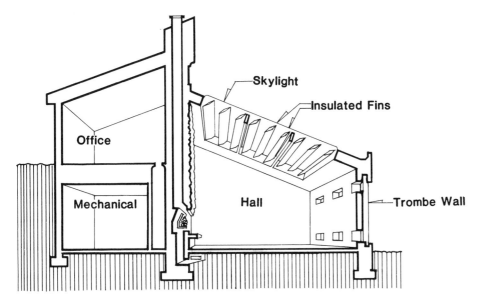

Friendship Federal Savings and Loan Association
Butler, Pennsylvania
Architects: Burt Hill Kosar Rittlemann Associates

Indirect Gain Systems

In indirect gain systems sunlight strikes a thermal mass located between the sun and the space. The sunlight absorbed by the mass is converted to thermal energy and transferred into the conditioned spaces. Because conditioned spaces do not receive solar radiation immediately, indirect gain systems offer greater control over temperature swings and overheating. At the same time, because the thermal mass is confined to the wall and not evenly distributed throughout the space, as that is in direct gain systems, the effective reach of *radiant* heat (but not convective heat) from the wall is 15 to 20 feet.

☐ The two basic types of indirect gain systems are thermal storage walls and roof ponds. The difference between the two systems is the location of the mass; one is contained in a wall and the other on the roof over the space being heated.

Thermal Storage Walls

☐ Thermal storage walls are composed of masonry or water. Typically the south-facing side is covered with glazing to prevent the escape of thermal radiation and painted a dark color for better absorption of the sunlight (as discussed in the section on direct gain). The selection of a material and its thickness determines the wall's ability to store and distribute heat to the living spaces during the desired time period. Radiant distribution from the wall can be delayed up to 12 hours, depending on the depth of the wall and the heat-storing properties of the wall's construction.

☐ Masonry wall designs range from solid, unvented masonry walls that supply only radiant heat to the building to walls with a number of openings or vents to allow light into the living spaces and facilitate the distribution of heat to the building by convection from the cavity between the wall and the glazing.

☐ The Trombe wall, a distinct type masonry or water thermal storage wall, combines radiant distribution with a convection loop that draws cool air from inside the building through low wall vents and delivers warmed air back to the building through upper wall vents. This convective heating is almost immediate, and can provide warmth to the space during the day even though radiant heat is not released by the wall until nighttime.

☐ An air space of 3½ inches or so must exist between the wall and either double glazing with movable nighttime insulation (assumed R-9) or triple glazing—which is comparable to nighttime insulation.

☐ Recent studies indicate that the optimal vent size depends primarily on the percentage of the heating load the designer wants to satisfy with the Trombe wall. Recommended vent areas

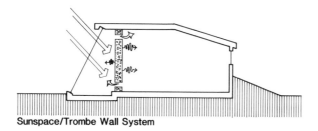

Sunspace/Trombe Wall System

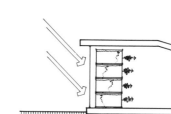

Trombe Wall System

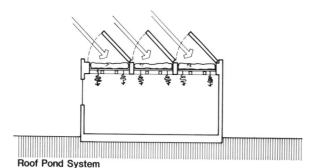

Roof Pond System

Water Wall System

Indirect Gain Systems

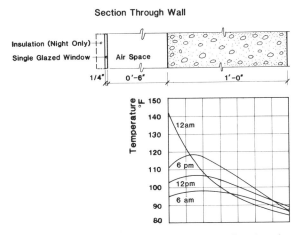

Section Through Wall

Insulation (Night Only)
Single Glazed Window
Air Space

1/4"   0'-6"   1'-0"

Temperature of Glass-Covered Masonry Wall as Function of Time

are shown in the accompanying table. "Vent area" in this table is the area of the lower vents, which is equal to the area of the upper vents, measured as a percentage of the total Trombe wall area.

☐ Putting aside the issue of time of heat delivery for a moment, Trombe walls tend to perform slightly better than unvented thermal storage walls. For example, a building in Albuquerque that would have satisfied 70 percent of its heating load without vents would satisfy 76 percent with upper and lower vents, each equal to ½ percent of the wall area.

☐ The question of whether or not to place vents in the wall depends primarily on the timing of the need for heat. If heat is needed primarily during the day then the vents are needed. If not, the vents will lead to daytime overheating.

☐ Many designers prefer to use direct gain windows instead of vents to provide daytime building heating. This can distribute heat gains more evenly and avoid the overheating possible with vented thermal storage walls.

☐ In water thermal storage walls the water can be placed in a variety of containers, each with different ratios between heat-exchange surfaces and storage mass. Larger containers provide greater and longer-term heat storing

capacity, while smaller containers provide greater heat-exchange surfaces and thus faster distribution. Many container variations are available, including tin cans, bottles, tubes, bins, barrels, drums, bags and complete water walls.

☐ The primary advantage of using a water wall is the ability to obtain a very high thermal storage value within a reasonable space. It is impractical to achieve thermal storage values as high as 90 BTU/deg. (F.)/sq.ft. with a masonry wall because it would need to be 3 feet thick. This would be not only awkward and uneconomical, but also ineffective, because of the inability of heat to pass through such a thick wall. However, a water wall having this heat storage capacity could be made only 18 inches thick. It would perform well and provide for any small temperature swings.

☐ Sizing a thermal storage wall has major cost implications. Not only is the wall itself expensive, but the space it takes up within the building is valuable. Sensitivity studies show that performance increases markedly with increasing thermal storage mass up to but not beyond the point where the mass is sufficient to carry over excess daytime solar heat to supply the building heating load during the night. In commercial buildings periods of occupancy and night setback temperature are especially important in determining the optimum amount of thermal mass.

☐ Regardless of the type of mass system chosen, the size or surface area of a thermal storage wall depends on the absorptivity of the wall's south-facing surface (as discussed in the section on direct gain), the heat loss from the conditioned spaces, climate and amount of incident solar radiation. The rate of heat loss from a space is largely determined by the difference between indoor and outdoor air temperatures. The larger this difference, the faster the rate of building heat loss. Therefore, in cold climates, a larger thermal storage wall is needed to keep a space at close to 70 degrees (F.). Local climate and latitude changes the solar energy incident on a south-facing wall during the winter. For

Percentage of heating load to be provided by thermal storage wall	Recommended Vent Area	Comment
25%	3%	Performance levels off above 3%
50%	1%	Performance levels off above 1%
75%	½%	Performance decreases above 1%

Recommended Vent Areas

example, at 36 degrees North latitude (Tulsa, Oklahoma) each square foot of thermal wall intercepts approximately 1,883 BTUs during a clear January day, while at 48 degrees North (Seattle) the same wall receives only 1,537 BTUs. As a general rule, then, a thermal storage wall needs to be larger the farther north (or the more severe the winter climate in which) a building is located.

☐ The accompanying tables provide rules of thumb for sizing double-glazed thermal storage walls to maintain space temperatures at 65 to 70 degrees (F.) without any additional heating source. If a wall is too thick, heat will dissipate within it before it can reach the conditioned spaces; if it is too thin, the heat will reach conditioned spaces during the day, dissipating within the space before the heat is needed during the night and, possibly, causing the space to be overheated during the day. If the surface area of a wall is too great or too small, the spaces will be too cold or too hot, respectively.

Controls

☐ As in the direct gain systems, controls for the operation of thermal storage walls are important, though less so than in direct gain systems, because the space is not directly influenced by solar gain. For optimal efficiency in the winter, external movable insulation or other insulation should be provided to protect the storage mass from wasteful heat loss to the overcast or night sky. In the summer, unwanted heating of the storage mass can be pre-vented by shading the glazed area with overhangs or closing the external insulation. (The use of Trombe walls to induce ventilation in the summer is discussed in the section on direct cooling in this monograph.) With a water wall, thermal transfer across the water is rapid, and radiant distribution from the wall to the interior space is rapid, in contrast to the longer time lag of a masonry wall. Therefore, if heat is less desirable until the cooler evening hours, a water wall requires some storage-distribution control. Insulation between storage and the space can keep heat in the wall until needed. With water walls, such insulation would not interfere with the system's ability to heat the space convectively during the day through the vents.

Roof Pond

☐ A second indirect gain system is the roof pond. In the roof pond system, the passive collector-storage mass is moved from the floor and wall of the building to the roof.

☐ The roof pond system requires a body of water on the roof, exposed to direct solar gain, which it absorbs and stores. Since thermal storage is in the ceiling of the building, it will radiate uniform, low-temperature heat to the entire building in both sunny and cloudy conditions. Because distribution of solar heat from the roof pond is by radiation only, the ceiling must be close to the individuals being warmed, because radiation density drops off with distance. This suggests that the storage mass be uniformly spread over all spaces and that ceiling heights not be raised from the normal. Movable insulation is generally required to reduce unwanted heat losses to the environment on sunless winter days and nights and unwanted heat gain in summer. (The use of roof ponds to draw heat from a building in the summer is discussed in the section on indirect cooling in this monograph.)

Material	Recommended Thickness
Adobe	8–12 inches
Brick (common)	10–14 inches
Concrete (dense)	12–18 inches
Water	6 inches or more (0.5 cu.ft/sq.ft. of south-facing glass)

Storage Wall Thicknesses

Average Winter Outdoor Temperature (°F) (degree-days/coldest month)	Square Feet of Wall Needed for Each One Square Foot of Floor Area to be Heated	
	Masonry Wall	Water Wall
15° (1,500)	0.72–>1.0	0.55–1.0
20° (1,350)	0.60–1.0	0.45–0.85
25° (1,200)	0.51–0.93	0.38–0.70
30° (1,050)	0.43–0.78	0.31–0.55
35° (900)	0.35–0.60	0.25–0.43
40° (750)	0.28–0.46	0.20–0.34
45° (600)	0.22–0.35	0.16–0.25

Thermal Storage Wall/Floor Area Ratio

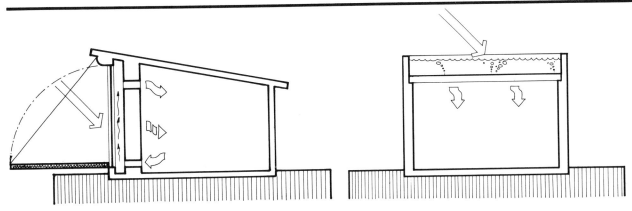

Control of Heat Distribution in a Masonry Trombe Wall

Roof Pond

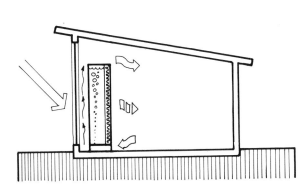

Control of Heat Distribution in a Water Thermal Storage Wall

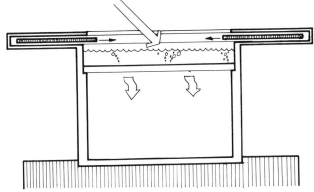

Movable Insulation on a Roof Pond System

☐ Since the roof *is* the collector, this system is most suitable for heating one-story buildings, or the upper floor of a two- or three-story structure. Although the system is somewhat restrictive as to building height, it does not dictate a building shape or orientation and allows complete freedom with regard to the arrangement of indoor spaces. In addition, the roof pond is invisible from the street level.

☐ The area of roof pond required varies according to whether movable insulation is used and the type of glazing, as well as climate and

building load. The recommended ratios of roof pond area to the floor area heated are given in the accompanying table.

☐ Roof pond heating is characterized by stable indoor temperatures and high levels of comfort because of the large area of radiative surface (usually the entire ceiling). Daily fluctuations of space temperature range from only 5 degrees to 8 degrees (F.) in a masonry building, and 9 degrees to 14 degrees (F.) in a building constructed of lightweight materials.

Average winter outdoor temperature (°F)	15 to 25 degrees (F.)	25 to 35 degrees (F.)	35 to 45 degrees (F.)
Double-glazed ponds w/night insulation	—	0.85–1.0	0.60–0.90
Single-glazed ponds w/night insulation and reflector	—	—	0.33–0.60
Double-glazed pond w/night insulation and reflector	—	0.50–1.0	0.25–0.45
South-sloping collector cover w/night insulation	0.60–1.0	0.40–0.60	0.20–0.40

Roof Pond Area/Floor Area Ratios

Night Insulation

☐ Night insulation provides the means for controlling the heat flow from the pond to the space. The most common movable insulation panels are 2-inch polyurethane foam reinforced with fiberglass strands and sandwiched between aluminum skins. This is a standard item marketed as "metal building insulation." This insulation has been used successfully for up to 40-foot spans before requiring support by metal channels. In the flat roof pond system, the metal frames that support the insulation panels should be designed so that they do not form a straight heat-conducting path from the ponds to the exterior.

☐ For a flat roof pond with horizontal sliding panels, the panels should be as large as possible to reduce the amount and cost of hardware (such as tracks, seals). The tracks for the panels must be able to withstand deflection, and the panels should seal tightly over the ponds when closed. This requires careful detailing, especially for the sliding panels generally applied to flat roofs. Sometimes the tightness needed may require neoprene curtains and seals that ride along the panels. A study performed in 1973 showed that 24 percent of the energy striking the ponds on an average winter day was lost back through the insulation at night because of inadequate seals. The efficiency of this system can be increased by designing the insulating panels to act as reflectors when in the open position, using either a bifolding or solid panel hinged along its north edge and covering the surface of the panel with a reflective material.

Dove Publications Building
Benedictine Monastery
Pecos, New Mexico
Designer: Mike Hansen

The south elevation of the Dove Publications building is dominated by three 140-foot-long rows in insulated glass windows encompassing a total of 1,500 square feet of double-glazing. Practically the entire energy performance of the building rests on this glass-covered elevation. An upper-level, set-back clerestory admits sunlight to heat and illuminate the warehouse space at the back of the building. The middle row of glazing warms the office space in front, and also allows the sun to strike the heat-retentive central masonry wall between the office and warehouse spaces. The sunlight passing through this direct gain glazing provides almost all the heat needed during working hours. The lowest band of glazing fronts a wall of water-filled thermal storage barrels. The drums from the water wall protrude up into the office area but are enclosed in insulated cabinets that double as counter-height working areas.

The water wall consists of 138 standard 55-gallon steel barrels filled with water. To prevent freezing and fungus growth, the water is actually a mixture of water and propylene glycol, with 8 ounces of 10-weight oil added as a rust inhibitor. To allow for thermal expansion, the drums are only 90 percent full, containing approximately 50 gallons of liquid per drum. The steel drums themselves are painted black to increase solar absorption and inhibit rust build-up on the exterior.

The water in the drums is warmed by solar energy passing through the lower row of glazing. The insulated cabinet enclosures prevent the heat from being transferred to the office space unless ventilating louvers are opened. As long as the louvers are closed, heat is merely stored by the water mass. When the louvers are opened, however, air moves into the cabinet space through floor vents by natural convection, and is warmed by the water drums. The warm air then rises, passes through a second set of vents along the upper edge of the cabinet wall, and flows into the office space.

Dove Publications Building
Benedictine Monastery
Pecos, New Mexico
Designer: Mike Hansen

Normally the louvers are closed during the day and opened only during the night to maintain adequate interior temperatures until the next morning. During the day, the upper row of windows provides enough direct-gain heating for the offices to maintain comfortable temperatures without the use of heat from the water wall. In fact, during the day direct gain is so plentiful that curtains had to be installed to control it. By necessity, however, because they were a last-minute addition, they had to be located on the inside of the glazing, making them more useful for controlling glare than for screening out the sun's heat during summer months. To be truly effective for heat control, shading devices should be located on the outside of the glazing or at least made of highly reflective materials. Winter overheating is, however, rare enough not to cause any major user complaints.

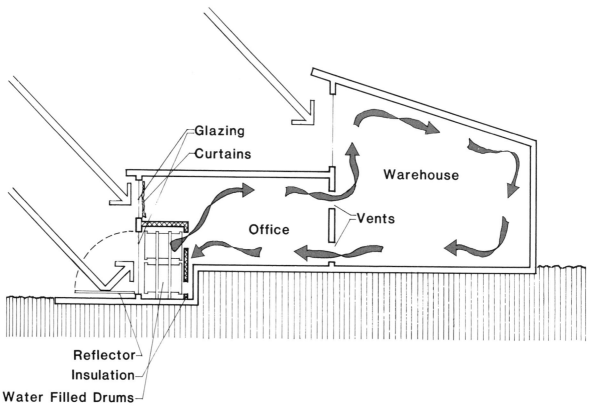

Dove Publications Building
Benedictine Monastery
Pecos, New Mexico
Designer: Mike Hansen

Isolated Gain Systems

In isolated gain systems, the solar collection and storage elements are in a "sunspace" separate from the spaces they heat.

☐ Solariums, greenhouses, and atriums are common examples of sunspaces in isolated gain systems. These terms are used somewhat interchangeably in the passive solar literature. Loosely defined, a solarium is often a narrow, one- or two-story space running the length of all or part of the south side of the building, or is an attached room, as in a sunporch or sunroom. In contrast, an atrium is a more integral part of the building, adjacent to the majority of spaces in the building. Greenhouses, totally glazed attached rooms, are used predominantly for plant growing and are usually located off one or several of the main spaces on the south side of the building.

☐ In all these variations the sunspace itself is a direct gainspace. Sunlight enters the sunspace and strikes an absorber surface. Lightweight materials reradiate the sunlight as heat almost immediately, whereas thermal mass materials store it. Storage materials and location vary and include masonry walls, water-filled drums, concrete or rock floors and pools. Because sunspaces can reach high daytime temperatures, provision is often made for ducting heat to a storage area somewhere in or below the building; a rock bed below the first floor is a common example of this technique. The sizing and location of storage depends on whether the sunspace is used during the evening hours and whether the storage is used to heat the building at night.

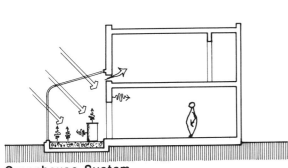

Greenhouse System

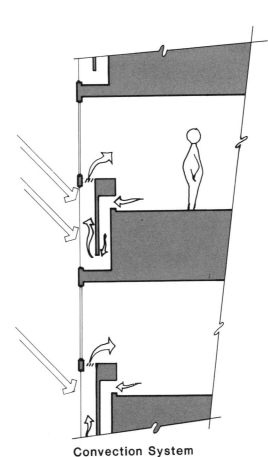

Convection System

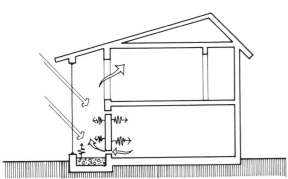

Solarium/Sunspace System

Isolated Gain System

☐ Distribution schemes also vary in isolated gain systems. Vents, windows and doors can be opened during the day to allow a convective flow of heat from the sunspace into the conditioned spaces. Radiant distribution of heat stored in the common walls between the sunspace and main spaces is also common. Controls depend on the use of the sunspace. Insulation should be used on the glazing at night if the space is used. Otherwise, night insulation is sometimes used on glazed areas between the sunspace and the main spaces. In the summer, shading and ventilation are particularly important controls; with minimal adjustments the secondary space can also often be used to drive a convective ventilation system that cools the entire building.

☐ Isolated gain systems can be used in most climate regions, because the separate collection-storage space allows solar heat gain to be used or shut off at will.

☐ The complicated nature of thermal energy flow between sunspace and building makes it difficult to give rules of thumb to accurately size a sunspace. A well designed sunspace with low heat losses and good thermal connection to the building can be as good as direct gain or thermal storage wall systems, whereas a thermally "leaky" sunspace can be much poorer.

☐ The major construction material in the sunspace is double glass or transparent rigid plastic. (Plastic sheet has a short life, however, and its appearance can deteriorate.) In cold climates 1.4 to 2.0 square feet of south-facing double glass are needed for each square foot of building floor area to be heated. In temperate climates, 0.8 to 1.4 square feet of glass area are sufficient.

☐ The nature of the thermal connection between the sunspace and building will determine the effectiveness of the sunspace as a heating source.

Controls

☐ The temperature of the sunspace can be effectively controlled within a predictable range by properly sizing the collector area (glazing) and thermal mass. Temperature control in adjoining spaces is the same as for a thermal storage wall system.

☐ The surface of a thermal storage wall (sunspace side) should be highly absorptive, as discussed in connection with direct gain. In cool and cold climates, thermocirculation vents or operable windows should be located in the wall, and the sunspace should be thermally isolated during extended cloudy periods.

☐ An attached sunspace has the following characteristics:
—because the occupied space is buffered by the sunspace, temperature swings in the occupied space are small
—thermal control (primarily through shading and natural ventilation) is critical to reduce overheating in the summer
—hot air from the top of the sunspace can be drawn through ducts by a fan to heat rock bed storage and back to the sunspace—this will improve the system efficiency and reduce overheating in the sunspace.

☐ One design strategy for sunspaces that can be suitable for residential applications is to divide the building into two thermal zones and accept fairly large temperature swings in one zone in order to stabilize temperatures in the other zone.

☐ In the accompanying figure, large temperature swings can be expected in the sunspace because there is a large excess of heat. Heat storage is in the mass separating the zones and in the floor of the sunspace. Depending on the size of the sunspace, its mass volume, and the glazing area, temperature swings of 25 to 35 degrees (F.) can be anticipated. The sunspace could be used as greenhouse, sunroom, atrium, transit area, vestibule or airlock entry.

☐ A principal advantage to this approach is reduced temperature swings in the main building, which is protected from the extremes of the sunspace by the time delay and heat capacity effects of the mass wall. With a little care in the design, one can phase the time of heat arrival into the building so as to maintain a nearly constant interior temperature.

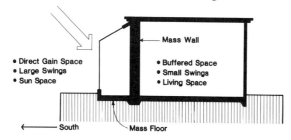

Two-Zone Approach to Passive Heating

Balcomb Residence
Santa Fe, New Mexico
Designers: Susan Nichols and William
Lumpkins, of Communico

The Balcomb residence in Santa Fe, New Mexico, is an example of the effective use of the two-zone approach. Temperatures experienced in the two-story greenhouse typically range from 52 to 85 degrees (F.) in winter and from 65 to 87 degrees (F.) in summer, with a winter low of 43 degrees (F.) and a summer high of 95 degrees (F.). Ambient outside temperatures range from a winter low of −14 degrees (F.) to a summer high of 95 degrees (F.). There is no auxiliary heat in the greenhouse.

A major mechanism for transfer of heat from the sunspace to the main building is usually by convection of hot air during the day. Heat is stored in the main building wells and other materials. The convection can be through doorways through the common well separating the sunspace from the main building. These can be closed at night to prevent reverse flow of heat.

The living space is separated from the greenhouse by an adobe mass wall (14 inches thick downstairs and 10 inches thick upstairs). Heat takes 7 to 8 hours to travel through these walls. In addition, most rooms in the house have

Photo: John R. Hoke, Jr., AIA

Balcomb Residence
Santa Fe, New Mexico
Designers: Susan Nichols and William Lumpkins, of
Communico

doors opening to the greenhouse for direct convective heating as needed. Temperatures in the downstairs living room range from 63 to 75 degrees (F.) in the winter, with a typical daily swing of 6 to 7 degrees (F.), and from 70 to 78 degrees (F.) in the summer, with a typical daily swing of 4 to 5 degrees (F.). This small swing in winter is partly due to the stabilizing effect of underfloor rock beds, which are heated by warm air removed from the peak of the greenhouse, where it would otherwise be largely lost. This results in a decrease in maximum winter greenhouse temperatures from 95 to 85 degrees (F.), thus improving the comfort there. The house has been carefully monitored and evaluated; the solar heat contributes 57 million BTU per year or 89 percent of the annual heating requirement of the house that are not satisfied by normal internal gains.

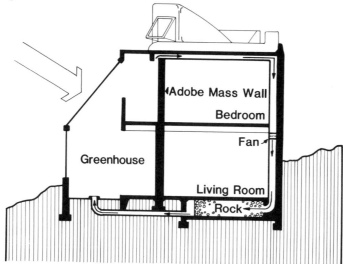

Balcomb Residence
Santa Fe, New Mexico
Designers: Susan Nichols and William Lumpkins, of
Communico

Thermosiphons

☐ Thermosiphons are passively driven by temperature differentials. These systems take advantage of the tendency of warm fluids and gases to rise and cold fluids and gases to fall. Air heated by the sun is allowed to rise, flowing to either conditioned spaces or storage. As the heated air leaves the collector area it draws in cool air from below to replace it, creating a convective loop that functions as long as heat is available.

☐ Air thermosiphon systems in many ways come closest to conventional mechanically driven hot air systems and active solar systems. The accompanying figure shows a thermosiphon system.

—Collector depth (CD) should be at least ¹⁄₁₅ collector length (CL).

—Overall collector height (CH) should be at least 6 feet to generate adequate air pressure to drive the system.

—Insulate storage box with the thermal equiv-

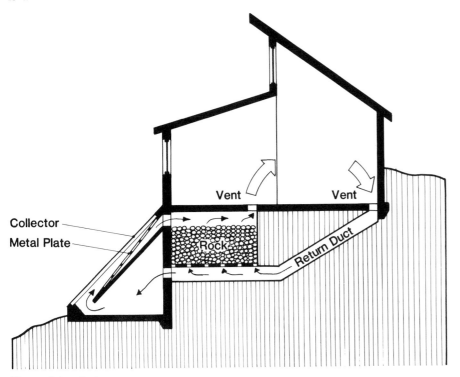

Thermosiphon System

☐ When coupled with remote storage, thermosiphons can maximize the usefulness of the heat collected because delivery can be totally controlled. Because large expanses of windows in conditioned spaces are unnecessary, heat loss through windows during nongain periods can be reduced, making thermosiphons particularly attractive for harsh climates. The ability to direct the heat to either integrated or isolated storage also gives a great deal of flexibility in the heating design of a building. Furthermore, the construction and installation of simple air heat collectors of this type are relatively easily and inexpensively accomplished, and make them an excellent choice for retrofit designs (primarily residential).

alent of at least 6-inch batt insulation.

—The cross-sectional area of the ducts should be ¹⁄₁₅ to ¹⁄₂₀ the area of the collector—this size allows a minimum of friction losses; no dimensions should be less than 5½ inches.

—Avoid corners in flow channels.

—Storage cross sections should be at least ⅔ of collector area.

—Insulate between downflow and upflow with at least 1-inch duct board.

—Use clean rock to avoid layers of dirt in bin.

—to avoid reverse thermosiphoning dampers can be used. Alternatively the *bottom* of the storage bed should be *above* the top of the collector—both the inlet and outlet should be placed at the top of the collector; as a result, a cold

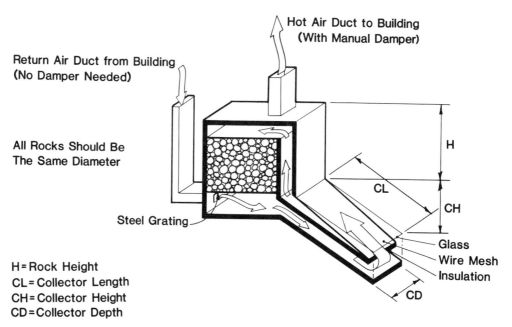

Return Air Duct from Building
(No Damper Needed)

Hot Air Duct to Building
(With Manual Damper)

All Rocks Should Be
The Same Diameter

Steel Grating

H = Rock Height
CL = Collector Length
CH = Collector Height
CD = Collector Depth

H
CL
CH
Glass
Wire Mesh
Insulation
CD

Thermosiphon system

air "plug" will develop at night, with both columns of cold air of the same length, tending not to move.
—Locate heated space above storage bin.
—Build vent flap at top of collector to open during summer to prevent overheating.

☐ Because the thermosiphon will not be working at night, there will be no heat loss at that time. Therefore, double glazing of collectors may not be advantageous·unless the climate has at least 7000 heating degree days or more.

☐ Thermosiphon collectors mounted at a flat angle are self-stagnating. A tilt between 45 degrees and 90 degrees from the horizontal optimizes the thermal chimney effect. However, vertical collectors often integrate into building forms more easily.

☐ Black expanded metal lath mesh—five to six layers—has been a very successful thermal collector and exchange surface for thermosiphons. Each square foot, counting all surfaces of each layer, has about 0.75 square feet of actual transfer surface.

☐ A thin metal plate at the back of the collector can improve performance significantly—approximately 15 percent—by catching light and adding another square foot of transfer area. The mesh is placed diagonally across the air passage, so that air must pass through the mesh completely at least once during a pass. When

flat plates or corrugated plates are used for the thermal collector and exchange surfaces, they should be mounted in the *center* of the collector air passage. The heat transfer coefficient of such a system is less than 2.

☐ All ducts and unglazed portions of the collector system should be well insulated. Polystyrene, which melts at approximately 180 degrees (F.), should not be used. Clearance should be allowed around all glazing, and sealant should be used for airtight construction that can also accommodate expansion and contraction.

☐ Well-designed and well-constructed systems collect about 40 percent of the available solar energy in cold climates. Twenty-five percent probably represents the lower edge of expected performance in less well designed and constructed systems. In milder climates, system efficiencies of 40 percent and 50 percent can be expected. For example, in Kansas City, the clear-day incident solar radiation on 21 January for a south-facing collector is 1907 BTU/sq.ft./day. The energy collected would range between 477 BTU/sq.ft. (25-percent efficiency) and 763 BTU/sq.ft. (40 percent) of collector per day.

Heat Pipe

☐ Thermosiphon heat pipes have been used for many years, with applications from spacecraft to the Trans-Alaska Oil Pipeline, where they prevent melting of the permafrost.

124

☐ A heat pipe has very high effective thermal conductivity. A small quantity of liquid is placed in a tube from which the air is then evacuated, and the tube is sealed. When the lower end of the tube is heated, the liquid vaporizes and the vapor moves to the top or cooler end where it is condensed, transferring its latent heat. The condensate then returns to the warm end by gravity. Since the latent heat of evaporation is large, considerable quantities of heat can be transported with a very small temperature difference.

☐ Heat pipes typically use standard copper pipe and freon 12 as the working fluid. They operate at temperatures as low as 51 degrees (F.) and have a thermal conductivity more than a 100 times that of a solid copper rod of the same diameter. The accompanying figure shows a heat pipe used to extract heat from below grade to temper the envelope of a building.

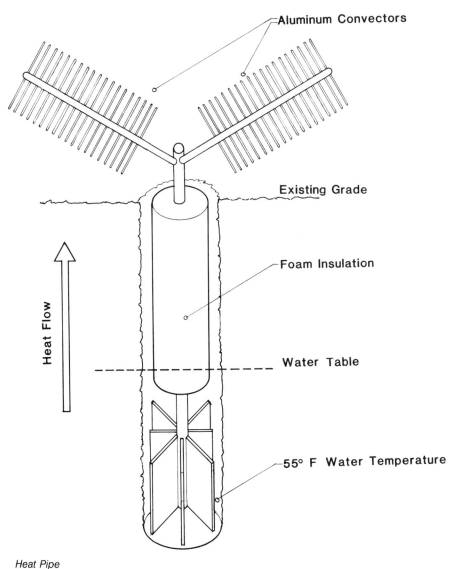

Heat Pipe

Passive Cooling

As with passive heating strategies, passive cooling techniques are better defined for residential and small-scale buildings than for large-scale commercial buidlings. However, if environmental conditions are right, it is possible to take advantage of natural cooling forces in the environment to reduce the large cooling requirements of most commercial buildings.

☐ As with heating systems, passive cooling systems can be categorized as direct, indirect and isolated. *Direct cooling* involves both avoiding heat gains and cooling a space by exposing it directly to environmental heat sink(s).

☐ *Indirect cooling* involves cooling a space by spontaneous radiation of thermal energy to storage (or some exchange surface) that is in turn cooled by exposure to environmental heat sink(s).

☐ *Isolated cooling* involves cooling a space with air that is conditioned passively at a remote location.

☐ Many of the factors that result in passively heated buildings also work in favor of natural cooling. Good insulation, for example, keeps heat out of as well as in a building.

☐ The design of passive cooling systems requires the identification of an environmental heat sink to which excess heat from a structure can be rejected. Four commonly available heat sinks are:
—the sky, especially on clear nights
—the heat absorptance that occurs during evaporation
—cool night air
—cool temperatures of the ground.

☐ The accompanying chart indicates the primary cooling techniques and their ability to affect air temperatures, movement, and humidity and mean radiant temperature.

Design Strategies	Air Temperature	Air Movement	Humidity	Mean Radiant Temperature
Shading	●			●
Underground Construction	●			●
Thermal Mass	●			●
Night Sky Radiation	●			
Earth-Air Heat Exchange	●	●	●	
Thermosiphon	●	●		●
Evaporative Cooling	●		●	
Night Ventilation			●	
Day Ventilation	●	●	●	●

Passive Cooling Strategies Affecting Comfort Variables

126

Princeton Professional Park
Princeton, New Jersey
Architects: Harrison Fraker, Architects
Princeton Energy Group

The Princeton Professional Park in Princeton, New Jersey, is a 64,000-square-foot trio of speculative office buildings. The design embeds offices in a garden environment, with the three buildings linked by wandering paths.

An atrium in each building serves as a thermally isolated space where heat is collected during the day in the heating season. It is a buffer zone that lessens the number of office walls exposed to the outside air, improving the skin-to-volume ratio.

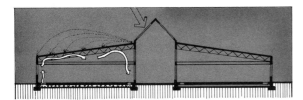

Princeton Professional Park
Princeton, New Jersey
Architects: Harrison Fraker, Architects
*   Princeton Energy Group*

For storage, an inexpensive horizontal rock bed is used. A draw-down air-handling system supplies the rock bed with heat from the atrium. Heat stored during the day radiates through the slab at night.

About half the heating energy for each building is provided by internal gains, with another 40 percent from solar. Each office module is supplied with one standard heat pump package as auxiliary, and tenants have individual controls. Mechanical heating is estimated to be only 30 percent that of similar conventional buildings.

The rock bed and atrium, together with natural ventilation and a wet-roof evaporation system, also reduce the annual cooling load of each building by 80 to 90 percent.

Climate analysis shows that natural ventilation can cool the building from April through June, and from mid-September through October—a considerable portion of the airconditioning season. The atrium assists here. The hot air building up at the top of the atrium creates a thermal chimney effect, pulling air from the offices into the atrium and out the ridge vent. Winds, which are consistent in the swing seasons, come out of the northwest and southwest to provide good cross ventilation through the operable windows on the outside and atrium walls.

July and August are hot and humid. Because these are one-story buildings they use a spray system on the roof to achieve evaporative heat loss. Controlled intermittent spraying of the roof, with pauses for complete evaporation, lowers 3 PM peak surface temperatures from 180 degrees (F.) to close to 90 degrees (F.). Because the airconditioning equipment does not have to handle the major skin load at peak times, the reduction in airconditioning costs alone almost justifies the spray system's cost.

By coupling the spray roof system and the rock bed, the roof can also be used to reject heat at night. Air circulating behind the spray roof, cooled to as low as 60 degrees (F.), circulates down to the rock bed, which in turn is cooled to near 65 degrees (F.).

When the building is shut during the day in the cooling season, return air from the offices is circulated through the rock bed for pre-cooling and then goes to the airconditioning unit, which, if the air is cool enough, simply circulates it.

Princeton Professional Park
Princeton, New Jersey
Architects: Harrison Fraker, Architects
*   Princeton Energy Group*

Direct Cooling

Direct cooling has four major components: keeping heat out, providing ventilation, underground construction and evaporative cooling. Most of the strategies for keeping the heat out of a building are the opposite of those for admitting direct solar gain, and include:
—orientating the building away from intense solar exposure
—using indirect daylighting instead of artificial lighting
—shading roofs, walls and windows with overhangs, wing-walls and vegetation
—adjusting surface-area-to-volume ratios.

These and related strategies for reducing heat gain are discussed in other monographs of this handbook.

Natural Ventilation

☐ If cooling load is still an issue when the designer has controlled as much heat gain as possible, natural and induced ventilation can be used to increase comfort in the face of temperature and humidity levels that would otherwise be uncomfortable. Human comfort is primarily a function of four variables: air temperature, air movement, humidity, and the mean radiant temperature of interior surfaces. Ventilation is considered direct cooling because air movement past the body increases heat transfer from the skin and because comfort conditions are immediately improved when outdoor air replaces indoor air that is warmed or more humid.

☐ As the accompanying graph indicates, ventilation rates of 200 feet per minute (fpm) provide comfortable conditions even with 85-degree (F.) temperatures and 50-percent relative humidity. It is generally recommended that ventilation rates should be between 200 and 400 fpm to provide comfortable conditions without the assistance of mechanical cooling. Note, however, that airspeeds above 200 fpm can disturb loose papers and should be avoided if this is the problem.

☐ Natural air movement is caused by differences in temperature, and the other differences in pressure. Vertical currents of air carrying the dust of a field up into the sky are frequently observed. These vertical currents, called "thermals," are composed of relatively hot air that rises above the cooler air surrounding it. The wind, an example of the second phenemonon, is simply a large mass of air moving from a high pressure area in one geographical location to a low pressure area in another.

☐ Designing to maximize natural ventilation requires data on wind speed and direction and terrain and landscaping at the site and airflow patterns in rooms for various building and aperture geometries. Note that adjacent structures, both existing and those that might be built in the future, can affect wind speed and direction significantly. To integrate natural ventilation design with fans, daylighting, mechan-

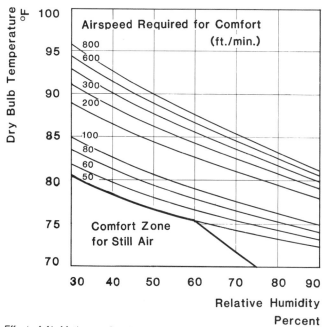

Effect of Air Motion on Comfort

ical airconditioning, heating requirements, etc., one also needs airchange rates, levels of internal heat gains, and building envelope heat transfer coefficients.

☐ Orientating a building to take advantage of the prevailing wind direction during the cooling season need not conflict with other design requirements. Often, room airspeeds are not significantly reduced even when the wind direction is as much as 45 degrees away from normal incidence and in many cases, e.g., long narrow openings, they may be enhanced. Therefore, it is possible to face the long wall of buildings up to 45 degrees away from the prevailing wind direction to take advantage of shading and ventilation simultaneously. In addition, landscaping can be strategically planned to channel winds in preferred directions.

☐ To optimize natural ventilation buildings should ideally be long and narrow, with rooms one or at most two rows deep. Cross ventilation can be encouraged by providing interior doors with louvers. Buildings can be elevated to take advantage of the faster windspeeds higher up. Larger structural cooling can also result if all sides of the building are exposed.

☐ In rooms with windows on only one wall, the average room airspeed can reach only about 15 percent of the external value because the ventilation in this case depends on the turbulent fluctuations of the wind pressure. The ventilation could be increased, however, to about 35 percent by adding vertical wingwalls on window sides if the wind is at an oblique incidence. In general, airspeeds in cross-ventilated rooms with fairly large (approximately 33 percent of wall area) windows on either opposite or adjacent walls can reach 35 to 45 percent of the external wind.

☐ Window design can be crucial to effective ventilation. Horizontal pivot windows such as projection, awning or jalousies are the best kinds, as they reduce the effective aperture area only 25 to 33 percent, compared to 50 percent of double- or single-hung windows or horizontal sliders, and allow free control of airflow direction.

☐ Mesh screens can reduce the overall ventilation rate 25 to 50 percent for windspeeds in the 2 to 10 mph range. Screening an entire balcony in front of the windows produces better ventilation than screening the windows individually.

High Pressure Areas

☐ A stationary obstacle in the path of the

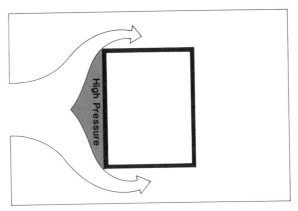

High Pressure Areas

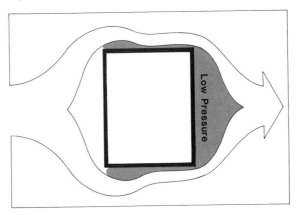

Wind Shadows

wind will repel the moving air and cause it to pile up and slow down until it finds a new path in which to flow. The area affected has a relatively high pressure. This is illustrated in the accompanying figure. The gray area has a high pressure. Generally, ventilation inlets should be placed in the wall adjacent to the high pressure area. Extended eaves, canopies and wingwalls can be used to encourage high pressure zones near an inlet that must be placed in an otherwise low pressure zone.

Wind Shadows

☐ When the flow of air completely envelops the building, wind shadows are created. The wind shadows are shown in gray in the accompanying figure. The size and shape of the wind shadows do not vary with the wind speed but are determined by the geometry of the building. The illustration is a plan view, but the same effect occurs in the cross section as well. When the wind is diverted by the building, the moving air "hops" over and around the building and creates these wind shadows. The wind shadows are relatively low pressure areas. It is therefore desirable to provide outlet openings in the walls adjacent to them so that the air can be "pulled" out of the building.

Inertia

□ If there is an opening in a wall facing the wind, the air will flow through the opening (provided, of course, there is another opening for its exit) and will tend to travel inside the building in the same direction as it travels outside of the building, as a result of air's inertia. Because of inertia, the air flow patterns in a building situated 45 degrees with the wind will be quite different from those in a building which is perpendicular to the wind.

Pressure Differences

□ Air flows out of an area of greater pressure into an area of lower pressure, as shown in the accompanying figure. The exact pattern of air flow in this particular situation will be determined by the inertia as well as by the pressure differences. The speed of air flow within the building will be directly proportional to the speed of the wind.

Changes in Direction of Air Flow

□ Changes in direction of air flow within a building tend to make speeds comparable to outside air difficult to obtain.

□ A change in direction at a place where air speed is high uses much more of the available energy than if the same change in direction were made at a place where the air speed is low. Abrupt changes in direction of air flow caused by obstacles such as partitions create a piling-up effect that slows down the speed. For example, if the partition immediately opposite the inlet opening in room A in the accompanying figure were eliminated, as in the case of room B, the air can enter the room with only a slight change in direction, and better speeds can be obtained. Therefore, to achieve maximum air flow, abrupt directional changes should be kept to a minimum.

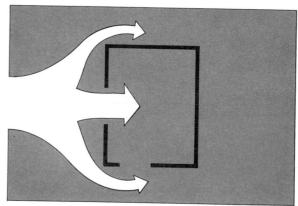

Inertia

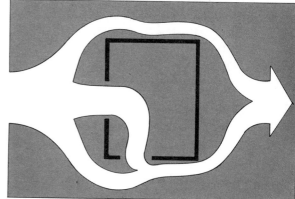

Pressure Differences

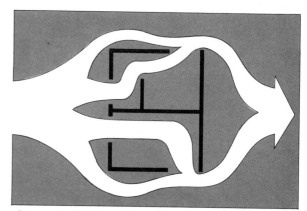

Changes in Direction of Air Flow

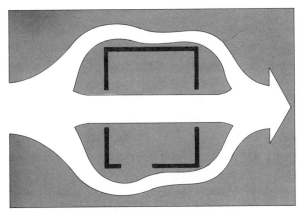

Maximum Air Changes

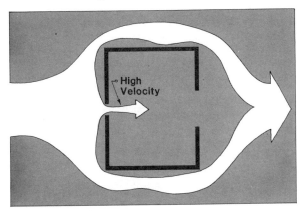

Maximum Speed

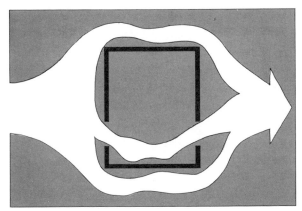

Location of Openings

☐ On the other hand, moderate directional changes in a room can improve ventilation, because the resultant recirculation motion in the room creates a more uniform air flow and enhances heat removal from room surfaces.

Maximum Air Changes

☐ If maximum air changes at a given wind speed are desirable, openings on the inlets and outlets should be as large as possible. In the case of a simple rectangular plan, the inlet and outlet openings should be opposite each other for maximum air changes to benefit from the previously mentioned characteristics of air flow.

Maximum Speeds

☐ Like the flow of water, the flow of air will dam up when blocked by an object, such as a wall, and will exert pressure on that wall. If the wall is punctured with any opening, the air will flow out at a relatively high speed. In the accompanying figure the air flow dammed up outside the building is being forced through the inlet opening. Consequently, there is relatively high speed within the building. If the direction of the wind were reversed, the "dam" would form at the opposite wall, and the increased speed would be on the outside of the building. Therefore, if speed within the room is desirable, the outlet opening should be larger than the inlet.

Locations of Openings

☐ The air flow pattern within a room is also affected by the placement of inlet openings with respect to wall areas. In the accompanying figure the inlet opening is placed asymmetrically with reference to the face of the buidling, and the air enters the building at an oblique angle. Had the opening been in a symmetrical arrangement, the air pattern within the building would have been in the same direction as the outside air flow.

Assume a simple single-room building having a low window on the windward side and a high window on the leeward side. The ground is level, and the wind is blowing perpendicularly to the building.

When the wind is blowing against the building and piles up on the windward face, the inertia of the air will tend to carry it on through the opening in the same direction as the outside air flow. The low inlet opening is located next to a high pressure area; therefore, the air should flow through this opening, even without the benefit of the inertia consideration. Consequently, because of both inertia and pressure differences, there will be a strong flow of air into the low inlet opening, provided there is an effective outlet opening.

From the accompanying drawing of example A, it can be seen that change in direction is slight; therefore, no difficulties should be encountered. If greater air changes are desired, both inlet and outlet openings should be increased. If greater speeds are desired, the size of the outlet should be increased.

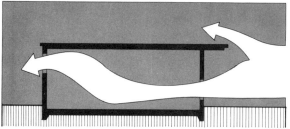

Natural Ventilation Example (A)

Assume the same building with the following exception: the high opening is the inlet and the low opening is the outlet. In this case, shown as example B, there will be a very noticeable difference in air flow patterns from those found in the previous situation. First, there is a considerable amount of wall area between the inlet opening and the ground. When the wind flows along the ground and hits this large wall area, it must change direction, and by the time the air flow reaches the inlet opening, it is going in an almost vertical sweep. The inertia of the air will then tend to carry it on past the opening. The speed of the air passing the opening is also fairly high, resulting in relatively low pressure outside that opening. Very little movement of air will flow from the high opening on the windward side to the low opening on the leeward side.

The most obvious way to get air to enter this room is to use an overhang, as in example C. The size and shape of the overhang will largely determine how much air will flow into the room. Assuming the overhang to be the size and shape as shown in the drawing, the flow of air will assume approximately the pattern shown. Although there is cross ventilation in the room,

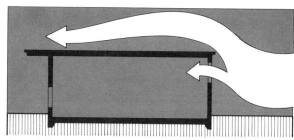

Natural Ventilation Example (B)

however, the strong air movement is not in the occupied zone near the floor.

The air in this situation can be diverted to the floor using projected-type windows as shown in example D. The air flow is diverted down toward the floor and exhausted at the low window. In general, allowing air to flow into the building at low openings and to leave at high openings is probably the most efficient way to ventilate this type of building. This is especially true in rooms with high ceilings, because the effects of air flow caused by temperature differences are superimposed on the effects of air flow caused by pressure differences, and a strong movement of air is assured.

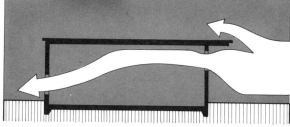

Natural Ventilation Example (C)

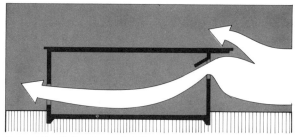

Natural Ventilation Example (D)

The same air flow characteristics can be used to analyze a more complicated building. For example, assume a four-room building as shown in example E. All rooms have floor-to-ceiling openings, all openings are of the same size, and there are no louvers, deflecting vanes or casement type windows. The prevailing wind is from the direction as indicated, and the site is level.

The characteristics of air flow suggest that the ventilation for room A is very good, because the inertia of the air tends to carry it on through the inlet and because the inlet joins a low pressure area.

Room B does not appear to be as well ventilated as room A, because the inertia of the air tends to carry it past the opening. If the openings in room A are relatively large, as compared to the wall area facing the wind, the ventilation in room B may be minimal. On the other hand, if the openings are small, as compared to the wall facing the wind, there will be enough pressure developed to divert an appreciable amount of air into room B. Since the outlet opening of room B adjoins a wind shadow and has relatively low pressure, cross ventilation will be good. Probably the greatest air movement will be on the downward side of the room. Because of the floor plan, there will be some, but very little, air movement caused by a slow moving eddy in the U-shaped portion.

Air movement through room C is less than that likely to pass through room B because of the two changes in direction that occur. However, both changes take place where speeds are relatively low, and a noticeable amount of ventilation can be expected.

Room D is not located advantageously from the standpoint of natural ventilation. It cannot benefit by the effects of inertia, and both openings adjoin wind shadows and are in regions of about equally low pressure.

These situations can be altered considerably if the rooms remain the same, but the location, size, and types of openings are changed. For example, there is even the possibility of obtaining air flow in room D if a fin, such as in a large casement type window, were installed in the opening parallel to the prevailing breeze. If large enough, the fin could scoop the breeze into the room. Room C would have more effective ventilation if the inlet opening were located on the windward wall and the outlet opening were located on the leeward wall.

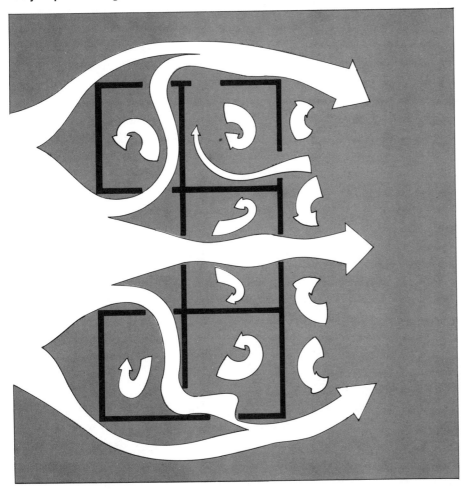

Natural Ventilation Example (E)

133

Induced Ventilation

☐ Where prevailing winds are not suitable for natural ventilation, a building can be designed to induce its own ventilation by duplicating the temperature and pressure stratifications that are the source of wind itself.

☐ As air warms, it becomes lighter and rises, seeking its way out of an enclosed space and drawing cooler replacement air from below. By using sunlight to heat an isolated pocket of interior air to greater than ambient temperatures and controlling its escape, a building can generate air circulation and maximize the influx of cooler air.

☐ The most effective application of this is a solar-exposed enclosure tall enough to generate maximum air flow and massive enough to retain heat to power the system into the evening hours. Many solar design elements usually associated with passive heating—thermosiphon systems, indirect gain sunspaces, and Trombe walls—can be used to produce the same cooling effect. The optimal system draws its replacement air from the coolest possible location, a planted, shaded area to the north or an underground air pipe or storage chamber.

☐ Note that design modifications are often needed to allow passive heating elements to provide both heating and cooling. In Trombe walls for heating, for example, both the top and vents open into the interior to provide it with warmed air. For cooling, the top vent must be shut and a second top vent, opening to the outside, must be provided to exhaust the warm air.

Underground Construction

☐ As discussed in the "Building Envelope" monograph in this handbook, underground temperatures below the frostline remain stable at approximately 56 degrees (F.). The mass of the earth takes so long to heat up and cool down that it approximates this average temperature year-round, with only slight increases at the end of summer and slight decreases at the end of winter. In climates with severe winter or summer temperatures, underground construction provides a more comfortable outside design temperature.

☐ At shallow depths, ground temperatures fluctuate somewhat with the seasons, but as much as three months behind schedule. Thus the earth not only attenuates extreme air temperatures, but acts as a time lag device, carrying winter coolness well into late spring and summer warmth into late fall.

☐ Degree days for cooling and heating can be significantly reduced for an underground building. The accompanying chart shows the differences between a 2-to-12 feet profile and a 2-to-26 feet profile for Minneapolis. The need for cooling is eliminated and the heating degree days, at base 65 degrees (F.), are reduced 26 percent. An identical profile for Temple, Texas, shows that the 2-to-12 feet profile reduced heating degree days by 91 percent and cooling degree days by 15 percent, while the 2-to-26 feet profile eliminated the heating degree days entirely and reduced the cooling degree days 21 percent.

☐ These reductions in degree days are a result of the ground's keeping sunlight away from a building's envelope in summer and keeping

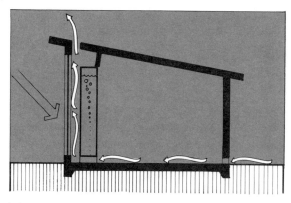

Induced Ventilation for a Water Thermal Storage Wall

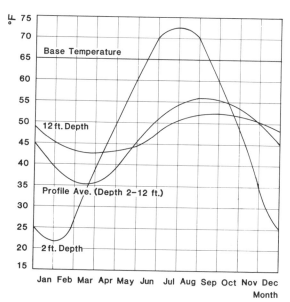

Underground Temperatures for Minneapolis

cold air away from the building's envelope in winter. Underground construction also cools in the summer directly by allowing the ground to serve as a direct heat sink for heat flowing from the building envelope.

☐ In the accompanying map, the United States is divided into three zones. In zone 1, underground construction reduces heating needs significantly but reduces cooling needs less. In fact, the summers in the northern portion of this zone are sufficiently cool that heating would be required during the summer to take the chill off underground rooms.

☐ In zone 2, both heating and cooling loads are reduced. However, because of the high relative humidities in this zone, mechanical air-drying would be required to prevent condensation on walls and floors.

☐ In zone 3, underground construction is not recommended, either because the climate is moderate or because of the complications created by extreme relative humidities.

Evaporative Cooling

☐ Swamp coolers, fountain courts, atrium pools and roof sprays are all applications of evaporative cooling.

☐ When a body of water is placed in a hot and relatively dry space, the water evaporates into the air and increases humidity. In the process it absorbs heat from the air at a rate equivalent to about 1,000 BTUs for every pound of water evaporated, because this much energy is needed to initiate the phase change of water from liquid to vapor (evaporation) and the only source of this energy is the air itself.

☐ Interior evaporative coolers are effective in reducing the sensible temperature in buildings in hot, dry climates if the ambient humidity is low enough, but they present two drawbacks: interior humidity can be increased to a point where discomfort occurs, and water requirements for their use can be a problem in some arid regions. Efficient evaporative cooling systems should be designed to not increase internal air humidity too much and to be economical in water consumption.

☐ Evaporative cooling can also be put to work to cool a radiative roof deck or any other radiative surface in contact with interior spaces. If a roof is sprayed with water, evaporation cools the roof surface, encouraging its absorption of heat from the interior and the dispersal of that heat into the atmosphere.

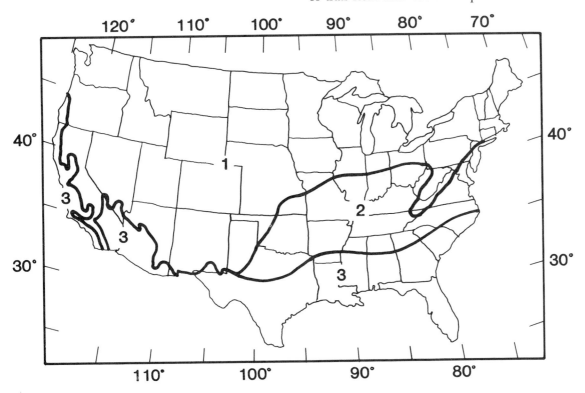

Underground Construction Zones

135

Indirect Cooling

As with direct cooling systems, indirect cooling systems parallel their heating counterparts. In fact, many indirect passive heating elements can be adjusted to provide cooling as well. The primary techniques are night sky radiation and night ventilation.

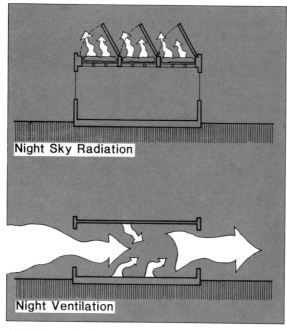

Indirect Loss Systems

Night Sky Radiation

☐ Night sky radiation is an indirect heat-loss process in which interior spaces are exposed to the heat sink of a massive body of water or masonry on the roof of a building. At night the mass is exposed in turn to the heat sink of a cool, clear night sky. The mass is covered by insulation during the day to ensure it will reheat by drawing heat from the building and not the sun.

☐ Night sky radiation is most effective where the diurnal (day-night) temperature swing is in excess of 20 degrees (F.) and where the night sky is relatively clear (radiative losses to the vast heat sink of the sky are impeded by the greenhouse effect of cloud cover).

☐ Masonry mass was used in such historic examples of radiative design as the pueblos and Spanish missions of the Southwest, but recent design efforts have focused on using roof-sited water as the radiative mass. In a typical roof-pond (or thermo-pond) building, bags or bins of water on the roof are covered with movable insulation during the day to absorb heat from the interior spaces below. At night the insulation is removed and the heat stored in the water is released to the cool skydome. Other systems designed along the same lines use floating insulation that can be immersed in the roof pond at night, or stationary insulation over which the water is piped at night. In any configuration, radiative cooling can also provide heating in winter; the exposed mass absorbs solar radiation by day and, insulated from the sky, transmits heat to the interior spaces by night.

☐ Up to 20 or 30 BTUs per square foot of pond surface per hour can be dissipated under very clear skies with low humidity and cool nighttime temperatures. If greater cooling is needed and/or climatic condiions are not optimal, the outside surface of the enclosed ponds can be sprayed with water or flooded to increase cooling by evaporation as well as by nocturnal radiation and convection. About four times as much heat can be dissipated from the roof pound by evaporation as by radiation.

☐ Four passive cooling systems using the roof as a heat dissipator are illustrated in the accompanying figures.

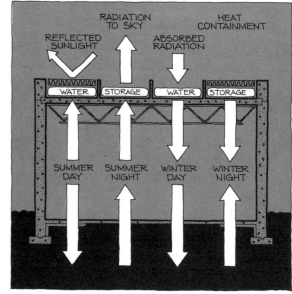

Night Sky Radiation

Type of Pond	Hot-Humid Climate	Hot-Dry Climate
Single-glazed pond	1.0	0.75–1.0
Single-glazed pond augmented by evaporative cooling	0.75–1.0	0.33–0.50

Roof Pond Area/Floor Area Ratios

□ System A is a roof pond building with movable exterior insulation. Bags containing 2 to 6 inches of water are placed on a sheetmetal deck and covered during the day by movable insulation panels. Much of the cooling is produced by infrared radiation to the night sky. When required, enhanced cooling is obtained by flooding or spraying the roof with water. The water bags provide the principal thermal storage and are thermally coupled to the space by radiation and convection through the conducting ceiling. The position of storage in the ceiling provides intimate thermal contact with the dissipating surface and the space to be cooled. The radiant ceiling not only cools other surfaces, and the air indirectly, but also directly cools the occupants.

□ System B has a lightweight metal deck covered with movable insulation. Thermal storage is provided by high thermal mass exterior and interior walls and the floor slab. The roof is exposed at night and is cooled by radiation (and evaporation if required). Heat is transferred from storage to the roof by radiation and natural convection. During daylight hours this ceiling does not provide the benefits of radiant temperature control. The additional thermal resistance introduced by the separation of the dissipating surface and thermal storage reduces system performance. Its advantage lies in the fact that it is more economical to construct massive floors and walls than to construct roof structures to support a significant roof load.

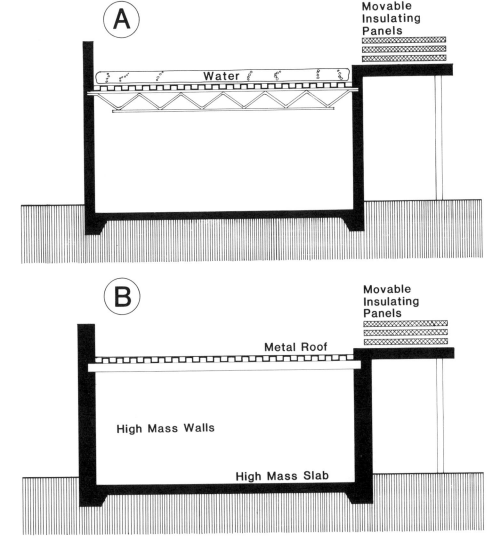

Passive Cooling Systems Using the Roof as a Heat Dissipator

☐ In system C water is passed through pipes in the slab and then trickled uniformly over the roof (which is insulated and could have a moderate pitch). The slab and earth beneath provide the thermal storage. Although convection is significant, the slab couples to the space and secondary storage mass in the walls primarily by radiation. System C has the advantage of replacing the need for moving insulation panels over fixed water by moving water around fixed insulation. If sufficient pipe wall area and flow rate is provided in the slab, the increased thermal resistance between the dissipating surface and the storage mass is not a significant handicap. However, cooling from the floor is not as effective as cooling from above.

☐ System D consists of a metal roof forming an air plenum above fixed interior insulation. As room air is circulated through the plenum, energy stored in the walls and floor is transferred to the uninsulated metal roof deck by forced convection only. Sharing the structural advantage with system C of a lightweight roof system with fixed insulation, but avoiding elaborate plumbing requirements, this system allows an economic integration of a passive cooling technique into standard construction. However, the relatively poor coupling between air as a heat transfer fluid and the uninsulated

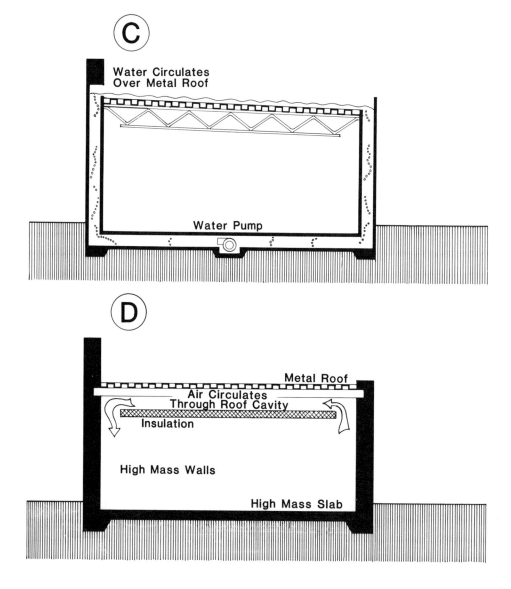

roof deck, the higher associated parasitic energy requirements for air movement as opposed to water movement, and the lack of radiant cooling of people or storage result in poor thermal performance.

Night Ventilation

☐ Like radiative cooling, night ventilation takes advantage of the thermal absorption, and lag characteristics of mass, and requires the same 20-degree (F.) diurnal temperature swing to be effective.

☐ The principle is that the transmission of heat through mass—stone, concrete, adobe—is both delayed and attenuated over time. Depending on the material and the thickness of a massive wall, the delay can stretch from 2 to 12 hours, and the greater the lag the greater the attenuation of heat transmitted. Thus less heat reaches the interior spaces, and it doesn't arrive until late evening or night, when ambient temperatures have dropped and the exterior wall is radiatively cooling. By night's end the wall is again a cold barrier to the daytime onslaught of insolation. Exterior sheating, insulation, or shady vegetation can add to that barrier, further flattening the diurnal curve.

☐ Night ventilation can complement thermal storage systems used in the winter for heat collection. During the day, the building is closed to outside air circulation, while the storage mass acts as a heat sink. At night, the interior of the building is "flushed out," with the warm air escaping to the cool night. Cool night air is thus induced into the building.

☐ The cooling capacity of night ventilation systems is limited to the minimum outdoor air temperature. They are most effective in hot, arid climates that have a diurnal swing of 20 degrees (F.) or greater. The performance of a night cooling system also depends on the capacity of the thermal storage mass. Night air can provide instantaneous cooling, but the extent to which the system can be used to offset warmer daytime temperatures depends on the heat-sink capacity of the structure. The amounts of mass recommended earlier in this monograph for passive heating generally apply as well to cooling.

☐ Rock beds can also be used as thermal storage for night ventilation systems. The rock bed is cooled by outdoor air at night and, during the day, air from interior spaces can be directed through the rocks to be cooled. Rock beds have the advantage of a large surface area, allowing for rapid heat exchange.

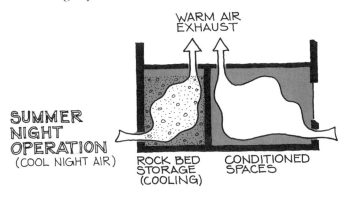

WARM AIR EXHAUST

SUMMER NIGHT OPERATION (COOL NIGHT AIR)   ROCK BED STORAGE (COOLING)   CONDITIONED SPACES

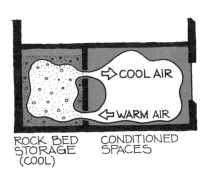

SUMMER DAY OPERATION (WARM DAY AIR)   ROCK BED STORAGE (COOL)   CONDITIONED SPACES

COOL AIR
WARM AIR

Night Ventilation

Showcase Building
McClellan Air Force Building
Sacramento, California
Architects: Sol-Arc

The Showcase Building at McClellan Air Force Base in Sacramento, California, is designed to demonstrate the practicality of using solar in a commercial building on the base. A focal point for visitor instruction and demonstration, the building houses an energy library, a small auditorium, and a display and atrium area, as well as office space and the computer terminals for the base's energy management control system. The building is located at the main gate, where visitors start their tours of the energy-saving installations around the base.

Sol Arc, a Berkeley-based architectural and energy consulting firm, was commissioned to design the 7,600-square-foot building.

Though Sacramento is inland, its climate is influenced by cooler air from the Pacific. Summers are warm and dry; winters are cool and short. Daily temperatures in the summer can swing up to 105 degrees (F.) and drop below 70 degrees (F.) at night.

Thermal mass is integrated into the building's walls, roof, and floor. The exterior walls are concrete block painted on the inside and finished on the outside with R-11 rigid insulation and plaster.

The building is set 2 feet into the ground, and most of the walls are bermed an additional 5 feet. The roof is made of steel decking filled with concrete and covered with R-19 insulation and roofing. The steel decking is exposed to the interior to promote heat transfer between the roof mass and the interior air.

Twenty steel water tubes assist the building mass in meeting the heating and cooling loads. The custom-fabricated, 2-foot-diameter, 10-foot-tall tubes are vertical elements in the structural system. Most of the tubes line both sides of the atrium; three are in the briefing room.

On summer days the cool water in the water tubes absorbs heat from the warmer room air. At night the water in the tubes is pumped up to the roof, where it is circulated through a rooftop evaporative cooling tower. After this has lowered the water's temperature 5 to 10 degrees, it returns to the tubes. The temperature of the water in the tubes is computer-controlled to help limit condensation. Cooler outside air is introduced into the building on summer evenings.

Showcase Building
McClellan Air Force Base
Sacramento, California
Architects: Sol Arc

State Office Building
San Jose, California
Architects: Els Design Group
and Sol-Arc

California's new State Office Building is located in a central San Jose redevelopment area. The building is organized on a checkerboard pattern of open courtyards and enclosed office spaces.

The San Jose climate is so mild that most of its heating needs can be met by warm air drawn off the interior lighting fixtures by the mechanical air-handling system. The real loads for this building are cooling ones, which the designers reduce by a variety of passive solar means: shading that reduces the amount of heat entering the building, natural lighting that reduces the amount of internally generated heat; and heat sinks, in the form of the building's concrete mass and a rock bed, that remove heat from within the building. The mechanical system and the solar systems are computer-coordinated.

At night the building's computer directs the HVAC system to flush San Jose's cool night air through the building and the rock bed. This cools both the mass of the building's concrete structure and the rocks, leaving them ready to absorb heat during the day. The result is a significant reduction in the building's cooling load.

Computer simulation indicates that coordinated performance of all the energy and lighting strategies consumes 70 percent less energy per year than a conventionally designed building of the same size and program.

State Office Building
San Jose, California
Architects: ELS Design Group and Sol Arc

Isolated Cooling

Isolated cooling involves cooling a space with air that is passively conditioned at a remote location.

☐ In many areas, notably the southeastern United States, the earth offers the only sink available at temperatures amenable to passive cooling. Earth cooling tubes or cool pipes, provide one method of using the earth as a heat sink. Such tubes affect building design only slightly and offer retrofit possibilities as well. Furthermore, they allow the building to be alternately thermally coupled to the earth or isolated from it in response to the building's cooling requirements.

☐ Cool pipes are simple and require low operating energy. They are often more applicable to commercial rather than residential applications. Other cooling schemes for residences, such as nighttime ventilation of thermal mass, are simple and more cost-effective since they moderate indoor temperature year-round. In addition, it can be difficult to find room for an optimal length cool pipe on a residential lot. Commercial lots, on the other hand, are generally larger, and installation costs can be reduced if excavation is necessary for other reasons as well.

☐ Cool pipes can be either open systems, which precool ventilation air or closed systems, which precool return air for a mechanical system. Cool air drawn through these pipes can also be stored in rock bed storage.

☐ The performance of a cool pipe is strongly related to the temperature differential driving the heat transfer. Inlet temperatures, whether return air or outside air is used, are readily quantified. In most locations, earth temperatures at depths greater than 20 to 25 feet remain relatively stable, roughly 2 to 3 degrees (F.) above the average annual air temperature. Values at lesser depths will be somewhat higher during the cooling season. Most sources recommend placing cool pipes at a depth of 6 to 12 feet.

☐ Cool pipes should be pitched down to the building. Near the bottom end of the pipe, a condensation drain or humidification pan can be used to adjust humidity level. Cool pipes commonly used are 4 to 12 inches in diameter and constructed of clay tile or noncorrosive metal. In most cases, corrugated tube walls improve performance significantly. In any system, reduced cooling capacity will be encountered at flow velocities less than 400 feet per minute.

☐ Longer pipe runs generally result in more effective heat exchange. For example, a simulation of a cool pipe system of 6-inch diameter polypropylene pipe, with an inlet temperature of 85 degrees (F.) and ground temperature of 65 degrees (F.) yields the results shown in the accompanying table.

☐ High installation and materials cost can make cool pipes more expensive than airconditioners, evaporative coolers, and passive solar design except perhaps in some commercial applications.

Length (Ft.)	Air Temp (F.)	Exchanger Efficiency (%)
20	80.1	24
40	76.4	43
60	73.6	57
80	71.5	67.5
100	69.9	75.5

Cool Pipes—Variations in Efficiency

SHADING AND SUN CONTROL

Introduction

Windows can have profound effect on indoor thermal conditions. Heat gain through a sunlit glass area is many times greater than through an equal area of ordinary wall, and its effect is usually felt almost immediately, with no appreciable time lag. But shading devices can modify the thermal effects of windows to a very great extent.

Shading devices can be applied either externally, internally or between double glazing. They can be fixed, adjustable or retractable and of a variety of architectural shapes and geometrical configurations. Internal shading devices include venetian blinds, roller blinds, curtains and films. Most are retractable, that is, the devices can be lifted, rolled, or drawn back from the window, but some are only adjustable in their angle. External shading devices include shutters, awnings, overhangs and a variety of louvers: vertical, horizontal and a combination of both (eggcrate). Shading between double glazing includes venetian blinds, pleated paper and roller shades. They are usually adjustable or retractable from the inside. Special glasses also control the thermal effect of windows, though to a lesser degree than shading.

Shading devices can control heat gain either constantly or selectively, eliminating the sun in overheated periods admitting it in underheated periods. They can also affect daylight, glare, view and ventilation. The relative importance of these various factors varies under different climatic conditions and in different applications. Thus, in certain buildings, direct sunlight may be welcomed in winter and undesirable in summer, and in others it may be disturbing regardless of the climatic conditions. Sometimes requirements may seem contradictory, e.g., good lighting for seeing but minimal solar heat gain, but solutions can often be found that fulfill all requirements.

Adjustable and retractable shading devices can be adjusted to fulfill changing requirements at will, but fixed devices exert their effect in a predetermined fashion, depending on the interplay between their geometrical configuration, orientation and the diurnal and annual patterns of the sun movement.

Efficient shading, such as external shutters, eliminate more than 90 percent of the heating effect of solar radiation. Inefficient shading, such as dark-colored internal devices, allows 75 to 89 percent of the solar radiation impinging on the window to enter the building.

Sun Motion

The earth rotates around the sun at a constant 23.5 degree tilt. As a result, a given building site is closer to the sun in certain seasons, and gets more sunlight at certain times.

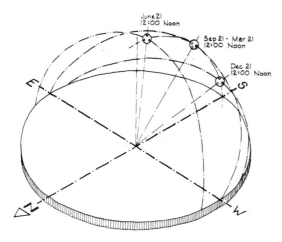

Seasonal Variations in Positions of the Sun

☐ The sun's path across the sky determines the number of hours a window receives direct sunlight and at what angle. This path varies with the seasons and with the latitude. The summer sun rises north of east and sets north of west. The winter sun rises south of east later in the morning, travels in a lower arc, and sets south of west earlier in the evening. The farther north a site is, the greater the northerly and southerly shifts of sunrises and sunsets each season. When the site is very far north the sun travels in a low arc across the sky, and days are very long in summer, very short in winter.

☐ Because of the lower and more southerly path of the winter sun across the sky, a window facing south receives sunlight in winter at a more direct angle and for more hours of the day than a window facing east or west.

☐ Because of the higher and more northerly path of the summer sun across the sky, a window facing south gets no direct sun at sunrise or sunset, and in the middle of the day the sun strikes the windows at a glancing angle. As a result, the high position of the summer sun permits modest building projections to totally shade the window (while permitting the lower winter sun to penetrate). East and west exposures get summer sun for more hours of the day and a more direct angle than south exposures. Hence, east and west are more difficult to shade. The north exposure also receives summer sun, but for only a short period of the day and at very oblique angles. North-facing windows therefore have minimal thermal consequences in summer.

Latitude	Date	South	East or West	North
Boston				
42° N	June 22	786	1026	638
42° N	Dec. 22	757	286	143
Atlanta				
34° N	June 22	681	1105	681
34° N	Dec. 22	1050	458	220

Average Daily BTU/Sq. Ft./Day in Boston and Atlanta

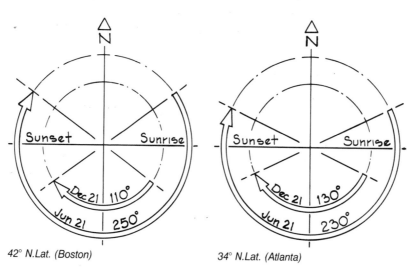

42° N.Lat. (Boston)   34° N.Lat. (Atlanta)

Seasonal Variations in Solar Azimuth for Boston and Atlanta

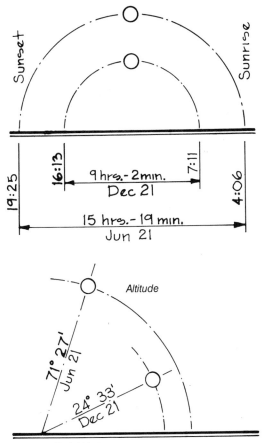

Boston 42°21' N.Lat.

Atlanta 33°45' N.Lat.

Seasonal Variations in Hours of Available Sunlight and Solar Altitude in Boston and Atlanta

□ The farther north a site is, the more winter sunlight the south exposure receives in comparison to the east or west exposures. The farther south a site is, the less summer sunlight the south exposure receives in comparison to the east or west exposures.

□ The amount of incident solar energy a window transmits any given day depends on the angle at which sunlight strikes the window and how many hours it does so. The angle of sunlight affects the amount of solar energy transmitted in two ways: by determining the proportion of light reflected, absorbed and transmitted, and by determining the projected width of the window measured perpendicular to the rays of light. The effect of the sunlight angle on reflection is minimal until it becomes less than 55 degrees and even down to twenty degrees it is of little consequence.

□ The projected width is the width of a window projected onto a plane perpendicular to the rays of light. This width narrows as the angle at which the light intercepts the glass becomes smaller. Less light is transmitted as less area is exposed.

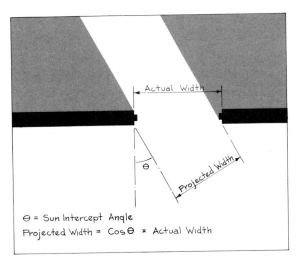

Projected Window Width

147

Solar Angles

The position of the sun, as represented by the altitude and azimuth angles, is a function of specific geographic location, season, and time of day. Solar path diagrams allow designers to compute the sun's position by depicting the path of the sun within the sky vault as projected onto a horizontal plane.

☐ The altitude angles are represented at 10-degree intervals by equally spaced concentric circles; they range from 0 degrees at the outer circle to 90 degrees at the center point.

☐ The azimuth angles are represented at 10-degree intervals by equally spaced radii; they range from 0 degrees at the south meridian to 180 degrees at the north meridian.

☐ The elliptical curves in the diagrams rep-

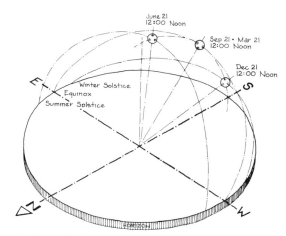

Position of the Sun

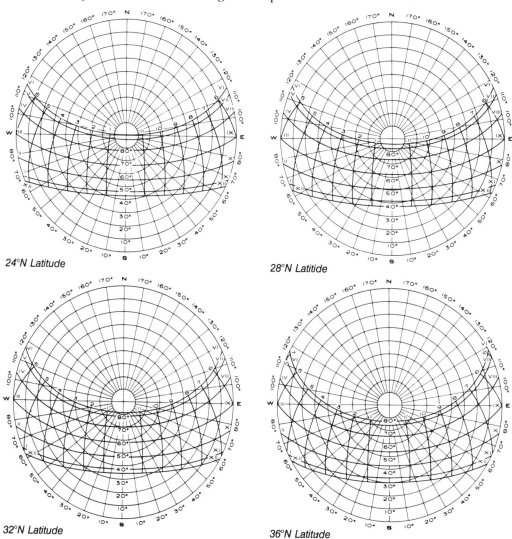

24°N Latitude

28°N Latitide

32°N Latitude

36°N Latitude

Source: The American Institute of Architects, *Architectural Graphics Standards*, Seventh Edition, © 1981. Reprinted by permission of John Wiley & Son, Inc., New York, New York.

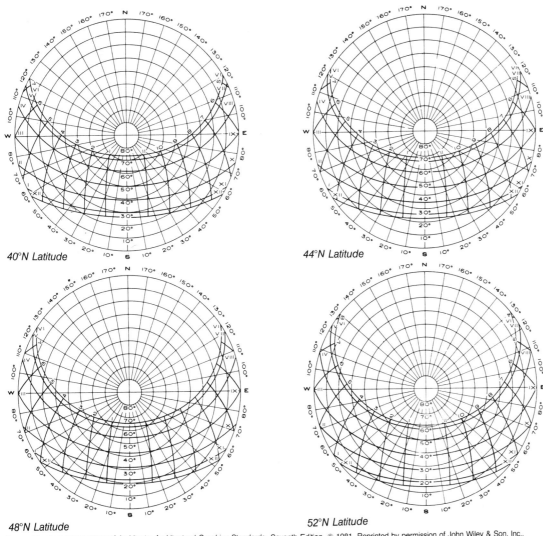

40°N Latitude

44°N Latitude

48°N Latitude

52°N Latitude

Source: The American Institute of Architects, *Architectural Graphics Standards*, Seventh Edition, © 1981. Reprinted by permission of John Wiley & Son, Inc., New York, New York.

resent the horizontal projections of the sun's path on the 21 day of each month.

☐ The months are designated by roman numerals.

☐ The hours of the day are indicated in arabic numerals.

Find the sun's position in Columbus, Ohio, on February 21 at 2 P.M.

1. **Locate Columbus on the map. The latitude is 40 degrees N.**

2. **In the 40 degrees sun path diagram select the February path (marked with II) and locate the 2 P.M. line.**

3. **The intersection of these two lines is the position of the sun. The altitude on the concentric circles is 32 degrees, and the azimuth along the outer circle is 35 degrees, 35 minutes, W.**

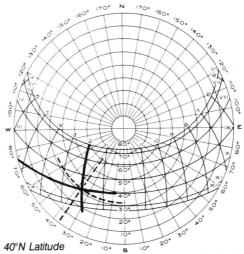

40°N Latitude

Source: The American Institute of Architects, *Architectural Graphics Standards*, Seventh Edition, © 1981. Reprinted by permission of John Wiley & Son, Inc., New York, New York.

149

Solar Radiation

To evaluate the importance of solar shading the designer must know the amount of solar energy falling on the exposed surface.

☐ The upper half of the radiation calculator charts the direct solar radiation falling on a horizontal plane under clear sky conditions.

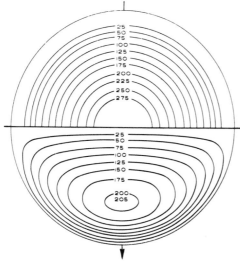

Solar Radiation Calculator

Source: The American Institute of Architects, *Architectural Graphics Standards*, Sixth Edition, © 1970. Reprinted by permission of John Wiley & Son, Inc., New York, New York.

☐ The lower half charts the direct solar radiation falling on a vertical surface.

☐ The radiation lines are indicated at BTU/sq. ft./hour intervals.

☐ The calculator is on the same scale as the solar path diagrams described under Solar Angles. The calculator can be transferred to a transparent overlay and superimposed on the solar path diagrams. When it is placed in the desired orientation, radiation values can be easily read.

To evaluate the need for solar control, the amount of direct solar energy falling on the glass surface should be calculated.
Location: 40 degrees N
Building orientation: 15 degrees east of south
Glass exposures: north/south facades
Superimpose the solar radiation calculator over the solar path diagram and orient the calculator 15 degree east of south. Since the most penetrating sun angles occur on June 21, the solar radiation values are read directly along the June 21 sun path.

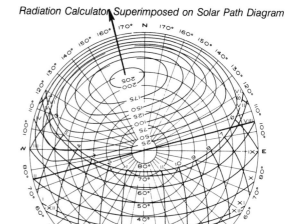

Radiation Calculator Superimposed on Solar Path Diagram

40°N Latitude

North Glazing

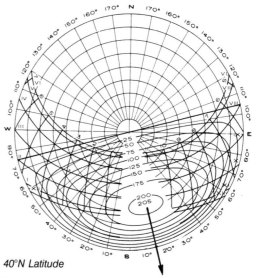

40°N Latitude

South Glazing

Source: The American Institute of Architects, *Architectural Graphics Standards*, Sixth Edition, © 1970. Reprinted by permission of John Wiley & Son, Inc., New York, New York.

The resultant values are displayed. One can see that the south side receives eight hours of insolation, with energies over 90 BTU/sq. ft./hour around 11 A.M. The north side receives negligible energy in the morning, but a considerable amount around 6 P.M.

Southern side

Radiation on south facing vertical surface

Northern side

Radiation on north facing vertical surface

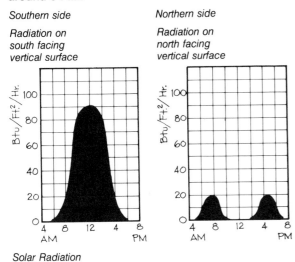

Solar Radiation

Champion Plaza
Stamford, Connecticut
Architect: Ulrich Franzen

The Champion Corporation headquarters is designed with vertical louvers for the east and west facades and horizontal louvers for the south facade. These louvers act as a sunshade and daylight reflector that illuminates the interior ceiling, eliminating the need for window-wall perimeter lighting.

Shading Masks

The effect of shading devices can be plotted in the same way as the solar path. Any building element defines a characteristic form known as a "shading mask."

☐ Masks of horizontal devices create a segmented pattern.

Derivation of Solar Masks

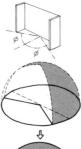 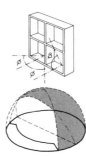

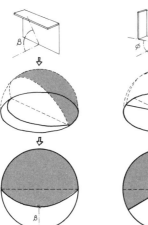

Segmental Mask   Radial Mask   Combination Mask

☐ Masks of vertical devices create a radial pattern.

☐ Masks of eggcrate devices create a segmental and radial pattern.

☐ Shading devices can be designed by following certain steps:

1. Determine the times when shading is needed. During warm periods ("overheated period") shading is needed to improve comfort conditions. For practical purposes, 70 degrees F is a good dividing line between overheated periods and underheated periods.

2. Plot the overheated period on the solar path diagram for the appropriate latitude (solar path diagrams are found under Solar Angles).

3. Construct a shading mask by laying the shading mask protractor over the solar path diagram in the proper orientation. The types determine the shading devices (horizontal, vertical, eggcrate) whose masks will cover the overheated period.

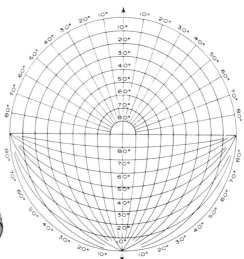

Shading Masks Protractor

Source: The American Institute of Architects, *Architectural Graphics Standards*, Seventh Edition, © 1981. Reprinted by permission of John Wiley & Son, Inc., New York, New York.

4. Design of shading devices can be accomplished by reading the appropriate angles off the shading mask protractor.

—β is the angle between the window and the edge of the horizontal device. The angle is read from the radial lines located on the bottom half of the shading mask protractor.

—θ is the angle between the window and the edge of the vertical device. The angle is read from the segmental lines located on the top half of the shading mask protractor.

—β and θ angles are used for the design of eggcrate devices.

5. Shading masks can be drawn for full shade (100 percent mask) when the observation point is at the lowest point of the surface needing shading; or for 50 percent shading when the observation point is placed at the halfway mark on the surface.

Location: 40 degrees N
Building orientation: 15 degrees east of south
Glass exposures: north/south facades

1–2. The contours of the overheated period for the site is plotted on a solar path diagram for 40 degrees N.

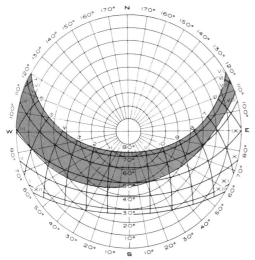

Overheated Period Superimposed on Solar Path Diagram

3. The shading mask protractor is superimposed over the solar path diagram. From this one can see that, for the south, devices with segmental character (horizontal overhangs) will provide shading during the overheated period. For the north side the use of devices with radial mask patterns (vertical fins) will be effective. The darker tone shows the area where the shading device coincides with the overheated period.

4. On the south side one could apply a 60 degree (100 percent shading) solid overhang. On the north side, the required angles in the shading mask are different toward the west (45 degrees for 50 percent), and the east (72 degrees for 50 percent). The device should be oblique to the wall surface. The plan and section of the designed shading devices are shown.

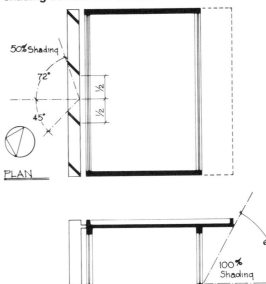

Design of Shading Devices

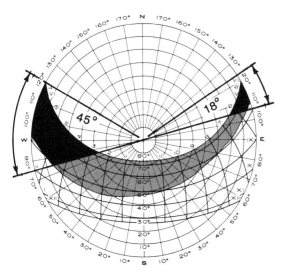

North Glazing:
Coincidence of 50% shading mask with overheated period.

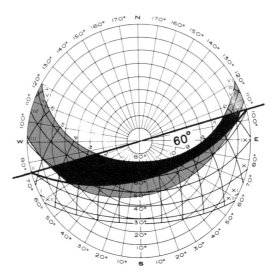

South Glazing:
Coincidence of 100% shading mask with overheated period.

Other Considerations in Shading Design

A number of considerations should be taken into account when designing or selecting a shading device.
These include:
—structure
—durability
—maintenance of the device
—replacement or retrofit
—effects on cleaning
—accumulation of precipitation
—fire safety
—acoustics
—internal visual effects
—external visual effects
—thermal effect on the glazing material

☐ The designer will want to consider how much a shading device weighs and what kind of support it offers the building structure. Horizontal overhangs, for example, can function as cantilevers and thus increase structural efficiency. Certain external shading devices can be used for lateral bracing or shear stiffening.

☐ The durability of shading devices may be difficult to determine. Ruggedness of the operating mechanism sometimes determines durability of interior devices. Gradual or accidental loss of efficiency often governs the useful life of some glazing systems. With external devices, the resistance to physical and chemical damage or deterioration may influence durability.

☐ The maintenance requirements of various devices are quite different. Some devices may require replacement every few years—others, periodic refinishing; some may require annual maintenance—others only require periodic cleaning.

☐ Some shading devices are easier to replace or retrofit than others. Some external appendages require modification of the building structure; others are more easily installed. Some glazing devices require replacement of the existing glazing with the new material. Most interior devices are more easily replaced.

☐ Some shading devices make cleaning windows difficult. There are two ways to clean exterior window glass equipped with exterior shading. Either the device is removable to facilitate the use of a window-cleaning scaffold (vertically or horizontally operated), or the shade itself is used as a platform or support during window-cleaning. With interior shading devices, the ease of removal or relocation of the device should be considered. The only consideration with glazing is that certain chemicals and cleaning tools may be damaging to the glazing surfaces and must be avoided.

☐ Several shading devices may collect precipitation (snow, ice and rain), leading to leakage, accelerated weathering or simply increased load on the structural design at certain times in the year. To avoid this problem, make flat surfaces slope slightly away from the building to drain the precipitation and install drips or gutters on the underside to shed water.

☐ The presence of a shading device can have certain effects on a building in case of fire. Some external devices can theoretically incorporate emergency rescue facilities (such as access platforms, safety ladders, etc.) Others actually impede the exit or entrance of persons during a fire. Exterior devices can act as flame deflectors, whose dimensions can coincide nicely with typical horizontal overhangs. In selecting shading devices, fire safety must be kept in mind and care taken that devices have no potential for spreading flames or producing toxic fumes or smoke.

☐ Shading devices can have several influences regarding acoustics. Some external devices can reflect sound onto the glass, while others can deflect sound away from the glass; some can absorb sound, while others can create structure-borne noise within the building. Internal devices (like external treatments) may affect sound reflection, absorption, dispersion or reverberation. Shading devices generally restrict the entry of outside noise created by traffic, industry or recreation.

☐ The esthetic appeal of the shading system can change the whole character of a room. Interior devices have the greatest effect, but some exterior shades are visible from the inside. The style of the shading system can have influence the building's interior design. The directional character and proportions of the shade can perceptibly enhance the look of the interior. Kinetic qualities, such as the changing play of light penetrating the interior, can also add a dynamic dimension to an interior.

☐ The shading device should be visually pleasing to passersby both during the day and at night. Stylistic factors, directional and proportional aspects and the kinetic qualities of interior devices are equally important to the exterior of the buildings. The rhythmic or textural qualities of several devices can aid the surface articulation of the facade. Visual weight and means of support can affect on the buildings perceived mass. The play of artificial light at night (both interior lights and exterior lighting patterns) can enhance the building's style.

☐ The use of shading devices, in combination with today's tinted and coated glass products, requires careful attention to the potential thermal stresses that may occur in the glass. A lack of consideration can lead to excessive and costly glass breakage.

Horizontal Projections

Horizontal plane(s) projecting in front of or above a window can intercept the summer sun, admit much if not all of the winter sun, and yet allow a view. A single projection may suffice if the plane projects far enough from the building, as do generously overhanging roofs of deeply recessed windows. Alternatively, more modest projections can be equally effective in shading, but they must be more closely spaced.

☐ South-facing windows are more effectively shaded by horizontal projecting planes. In hot climates of the lower latitudes, long verandas, movable horizontal louvers and roof overhangs work well. In the middle latitudes, longer overhangs are required on south elevations, creating possibilities for using pergolas with slatted trellis-work or even movable canvas awnings. At higher latitudes, horizontal elements on southern windows begin to en-

croach significantly on the view; ranks of louvers hung from solid horizontal overhangs can drop down almost to the horizon. Fortunately at high latitudes natural ventilation through operable windows will usually eliminate overheating. This means that internal sun shades can be used to control glare.

☐ For shading effectiveness, the color of the projection should be dark on the underside to reduce the light reflected off the projection and through the window. The light absorbed by this dark color is converted to heat and then dissipated to the outside air without becoming an airconditioning load. A separating gap between the shading device and the window is important to vent the trapped hot air.

☐ For daylighting effectiveness the underside of horizontal projections should be light in color to reflect indirect light from the ground into the room.

Horizontal Projections

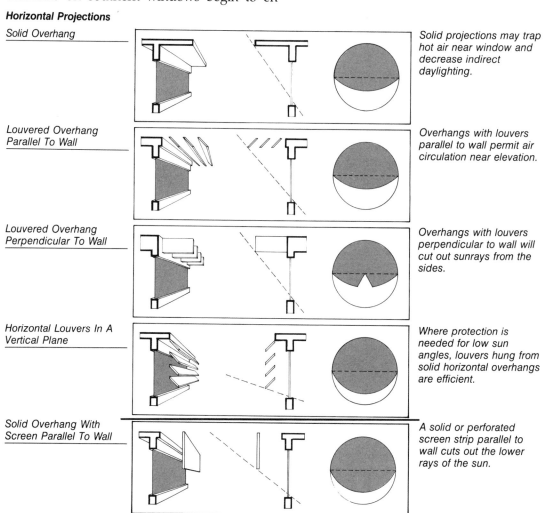

Solid Overhang

Solid projections may trap hot air near window and decrease indirect daylighting.

Louvered Overhang Parallel To Wall

Overhangs with louvers parallel to wall permit air circulation near elevation.

Louvered Overhang Perpendicular To Wall

Overhangs with louvers perpendicular to wall will cut out sunrays from the sides.

Horizontal Louvers In A Vertical Plane

Where protection is needed for low sun angles, louvers hung from solid horizontal overhangs are efficient.

Solid Overhang With Screen Parallel To Wall

A solid or perforated screen strip parallel to wall cuts out the lower rays of the sun.

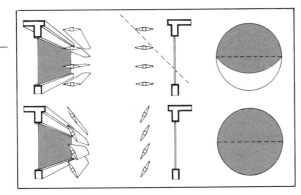

Movable horizontal
louvers allow the flexibility
of changing mask
characteristics through
positioning, but they can
be costly and
complicated.

The following technique can be used to determine quickly the size off a horizontal overhang for vertical windows which have azimuths *within 10 degrees of due south*. To use the nomograph, the designer needs to know window height and site's latitude, as well as how many days the window is to be totally shaded in summer and how many days it is to be unshaded in winter.

☐ The window is defined by its height, h.

☐ The overhang is defined by its projection, p.

☐ The distance (gap) between the top of the window and the edge of the overhang is defined as g.

☐ The results from the nomograph are the ratio of the overhang projection to the window height, p̄ and the ratio of the overhang gap to the window height, ḡ.

The method for the technique is as follows.

1. Locate the latitude line for the site (interpolate if necessary).

2. Draw a line from B through the intersection of the latitude curve and the number of days the window is to be *shaded* before and after the summer solstice. The result is the summer shading line.

3. Draw a line from T through the intersection of the latitude curve and the number of days the window is to be *unshaded* before and after the winter solstice. The result is the winter shading line.

4. The intersection point of the summer and winter shading lines gives the p̄ and ḡ values.

5. Multiply the value of p̄ by the window height to calculate the overhang projection length.

6. Multiply the value of ḡ by the window height to get the distance between the top of the window and the edge of the overhang.

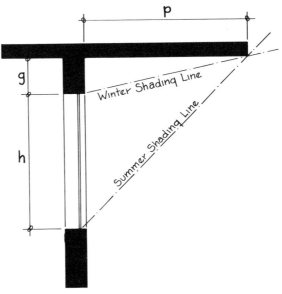

Horizontal Overhang

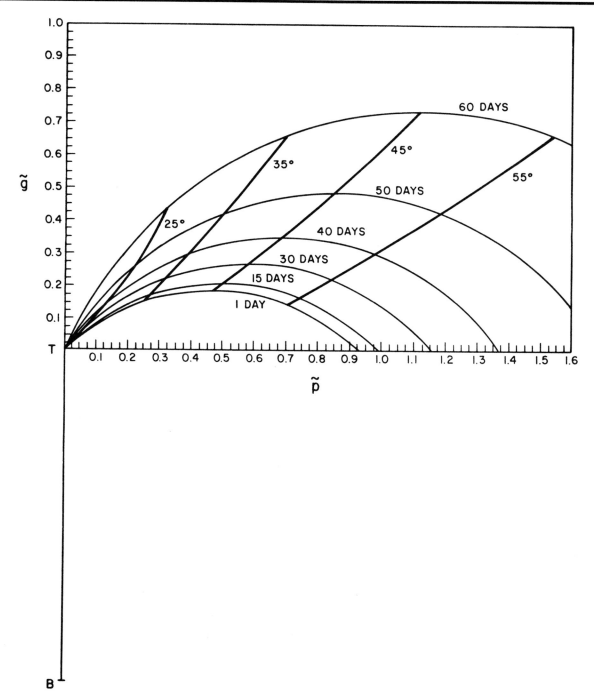

Nomograph for Sizing Overhangs

Source: Michael Utzinger, *Solar Age*, © 1981. Reprinted by permission of *Solar Age Magazine*, Harrisville, New Hampshire.

Location: 45 degrees N
Window height (h): 6′
Number of days to be shaded before and after summer solstice: 40 days
Number of days to be unshaded before and after winter solstice: 60 days
Results

$$\tilde{p} = .775$$
$$\tilde{g} = .475$$

Therefore:

$$.775 \times 6′ = 4.65′$$
$$.475 \times 6′ = 2.85′$$

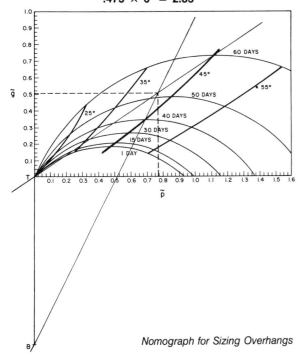

Nomograph for Sizing Overhangs

Source: Michael Utzinger, *Solar Age*, © 1981. Reprinted by permission of *Solar Age Magazine*, Harrisville, New Hampshire.

The table below can be used to determine the approximate amount of shade from horizontal projections. The values in the table are averages for the 5 hours of maximum solar intensity on August 1 for a given wall orientation. To find the depth of shade(d), multiply the width of overhang(x) by the value(k) from the table.

$$d = kx$$

where x = width of overhang in feet
d = depth of shade in feet
k = multiplier value from table (no units)

	Glass Exposure			
°Latitude	E and W	SE and SW	NW, N and NE	S
50	0.79	1.01	1.24	1.70
45	0.80	1.13	1.44	2.05
40	0.81	1.25	1.67	2.60
35	0.82	1.41	1.79	3.55
30	0.83	1.63	2.89	5.40
25	0.83	1.89	4.63	10.10

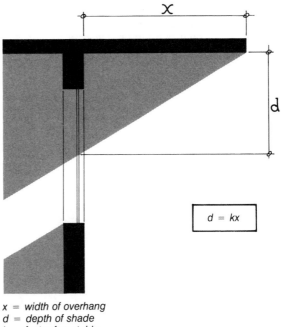

x = width of overhang
d = depth of shade
k = factor from table

$$d = kx$$

Horizontal Projection Calculation Technique

Source: M. David Egan, *Concepts in Thermal Comfort*,
© 1975. Reprinted by permission of Prentice-Hall, Inc., Englewood Cliffs, New Jersey.

Western Life Insurance Headquarters
Woodbury, Minnesota
Architects: Ellerbe Associates

Trapezoidal in plan, the Western Life Insurance Headquarters building in Minnesota covers 350,000 square feet on the south east corner of a 55-acre site. The building houses the company's computer center, and is entirely heated by recapturing heat generated by the computers.

The building envelope was carefully designed for solar orientation. Each facade has a different configuration, both to take advantage of the sun for natural lighting and to control heat gain. Each floor of the southeast side is cantilevered over the floor below. This arrangement of floors protects against too much summer sun and yet admits the low rays of the winter sun. The top floor has a steel sun louver of its own. In contrast, the northwest windows are dramatically recessed in the precast concrete facade to screen them from the prevailing winter winds; this in turn protects the air film adjacent to the windows. Both east and west facades are windowless, precast concrete.

The building not only responds to climate and weather, it is heated in winter entirely by waste heat from its own computers. Underground tanks are used to store surplus hot water, as well as the chilled water needed to supplement the airconditioning system. Other energy-conserving devices include solar blinds controlled by the angle of the sun's rays, mirrored and bronze-tinted glass and task lighting.

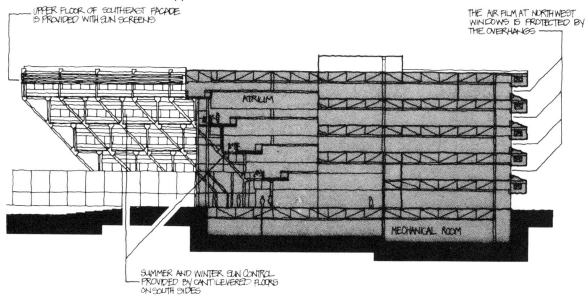

UPPER FLOOR OF SOUTHEAST FACADE IS PROVIDED WITH SUN SCREENS

THE AIR FILM AT NORTHWEST WINDOWS IS PROTECTED BY THE OVERHANGS

ATRIUM

MECHANICAL ROOM

SUMMER AND WINTER SUN CONTROL PROVIDED BY CANTILEVERED FLOORS ON SOUTH SIDES

Western Life Insurance Headquarters; Woodbury, Minnesota. Architects: Ellerbe Associates

Western Life Insurance Headquarters; Woodbury, Minnesota. Architects: Ellerbe Associates

Vertical Projections

Fins and other vertical projections most successfully shade easterly and westerly orientations.

☐ Vertical elements can be designed to vary their angle according to the sun's position. Movable vertical louvers provide shading coefficients from 0.15 to 0.10 but icing problems make them impractical in cold climates. On cloudy days, a photocell control device can set movable louvers to the perpendicular position for maximum light penetration.

Vertical Projections

Vertical Perpendicular Fins

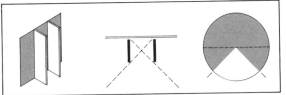

Fins perpendicular to the wall create a critical horizontal shadow angle beyond which total shading occurs.

Vertical Angled Fins

Fins oblique to the wall results in an asymetrical shading mask.

Adjustable Vertical Fins

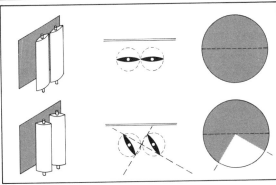

Adjustable vertical fins can be adjusted to exclude light entirely or to permit penetration of the sun from any angle. They can be costly and complicated.

Los Angeles Hall of Records; Los Angeles, California. Architects: Richard Neutra

Eggcrate Shading Devices

The eggcrate shading device combines vertical and horizontal elements. The device works well on walls facing southeast, and is particularly effective for a southwest orientation. Because of its high shading efficiency (e.g., shading coefficient 0.10), the eggcrate device is often used in hot climates. The horizontal elements also control ground glare from reflected solar rays.

Combination Shading Devices

Fixed Eggcrate

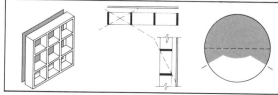

Fixed eggcrates do not allow for seasonal variation in critical shading angles, and can prevent sun penetration in winter.

Angled Eggcrate

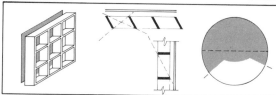

Eggcrates with slanting vertical fins create asymetrical shading masks.

Adjustable Eggcrate

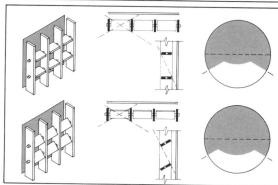

Eggcrates with movable horizontal elements allow for adjustable shading mask characteristics.

Carpenter Center for the Visual Arts
Harvard University
Cambridge, Massachusetts
Architect: Le Corbusier

Le Corbusier used an eggcrate facade for systematic solar shading of the window wall. While reducing direct penetration of solar heat into the building, the concrete "brise-soleils" also inevitably reduces the amount of daylight that enters the interior.

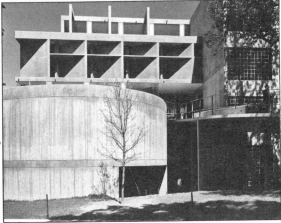

Carpenter Center for the Visual Arts; Cambridge, Massachusetts. Architect: Le Corbusier

Federal Home Loan Band Board Building
Washington, D.C.
Architects: Max O. Urbahn Associates

The Federal Home Loan Bank Board Building was designed within the energy guidelines of its client, the General Service Adminstration. The bays of glass are outlined and shaded by exposed concrete ledges and limestone fins. The building's fenestration is composed of double-glazed clear glass, 65 percent of which is backed by panels of rigid insulation and gypsum board to further reduce solar gain. On exposed elevations, venetian blinds permit occupants to "control" sunlight. Sliding doors to the balconies are more deeply recessed and shielded by ledges above.

Federal Home Loan Bank Board Building; Washington, D.C. Architects: Max O. Urbahn Associates

163

Sun Screens

A sun screen's effectiveness in shading a window depends on how well it absorbs light and on its geometry. The more a sun screen reflects light, the less effective it may be. If its slats have a reflective surface, part of the light striking the top of one slat will be reflected directly through the window; part of the light will be directed to the underside of the slat above and, from there, through the window. Thus, highly absorptive surfaces improve the effectiveness of sun screens.

☐ An external sun screen close to a window creates a layer of virtually still air. This reduces the winter U-value of a single-glazed window from 1.13 to 0.85.

☐ An external sun screen blocks a window's exposure to the winter night sky, which tends to be colder than ground surfaces.

☐ Visibility for occupants of the building can be as much as 86 percent of the visibility of an unprotected window.

☐ Certain types of sun screen are equivalent to and suitable for insect screening.

☐ Sun screens block light reflected from the ground or adjacent buildings more effectively than awnings, roof overhangs or wall fins.

☐ Sun screens allow for a high percentage of diffuse solar radiation for daylighting, while blocking direct radiation that can create glare problems.

☐ Sun screens can, however, interfere with outswinging windows and fire access.

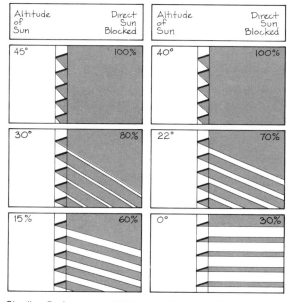

Shading Performance of 17 Degree Horizontal Blinds

Shutters

An exterior shading device that effectively blocks all direct sunlight can reduce solar heat gain through a window up to 80 percent. The effect of closed exterior shutters, however, depends upon how well the heat absorbed by the shutter itself is dissipated to the outside air. Shutters with operable louvers that can be adjusted to block the sun but let air circulate can keep out more heat, as can light-colored shutters which reflect much of the sunlight rather than absorb it.

☐ Shutters with pivoting louvers that can be closed can make the space between shutters and glass air tight, and thus reduce heat loss.

☐ Shutter operation requires reaching outside the window. This means that the insect screen or the storm sash must be mounted inside the window and must not be sealed shut.

☐ Wind can damage shutters if they are not secured properly.

Terman Engineering Center
Palo Alto, California
Architects: Harry Weese & Associates

The Stanford University Engineering Center uses a window shutter system. The floor-to-ceiling openings and sliding shutters are similar to examples of European 13th and 14th century domestic architecture. Operable glazing for the perimeter spaces consists of floor-to-ceiling French doors which are set back to provide shade and a small balcony for each office. Each window is provided with operable louvered shutters which move on a standard hanging track commonly used as barndoor hardware. These are located on the exterior side of the glazing to block the sun before it is transmitted through the glass. The louvered shutters, larger than standard dimensions, are custom-made. These can either be opened to allow sun and breezes to go through or be closed to keep the sun out while still allowing breezes to pass through.

Photo: Hedrick-Blessing

Photo: Hedrick-Blessing

Terman Engineering Center; Palo Alto, California. Architect: Harry Weese & Associates

Roller Blinds/Shades

Roller blinds or shades at the head of a window can be lowered to provide an opaque barrier to the summer sun, blocking both direct and diffuse sunlight. Up to 35 percent reduction in air conditioning costs have been associated with the use of roll blinds.

Glass Type	Season	Glass Alone	Glass + ½″ × 2″ Roll Blind Slats	Glass + ⅛″ × 1⅜″ Roll Blind Slats
Single	Winter	1.13	0.405	0.568
	Summer	1.04	0.395	0.550
Double (1/2″ air space)	Winter	0.49	0.301	0.384
	Summer	0.56	0.297	0.376
Single + storm sash	Winter	0.56	0.297	0.376
	Summer	0.54	0.290	0.366

Roller Blind U-Values

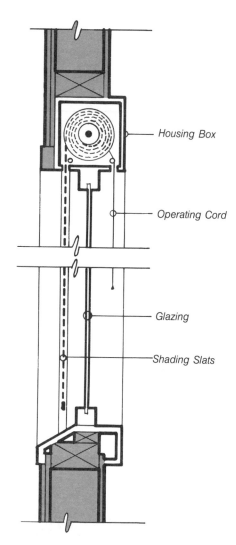

Housing Box

Operating Cord

Glazing

Shading Slats

☐ When the slats are in the lowered position but not completely closed, the horizontal openings between the slats permit air to circulate through the blind.

☐ If the roller blind tracks are hinged, the entire lowered blind can be projected from the window during the day to give both natural ventilation and shading.

☐ Light-colored roller blinds keep a room cooler, because they reflect incident sunlight and remain cooler than dark-colored blinds.

☐ Exterior roller blinds provide the most effective insulating air space of all exterior devices, due to the tight joints between the slats and the seal provided at the top and sides.

☐ Noise transmission can be reduced with lowered blinds. Noise reductions from 100 DBA to 60 DBA have been associated with lowered roller blinds.

☐ Roller blinds can delay access in the event of a fire, but if they are metal, may also delay spread of flames out the window and up the side of the building.

☐ Roller blinds are usually limited to a maximum single span of 12′ for vertical windows (less for sloped windows) and a maximum height of approximately 10′. Large exterior roller shades should be motor operated.

California State Office Building
Sacramento, California
Architects: Office of the California State Architect

The envelope of the California State Office Building "Site 1" is 80 percent glazing. Exterior roller shades on the east and west reduce solar radiation that hits the glass. These fabric screens are used extensively in Europe but have previously not been used in the United States on a project of this scale. The roller shades will be operated by a combination of time clocks and photo sensors. The shades will be rolled down only when the sun strikes directly the east or west side of the building. At other times they will be up so as not to block the views of the building occupants.

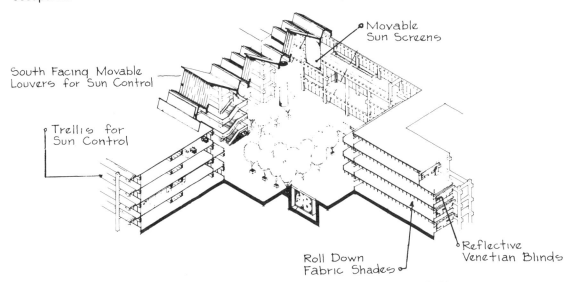

Movable Sun Screens

South Facing Movable Louvers for Sun Control

Trellis for Sun Control

Roll Down Fabric Shades

Reflective Venetian Blinds

California State Office Building; Sacramento, California. Architect: Office of California State Architect

Awnings

Awnings can reduce summer solar heat gain up to 55 to 65 percent on south-facing windows and 72 to 77 percent on west-facing windows. How well an awning shades a window depends on how opaque the material is to both direct sunlight and diffuse light from the sky.

Material	% Direct Transmittance	% Diffuse Transmittance
Canvas	0	0
Plastic	25	15
Aluminum (separated slats)	0	20

Solar Transmittances of Awning Materials

☐ The surfaces of the awning exposed to the sun should be light in color to minimize the amount of sunlight absorbed and transferred to the window by radiation and convection. A white canvas awning or slatted, white aluminum awning reflects 70-90 percent of the sunlight—more if it is clean, less if it is dirty, as dirt absorbs light. By comparison, a dark-green canvas awning reflects only 20 percent, and a dark-green plastic awning reflects only 27 percent.

☐ Fabric awnings are usually installed with a continuous narrow gap between the top of the awning and the wall to prevent hot air from being trapped under the awning. Slatted aluminum awnings have gaps (ranging from ¼" to ¾" between the horizontal slats) that provide air circulation.

☐ A south-facing window requires only a minimal horizontal projection to be completely shaded all day, all summer. A window facing east or west needs an awning that extends down a substantial percentage of the window height to protect against the low angles of early morning and late afternoon sun. In addition, the sides of the awning should be closed to prevent sunlight from angling in behind the awning on south-facing windows.

☐ Fabric awnings are susceptible to wind damage and other "weathering," and must be periodically replaced.

☐ The net effectiveness of an awning in protecting against the summer sun is given for a design day representing August 1 at 40 degrees N latitude. Heat gain is totaled for the period from 8 A.M. to 4 P.M. for the south exposure and noon to 5 P.M. for the west exposure. The awnings have a 70 percent drop and provision to vent air at the top. A dark foreground is assumed. For a light foreground the heat gain could be as much as twice the amount shown, due to the light reflecting up beneath the awning.

Orientation	Solar Time	With Side Panels % Awning Drop			Open Sides % Awning Drop		
		0.65	0.60	0.55	0.65	0.60	0.55
South	8 A.M. 4 P.M.	4	8	13	7	14	22
	9 A.M. 3 P.M.	2	4	7	5	11	18
	10 A.M. 2 P.M.	—	2	5	2	5	7
East	7 A.M. 5 P.M.	7	13	22	7	13	22
West	8 A.M. 4 P.M.	—	7	15	—	7	15

Percentage of Glass Area Sunlit for Various Awning Configurations (Awning drop equals the distance the awning extends down by the total window height.)

**Residence on Long Island Sound
Architect: Donald Watson, FAIA**

This house features a shading trellis on the west side, permitting the winter sun to enter the house but providing summer shade. Other design features include solar heating, a roof garden patio, and an in-ground rock bed for passive solar heat storage.

Multiple Glazing

Glass conducts heat well—nine times better than plywood in fact. Heat flows easily through glass, escaping out doors in winter and penetrating indoors in summer. This rate of heat flow is so great that even several layers of glass in contact with each other have negligible thermal benefit. Air spaces between the layers of glass, however, interrupt the path of conduction, and significantly reduce the rate of heat flow. To move through air spaces, heat must be transferred by radiation and convection.

☐ The width of the air space affects its thermal performance. Up to approximately ⅝", the wider the air space, the greater the reduction in heat flow. An air space narrower than ³⁄₁₆" begins to be ineffective. At the other extreme, increasing the air space beyond ⅝" does not substantially reduce the U-value below that of the ⅝" separation. U-values for different air-space widths are shown.

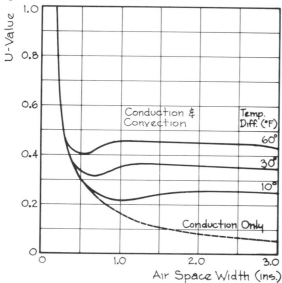

Effect of Air Space Width on Double Glazing U-Value

☐ Because the heat flow across multiple glazing is substantially reduced, the temperature of the glazing surface facing the room is much closer to room temperature than is the case with single glass. Discomfort near windows, ice formation and condensation are thereby alleviated.

☐ Three layers of glass separated by air spaces are more effective than two separated layers of the same overall width. Triple glazing with two ¼" air spaces has a U-value of 0.47, compared to 0.58 for double glazing with a single ½" air space.

☐ The heat-absorbing and radiating properties (characterized by the term "absorptances" and "emittance") of the two glass surfaces facing toward the air space will affect the rate at which heat is radiated across the cavity. A coated film such as tin oxide or indium oxide, or a pure metal such as gold, silver or copper, applied to either of the glass surfaces facing the cavity will reduce heat transfer by radiation. Examples of the effectiveness of such coatings are given.

Effective Emittance	Winter U-value
0.8 (untreated)	0.58
0.60 (treated)	0.52
0.40 (treated)	0.45
0.20 (treated)	0.38

Effective Emittance and U-Values of Treated and Untreated Double Glazing with ½" Air Space

☐ Multiple glazing can reduce the amount of sunlight transmitted. Because glass is not 100 percent transparent, some of the sunlight is absorbed and converted to heat within the glass. This heat is then dissipated to the air by radiation from both surfaces.

☐ There can be a substantial difference in glazing costs when multiple glazing is specified. Typically, a total window unit consisting of frame, sash and glazing costs approximately 50 percent more for double versus single glazing.

Hooker Office Building
Niagara Falls, New York
Architects: Cannon Design Inc.

This building has two skins and sophisticated control features. To supplement artificial light with natural lighting an extraordinary exterior membrane was designed for the building. Because standard glazing did not meet their needs, the designers used both an inner glass skin and an outer glass skin, 4' apart.

The 4'-space between the glazing allows heat to buildup, in cold weather. But when heat is not needed, a set of temperature-controlled sensors operates venting dampers at the top and bottom of the cavity, releasing warm air at the top through convection.

Description	Thickness	U-Value (Winter)	U-Value (Summer)	Visible	Solar	S.C.
Single, Clear	⅛″	1.16	1.04	.90	.84	1.00
	¼″	1.13	1.04	.89	.78	.95
	⅜″	1.11	1.03	.88	.72	.90
	½″	1.09	1.03	.86	.67	.86
Single, heat absorbing	¼″	1.13	1.10	.52	.96	.71
Double	³⁄₁₆″ air space	.62	.65		.71	.88
	¼″ air space	.58	.61			
	½″ air space	.49	.57	.80		.82
	½″ air space Low e Coating e = .20	.32	.38			
	e = .40	.42	.49	.14		.25
	e = .60	.43	.51			
Triple	¼″ air space	.39	.44			.71
Acrylic, single glazed	¼″ air space	.96	.89	.92	.85	.98
Acrylic, w/reflecting coating	¼″ air space	.88	.83	.14	.12	.21

Shading coefficients and U-Values for Various Types of Glazing

Convection will also occur around the building as warm air flows from warmer to cooler exposures. Facades will also have separately controlled louvers between the glazing surfaces to allow for specific thermal and lighting needs for the building.

Hooker Office Building; Niagara Falls, New York. Architects: Cannon Design Inc.

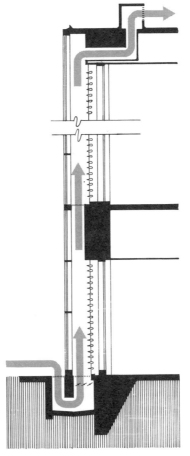

Hooker Office Building; Niagra Falls, New York. Architects: Cannon Design Inc.

Heat-Absorbing Glass

Solar energy at sea level is composed of approximately 3 percent ultraviolet radiation, 44 percent visible light and 53 percent thermal infrared radiation. In addition to this infrared energy, visible light is converted to heat whenever it strikes an opaque surface. Therefore, the amount of total solar energy transmitted determines the amount of heat gain. Adding a metallic oxide to the ingredients of glass increases its absorptivity of ultraviolet, visible and near-infrared solar energy, especially the latter. This characteristic distinguishes heat-absorbing glass from glass that is merely tinted.

☐ The solar energy absorbed by heat-absorbing glass is converted to heat, which is radiated and convected to the outdoors and indoors, proportional to the temperatures, air movements and the surface characteristics of either side of the glass. On a summer day more heat is dissipated indoors because the interior of an air conditioned building is cooler. But in winter more heat is dissipated to the outdoors because the outside temperatures are lower. Heat-absorbing glass is an improvement over single glass plate but it still admits much of the summer sun's heat. The percentages shown will vary with the sun's angle.

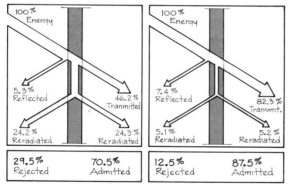

Solar Energy Transmission through Heat-Absorbing Single Glazing vs. Clear Glass

☐ Heat-absorbing glass reduces fading of interior fabrics better than clear glass because it absorbs more ultraviolet solar radiation. At the same time, heat-absorbing glass radiates more heat thus creating discomfort for occupants near windows.

Double Glazing:
Composite of ¼" Heat-Absorbing and ¼" Plate Glass

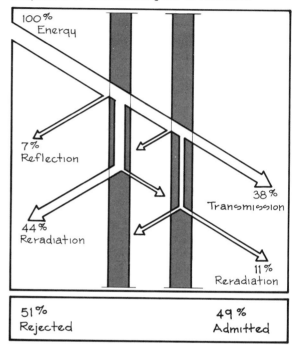

Solar Energy Transmission through Heat-Absorbing Double Glazing

☐ Heat-absorbing glass used as the outer sheet of glass in double glazing performs much better than it does as a single glazing. Heat in the glass enters the building only after it bridges the trapped air space by radiation and convection; more heat will be dissipated to the outside air because it is in direct contact with the heat-absorbing glass. Furthermore, heat will dissipate into the outdoors much more quickly if there is any wind.

Glass Type	Glass Width	% Visible Transmission	% Total Solar Transmission	Shading Coefficient
Clear single glazed	¼"	89	78	0.95
Heat absorbing (double)	¼"	75	47	0.69
Clear insulating (double)	1"	80	59	0.82
Heat absorbing insulating (double)	1"	67	36	0.55

Performance of Heat-Absorbing Glass

☐ If heat-absorbing, double glass is installed in reversible sash, the heat-absorbing sheet of glass can face outside in summer to dissipate heat outward, and inside in winter to dissipate heat inward. This configuration can be even more effective if closable vents are installed above and below the heat-absorbing glass. In winter, during the day the vents are opened to circulate the heated air between the two sheets of glass into the building interior, then closed at night to preserve the insulating value of the air space. In summer, with the sash reversed, the heated air between the glass sheets is discharged outdoors, further reducing the amount of heat entering the building.

☐ Interior draperies, roll shades or blinds can be used to reflect back to the glass much of the sunlight that has penetrated heat-absorbing glass. The double exposure of the heat-absorbing glass to sunlight substantially increases the glass temperature. Similarly, when heat-absorbing glass is used in double glazing, the inner sheet of clear glass reflects part of the sunlight back to the outer sheet of the heat-absorbing glass, increasing its temperature. These high temperatures create large stresses within the glass, so the strength of the glass at its edges can be critical.

☐ The thickness of heat-absorbing glass will affect its color, since tinting is caused by an ingredient dispersed throughout the glass, rather than occurring only at the surface, as with reflective glass. If various window sizes dictate different glass thicknesses for reasons of strength, the color-density variation (viewed from the outside) and the brightness variation (viewed from the inside) must be considered. The view out through heat-absorbing glass, however is brighter than that through most reflective glass.

Summer Operation   *Winter Operation*

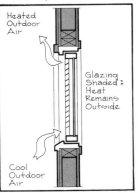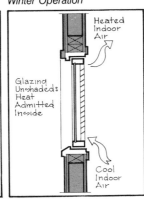

Reversible Double-Glazed Sash with Heat-Absorbing Glass and Adjustable Blinds

Reflective Glass

Reflective glass, which has a coating of metallic oxide or other material, increases the amount of solar energy reflected at the window, thus reducing the cooling load within the building.

☐ Reflective glass used as the outer sheet of double glazing is more effective in keeping out the sun's heat than reflective glass used as single glazing. The trapped air space between the two layer of glass acts as insulation, impeding the inward flow of heat.

Glass Type	Glass Width	% Visible Transmission	% Total Solar Transmission	Shading Coefficient
Clear single glazed	¼"	89	78	0.95
Gray reflective single	¼"	34	25	0.60
Clear insulating (double-glazed)	1"	80	59	0.82
Gray reflective insulating	1"	30	29	0.47

Performance of Reflective Single and Double Glazing

☐ If the reflective coating or film is placed on the outer sheet of double glazing, not on the inner sheet, heat admitted through glass can be reduced. This is because reflective glass absorbs more sunlight—and heat——than clear glass. When this heat is concentrated in the outer sheet of insulating glass it is more easily dissipated to the outside air, especially if there is a breeze.

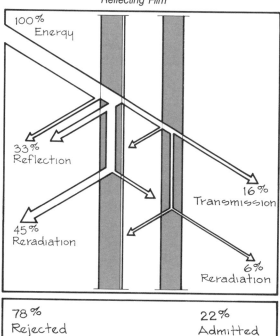

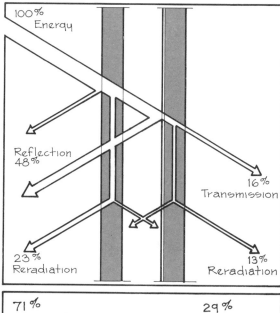

Effect on of Reflecting Film Location on Heat Transmission Through Double Glazing

☐ Certain types of reflective coatings on either one of the sheets of double glazing can reduce heat losses in winter. The winter U-value of clear double glazing with ½″ air space is 0.58 versus as low as 0.28 for double glazing with an outer sheet of reflective glass.

☐ Proper adhesives should be used in single glazing to ensure stable bonding of reflective coating to the glass.

☐ Proper detailing of reflective glass is important to avoid thermal breakage because of the higher solar absorptivity of reflective glass. If the glass is installed in a high-mass material such as concrete, the lag in the time it takes the concrete to heat up in comparison to the glass will result in extreme center-to-edge temperature differences and edge stresses in the glass.

☐ Distortion of image is more critical with reflective glass because the outside viewer sees a reflected image, rather than seeing through the image as in clear glass. Mock-ups on the site are worthwhile to study the visual appearance of reflective glass and the effects of distortion.

☐ Reflective glass can create a glare for the occupants of adjacent buildings, pedestrians and drivers.

☐ Reflective glass darkens the view out by reducing light transmission. Bronze or other tinted reflective glasses can also distort the colors of the view.

Photo: Gordon H. Schenck, Jr.

Crystal Cathedral; Garden Grove, California. Architect: Johnson/Burgee Architects

Photo: Gordon H. Schenck, Jr.

R. J. Reynolds Headquarters; Winston-Salem, North Carolina. Architects: Odell Associates, Inc.

175

Glass Blocks

Glass blocks are hollow masonry units molded in two halves that are fused together at a high temperature. The permanently sealed air is exceptionally dry, preventing condensate from forming within the cavity. This air space gives the glass blocks a low U-value, yet they admit approximately 50 to 60 percent of the incident solar energy, including 78 to 84 percent of the visible light. Glass blocks are available with double cavities with the same overall block depth—usually a nominal 4".

☐ The larger the block face dimensions, the lower is the U-value of the wall. Heat loss is greatest at the edges of a block because the glass bridges the air space.

Nominal Size (inches)	U-Value (single cavity)	U-Value (double cavity)
4 × 12	0.60	0.52
6 sq.	0.60	—
8 sq.	0.56	0.48
12 sq.	0.52	0.44

Glass Block U-Values

☐ Because glass block has greater mass than window glass, a time lag occurs between the moment the sun first falls on the block and the moment the room temperature rises. To approximate this lag in calculating heat gain, use the solar heat gain factor from the previous rather than the current hour. This product plus the heat gain or loss through the block (U-value multiplied by the inside/outside temperature difference) equals the net heat gain or loss.

☐ The shading coefficient of glass block can be lowered by contouring the glass surface(s) and/or by fusing various types of inserts between the two halves before they are joined in the manufacturing process.

☐ Various types of inserts can reduce glare from glass blocks. White opal glass is an example of a glare-reducing insert that has the added benefit of giving the block a more uniform brightness. A grid surface pressed into the glass can also reduce glare by diffusing the light.

☐ Sound transmission is less than with glass, ranging from 35.3 db at 128 cycles per second to 47.5 db at 2048 cycles per second.

☐ Many projectiles that would shatter window glass are deflected by glass block. This deters vandalism and forced entry.

☐ Glass blocks are fire-rated at up to 1-1/2 hours.

☐ Overheating is possible in summer or even spring and fall in rooms with large expanses of unshaded glass block and inadequate provision for natural ventilation.

☐ The view through most glass block types, in and out, is distorted or completely obscured.

☐ The displayed chart shows the light penetration of glass block on a south exposure, compared to glass block on both a south and north exposure 90' apart.

	Shading Coefficient		
Type	Exposed to Sun	Shaded N, NW, W, SW	Shaded NE, E, SE
Window glass	1.00	—	—
Clear block	0.65	0.40	0.60
Clear with glass fiber insert	0.44	0.34	0.51
Contoured outer surfaces, prismatic inside surfaces and glass fiber insert	0.33	0.27	0.41
Same as above plus ceramic coating on insert or gray glass used for block or prismatic glass fiber insert	0.25	0.18	0.27

Shading Coefficients of 8" × 8" Glass Blocks (shading coefficients for 12" × 12" and 6" × 6", multiply by 1.15 and .85, respectively.)

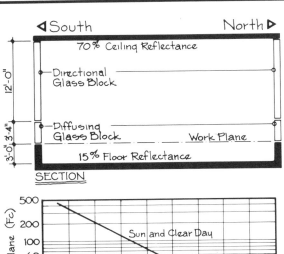

◁ South   North ▷

70% Ceiling Reflectance

Directional Glass Block

0% Wall Reflectance

Diffusing Glass Block

Work Plane

15% Floor Reflectance

12'-0" 3'-0" 3'-4"

SECTION

◁ South   North ▷

70% Ceiling Reflectance

Directional Glass Block

Diffusing Glass Block   Work Plane

15% Floor Reflectance

12'-0" 3'-0" 3'-4"

SECTION

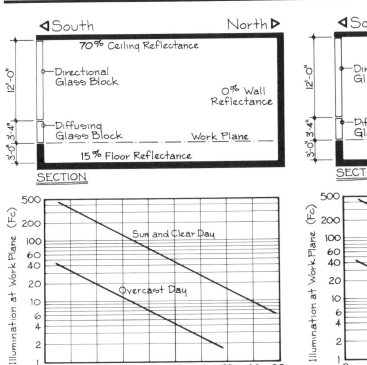

Illumination at Work Plane (Fc) — Sun and Clear Day / Overcast Day — Distance from South Fenestration (Ft)

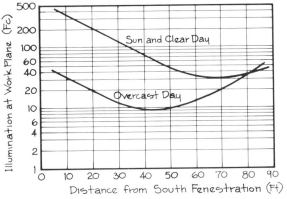

Illumination at Work Plane (Fc) — Sun and Clear Day / Overcast Day — Distance from South Fenestration (Ft)

*Illumination from Glass Block on One and Two Exposures
(Note: 40 degrees N on March 21, 10 A.M. and 2 P.M.)*

Glassell School of Art
Houston, Texas
Architects: S.I. Morris Associates

The Glassell School of Art has exterior walls of clear glass block that provides a semiobscured view of the outside, yet admits daylight and some direct sun. The glass block resists convected heat.

Photo: Nick Wheeler

Training Facility, New London Submarine Base; Groton, Connecticut. Architects: Hartford Design Group

Photo: Rick Gardner

Glassell School of Art; Houston, Texas. Architects: Morris-Aubry Architects

177

Window Tilt

Reflection of sunlight at the surface of glass varies considerably, depending on the incident angle at which the light strikes the glass (e.g., the angle between the light ray and a perpendicular line from the surface of the glass). At incident angles less than 57 degrees, the amount of direct sunlight reflected increases at an increasing rate, with the amount of transmitted light decreasing correspondingly.

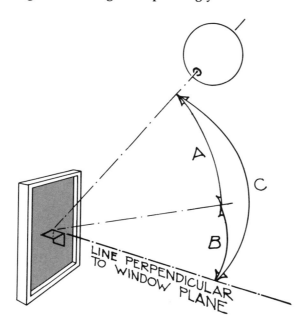

ΔA = Angle Between Sun and Window in Plan View

ΔB = Angle Between Sun and Ground Plane (Altitude)

ΔC = Incident Angle

Incident Angle Between Sun Ray and Glazing

☐ A tilted window, projecting horizontally outward, further reduces transmission of summer sunlight by reducing the area of glass exposed to the sun. The geometry is the same as if there were a horizontal projection shading vertical glass. The shading effect becomes negligible in winter when the sun travels at a lower angle across the sky.

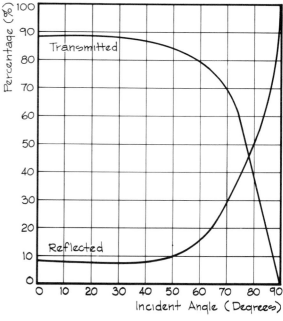

Correlation Between Incident Angle and Light Transmission Through Glazing

☐ Closer to the equator (e.g., 34 degrees N latitude) the sun is higher in the sky, both summer and winter. Thus, less tilt of the window is required to achieve the same reduction in summer sun transmission than in latitudes further north.

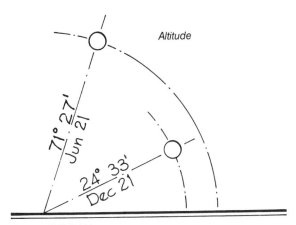

Altitude

71°27'
Jun 21

24°33'
Dec 21

Boston 42°21' N.Lat.

Solar Altitude in Boston and Atlanta

☐ The incident angle of the sun on vertical glass in the summer is likely to be well above 57 degrees. For example, at 42 degrees N latitude at noon on June 22, the incident angle of sunlight on a vertical plane of glass facing south is 71.45 degrees. This is so far in excess of 57 degrees that any increase in the incident angle (i.e., tilting the top of the glass outward), will greatly increase the amount of light reflected and correspondingly reduce solar heat gain.

☐ The incident angle of sunlight on vertical glass in winter is likely to be less than 57 de-

grees. For example, at 42 degrees latitude at noon on December 22, the incident angle between the sun and a south-facing window is 24.55 degrees. At this low sun angle, a slight tilt to the glass will not appreciably decrease the amount of sunlight transmitted in comparison with vertical glass.

IBM Regional Office
Southfield, Michigan
Architects: Gunnar Birkerts & Associates

Only 20 percent of this IBM building's envelope is glass. Horizontal ribbons of the glass slope inward, reducing the solar radiation entering the building. The glass picks up light from a curved reflecting surface running along the bottom of the building. The light bounces upward where it is diffused and thrown into the interior.

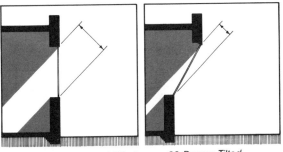

Sun Exposure of Vertical Window vs. 30 Degree Tilted Window

Prefinished
Insul. Mtl.
Wall Panel

Suspended Accoustical
Tile Ceiling

Flour. Lighting

Prefinished Mtl.
Lt. Reflector Shield

1" Insul. Clear Glass
in Extruded Alum.
Thermal Break Frame

Insul. St. Stl.
Sill Panel
Reflector

Carpet

4'-0"
3'-9"
2'-4"
2'-5"
12'-6"

IBM Regional Office; Southfield, Michigan. Arhcitect: Gunnar Birkerts & Associates

IBM Regional Office; Southfield, Michigan. Architect: Gunnar Birkerts & Associates

Applied Films

Metallic oxides deposited on transparent plastic films reflect much of the incoming solar energy while still permitting a view out. The shading coefficient of such reflective films can be as low as 0.24.

Certain types of film coating enhance the window's reflection of infrared heat, yet only minimally reduce the window's transparency to the incoming light. These "low-emissivity" films reduce the winter U-value of the window from 1.13 to as low as 0.74.

☐ Reflective films and to a lesser extent low-emmissivity films have the disadvantage of reducing the aspect of incoming solar energy in the winter. The displayed chart illustrates the seasonal benefit (+) or detriment (−) of single glazing compared to glazing with applied low-emissivity or reflective films in a southern and northern city. The energy effectiveness of applied films depends on whether airconditioning or heating is dominant, and which direction a window faces.

☐ Films can be applied to existing windows. Replacement of film however, is costly, difficult and probably necessary after 9 to 12 years. Film applied to single glazing has reduced effectiveness because a protective coating over the film is needed to prevent abrasion.

☐ Films reduce fabric fading.

☐ Films can hold glass together in event of shattering, if film thickness is adequate.

☐ A reflective film applied to windows in an office building in Silver Spring, Maryland, reduced the airconditioning load by 50 percent. The average airconditioner operation cycle was reduced from 24 hours a day during peak summer periods to 12 hours a day. Winter heat loss reductions were also observed but not quantified.

☐ Film applied to double-glazed reflective glass or heat—absorbing glass can increase the thermal stresses on the glass.

City	North		East		South		West	
	Winter	Summer	Winter	Summer	Winter	Summer	Winter	Summer
Dallas								
No Film	−24	−95	+26	−156	+102	−118	+26	−185
Low-emissivity	−7	−80	+35	−135	+107	−101	+38	−161
Reflective	−46	−41	−33	−56	−14	−46	−33	−63
New York								
No Film	−84	−43	−38	−76	+29	−59	−39	−81
Low-emissivity	−43	−39	−2	−68	+58	−53	−2	−73
Reflective	−105	−11	−93	−19	−76	−15	−93	−20

Window Energy Expenditure by Orientation (KBTU/sq. ft.)
(− denotes energy input required from mechanical system.)

		Transmission						Winter "U" Value	
Film	Type of Glass	% Total Visible	% Total Solar Energy	% Total Solar UV	% Total Solar Reflection	Shade Coefficient	Max. Heat BTU/ Hr./Sq. Ft.	In Sunlight	Night-time
R-18 applied to:	⅛" or ¼" Clear	15	12	2	48	.26	56	.80	.93
	¼" Grey or Bronze	8	6	1	17	.30	65	.91	.92
Without film	⅛" Clear Glass	90	85	77	7	1.00	216	1.05	1.08
	¼" Clear Glass	88	77	68	7	.94	203	1.03	1.06
	¼" Grey Glass	42	45	31	5	.69	149	1.01	1.06
	⅛" Bronze Glass	51	45	21	5	.69	149	1.01	1.06

Film and Glass Comparisons

Insulating Shutters

An insulating panel that reduces a single glazed window's U-value to 0.38 or less is twice as insulating as residential double glass (1/4" air space) with a U-value of 0.65. Thus, if the panels are closed only during the hours of darkness, approximately 12 hours per day, they achieve energy savings comparable to insulating glass. Furthermore, the difference between outside day and night temperatures is likely to be greater than the difference between day and night thermostat settings. Therefore, even if the nighttime thermostat is set back, the insulating shutters can effectively conserve heating energy.

☐ The displayed chart lists several common rigid insulating materials, their resistances and the winter U-value of a single-glazed window with the panel in contact with the glass.
☐ Polystyrene and polyurethane foam panels should be clad to protect against the toxic fumes they give off if ignited. This also protects the easily crushable foam.
☐ The winter heat loss through a window can be reduced by covering the window with an insulating panel in contact with the glass. The heat loss is then reduced in proportion to the insulating value of the panel, measured as resistance to heat flow per inch thickness of material. The U-value for a window with a 1" insulating panel against it can be approximated as follows:

$$U_{total} = \left(\frac{1}{U_{glass\ alone}} + R_{panel} \right)^{-1}$$

This formula assumes equivalent values for the air film at the surface of the panel and at the interior surface of the glass, or an R-value of 0.68 in both cases.

Material	Resistance (for 1" thickness)	U-value of Window with 1" Panel	U-value of Window with 2" Panel
Expanded polystyrene, extruded, plain	4.00	0.20	0.11
Expanded polystyrene, molded beads	3.57	0.22	0.12
Expanded polyurethane	6.25	0.14	0.07
Cork (¾")	1.68	0.39	—
Cork/paper board/ cork (¾")	2.56	0.29	—
Plywood (¾")	0.93	0.55	—

U-Values of Various Insulating Panel Materials

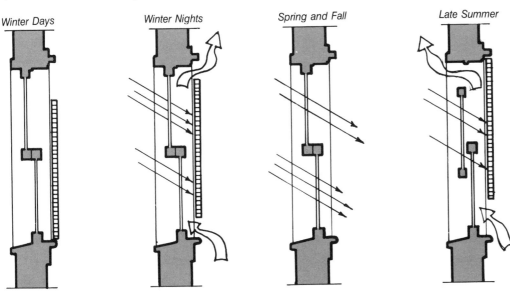

Winter Days   Winter Nights   Spring and Fall   Late Summer

Insulating Panel Management

Opaque Shades

Opaque shades are similar to film shades and are available in most of the configurations discussed in the section on film shades.

☐ Summer solar heat gain through windows can be reduced by an opaque, white shade that reflects much of the incoming solar energy back out through the glass. The color of the shade and its opacity greatly affect performance.

Color	% Transmitted	% Reflected	% Absorbed
Light-color, translucent	25	60	15
White, opaque	0	80	20
Dark, opaque	0	12	88

Solar Energy Transmission through Opaque Shades

☐ The light absorbed by the shade raises its temperature. Heat is then dissipated into the room by radiation to room surfaces and by convection of room air in contact with the warm shade surface.

☐ Opaque shades reduce heat flow through a window in both winter and summer. An opaque roll shade with a moderately close fit to the window opening in the wall will achieve a summer U-value of approximately 0.88.

☐ An opaque shade can have a dark color on one side that absorbs sunlight and a white surface on the reverse side that reflects sunlight. By simply reversing the shade from dark side facing out in winter to reflective side facing out in summer, the shade can perform either as an effective solar collector or as a shading device.

Hypothetical calculations have been made for the summer and winter energy benefit or expenditure in New York City for one square foot of window, with and without a roll shade. Three orientations were calculated, with west being assumed similar to east.

The following values are used in the calculation:

Type of Glazing	Winter U-Values	
	Shade up	Shade down
Single glass	1.13	0.88
Storm double	0.55	0.49

The shading coefficient for double glazing was assumed to be 0.88.

Heat loss for the winter was calculated with the shade lowered 12 hours per day. The heating season used was 4714 degree days (d) for a period from October to April.

$$Q = (WSHG \times SCO - (12 \times U_{shade} \times d) + (12 \times U_{no\ shade} \times d)$$

The results of this calculation are shown.

Type of Glazing	Winter Solar Heat Gain (WSHG) (KBTU/winter, sq. ft.)		
	N	E, W	S
Single	45	91	159
	39.6		139.9
Double		80.1	

182

Glass	% Solar Trans-mission	Shading Coefficient		
		Opaque Dark	Opaque White	Translucent Light
Single clear	87	0.59	0.25	0.39
Single heat-absorbing	35	0.45	0.30	0.36
Double clear	69	0.60	0.25	0.37
Double heat-absorbing	28	0.40	0.22	0.30

Solar Energy Transmission through Opaque Roll Shades

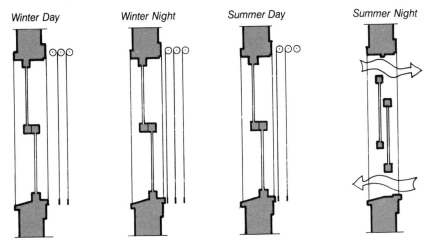

Winter Day   Winter Night   Summer Day   Summer Night

Multiple Shade System Management

Glazing	Shading	North		East		South	
		Winter	Summer	Winter	Summer	Winter	Summer
Single	None	−84	−43	−38	−76	+29	−59
Single	Roll Shade	−69	−15	−23	−26	+45	−20
	Savings	15	28	15	50	16	39
Storm/double	None	−25	−37	+14	−65	+71	−51
Storm/double	Roll Shade	−19	−13	+21	−23	+81	−18
	Savings	6	24	7	42	10	33
Net benefit of double glazing with roll shade vs. single glazing with no shade		65	30	17	53	52	41

Seasonal Energy Expenditure for a Window in New York City (KBTU/sq. ft.) (− denoted energy input from mechanical system.)

Film Shades

Film shades, like opaque shades, are available in various configurations. They can be fixed to the window or attached to fixed or movable frames or movable rollers. Further, film shades with different transmission characteristics can be used in flexible combinations to respond to daily or seasonal changes in temperature.

☐ A film shade sealed against the perimeter of a window frame will create an insulating layer of air. This effect can be multiplied by providing several consecutive layers of shades and air spaces. One such system is reported to provide U-values of 0.55 for the window with one shade pulled down, 0.31 with two shades pulled down, and 0.18 with three shades pulled down.

☐ A shade sealed at the edges impedes infiltration.

☐ A *reflective* film shade can reflect as much as 60 percent of the incoming sunlight back out through the window.

☐ A *low-emissivity* or other selective transmissivity film shade can reduce the window's absorption of heat radiated from interior wall surfaces, furniture and people. This can result in a heat-loss reduction of 57 to 64 percent from single-glazed windows without a shade.

☐ Installed to reduce heat losses, low-emissivity film shades have the disadvantage of also reducing winter solar heat gain. Calculation of the net heat gain or loss for a given location suggests that they are effective on north, east and west orientations and that transparent uncoated film shades are effective on south orientations.

☐ Heat-gain reductions are possible with selective transmissivity film shades that transmit 75 percent of the visible light but only 55 percent of the total solar radiation.

Other uses and characteristics of film shades include:

—Lack of privacy at night with reflective shades; conversely, night visibility into buildings requiring security surveillance.

—Elimination, with selective transmission films, of ultraviolet radiation that fades fabrics.

—Difficult installation on non-vertical or curved glazing.

—Unattractive appearance after several years due to scratches and wrinkles, especially at shade edges. The film can be replaced however, at much less cost than the initial installation cost.

☐ Tests have been conducted on a low-emissivity film shade with a magnetic edge tape that seals the perimeter to an iron oxide tape adhered to the jamb and sill. Measurements were taken on five adjacent windows in using an infrared temperature sensor and thermocouple. One window was uninsulated while the other four received various retrofit options. Results of this test are displayed.

Type	% Heat Loss Reduction (comparison to single glazed windows)
Conventional roll shade plus a blackout shade for movie projecting	28–36
Clear plastic film shade with all perimeter sealed	36–43
Wooden frame exterior storm window	50–57
Low heat emitting film shade sealed on bottom and sides only	57–64

Heat Loss Reductions of Various Shades

Draperies

A window tightly fitted with draperies reduces heat loss much better than an uncovered window. But a closed drapery is an effective insulator only when conditioned air is kept from circulating freely between the drapery and the window. When room air comes in contact with the cold glass, it is cooled and cascades back into the room at the bottom of the drapery. Under such conditions, the winter U-value of a single-glazed window is only reduced from 1.13 to 1.06. By contrast, the winter U-value of a tight-fitting, tight-weave closed drapery and single-glazed window can be as low as 0.88.

Glass Type	Width of Air Space (inches)	No Shading	Interior Shading
Single Glazing	0	1.06	0.81
Double Glazing	3/16	0.66	0.54
	1/4	0.65	0.52
	1/2	0.59	0.48

U-Values of Double Glazing With Draperies

☐ Drawn draperies improve comfort near windows, because they are much closer to room temperature than the glass, with a corresponding reduction in body heat loss by radiation.

☐ The drapery track should extend far enough to either side of the window to permit the draperies to be drawn clear of the window, thus allowing all available sunlight into the room when desired.

☐ Summer heat gain can be reduced with draperies. The effectiveness of the drapery is determined by three main factors: the amount of incoming solar energy reflected back to the glass, the amount of solar energy absorbed and held by the fabric and the amount of solar energy transmitted from the fabric and through the openings of the weave. For single-glazed windows with tight-fitting draperies, the summer U-value can be as low as 0.81 compared to 1.06 for the uncovered window. The shading coefficient of single-glazed windows (1/4" plate) with draperies ranges from 0.80 down to 0.35, the low value representing a highly reflective tightly woven drapery material.

☐ The window heat gain can be calculated by adding the solar heat gain and the conducted heat gain. The solar heat gain equals the amount of solar energy transmitted plus the amount of solar energy absorbed by the configuration and dissipated into the building interior. The conducted heat gain equals the U-value multiplied by the inside/outside temperature difference.

☐ Double draperies (two layers of draperies separated by an air space) further improve the thermal performance of windows. A summer U-value of 0.65 is possible for single-glazed windows, assuming the same degree of air tightness for both layers of trapped air. If the two layers of drapery are even more air-tight than the drapery and the window, the calculated U-value is even lower—0.57.

☐ Noise within a room is absorbed by draperies rather than reflected as with uncovered glass. Also, outside noise transmitted through the glass is partially absorbed. The denser the weave and weight, the more effective are draperies in reducing noise transmission. The effect of the openness of the weave on sound reduction is displayed.

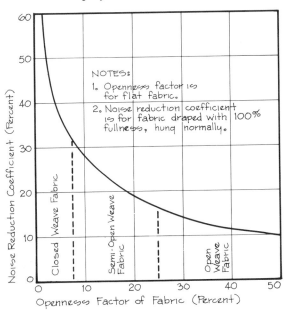

Effect of Drapery Fabric Weave on Noise Reduction

185

Venetian Blinds/Interior Louvers

Interior horizontal or vertical louvers are an effective means of variably controlling the amount of daylight admitted into a room. The slats can be tilted to provide maximum reflection of sunlight back out a window in the summer or to block all direct-beam sunlight while admitting diffuse daylight. With a light-colored ceiling, the slats can be tilted to reflect part of the direct-beam sunlight up to the ceiling, where it can be reflected back down to work surfaces. The amount of light reflected to the work surface is greatly diminished, but glare is eliminated. Automated control systems can be used to adjust the tilt and even raise and lower the louvers as the outdoor light level varies.

Color	Type	% Transmission	% Reflection	% Absorption
Light-colored	horizontal	5	55	40
Medium-colored	horizontal	5	35	60
White	vertical (closed)	0	77	23

Transmission, Reflection and Absorption Characteristics of Venetian Blinds (Figures are for blinds at a 45 degree tilt with sunlight perpendicular to the slats.)

Glass Type	Solar Transmission	Medium Horizontal	Light Horizontal	White[1] Vertical
Single clear	0.87	0.64	0.55	0.29
Single heat-AB	0.46	0.57	0.53	—
Single reflective[2]				
SC = 0.30	—	0.25	0.23	—
= 0.40	—	0.33	0.29	—
= 0.50	—	0.42	0.38	—
= 0.60	—	0.50	0.44	—
Double clear	—	0.57	0.51	0.25
Double heat-AB[3]	—	0.39	0.36	0.22
Double reflective				
SC = 0.20	—	0.19	0.18	—
= 0.30	—	0.27	0.26	—
= 0.40	—	0.34	0.33	—

Shading Coefficients of Venetian Blinds

NOTES: 1. White vertical blind performance is rated for tightly closed blinds in conjunction with glass having a solar transmittance between 0.71 and 0.80.

2. Shading coefficients (SC) under the reflective glass column indicate the performance of the glass without interior shading for the purpose of identifying glass types.

3. Heat absorbing glass for outer sheet of glass, clear glass for inner sheet of glass.

DAYLIGHTING

Introduction

The use of daylight in modern architecture had its beginnings with great architects like Frank Lloyd Wright, Alvar Aalto, Louis Kahn and, to a lesser extent, Corbusier. Many of the designers who followed them also created beautiful daylit buildings—until the 1950's, when an abundant supply of fossil fuel made artificial light inexpensive. At that time, except for a few leaders who retained an appreciation of natural light in building design, architects began to rely almost exclusively on artificial light.

Designers, reawakened to daylighting's tantalizing potential for conserving a scarce and expensive resource, are again designing energy-conserving, cost-effective buildings that are also pleasing. Until we learn how to evaluate the amenities associated with daylighting, it is difficult to quantitatively evaluate daylighting designs. Yet no designer needs to feel trapped between designing an inexpensive, unexciting box, on the one hand, and an esthetically and psychologically pleasing cathedral, at very high cost, on the other.

The designer can determine which parts of the design will contribute to savings from reduced use of artificial lighting and which will not. Current evaluation techniques cannot predict absolute savings from the use of daylight; however, they can determine the relative performance of design alternatives.

Natural light has good modeling shadows, minimal ceiling reflections and good vertical illumination, as well as gradual but almost infinite variability. And natural light, especially if there is also a view, fulfills a psychological desire for contact with the outdoors. It is no wonder that research has repeatedly confirmed a preference by building users for natural over artificial light.

Sky Conditions

Probably the most outstanding characteristic of daylight is variability. Variability caused by diurnal and seasonal patterns of the sun is predictable, but variability caused by weather is not. Because of this unpredictability and the lack of data, the precise quantities of daylight available for illumination are, for most places, unknown.

☐ On the other hand, available data on cloud cover can be used in analyzing daylighting schemes. The National Climatic Center of the National Oceanographic and Atmospheric Administration (NOAA, Asheville, NC 28801), has data in their Local Climatological Data summaries presented in terms of the average number of days, per month, of partly cloudy, overcast, and clear skies.

☐ Researchers at the U.S. National Bureau of Standards working on a sophisticated computer program for determining the energy savings of daylighting, are using weather data normally collected by NOAA to predict the amount of illumination in the sky.

☐ Predictions of energy savings depend on the correlation that exists between total solar radiation and diffuse illumination or "cloud ratio," if the percentage of the sky obstructed by the clouds is taken into account.

☐ Cloud ratio is the ratio of diffuse radiation to total solar horizontal radiation. By using existing weather data, designers may soon be able to predict the amount of daylight or diffuse illumination available wherever NOAA has tabulated weather data.

☐ There are three principal sky conditions:
—clear sky with sunshine
—overcast sky
—partly cloudy sky

☐ Of all the sky conditions, the overcast sky provides the most uniform illumination, generally lasting for hours at a time. Overcast sky, about three times as bright at the zenith as it is near the horizon, is the sky condition used most frequently in evaluating design decisions for daylighting because it generally represents the minimum sky condition to be encountered.

☐ A clear sky is generally not as bright as an overcast sky and is about three times brighter at the horizon than at the zenith. Except in the vicinity of the sun and along the horizon, a clear sky has relatively uniform luminance that varies gradually throughout the day.

☐ Clouds, on the other hand, move and change rapidly. Because white clouds have high reflectivity, a partly cloudy sky often provides the highest levels of illumination.

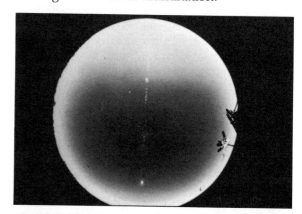

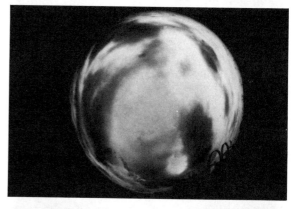

Sky Illumination

Site

Before beginning to design, the designer needs to examine the site for features that will help in using daylight. To ensure that the building is well integrated with the site and, in that sense, responsive to its context, the designer should identify these features:

—vegetation that will filter sunlight, reduce glare or otherwise make sunlight usable for visual tasks in the building

—built features of the site or adjacent to the site that will increase or decrease the introduction of daylight into the building, unless they can be minimized

☐ By manipulating trees, shrubs, vines and ground surfaces, a designer can control the quality and quantity of daylight entering a building and better integrate the building with its site. These elements of the site are probably some of the first things a designer should think about as he seeks a design solution.

—Vegetation filters daylight and thus eliminates glare and excessive thermal gain if it is properly used.

—Ground surfaces can be used to reflect daylight into the building, once their approximate reflectivity has been calculated by following the accompanying chart.

—Highly reflective surfaces near the site (such as buildings with reflective surfaces) can create unwanted glare.

Ground Surfaces	%
Grass fields, lawns	6
Snow, fresh	74
Snow, old	64
Wild fields	25
Concrete	55
Macadam	18
Gravel	13
Bare earth	7

Reflectance Values of Ground Surfaces

—Adjacent buildings on the east, west and north can be used to reflect sun and skylight into the building.

—Daylight reflected off the ground or other surfaces can be filtered by placing plants to block light, either before it strikes the reflecting surface or after it is reflected.

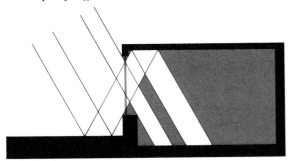

Ceiling Reflected Ground Light

Building Form

If daylighting were the designer's sole objective, it would be best to increase daylighting by extending the perimeter of the building. Often, however, a designer must also satisfy a competing need for reduced heat gain and heat loss through glazing.

☐ In manipulating the building's overall form and geometry, the designer controls the esthetic effect of daylight in the building. When the building's form has been chosen, the quantity of daylight entering can be roughly approximated. Precise calculations are made by manipulating controls at the building envelope once the overall form has been achieved.

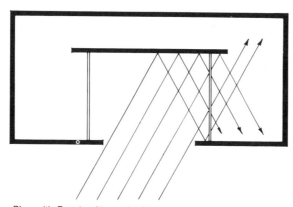

Plan with Exterior Alcove for Daylighting

☐ Clerestories, sawtooth roofs and light wells can be used to bring light in high and let it wash down the walls. Bringing daylight obliquely into a room in this way creates a soft ambiance to the space.
☐ Ceiling height and window height can be raised in a room to bring in more daylight.
☐ Room depth can be reduced to get greater illumination toward the rear of a room.
☐ Daylight controls (light wells with shading, eggcrate diffusers, louvers, diffuser shades) can be used to get light from any orientation as soft and diffuse as north light.

☐ Interior courtyards and open light wells can be used to bring light into the interior of buildings with deep plans; a designer can use these to enhance view and natural ventilation.

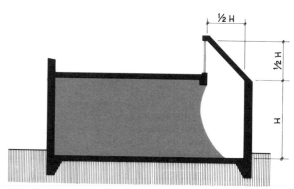

Effective Proportions for Clerestory Wall Wash, Using Daylight

☐ The perimeter of the building can be extended to gain increased exposure for daylighting.
☐ When overcast skies predominate during occupied periods, room depth should be limited to 2½ times window height if continuous or nearly continuous windows are used.

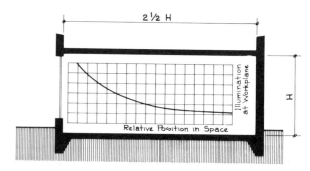

Relationship of Room Depth to Window Height for Overcast Sky Conditions

☐ When clear skies predominate during occupied periods, room depth should be limited to 3½ times window height if continuous or nearly continuous windows are used.

☐ Enclosed atria can be used to bring in light to a protected central core from which spaces within the building can gather light. Atria effectively increase the building perimeter.

☐ Windows can be located close to the ceiling or side walls to avoid strong brightness ratios.

☐ High-reflectance ceilings and walls can help light penetrate deep into a room.

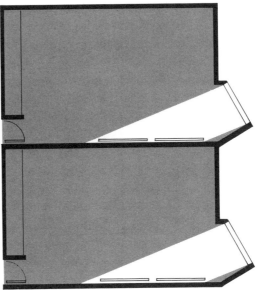

Sidelighting

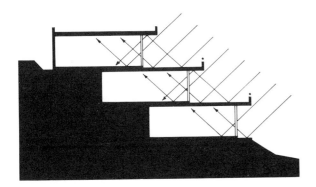

Stepped Roof with Reflective Surfaces

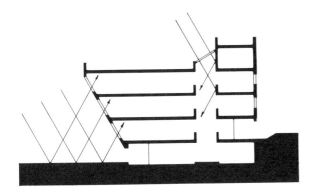

Stepped Facade with Reflective Surfaces

RECTANGLE 4:1 RATIO

ASSUMPTIONS: 126,000 sq.ft.
15'-0" Perimeter Zone
Lighting: 1 watts/sq.ft.
+ daylight in perimeter zone
Lighting: 2 watts/sq.ft. in core

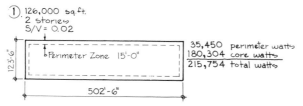

① 126,000 sq.ft.
2 stories
S/V = 0.02

Perimeter Zone 15'-0"

35,450	perimeter watts
180,304	core watts
215,754	total watts

12'-3"-6"   502'-6"

② 126,000 sq.ft.
5 stories
S/V = 0.03

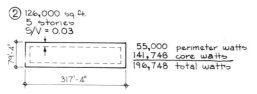

55,000	perimeter watts
141,748	core watts
196,748	total watts

79'-4"   317'-4"

③ 126,000 sq.ft.
10 stories
S/V = 0.04

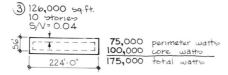

75,000	perimeter watts
100,000	core watts
175,000	total watts

56'   224'-0"

Building Shape and Lighting Power Requirements

SQUARE 1:1 RATIO

ASSUMPTIONS: 126,000 sq.ft.
15'-0" Perimeter Zone
Lighting: 1 watt/sq.ft
+ daylight in perimeter zone
Lighting: 2 watts/sq.ft. in core

① 126,000 sq.ft.
2 stories
S/V = 0.015

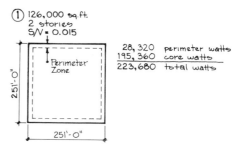

Perimeter Zone

28,320	perimeter watts
195,360	core watts
223,680	total watts

251'-0"   251'-0"

② 126,000 sq.ft.
5 stories
S/V = 0.025

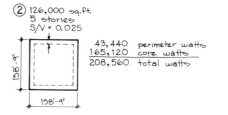

43,440	perimeter watts
165,120	core watts
208,560	total watts

158'-9"   158'-9"

③ 126,000
10 stories
S/V = 0.035

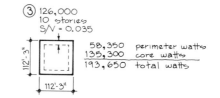

58,350	perimeter watts
135,300	core watts
193,650	total watts

112'-3"   112'-3"

194

S.C. Johnson and Son, Inc.
Racine, Wisconsin
Architect: Frank Lloyd Wright

Frank Lloyd Wright was the first architect to experiment with a mechanically controlled atrium space. In the S.C. Johnson and Son, Inc., Administration Building in Racine, Wisconsin, Wright used the atrium as an open office space. Sealed off visually from the outdoors and focusing inward, this interior is nonetheless flooded with natural light that enters from the ceiling and high on the walls.

Giant mushroom columns do not interfere with office functions. These round, organic-looking forms support a luminous ceiling through which natural light floods into the space. In addition, light that comes from high on the wall passes through Pyrex glass tubing, flooding the floor of the atrium space and the balconies; surrounding it with light.

The physical arrangement of the central space and the balconies around it expresses the company's philosophy. The secretarial pool of workers is on the floor of the atrium below, and the semiprivate offices of the managers are in the balconies opening to the central atrium space yet screened by the same glass tubing used on the ceiling. Light floods from the atrium into these offices to underscore their part of the communal work. This relationship contrasts to the closed, cubicle offices prevalent when Wright designed this building, and suggests a progressive approach by management that is only today becoming universal.

S. C. Johnson and Son, Inc., Racine, Wisconsin; Architect: Frank Lloyd Wright

Windows

Windows, clerestories and skylights transmit sunlight into the building, and it is here, at the building's envelope, that the problems of overheating and glare are most easily solved by appropriate glazing and lighting controls.

☐ Ideally, glazing permits light to enter the building without significantly changing its color, at the same time excluding weather and permitting a view outside. In practice, however, the glazing needed to control heat gain often obscures the view. Float glass, sheet glass, wire glass, acrylic and polycarbonate plastic sheet and glass block—tinted, untinted, or reflective—all have different transmittance values.

☐ Depending on exposure or orientation, daylight passing through windows, clerestories or skylights has different colors and modeling of shapes. Light from the north is generally cool in color and has a uniform, shadowless character. Light from the south, east or west is tremendously varied in both color and direction.

☐ Sidelighting through windows is an excellent source of lighting because its horizontal directionality provides good modeling shadows, minimal veiling reflections and excellent vertical surface illumination.

☐ Details of the window can have significant effects on both the quantity and quality of light that enters a building; window detail such as mullions, frames, heavy window supports and small glass lights can obstruct up to 20 percent of the available light. Dirt accumulation and wired glass further obstruct light.

☐ If windows are small relative to the wall surface, deep window wells, rounded jambs, or splayed window jambs can be used to soften brightness contrasts between interior and exterior surfaces.

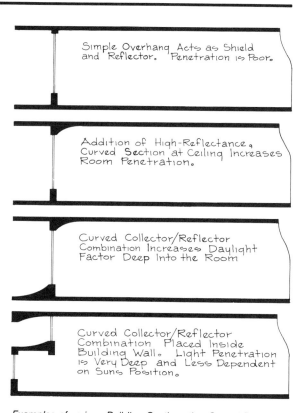

Simple Overhang Acts as Shield and Reflector. Penetration is Poor.

Addition of High-Reflectance, Curved Section at Ceiling Increases Room Penetration.

Curved Collector/Reflector Combination Increases Daylight Factor Deep Into the Room

Curved Collector/Reflector Combination Placed Inside Building Wall. Light Penetration is Very Deep and Less Dependent on Suns Position.

Examples of various Building Sections that Control Direct Sunlight and Permit Reflected Daylight to Enter

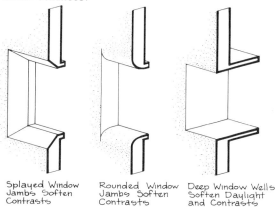

Splayed Window Jambs Soften Contrasts

Rounded Window Jambs Soften Contrasts

Deep Window Wells Soften Daylight and Contrasts

Effect of Various Window Forms on the Quality of Admitted Daylight

☐ Louvers, venetian blinds, curtains, over-hangs, or shading devices modify the intro-duction of sunlight into buildings, particularly east- or west-facing windows.

Roll Shades Venetian Blinds Shutters Louvers

Drapes Glass Block Low Transmittance Glazing Awnings

Sun Control Devices

☐ Too great a contrast between a window and a dark interior can be avoided by directing light toward the ceiling or interior wall in rooms with excessive room-depth-to-window-height ratios (e.g., about 2½ to 1).

☐ The light admitted to a space is propor-tional to the percentage of wall area occupied by windows.

☐ Windows on adjacent walls primarily light up these walls; windows on opposite walls not only give good bilateral lighting but illuminate adjacent walls as well.

☐ Tall, narrow windows generally give bet-ter penetration of skylight at points near the back of a room than long, low windows. When tall, narrow windows are widely separated, the distribution of daylight parallel to the window is uneven. Floor and wall area between the windows can appear rather dark.

☐ Windows on adjacent walls of square rooms give good penetration of daylight unless they are comparatively narrow and placed close to the corners of the room. They also reduce glare by lighting the area of wall surrounding the opposite window.

☐ Bay windows can fully illuminate the area itself, but not the rest of the room, unless they are very high.

☐ Windows on opposite sides of a compar-atively narrow room throw light onto the op-posing walls and hence reduce the brightness contrast. However, in certain cases, e.g., a classroom with fixed seating and a chalkboard on one wall, bilateral lighting, unless properly controlled, could be distractingly bright for per-sons at the back of the room.

☐ Large windows extending the full width of a wall distribute daylight more uniformly than windows separated by substantial wall areas, but they also create glare under bright skies unless they are covered with suitable blinds, screens, or overhangs.

Clerestories and Sawtooth Roofs

Clerestories introduce light deep into a space without creating the excessive brightness that a direct view of the sky or sun produces.

☐ Overhangs or horizontal louvers protect against the thermal effects of the sun, just as windows do.

☐ Clerestories can be used on one side of a building for nondirectional light and on two sides of a building for bidirectional lighting.

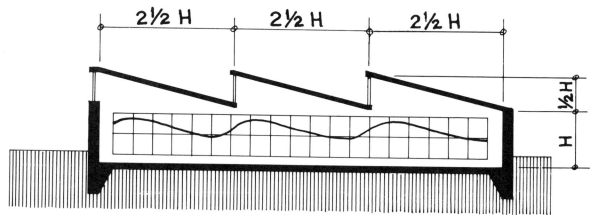

Sawtooth Roof

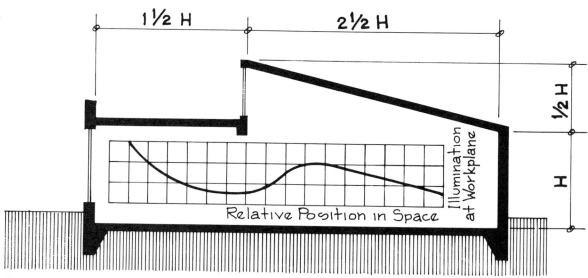

Clerestory
Effective Proportions for Sawtooth Roofs and Clerestories

Joan Miró Foundation/Center for Studies of Contemporary Art
Barcelona, Spain
Architect: José Luis Sert, FAIA

José Luis Sert's deep understanding of the Mediterranean climate, Catalonian architecture, and the art of his lifelong friend, Joan Miró, are well expressed in this Joan Miró Foundation/ Center for Studies of Contemporary Art in Barcelona, Spain. This building realizes the goals that Sert called for in 1934: a regional architecture that responds to the intense sun, a limpid atmosphere, and the friendly countryside of the Mediterranean climate, and links together the spirits of different ages.

On a beautiful site jointly chosen by Sert and Miró, this low, one-story building overlooking Barcelona uses natural ventilation and light introduced through large glazed areas. Influenced by Mediterranean architecture of earlier periods, Sert has opened courtyards onto gardens and created octagonal workrooms.

In and out of doors, contemporary paintings and sculptures are displayed in the gallery spaces formed by the interior glass core and by the building form. Clerestories, thrust through the roof of the building and set close to one another, diffuse light into the interior galleries. These half-barrel clerestories create the openness of the galleries—a spaciousness that is enhanced as one walks around the building and sees the art works reflected in the glass.

Joan Miró Foundation/Center for Studies of Contemporary Art, Barcelona, Spain; Architect: José Luis Sert, FAIA

Skylights

One of the most efficient means of introducing light deep into a building is through skylights, because the amount of light falling on the horizontal plane can be two times that on the vertical plane with overcast sky. Skylights must be used with caution, however, because they can also introduce direct sun into the building in the summer and cause excessive heat loss in winter. This can be avoided through the careful use of shading and insulating controls or by limiting the skylight area to approximately 5 percent of the total roof area.

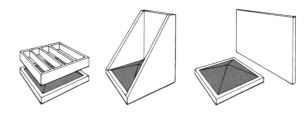

Shading Devices for Skylights

☐ The most effective use of skylights is on the top floor of a building. Lightwells and other devices can bring light into the lower levels, but they are not always cost-effective.

—Clear glazing can be used in skylights, with an exterior screen to intercept unwanted direct sun; clear glazing permits a view of the changing sky.

—Skylights bring light deep into an interior space. They must be cleaned periodically to maintain their prime transmission qualities. Roof openings and skylights are useful in deep rooms with short windows where room-depth-to-window-height ratios exceed 2 to 1.

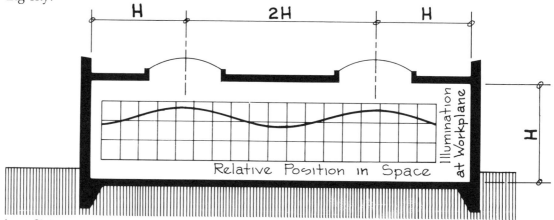

Large Skylights (3/4H in diameter)
Effective Proportion for Skylights

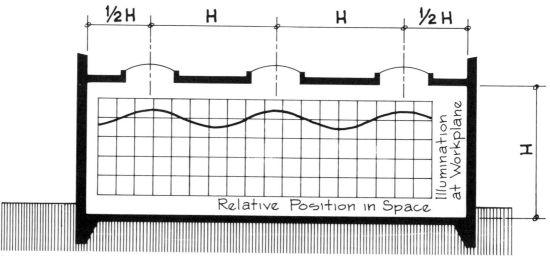

Small Skylights: (3/8H in diameter)

Kimball Art Museum, Fort Worth, Texas; Architect: Louis I. Kahn, FAIA

Kimball Art Museum
Fort Worth, Texas
Architect: Louis I. Kahn, FAIA

Light was vitally important in Kahn's design of the Kimball Art Museum in Fort Worth, Texas, where art is effectively illuminated and where visitors are made to feel a part of the changing, rotating universe by catching glimpses of sky, sun, foilage, and water. This effect was achieved only after many experiments and difficulties. The building was almost complete when the breakthrough was made and the design solution found. The long axis of each vault has a central skylight with a partial reflector below it. Most light coming through the 2½-foot opening in the vault is reflected back onto the vault to articulate its curvature by the curved partial reflector below it. To reduce contrast, the reflector is perforated with tiny holes. Art works are protected from direct sun by eliminating these holes directly beneath the 2½-foot opening in the vault in areas where art works are displayed. In public areas, entry halls, auditorium, banquet area and bookstore, perforation allows diffuse light to enter.

Light Shelves

Light shelves, or horizontal projections at the building interior, bring light deep into a room by reflecting incoming light off the ceiling. If these shelves are placed near the ceiling, a soft, diffuse light spreads out through the entire room as the light bounces off the ceiling.

☐ Through the use of cold mirrors, the infrared part of the spectrum can be separated from the visible. The infrared can then be used to generate heat, with the visible light directing various kinds of mirrors to produce diffuse or direct light.

Light Shelf

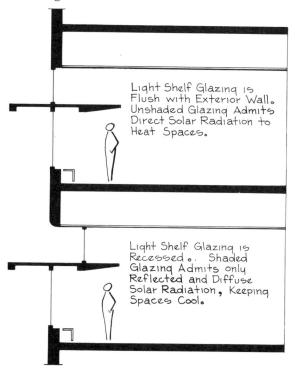

Light Shelf Glazing is Flush with Exterior Wall. Unshaded Glazing Admits Direct Solar Radiation to Heat Spaces.

Light Shelf Glazing is Recessed. Shaded Glazing Admits only Reflected and Diffuse Solar Radiation, Keeping Spaces Cool.

Location of Glazing in Light Shelves Affects Heat Gain

☐ Because daylighting relies completely on fixed openings, the designer confronts two problems. First, as the sun moves across the sky, its most concentrated rays can be gathered only when they happen to be perpendicular to the fixed opening. Second, unless the building has only one story, it can be difficult to get light deep into the building interior without a huge opening such as an atrium.

202

□ Although still experimental, solar optics can be used to transmit concentrated quantities of sunlight deep into the interior of a building by using only a small amount of interior space. To do this, a mechanical sun-tracking instrument, or heliostat, follows the sun and projects its rays through a small opening in the building envelope, guiding it down a narrow passageway such as a stair tower or pipe chase with a system of lenses and mirrors. From these vertical shafts the sunlight can be brought into a room along the ceiling.

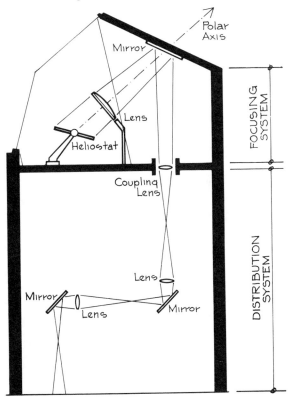

Heliostat Sun Tracking and Distribution Systems

Skylight Sculpture
Chapel at the Harvard Business School
Cambridge, Massachusetts
Architect: Moshe Safdie
Sculptor: Charles Ross
Prism steering design and installation:
Thomas Hooper

The prisms in this sculpture by Charles Ross are computer controlled to track the sun and constantly reflect and refract daylight into the chapel below.

Lockheed Missiles and Space Company Building
Sunnyvale, California
Architect: Leo A. Daly

In this 600,000 square-foot engineering office for Lockheed Missiles and Space Co., a central core brings light to the center of the space. Elevator cores at the building's east and west ends allow bilateral daylighting on north and south facades.

On the inside of the north and south facades, 12-foot light shelves direct light back onto a sloped ceiling and deep into the space. Well-integrated with other environmental controls, the shelves contain the HVAC duct work, and even the fluorescent lights, which reflect artificial light off the ceiling, making it appear to originate where the daylight does. In addition, on the exterior south facade, a shiny white light shelf both reflects indirect light and shades the glazing below it.

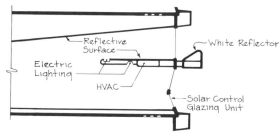

Lockheed Missiles and Space Company Building, Sunnyvale, California; Architect: Leo A. Daly

Lockheed Missiles and Space Company Building, Sunnyvale, California; Architect: Leo A. Daly

Civil/Mineral Engineering Building, University of Minnesota
St. Paul, Minnesota
Architect: Myers and Bennett Architects/BRW

The Civil/Mineral Engineering Building at the University of Minnesota is an experiment in solar optics. It will use a heliostat that tracks the sun and a system of lenses and mirrors that focus the light through a small hole in the building envelope to project concentrated sunlight into the building. Once inside, the light is split into its infrared and light components.

All but 5 percent of the 145,000-square-foot building is below ground; of this, 30,000 square feet is office and laboratory space 100 feet below the surface. On the roof of this building, ten heliostats in two glass penthouses will send light streams into the building. Each heliostat reflective surface is 16.5 square feet and will be able to light 412 square feet in the building with almost 100 footcandles. Different mirrors within the building will produce a variety of light effects, ranging from an image of the sun on the wall, a band of light on the ceiling or light uniformly distributed over the floor.

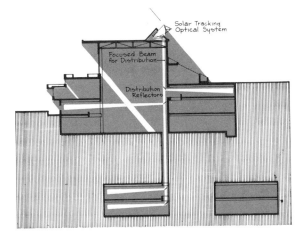

Civil/Mineral Engineering Building, University of Minnesota; Architect: Myers & Bennett Architects/BRW

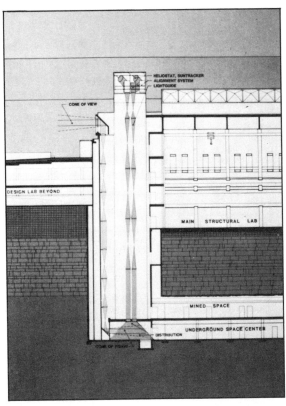

Civil/Mineral Engineering Building, University of Minnesota; Architect: Myers & Bennett Architects/BRW

Interior Surfaces

Visual acuity is proportional to an object's physical size, perceived brightness and contrast. In general, the brighter the object, the easier it is to see. But our ability to see an object depends largely on its background. The greater the contrast between the object and its immediate surroundings, the easier it is to see.

☐ Once daylight enters a building it can be controlled to some extent by the interior surfaces. Rooms with dark-colored fabrics and wall surfaces have less daylight than rooms full of diffusely reflecting, light-colored surfaces. Highly reflective surfaces cause concentration of light which can be distracting if in the field of view. They may also interfere with task performance if excessive brightness on the task reduces contrast.

—Light-colored, diffusely reflecting surfaces facilitate the distribution of light.

—Reflectance of ceiling should be 80 percent or higher.

—Reflectance of walls should be 50 to 60 percent.

—Light finishes on floors and interior furnishings add brightness and liveliness to interiors.

—Interior surface finishes have a significant effect on the amount of illumination reaching a task. The diagrams show the effect that painting various surfaces black has on the illumination at point X. In a room with all white surfaces, illumination at X is assumed to be 100 percent. The percentages given are the amount that illumination was reduced as a result of painting the room surfaces black. In the left-hand diagrams, the window wall is in the foreground and is removed for purposes of the illustration. In the diagrams, additional windows have been placed in the back of the room.

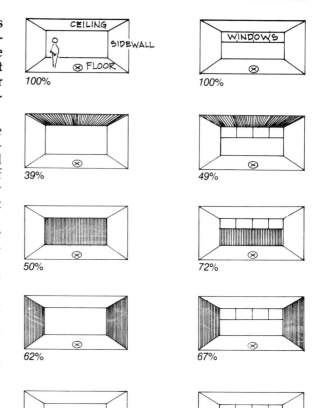

The two uppermost diagrams depict rooms in which all interior opaque surfaces are white and the available light at point x is 100%. The diagrams show the same rooms after selected surfaces have been painted black, and their corresponding lighting levels at point x. The ceiling, therefore, is the most effective in supporting level illumination

Surface Reflectance Performance
SOURCE: Evans, Banjamin H., *Daylight in Architecture,* © 1981. Reprinted by permission of McGraw-Hill Book Co., New York.

Medium Value Colors	%
White	80–85
Light gray	45–70
Dark gray	20–25
Ivory white	70–80
Ivory	60–70
Pearl gray	70–75
Buff	40–70
Tan	30–50
Brown	20–40
Green	25–50
Olive	20–30
Azure blue	50–60
Sky blue	35–40
Pink	50–70
Cardinal red	20–25
Red	20–40

Approximate Reflection Factors

Color	Reflection Factor (%)
White	80 to 90
Pale yellow	80
Pale beige, lilac	70
Pale blue, green	70 to 75
Mustard yellow	35
Medium brown	25
Medium blue, green	20 to 30
Black	10

Reflective Factors of Colors

Surface	Reflection Factor (%)
Ceilings	80
End walls:	
in poorly lighted rooms	70
in well lighted rooms	25
Walls containing window(s)	80
Floors	25

Desirable Reflection Factors for Interior Surfaces

Crystal Cathedral, Garden Grove, California;
Architects: Johnson/Burgee Architects

Artificial Lighting

When natural and artificial lighting are properly integrated, daylight minimizes the use and expense of artificial light, while artificial lighting compensates for inadequate daylight.

☐ In some daylighting designs, electric lighting is not needed at all and is not even installed. Normally, however, daylighting does not save energy unless controls on the artificial lighting system—"on/off" or "dimming" controls, manual or automatic—restrict electricity use when daylight is sufficient.

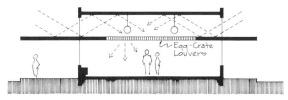

Integrated Artificial Light and Daylight

☐ The following are some ways to enhance the "natural" effect of artificial lighting and make it compatible with natural lighting:

—Use artificial lighting that is close in color to daylight.

—Avoid artificial lighting of different colors (e.g., a "warm" and a "cool" wall of a single color). If different colors of artificial light are played on a wall, the wall should be different colors itself, with each color compatible with its artificial light source; thus, "warm" color with a "warm" light and "cool" color with a "cool" light.

—Place skylights and clerestories out of the line of vision to avoid glare and to better integrate daylight with artificial light.

—Use indirect electrical lighting to mimic the directional aspects of daylighting.

Unity Temple
Oak Park, Illinois
Architect: Frank Lloyd Wright

In the Unity Temple in Oak Park, Illinois, Frank Lloyd Wright skillfully integrated artificial lighting and daylighting. In much of Wright's work artificial lighting is concealed and allowed to wash the ceiling and walls from on high as though it is a wash of natural light. If light fixtures are visible at all, they are usually placed where natural light originates. In Unity Temple, Wright placed the lighting fixtures overhead. When turned on, they shine down in the same way as does daylight from the ceiling overhead and windows high on the congregation hall walls.

Unity Temple, Oak Park, Illinois;
Architect: Frank Lloyd Wright

Photo: Fred Leavitt

Integration Of Natural Ventilation, Solar Heating And View

Lighting, heating, cooling and ventilation, and the esthetic satisfaction of a good view, can not always be accomplished through the same piece of glazing, especially if we wish to maximize the benefit of these natural forces. Sometimes these functions must be separated.

☐ In placing windows and other types of glazing, the designer cannot afford to neglect one function entirely in satisfying another. Providing a view, for example, may preclude natural ventilation, because window placement is poor, or causes glare.

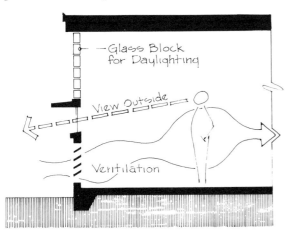

Daylight and Ventilation Control Can Conflict with View

☐ The following are guidelines for integrating the various functions of lighting, heating, cooling and ventilation:

—Where possible, use different glazings to satisfy different building needs.

—Direct the light that accompanies solar heating away from task areas to avoid glare.

—In designing windows, take into account the acoustic problems they may create.

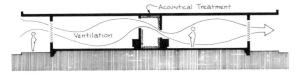

Daylighting, Ventilation and Acoustic Control

Physical Models

Procedures for evaluating daylighting designs should reflect the nature of information available at each phase of design. Thus, as the design proceeds, and decisions become more refined, so should the means of evaluating these decisions.

☐ Scale models are useful in making the qualitative assessment that is the final arbiter of any good design. Light behaves in scale models exactly as it would in full-sized buildings. Because accurate data on available daylight are not available in all locations in the United States, scale models are one of the better means of evaluating a design for daylighting. Models are of particular value in "observing" the effects of daylight in a space, either with the naked eye or with a camera. An additional reason for using models is that there is no predictive technique that can evaluate the amount of illumination on a work surface when direct sun shines into a space.

☐ During the schematic phase of design, a rough scale model, with openings cut for daylighting, can provide a rough estimate of the amount of illumination (footcandles) available on a work surface. Since these models can be constructed relatively quickly, several different concepts, as well as the same concept with the windows in different places, can be compared.

☐ In the development phase of design, a more detailed scale model finalizes window sizes and locations. The model measures the amount of illumination on the work surface with an accuracy sufficient for this design stage.

☐ Finally, a full-scale mock-up of key sections of the design can be made to finalize daylighting decisions.

☐ *Model Geometry*
—In any daylighting model the size of openings should be accurate, as should window frames, mullions, sills, jambs and skylight wells. Louvers must be represented if they block or reflect light

—Thickness of walls in the model is generally not important.

—Depth and reflectivity of window sill must be accurately represented.

—For blinds or louvers, the proportions of width to opening must be the same.

—In buildings with very large interior spaces uninterrupted by floor-to-ceiling walls, a typical bay or section can be simulated by enclosing the typical space with mirrored side walls.

—In comparing design changes in spaces with daylight openings on more than one wall, detect changes resulting from one opening by blacking out the other. The secondary opening can be covered with an opaque material painted black to simulate the light from inside that would be absorbed through the opening when it is in operation, unless it has shades or venetian blinds.

☐ *Materials*
—Materials used in the model should have the same opacity, transparency, reflectance and texture as those to be used in the building. Paint can be used to simulate most wall surfaces.

—Color has little significance, since the instruments measure only quantity of light reflected. Use gray paints on dark and light paper to simulate surfaces.

—Construct walls of plywood or cardboard, and then paint appropriately. If foamboard is used it must be painted or covered with opaque material.

—Glass can be simulated with real glass of float glass quality.

—For overcast skies, simulate plastic dome skylights with a flat covering of translucent or transparent material approximating the transmission properties of the dome material. Simulate sunny conditions with a plastic tent using the same angle of acceptance of the sun as the dome would have.

—To determine the normal transmission of transparent or translucent materials, place a light cell in an opaque box opposite a small opening (about 2" square) with some type of constant, relatively small, diffuse source light just outside the box (about 10 to 12 inches). With the light burning, the illumination on the light cell is recorded. Next, place the material to be tested over the opening in the box and record the illumination on the cell again. Calculate the material transmission by dividing the first measurement (box without material) with the second (material to be tested in place). Example: 144/180 × 100 = 80 percent transmission.

☐ *Scale*
—Models can be constructed at any convenience scale; however, they should be large enough to reproduce details accurately, and to accommodate the illumination meter probe without causing excessive reflection.

—A scale of 3/4 inches to 1 foot is convenient for daylighting studies of a room but 1/2 inch or 3/8 inch scale can be used if care is exercised in construction and measurement.

□ *Instrumentation*

—Many kinds of photometers (light meters) and photocells are available for daylighting studies.

—Most suitable photometers use a photovoltaic power cell; however, battery-operated photometers are also available.

—For measuring actual illumination levels, the photocell should be adapted with a color corrector (a "Viscor Filter") to screen out measurement of portions of the spectrum other than the visible.

—Because photocells are not as sensitive to light striking them from a low angle (as opposed to direct or high angles), they must also be fitted with a cosine correction device.

—A photometer should provide a range in measurement of 1 to 12,000 footcandles.

—Caps can be made to adjust the percentage of light admitted to the photocell. For example, if the maximum range of the scale is 1,000 footcandles, and one wishes to measure a lighting level of 2,000 footcandles, the cell can be covered with a cap allowing 50 percent of the light to penetrate; the indicated level is then multiplied by two. The cap is made by drilling holes equal to 50 percent of the total photocell area.

—Photometers with a photocell built into the display meter case are not suitable for model studies.

□ *Model Testing*

—The outdoor location should approximate the sky and ground conditions for the proposed building.

—Ground conditions can make a large difference in interior illumination levels and distribution, because much of the light entering the building can be reflected from the ground.

—Exterior sky conditions must be measured at the beginning, during and at the end of model daylight tests. These measurements give a basis for test comparison and indicate changing sky conditions. They are especially important if design schemes are being compared.

—For the designer, two reference measurements—Ev and Eh—are important.

□ Ev = illumination from the sky one the plane of the vertical fenestration or window wall and parallel to the wall (a few inches immediately outside the window but beyond any obstructing parts of the building, such as overhangs and louvers. This measurement is made by placing the photocell on the center of the vertical window wall of the model if there are

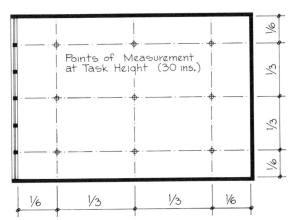

Suggested Locations for Measurement of Daylight in Models

no protruding building parts to restrict the light reaching the cell. This measurement provides an indication of the total light from the sky, plus the light reflected from the ground and surrounding objects near window openings. If the ground surface is to be altered in any way, the Ev reference measurement should include only the light from the sky, by attaching a horizontal black shield to the light cell.

□ Eh = total hemispheric illumination on the unobstructed plane of the ground from both the sun and sky (any distance from the ground up to several hundred feet will suffice; usually the roof of the model is an appropriate place). This measurement is necessary when the model has horizontal openings. The measurement is made by placing the light cell on a flat surface, such as the model roof, where light from the sky will not be obstructed. This measurement provides an indication of the total light from the sky that is available to pass into a horizontal opening such as a skylight.

—Standard points for measurement in rectangular rooms are shown in the accompanying figure. If the designer considers other points in the room particularly significant to the design, they can be used as reference points instead.

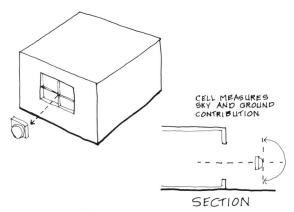

CELL MEASURES
SKY AND GROUND
CONTRIBUTION

SECTION

Measurement of Illumination on Vertical Surfaces

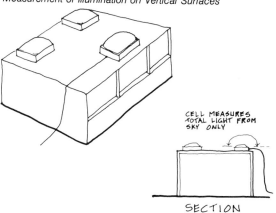

CELL MEASURES
TOTAL LIGHT FROM
SKY ONLY

SECTION

Measurement of Illumination on Horizontal Surfaces

SOURCE: Evans, Benjamin H., *Daylight in Architecture*, © 1981. Reprinted by permission of McGraw-Hill Book Co., New York.

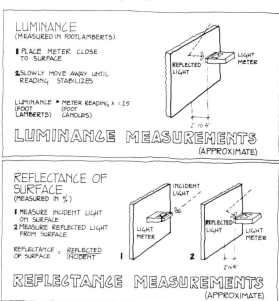

LUMINANCE
(MEASURED IN FOOTLAMBERTS)

1 PLACE METER CLOSE
TO SURFACE

2 SLOWLY MOVE AWAY UNTIL
READING STABILIZES

LUMINANCE = METER READING x 1.25
(FOOT   (FOOT
LAMBERTS)   CANDLES)

REFLECTED
LIGHT

LIGHT
METER

2" TO 4'

LUMINANCE MEASUREMENTS
(APPROXIMATE)

REFLECTANCE OF
SURFACE
(MEASURED IN %)

1 MEASURE INCIDENT LIGHT
ON SURFACE
2 MEASURE REFLECTED LIGHT
FROM SURFACE

REFLECTANCE = REFLECTED
OF SURFACE   INCIDENT

INCIDENT
LIGHT

LIGHT
METER   1

REFLECTED
LIGHT

LIGHT
METER

2" TO 4'

2

REFLECTANCE MEASUREMENTS
(APPROXIMATE)

Measurement of Luminance and Reflectance

Note: Do not allow body to block any light when taking measurements.

Lumen Method

The *Lumen Method,* which is the method most widely used in the United States, was developed by J. W. Griffith for Libbey-Owens-Ford Company. In this method, many different variables are taken into account, including sky conditions, position of sun, room size, glazing area and transmission characteristics such as overhangs, shades and blinds. The calculation technique is limited to predicting amount of illumination on a centerline five feet from the window, five feet from the back wall, and a point midway between, but can be modified by combining with area source comparative calculations to give reasonable values anywhere on a horizontal work plane.

☐ The Lumen Method is as follows:

1. Determine solar altitude from table 1 or a sun angle calculator.

2. Choose sky conditions. Determine illumination on window (Ekw) and illumination on horizontal surfaces (Ekg) from table 2.

3. Determine solar illumination value (Euw and Eug) from table 3. Add to illumination on window (Ekw) and illumination on horizontal surfaces (Ekg).

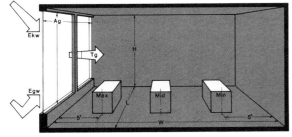

Lumen Method Factors

—Illumination on ground (Ekug) = illumination from sky on ground (Ekg) + illumination from sun on ground (Eug).

—Illumination on Window (Ekuw) = illumination from sky on window (Ekw) + illumination from sun on window (Euw).

4. Multiply the illumination on the ground by the reflectance factor of the ground (Rg) and the field proportion factor 0.5 to obtain the illumination on the window from the ground (Egw).

—Illumination from ground on window (Egw) = illumination on ground (Ekug) × reflectance of ground surface (Rg) × 0.5.

5. Determine the total transmitting area (Ag) of the window, taking into account the metal frame. From manufacturer's product data, find the transmittance factor of the glass itself (Tg) or use table 4.

6. Determine room dimensions and reflectance of wall surfaces. Determine coefficients of utilization (C and K) from tables 5 and 6. For diffusing shades use 1/2 total incident illumination from sun, sky and ground on window, or 1/2 × (Ekuw + Egw).

7. Multiply the values of illumination on the window by the window factors and the coefficients of utilization, separately for light from the ground and light from the sky (Ekwp and Egwp).

—Illumination from sky on work plane (Ekwp) = illumination on window (Ekuw) × window area of transmittance (Ag) × transmittance of glass for average daylight (Tg) × coefficient of utilization (C) × coefficient of utilization (K).

—Illumination from ground on work plane (Egwp) = illumination from ground on window (Egw) × area of transmittance (Ag) × transmittance of glass for average daylight (Tg) × coefficient of utilization (C) × coefficient of utilization (K).

8. Add the values found in step 7 in order to obtain the total illumination of the work plane in foot-candles.

—total illumination on work plane = illumination from sky on work plane (Ekwp) + illumination from ground on work plane (Egwp).

26° N. Latitude

June 22 A.M.	P.M.	Solar Altitude	Solar Azimuth (from South)
6	6	10.05	111.30
7	5	22.82	105.97
8	4	35.93	101.15
9	3	49.24	96.45
10	2	62.69	88.83
11	1	76.15	82.61
12		87.45	0.00

March 21, Sept. 24 A.M.	P.M.	Solar Altitude	Solar Azimuth (from South)
6	6	0.00	90.00
7	5	13.45	83.30
8	4	26.70	75.80
9	3	39.46	66.33
10	2	51.11	52.79
11	1	60.25	31.44
12		64.00	0.00

December 22 A.M.	P.M.	Solar Altitude	Solar Azimuth (from South)
7	5	2.23	62.48
8	4	13.76	54.88
9	3	24.12	45.30
10	2	32.66	33.01
11	1	38.46	17.65
12		45.55	0.00

30° N. Latitude

June 22 A.M.	P.M.	Solar Altitude	Solar Azimuth (from South)
6	6	11.48	110.59
7	5	23.87	104.30
8	4	36.60	98.24
9	3	49.53	91.79
10	2	62.50	83.46
11	1	75.11	67.48
12		83.45	0.00

March 21, Sept. 24 A.M.	P.M.	Solar Altitude	Solar Azimuth (from South)
6	6	0.00	90.00
7	5	12.95	82.37
8	4	25.66	73.90
9	3	37.76	63.44
10	2	48.59	49.11
11	1	56.77	28.19
12		60.00	0.00

December 22 A.M.	P.M.	Solar Altitude	Solar Azimuth (from South)
7	5	0.38	62.40
8	4	11.44	54.15
9	3	21.27	44.12
10	2	29.28	31.73
11	1	34.64	16.77
12		36.55	0.00

34° N. Latitude

June 22 A.M.	P.M.	Solar Altitude	Solar Azimuth (from South)
5	7	1.47	117.57
6	6	12.86	109.78
7	5	24.80	102.54
8	4	37.07	95.28
9	3	49.49	87.10
10	2	61.79	76.00
11	1	73.17	55.11
12		79.45	0.00

March 21, Sept. 24 A.M.	P.M.	Solar Altitude	Solar Azimuth (from South)
6	6	0.00	90.00
7	5	12.39	81.48
8	4	24.49	72.11
9	3	35.89	60.79
10	2	45.89	45.92
11	1	53.21	25.60
12		56.00	0.00

December 22 A.M.	P.M.	Solar Altitude	Solar Azimuth (from South)
8	4	9.08	53.57
9	3	18.38	43.12
10	2	25.86	30.65
11	1	30.81	16.05
12		32.55	0.00

Lumen Method: Table 1

38° N. Latitude

June 22 A.M.	P.M.	Solar Altitude	Solar Azimuth (from South)
5	7	3.32	118.42
6	6	14.18	108.87
7	5	25.60	100.70
8	4	37.33	92.25
9	3	49.13	82.47
10	2	60.58	69.06
11	1	70.61	45.67
12		75.45	0.00

42° N. Latitude

June 22 A.M.	P.M.	Solar Altitude	Solar Azimuth (from South)
5	7	5.15	117.16
6	6	15.44	107.87
7	5	26.28	98.78
8	4	37.38	89.19
9	3	48.45	77.96
10	2	58.95	62.79
11	1	67.64	38.62
12		71.45	0.00

46° N. Latitude

June 22 A.M.	P.M.	Solar Altitude	Solar Azimuth (from South)
5	7	6.97	116.78
6	6	16.63	106.77
7	5	26.82	96.80
8	4	37.22	86.15
9	3	47.47	73.66
10	2	56.95	57.25
11	1	64.40	33.33
12		67.45	0.00

Lumen Method: Table 1

38° N. Latitude

March 21, Sept. 24 A.M.	P.M.	Solar Altitude	Solar Azimuth (from South)
6	6	0.00	90.00
7	5	11.77	80.63
8	4	23.20	70.43
9	3	33.86	58.38
10	2	43.03	42.16
11	1	49.57	23.52
12		62.00	0.00

December 22 A.M.	P.M.	Solar Altitude	Solar Azimuth (from South)
8	4	6.69	53.12
9	3	15.44	42.30
10	2	22.40	29.75
11	1	26.96	15.45
12		28.55	0.00

42° N. Latitude

March 21, Sept. 24 A.M.	P.M.	Solar Altitude	Solar Azimuth (from South)
6	6	0.00	90.00
7	5	11.09	79.84
8	4	21.81	68.88
9	3	31.70	57.81
10	2	40.06	40.79
11	1	45.88	21.82
12		48.00	0.00

December 22 A.M.	P.M.	Solar Altitude	Solar Azimuth (from South)
8	4	4.28	52.82
9	3	12.46	41.63
10	2	18.91	29.01
11	1	23.09	14.96
12		24.55	0.00

46° N. Latitude

March 21, Sept. 24 A.M.	P.M.	Solar Altitude	Solar Azimuth (from South)
6	6	0.00	90.00
7	5	10.36	79.09
8	4	20.32	67.45
9	3	29.42	54.27
10	2	36.98	38.75
11	1	42.14	20.43
12		44.00	0.00

December 22 A.M.	P.M.	Solar Altitude	Solar Azimuth (from South)
8	4	1.86	52.65
9	3	9.46	41.12
10	2	15.41	28.41
11	1	19.23	14.56
12		20.55	0.00

Lumen Method: Table 1

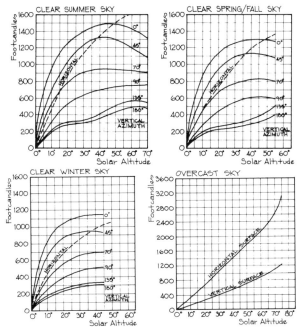

Lumen Method: Table 2
Source: Libbey-Owens-Ford Company, Toledo, Ohio

Lumen Method: Table 3
Source: Libbey-Owens-Ford Company, Toledo, Ohio

215

Glass	Thickness in.	Thickness mm.	Transmittance Average Daylight %	Transmittance Total Solar %
Sheet	SS	2.5	90	85
	DS 3	3	89	80
	3/16	5	89	78
Clear	1/8	3	89	80
	3/16	5	88	78
	1/4	6	87	75
	5/16	8	86	70
Clear Heavy duty	3/8	10	84	67
	1/2	12	82	61
	5/8	15	80	56
	3/4	19	78	51
	7/8	22	75	48
Blue-green	1/8	3	83	63
	3/16	5	79	55
	1/4	6	75	47
Grey	1/8	3	61	63
	3/16	5	51	53
	1/4	6	44	46
	5/16	8	35	38
	3/8	10	28	31
	1/2	12	19	22
Bronze	1/8	3	68	65
	3/16	5	59	55
	1/4	6	52	49
	5/16	8	44	40
	3/8	10	38	34
	1/2	12	28	24

Monolithic Glass Clear and Tinted

Lumen Method: Table 4
Source: Libbey-Owens-Ford Company, Toledo, Ohio

Glass	Thickness in.	Thickness mm.	Transmittance Average Daylight %	Transmittance Total Solar %
Clear	1/8	3	80	69
	3/16	5	79	52
	1/4	6	77	59
Blue-green	1/8	3	75	52
	3/16	5	70	43
	1/4	6	66	36
Grey	1/8	3	55	52
	3/16	5	45	42
	1/4	6	39	35
Bronze	1/8	3	61	54
	3/16	5	53	43
	1/4	6	46	38

Thermopane Insulating Glass (inboard light clear)

Lumen Method: Table 4
Source: Libbey-Owens-Ford Company, Toledo, Ohio

Glass	Thickness in.	Thickness mm.	Vari-Tran Coating Color	Vari-Tran Coating Number	Transmittance Average Daylight % Tol	Transmittance Total Solar %
Clear	1/4	6	Silver	1–108	8 ± 1.5	9
				1–114	14 ± 2.0	15
				1–120	20 ± 2.5	19
	1/4	6	Golden	1–208	8 ± 1.5	8
				1–214	14 ± 2.0	13
				2–220	20 ± 2.5	20

Laminated Safety Glass with Vari-Tran Coating

Lumen Method: Table 4
Source: Libbey-Owens-Ford Company, Toledo, Ohio

Glass	Thickness		Vari-Tran Coating		Transmittance	
Clear	1/4	6	Silver	1–108	8 ± 1.5	9
				1–114	14 ± 2.0	16
				1–120	20 ± 2.5	20
	1/4	6	Golden	1–208	8 ± 1.5	9
				1–214	14 ± 2.0	14
				1–220	20 ± 2.5	21
B-Green	1/4	6	Blue	2–350	50 ± 5.0	35
Grey Tuf-Flex	1/4	6	Grey	3–108	8 ± 1.5	11
				3–114	14 ± 2.0	17
				3–120	20 ± 2.5	24
Grey	1/4	6		3–134	34 ± 4.0	36
Bronze Tuf-Flex	1/4	6	Bronze	4–108	8 ± 1.5	9
				4–114	14 ± 2.0	14
				4–120	20 ± 2.5	20
Bronze	1/4	6		4–134	34 ± 4.0	31

Monolithic Glass with Vari-Tran Coating

Lumen Method: Table 4
Source: Libbey-Owens-Ford Company, Toledo, Ohio

Glass	Thickness		Vari-Tran Coating		Transmittance	
Clear	1	25	Silver	1–108	7 ± 1.5	7
				1–114	13 ± 2.0	14
				1–120	18 ± 2.5	16
	1	25	Golden	1–208	7 ± 1.5	7
				1–214	13 ± 2.0	12
				1–220	18 ± 2.5	17
Blue-green	1	25	Blue	2–350	45 ± 5.0	28
				2–350–2	38 ± 5.0	20
Grey Tuf-Flex	1	25	Grey	3–108	7 ± 1.5	9
				3–114	13 ± 2.0	14
				3–120	18 ± 2.5	20
Grey	1	25		3–134	30 ± 4.0	29
Bronze Tuf-Flex	1	25	Bronze	4–108	7 ± 1.5	7
				4–114	13 ± 2.0	11
				4–120	18 ± 2.5	15
Bronze	1	25		4–134	30 ± 4.0	25

Thermopane with Vari-Tran Coating

Lumen Method: Table 4
Source: Libbey-Owens-Ford Company, Toledo, Ohio

Coefficient of Utilization (C)
Overcast Sky

Room Length		20'		30'		40'	
Wall Reflectance		**70%**	**30%**	**70%**	**30%**	**70%**	**30%**
	Room Width						
Max	20'	.0276	.0251	.0191	.0173	.0143	.0137
	30'	.0272	.0248	.0188	.0172	.0137	.0131
	40'	.0269	.0246	.0182	.0171	.0133	.0130
Mid	20'	.0159	.0117	.0101	.0087	.0081	.0071
	30'	.0058	.0050	.0054	.0040	.0034	.0033
	40'	.0039	.0027	.0030	.0023	.0022	.0019
Min	20'	.0087	.0053	.0063	.0043	.0050	.0037
	30'	.0032	.0019	.0029	.0017	.0020	.0014
	40'	.0019	.0009	.0016	.0009	.0012	.0008

C_{os} Coefficients of utilization (C) for room length and width, illuminated by overcast sky.

Lumen Method: Table 5
Source: Libbey-Owens-Ford Company, Toledo, Ohio

Coefficient of Utilization (C)
Clear Sky

Room Length		20'		30'		40'	
Wall Reflectance		**70%**	**30%**	**70%**	**30%**	**70%**	**30%**
	Room Width						
Max	20'	.0206	.0173	.0143	.0123	.0110	.0098
	30'	.0203	.0173	.0137	.0120	.0098	.0092
	40'	.0200	.0168	.0131	.0119	.0096	.0091
Mid	20'	.0153	.0104	.0100	.0079	.0083	.0067
	30'	.0082	.0054	.0062	.0043	.0046	.0037
	40'	.0052	.0032	.0040	.0028	.0029	.0023
Min	20'	.0106	.0060	.0079	.0049	.0067	.0043
	30'	.0054	.0028	.0047	.0023	.0032	.0021
	40'	.0031	.0014	.0027	.0013	.0021	.0012

C_{cs} Coefficients of utilization (C) for room length and width, illuminated by clear sky (with or without direct sun).

Lumen Method: Table 5
Source: Libbey-Owens-Ford Company, Toledo, Ohio

Coefficient of Utilization (C)
Ground

Room Length		20'		30'		40'	
Wall Reflectance		**70%**	**30%**	**70%**	**30%**	**70%**	**30%**
	Room Width						
Max	20'	.0147	.0112	.0102	.0088	.0081	.0071
	30'	.0141	.0112	.0098	.0088	.0077	.0070
	40'	.0137	.0112	.0093	.0086	.0072	.0069
Mid	20'	.0128	.0090	.0094	.0071	.0073	.0060
	30'	.0083	.0057	.0062	.0048	.0050	.0041
	40'	.0055	.0037	.0044	.0033	.0042	.0026
Min	20'	.0106	.0071	.0082	.0054	.0067	.0044
	30'	.0051	.0026	.0041	.0023	.0033	.0021
	40'	.0029	.0018	.0026	.0012	.0022	.0011

C_{ug} Coefficients of utilization (C) for room length and width, illuminated by uniform ground light.

Lumen Method: Table 5
Source: Libbey-Owens-Ford Company, Toledo, Ohio

218

Coefficient of Utilization (C)
Diffuse Shade
Sky

Room Length		20'		30'		40'	
Wall Reflectance		70%	30%	70%	30%	70%	30%
	Room Width						
Max	20'	.0247	.0217	.0174	.0152	.0128	.0120
	30'	.0241	.0214	.0166	.0151	.0120	.0116
	40'	.0237	.0212	.0161	.0150	.0118	.0113
Mid	20'	.0169	.0122	.0110	.0092	.0089	.0077
	30'	.0078	.0060	.0067	.0048	.0044	.0041
	40'	.0053	.0033	.0039	.0028	.0029	.0024
Min	20'	.0108	.0066	.0080	.0052	.0063	.0047
	30'	.0047	.0026	.0042	.0023	.0029	.0020
	40'	.0027	.0013	.0022	.0012	.0018	.0011

C_{us} Coefficients of utilization (C) for room length and width, illuminated by uniform sky light through diffuse window shade.

Lumen Method: Table 5
Source: Libbey-Owens-Ford Company, Toledo, Ohio

Ground

Room Length		20'		30'		40'	
Wall Reflectance		70%	30%	70%	30%	70%	30%
	Room Width						
Max	20'	.0147	.0112	.0102	.0088	.0081	.0071
	30'	.0141	.0112	.0098	.0088	.0077	.0070
	40'	.0137	.0112	.0093	.0086	.0072	.0069
Mid	20'	.0128	.0090	.0094	.0071	.0073	.0060
	30'	.0083	.0057	.0062	.0048	.0050	.0041
	40'	.0055	.0037	.0044	.0033	.0042	.0026
Min	20'	.0106	.0071	.0082	.0054	.0067	.0044
	30'	.0051	.0026	.0041	.0023	.0033	.0021
	40'	.0029	.0018	.0026	.0012	.0022	.0011

C_{ug} Coefficients of utilization for room length and width, illuminated by uniform ground light through diffuse window shade.

Lumen Method: Table 5
Source: Libbey-Owens-Ford Company, Toledo, Ohio

Coefficient of Utilization (C)
Horizontal Louvers
Sky

Room Length		20'		30'		40'	
Wall Reflectance		70%	30%	70%	30%	70%	30%
	Room Width						
Max	20'	.0556	.0556	.0392	.0397	.0298	.0317
	30'	.0522	.0533	.0367	.0389	.0278	.0311
	40'	.0506	.0528	.0359	.0381	.0270	.0306
Mid	20'	.0556	.0556	.0418	.0411	.0320	.0364
	30'	.0372	.0339	.0278	.0286	.0220	.0256
	40'	.0217	.0211	.0192	.0186	.0139	.0164
Min	20'	.0556	.0556	.0422	.0456	.0320	.0409
	30'	.0294	.0233	.0222	.0203	.0189	.0194
	40'	.0139	.0110	.0133	.0108	.0120	.0100

C_{sv} Coefficients of utilization (C) for room length and width, illuminated by sun and sky through horizontal louvers.

Lumen Method: Table 5
Source: Libbey-Owens-Ford Company, Toledo, Ohio

Ground

Room Length		20'		30'		40'	
Wall Reflectance		70%	30%	70%	30%	70%	30%
	Room Width						
Max	20'	.0556	.0556	.0392	.0426	.0303	.0348
	30'	.0528	.0539	.0370	.0433	.0289	.0337
	40'	.0506	.0544	.0359	.0426	.0278	.0344
Mid	20'	.0556	.0556	.0414	.0459	.0320	.0381
	30'	.0367	.0356	.0274	.0308	.0217	.0270
	40'	.0239	.0233	.0192	.0222	.0153	.0181
Min	20'	.0556	.0556	.0430	.0486	.0328	.0398
	30'	.0261	.0228	.0217	.0211	.0170	.0192
	40'	.0128	.0108	.0119	.0107	.0098	.0097

C_{gv} Coefficients of utilization for room length and width, illuminated by ground light through horizontal louvers.
Lumen Method: Table 5
Source: Libbey-Owens-Ford Company, Toledo, Ohio

Coefficient of Utilization (K)
Overcast Sky

Ceiling Ht.		8'		10'		12'		14'	
Wall Reflectance		70%	30%	70%	30%	70%	30%	70%	30%
	Room Width								
Max	20'	.1250	.1290	.1210	.1230	.1110	.1110	.0991	.0973
	30'	.1220	.1310	.1220	.1210	.1110	.1110	.0945	.0973
	40'	.1450	.1330	.1310	.1260	.1110	.1110	.0973	.0982
Mid	20'	.0908	.0982	.1070	.1150	.1110	.1110	.1050	.1220
	30'	.1560	.1020	.0939	.1130	.1110	.1110	.1210	.1340
	40'	.1060	.0948	.1230	.1070	.1110	.1110	.1350	.1270
Min	20'	.0908	.1020	.0951	.1140	.1110	.1110	.1180	.1340
	30'	.0924	.1190	.1010	.1140	.1110	.1110	.1250	.1260
	40'	.1110	.0926	.1250	.1090	.1110	.1110	.1330	.1300

K_{os} Coefficients of utilization (K) for ceiling height and room width, illuminated by overcast sky.
Lumen Method: Table 6
Source: Libbey-Owens-Ford Company, Toledo, Ohio

Coefficient of Utilization (K)
Clear Sky

Ceiling Ht.		8'		10'		12'		14'	
Wall Reflectance		70%	30%	70%	30%	70%	30%	70%	30%
	Room Width								
Max	20'	.1450	.1550	.1290	.1320	.1110	.1110	.1010	.0982
	30'	.1410	.1490	.1250	.1300	.1110	.1110	.0954	.1010
	40'	.1570	.1570	.1350	.1340	.1110	.1110	.0964	.0991
Mid	20'	.1100	.1280	.1160	.1260	.1110	.1110	.1030	.1080
	30'	.1060	.1250	.1110	.1290	.1110	.1110	.1120	.1200
	40'	.1170	.1180	.1220	.1180	.1110	.1110	.1230	.1220
Min	20'	.1050	.1290	.1120	.1300	.1110	.1110	.1110	.1160
	30'	.0994	.1440	.1070	.1260	.1110	.1110	.1070	.1240
	40'	.1190	.1160	.1300	.1180	.1110	.1110	.1200	.1180

K_{cs} Coefficients of utilization (K) for ceiling height and room width, illuminated by clear sky (with or without direct sun).
Lumen Method: Table 6
Source: Libbey-Owens-Ford Company, Toledo, Ohio

Ceiling Ht.		8'		10'		12'		14'	
Wall Reflectance		70%	30%	70%	30%	70%	30%	70%	30%
	Room Width								
Max	20'	.1240	.2060	.1400	.1350	.1110	.1110	.0909	.0859
	30'	.1820	.1880	.1400	.1430	.1110	.1110	.0918	.0878
	40'	.1240	.1820	.1400	.1420	.1110	.1110	.0936	.0879
Mid	20'	.1230	.1450	.1220	.1290	.1110	.1110	.1000	.0945
	30'	.0966	.1040	.1070	.1120	.1110	.1110	.1100	.1050
	40'	.0790	.0786	.0999	.1060	.1110	.1110	.1180	.1180
Min	20'	.0994	.1080	.1100	.1140	.1110	1110	.1070	.1040
	30'	.0816	.0822	.0984	.1050	.1110	.1110	.1210	.1160
	40'	.0700	.0656	.0946	.0986	.1110	.1110	.1250	.1320

K_{ug} Coefficients of utilization (K) for ceiling height and room width, illuminated by uniform ground light.
Lumen Method: Table 6

Source: Libbey-Owens-Ford Company, Toledo, Ohio

Ceiling Ht.		8'		10'		12'		14'	
Wall Reflectance		70%	30%	70%	30%	70%	30%	70%	30%
	Room Width								
Max	20'	.1450	.1540	.1230	.1280	.1110	.1110	.0991	.0964
	30'	.1410	.1510	.1260	.1280	.1110	.1110	.0945	.0964
	40'	.1590	.1570	.1370	.1270	.1110	.1110	.0973	.0964
Mid	20'	.1010	.1160	.1150	.1250	.1110	.1110	.1010	.1100
	30'	.0952	.1130	.1050	.1220	.1110	.1110	.1100	.1220
	40'	.1110	.1050	.1240	.1070	.1110	.1110	.1300	.1240
Min	20'	.0974	.1110	.1070	.1210	.1110	.1110	.1120	.1190
	30'	.0956	.1250	.1030	.1170	.1110	.1110	.1150	.1250
	40'	.1110	.1050	.1250	.1110	.1110	.1110	.1330	.1240

K_{us} Coefficients of utilization (K) for ceiling height and room width, illuminated by uniform sky light through diffuse window shade.
Lumen Method: Table 6

Source: Libbey-Owens-Ford Company, Toledo, Ohio

Ceiling Ht.		8'		10'		12'		14'	
Wall Reflectance		70%	30%	70%	30%	70%	30%	70%	30%
	Room Width								
MAX	20'	.1240	.2060	.1400	.1350	.111	.111	.0909	.0859
	30'	.1820	.1880	.1400	.1430	.111	.111	.0918	.0878
	40'	.1240	.1820	.1400	.1420	.111	.111	.0936	.0879
MID	20'	.1230	.1450	.1220	.1290	.111	.111	.1000	.0945
	30'	.0966	.1040	.1070	.1120	.111	.111	.1100	.1050
	40'	.0790	.0786	.0999	.1060	.111	.111	.1180	
MIN	20'	.0994	.1080	.1100	.1140	.111	.111	.1070	.1040
	30'	.0816	.0822	.0984	.1050	.111	.111	.1210	.1160
	40'	.0700	.0656	.0946	.0986	.111	.111	.1250	.1320

K_{ug} Coefficients of utilization (K) for ceiling height and room width, illuminated by uniform ground light through diffuse window shade.
Lumen Method: Table 6

Source: Libbey-Owens-Ford Company, Toledo, Ohio.

Coefficient of Utilization (K)
Horizontal Louvers
Sky

Ceiling Ht.		8'		10'		12'		14'	
Wall Reflectance		70%	30%	70%	30%	70%	30%	70%	30%
	Room Width								
Max		.1540	.1700	.1290	.1310	.1070	.1120	.0910	.0910
Mid	20'	.1000	.1060	.1010	.1060	.0990	.1020	.0910	.0910
	30'	.0740	.0800	.0860	.0900	.0910	.0930	.0910	.0910
	40'	.0700	.0740	.0790	.0840	.0880	.0910	.0910	.0910
Min	20'	.0800	.0800	.0910	.0910	.0930	.0930	.0910	.0910
	30'	.0680	.0680	.0790	.0790	.0870	.0870	.0910	.0910
	40'	.0640	.0640	.0760	.0760	.0840	.0840	.0910	.0910

K_{sv} Coefficients of utilization (K) for ceiling height and room width, illuminated by sun and sky through horizontal louvers.
Lumen Method: Table 6

Source: Libbey-Owens-Ford Company, Toledo, Ohio

Ground

Ceiling Ht.		8'		10'		12'		14'	
Wall Reflectance		70%	30%	70%	30%	70%	30%	70%	30%
	Room Width								
Max		.1740	.2000	.1420	.1570	.1170	.1230	.0910	.0910
Mid	20'	.1040	.1160	.1100	.1210	.1060	.1120	.0910	.0910
	30'	.0740	.0820	.0920	.0990	.0990	.1060	.0910	.0910
	40'	.0580	.0620	.0790	.0830	.0920	.0960	.0910	.0910
Min	20'	.0780	.0820	.0930	.0970	.0990	.1020	.0910	.0910
	30'	.0580	.0600	.0740	.0760	.0900	.0920	.0910	.0910
	40'	.0520	.0560	.0700	.0710	.0860	.0870	.0910	.0910

K_{gv} Coefficients of utilization for ceiling height and room width, illuminated by ground light through horizontal louvers.
Lumen Method: Table 6

Source: Libbey-Owens-Ford Company, Toledo, Ohio

Location: Kansas City, Missouri (38°N)

Average Ground Reflectance: 6%

Floor Area: 480 square feet

Height of window: 7 feet

Width of window: 24 feet

Room width: 20 feet

Room length: 24 feet

Ceiling height: 12 feet

Point of illumination: Min (5 feet from back of wall)

Time of day: 12:00 p.m.

1. Solar Altitude = 75.45° from table 1.
2. Ekw = 1200 fc from table 2 for overcast sky
Ekg = 3100 fc from table 2 for overcast sky.
3. Euw = 0, overcast sky
Eug = 0, overcast sky
Ekug = Ekg + Eug = 3100 + 0 = 3100 fc
Ekuw = Ekw + Euw = 1200 + 0 = 1200 fc.
4. Egw = Ekug × 0.06 × 0.50 = 3100 × 0.06 × 0.50 = 93 fc.
5. Ag = 24 feet × 7 feet = 168 sq. ft.
Tg = 0.50
6. Floor area = 480 sq. ft.

Reflectance = 0.50
C = 0.0063 for overcast sky (by interpolation) from table 5
C = 0.0081 for ground (by interpolation) from table 5
K = 0.111 for overcast sky from table 6
K = 0.111 for ground from table 6
7. Ekwp = Ekuw × Ag × Tg × C × K
Ekwp = 1200 × 168 × 0.50 × 0.0063 × 0.111
Ekwp = 71 fc.

Egwp = Egw × Ag × Tg × C × K
Egwp = 93 × 168 × 0.50 × 0.0081 × 0.111
Egwp = 7 fc.
8. Total illumination on work plane
= Ekwp + Egwp
= 71 + 7
= 78 fc.

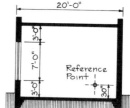
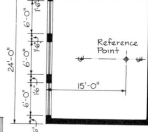

Sample Problem

Daylight Factors Method

The *Daylight Factors Method* delivers a factor—dependent on such variables as floor area, height of windows above reference plane, width of window, area of glass, and perpendicular horizontal distance of reference point from window, — which is multiplied by the available daylight to determine the amount of light reaching the work surface.

☐ The Daylight Factor Method is as follows. For uniform layout of *toplighting*, Average Daylight Factor (DF) (%) =

$$\frac{(F) \times (u) \times (Ag)}{Af}$$

Where:

F = the window factor, given the amount of skylight incident on the roof. F is equal to 1 for an unobstructed site.

u = the coefficient of utilization—ratio of light reaching the reference plane.

Ag = area of glazing

Af = area of floor

U Values	Average Interior Reflectance	
	50%	20%
Horizontal to 30°		
Monitors	0.4	0.3
Monitors at 60°	0.25	0.2
Vertical Monitors	0.15-0.2	0.1-0.15

Coefficients of Utilization

For *sidelighting*, Daylight Factor (DF)(%) = (Sky Component) + (Internal Reflective Component) =

$$\frac{10\, WH^2}{D\,(D^2 + H^2)} + \frac{4\, GR}{F\,(1 - R)}$$

Where:

F = floor area

H = height of window above reference plane (distance from reference plane to top of window)

W = width of window

D = perpendicular horizontal distance of reference point from window

G = net area of glass

R = reflectance of walls in % (typically, a ceiling is 75%; floor and furniture, 15%, walls, 50%)

☐ The daylight factor is multiplied by the available exterior illumination on a horizontal surface from the light intensity graphs to get the daylight illumination in footcandles. It is important to note that the daylight factor method was developed for overcast sky conditions. The available exterior illumination during cloudy or overcast sky conditions should be used. This will give the minimum daylighting that is available, thus allowing the designer to understand the maximum artificial lighting that will be needed.

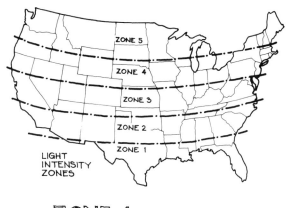

LIGHT
INTENSITY
ZONES

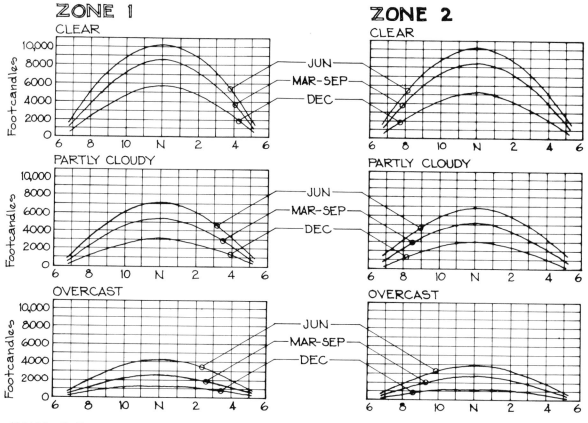

ZONE 1

CLEAR

JUN
MAR-SEP
DEC

PARTLY CLOUDY

JUN
MAR-SEP
DEC

OVERCAST

JUN
MAR-SEP
DEC

ZONE 2

CLEAR

PARTLY CLOUDY

OVERCAST

Light Intensity Zones
Source: Naturalite, Inc., Dallas, Texas

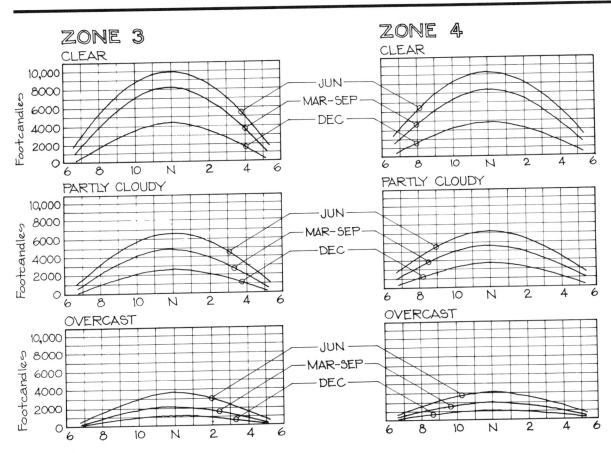

Light Intensity Zones
Source: Naturalite, Inc., Dallas, Texas

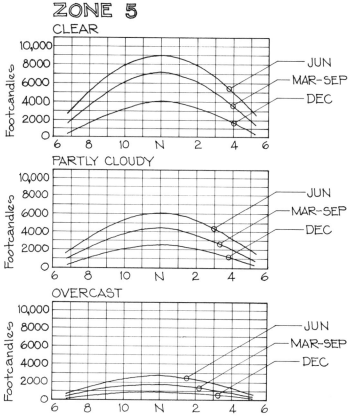

ZONE 5

CLEAR

— JUN
— MAR-SEP
— DEC

PARTLY CLOUDY

— JUN
— MAR-SEP
— DEC

OVERCAST

— JUN
— MAR-SEP
— DEC

Light Intensity Zones
Source: Naturalite, Inc., Dallas, Texas

Location:	**Kansas City, Missouri (zone 3)**
Floor Area (F):	**480 square feet**
Height (H) of window above reference plane:	**7 feet**
Width (W) of window:	**24 feet**
Distance of Reference Point from Window (D):	**15 feet**
Net Area of Glass (G):	**168 square feet**
Reflectance (R):	**50 percent**

Daylight Factor =

$$\frac{10 \ WH^2}{D \ (D^2 + H^2)} + \frac{4 \ GR}{F \ (1 - R)}$$

$$= \frac{10 \ (24 \times 7^2)}{15 \ (15^2 + 7^2)} + \frac{4 \ (168 \times 0.50)}{480 \ (1 - 0.50)}$$

$$= 4.26\%$$

For overcast days at noon during:

June	= 3800 × 0.04 =	**152 fc**
March-Sept.	= 2000 × 0.04 =	**80 fc**
December	= 1000 × 0.04 =	**40 fc**

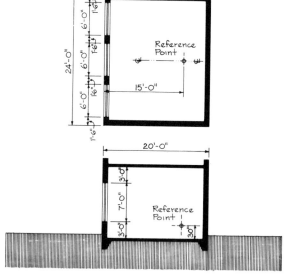

Sample Problem

Economic Analysis

Natural daylighting in place of artificial lighting in a building may increase capital costs. Additional or more sophisticated luminaire controls (e.g., manual or automated dimming or on/off switches), and additional glazing and other design requirements (e.g., clerestories) are the most obvious extra costs of daylighting. Heating loads in winter can grow because of reduced internal heat gain from luminaires—although this can be offset by solar heat gain through increased glazing. And, cooling loads in summertime can be increased if this glazing is not adequately shaded.

☐ On the other hand, savings from daylighting can be considerable. Daylighting not only lowers electricity consumption, it also reduces summer cooling loads—a major energy user—because of reduced heat gain from luminaires.

☐ Life-cycle cost/benefit analysis considers both the initial and long-term costs of daylighting designs. For daylighting, the analysis focuses on savings in electricity for lights, increased heating loads in winter and reduced cooling loads in summer.

☐ Although life-cycle cost/benefit analysis cannot be dealt with comprehensively here, the following sample problem indicates how it can be used.

A physical model of an office building shows that 50 footcandles of illumination on the work surface is available up to 15 feet away from the south window wall when the illumination on the vertical, southfacing facade is 2,400 footcandles. The building is occupied 8:00 A.M. to 5:00 P.M., 5 days a week, 12 months a year. When there is a level of 50 footcandles of illumination on the work plane, all perimeter lighting (30 percent of the building's total) will turn off. The lighting fixtures are all located in a 15-foot band next to the window wall.

Using the Libbey-Owens-Ford Sun Angle Calculator for the required latitude (in this case Denver, Colorado, 40 degrees N. Lat.), for the 21st day of each month between the hours of 8:00 A.M. and 5:00 P.M. (hours of occupancy for the office building), determine the altitude and azimuth of the sun in relation to a south-facing facade. From the illumination curves by Libbey-Owens-Ford the illumination on the vertical south-facing wall can be determined for each month for clear sky and for solar illumination. This information can be charted as shown for each hour examined.

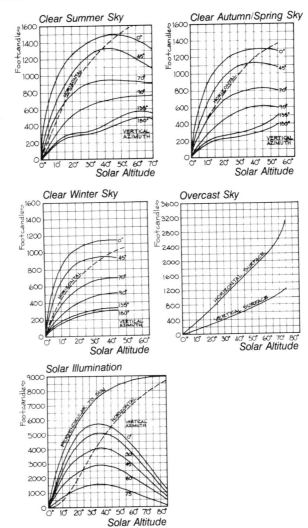

Illumination Graphs
Source: Libbey-Owens-Ford Company, Toledo, Ohio

Graphs for predicting the illumination on the horizontal and vertical surfaces under various types of skies. Illumination from the sun is considered separately.

		9:00 A.M.				
		True Alt. Degrees	Azimuth Degrees	F.C. (Sky)	F.C. (Sun)	F.C. (Total)
Winter	Dec 21	14	42	790	3000	3790
	Jan 21	17	44	810	2900	3710
Spring	Feb 21	24	50	900	3200	4100
	Mar 21	33	58	925	3100	4025
	Apr 21	41	68	810	2100	2910
Summer	May 21	45	77	840	1210	2050
	Jun 21	48	80	810	1200	2010

Denver, Colorado; 40° N. Lat.
South Facing Vertical Glazing
Illumination Values—Sample Problem

Then, the total footcandles available on the south-facing wall for each hour of office occupancy for the 21st day of each month can be recorded. Those hours above and below the 2,400 footcandles that will provide sufficient daylight inside to turn off the artificial perimeter lighting can be distinguished.

	8:00 A.M.	9:00 A.M.	10:00 A.M.	11:00 A.M.	12:00 A.M.	1:00 P.M.	2:00 P.M.	3:00 P.M.	4:00 P.M.
Dec	1370	3790	5110	6110	6950				
Jan	2825	3710	5550	6215	7250				
Feb	2340	4100	5900	6670	7110				
Mar	2090	4025	5250	6140	6500				
Apr	2080	2910	3975	4900	5375				
May	720	2050	3150	3780	4310				
Jun	700	2010	2690	3325	4240				
Jul	720	2050	3150	3780	4310				
Aug	2080	2910	3975	4900	5375				
Sep	2090	4025	5250	6140	6500				
Oct	2340	4100	5900	6670	7110				
Nov	2825	3710	5550	6215	7250				

Denver, Colorado 40° N. Lat.   *Bold line outlines those hours of a typical day for each month during which there is insufficient*
South Facing Vertical Glazing   *daylight to turn off artificial lighting. Right side of chart is symmetrical with left side.*

1. Annual hours of operation: 52 weeks × 5 days/week × 9 hours/day = 2,340 hours/year.
2. Vertical illumination on south wall below 2,400 fc: 26 months/hour periods × 20 days (4 weeks) per month = 520 hours/year.
3. Vertical illumination on south wall above 2,400 fc: 2,340 − 520 − 1,820 hours/year.

Finally, this result can be adjusted on the basis of NOAA's LCD data on sky cover (see section on climate data). The LCD data on average number of clear, partly cloudy and overcast days per month show that the sky is overcast 34 percent of the time and partly cloudy 31 percent of the time.

	% Possible Sun	Mean Sky Cover Sunrise-Sunset (Hrs.)	Sunrise to Sunset (Days)		
			Clear	Partly Cloudy	Overcast
Jan	72	5.4	11	7	13
Feb	80	5.6	12	4	13
Mar	79	5.1	10	13	8
Apr	66	6.5	6	11	13
May	65	7.0	5	9	17
Jun	77	4.7	12	13	5
Jul	75	4.8	11	15	5
Aug	73	5.2	10	12	9
Sep	65	5.8	11	4	15
Oct	78	3.5	17	6	8
Nov	70	5.6	9	9	12
Dec	87	4.4	14	9	8
Year	74	5.3	128	112	126
Percent			35%	31%	34%

Sky Cover—Sample Problem

4. Hours of daylighting lost under overcast sky: 1,820 − (34% × 1,820) = 1,201 hours/year remaining.

5. Hours of daylighting lost under partly cloudy sky: 1,201 − (31% × 50% × 1,201) = 1,015 hours/year remaining. (It is assumed that 50 percent of hours of partly cloudy skies are above 2,400 fc and 50 percent below.)

This is a conservative estimate because it does not consider ground illumination and on overcast days there is probably enough illumination to turn off the lights.

Thus, daylighting can supply the perimeter's lighting needs 1,015 hours of the annual 2,340 operating hours, or 43 percent. This result, when considered with the reduced cooling and increased heating of natural compared to artificial lighting, gives the total difference in energy consumption between this daylighted building and one without daylighting. By comparing costs and benefits over the life of the building and its daylighted alternative, the designer can determine the wisdom of an extra investment in daylighting.

The Corcoran Art Gallery
Washington, D.C.

The design of this art museum replicates the top-lighting oculus of the Pantheon, including the exposed structural ribbing, which serves to reflect and diffuse the daylight.

HVAC SYSTEMS

Introduction

Fifty years ago, the American Society of Heating and Ventilating Engineers (ASHRAE) defined comfort airconditioning as "the process of treating air so as to control simultaneously its temperature, humidity, cleanliness and distribution." As buildings have become more complex and varied, HVAC systems have become more precise and refined—but their basic goal remains the same. This monograph seeks to provide a conceptual understanding of HVAC systems and energy conscious design. In analyzing a system's needs, the designer should consider:
—level of energy redundancy
—level of control capability
—flexibility
—appearance
—cost

☐ *Redundancy* refers to the once-prevalent practice of achieving precise temperature control by expending competing energy to condition the same air twice, first to cool it and then to reheat it.

☐ *Control capability* refers to issues such as occupant access to thermostats and operable windows, both during occupied and normally unoccupied periods. Designers should make owners aware that when occupants are given control of thermostats, they also have a responsibility to exercise it sensibly. A number of major conservation successes have paid close attention to occupant use patterns, including feedback and reminder systems.

☐ *Flexibility* refers to the ability to accommodate space rearrangement as well as space functional changes. To determine the extent and value of possible future system changes at the time of original installation is a complex matter.

☐ *Appearance* of both the interior and exterior of a building can be significantly affected by the HVAC system installation. While many of these design problems can be resolved, some systems present more severe architectural design restraints than others.

☐ *System costs* must be addressed both as initial and as annual costs. Cost figures are generally available from local contractors on a dollar/net ton basis for various types of systems.

| System | Cost and Comfort Characteristics | | |
	Installation Cost	Operating Cost	Comfort Performance
Single duct	High	Medium	Medium
Double duct	High	High	High
Multi-zone	Medium	Medium	High
4-pipe	High	Medium	Medium
3-pipe	Medium	High	Low
2-pipe (Fan-coil)	Low	Medium	Low
2-pipe (Induction)	Medium	Medium	Medium
Packaged terminal air conditioner	Low	Medium	Medium

Cost and Comfort Characteristics of HVAC Systems

Psychrometric Fundamentals

The ASHRAE Systems handbook states that the following factors have the greatest effects on human comfort:
—space temperature
—space humidity
—quantity and quality of temperature control
—air motion control
—mean radiant temperature
—noise level
—odor level
—air cleanliness

☐ Of these, temperature and humidity are of fundamental importance. The psychrometric chart graphically represents the interrelation of air temperature and moisture content. This chart is a basic design tool for mechanical engineers and merits considerable attention from all designers. Several terms must be explained before the charts can be fully appreciated.

☐ Of primary importance for HVAC design is the "enthalpy" or total heat content of the air. This quantity is plotted on the psychrometric chart diagonally from lower left to upper right. Enthalpy is the sum of sensible heat and latent heat. Sensible heat is heat represented by the dry-bulb temperature of the air. Dry-bulb temperature is plotted horizontally on the chart.

☐ In contrast to dry-bulb, "wet-bulb temperature" is one of several terms that describes the latent heat content of the air. Wet-bulb temperature is measured by a "sling psychrometer". The two temperatures allow one to determine the relative humidity using the psychrometric chart.

☐ As air heats, its capacity to hold water vapor increases. The amount of moisture in a given volume of air is expressed in either grains or pounds of moisture per pound of dry air (7,000 grains weigh 1 pound). These values for an absolute quantity of moisture, also called specific humidity, are plotted vertically on the psychrometric chart. Air is saturated when it can no longer absorb additional moisture. This

point is referred to as the "saturation point", the "dewpoint", or the condition of "100-percent relative humidity". The dewpoint is quite significant. At this point, if more moisture is added or the air is cooled, as by a cold surface, condensation occurs. An important consideration for architectural or HVAC design, dewpoint affects window design, placement of insulation, vapor barriers and the space required for condensate drain piping for chilled water systems.

From any given point on the chart (e.g., Point C) the dewpoint of the given temperature/moisture combination can be determined by reading horizontally in either direction. The curved line on the far left is the plot of temperature moisture combinations at which wet bulb and dewpoint (100-percent relative humidity) converge.

Given:	84 degrees (F.) (dry bulb)
	68 degrees (F.) (wet bulb)
	Relative Humidity = 45 percent

From the chart one can also determine the following:

59 degrees (F.) = dewpoint
76 grains of moisture
33.5 BTU/lb. of dry air (enthalpy)

Air reaches its dewpoint when it can no longer absorb additional moisture.

☐ "Latent heat" is the quantity of heat required to change water from a liquid to a gas (vapor). This quantity of heat is also called the "heat of vaporization."

☐ Latent heat can involve significant amounts of energy. "One British Thermal Unit (BTU)", by definition, is the quantity of heat required to raise the temperature of one pound of water from 59 to 60 degrees (F.). The heat of vaporization, or the latent heat required to turn that same pound of water into vapor, is 970.3 BTUs—a factor of almost a thousand.

☐ Virtually all cooling technology, and much HVAC design, manipulates these phase changes, and the associated heat transfers, to enhance human comfort.

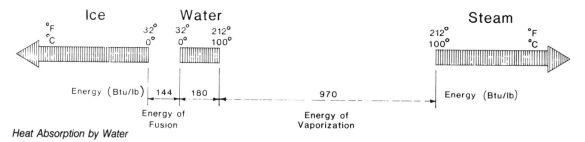

Heat Absorption by Water

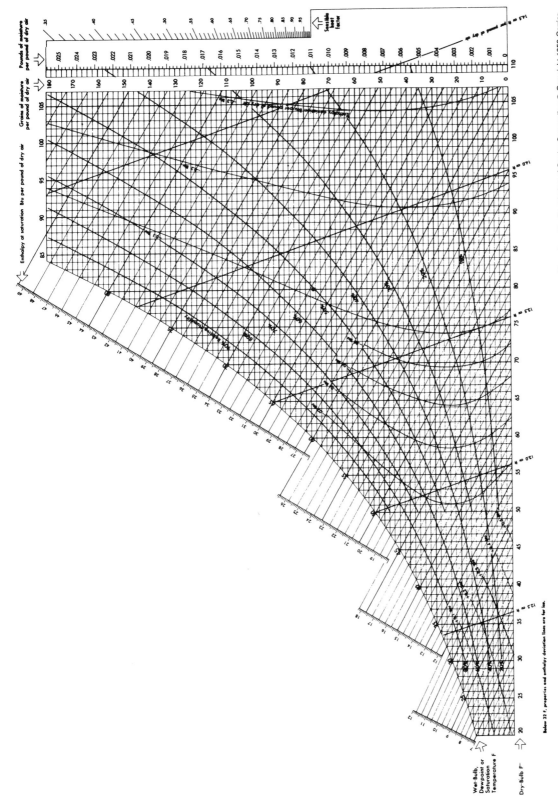

Psychromatic Chart

Reproduced by Permission of Carrier Corporation © Copyright 1959 Carrier Corporation

Psychrometric Chart-Processes

HVAC design begins with the range of temperature-humidity conditions called the human comfort zone. Based on extensive research, HVAC professionals define the human comfort zone as a minimum of 20-percent relative humidity (RH) from 68 to 80 degrees (F.) and a maximum of 80-percent RH from 68 to 75 degrees (F.), decreasing to 50-percent RH at 80 degrees (F.).

☐ The psychrometric chart shows this human comfort zone and the various processes that change the physical properties of air. The environmental systems are the means to accomplish such a change. The designer, by knowing what requirements must be satisfied, can identify the various processes needed in different portions of the system to change temperature-humidity conditions to make them fall within the human comfort zone. It is then possible to determine which space-conditioning techniques can accomplish the necessary results. The process vectors shown on the accompanying psychrometric chart are as follows:

—*Cooling and dehumidification* is accomplished by passing air over a cold surface that has a temperature below the dewpoint of the air.

—*Dehumidification* (only) can be accomplished by passing the cooled, dehumidified air through a heat exchanger to precool incoming air, which in turn heats the outgoing air.

—*Sensible cooling* (only) is accomplished by ensuring that the temperature of the cold surface is above the dewpoint of the air.

—*Evaporative cooling* occurs when water is caused to evaporate into the airstream (the heat of vaporization being removed from the sensible heat content of the air).

—*Humidification* can be accomplished by passing air over warmed water or by spraying either steam or a fine water mist into the airstream.

—*Heating and humidification* is the humidification process with the addition of a hot surface to preheat the air.

—*Heating* (only) is accomplished by simply passing air over a hot surface.

—*Chemical Dehydration or Dehumidification* is accomplished by passing moist air through either beds of various dessicants or filters wetted with moisture-absorbing chemicals. A small decrease in enthalpy is caused by the heat of chemical mixing, but the large increase in sensible heat is caused by the heat of vaporization being released back into the airstream as the moisture condenses.

☐ Plotting the human comfort zone on the psychrometric chart provides a ready indication of possible processes to be pursued. The configuration of the vectors is constant, but the central point is determined by the intersection of dry bulb and wet bulb temperatures of the air, whether it be outside air, return air, or a mixture. In the example, where point A is 80 degrees dry bulb, 50 percent RH or 67 degrees wet bulb, the four vectors that fall into the comfort zone indicate relevant processes—evaporative cooling, sensible cooling, cooling and dehumidification, and dehumidification. Had the center of the vectors fallen at the bottom-left corner of the comfort zone, Point B, the other four processes would be considered.

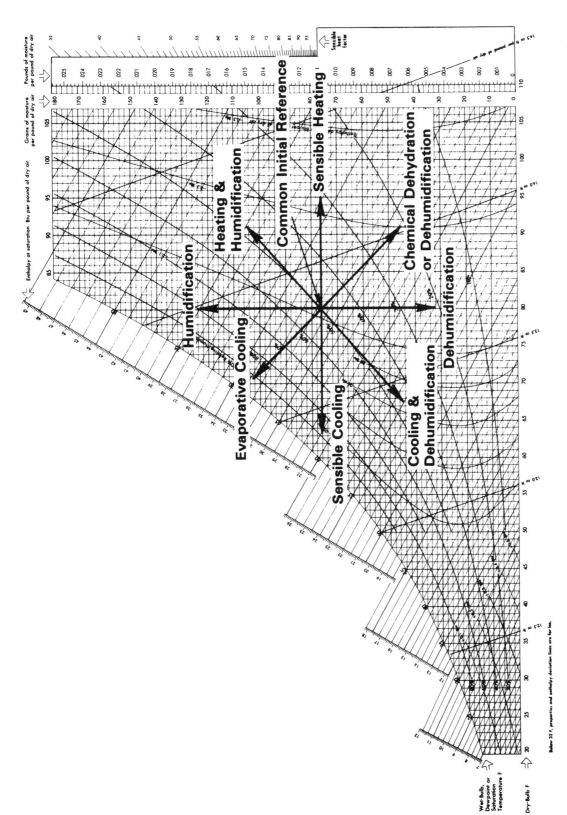

Psychrometric Chart—Processes

William G. Eads, *Testing, Balancing and Adjusting of Environmental Systems*, © 1979. Reprinted by permission of Sheet Metal and Air Conditioning Contractors National Association, Inc., Vienna, Virginia.

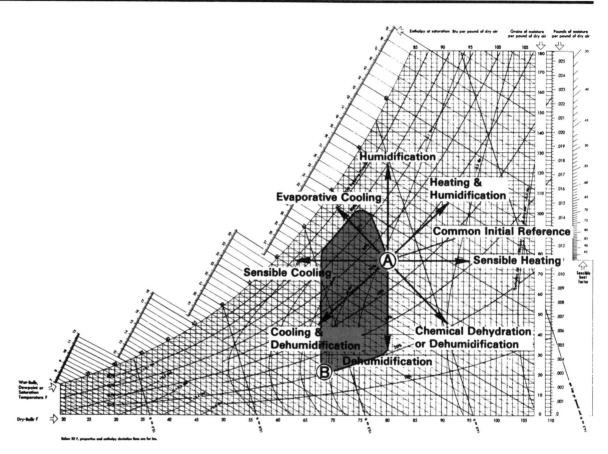

Psychrometric Chart—Processes

The following problem will demonstrate how a designer can use the psychrometric chart. The example describes a cooling load, but a similar process is used for heating systems.

Given:	Supply Air Temperature	55 degrees (F.) dry bulb Point A
	Supply Air Relative humidity	95 percent
	Return Air Temperature	78 degrees (F.) dry bulb Point B
	Return Air Relative humidity	50 percent
	Outside Design Conditions (Summer)	95 degrees (F.) dry bulb Point C
		70 degrees (F.) wet bulb
	Final Air Mixture to be delivered to the space	= 25 percent outside air Point D
		75 percent return air

Point D falls one fourth on the way up the line B-C because 25 percent outside air is used. The total heat to be removed from every pound of dry air can now be determined by the difference of the enthalpy at Point D and Point A.

31.5 BTU/lb.	Point D
−22.6 BTU/lb.	Point A
8.9 BTU/lb.	

As explained earlier, the psychrometric chart plots dry-bulb temperature horizontally and moisture content vertically. Therefore the representative portions of the total heat can be determined using the enthalpy at Point E.

Sensible Heat		= Latent Heat	
28.7 BTU/lb.	Point E	31.5 BTU/lb.	Point D
−22.5 BTU/lb.	Point A	−28.7 BTU/lb.	Point E
6.2 BTU/lb.		2.8 BTU/lb.	

The latent heat portion of the total cooling load (2.8 BTU divided by 8.9 BTU) is therefore 31.5 percent—a very significant portion. The following example is given to further illustrate the use of the

238

psychrometric chart and to emphasize the
significance of latent heat.

If in the previous example 100 percent outside
air was used rather than 25 percent, the total heat
would be considerably larger:

41.4 BTU/lb.	Point C
22.6 BTU/lb.	Point A
18.1 BTU/lb.	Total heat with 100-percent outside air
32.8 BTU/lb.	Point F
22.6 BTU/lb.	Point A
10.2 BTU/lb.	Sensible heat
41.4 BTU/lb.	Point C
32.8 BTU/lb.	Point F
8.6 BTU/lb.	Latent Heat

The latent heat (8.6 BTU/lb. divided by 18.8 BTU/lb.)
now represents 45.7 percent of the total cooling
load.

So far our results have been in BTUs per pound.
To complete the sizing of this mechanical system
the designer must also determine air density and
building volume. This will give the total number of
pounds of air.

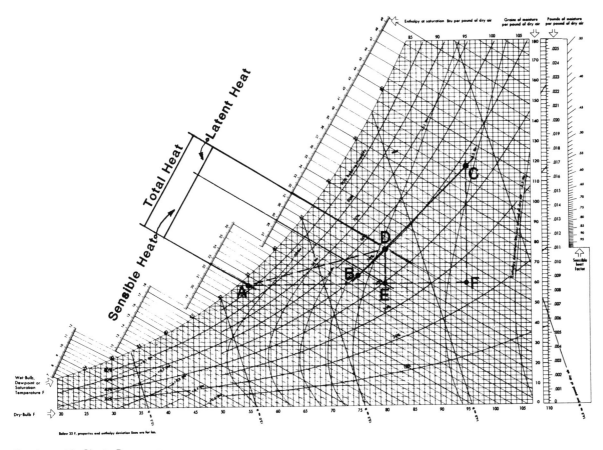

Psychrometric Chart—Processes

Building Types

The selection of a particular HVAC system is influenced by many factors, including economics, design temperatures, physical space availability, the need for maintaining separate thermal temperature zones, the availability of energy (particularly of the source of energy), esthetics, hours of operation and occupancy. Certain air-conditioning systems are appropriate for certain structures. Hospitals, factories, office buildings each tend to use its own type of air-conditioning systems.

Office Buildings

☐ Office buildings should be designed for a shifting tenant occupancy. They should have many independent zones of control and great flexibility to permit rearrangement of these zones as the population shifts. Small one-or-two-story offices can be served by rooftop, packaged, air-cooled units. These lack some flexibility, but the capital cost is low and other types of zoning systems become quite expensive in small increments.

☐ The use of double-duct or multizone units is decreasing. Double-duct systems provide great flexibility, however, both in zoning and in revising the system, and have been widely applied to office structures in the past.

☐ Highrise buildings are frequently served by induction-type systems for the skin and either variable volume or double-duct for the core. Normally, the core of such a structure requires no heat. Induction systems call for a minimum of shaft space and relatively small ducts and pipes. The system can be very flexible and has a great potential for zoning.

☐ Fan-coil units, either two- or four-pipe or water-to-air heat pumps are also suitable for large office buildings. These types may not have the flexibility of the induction system or the double-duct system; however, some of the capital cost can be deferred until tenant space is leased. This advantage is particularly noticeable with heat pumps.

Theaters

☐ Although they need not be zoned for temperature, theaters must be quiet, well-ventilated and low in humidity. They are frequently air-conditioned with single-zoned fan coil units using chilled water or direct expansion refrigeration. This system is not noisy and uses outside air or ventilation. It also has a high dehumidifying capacity essential to theaters where many people assemble in a relatively small space and would create high latent heat loads with air-conditioning.

Factories

☐ Factories are most often single-story structures with a large, clear span height. Most factories are heated and ventilated only, although there is a growing trend toward more comfort cooling. Temperature and humidity in textile and color printing factories must be controlled to maintain production or quality. If, as seems to be the case, workers produce more and make fewer errors in comfort-controlled atmospheres, air-conditioning may be economically feasible in factories. Separate thermal zones, if they exist at all, are usually large and can be handled by independent units. Both large, self-contained air-conditioners and central chilled water plants with fan coils have been effectively used in factories.

Hospitals

☐ Comfort systems for hospitals are under severe regulatory code restrictions. Normally outside air must be used in surgical suites to flush out odors and hazardous vapors. Exhaust openings are usually located near the floor of surgical suites to capture heavy gases, and humidity control is essential because of the presence of static electric discharges that might ignite explosive vapors.

☐ Nurseries, delivery rooms, intensive care areas, and cardiac areas are all subject to special temperature and humidity control requirements.

☐ To keep hazardous organisms from spreading, pressure differentials between different parts of the hospital must be maintained. This is especially important for isolation wards, which are often airconditioned using induction units or individual fan-coil units for each unit. Central air-handling systems can be used for patient areas, provided adequate air filtration is included. Fiberglass ductwork is usually not specified for hospital airconditioning, since duct work provides good breeding grounds for microorganisms.

Schools

☐ As classrooms require separate zoning, they are usually served by fan coil units or heat pumps located in the room under the windows or operated by remote control. Rooms must be adequately ventilated and free of noise.

Stores and Shopping Centers

☐ Some large shopping malls use central water chilling and water heating systems. Individual stores are airconditioned using separate fan-coil units served by chilled and/or hot water for each store. Smaller shopping centers and individual stores that are not a part of a shopping center usually are airconditioned with self-contained rooftop packages. Air distribution is less critical in commercial establishments than in office buildings and hospitals, because shoppers are moving about and are not as sensitive to drafts.

Multi-residential Buildings

☐ Lowrise apartments, of one-to-three stories, can be served from forced-air furnaces located in each apartment, with cooling coming from a remote air-cooled condenser, usually mounted on the roof. Central chilled water plants have been applied to such buildings with individual fan coils for each apartment. Water-to-air heat pumps with a circulating heat sink from which the individual heat pumps can either accept or reject heat have also been successfully applied to apartments.

☐ Highrise structures for housing are most likely to use central water chilling and water heating plants with individual fan-coil units for each apartment. Water-to-air heat pumps are also a suitable choice.

☐ Every tenant expects to control the heating and air-conditioning of his own apartment—not only the precise temperature, but also the hours of operation.

Detached Single-Family Residences

☐ Most detached residences are heated with forced air furnaces that force air through a direct expansion cooling coil. This coil is connected by refrigerant piping to a remote air-cooled condensing unit to furnish the cooling. In larger residences, it is often desirable to separate the house into separate zones, usually into sleeping areas and living areas. The possibility of a natural gas shortage has induced many designers to use heat pumps for heating and cooling of residences, and this trend will no doubt accelerate. Radiant electric heating panels and units are often used for low first-cost applications.

Denver Square Office Tower
Denver, Colorado
Architects: Skidmore, Owings & Merrill
Engineers: Flack & Kurtz

The Denver Square Office Tower is a new highrise office building designed by the Denver office of Skidmore, Owings, & Merrill and Flack & Kurtz Mechanical Engineers. Its anticipated energy consumption is only 69,000 BTU/sq.ft./yr. Much of the success of the energy conservation is attributed to the integral design approach taken

Denver Square Office Tower
Denver, Colorado
Architects: Skidmore, Owings and Merrill
Engineers: Flack and Kurtz

by architects and mechanical and illuminating engineers.

The reflective double glazing is calculated to reduce transmission losses by 45 percent and solar gains by 40 percent. The lighting requirements of 60 to 70 foot-candles is achieved with approximately 2 watts/sq.ft. The HVAC system is variable-air-volume with interior and perimeter zones of each floor on the same system. This 100-percent outside air capability allows free cooling to begin at 60 degrees (F.), given the dry Denver climate. Heat-reclaiming light fixtures are used throughout. Central chillers are modular units with separate pumps for each unit.

241

Energy Simulation

A graphic depiction, or flowchart, of the full step-by-step process of energy simulation is required to fully understand a complete HVAC system. Annual computer simulations proceed through this entire flowchart (or one similar to it) 8,760 times, once for each hour of the year. Building descriptive data, together with weather, occupancy and operating profiles are the first inputs. Building base loads and external shading patterns are then calculated and applied to the appropriate zones. Each zone load is then calculated to include wall, roof and glass transmission, solar heat gain, and heat gains from light, people, infiltration and equipment. When the zone analyses are complete, the zones are assigned to the appropriate distribution system. The total load seen by the distribution system is then calculated, a system operating mode (response) determined, and the resulting system's operation analyzed. When all distribution systems are analyzed, they are then assigned to the appropriate central plant equipment. The primary system load is calculated and the response analyzed. When all primary systems have been analyzed, the energy usage is cumulated by major components: lighting, distribution systems, base loads and central equipment.

☐ Such energy simulation flowcharts provide a graphic conception of HVAC systems—a building envelope enclosing a set of discrete thermostatically controlled zones served by secondary distribution systems that in turn rely on primary central equipment for heating and cooling.

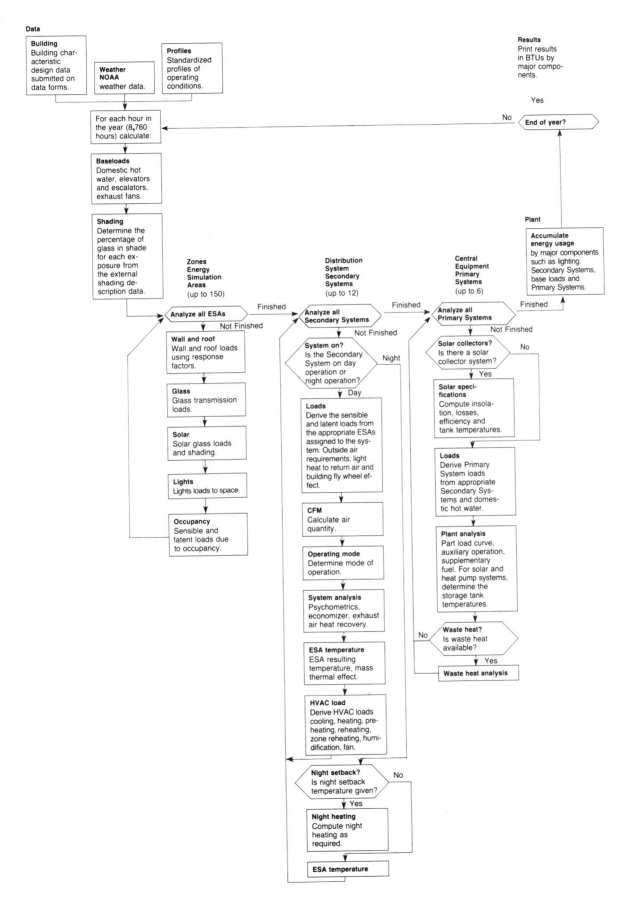

Data

Building
Building characteristic design data submitted on data forms.

Weather
NOAA weather data.

Profiles
Standardized profiles of operating conditions.

Results
Print results in BTUs by major components.

For each hour in the year (8,760 hours) calculate:

End of year? — Yes / No

Baseloads
Domestic hot water, elevators and escalators, exhaust fans.

Shading
Determine the percentage of glass in shade for each exposure from the external shading description data.

Plant

Accumulate energy usage by major components such as lighting, Secondary Systems, base loads and Primary Systems.

Zones
Energy
Simulation
Areas
(up to 150)

Distribution
System
Secondary
Systems
(up to 12)

Central
Equipment
Primary
Systems
(up to 6)

Analyze all ESAs — Finished → **Analyze all Secondary Systems** — Finished → **Analyze all Primary Systems** — Finished

Not Finished / Not Finished / Not Finished

Wall and roof
Wall and roof loads using response factors.

System on?
Is the Secondary System on day operation or night operation? — Night

Solar collectors?
Is there a solar collector system? — No

Glass
Glass transmission loads.

Day

Yes

Solar
Solar glass loads and shading.

Loads
Derive the sensible and latent loads from the appropriate ESAs assigned to the system. Outside air requirements, light heat to return air and building fly wheel effect.

Solar specifications
Compute insolation, losses, efficiency and tank temperatures.

Lights
Lights loads to space.

Occupancy
Sensible and latent loads due to occupancy.

CFM
Calculate air quantity.

Loads
Derive Primary System loads from appropriate Secondary Systems and domestic hot water.

Operating mode
Determine mode of operation.

Plant analysis
Part load curve, auxiliary operation, supplementary fuel. For solar and heat pump systems, determine the storage tank temperatures.

System analysis
Psychometrics, economizer, exhaust air heat recovery.

ESA temperature
ESA resulting temperature, mass thermal effect.

Waste heat?
Is waste heat available? — No / Yes

HVAC load
Derive HVAC loads cooling, heating, preheating, reheating, zone reheating, humidification, fan.

Waste heat analysis

Night setback?
Is night setback temperature given? — No

Yes

Night heating
Compute night heating as required.

ESA temperature

243

Fluor Office Building
Los Angeles, California
Architect: Welton Beckett Associates
Engineers: James A. Knowles and Associates

The new office building for Fluor Engineers and Constructors, designed by Welton Beckett Associates, Architects, and James A. Knowles and Associates, mechanical engineers, provides a case study of a simple, energy-efficient and climate-sensitive design. Analysis of the southern California climate and the building program revealed a clearly predominant cooling load. The only heating provided other than the natural heat recovered from lighting and occupants, is from perimeter electric radiant panels, which are used only for start-up and on the rare cold days. Highly reflective single glazing was used throughout. To reduce noise, unattractive mechanical equipment was tucked above exterior concrete stair towers.

Air handlers, both supply and return, have variable pitch and axial flow. A central computer monitors enthalpy and controls normal operation.

Fluor Office Building
Los Angeles, California
Architects: Welton Beckett Associates
Engineers: James A. Knowles and Associates

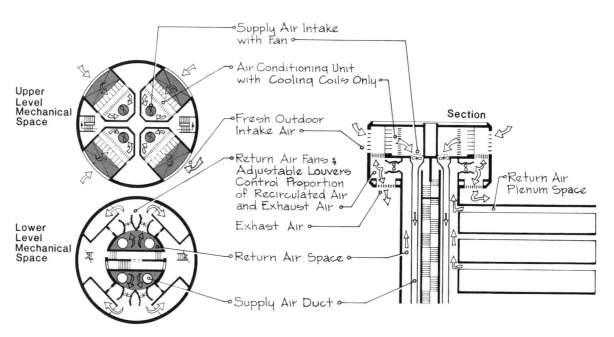

Upper Level Mechanical Space

Lower Level Mechanical Space

Supply Air Intake with Fan

Air Conditioning Unit with Cooling Coils Only

Fresh Outdoor Intake Air

Return Air Fans & Adjustable Louvers Control Proportion of Recirculated Air and Exhaust Air

Exhaust Air

Return Air Space

Supply Air Duct

Section

Return Air Plenum Space

Fluor Office Building
Los Angeles, California
Architects: Welton Beckett Associates
Engineers: James A. Knowles and Associates

244

Load Control

A main objective of energy-conscious design is to reduce annual system load. Care should be taken that such strategies do not raise the peak loads on a system or cause wide fluctuations in system loading. Large areas of south-facing glazing, for example, can significantly reduce heating loads in winter. Shadows from neighboring buildings, however, can cause large variations in the heating loads in specific spaces. A centralized HVAC system would have difficulty maintaining comfort and economy where this large load variation exists. Summer heat gains through glazing can also increase peak cooling loads unless adequate sunshading is provided.

Reducing Peak Loads

☐ Reducing peak loads on systems permits a reduction in the size and quantity of system elements. A double economy of energy and material is achieved. The best opportunities for peak load reduction are found with HVAC and lighting systems. The two basic strategies for reducing peak loads are:

—*Basic system load reduction.* This includes most energy design strategies; examples are insulation to reduce heating and cooling loads and daylighting to reduce illumination loads.

—*Peak load shedding:* By deferring loads from peak load periods to periods of low loads it is possible to flatten the system load schedule. Maintaining a constant occupancy schedule for a space or building is one strategy for shedding peak loads. The peak heating and cooling loads may also be reduced by avoiding reheat and recool periods associated with varying occupancy.

Storage Systems and Peak Heating/Cooling Load

☐ Occupancy scheduling and heat- and cold-storage systems can be used to supplement HVAC heating and cooling loads during peak periods. During off-peak periods, central HVAC systems can divert some of their heating and cooling capacity to mass storage systems. As the heating or cooling load rises above the capacity of the system, the heated or cooled storage system is used to supply extra capacity. Thermal storage systems have the following advantages:

—More efficient system because heating and cooling plants operate closer to maximum capacity and, therefore, maximum efficiency, for longer periods of time;

—Potential integration of solar heating and cooling by using a common storage system.

Load Variation Over Time

☐ Many of the concepts that apply to peak load shedding also apply to load variation over time. Energy-conserving buildings tend to reduce system load variation. Large variations in system load due to occupancy and climate can adversely affect the effectiveness and efficiency of energy-consuming systems.

☐ The rate and cycle period over which these loads change is just as important as the size (scale) of load variation. HVAC and lighting systems can be especially sensitive to system load variations.

☐ In HVAC systems, fluctuating thermal loads in spaces mean that HVAC systems will run at significantly less than 100-percent capacity for long periods. HVAC systems, however, are usually less efficient when operating at these reduced loads. The rate at which thermal loads change can also tax the ability of the system to adjust efficiently and effectively to demands.

☐ Seasonal variations in thermal load are characterized by a low rate of change over a yearly cycle. The magnitude of the load variation can be large, however. Since thermal loads in the intermediate seasons (spring and fall) can be far less than the peak loads of winter

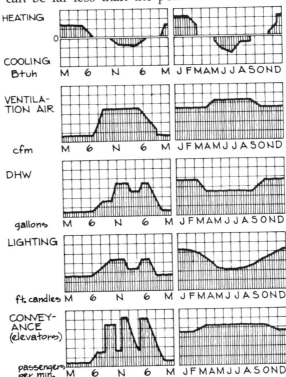

System Load Profiles

245

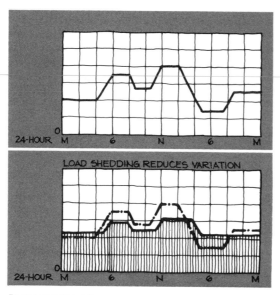

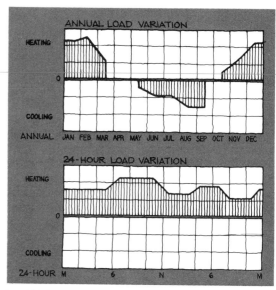

Peak Load Shedding

Load Variation Over Time

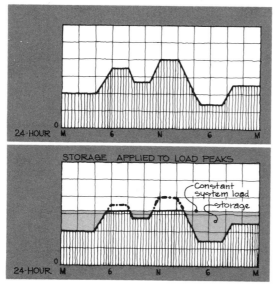

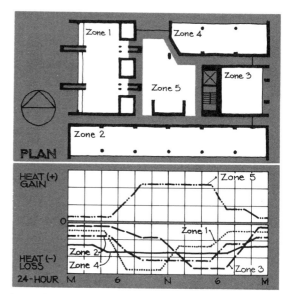

Effect of Storage

Load Variation Between Spaces

and summer, inefficiencies might be expected during these intermediate seasons. Some central HVAC systems have modular or incremental heating and cooling plants to overcome these load variations. These systems are made up of a number of smaller modular units connected in series. Modular units always operate at or near 100-percent capacity; as heating or cooling loads fluctuate, units are turned on or off to meet the demand. Decentralized HVAC systems and electrically driven systems tend to maintain efficiency during off-peak thermal load conditions.

☐ Rapid thermal load variations in a building are characteristic of the hourly and daily cycles of occupancy and climate. A passive strategy for retarding and reducing thermal fluctuations is the addition of thermal mass to the envelope and interior. If wide thermal load variations remain (usually due to occupancy), HVAC systems should be selected so as to minimize the time lag between the actual load change and the system's ability to sense and provide for this change. All-water systems usually have long time lags, whereas all-air HVAC systems have shorter time lags. Decentralized (unitary) HVAC equipment located in the space it serves can often react very quickly to load variation.

Load Variation Between Spaces

☐ At a given time, system loads can vary widely between different spaces and zones. Both the occupancy schedules of specific spaces and climate-related factors contribute to this load variation. It is often possible to arrange spaces and zones so that both occupancy and climate-related system loads are accommodated.

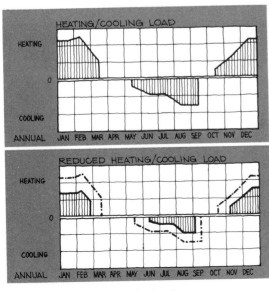

Reducing Heating and Cooling Loads

Zoning

Heating, lighting, dehumidifying and cooling are interrelated activities that not only affect each other but vary considerably in different spaces and at different times of the day and year. They challenge the designer to create an energy-efficient, cost effective system that satisfies all these interrelated and changing needs.

Occupancy

☐ Space conditioning (HVAC) and the lighting, hot water and circulation needs of a building are determined by the varying schedules of its occupants. Schedules can be developed in the preliminary phase of design. Depicted graphically, occupancy schedules describe the dynamic nature of occupancy-related loads over a period of time. Internal heat gains due to lights, machines, and people are proportional to occupancy. During periods of low or zero occupancy, space conditioning and building service requirements are at a minimum. Therefore, occupancy becomes a major determinant of loads. Occupancy schedules are necessary before accurate load schedules can be derived.

☐ In developing occupancy schedules, it can be useful to group together individual spaces with similar occupancy characteristics, since different spaces or zones often have widely diverse occupancy schedules. Zoning strategies based on occupancy can have beneficial impacts on energy use.

☐ Variations in the system loads of these spaces can then be handled more economically. Occupancy characteristics are the primary determinants of whether central system or decentralized (unitary) HVAC systems are more efficient.

☐ Individual control of zones with similar occupancy characteristics can also be applied to lighting, hot water, elevators and other services. An energy management system can be used to control equipment on a predetermined schedule or on the basis of sensors in individual zones. Controls can also be located in the zone or space.

Climate

☐ Variations in climate can also affect load schedules. Climate varies over 24-hour and annual cycles. Climate schedules indicate how temperature, humidity, solar insolation, and wind vary over time. The effect of climate on system loads will change according to:

—The degree to which the building envelope insulates against and controls the external climate. A well-insulated building tends to reduce the impact of climate variation on system loads. Buildings with minimum exposed areas, such as buildings in urban sites, tend to be affected less by climate than freestanding buildings. Climate will play a larger role in poorly insulated buildings or buildings with operable windows and vents. It should be emphasized, however, that good design can often use the external climate to reduce system loads.

—The quantity of ventilation air required of the HVAC system. If outdoor ventilation air needs to be heated/cooled or humidified/dehumidified, it represents a load on the HVAC system. Often, however, outdoor air is more economical to use than recycled return air. Free cooling, in buildings with large internal loads, can be accomplished using outdoor air up to 75 degrees (F.) within an acceptable humidity range. An air economizer control on an HVAC system considers the temperature and humidity of both return and outdoor air to determine which is more energy-conserving. Operable windows and vents do not offer this type of sensitive control and are often misused.

☐ HVAC systems are often zoned by orientation where external climate causes variations in thermal loading. HVAC systems have trouble meeting widely varying thermal loads within a zone efficiently. The type of HVAC system selected will depend on the "thermal flexibility" that can be tolerated while maintaining efficiency. If it is not possible for a centralized HVAC system to provide for thermal load variation efficiently, decentralized HVAC systems should be considered.

☐ HVAC systems should be zoned to account for climate and occupancy wherever possible. HVAC systems are zoned according to orientation in perimeter spaces (spaces with exterior wall or roof), where thermal-load variation between these orientations exceeds the efficient "flexibility" of the system. Internal spaces (spaces with no outdoor exposure) are very often zoned separately from peripheral zones. Internal zones usually require only cooling. For this reason, buildings that require interior cooling and ventilation usually divide HVAC systems into "internal" and "perimeter" zones.

☐ Tall buildings must often be separated into vertical zones as well, because of the "stack effect" phenomenon, in which hot air rises through elevator shafts and stairwells, increasing exfiltration at the top and infiltration at the bottom of the building.

248

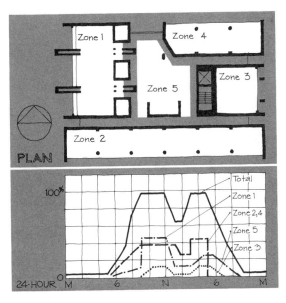

Occupancy Zoning

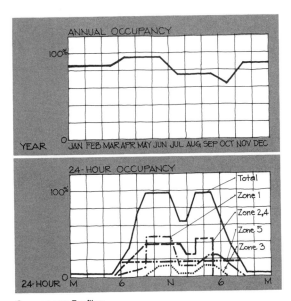

Occupancy Profiles

Exfiltration at Top

Warm Air Rises up Vertical Shaft

Dense Cool Air Infiltrates at Bottom

Stack Effect

Hooker Office Building
Niagara Falls, New York
Architects: Cannon Design, Inc.

The 200,000-sq.ft. corporate office headquarters of the Hooker Chemicals and Plastics Corp., designed by Cannon Design, Inc., is a special effort on the part of both the client and the architect to promote energy conservation. Located in downtown Niagara Falls, N.Y., the building makes use of a unique combination of glazing, shading, daylighting and a sophisticated HVAC control system.

The building contains a 15′ perimeter lighting zone, which uses two-stage controls for maximum daylighting. Inside this zone, localized task and ambient lighting are used. Reconciling the conflicting needs for adequate daylighting and protection against a severe climate, the designers have created a unique envelope consisting of an inner skin and an outer one, 4′ apart, on all four facades.

Between the two membranes are huge insulated louvers. Light sensors on the louvers allow a motorized system to turn the blinds horizontal for facades in shade, down 45 degrees in full sun, or position them in between. When louvers are in the full-sun position, daylight will be refracted into the space by the white louver surfaces.

In addition to the louver controls, the building uses temperature sensors to operate venting dampers to release undesired heat from the cavity out of the top of the building. These sensors are part of a complex central computer control system that monitors not only thermal conditions but also security points and fire safety information. This control system also "watches over" the variable-air-volume system and allows for precise pinpointing of operating conditions. As a result of this dynamic control system, the four separate facades will vary constantly according to weather, time of day and time of year.

A computerized simulation of annual energy use indicates that this building, designed completely with off-the-shelf equipment, will consume approximately 16,000 BTU/sq.ft./yr.

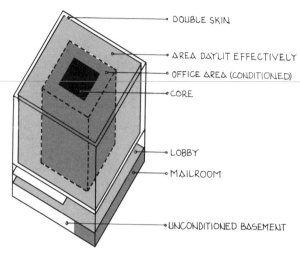

Hooker Office Building
Niagara Falls, New York
Architects: Cannon Design, Inc.

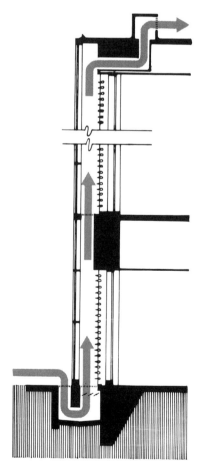

Hooker Office Building
Niagara Falls, New York
Architects: Cannon Design, Inc.

250

Hooker Chemical Building
Niagara Falls, New York
Architects: Cannon Design, Inc.

Photo: Patricia Layman Bazelon

Heat Recovery

Cascading energy systems recover thermal energy generated by building operation to satisfy part of the building's energy needs. Sources of heat include machines, lights, process energy and people. Space heating is the most obvious application of a cascading energy system, although many other applications can be easily integrated into conventional building systems.

☐ Heat energy is available in varying concentrations or energy levels. Cascading energy systems generally are more cost-effective when they can collect higher concentrations of waste heat. An air handling HVAC system will collect hotter air if heat-generating activities are concentrated in one space.

☐ Some systems are specifically designed to cool machinery and lighting fixtures before their heat is released into the space. Water-cooled equipment reduces the cooling load in this way and provides a high-level source of waste heat. The hot water generated can be applied to space heating, absorptive refrigerant space cooling and domestic hot water systems.

☐ The major method for recovering lighting heat is plenum-return systems. Ducted-air systems can provide a direct means of controlling and redistributing heat dissipated by lighting fixtures. A lighting fixture provided with slots, through which return air is drawn into the ceiling plenum, is one approach. As air passes over the lamps, ballasts and sheet metal of the luminaire, it picks up as much as 80 percent of the electrical energy used by the light as dissipated heat and carries it into the plenum.

☐ Plenum heat can be used in space conditioning systems in many ways. In some systems the plenum can be the source of heat for air supply, with supplementary heat supplied by duct heaters or water coils piped to the water side of a double-bundle condenser.

☐ Heat from air-return lighting fixtures can be drawn off and discharged outdoors rather than being used to heat occupied space. This approach reduces the cooling load for the building and can result in economies in distribution ductwork and refrigerator equipment. Another advantage is that removing heat from the lighting fixtures can increase their efficiency 10 to 20 percent.

☐ The integration of heat recovery strategies, localized and variable airconditioning, and lighting needs, and potentially rapid fluctuations in outdoor conditions can create the need for automated control of energy-related systems. Energy management systems currently available range from relatively simple devices that offer peak-demand control, load cycling and time-of-day scheduling to highly sophisticated computerized systems that monitor indoor and outdoor temperature, humidity and light levels, and respond accordingly. The latter systems have already demonstrated their effectiveness in providing comfort control, energy conservation and facilities maintenance functions in larger buildings. Doubtless reductions in the cost of microcircuitry will soon make these systems useful and cost-effective for smaller, less complex buildings as well.

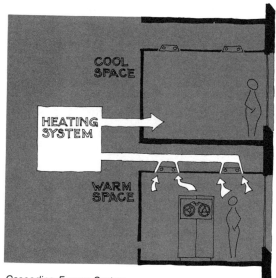

Cascading Energy System

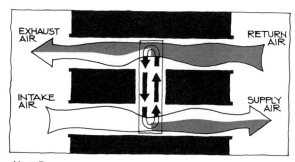

Heat Recovery

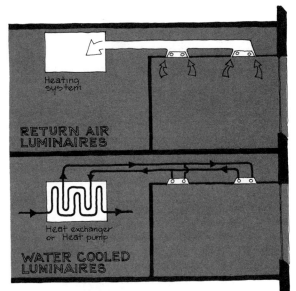

Heat Recovery from Lighting Systems

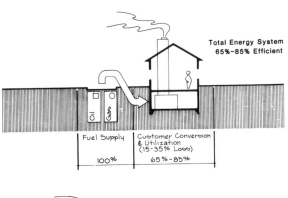

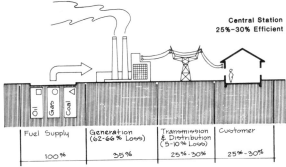

Total-energy and Central-station Efficiencies

Total Energy

□ Total Energy (TE) is the term used for systems that use fossil fuels to generate electricity on site and use the heat of generation for space conditioning, domestic hot water or other purposes. The appeal of TE systems is that they avoid the considerable conversion and transmission losses which occur when fossil fuels are used to produce electricity at a central utility, and are able to beneficially use the thermal by-product of electrical generation. In contrast, the thermal by-product of electrical generation at central power plants can become a thermal pollutant as it is discharged into the atmosphere or streams.

□ As with district heating and cooling, TE systems have found most use in large installations with consistently high loads like shopping centers, universities and hospitals. Consideration of TE systems for any application should follow careful analysis of the loads to be met, the local fuel situation, the added investment required by a TE plant, and service and maintenance costs, as well as federal regulations concerning power generation.

□ District systems, which provide steam or chilled water produced outside the building, have long existed in cities and on campuses and military installations. Today, however, when we seek opportunities to integrate our energy usage patterns, the economies of scale possible with district systems merit consideration for a greater variety of applications.

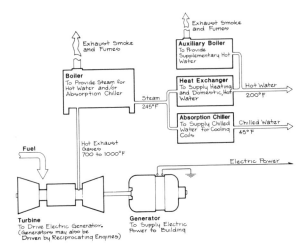

Total Energy

253

Santa Clara County Service Center
San Jose, California
Architects: Hawley and Peterson
Engineers: Weston Associates

The County of Santa Clara Service Center, in San Jose, Calif., designed by architects Hawley & Peterson and by Weston Associates, mechanical/electrical engineers, is composed of three buildings—a main office building and two smaller support structures. The design takes maximum advantage of air once it is conditioned, using it three separate times.

Conditioned air is first delivered to the office of the main office building. Two vertical utility shafts that house air duct risers and hot and chilled water pipes, also serve as warm air plenums, and maximize usable floor area. The conditioned air reaches the offices through air-handling luminaires and is returned through the lamp compartments of the luminaires to an above-ceiling plenum. From the plenum, the return air is pulled through slotted concrete fascia beams into a large central court. This court is designed for temperature differentials larger than the office space, yet not extreme enough to cause discomfort.

The air in the court space, having been used a second time, is then drawn through wooden grilles lining the floor of the court. (The fan room under the main building also serves as a plenum for the complex.) Pressure from the exhaust return fan forces air through the two utility tunnels, where it is used for general ventilation and equipment exhaust.

Automatically controlled dampers direct varying quantities of air through the utility tunnels, exhaust fans and to the supply system of the main building. Both support buildings have HVAC equipment for their office spaces.

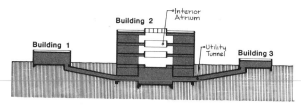

Santa Clara County Service Center
San Jose, California
Architects: Hawley and Peterson
Engineers: Weston Associates

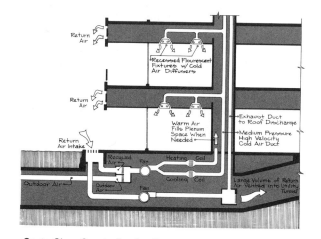

Santa Clara County Service Center
San Jose, California
Architects: Hawley and Peterson
Engineers: Weston Associates

"Free" Cooling

The hourly and daily changes in the temperature and humidity of outdoor air can also be put to advantage in the design of HVAC systems. Unlike strategies for recovering waste heat from energy already expended, these designs avoid expending it in the first place.

☐ An enthalpy optimizer control is used in hot weather to sense both dry- and wet-bulb temperatures of the outside air and the return air. The optimizer uses this information to determine the enthalpy or total heat content (sensible plus latent heat) of the two air-streams. In this way, the optimizer can select whichever requires the least heat removal. This control is the basis of the economizer cycle.

☐ The economizer cycle is often used in HVAC systems to avoid unnecessary cooling of air in cool weather. A sensor registers the dry-bulb and wet-bulb temperatures of outside and return air. If outside air is appropriately cool, it regulates how much outside air should be taken in. For example, the outside air may have a higher dry bulb temperature than return air, but may also contain much less moisture, i.e., have lower overall heat content. It will require less energy to cool the outside air than to dehumidify the return air.

☐ Balance and changeover temperatures also can help the designer integrate HVAC systems with the local elements. The balance temperature is the outside air temperature at which mechanical heating is no longer required because the internal gains from people, lights and equipment and solar heat gains are exactly equal to the losses from infiltration, ventilation and conductance through the envelope. The changeover temperature is the outside air temperature at which mechanical cooling is no longer required because the combination of infiltration, transmission losses and ventilation using 100-percent cold outside air is just equal to the internal gains.

☐ Usually no heat is required above the balance temperature and no cooling is required below the changeover temperature. However, some buildings with high internal gains, such as hospitals, have balance points as low as 10 degrees (F.). While a summation of total gains and total losses may be zero, substantial perimeter zone heating and make-up air heating will exist.

☐ The composite room load profiles shown for typical interior and perimeter areas have been based on occupied conditions. Composite room load profiles can also be drawn for un-

occupied daytime periods, night periods or other combinations of operational periods and load factor combinations to determine room heat flow characteristics under different sets of operating conditions. The actual loads used for constructing room load profiles may be expressed in terms of total BTU/hr. or BTU/hr./sq.ft. or floor area of the space being analyzed, for quantifying heat flow at partial load operation.

☐ The thermocycle economizer avoids use of the mechanical compressor—the single largest energy consumer in a refrigeration machine—when the outdoor wet-bulb temperature is suitable. If the design temperature for

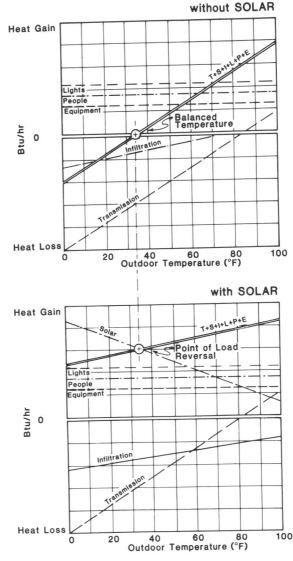

Room Load Profile (Composite)—North Exposure

Room Load Profile (Composite)—South Exposure

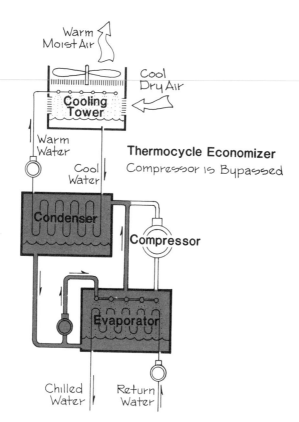

Operation of Thermocycle Economizer

feasibility of thermal storage, cost/benefit of various heat recovery strategies and, perhaps most important, the relative weight on an annual basis of the heating and cooling loads. For example, a design with a balance temperature of 38 degrees (F.) would need an investigation of weather data to see how much of the time the temperature falls between 51 and 42 degrees (F.). The larger this period of time, the more beneficial the system with the higher changeover becomes. If the period is relatively short, then the choice of system can be made on other grounds.

☐ The worst-weather conditions (the coldest day in winter and hottest, humid day in summer) can be dealt with in a relatively straightforward manner by simply sizing the system to meet these loads. The real challenge and potential for energy conservation lies in the varied, considering 363 days between the extremes.

the chilled water is 55 degrees (F.), for example, whenever outdoor wet-bulb temperature is around 45 degrees (F.), it is possible to turn off the compressor but still use the evaporative cooling cycle. This is done by using the cooling tower to cool the condenser water down close to the outside wet-bulb temperature, in effect reversing the temperature differential of the refrigerant cycle.

☐ The condenser water causes the refrigerant to condense. By installing a pipeline for the refrigerant to bypass the compressor, and a small pump sufficient to move the refrigerant to spray nozzles above the evaporator coils, the relatively warmer chilled water will cause the refrigerant to evaporate just as it would if the compressor with its much larger motor were in operation.

☐ The basic requirement of the thermocycle economizer, that the outside wet-bulb temperature be 5 to 10 degrees cooler than the design temperature for the chilled water, occurs frequently in many parts of the country.

☐ These concepts can give insights into such decisions as the type of distribution system,

256

All-Air Systems

HVAC systems are generally classified according to the fluid delivered to the occupied space: air, air and water, water, or refrigerant. This convenient method of classification will be used in the discussion that follows.

☐ All-air systems have the following advantages and disadvantages.

Advantages:

—Adaptable to humidification, heat-recovery systems and automatic seasonal changeover

—Adaptable to complex zoning schemes, with ability to provide year-round heating and cooling

—Adaptable to close control of temperature and humidity, e.g., in computer rooms.

—Can use untreated outside air instead of mechanically cooled air more often in summer

Disadvantages:

—Special care required with terminal device placement and surrounding structural elements to ensure accessibility to terminal units for maintenance and repair

—In cold climates, radiation heating needed at perimeter during unoccupied hours to avoid having to heat entire building

—Higher structural costs and increased HVAC loads, due to large duct spaces that increase building volume

☐ The available all-air systems can be classified as single-path or dual-path:

—Single duct, constant-volume

—Single duct, variable-volume

—Single duct, reheat (constant-or-variable-volume)

—Dual-duct (including dual-duct variable-volume)

—Multizone.

☐ The single-duct, single-zone system can be quite effective but its range of application is somewhat limited. The single-duct, variable-volume system is clearly superior to the remaining all-air systems designed to deliver constant temperature air. This system satisfies the severest zone load and gives smaller volumes of the same constant-temperature air to other zones with lesser loads. This system is especially effective for groups of interior zones where loads do vary but generally not rapidly nor

frequently. The most serious problems would occur in zones with lesser heat loads but which produce larger quantities of moisture, dirt or odor that are too large to be eliminated by low volumes of air. Spaces with no cooling loads, but a minimum air supply volume can become too cool.

☐ Constant-volume, multizone systems can satisfy different loads by varying air temperature only. Unfortunately, the normal control strategy is to cool all of the air to the level required by the severest load and to reheat the air delivered to all zones with lesser loads as necessary. This technique offers finely tuned control but can waste energy.

☐ The variable-volume systems, in addition to eliminating wasteful reheating, have other energy conservation benefits. Controls can be designed so that as the total of all the various zone loads decreases and as more VAV dampers reduce the volume, the delivery air temperature can be increased and/or the system air volume reduced. This significantly reduces fan power consumption.

☐ In general, all-air systems' energy use can be ranked as shown.

Systems	Energy Use
Variable-volume interior with perimeter radiant heating VAV and perimeter heating can often oppose each other in perimeter zones with varying solar exposures. It may be necessary to control the perimeter system with an outside air anticipator and solar compensator but these are difficult to coordinate with the VAV system	Lowest
Variable-volume interior with perimeter constant volume VAV with perimeter constant volume theoretically uses a little more energy, but actually uses less by avoiding simultaneous heating and cooling.	Low
Variable-volume, dual-duct	Medium
Variable-volume, with terminal reheat	Medium
All-air induction with perimeter reheat	Medium
Constant-volume, dual-duct and multizone	High
Constant-volume perimeter induction	Very High
Constant-volume single-zone and terminal reheat	Highest

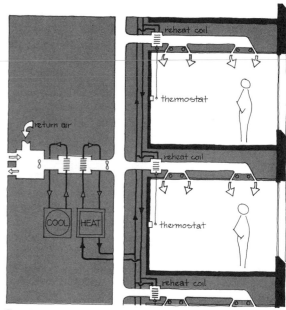

Single-duct, Single-zone System

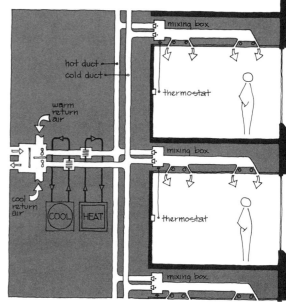

Terminal Reheat System (May Also Be Electric Resistance)

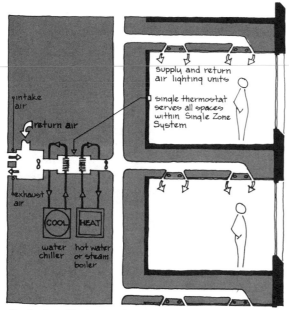

Single-duct, Variable-air-volume System

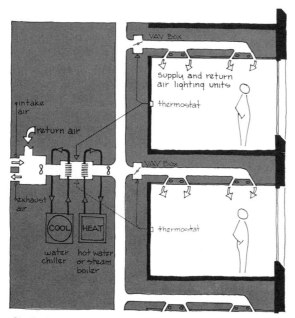

Dual Duct System

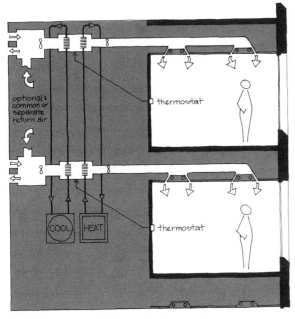

Constant-volume, Multi-zone System

☐ Other general advantages and disadvantages of all-air systems are:

Advantages:

—Well-suited to laboratories or other applications requiring abnormal exhaust makeup

—Provides least infringement on rentable floor space

—Provides flexible control of air motion

—Does not interfere with window drapes; minimum damage risk to furnishings

Disadvantages:

—Perimeter systems not available for use as rapidly as radiation systems during building construction

—Absence of built-in automatic zone devices for rapid easy balancing when a single air system serves areas which are not rented simultaneously

—Sometimes difficult to prevent unwanted air noise and motion

—Often difficult to provide for proper fire safety separations

Federal Home Loan Bank Board
Washington, D.C.
Architect: Max O. Urbahn Associates, Inc.
Engineers: Syska and Hennessy, Inc.

The Federal Home Loan Bank Board building occupies a prestigeous site across from the Executive Office Building in downtown Washington, D.C. Architect Max Urbahn carefully adhered to the General Service Administration's energy budget guidelines of 55,000 BTU/sq.ft./yr.

Energy conservation in the building began with HVAC planning by Urbahn and consulting engineers Syska & Hennessy. The building was designed with three thermal zones, rather than the traditional two. Each thermal zone has a separate air distribution system, chosen to meet its particular needs efficiently. For the exterior wall, the first zone, a constant-volume reheat system (reheat coil at air handlers) is used to create a curtain of air and thus reduce conducted loss or gain at the windows. The exterior system is not required when the outdoor temperature falls between 60 and 80 degrees (F.). The second, perimeter zone extends from the exterior wall to 12 to 15 feet inside. It uses a variable-air-volume system that balances interior loads from people, lights and direct solar gain. The third, interior zone uses air-powered, above-ceiling induction boxes that reduce the amount of air delivered through diffusers as the load diminishes.

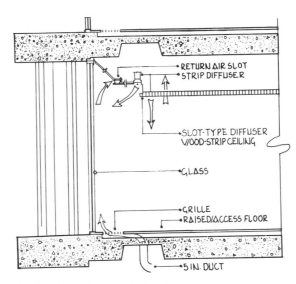

Federal Home Loan Bank Board
Washington, D.C.
Architects: Max O. Urbahn Associates, Inc.
Engineers: Syska and Hennessy, Inc.

Air-Water Systems

Air-water systems combine the cost and energy-efficiency of water systems with the flexibility of air systems, to provide forced-air ventilation, central control humidity and rapid response to load fluctuations in a variety of zones.

☐ In these systems both air and water are delivered to each space, and heating and cooling functions are carried out by changing the temperature of one or both media to control space temperatures year-round.

☐ Water's high specific heat allows it to deliver a given amount of heating and cooling capacity in a much smaller volume than air requires. This results in distribution pipes much smaller than comparable air ducts, a feature that makes water attractive in highrise and other buildings where space is at a premium.

☐ Further, the pumping necessary to circulate the water throughout the building is usually about ⅙ the fan power that would be required for an all-air system. The savings on operating cost can be quite substantial when compared with medium- or high-pressure all-air, constant-volume systems.

☐ When water is the primary conditioning medium, the system can be designed so that the air supply is equal to ventilation or exhaust requirements, eliminating the need for return air ducts and fans.

☐ Air-water systems are primarily applicable to multiple perimeter spaces where a wide range of sensible loads exists and where close control of humidity is not required. Where significant fluctuations in airconditioning requirements can occur at the same time on a given exposure, individual room control is available.

☐ For all systems using outdoor air, there is an outdoor temperature, the changeover temperature, at which mechanical cooling is no longer required. At this point, the system can accomplish cooling through the use of outdoor air; at lower temperatures, heating rather than cooling is needed. With all-air systems capable of operating with up to 100-percent outdoor air, mechanical cooling is often not required at outdoor temperatures below 50 to 55 degrees (F.) An important characteristic of air-water systems, however, is that refrigeration for secondary water cooling may continue to be needed even when the outdoor temperature is considerably less than 50 degrees (F.)

☐ Systems of this type have been commonly applied to office buildings, hospitals, hotels, schools and better apartment houses.

☐ Air-water systems generally have the following advantages and disadvantages:
Advantages:
—Ability to handle a variety of loads by separate sources of heating and cooling in each space
—Capacity for centralized humidification, dehumidification and filtration
—Smaller central air handler needed because of reduced air volume
—Capacity for space heating by water system alone, without fans, at night or during power emergencies if wall units are located under window
Disadvantages:
—Air at low dewpoint is necessary when primary system accomplishes all dehumidification
—Inability to prevent condensation caused by open windows or other sources of humidity
—Humidity control requires water chilled to low temperatures or even chemical dehumidification
—Reliance on mechanical cooling even when the outdoor temperature is considerably less than 50 degrees (F.)

☐ As illustrated, the inspace equipment will generally be either induction units or fan-coil units.

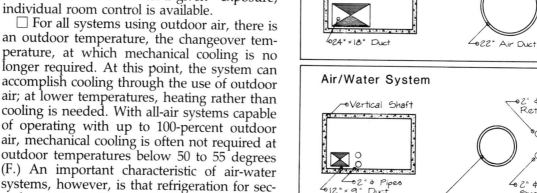

Comparative Space Requirements

260

Air-Water Induction Systems

☐ In an air-water induction unit, centrally conditioned air is supplied to the unit plenum at high pressure. It then flows through induction nozzles and induces air from the room to flow over the water coil and become heated or cooled. The primary and secondary air are mixed and discharged to the room.

☐ A wide variety of induction unit configurations is available, including units with low overall heights or with extremely large coil face areas, to suit the particular needs of space or load.

Fan-Coil Conditioner System with Primary Air

☐ Fan-coil conditioner units are versatile room terminals that can be used with both air-water and water-only systems. Despite the shortcomings in the quality of airconditioning achieved with water-only systems, the fan-coil units have been more commonly associated with that type of system than with air-water systems. Many of the standard features of the units are accordingly used for the water-only applications.

☐ The basic elements of fan-coil units are a finned-tube coil and a fan. The fan recirculates air continuously from within the perimeter space through the coil, which is supplied with either hot or chilled water. In addition, the unit can contain an auxiliary heating coil, which usually functions by electric resistance, steam or hot water. The primary air system for areas using fan-coils units need not be integrated with the fan-coil system.

☐ Air-water systems are categorized as two, three, and four-pipe systems. Incorporating both cooling and heating capabilities for year round airconditioning, they all function in the same way, although the details of system design differ significantly.

Two-Pipe Systems

☐ Two-pipe systems distribute water through one supply pipe and one return pipe. Each unit is supplied with water from the pipes and with conditioned air from a central apparatus. Two-pipe systems have the major disadvantage of not being able to provide heating and cooling to different parts of the building at the same time.

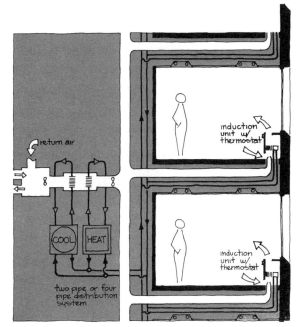

Air-water Induction System

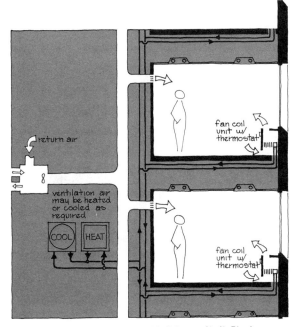

Fan-coil Conditioner System with Primary Air (2 Pipe)

261

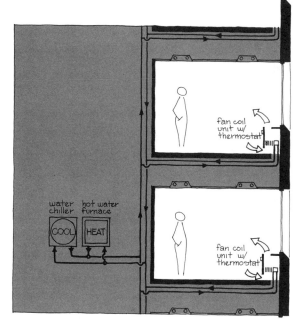

Two-pipe System

☐ The water-coil output of each terminal is controlled by a local space thermostat, and can vary from 0 percent to 100 percent of capacity as required to maintain space temperature. Two-pipe systems are generally satisfactory during the winter and summer seasons. The intermediate seasons, however, can create problems because of the system's inability to provide simultaneous heating and cooling to different parts of the building. Primary air temperatures must be reset as outside air temperature changes and thus both a temperature reset schedule and calculation of primary air quantities become critical to the design.

Three-Pipe Systems

☐ Three-pipe systems have three pipes to each terminal unit: a cold water supply, a hot water supply and a common return. Hot and cold water are usually used in the unit selectively, depending on temperature requirements.

☐ Three-pipe systems are not widely used. They can be wasteful of energy, especially when there are wide variations between zone loads, because as with all-air systems the mixing is actually heating and cooling the same space at the same time. Also, there are only minor savings from deleting one pipe, but major control problems.

Four-Pipe Systems

☐ Four-pipe systems have four pipes to each terminal unit: one each for chilled water supply and return, and two more for warm water supply and return. As four-pipe systems do not mix the hot and chilled water in a common return pipe, they are superior to three-pipe systems in reducing the energy needed to reheat and rechill the water after it returns to the central unit.

☐ The controls for four-pipe systems are generally simpler than for two- or three-pipe systems, and the first-costs often work out to be quite close. Energy and operating costs for four-pipe systems are generally comparable as well.

☐ As with all-water and refrigerant systems, a major consideration with air-water systems is the need for condensation drain pans or drain piping. During the cooling season all latent heat removal should be accomplished by central equipment in the primary air system. If not, then the temperature of the water coil will fall below the dewpoint of the room air and condensation will occur, with possibly annoying or damaging results. The energy and cost tradeoffs involved should be carefully analyzed.

☐ Increased energy conservation for air-water systems can be achieved by careful attention to the following:

—Zoning the primary air by solar exposure can reduce primary air reheat.

—The northern building exposures can be on a separate air-and-water zone so that north zone changeover can occur at higher outdoor temperatures.

—Primary air preheat energy can be obtained by heat recovery systems or exhaust air heat transfer.

—The need for simultaneous primary air dehumidification and reheat can be reduced by installation of a condensate drain system and other provision for wet-coil room unit operation.

☐ Air-water systems have other advantages and disadvantages.

Advantages:

—Pipework and ducting that lasts as long as 20 to 25 years

—Positive ventilation air supply

—Recirculation that occurs only within each room when all primary air is outdoor air, and thus reduced cross-contamination

—High quality air filtration

—Reduced cooling capacity, with the building load rather than the sum of room peaks determining capacity requirements

Disadvantages:

—Applicable only to the perimeter of most buildings

—Frequent cleaning or room units required

—Usually not possible to shut off primary air supply in individual rooms

—Supplementary ventilation air needed for spaces with high exhaust requirements

☐ All-water systems use fan-coils or unit ventilators with unconditioned ventilation air supplied by an opening through the wall or by infiltration. Cooling and dehumidification are provided by circulating chilled water or brine through a finned coil in the unit. Heating is provided by supplying hot water through the same or a separate coil, using two-, three-, or four-pipe water distribution from central equipment. Electric heating at the terminal can be used to enhance system flexibility.

☐ All water systems can be especially economical and compact, but their effectiveness as space conditioners is limited to buildings with small interior spaces, such as motels, apartments, and small office buildings.

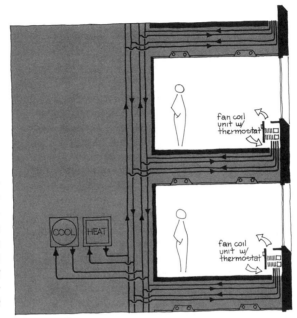

Four-pipe System

Government of Canada Building
Toronto, Canada
Architects: Dubois Plumb Associates
Shore, Tibe, Henschel, Irwin,
Peters
Engineers: Engineering Interface Limited

The energy-conserving features integrated into the design of the Government of Canada Building in Toronto have reduced consumption to 66,600 BTU/sq.ft./yr. Designed by architect Macy Dubois, the building achieves a high quality work space while complying with a low first-cost construction budget. The 825,000-sq.ft. building integrates the following features.

The 100-footcandle illumination required by union contract is achieved using 2 watts/sq.ft. A unique ceiling grid system accommodates acoustic tile, luminaires, air supply/return, power drop and sprinkler heads.

HVAC distribution is by variable-air-volume using 26 on-floor air handlers that substantially reduce duct friction loss. Heat of lighting is recovered and delivered at 100 degrees (F.) to perimeter fin-coil radiators.

Four 75,000-gallon storage tanks are expected to reduce heating costs by 60 percent and cooling costs by 20 percent. This storage capacity allowed a 30 percent reduction in chiller size. Chilled water temperatures low enough for dehumidification make it unfeasible to mix supply and return water, creating a design problem for the storage system. The ingenious invention of engineer Robert Tamblyn was a plastic membrane within the tank that expands as it receives warmer return water during the day and contracts at night. At off-peak hours the water is chilled for the next day's use.

Government of Canada Building
Toronto, Canada
Architects: DuBois Plumb Associates
Shore, Tibe, Henschel, Irwin, Peters
Engineers: Engineering Interface Limited

Government of Canada Building
Toronto, Canada
Architects: DuBois Plumb Associates
Shore, Tibe, Henschel, Irwin, Peters
Engineers: Engineering Interface Limited

Unitary Systems

All of the mechanical distribution systems discussed thus far are designed to take advantage of the performance efficiencies of large central plant equipment. Most refrigerant systems, on the other hand, are designed for decentralization. Inefficiencies in performance are offset by the following advantages:

—Individual room control, air distribution and ventilation system for each room, usually with simple adjustment by the occupant

—Heating and cooling capability always available independently of operation of other spaces in the building

—Only one terminal zone or conditioner affected in the event of equipment malfunction

—Usually low initial cost

—Reliable, manufacturer-matched components (usually with certified ratings and published performance data), assembled by manufacturer

—Ability to shut down equipment in unoccupied rooms for extended periods

□ Unitary systems rarely have the variations of coil configurations, evaporator temperatures, air-handling arrangements and refrigerating capacities available in central systems. Thus, unitary equipment often requires a higher level of design ingenuity and performance to develop superior system performance. Yet, because of factory control in component matching and of quality control in interconnection, application of unitary equipment seldom leads to serious breakdowns.

□ Multiple units come either as window air conditioners or thru-the-wall units, also called packaged terminal air conditioners (PTACs). PTACs generally include a heating section, while window air conditioners do not.

□ Unitary systems are generally located on the roof. At least the fan and evaporator of a rooftop system is mounted on the roof. The air distribution ductwork penetrates the roof. The compressor and condensing section can be mounted remotely, but they are more often packaged with the fan and evaporator. The complete system consists of the unitary equipment, air distribution and air delivery system(s), interlocking controls, structural supports and vibration-isolation system.

□ Unitary systems can also be equipped with variable-volume terminals, either the by-pass or squeeze-off type. Unitary systems are designed for constant-air-volume control units and do not have the capacity for adjusting fan speeds. For small outside air percentages, by-

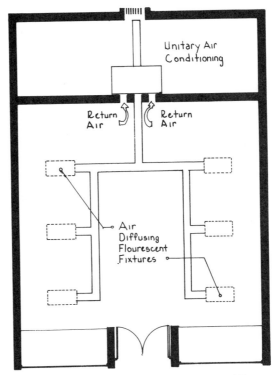

Single Packaged Unit with Variable Air Volume and Bypass

pass terminals avoid increases in duct static pressure and do not allow the cooled air to mix with warm room air before circulating it again.

□ As indicated earlier, unitary systems are well suited to logical zoning, with one unit per zone. A variation on this theme is the use of a single unitary system to supply preconditioned air to other unitary systems in the building. Under mild weather conditions, such a unit continues in operation even if the zone thermostats have one or more other units off. This prevents the introduction of hot, humid air into the conditioned spaces under periods of light loading. This strategy can also be adapted to highrise buildings.

□ Direct-expansion, water-loop heat pumps deserve special attention because heat recovery and redistribution—prime energy-conserving tactics—are among their inherent characteristics.

□ The direct expansion, water-loop heat pump is used as terminal equipment to heat and cool a zone when connected to a closed-loop piping circuit with means for adding heat to, or rejecting heat from, the water circuit. With supply loop water temperature maintained between 60 and 90 degrees (F.), and with a water flow rate of 2 to 3 gallons per minute (g.p.m.) per ton, the terminal equipment can operate on either heating or cooling to maintain temperature in its zone.

☐ Water circulated within the closed loop becomes either a sink or a source of heat. Units on the heating mode extract heat from the water. Units on the cooling mode reject heat to the water. Heat rejected from the central core units is carried in the loop water to perimeter units for use in the heating season. Unlike air-source heat pumps, heat available for units of this system does not depend on outdoor temperature, since the water loop is the primary source, and a secondary source of heat is usually provided.

☐ In the cooling mode, the heat pump operates as a water-cooled air-conditioner. In the heating mode, the functions of the evaporator and the condenser are reversed so that the equipment operates as a water chiller. Heat is

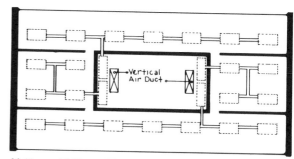

Multiroom Multistory Office Building with Unitary Air-conditioners

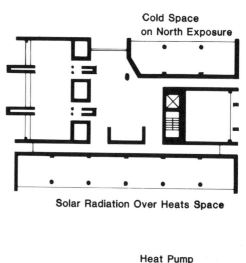

Cold Space on North Exposure

Solar Radiation Over Heats Space

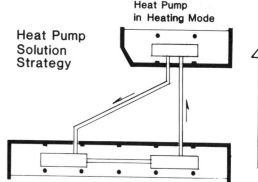

Heat Pump Solution Strategy

Heat Pump in Heating Mode

System Heat Flow

Heat Pumps in Cooling Mode

Closed Loop Water-loop Heat Pump System

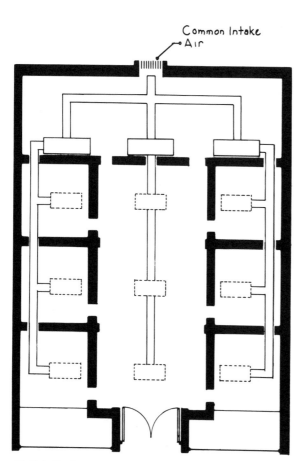

Common Intake Air

Multiple Packaged Units with Separate Central Outdoor Makeup Unit

removed from the water in the water-to-refrigerant heat exchanger, which then acts as the evaporator. That heat, plus the heat from the compressor, is rejected through the refrigerant-to-air heat exchanger (acting as the condensor) and heats the room.

☐ The multiple water-loop heat pump system offers zoning capability, since terminal equipment can be selected with cooling capacity as low as 7,000 BTU/hr. Since equipment can be placed in interior areas, the system can accommodate future relocation of partitions with a minimum of modifications.

☐ This system is twice as efficient in heating than in cooling, because waste heat entering spaces from the terminal compressors enhances the system's heating capacity, but detracts from its cooling capacity.

☐ Many applications of this system lend themselves well to heat storage. Installations that operate in winter on the cooling cycle most of the day and the heating cycle at night (such as a school) are excellent candidates for heat storage. This can be accomplished by installing a large storage tank in the closed loop circuit ahead of the boiler and adjusting the controls of the heat rejector to allow the loop temperature to build up to 95 degrees (F.) during the day. The volume of water at 95 degrees (F.) can be used during unoccupied hours to maintain heat in the building, allowing the loop temperature to drop from 95 to 65 degrees (F.) (instead of 70 degrees (F.) minimum without storage). The boiler would not be called on until the loop had dropped the entire 30 degrees (F.). The storage tank operates as a flywheel to prolong the period of operation between the limits where neither heat makeup nor heat rejection is required.

☐ Terminal units are available in a variety of sizes and types, including the following:

—Finished console cabinets for window or wall flush mounting

—Floor-mounted vertical units for concealed installation

—Ceiling-concealed models hung from floors above and connected to duct-work

☐ Selection of terminal equipment will require close coordination of architectural, engineering and lighting details. Access for service and maintenence must be provided for ceiling units.

☐ A secondary heat source (boilers—gas, oil or electric) and heat rejection equipment (usually closed-circuit evaporative cooling) are required when the water loop temperature goes out of the 10–95 degree (F.) range.

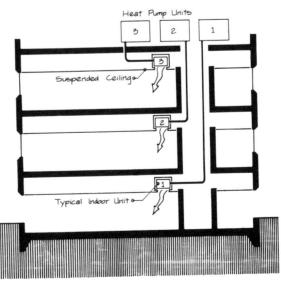

Winewood Office Park
Tallahassee, Florida
Architects: Clemons, Rutherford and Associates

Chillers And Boilers

Chillers

☐ As stated earlier in the section on psychrometric fundamentals, most cooling technology depends on taking advantage of the heat transfer, called the heat of vaporization, involved when refrigerant substances change from liquid to vapor, and vice versa. Acceptable refrigerants, such as the commonly used freon must be nontoxic, nonexplosive, noncorrosive, and change state at convenient temperatures and pressures. The beneficial effects of manipulating this process have their cost. It takes energy, first, to force the vaporized refrigerant back into a liquid state after it has absorbed heat so that it can be evaporated again. It takes additional energy to move the heat transport fluids (air or water). In most large central systems, circulated water carries heat from the room air-handling unit to the refrigeration unit, and a similar water circuit disposes of it in the cooling tower.

☐ Variations in coefficients of performance (COP) vary among refrigerating units, depending on the type of compressor (reciprocating, centrifugal or rotary screw) and on the way fluids are transported (water-to-water, air-to-air, or air-to-water). The COP of refrigeration systems is the ratio of the net heat removal by the evaporator to the total energy input to the compressor. Central plant chillers are generally water-cooled centrifugal compressors powered by electric motor or occasionally by steam turbine or diesel engine.

Equipment COP	COP
Single stage absorption	0.67
Two stage absorption	1.25
Turbine drive centrifugal	1.0
Turbine drive chiller with piggy back absorption chiller	1.6
Electric driven reciprocating chiller	3.5
Electric driven centrifugal chiller	4.0

Coefficients of Performance

☐ An absorption chiller is both more complicated and less efficient than compressive refrigeration, but it has become more important because it can take advantage of high waste heat-temperatures above 185 degrees (F.)—when these are available. This cooling cycle depends again on manipulating the heat of vaporization, but water, rather than freon, is vaporized as the refrigerant.

☐ Absorption chillers have fewer moving parts, are quieter, and demand somewhat less attention than compression machines. Absorption chillers are often economically competitive with vapor compression machines, but because the repertoire of waste water heat recovery and energy cascading techniques has expanded in recent years, absorption chillers are now frequently viewed as appropriate supplements to other equipment.

Evaporator and absorber

—Consider two connected, closed tanks with a salt solution (lithium bromide) in one and water in the other. The salt solution in the absorber soaks up some of the water in the evaporator. The water remaining is thereby cooled by evaporation.

Compressive Refrigeration Cycle

Evaporator coil and pump added

—This refrigeration effect is used by putting a coil in the evaporator tank. Water from this tank is pumped to a spray header that wets the coil. The spray's evaporation chills water in the coil as it circulates to the refrigeration load. Solution pumped to spray in absorber raises efficiency.

Solution pumps and generator added

—In an actual operating cycle, the salt solution is continuously absorbing water vapor. To keep the salt solution at proper concentration, part of it is pumped directly to a generator where excess water vapor is boiled off. The reconcentrated salt solution is returned to the absorber tank where it mixes with the solution sprayed to absorber in step 2.

Condenser and heat exchanger added

—Water vapor boiled off from the weak solution is condensed and returned to the evaporator. A heat exchanger uses the hot, concentrated salt solution leaving the generator to preheat the cooler, weak solution coming from the absorber. Finally, condensing water circulating through the absorber and condenser coils removes the waste heat.

Absorption Refrigeration Units

Boilers

☐ Boilers are used in the vast majority of HVAC systems. They should be selected to provide high average efficiency for the predominant load range. Large boilers with modulating burners can operate at constant efficiency down to 25 percent of their maximum rated outputs. The use of two or more boilers in sequential operation can increase boiler operating efficiency when system loads are below 25 percent of peak load, with each boiler operating as its highest average efficiency and responsive to its incremental portion of the load.

☐ For small boilers with fixed-firing-rate burners the most efficient boiler arrangement is a modular boiler assembly consisting of multiple boilers. Each boiler is able to respond to a small increment of load and operate at peak efficiency. Under part-load operation such boiler modules will start and stop in sequence to match the load.

☐ For most commercial applications heating is accomplished by circulating air over fin coils supplied with boiler-heated water. The variations primarily involve coil location.

☐ Boilers can be heated by oil, natural gas, coal, or electricity. Oil comes in several varieties. The lighter oils, No. 1 and No. 2, ignite and burn at lower temperatures and are more satisfactory than heavier oils for intermittent, automatically controlled heating systems. The lighter fuels are also more expensive, and as prices have risen, burners have been developed to make use of the heavier No. 5 and No. 6 oils. These oils often must be preheated and atomized by being forced under pressure through a nozzle. Gas burning is relatively straightforward. Given the supply uncertainty we have faced in recent years, multifuel boilers have been developed.

Manchester Federal Building
Manchester, New Hampshire
Architects: Isaak and Isaak, Architects
Engineers: Richard D. Kimball Co.
Dubin- Bloome Associates

The Manchester Federal Building in Manchester, N.H., was designed by Isaak & Isaak, Architects, Richard D. Kimball Co., mechanical engineers, and Dubin-Bloome Associates, solar design and energy conservation consultants, as an energy conservation laboratory. The 176,000 sq.ft. building houses a ground floor of public service spaces and six upper floors of more typical office space. It was decided quite early in the planning stage that the north wall would be completely opaque, and glazing on orientations would be restricted to 12 percent of the summer sun on the east and west and 100 percent on the south. Average U-values were .06 for walls, roof and floor slab above the garage and .55 for the glazing.

The heat pumps are zoned as either perimeter or interior. With the exception of under-window units on the daylighted second floor, all heat pumps are located remotely. Distribution is by variable-air-volume boxes with bypass; return is from ceiling plenum space. The exterior zones on the fourth and fifth floors are served by on-floor air handlers with capacity for variable-volume control and recovery of heat from lighting. Perimeter zones on the sixth and seventh floors are provided with separate fan-coil handling units that can recover heat of lighting from the ceiling plenum. The units are supplied with four water pipes but only two pipes need be used.

All outdoor air, as well as air for the interior zones for the upper four floors, is provided by an air handler in the penthouse. This central air system is provided with an enthalpy controller, permitting outdoor air to be used in an economizer cycle.

The chilled water storage capability allowed a 15-ton undersizing of chiller capacity for peak load conditions on the upper four floors.

The solar system consists of 4,000 sq.ft. of flat-plate collectors with adjustable tilt from 20 to 80 degrees. Winter freeze protection is provided by a mixture of 50-percent ethylene-glycol and 50-percent water passed through a heat exchanger. In summer the glycol mix is drained to storage and water is passed directly through the collectors allowing higher temperatures for use in the absorption chiller. This is important, as the absorption chiller output falls off rapidly at low generator temperatures.

The components and subsystems of the mechanical design, regarded individually, are not unique to this building, with the possible exception of the full-time use of the emergency generator. While it would be difficult to single out any item that would not have been used in conventional design, their collective use in the total system reflects a high degree of care in planning a unique combination of available equipment and systems to achieve the primary goal of conserving energy.

Manchester Federal Building
Manchester, New Hampshire
Architects: Isaak and Isaak, Architects
Engineers: Richard D. Kimball Co.
　　　　　　Dubin-Bloome Associates

Photo: K. Daucella

Pumps, Motors And Fans

Pumps

☐ Properly selected, pumps offer high efficiency under part load conditions. With automatic-throttling-type control valves and multiple pumps that can be started and stopped in sequence, the quantity of fluid in circulation can be reduced to match the load and still maintain high-efficiency operation. This can be especially useful in multiple heat pump systems.

Motors

☐ Alternating current motors vary from low efficiencies at fractional horsepower outputs to higher efficiencies of larger motors. In the last few years, higher-efficiency motors offering significant energy savings have become widely available. Above 3 horsepower, squirrel-cage motors operating at ½ to ¾ part loads are slightly less efficient than at full-load rating. Below 3 horsepower, for similar load comparisons, losses in motor efficiency are greater.

Fans

☐ Fans should be selected for the highest operating efficiency at predominant operating conditions to minimize energy consumed for air circulation. Centrifugal fans include the air-foil, backward-inclined, and forward-curved types. The air-foil and backward-inclined types have similar efficiencies, with the air foil more efficient in larger sizes. Efficiency of the forward-curved type is lower than the other two centrifugal types.

☐ Vaneaxial fans are available with either fixed or adjustable pitch blades. At full-load operation, their efficiencies are comparable to centrifugal fans. At part-load operation, the position of adjustable pitch fan blades can be automatically reset to reduce air quantity and maintain high operating efficiency. Variable inlet vanes used with fixed blade vaneaxial fans can vary the quantity of air flow for efficient part load operation.

Heat Exchangers

Thermal Wheels

☐ Thermal wheels, also called heat wheels, are packed with a heat-absorbing material such as aluminum or stainless steel wool. The wheels transfer energy from one airstream to another or, for large boiler plants, from flue gas to combustion air. The thermal wheel can only be installed when the hot and cold airstreams are immediately adjacent and parallel. Two types of thermal wheel are available: one transfers sensible heat only, the other transfers both sensible and latent heat.

☐ Thermal wheels are driven by electric motors, which use energy and decrease summer efficiency because of motor-generated heat. Efficiencies are generally 60 to 80 percent for sensible heat transfer and 20 to 60 percent for latent heat transfer.

Heat Pipes

☐ Heat pipes running through the adjacent walls of inlet and outlet ducts can be an efficient means of transferring heat from the warmer duct to the cooler one. The heat pipes are short lengths of copper tubing, sealed tightly at the ends with wicks or capillaries and containing a charge of refrigerant. For single direction heat flow, the refrigerant moves by capillary action to the warmer end of the tube and evaporates, absorbing heat in the process. The warmer end of the pipe is slightly lower than the cooler end, where it condenses, releases its heat to the cooler duct, and re-migrates to the lower end. For dual-direction heat flow (summertime cooling recovery) heat pipes must be installed level. All liquid flow is then by capillary action only.

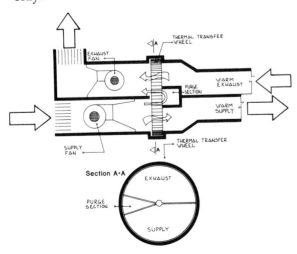

Thermal Wheels

Runaround-Coils

☐ A runaround coil system is composed of two or more extended surface fin coils installed in air ducts and interconnected by piping. A heat-exchange fluid of ethylene glycol and water is circulated through the system by a pump; the fluid absorbs heat from the hot air stream and releases it into the cold air stream (or vice versa). A runaround-coil system can be used in winter to preheat cold outdoor air and in summer to cool hot outdoor air. Where there is no possibility of freezing, water can also be used as the heat transfer medium. Runaround coils are most often used when it is physically difficult to locate the exhaust air duct in close proximity to the make-up air duct. They are substantially less efficient than heat wheels and heat pipe heat exchangers.

☐ When double bundle condensers are used for heat recovery, a coiling coil can be placed in the exhaust air duct to remove the heat before dumping to the outside. This heat is transferred via the chiller to the condenser side. This is one of the most efficient forms of exhaust air heat recovery possible. It should be considered if other system requirements support it.

Air-To-Air Heat Exchanger

☐ An air-to-air heat exchanger transfers heat directly from one air stream to another through either side of a metal transfer surface. This surface can be convoluted plates (for low-temperature use in HVAC systems) or tubes (for boiler flue gas heat transfer). The heat exchangers are available as packaged units or custom-made. Efficiencies tend to be lower than 50 percent, but these exchangers are relatively inexpensive, have low resistance to air flow, require no power input, and are durable.

☐ Extreme care should be used in the design of flue gas heat recovery systems. Improper design can lead to cooling flue gases below their condensation point. Flue gas condensate, particularly from oil-filtered boilers, is extremely corrosive.

Heat Pumps

☐ Heat pumps can also be used as heat exchangers that are most effective in the heating mode. Heat pumps can be configured in all possible combinations of air and water.

Shell/Tube Heat Exchanger

☐ Shell and tube heat exchangers can be used when configured to transfer heat to liquid from liquid, steam or gas. They are especially effective where large temperature differentials exist.

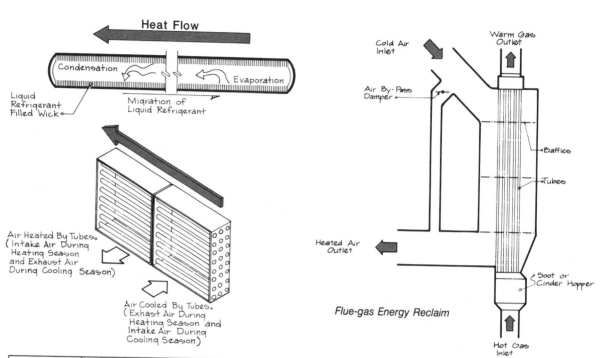

Heat Flow

Condensation   Evaporation

Liquid Refrigerant Filled Wick

Migration of Liquid Refrigerant

Air Heated By Tubes. (Intake Air During Heating Season and Exhaust Air During Cooling Season)

Air Cooled By Tubes. (Exhaust Air During Heating Season and Intake Air During Cooling Season)

Cold Air Inlet

Warm Gas Outlet

Air By-Pass Damper

Baffles

Tubes

Heated Air Outlet

Soot or Cinder Hopper

Flue-gas Energy Reclaim

Hot Gas Inlet

Heat Reclaim Sources	Temper Ventilation Air	Preheat Domestic Hot Water	Space Heating	Terminal Reheat	Temper Makeup Air	Preheat Combustion Air	Heat Heavy Oil	Internal to External Zone Heat Transfer
Exhaust air	1a, 1b, 1c, 2, 3, 4, 5				1a, 1b, 1c, 2, 3, 4, 5	Direct		5, Direct
Flue gas	1b, 3, 4		3, 4		1b, 3, 4	1b, 2, 3, 4		
Hot condensate	3, 6	3, 6	3, 5, 6	3, 6	3, 6	3, 6	6	
Refrigerant hot gas	6	6		6	6			
Hot condenser water	3, 6	3, 6	3, 5, 6	6	3, 5, 6	3, 5, 6	6	5
Hot-water drains		6						
Solid waste	7	7	7	7	7	7	7	
Engine and exhaust cooling systems	6, 8	6	6, 8	6	6, 8	6, 8	6	
Lights Air-cooled condensers	5, 9		5, 9 Direct	5, 9	5, 9			5, 9

Heat Reclaim Devices:
1. Thermal wheel
   a. Latent
   b. Sensible
   c. Combination
2. Runaround coil
3. Heat pipe
4. Air-to-air heat exchanger
5. Heat pump
6. Shell/tube heat exchanger
7. Incinerator
8. Waste heat boiler
9. Heat-of-light

Applications of Heat Reclamation Devices

Fred S. Dubin and Chalmers G. Long, Jr., *Energy Conservation Standards*, © 1978. Reprinted by permission of McGraw-Hill Book Company, New York, N.Y.

ACTIVE SOLAR SYSTEMS

Introduction

Active solar systems capture solar energy in order to deliver heat at moderate temperatures, generally between 90 and 200 degrees (F.).

Active solar systems use mechanical means to transport heat from the location where it is collected to the locations where it is either stored or used. The term *active* is used in contrast to *passive*, which refers to solar systems in which collection, storage and use are integrated spatially or heat transport is accomplished by either gravity convection, radiation or conduction. Passive solar applications are addressed in a separate monograph in this handbook.

Active systems are designed and applied to both residential- and commercial-scale buildings. A primary difference between the two applications is that a residential system, though requiring auxiliary backup, tends to be designed as the building's primary system, while a commercial solar system is generally only an increment to the building's larger, more conventional mechanical systems.

Active solar systems can be applied to a variety of needs, including space heating, domestic or service (e.g., restaurant) hot water, space cooling, swimming pool heating and industrial process hot water. All involve solar collectors to absorb and retain solar energy (*insolation*). All involve a transport fluid, either

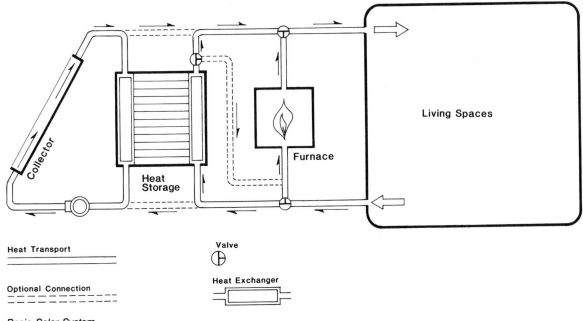

Heat Transport

Optional Connection

Valve

Heat Exchanger

Basic Solar System

air or a liquid (generally water or a water-antifreeze solution). The transport fluid requires a network of ducts and fans for air, or piping and pumps for liquid. If heat collected by the system is to be used at a later time, a method of storing heat is required. If the heat is to be transferred from one fluid to another (e.g., from antifreeze solution to water or from water to air) heat exchangers will be required. These elements—collection, transport, heat exchange, distribution and storage—make up what is normally considered a complete active solar system.

A major factor affecting solar systems is the delivery temperature required. Space heating can be accomplished at lower temperature than domestic water heating, for example, and space cooling usually at lower temperatures than industrial process water heating. This affects a wide range of design decisions (e.g., collector type, amounts of insulation, fluid flow rates, system pressure tolerance).

The following symbols are used to display various pieces of equipment and their location in the graphic illustrations presented throughout this monograph.

SYMBOLS

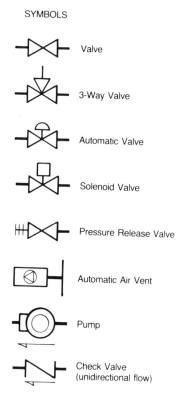

Valve

3-Way Valve

Automatic Valve

Solenoid Valve

Pressure Release Valve

Automatic Air Vent

Pump

Check Valve (unidirectional flow)

Feasibility Considerations

The feasibility of using an active solar system is best addressed with a focus on the problem to be solved and not a predetermined solution. For example, active solar systems are usually thought of as including collectors, transport systems, storage and, perhaps, heat exchangers. Many solar applications, however, do not require all of these elements. Any application in which it is physically possible to collect and use solar energy is, theoretically, feasible. If it is also possible to reduce first costs without either increasing operating costs or decreasing efficiency, feasibility is improved.

☐ An example illustrates the point. The owner of a building in Reno, Nevada, approached a design firm to investigate the possibility of adding a solar system. He was told that his building was well sited and structurally able to support roof-mounted collector arrays, but that a solar system would require an area of collectors four times the size of his roof and an addition to house heat storage. This design response is clearly based on a presumption that the solar system had to satisfy a certain percentage of the total load.

☐ Without that assumption a different design might have been offered. Given the building's relatively constant daytime usage, it would have been possible to limit the number of collectors only to those needed to preheat incoming water for the existing boiler, with fluid transport accomplished by city water pressure. This solution would yield maximum possible collector efficiency and eliminate the first cost for heat exchange and storage.

☐ *Economic feasibility* is defined here as lower life cycle cost; that is, over the life of a solar system the sum of all costs minus energy savings must be less than the sum of costs for a conventional system plus its energy costs.

☐ Analysts at the National Bureau of Standards have identified five basic energy economic analysis approaches: *net benefits or savings, savings-to-investment ratio, internal rate of return, discounted payback* and *life-cycle costs*.

☐ Life-cycle costs (LCC), net benefits (B-C) and savings-to-investment ratio (SIR) analysis tools provide virtually the same information but in different terms. The net benefits (B-C) tool should give precisely the same dollar result as would be arrived at by comparing LCC compilations. The SIR expresses not the dollar amount, but the ratio of savings per dollar of cost for the entire system.

☐ The internal-rate-of-return (IRR) on additional investment is expressed as a percentage. For IRR, only differences in savings and costs are considered. These four analysis tools are all comprehensve life-cycle cost methods that consider the time value of money over the life of a system.

☐ The last method, discounted payback, again considers the time value of money, but only up to the point at which energy savings pay for all initial costs and replacement/maintenance cost incurred to that point.

☐ The shorter the time frame in which specific clients operate, the more likely they are to prefer internal-rate-of-return and discounted-payback.

Site/Climate Analysis

A site and climate analysis for a solar system is performed to ensure that a sufficient quantity of solar radiation falls upon the given location and that it will not be shaded by existing or anticipated obstructions. More extensive information on this topic appears in the "Climate and Site" and "Shading and Sun Control" monographs in this handbook.

☐ The two primary climatic factors to be considered are the amount of solar radiation at the site and the geometric relationship (angle of incidence) between the sun rays and the absorbing collector surface. This amount of solar radiation varies depending on latitude and season, with higher values closer to the equator and the highest annual values around June 21 (see accompanying tables).

☐ The incident angle determines percentages of radiation transmitted, reflected and absorbed by collector materials. The incident angle varies with altitude, which is the angle of the sun above the horizon, and with azimuth, which is the angle between the sun's position and true south. Collectors, other than motorized tracking collectors, are fixed in one plane. Thus as the sun moves across the sky and its azimuth and altitude change, the angle of incidence also changes. Less solar energy is reflected away from the collector absorber surface as the solar rays come closer to being perpendicular to the plane of the collector.

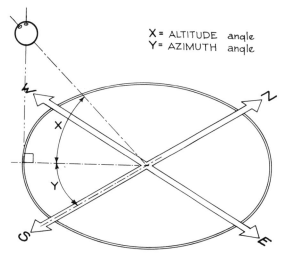

Sun Position

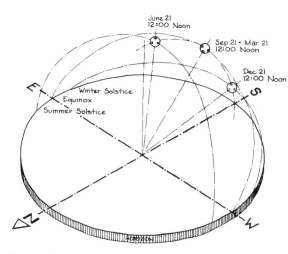

Seasonal Variations in Sun Position

☐ Any strategy that increases the amount of time that collectors are more nearly perpendicular to the sun's rays will increase system efficiency. Tracking collectors move continuously to follow the path of the sun. Flat-plate collectors can be mounted with adjustable tilt to be changed seasonally or even monthly. Fixed flat-plate collectors are set at the tilt that optimizes the overall amount of heat collected. As a rule of thumb, fixed flat-plate collectors used year-round should be mounted to true south and at a tilt equal to latitude plus 5 degrees. If the solar system is designed for use in the heating season only, a higher tilt, of latitude plus 15 degrees, will be more nearly perpendicular to the winter sun.

☐ Site shading patterns and local climatic patterns will determine whether the collectors will see an asymmetrical solar day. If there is a persistent pattern of morning cloudiness or morning shading, for example, then the designer can consider orienting the collectors west of south to maximize collection of afternoon sun.

☐ Existing shading conditions can be subject to changes caused by subsequent growth of trees or construction on adjacent land. "Sun-rights" and solar access are discussed in the following section on codes and standards.

Shenandoah Solar Recreational Center
Shenandoah, Georgia
Architects: Taylor and Collum, Architects
Engineers: Newcomb & Boyd

This two-story, 54,000-square-foot building houses an assortment of spaces, including office, lounge, meeting room, gymnasium, game room and ice-skating rink. The mechanical room forms part of the lobby so that visitors can view components of the solar system, which provide space heating, cooling, DHW, ice-rink resurfacing and swimming pool heating. The building is constructed of poured concrete with sloping sides covered with earth. Window areas are small, single-glazed, and completely shaded.

The solar system consists of 11,200 square feet of flat-plate collectors. The collectors are double-glazed (low-iron glass), with a selective black chrome surface (α/e ratio of .95/.07 or 13.6). Heat transport fluid is water, protected from freezing by recirculation of warm water. The saw-tooth configuration allows for bands of polished aluminum reflectors totaling 26,000 square feet facing each row of collectors. Hot water storage is provided by a 15,000-gallon water tank buried outside and insulated with 2 feet of sod and a 2300-gallon buffer tank with 9 inches of insulation.

Collector water at 190 degrees (F.) or above is supplied to the 94-ton absorption chiller. Cold water storage is provided by two 30,000-gallon storage tanks. The hot water buffer tank is used in the primary loop to reduce on-off cycling of the chiller. This system provides 65 percent of the cooling energy requirements.

Shenandoah Solar Recreational Center
Shenandoah, Georgia
Architects: Taylor and Collum, Architects
Engineers: Newcomb & Boyd

Codes and Standards

State and local codes and standards can have important effects on solar system design. With the exception of the collectors, the equipment involved is not unique to solar systems, and it will be subject to plumbing codes, building codes, mechanical codes, and boiler and pressure-vessel codes. Many jurisdictions have adopted solar codes to govern collector design and other factors unique to solar systems. Others subject collectors to the provisions of sign ordinances. When local codes include no specific solar provisions, code officials can be consulted.

☐ Local zoning ordinances can impose minimum setbacks from property lines, maximum possible lot coverage and height restrictions. Architectural review committees or similar local groups sometimes have a role in approving building appearance and other design elements, especially in historic districts and planned communities. Variances from existing codes and zoning restrictions are often possible with relatively new issues like solar technology.

☐ Not all community legislation concerning solar design is prohibitive. Some communities, notably in Florida and California, have passed legislation requiring either solar hot water systems or the hook-up for them in any new residential construction.

Standards

☐ Private organizations, the federal government, and many state and local governments have established standards for solar hot water systems. Most organizations providing grants or tax benefits require that projects adhere to recognized standards. The U. S. Department of Housing and Urban Development has published *Intermediate Minimum Property Standards for Solar Heating and Domestic Hot Water Systems*.

☐ The U. S. Department of Energy and the National Bureau of Standards, through their "Model Solar Document," are developing standards for components and design methods. Professional societies such as the American Society of Heating, Refrigerating and Air-Conditioning Engineers and trade associations such as the Sheet Metal and Air Conditioning Contractors' National Association have published guidelines for solar system design and installation. In addition, the International Association of Plumbing and Mechanical Officials has developed a *Uniform Solar Energy Code*, which has been adopted by some communities.

"Sunrights" and Solar Access

☐ The question of "sunrights" has become the subject of considerable legal debate in recent years. It is generally agreed that owners have full rights to sunlight falling vertically on their property. However, our legal system does not generally recognize the right to sunlight that might be blocked by activities or objects on another site.

☐ Some owners have obtained legally enforceable *easements* of solar access from adjoining landowners. Developers of large tracts of land can place a *restrictive covenant* on the property that gives neighbors easements over each other's lots, either by specifying the restriction or creating a controlling body to rule on situations as they arise. Zoning ordinances can approach the problem in several ways. Access to direct sunlight can be incorporated into height and use restrictions, for example.

System Types

In active systems, either air or a liquid can be used to collect solar heat. The heat can subsequently be transferred to another fluid using heat exchangers, allowing the manner of supplying heat to the load to be independent of the nature of the heat collection medium.

☐ A solar collector of the liquid- or air-heating type, in combination with an insulated storage reservoir with associated pumps (or blowers), piping (or ducting) and a control system are the components necessary for solar heating a space-or heating domestic or service hot water.

☐ The collectors can be of the flat-plate, evacuated tube, or concentrating type, depending on the temperatures required by the load. Storage can be by a hot-water tank, a rock bed (for air systems), or phase-change material.

☐ In residential applications a control system consisting of thermostats and relays controls the solar collection system, the heat distribution system, and their interaction with the auxiliary heating or cooling system. In commercial applications the solar system itself is more likely to be an auxiliary system, controlled by the controls for the larger HVAC system.

☐ Several additional subsystem components common to most conventional heating, ventilating and airconditioning systems, but designed specifically for the requirements of solar systems, are heat exchangers, pumps and blowers, valves, dampers, air vents and expansion tanks.

☐ In the simplest analysis, there are two system types, *air* and *liquid* (primarily water). The major differences in these two approaches are that liquids transport and store heat more efficiently than air, and that water freezes.

☐ Using air as the transport medium avoids the freezing problem associated with water collectors, but creates a substantial penalty in additional space requirements. Forced convection of air transfers 5 to 50 BTU/hr. sq. ft. degree (F.), while the same value for water is 50 to 100 BTU/hr. sq. ft. degree (F.). Air systems also generally use rock storage, which has a similar space penalty. Rocks are 50 percent more dense than water but will hold only 20 percent as much heat per pound; three times as much space is required.

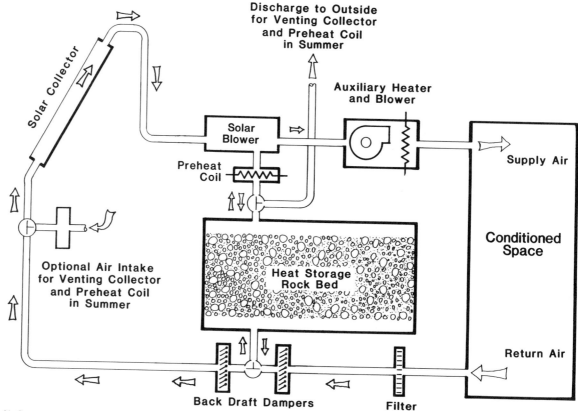

Discharge to Outside
for Venting Collector
and Preheat Coil
in Summer

Air System

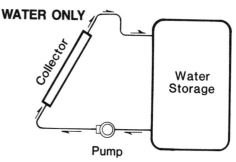

WATER ONLY

Solar System—Water

☐ There are freezing problems associated with water systems. Most of the conventional means of providing freeze protection diminish system efficiency and increase power requirements.

☐ One common solution to the freezing problem is to circulate an antifreeze solution, rather than water, through the collectors. The antifreeze is less efficient than water as a heat transfer fluid and requires the use of a heat exchanger (double-jacketed for domestic hot water systems to preserve purity) and the use of two pumps rather than one. Hydrocarbon and silicon fluids also can be used but are less efficient. These systems are referred to as indirect (double loop) systems.

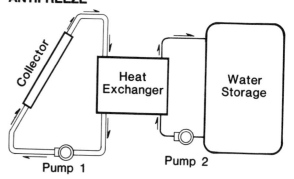

ANTIFREEZE

Solar System—Antifreeze

284

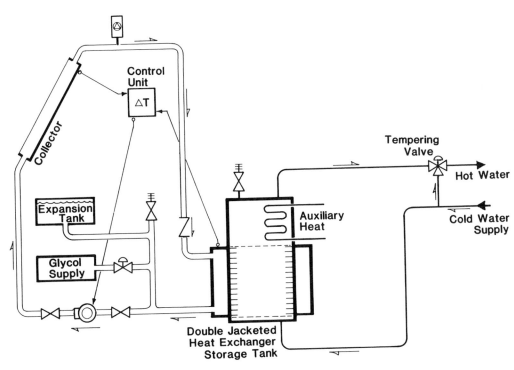

Control Unit △T

Collector

Tempering Valve

Hot Water

Expansion Tank

Glycol Supply

Cold Water Supply

Auxiliary Heat

Double Jacketed Heat Exchanger Storage Tank

Indirect, Single Tank Liquid System

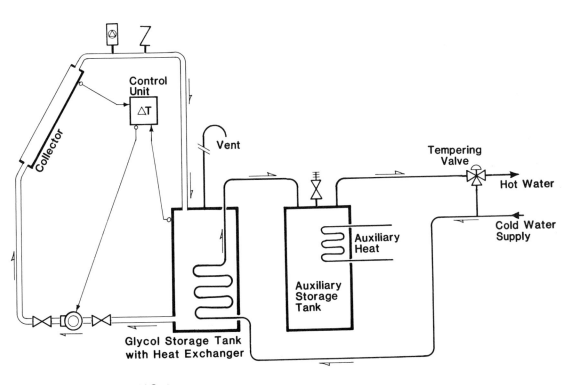

Control Unit △T

Collector

Vent

Tempering Valve

Hot Water

Cold Water Supply

Auxiliary Heat

Auxiliary Storage Tank

Glycol Storage Tank with Heat Exchanger

Indirect, Double Tank Liquid System

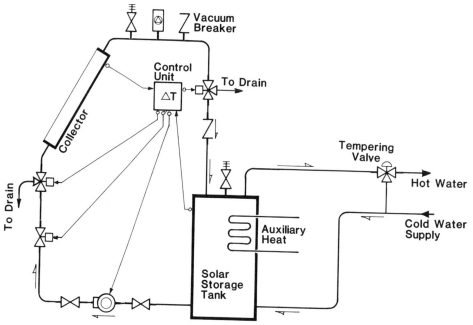

Direct, Single Tank Liquid System

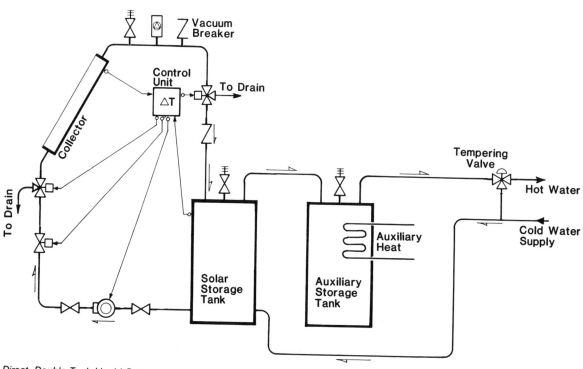

Direct, Double Tank Liquid System

286

□ Direct systems (single loop) generally circulate water through the collectors only during heating periods. A means for draining the collectors during freezing weather must be provided. This generally introduces air into the system each time it is drained, requiring vacuum breakers, air vents, additional sensors and valves. Another method is to recirculate warm storage water to heat the collectors above freezing, which often causes only small heat losses.

□ There are few variations on the air system and because of its significant space requirements it is used widely only in the residential market. However, due to internal loads, less collector area is needed for commercial buildings. Thus air systems can be effectively used when combined with forced air duct systems.

□ In commercial and industrial applications, systems tend to be large, so the compactness of water systems can be an advantage.

□ Commercial and industrial buildings in nearly all climates require airconditioning, so the use of air-type solar heating would require, under present conditions, conventional cooling facilities as well. Current development efforts may lead to practical cooling systems that use the higher temperature possible with water-type solar heating systems to drive rankine engines or to regenerate dessicant cooling systems. The probable outcome of this work is not yet clear, so commercial and industrial buildings in freezing climates are candidates for either system type. Existing buildings heated by warm air often adapt easily to solar air systems, whereas those using hot water heat at temperatures below 140 degrees (F.) are often well suited to solar hot water systems.

□ In summary, air and liquid systems offer the following advantages and disadvantages:

Liquid	Air
Collectors generally more efficient.	Collectors generally operate at slightly lower temperature.
Can be combined with domestic hot water system and air-cooling systems possible in the future.	Simpler; space heat can be supplied directly. Can preheat domestic hot water. Does not adapt easily to air cooling.
Freeze protection can require antifreeze and heat exchangers; costlier and less efficient.	No freeze protection required.
Precautions must be taken against corrosion, leakage and boiling.	Low maintenance requirements. Leaks easily repaired with duct tape; however, they may be difficult to find.
Insulated pipes take up nominal space. Usually higher installation costs for collectors and storage components.	Ductwork and rock storage bed are bulky. Lower equipment costs.
	More energy required to drive fans than pumps. Noisier in operation.

Towns Elementary School
Atlanta, Georgia
Architects: Burt Hill Kosar Rittlemann Associates
Engineers: Dubin, Mindell and Bloome Associates

This active solar heating and cooling system is a 1977 retrofit to the one-story, 32,000-square-foot school, constructed in 1962. The school which accommodates approximately 200 students, has approximately equal winter heating and summer cooling loads.

The 10,400 square feet of collectors are mounted in sawtooth fashion on the existing roof. The flat-plate collectors have tempered double glazing and selective surface absorbers, and circulate water with inhibitors added. Collector freeze protection is provided by draining the water and replacing it with nitrogen gas.

The backside of each collector sawtooth is a mylar-covered reflector, mounted at 36 degrees from the horizontal. Totaling 12,000 square feet, the reflectors are calculated to increase the summer gain by about 30 percent. The typical collection temperature in midwinter is 140 degrees (F.); in midsummer it is 200 degrees (F.).

The system storage consists of three insulated, underground 15,000-gallon steel tanks, which store either hot or cold water. An existing gas furnace provides backup heat in both winter and summer. Cooling is provided by a 100-ton lithium bromide absorption chiller. The system furnishes more than 60 percent of the building's heating and cooling loads, including domestic hot water heating.

Towns Elementary School
Atlanta, Georgia
Architects: Burt Hill Kosar Rittlemann Associates
Engineers: Dubin, Mindell and Bloome Associates

Towns Elementary School
Atlanta, Georgia
Architects: Burt Hill Kosar Rittlemann Associates
Engineers: Dubin, Mindell and Bloome Associates

Terraset Elementary School
Reston, Virginia
Architects: Davis, Smith and Carter

Terraset was constructed by cutting away the top of a hill, casting the reinforced concrete structure on-site, and then backfilling with dirt around and over the building. It is equipped with a complex heat reclamation system with heat pump capability and uses 4,825 square feet of evacuated tube collectors mounted on a spaceframe over the entrance courtyard to the school for heating in the winter and absorption cooling during the summer.

The solar system instruments include a "Sunkeeper" microprocessor from Andover Controls that is accessed locally or by a remote terminal tied into a telephone line. The "Sunkeeper" software logic controls the operation of the solar system and provides, on demand, both instantaneous performance and average performance for each of the previous 32 hours. This remote monitoring, control and data logging capability applies only to the solar system, not to the school's conventional pneumatic HVAC. Additional measurements of flow power demand and temperature are needed for a complete performance determination.

The concrete roof and soil cover have been a mixed blessing. The massive roof and sheltered wall construction provides a dampening effect on diurnal temperature swings and reduces heating and cooling loads during the spring and fall. However, it provides little insulation during sustained winter periods when the temperature is below 35 to 45 degrees (F.) and the soil covering has been cooled to a steady state.

Terraset Elementary School
Reston, Virginia
Architects: Davis, Smith and Carter

Terraset Elementary School
Reston, Virginia
Architects: Davis, Smith and Carter

Collectors

The three major types of active solar collectors used in building applications are flat plates, evacuated tubes and various linear concentrator types. Flat plates are by far the most common type used for heating and hot water. Evacuated and concentrating collectors are more often used for applications requiring higher temperatures.

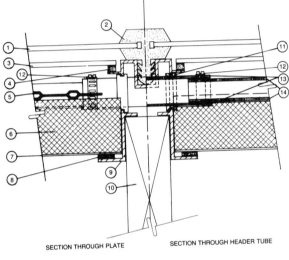

SECTION THROUGH PLATE   SECTION THROUGH HEADER TUBE

1	OUTER GLASS	8	SEALANT BEAD
2	NEOPRENE GLAZING GASKET	9	ALUMINUM EXTRUDED FRAME
3	INNER GLASS	10	SUBSTRUCTURE
4	HEAT RESISTANT GLAZING TAPE	11	GROMMET AND DESICCANT
5	FLUID CIRCULATING PLATE	12	HOSE CLAMP
6	RIGID FIBERGLASS INSULATION	13	FLEXIBLE HOSE
7	VAPOR BARRIER BACKING	14	HEADER TUBE

Solar Collector Detail

Flat-Plate Collectors

☐ A flat-plate solar collector consists of the following components.

☐ *Absorber plate*—metal (usually copper, steel or aluminum) or plastic surface covered with flat black paint or a special selective coating to maximize absorption and minimize reradiation.

☐ *Flow passages*—liquid flow is usually through tubes attached to or integral with the absorber plate; air flow occurs above and/or below the plate; the heat-transfer surface area is maximized by means of fins, slots or metal screening.

☐ *Cover plate(s)*—transparent cover (one, two or three) of tempered glass or various plastic materials are used to reduce convective and radiative heat losses to the outside air.

☐ *Insulation*—reduces conductive heat losses out the back and sides of the collector.

☐ *Enclosure*—a box to protect collector components from the weather.

☐ Fluid flow tubes in a flat-plate collector are spaced several inches apart, with the absorber surfaces between acting as fins that absorb heat and conduct it to the tubes. Tube spacing is an efficiency-versus-cost tradeoff. Copper tubes can be welded or soldered to copper plates or clamped to aluminum plates. The thermal conductance of the bond is critical and can vary by a factor of 200. A better technique is to extrude or otherwise form a tube pattern into the plate during manufacture. Tubes can be in parallel from inlet to outlet header or in a single serpentine. The latter technique eliminates the possibility of header leaks and ensures uniform flow but also increases pressure drop. When water is used as the heat-transport fluid, draindown freeze protection requires that flow passages be easy to drain.

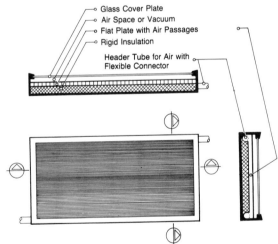

Solar Air Collectors

☐ Unlike liquid collectors, air-collector absorber plates do not require high thermal conductivity because air comes in contact with the entire surface. Routing the air flow beneath the absorber plate reduces thermal loss through the glazing. Heat transfer is enhanced by both increasing surface area and creating turbulent flow, but with a penalty of increased fan power requirements. Air collectors eliminate both freezing and boiling problems. Leaks are also not damaging, though they can degrade performance significantly.

Property or Material	Absorptance α	Emittance ε	$\dfrac{\alpha}{\varepsilon}$	Breakdown Temperature F (°C)	Comments
Black Chrome	.87–.93	.1	~9		
Alkyd Enamel	.9	.9	1		Durability limited at high temperatures
Black Acrylic Paint	.92–.97	.84–.90	~1		
Black Inorganic Paint	.89–.96	.86–.93	~1		
Black Silicone Paint	.86–.94	.83–.89	1		Silicone binder
Pbs/Silicone Paint	.94	.4	2.5	662 (350)	Has a high emittance for thickness > 10 μm
Flat Black Paint	.95–.98	.89–.97	~1		
Ceramic Enamel	.9	.5	1.8		Stable at high temperatures
Black Zinc	.9	.1	9		
Copper Oxide over Aluminum	.93	.11	8.5	392 (200)	
Black Copper over Copper	.85–.90	.08–.12	7–11	842 (450)	Patinates with moisture
Black Chrome over Nickel	.92–.94	.07–.12	8–13	842 (450)	Stable at high temperatures
Black Nickel over Nickel	.93	.06	15	842 (450)	May be influenced by moisture at elevated temperatures
Ni-Zn-S over Nickel	.96	.97	14	536 (280)	
Black Iron over Steel	.90	.10	9		

Characteristics of Absorptive Coatings

☐ The coating on the absorber plate determines in large part the plate's *absorptance* and *emittance*. Absorptance is the measure of how much energy is absorbed rather than reflected or transmitted. Emittance is the measure of how much is reradiated rather than contained. One would like to maximize the first and minimize the latter, or increase the ratio (α/e) between the two. Flat black paint is inexpensive and has a high absorptance (.95 to .98), but it also has a high emittance (.89 to .97), yielding an α/e ratio of 1. *Selective surface* is the term given to coatings with both high absorptance and low emittance. Black chrome, one of the more widely used selective surfaces, has an α/e ratio of 9 (α,0.9; e,0.1). Selective surfaces improve collec-

tor performance, but increase the cost; their long-term durability has not yet been determined.

Test	Poly-vinyl Fluoride	Poly-ethylene Tereph-thalate or Poly-ester	Polycar-bonate	Fiber-glass Rein-forced Plastics	Methyl Methacry-late	Fluori-nated Ethylene-Propyl-ene	Ordinary Clear Lime Glass (Float) (0.10–0.13% iron)	Sheet Lime Glass (0.05–0.06% iron)	Water White Glass (0.01% iron)
Solar Trans-mission (%)	92–94	85	82–89	77–90	89	97	85	87	85–91
Maximum Operating Temp. (F°)	227	220	250–270	200 produces 10% trans-mis-sion loss	180–190	248	400	400	400
Tensile Strength (psi)	13000	24000	9500	15000–17000	10500	2700–3100	1600 an-nealed 6400 tem-pered	1600 an-nealed 6400 tem-pered	1600 an-nealed 6400 tem-pered
Thermal Ex-pansion Coefficient (in/in/F° × 10⁻⁶)	24	15	37.5	18–22	41.0	8.3–10.5	4.8	5.0	4.7–8.6
Elastic Modulus (psi × 10⁶)	0.26	0.55	0.345	1.1	0.45	0.5	10.5	10.5	10.5
Thickness (in)	0.004	0.001	0.125	0.040	0.125	0.002	0.125	0.125	0.125
Weight (lb/sq ft) for above thick-ness	0.028	0.007	0.77	0.30	0.75	0.002	1.63	1.63	1.63
Greatest Load Area (psf:sq ft)	—	—	—	—	—	—	—	—	30:30 an-nealed 100:28 tempered
Length of Life (yr)	In 5 years retains 96% of total trans-mis-sion	4	—	7–20	—	—	—	—	—

Characteristics of Cover Plate Materials

Material	Density (Lb/Cu.Ft.)	Thermal Conductivity at 200 (°F) (BTU/Hr.Sq.Ft.°F/In.)	Temperature Limits (°F)
Fiberglass with Organic Binder	0.6 1.0 1.5 3.0	0.41 0.35 0.31 0.30	350 350 350 350
Fiberglass with Low Binder	1.5	0.31	850
Ceramic Fiber Blanket	3.0	0.4 at 400°F	2300
Mineral Fiber Blanket	10.0	0.31	1200
Calcium Silicate	13.0	0.38	1200
Urea-Formaldehyde Foam	0.7	0.20 at 75°F	210
Urethane Foam	2–4	0.20	250–400

Characteristics of Insulation Materials

□ Cover plates are normally of glass or one of several plastics. The two primary considerations are transmittance and durability. Window glass tempered to withstand high temperatures is most commonly used. Transmittance (T) of solar radiation is affected primarily by iron content. Transmittance can be .85 for an iron content of 0.12 percent and 0.92 for water white glass with an iron content of 0.01 percent. Glass is practically opaque to longwave, thermal radiation, which helps to trap the heat collected by the absorber plate. Plastics used as cover glazing are cheaper and lighter than glass and, because they are thinner, often have higher transmittance as well. Disadvantages of plastics are that they generally do not trap heat as well and degrade under both high temperature and ultraviolet radiation.

□ The number of cover plates depends on the type of application and involves a tradeoff between cost and performance. As a rule of thumb, the higher the differential between ambient and absorber temperatures the more cover plates are required, except that a single-glazed collector with a selective surface will often outperform a double-glazed one with a nonselective surface.

□ Various types of insulation are used in collectors to minimize heat losses out the back and sides. It is important that the insulation not outgas under stagnation conditions (that is, when heat builds up because the heat transport fluid is not flowing). Such gases can coat the inside of the glazing and greatly reduce transmittance. For this reason, fiberglass insulation is preferred over styrofoams and urethanes.

□ Collector enclosures are ordinarily made of steel, aluminum or fiberglass. The enclosure should allow for differential expansion while remaining air- and watertight. External pipe connections are particularly vulnerable; sealing compounds and gaskets must be able to withstand both stagnation temperatures and thermal cycling.

□ The performance of flat-plate collectors can be increased by an anti-reflective coating on cover plates, honey combs between absorber and cover to reduce convective heat loss, and exterior planar reflectors to increase incident radation.

□ Flat-plate collectors will not be economical for space cooling until both collector performance is improved and absorption units are produced that operate at 160 to 180 degrees (F.) There is a possibility that both will occur in the next 5 to 10 years.

□ For the present, however, advanced collector designs must be used for higher temperature applications.

Evacuated Tube Collectors

□ Evacuated tubes provide higher temperatures than flat-plate collectors because the vacuum surrounding the fluid-transport tube restricts convective heat loss. Evacuated tubes can collect both direct and diffuse radiation.

□ Several types of evacuated tubes are on

the market. Basic options are either two or three cylindrical glass tubes with the evacuated space between the outer and second tube. A selective surface is applied to the outside of the second cylinder. The three-tube version delivers fluid between the second and third tube and removes it within the third tube.

☐ Various configurations of reflectors can be used behind evacuated tubes to provide a small degree of concentration. Extremely high stagnation temperatures—over 600 degrees (F.)—make both thermal shock with cold water and boiling water during a power failure significant problems.

Parabolic Troughs

☐ Another way to cut down on heat losses and achieve higher temperatures is to concentrate the solar energy onto a smaller absorber surface. The most commonly used concentrator is a parabolic reflector trough with an absorber pipe located along the focal line. The concentrators require continuous tracking but only about a single axis. A parabolic dish will achieve higher concentration but only through the significant increase in mechanical complexity and cost required to track simultaneously in two planes (altitude and azimuth).

☐ Parabolic concentrators can collect only direct sunlight, not diffuse. As a result, they receive less of the available sunlight than flat plates, which in particularly cloudy climates can completely offset the gain in efficiency.

☐ Fresnel lens collectors also concentrate sunlight, but they do so by refracting (bending) the light instead of reflecting it as do parabolic concentrators.

☐ Fresnel lens applications are generally more expensive, but have the same advantages and disadvantages of parabolic troughs. One problem is the dust accumulation on specular and lens surfaces.

☐ The compound parabolic collector is a promising design still in the development stage. This collector essentially "funnels" the light down to the absorber surface rather than reflecting it. It requires only seasonal adjustment, accepts both direct beam and diffuse radiation over a wide angle, and does not require highly polished reflector surfaces, thereby tolerating dust and degradation better. The cost disadvantage is that a large amount of reflector surface is required.

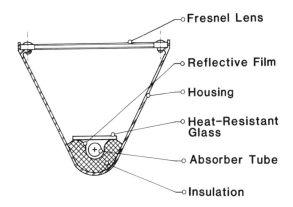

Linear Fresnel Lens Solar Concentrating Collector

Solar Concentrating Collector

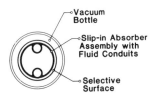

Vacuum Bottle with Slip-in Heat Exchanger

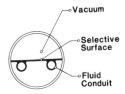

Flat Plate

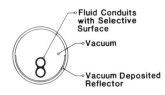

Concentrating

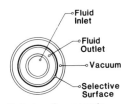

Tubular Concentric

Evacuated Tube Solar Collectors

293

New Mexico Department of Agriculture Building
Las Cruces, New Mexico
Architects: W.T. Harris and Associates
Engineers: Bridgers and Paxton

Energy-conscious design in this rectangular 25,000-square-foot, one-story laboratory begins with a tightly constructed envelope. Walls and roof have U-values of .1 and .05, respectively. The double-glazed windows make up only 5 percent of the wall area.

Two types of solar collectors are used on this building, both mounted at 30 degrees from the horizontal. Flat-plate collectors, with selective surface absorber plates (ratio of .9/.1) of mechanically clipped flow tubes total 626 square feet. Single cover plates (water-white, low-iron glass) is used. The remaining collectors are 540 square feet of tracking Fresnel lens units, which have 2-inch copper absorber plates with 3/8-inch copper tubes and non-selective coatings. The heat transport fluid is water with 40-percent propylene glycol for both collectors.

Solar heated water (175 to 185 degrees F.) is delivered to two absorption chillers. Storage is provided in two 14,000-gallon storage tanks. On a yearly basis, the solar system provides 80 percent of the energy required for space heating, cooling and hot water.

New Mexico Department of Agriculture Building
Las Cruces, New Mexico
Architects: W.T. Harris and Associates
Engineers: Bridgers and Paxton

Collector Efficiency

Collector efficiency is a measure of the percentage of available solar energy that the collector will transmit to the heat transport fluid. Two generic methods of measuring collector efficiency are the calorimetric and instantaneous methods.

☐ The calorimetric method uses a closed system consisting of collector and small storage tank and provides a good method for determining the day-long efficiency of a collector. It requires measurement of the quantity of incident solar radiation, the time period of measurement, and the temperature change of the system.

☐ The instantaneous method uses an open system, an isolated collector, and is performed at solar noon under steady-state conditions. The method requires measurement of the mass of transport fluid, fluid temperature change as it flows through the collector (air or liquid), and amount of solar radiation.

☐ The American Society of Heating, Refrigerating and Air-Conditioning Engineers, using a test method developed by the National Bureau of Standards (NBS), has adopted Standard 93–77, *Methods of Testing to Determine the Thermal Performance of Solar Collectors*. This standard uses the instantaneous method for determining collector efficiency based on gross collector area. Two procedures are used to determine the following:
—collector time constant
—instantaneous efficiency.

☐ The collector time constant is a measure of the thermal inertia of the collector, which is determined by its mass. The smaller the time constant, the more rapidly a collector will respond to short periods of insolation.

☐ The efficiency test is as described earlier. An incident angle modifier (see accompanying figure) adjusts for the decrease in collector efficiency that occurs as more of the incident solar radiation is reflected away from the absorber. This varies for different collectors, but, as a rule of thumb, the day-long modifiers for single and double glass can be given as 0.93 and 0.91, respectively.

☐ The U.S. Department of Housing and Urban Development (HUD) requires that efficiency tests of collectors be performed both before and after a 30-day stagnation test. This test is described both in HUD's *Intermediate Minimum Property Standards for Solar Heating and Domestic Hot Water Systems* and NBS's *Interim Performance Criteria for Solar Heating and Cooling*

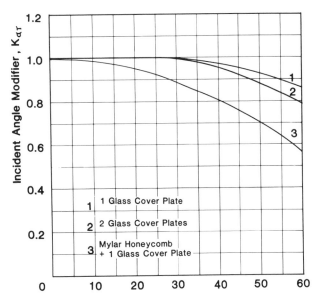

Assumptions : Glass Extinction Coefficient = 0.08/CM
Glass Refractive Index = 1.53
Absorber Plate Absorption = 0.9

1 Glass Cover Plate

2 Glass Cover Plates

Mylar Honeycomb + 1 Glass Cover Plate

Incident Angle Modifiers

Systems in Commercial Buildings. This test provides an indication of a collector's tolerance of the heat that builds up when no heat transport fluid is flowing.

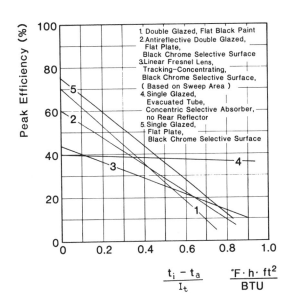

1. Double Glazed, Flat Black Paint
2. Antireflective Double Glazed, Flat Plate, Black Chrome Selective Surface
3. Linear Fresnel Lens, Tracking–Concentrating, Black Chrome Selective Surface, (Based on Sweep Area)
4. Single Glazed, Evacuated Tube, Concentric Selective Absorber, no Rear Reflector
5. Single Glazed, Flat Plate, Black Chrome Selective Surface

$$\frac{t_i - t_a}{I_t} \qquad \frac{°F \cdot h \cdot ft^2}{BTU}$$

Collector Efficiency Curves

☐ The accompanying figures indicate the efficiency of a variety of flat-plate and liquid collectors.

☐ Moving from left to right on the horizontal axis of these graphs, the temperature differential between the fluid temperature entering the collector (t_i) and outside air (t_a) increases. The curves show that for constant insolation striking the absorber plate (It), efficiency is inversely proportional to this temperature differential. As shown, the evacuated tube is less affected than the other collector types.

☐ Designers who have reached the stage of selecting collectors will know the weather patterns (the ambient temperature) and will also have made assumptions about the range of storage temperatures. Comparison of the efficiencies of different collectors within the limits dictated by these two temperatures enables designers to make tradeoffs among cost, efficiency, etc.

High Collector Heat Loss

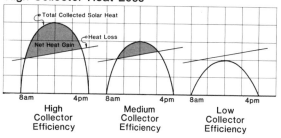

Low Collector Heat Loss

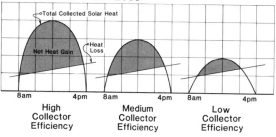

Importance of Low Operating Temperature to Collector Efficiency

☐ *Solar Heating Systems: Analysis and Design with the Sun Pulse Method* by Gordon F. Tully describes analysis and design of solar systems by the "sun-pulse method." This method changes the denominator of the plot of the above efficiency curves. Rather than plotting the insolation as single-point instantaneous value, it is graphed as a day-long sine function.

☐ The unshaded portion under the sine waves graphed here are conceptually equiva-

lent, though not precisely the same, as the numerator (t_i-t_a) in the preceding efficiency curves. Lowering the collector inlet temperature is a simple way to reduce heat loss from a collector. Presented this way, the curves show the importance of low operating temperature relative to collector efficiency.

Georgia Power Headquarters, Atlanta, Georgia
Architects: Heery & Heery, Architects and Engineers Inc.

The energy-conserving features of the Georgia Power Company headquarters in Atlanta, designed by Heery & Heery Architects and Engineers, Inc., limit its annual energy use to less than an estimated 49,000 BTU/sq. ft. for the total building and less than 35,000 BTU/sq. ft. for the tower. A field of 1,482 glass-mirror active solar collectors covers most of the 1.5-acre roof of the low-rise portion of the building. Design analysis indicates that these concentrating collectors will reduce by 15 percent the building's energy needs for airconditioning, heating and domestic hot water. The 360-degree (F.) water produced in the system will be run through an absorption chiller for the airconditioning system—in southern climates, the primary energy user. An electric chiller provides backup for the absorption chiller during the day, and is run at night to produce 300,000 gallons of chilled water for storage and use in the airconditioning system the next day—further reducing the building's electricity demands during peak afternoon periods.

Reflective glass covers the tower's entire exterior, but only the north and south sides have windows. The east and west walls are opaque ceramic-backed glass, lined with insulation. This covering reflects away more solar radiation than concrete, stone or most metals. Because glass also weighs less, the building requires less structural steel framework and concrete foundations.

The windows in the south and north walls are double-glazed to reduce heat gain through them. Windows in the south wall are completely shaded by the sun on June 21 by a combination of the wall's inward step-back and horizontal sunscreen tubes. Elevators, service systems, fire stairs and storage rooms are clustered on the windowless east and west sides; these areas require little heating and cooling, and serve as thermal buffers for the work areas. A specially designed high-pressure sodium fixture and an open plan in the work areas reduce the lighting requirement to one watt/sq. ft.

Georgia Power Headquarters
Atlanta, Georgia
Architects: Heery & Heery, Architects and Engineers, Inc.

Georgia Power Headquarters
Atlanta, Georgia
Architects: Heery & Heery,
Architects and Engineers, Inc.

Thermal Storage

Most active solar applications benefit from some form of thermal storage. Thermal storage enables the solar system to collect more heat than is immediately required and store it for later use. The size of the storage system depends on how long heat must be stored, which varies for different applications. Residential space heating storage may be sized for a period of two or three cloudy days. Commercial applications are often sized in relation to the diurnal (24-hour) cycle, though they can be designed for much longer periods.

□ The design tradeoffs involved in incorporating storage into energy delivery systems can be complex:
—storage temperature versus container and heat exchanger size
—power requirements versus heat exchanger size
—efficiency versus duration of storage
—efficiency versus storage and heat exchanger size
—energy density versus materials corrosion
—energy density versus container cost.

□ Thermal storage consists of a storage medium, a container and input-output devices. Containers must both retain the storage medium and prevent the loss of thermal energy. Stratification of the medium within the container causes vertical "layers" of different temperatures, which can be used by the designer to determine placement of inlets and outlets. Outlets high in the container will deliver the medium to the end use at a higher temperature. Return outlets to collectors placed low in the tank will return cooler medium, allowing the collectors to operate at higher efficiency.

Sensible-Heat Storage	Sp. Ht., BTU/Lb.°F	True Density, Lb./Ft.³	Heat Capacity, BTU/Ft.³°F	
			No Voids	30% Voids
Water	1.00	62	62	43
Scrap Iron	0.12	490	59	41
Magnetite	0.18	320	57	40
Scrap Aluminum	0.23	170	39	27
Concrete	0.27	140±	38	26
Stone	0.21	170±	36	25
Brick	0.20	140	28	20
Sodium (to 208 °F)	0.23	59	14	—

Heat Storage Materials

□ The capacity of thermal storage is proportional to the differences between storage input and output temperatures times the heat storage capacity of the particular medium used.

□ If water is the storage medium, the storage capacity will be the product of the volume, the specific heat of water and the operating temperature range. The specific heat of water, taken from the accompanying table, is 1 BTU/lb./degree (F.).

Highest temperature obtained 150 degrees (F.)
Lowest useful temperature 85 degrees (F.)
Operating range = 65 degrees (F.)

□ One cubic foot of water, again from the table, would give a storage capacity of $1 \times 62 \times 65 = 4030$ BTU. If the daily heat requirement of a house is 40 kWh (1 kWh = 3413 BTU) and two days' heat (273,040 BTU) is to be stored, the volume required will be:

$$\frac{40 \times 2 \times 3413}{4030} = 68 \text{ cubic feet.}$$

One gallon of water weighs approximately 8.3 pounds, which yields 7½ gallons per cubic foot of water (62/8.3 = 7.5). Thus the storage requirement, 68 cubic feet of water, is 508 gallons.

□ Often the recommended storage volume is related to the collector area. Rules of thumb are in the range of 10 to 20 pounds (1 to 3 gallons) of water for each square foot of collector.

□ If the storage medium is crushed rock or gravel, the heat storage capacity can be established as the product of the volume of container, the solidity ratio, the density and the

specific heat of the stone, and the operating temperature range. The solidity ratio may be typically around 0.7 (meaning there is 30 percent void between the solids). The density of stones, from the table, is then 110 lbs./cu. ft. with a specific heat of 0.21 BTU/lb./degree (F.). Thus the 68 cubic feet of storage in the above example, if filled with crushed stone instead of water, would give a storage capacity of:
68 cu. ft. × 110 pounds/cu. ft. × 0.21 BTU/lb./degree (F.) × 65 degrees = 102,102 BTU. which is aproximately 37 percent of the storage capacity of the water.

☐ To date, the majority of active solar storage systems have used water and rock beds. Water storage predominates in domestic hot water applications and rock-bed storage predominates in space heating applications.

☐ Insulated leak-proof tanks are the major cost component of water-based storage systems. Tanks can be steel, fiberglass or reinforced plastics, concrete or wooden. Characteristics, advantages, disadvantages and costs of such tanks are presented in the accompanying table.

☐ The cost ranges listed are approximate and are in 1979 dollars. Such costs depend on tank size, location, installation requirements, temperature ranges and insulation needs. The cost for much larger tanks for longer duration storages can be substantially lower.

☐ Rock beds are much simpler to construct than water tanks. Common materials can be used, and excessive insulation is not required because rock has rather low thermal conductivity. In addition, corrosion problems are eliminated, and small leaks cause little problem.

☐ Thermal stratification of storage will improve system performance significantly, from 5 to 10 percent. For water storage a temperature difference of up to 10 degrees (F.) can be maintained in a carefully designed system. Stratifi-

Type	Advantages	Disadvantages	Temperature limitations	Cost range ($1 gal)
Steel	• Can be pressurized • Much field experience • Easy plumbing connections	• Complete tanks difficult to install indoors • Subject to rust and corrosion	none	0.70–0.96
Fiberglass	• Factory insulated tanks available • Much field experience • No corrosion	• Maximum temperature is limited • Cannot be pressurized • Complete tanks difficult to install indoors	< 150–200°F	1.29–2.42
Concrete	• Can be precast or cast in place	• Possibility of cracks and leaks • Cannot be pressurized • Difficult to make leak-tight plumbing connections	< 210°F	0.69–0.92
Wooden	• Indoor installation easy	• Maximum temperature limited • Cannot be pressurized • Not suitable for underground installation	< 160°F	0.62–1.78

Water Storage Tank Characteristics

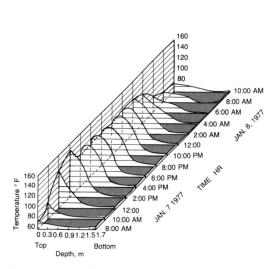

Temperature Profiles in Pebble Bed during Peak Heating

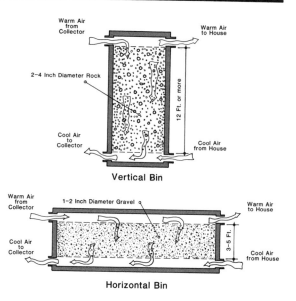

Rock-Bed Heat Storage

cation can be facilitated by the use of vertical tanks and baffles or anti-bending headers at the top and bottom of storage tanks.

☐ Ensuring stratification is much easier in rock beds than in water tanks because the rocks are immoble. Rock beds need an adequate plenum over the top to ensure that stratification is not upset by causing the hot injected air to move from top to bottom of the storage before spreading over the entire top surface of all the rocks.

☐ Storage efficiency, the ability to retard heat losses, can be increased by insulation—at a cost. The Sheet Metal and Air Conditioning Contractors' National Association recommends a maximum loss of 2 percent in 12 hours. The U.S. Department of Housing and Urban Development *Intermediate Minimum Property Standards* suggest a maximum loss of 10 percent in 24 hours. When the thermal losses supplement the building's heating load and overheating can be easily vented in summer, lower storage efficiencies are acceptable.

☐ Insulation is also a consideration for ducting and piping, which can lose thermal energy coming from collectors to the load or to storage and from storage to the load.

☐ The accompanying figure lists the variety of possible strategies for storing low-temperature thermal energy, a number of which are still in the research and development stage.

Location	Advantages	Disadvantages
Utility Room or Basement	● Minimal insulation requirement ● Insulation protected from weather ● Thermal losses contribute to building heat in winter ● Leaks easily detected ● Easy access for repairs	● Reduced living space ● Thermal losses increase summer air conditioning load ● Leaks possibly damaging to building interior ● Difficult to install steel or FRP tanks in an existing building
Unheated Garage	● Insulation protected from weather ● Leaks easily detected ● Easy access for repair ● Easy installation of steel or Fiber Reinforced Plastic tanks in an existing garage	● Reduced garage space ● Extra insulation required ● Freeze protection most often required ● Possible damage to garage from leaks ● Thermal losses not recovered
Crawl Space	● Insulation protected from weather ● Thermal losses may contribute to building heat in winter	● Thermal losses may add to summer airconditioning load ● Difficult access for retrofit or repairs ● Usual shaped tank may require extra insulation
Outdoors, above grade	● Easy access ● No increased airconditioning load from thermal loss ● No reduction in living space	● Extra insulation required ● Weather protection required ● No recovery of thermal losses ● Freeze protection usually required ● Possibility of vermin attacking insulation
Outdoors, below grade	● No increased airconditioning load from thermal losses ● No living space reduction	● Access for repairs difficult ● Several problems can be caused by contact with ground water ● Thermal losses not recovered ● Possibility of vermin attacking insulation ● Careful design required to ensure sufficient net positive suction head for the pump ● Cost for excavation

Storage Locations in Residences

☐ Annual cycle storages have a number of advantages. Solar energy collected on long, hot summer days can be used in the winter, reducing collector area, reducing summer stagnation problems, and greatly reducing if not eliminating backup energy needs. Sizing does become more critical, however.

☐ Solar ponds function as both energy collector and storage, which allows simplicity of design and can result in lower cost. Solar energy is trapped in the pond because the heavier salt water at the bottom counteracts the natural tendency to lose energy by convective currents. Salt-gradient solar ponds can be economically attractive in areas where land is readily available and little snow falls.

Phase-Changing Salts	Melting Point, °F	Heat of Fusion BTU per pound	Density Lb./Ft.
Calcium chloride hexahydrate	84–102	75	102
Sodium carbonate decahydrate	90–97	106	90
Disodium phosphate dodecahydrate	97	114	95
Calcium nitrate tetrahydrate	102–108	60	114
Sodium sulfate decahydrate (Glauber's salt)	88–90	108	97
Sodium thiosulfate pentahydrate	118–120	90	104

Salt Hydrates for Solar Heat Storage

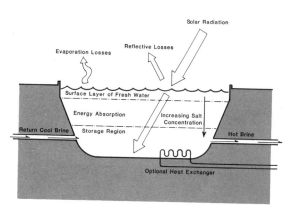

Solar Pond

Solution	Water: 1 Ft.³ 62 Lbs. Salt: 0.11 Ft.³ 10 Lbs.	Water: 1 Ft.³ 62 Lbs. Salt: 0.35 Ft.³ 32 Lbs.	Water: 1 Ft.³ 62 Lbs. Salt: 0.50 Ft.³ 45 Lbs.
BTU Stored	1240	4960	9300
Temperature Range (°F)	80°–100°	50°–130°	50°–200°
Temperature Difference	20°	80°	150°

Relative Volume of Water and Phase-Changing Glauber's Salts Required to Store Equal Amounts of Heat as the Usable Temperature Range Varies

☐ Larger sensible heat or phase-change storage generally have lower unit heat losses. Community systems offer the potential for use of only one backup system, statistical averaging of shared loads, and other economies of scale, although there will be increased distribution losses due to long distance runs. Annual storage may prove to be economical only in multifamily dwellings and large commercial applications.

☐ Latent heat-of-fusion storage for air systems is represented by eutectic salts. The heat storage principle of salts is that a material stores significant amounts of heat as it changes phase from solid to liquid (melts) and gives that heat up again as it solidifies. The advantage of these salts is that they change state at very convenient temperatures and require small volumes of space. After 30 years of investigation, the primary disadvantage continues to be that after a number of cycles the anhydrous salts tend to separate from the water, which slows down the reverse phase change, and makes the storage much less effective.

Heat Transport Fluids

Selection of the heat transport fluid dictates much of the remaining design. The primary advantages and disadvantages of air and water as heat transport fluids are discussed earlier in the section on system types.

☐ The larger the building, the more likely the use of liquid systems, since distribution piping consumes relatively small amounts of space. For air to be as efficient as liquid, large ducts and/or rapid air velocities must be used in combination with large fans. The larger ducts cost more and take up more space. The large fans required to provide higher air speeds through the ducts involve higher initial and operating costs. Higher air speeds also require higher air temperatures so that people will feel warm drafts rather than cool ones. One way to use air-type collectors effectively is to feed the air directly to ventilation equipment as pre-heated intake air, referred to as air tempering.

☐ Building designs that limit the location of solar collectors to the roof (rather than to the south-facing walls) are more likely to require the use of liquid systems because of the extra distance involved in transporting fluid to and from heat storage, which is usually located close to the ground because of its weight.

☐ The primary advantages of air as transport fluid are avoidance of the freeze problem and absence of damage from leakage. Leakage can, however, cause serious degradation of performance. Duct insulation (at least 1 inch) is recommended, even in heated spaces.

☐ Fan sizing will depend on the desired air flow rates and the cumulative pressure losses through collectors, ducts and rock bed storage. Factory-assembled air-handling units complete with automatic dampers and connections for auxiliary heat input are often effective solutions.

Collector Fluid Options	Heat Storage Options	Space Conditioning Options
air	rocks	forced warm or cool air
	small containers of water	air-warmed (or cooled) radiant panels
	small containers of phase-changing salts.	
water or other fluid such as oil or a water-anti-freeze solution	large containers (usually tanks) of water	forced hot or cold water, for example base-board or fan coil units
	large containers of water encir-cled by pebbles	hot or cold water radiant panels
		forced warm or cool air (this re-quires a heat exchanger to remove the heat or cool from storage and transfer it to the air)

Collector Fluid Options

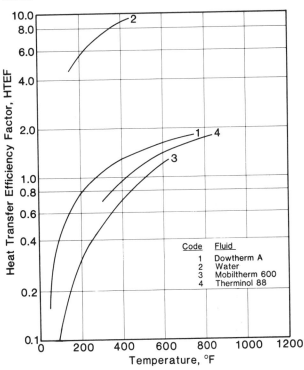

Heat Transfer Efficiency Factors

☐ The ideal heat transport liquid has good heat transfer capabilities, requires slow pumping power, remains in a liquid state at the range of possible temperatures and pressures, does not promote corrosion, is safe to use, and is inexpensive. Water can meet all these criteria with one exception—it freezes.

Characteristics	Water	50% Ethylene glycol/water	50% Propylene glycol/water	Silicone fluid	Synthetic hydro-carbon
Freezing Point	32	−33	−24	−120	−70
Boiling Point	212°F	230°F	225°F	400°F	550°F
Fluid Stability	requires pH or inhibitor monitoring	requires pH or inhibitor monitoring	requires pH or inhibitor monitoring	good	good
Corrosion	corrosive to iron and aluminum	corrosive to iron and aluminum	corrosive to iron and aluminum	non-corrosive	non-corrosive
Specific Heat (BTU/Lb.°F @ 100°F)	1.0	.83	.87	.30	.51
Viscosity (Lb./Ft.-Hr. @ 100°F)	1.66	2.5	3.0	17	11
Potability	potable	very toxic	non-toxic non-potable	non-toxic non-potable	non-potable

Collector Fluid Characteristics

□ One common solution to water's freezing is to mix glycol antifreeze (either ethylene or propylene) with water in a 50-percent solution. This degrades water's beneficial physical properties: the glycol-water solution has greater density, lower specific heat, and greater viscosity, all of which require increased pumping power. Several organic fluids can also be utilized as transport fluids.

Fluid	LD$_{50}$
Water	—
100% Ethylene Glycol (No inhibitors)	8.0
100% Propylene Glycol (No inhibitors)	34.6
100% Diethylene Glycol (No inhibitors)	30.
100% Triethylene Glycol (No inhibitors)	30.
100% Downtherm SR–1	4.
Mobiltherm Light	20.
SF–96(50) (Silicone)	50.
Q2–1132 (Silicone)	50.
Downtherm J	1.1
Therminol 44	13.5
Therminol 55	15.8
Therminol 60	13.0
Sun-Temp	No test info available

Toxicities of Heat Transfer Fluids

□ *Toxicity* is a significant problem in all situations in which heat transfer fluids can contaminate potable water. LD 50 values from the accompanying table refer to the quantity of substance (g/kg) that kills 50 percent of dosed test animals in 14 days.

□ For domestic hot water applications, the U.S. Department of Housing and Urban Development (HUD), National Bureau of Standards and many local codes require a double-walled heat exchanger whenever a toxic collector fluid is used. Fill locations should be carefully marked, designating the proper coolant to be used.

□ The various parameters involved in corrosion are well described in HUD's *Intermediate Minimum Property Standards for Solar Heating and Domestic Hot Water Systems.*

□ Corrosion is a more significant problem with aqueous solutions and tends to increase with high oxygen and chloride content, higher temperatures, and improper pH. Corrosion problems can take several forms: *Galvanic corrosion* is caused by the junction of two dissimilar materials in an electrolytic solution. Insulating couplings used between dissimilar metals can sometimes eliminate this problem; however, in many cases metal can still enter the fluid and travel to the site of another metal. *Pitting corrosion* involves rapid local metal loss. Aluminum and steel are susceptible to the presence of chloride ions. Aluminum is also susceptible to the presence of metal ions. *Crevice corrosion* is similar to pitting corrosion but occurs at crevices in the system, such as those at spot-welded joints.

Heat Transport Equipment

A heat exchanger is a device for transferring thermal energy from one fluid to another. Heat exchangers in active solar systems are used primarily to isolate collector piping loops containing toxic antifreeze solutions from storage and space heating or domestic hot water loops. They are also used to avoid use of the more expensive antifreeze solutions for storage.

☐ Heat exchangers can be used to reduce hydrostatic head on storage tanks when collectors are mounted at a considerable height above the water storage tank.

☐ Heat exchanger effectiveness is defined as the *actual* heat transfer rate divided by the *theoretical maximum* heat transfer rate.

☐ Effectiveness for typical liquid exchangers is 0.5 to 0.8. Sizing is usually done using manufacturers' literature. Most manufacturers will provide technical assistance in the selection process. Required information is:
—fluid inlet and outlet temperature
—heat transfer rate (in BTUs per hour) or fluid flow rate (in gallons per minute).

☐ A number of heat exchanger types are available. Remote heat exchangers are separate from the tank and require two pumps to circulate the fluids. More power is consumed, but, forced convection on both sides of the exchanger results in higher heat transfer. Tube-in-shell heat exchangers are widely used in solar hot water systems. They contain tightly packed tube bundles inside an outer jacket. The collector fluid is circulated across the tubes, while the storage fluid flows through tubes.

☐ The shell and double-tube heat exchanger is similar to the shell and tube except that a secondary chamber containing an intermediate fluid is located within the shell to surround the water tube in which potable water circulates. The heated toxic liquid circulates in the outer shell, transferring heat to the intermediate fluid, which in turn transfers heat to the tube carrying potable water. The exchanger should be equipped with a sight glass to detect leaks by a change in color—toxic liquid can contain dye—or by a change in the liquid level in the intermediate chamber, which would indicate a failure in either the outer shell or the intermediate tube lining.

☐ Double separation can be provided by using two separate heat exchangers between the collector and storage. The two heat exchangers may be of the same or different types and are generally of the shell and tube type.

☐ Jacket types of heat exchangers are either tubing or plate coils wrapped around and bonded to the outside of the metal storage tank.

☐ There is forced convection in the outer loop and natural convection between the wall of the tank and the storage liquid. They provide both excellent stratification in the storage tank and double separation.

☐ Immersion heat exchangers are either a coiled-tube bundle or a tank-within-a-tank. They have forced convection through the internal tubing or tank and natural convection into the storage liquid. The tube bundles come with or without fins and single- or double-sleeve construction. Tank-within-a-tank exchangers are metal tanks fitted with standard piping with the fluid circulating through them. Variations include finned tubes or discs on the piping.

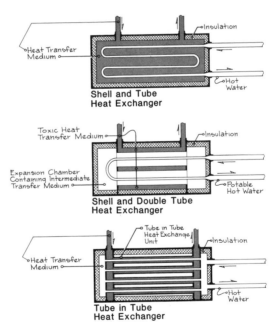

Shell and Tube
Heat Exchanger

Shell and Double Tube
Heat Exchanger

Tube in Tube
Heat Exchanger

☐ Double separation is possible with a continuous piping loop. Special provisions may be necessary on the storage tank so that it can accomodate these types of heat exchangers.

☐ The air-to-liquid heat exchanger (hydronic fin coil) is a standard item of HVAC equipment. It is used in a large portion of commercial buildings. In active solar systems it is used primarily for hot water preheat or delivery of heat from storage to load.

Pumps

☐ The efficiency of a pump is basically the work output divided by energy (electrical) input. The work is defined as flow rate times fluid head. *Head* is the combination of the pressure or resistance to flow within the piping loop and any height to which the fluid must be raised, expressed as a vertical column (in feet) of the given fluid. No more than the equivalent of 1 to 3.5 percent of the energy collected by the solar energy system should be consumed by the pump(s) used to circulate the fluids. This factor can be much higher (7 to 8 percent), degrading system efficiency.

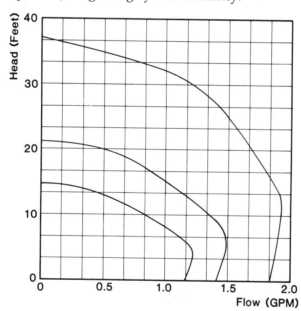

Typical Pump Curve

☐ The *flow* rate is the number of gallons of fluid or cubic feet of air per minute of heat transfer fluid that should flow through the collectors. The collector manufacturer will specify the most efficient flow rate.

☐ Flow/head requirements are critical to pump selection and can be highly significant for overall system design.

☐ Closed-loop systems are characterized by a continuous fluid loop with the pump installed in the fluid circuit. Since the fluid loop is continuous, the pump discharge pressure (or head pressure developed by the pump) must be sufficient to provide the proper flow characteristics to overcome the pressure loss of the entire loop, including exchangers. If the system is full and closed, there is no vertical head requirement due to the balance effect of fluid in the return line. This lack of a vertical head requirement means that pump power requirements are reduced and pumps with low discharge pressure can be used. Start-up head requirement must be available, however.

☐ Open-loop systems include a wide variety of configurations including drain-down and drain-back as well as loops that vent to the atmosphere. Certain collector loops create vertical pump-head requirements to lift fluid to the highest point in the collector system.

Pump Connections

☐ Strainers are advisable on the inlets of all pumps. Periodic maintenance is required to clean out impurities.

☐ Check valves should be located in pumping loops to prevent reverse thermosyphoning.

☐ Provisions for pump servicing should be made. Some methods are unions, bolted flanges, or flexible connections.

☐ Expansion tanks are designed into fluid loops to maintain required system pressures. For solar energy systems they require special consideration because of the volumes of liquid and wide temperature ranges involved.

☐ Piping design also involves sizing, configuration, fittings and insulation.

☐ Many engineering handbooks have pertinent tables. Standard pipe friction tables should be used. Pipe friction will vary with heat transfer fluid, flow rate and plumbing material.

☐ Drain-down and drain-back systems require substantially more pump pressure, to recharge the system (i.e. create a new siphon effect). This can require either multiple- or two-stage pump and control arrangements.

☐ Centrifugal pumps are generally preferred over the piston-type, positive-displacement pumps. They provide the safety feature of only creating pressures slightly above those rated if the fluid loop becomes blocked or a valve is inadvertently left closed.

☐ Pump materials that will come into contact with circulating fluid must be compatible with the fluid to ensure extended pump life. A bronze or stainless steel pump should be used when the pump is to be exposed to air. With antifreeze liquids (but not with glycols), a cast-iron pump can be used. Some antifreeze liquids or inhibitors can be harmful to pump seals and gaskets. Magnetic-drive pumps have no seals to wear and leak and can be used with any transfer fluid. Polyethylene and polypropylene seals interact with petroleum-based transfer fluids; pumps without seals or ones with special seals of elastomeric materials should be used.

☐ Pumps should be durable as they must run long periods of time at high temperatures and pressures. A pump failure will cause collector stagnation and can damage the entire system.

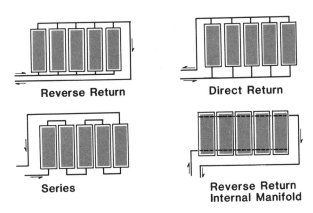

Collector Piping Configuration

☐ Collector piping and manifolding design should minimize installed cost, leakage, maintenance problems and heat losses. It should provide uniform flow to all collectors to maximize collector efficiency, minimize pump power requirements and provide for air purging. Internal manifolds using piping within the collector have great potential for reducing piping and insulation costs but require careful design to maintain proper flow to all collectors.

☐ Reverse-return arrangements are generally preferred because they provide equal flow to all collectors when low, uniform resistance is maintained in the manifolds—but generally require more piping and additional cost.

Expansion

☐ All pipes should be hung or anchored loosely enough to allow expansion and contraction with temperature changes. A 100-foot length of copper pipe will expand approximately 1 inch with a 100-degree (F.) temperature rise. This expansion can be compensated with silicone bulbs, bellows, braided wire, pipe elbows or swings. Silicone hoses are often used as expansion joints in arrays where there is little room for pipe expansion. Standard corrugated expansion joints made of copper alloy can also be used. Elbows also allow for some expansion, usually a sufficient amount for a small system.

☐ A primary source of parasitic losses in solar energy systems is the energy transport system (i.e. piping, fittings and pipe insulation). Significant thermal losses can occur if piping is incorrectly circulated or insufficiently insulated.

Controls

The controls of an active solar system—sensors, valves, dampers, differential thermostats, etc.—are the physical manifestation of the system's design logic. The controls should accomplish the following tasks:

—fluid-flow management to maximize collection of solar energy

—system protection from temperature extremes (e.g., freezing, overheating, malfunction)

—heat delivery; storage/auxiliary interconnections.

A control system has three major components: sensors, actuated devices and the "controller" or decision-making device.

Typically, sensors and visual monitors in an active solar energy system sense temperature, pressure, and flow rate. Common problems associated with sensors are improper or inadequate selection (mismatch of sensor and task), improper location and inaccessibility.

☐ Collector temperature sensors are critical to determining when solar energy is available. More accurate control is achieved when sensors are located directly on the absorber or on the outlet rather than in the return pipe above the collector. If located on the return pipe, no flow is allowed to pass the sensor prior to start-up, and it therefore relies on conduction and convection of heat from the collector and can give only an indirect measurement of the collector temperature. This can result in unnecessary delays in system start-up

☐ A loosely mounted sensor or one that is not well-connected to the collector can cause cooling of storage at the end of the day by retaining enough heat after the solar input drops off to indicate falsely that solar heat is still available.

☐ Storge tank sensors are generally placed as close to the outlet to collectors as possible. Attention should be paid to the effects of tank stratification; if sensors are placed in the hot portion of a storage tank they can erroneously indicate that collectors are not substantially warmer than storage—both delaying system start-up and causing premature shut-down.

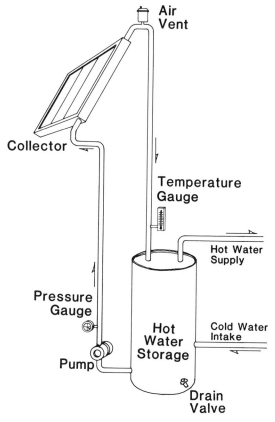

Monitoring Devices, Drains and Vents

☐ An actuated device is any component that executes the command of the control logic selectors. Pumps, fans, mixing valves, motorized dampers, flow switches and auxiliary water heater elements are examples. These devices control the fluid flow in the system and provide scale protection and auxiliary water heating. In drain-down or drain-back systems, their reliable operation is critical to providing freeze protection to the entire system.

☐ Valves control fluid flow, water pressure and air in the system. All of the valves necessary in a liquid solar system are common plumbing fixtures (see accompanying chart).

Type	Purpose	Location	Comment
Backflow Preventor	prevents mixing of potable water with non-potable fluid	on city water supply	required in some code jurisdictions, don't install near electrical components
Check Valve	permits liquid flow in only one direction	closed loop systems; between storage & collector to prevent reverse thermo-syphoning	be sure arrow on valve points in direction of flow
Pressure Relief Valve	allows fluid to escape closed loop if working pressure is exceeded	collector loop at return to storage	
Temperature and Pressure Relief	same as above (with temperature sensor attached)	top of storage tank and/or DHW tank	connect to container or waste drain required in most areas; don't use threaded fittings
Tempering or Mixing Valve	mixes cold water to water from storage tank when it exceeds set point	12″ below HW outlet with CW entering from bottom	remove temperature sensing element before soldering and replace afterwards; check position of fittings
Pressure Regulator	reduces incoming water pressure to prevent damage to components	drain-down	proceed by strainer; isolate with shut-offs for cleaning
Air Vent	eliminates air bubbles from system	high points of system (above collector manifold)	mount vent vertically; make sure cap is loose
Air Eliminator	removes air from heat transfer fluid	above expansion tank	
Balancing Valve	controls flow of fluids through system piping	system without reverse return piping; between manifold & each collector	can be square head cock, ball or globe valve; do not use a gate valve
Vacuum Relief Valves	permits system to drain by gravity	drain-down; above collector at high point; above CW inlet of storage to revent vacuum conditions to prevent collapse of tank	
Solenoid Valve	starts, stops or diverts flow of heat transfer fluid	drain-down systems	often 2 valves used; one for collector circulation; one for drain
Isolation (shut-off) Valves	permits components to be serviced without having to drain system	either side of pump and strainer; either side of external H_x; either side of pressure reg.	don't use globe valves; they restrict flow & reduce efficiency; don't isolate collector from relief valves
Fill Valve	manual fill-up with transfer fluid	high point of system (low point if transfer pump is used)	gate valve with open end facing up or quick connect valves
Drain Valve	draining & periodic cleaning	bottom of storage tank; one on collector loop for draining system	removing valve handles prevents tampering (store in a safe place)

Valves and Vents

☐ Early active solar systems experienced significant problems with leaking three-way valves. Problems can also arise from the substitution of check valves for approved back-flow preventors.

☐ As a rule, all valves in a pipeline should be the same size as the lines in which they are installed to permit a rapid drain-down, especially when using the drain-down freeze-protection method. Stop cocks should be the same size as their line.

☐ The controller uses sensors to determine whether the difference between the solar collector and storage temperatures is sufficient to justify pump operation. An adequate temperature dead band should be incorporated into the control design to prevent harmful cycling of the pump in the morning and evening and intermittently during cloudy periods. As a rule of thumb, pumps should be activated when a temperature difference of 8 to 10 degrees (F.) is detected between collectors and storage. Shutoff should occur when this differential drops 3 to 5 degrees (F.)

☐ If the collector is drained when not in use, the control should allow slight collector overheating before start-up and some thermal response lag in the collector sensor to avoid premature shutdown when the first cool water from the piping enters the collector.

☐ The control subsystem should ensure that temperatures and/or pressures developed in the solar energy system because of a power or system component failure do not damage any of the system components or the building. For example, high-temperature limiting devices should be installed to protect the system from damage resulting from rupture, etc., and a low-temperature limiting device should be installed to protect the system against free-up damage. Application of dampers is critical. Control dampers can be either proportional (regulating or balancing) or open/close (shut-off). Backdraft dampers control the direction of flow, like the check valves in liquid systems.

☐ Damper materials must be appropriate for prolonged exposure to dry, high-temperature air. Air leakage past dampers degrades system performance significantly. High-quality dampers designed for minimum air leakage and airtight inspection ports to facilitate maintenance and frequent inspection are required.

☐ An active solar system's controller receives output signals from the sensors, selects the desired control strategy, and transmits the appropriate order to the actuated devices, either directly or via relays.

☐ The central computerized energy management and control system (EMCS) installed in many large buildings can incorporate solar control, but this requires careful integration of the solar and conventional systems. For simpler systems a central control panel can be provided to consolidate the circuits, fuses and relays that provide the control functions.

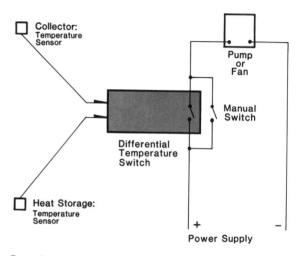

Basic Solar Differential Control System

☐ The model code for solar energy systems proposed by the U.S. Department of Energy calls for controls to prevent the following;
—the addition of energy to the storage medium when the temperature of the storage medium has reached its maximum design operating temperature
—thermosiphoning that will cause damage by freezing
—heat transfer fluids rising above the maximum design operating temperature of liquid systems; damage from thermal shock.

310

Hogate's Restaurant
Washington, D.C.
Engineers: Mueller Associates

Hogate's Restaurant, located in Washington, D.C., has 6,254 square feet of flat-plate collectors used for the hot water system which requires approximately 7,000 gallons of 150-degree (F.) water each day between 4 P.M. and 2 A.M. The solar energy system is a retrofit, and as such, the collectors face southwest instead of ideally facing south.

Collector tilt of 55 degrees from horizontal was dictated by architectural considerations. The solar collector loop uses a 60/40 mixture of propylene glycol and water as the heat transfer fluid. The potable water supply is isolated from the heat transfer fluid by a liquid-to-liquid heat exchanger. The collection and transfer of solar energy is controlled by the activation of two sets of pumps.

The solar energy system has been designed for three modes of operation: In mode 1, when there is a hot water demand and solar radiation is insufficient for operating the collector, cold water from the inlet is directed to the boiler where it is heated, if required, to 150 degrees (F.)

In mode 2, hot water from the collector goes to the load when there is sufficient solar energy to operate the collector and there is a demand for hot water.

In mode 3, hot water from the collector goes to storage when there is no hot water demand but there is sufficient solar energy for collector operation. This mode can be terminated either by lack of solar radiation or by the temperature of the water in the tank exceeding 180 degrees (F.).

Heat storage is provided in two 5,000-gallon tanks. Auxiliary energy is provided by a gas-fired boiler.

Hogate's Restaurant
Washington, D.C.
Engineers: Mueller Associates

Hogate's Restaurant
Washington, D.C.
Engineers: Mueller Associates

311

HVAC Integration

Residential air systems have three basic thermal operating modes: collector-to-storage, storage-to-load and collector-to-load. For liquid systems (especially commercial), operating modes are less straightforward, varying more with specific applications. A critical factor in every case is the manner in which auxiliary energy is integrated into the solar system, or vice versa. This can be done in many ways; no effort is made here to discuss them all, only to indicate relevant issues.

☐ The simplest active solar system would be one without storage that operated only when solar energy was available and the load demanded energy. The next level of complexity, as the accompanying diagrams for an air system illustrate, includes storage but keeps auxiliary heat entirely separate. Note diagram 3; this is not entirely satisfactory because in the intermediate seasons and on mild winter days it is possible that solar collection will suffice to meet the entire diurnal load.

☐ Systems increase in complexity as an attempt is made to integrate all of the components. For example, in large installations it is generally undesirable to have two separate heat delivery systems, one for the solar and the other for the backup. Integrating these two in one ducting system (for forced-air systems, for example) causes dampering and other control complications but can reduce the initial cost of heat delivery system. Several of the liquid systems in early federal active solar demonstration programs were found to be heating storage inadvertently with auxiliary energy. This is generally a question of whether the auxiliary is piped in series or in parallel. If designed in series the possibility exists that the return water temperature will exceed the storage temperature. If allowed to continue this condition will degrade collector efficiency.

1. Collector Heats Storage

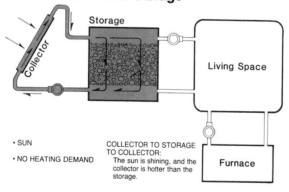

- SUN
- NO HEATING DEMAND

COLLECTOR TO STORAGE TO COLLECTOR:
The sun is shining, and the collector is hotter than the storage.

2. Collector Heats Storage, Storage and/or Furnace Heats Space

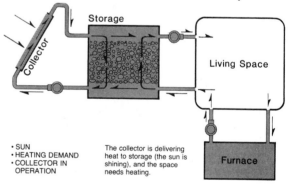

- SUN
- HEATING DEMAND
- COLLECTOR IN OPERATION

The collector is delivering heat to storage (the sun is shining), and the space needs heating.

3. Storage Heats Space

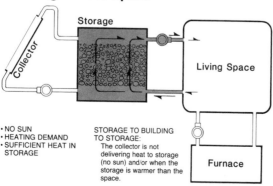

- NO SUN
- HEATING DEMAND
- SUFFICIENT HEAT IN STORAGE

STORAGE TO BUILDING TO STORAGE:
The collector is not delivering heat to storage (no sun) and/or when the storage is warmer than the space.

4. No Stored Solar Heat Furnace Heats Space

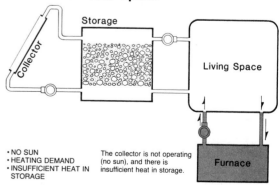

- NO SUN
- HEATING DEMAND
- INSUFFICIENT HEAT IN STORAGE

The collector is not operating (no sun), and there is insufficient heat in storage.

Collector—Storage Relationships

Auxiliary Heat In Series

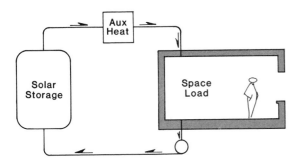

Auxiliary Heat In Parallel

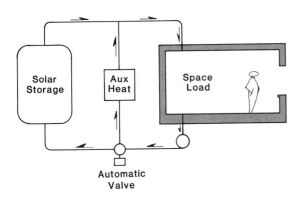

Auxiliary Heat Interfacing with Solar Storage

☐ Auxiliary fuel use is minimized if the auxiliary is in parallel with the load, using solar-heated water exclusively whenever the storage temperature exceeds the required heating coil temperature. When the storage temperature is too low, circulation of solar-heated water is discontinued and auxiliary heat is used exclusively. Piping and valving in such a system must be arranged so that the water bypasses the storage tank when auxiliary heat is in use; an automatic valve and single pump provide heat from the appropriate source. In severely cold weather, it can sometimes be better to leave comparatively warm water in storage unused for a time while the auxiliary supply is meeting the high demand in the building. The storage water would not be useful until the load is less severe or the storage temperature has been increased by addition of solar heat. This suggests the desirability of higher system operating temperatures at the same time that collector efficiency argues for lowering them.

☐ With air-delivery systems it is possible to solve this problem by using two separate hydronic coils in the air-stream—a lower-temperature one from solar-heated water and a higher-temperature one from auxiliary.

☐ A similar design problem is encountered with flat plate collectors used to activate absorption chillers. Promising research is underway attempting to lower the required temperatures, but at present the coefficient-of-performance (COP) of these units falls off rapidly as regeneration water temperatures drop below 170 degrees (F.).

☐ The system schematic and mode description for the Santa Clara Community Center, a case study presented later in this section, illustrates one design solution to the problem above. This system has three thermal operating modes.

☐ *Mode 1—Auxiliary or Storage to Load.* This mode is used when there is little or no solar energy available. Heating is supplied either from the stored hot water or from the boiler. Cooling is supplied from the cool storage which is maintained by the boiler/absorption chiller combination.

☐ *Mode 2—Collector to Storage Load.* This mode is used when the solar flux is sufficient to provide efficient building heating and hot water storage but is insufficient to drive the absorption chillers. The system operates in this mode during the early morning and late afternoon hours. Cooling is supplied as described for Mode 1.

☐ *Mode 3—Collector to Chillers.* This mode is used when the insolation is adequate to provide efficient firing of one or both absorption chillers. The active periods for this mode center on solar noon in summer. Chilled water is drawn from the bottom of the cold storage tank where it is coldest and deposited on the top of the tank on its return from the cold fan coils. If the temperature at the top of the cold reservoir rises above 55 degrees (F.), the boiler comes on to fire the absorption chillers.

☐ Because solar collector efficiency improves as collection temperatures are reduced, and conventional air-to-air heat pump system performance rises as heat-source temperature increases, a heat pump could be used advantageously to draw heat from storage, thus lowering the temperature of storage fluid fed to the collectors. Present indications are that such an operating mode can offer energy savings.

☐ The integration of solar and conventional HVAC systems is in several ways simpler for commercial than for residential buildings. A solar system in a commercial building is generally only a relatively small increment in an already complex mechanical system. More highly trained operating personnel are generally available, reducing maintenance problems. Solar applications are also generally consistent with current design and economic analysis efforts to diminish commercial peak loads by spreading them over larger time cycles, both diurnal and seasonal. On the other hand, cooling tends to be a much larger portion of the mechanical system load, and the solar cooling technology is not as advanced or cost-effective as solar heating.

Parameter	Recommended Design Value
1. Collector area	Determined by life-cycle cost analysis
2. Collector tilt	Lat +5° (water heating only) or Lat +15° (space and water heating)
3. Collector orientation	Due south
4. Storage mass	15 Lb.Water/Sq.Ft.$_c$ = 1.8 Gal/Sq.Ft.$_c$ (liquid system) or 15 BTU/Hr.°FSq.Ft.$_c$ = 75 Lb./Rocks/Sq.Ft.$_c$ (air system)
5. Heat exchanger heat transfer coefficient	10 BTU/Hr.°FSq.Ft.$_c$ (5–15 F approach)
6. Collector heat transfer	10 BTU/Hr.°FSq.Ft.$_c$ (liquid system) or 4 BTU/Hr.°FSq.Ft.$_c$ (air system)
7. Number of glazings	1
8. Collector surface absorptance	≥ 0.9 with selective surface
9. Collector coolant flow rate	10 Lb./Hr.Sq.Ft.$_c$ = 0.02 gpm water/Sq. Ft.$_c$ (liquid system) or 2 CFM/Sq.Ft.$_c$ (air system)
10. Collector back insulation	U = 0.1d BTU/Hr.°FSq.Ft.$_c$
11. Distribution pipe insulation	U = 0.15 BTU/Hr.°FSq.Ft.$_c$ of pipe

Recommended Solar System Design Parameters

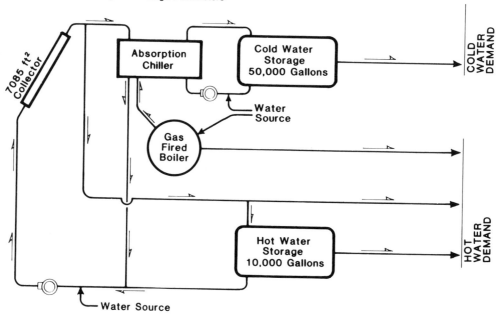

Solar System at the Santa Clara Community Center

Montgomery College
Germantown, Maryland
Architect: Silver Associates

Solar collectors are mounted on two of the three buildings on this campus. The active solar system has 8,854 square feet of flat-plate collectors integrated with the building's perimeter heating system, which is a series of locally controlled air-to-water heat pumps. Large areas of glass permit solar gain, and the heat pump units move this passive solar heat and internally generated heat from one place to another within the building. Large core areas of the buildings therefore have no heating system, requiring only ventilation.

Heat transport for the active solar system is by a glycol-water solution, which is passed through a heat exchanger. On cloudy days and during very cold periods, the system taps energy from 10,000 gallons of storage if the building heating demand exceeds the output from the collectors. If the storage is depleted a backup electric boiler is used.

The solar system was designed for the possible future addition of absorption chillers in order to use the collectors for cooling as well.

Projected solar contributions are 60 percent for space heating and 88 percent for domestic hot water. Operating costs have been 50 percent below a similar Montgomery Community College Campus located in the same area.

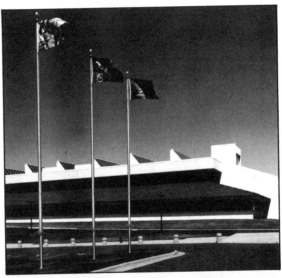

Montgomery College
Germantown, Maryland
Architect: Silver Associates

Montgomery College
Germantown, Maryland
Architect: Silver Associates

System Simulation

A variety of methods has been developed for the analysis and design of active solar heating, cooling, building service hot water, and industrial process heat systems. These include manual methods, hand-held calculator (programmable) methods and detailed computer simulations.

☐ There are three primary purposes to be served by these analysis and design methods. Foremost is the determination of an appropriate size for the collector array. Secondarily the components (e.g., storage, heat exchangers, etc.) must be selected and sized, and the system configuration and control strategy selected.

☐ The third purpose, which is circular and interactive with the two above, is the determination of economic feasibility. This involves assessing the costs of the solar system and the value of the fuel saved.

☐ Solar system performance and collector-sizing requirements differ from conventional systems in three significant respects. First, collection of solar energy and demand for its use do not always occur at the same time. Peak demand is generally at night or during cloudy weather. Sizing of solar system components is therefore based on overall system performance rather than on peak load calculations. Only auxiliary energy supply systems are sized for peak loads.

Second, both energy demand and thermal storage mass influence the operating temperature of solar collectors. This affects the amount of incident solar energy a given collector array can collect. The consequence is that seasonal building load variations strongly influence the annual performance of a solar energy system and must be considered.

Third, solar energy is typically collected and delivered over a wide range of temperatures, which influences the performance of heating coils and absorption chillers. Conventional "peak load" design methods are, therefore, not appropriate for solar systems.

☐ The performance of any solar heating or cooling system depends on the solar radiation available to the collector, the outside ambient air temperature and wind condition, the collector design, the inlet fluid temperature from storage, and the thermal load on the system. General understanding of how the above factors affect system performance in various locations requires a system simulation.

☐ A general schematic of how these variables are modeled is shown in the accompanying figure.

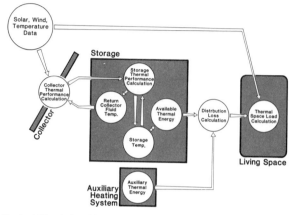

Typical Simulation Model

☐ Building loads vary somewhat but not to the extent or frequency of variations in both weather and solar incidence. Long-term system performance can only be accurately predicted with computer programs that perform hour-by-hour simulations (8,760 per year).

☐ Most of the simpler design and analysis methods are derived from statistical correlations of the results of these annual simulations. Many of the methods (from simple to complex) have been tested against actual installed solar systems. This is done by comparing predicted to monitored system performance.

☐ The advantages of the simplified manual methods are simplicity of use, low cost, computational speed, rapid turnaround and accessibility to persons with little technical experience. The simplified methods are generally more

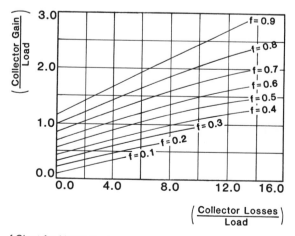

f-Chart for Liquid Systems

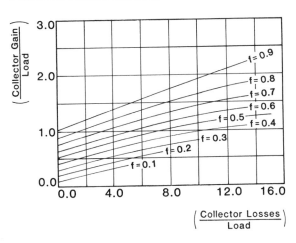

f-Chart for Air Systems

appropriate for use in design of hot water, residential, or small commercial buildings dominated by external loads.

☐ The most comprehensive and widely used simplified method is the f-chart method. It was developed using the TRNSYS program to simulate representative types of solar heating (air and water; space and hot water) systems in several different geographical locations. It is available on magnetic cards for programmable calculators, for microcomputers, and on time-sharing basis on large main frame computers. A manual f-chart user must calculate solar fractions for each month of the year for use in determining an annual solar fraction of the energy provided by the solar system.

☐ In the pursuit of even greater time savings several manual methods have been developed that yield an optimum collector area and an annual solar fraction directly. The Relative Areas program, developed at Colorado State University, and the GFL method are both such annual methods. Each was developed from correlations of f-chart results.

☐ The Solar Load Ratio (SLR) method for liquid systems was developed from the detailed hour-by-hour simulation results from a computer program developed at the Los Alamos Scientific Laboratory. It is a very simple design and sizing procedure originally developed for residential use but now extended to small externally dominated commercial buildings as well.

☐ The SLR results are presented in terms of the ratio of building load to collector area for liquid systems in the accompanying tables. These tables present the ratio in terms of the solar heating percentage of the total space heating requirement. The Load Collector Ratio (LC) is defined as:

$$LC = \frac{\text{Building Load (BTU/Degree Day}}{\text{Collector Area (ft}^2)}$$

☐ To use the Load Collector Ratio (LC) for determining the size of the collector for one of the cities listed (or an equivalent location), one must (1) determine the building's thermal load and (2) decide what percentage of solar heating the system is to provide.

☐ For example, a 2,000-square-foot building in Boise, Idaho, with a load of 6 BTU/Degree Day/S.F. for which a 50 percent solar fraction is desired will have a load collector ratio of 39. Using the above formula:

$$LC = \frac{\text{Building Load}}{\text{Collector Area}}$$

$$39 = \frac{2000 \times 6}{\text{Collector Area}}$$

Collector Area = 308 square feet

☐ One problem with both the SLR and f-chart methods is that their accuracy is limited to the reference solar systems originally modeled in the hour-by-hour simulations.

☐ The TRNSYS simulation program developed at the University of Wisconsin, and the DOE-2/CBS (Component-Based-Simulator-based on TRNSYS) are much more sophisticated than what has been discussed so far. Use of these simulation programs requires both engineering and computer training. Aside from the refined results made possible by the hourly integration of all variables, the significant advantage of these programs is that they allow users to build complete systems for simulation, mixing equipment and design strategies as desired.

☐ The DOE-2 program is far more complex than TRNSYS with the solar CBS only one component of the larger program, which simulates the complex interactions of multi-zoned multi-system commercial buildings.

☐ The accompanying tables demonstrate the wide assortment of design and analysis methods which are available.

Location	Degree Days	LC where solar provides 25%, 50%, 75% of heating load		
		25% BTU/DD Ft² collector	50% BTU/DD Ft² collector	75% BTU/DD Ft² collector
ARIZONA				
Page	6632	128	48	23
Phoenix	1765	300	118	59
ARKANSAS				
Little Rock	3219	126	48	24
CALIFORNIA				
Davis	2502	198	72	33
El Centro	1458	547	206	97
Fresno	2492	195	70	32
Los Angeles	2061	416	157	75
Riverside	1803	391	152	74
Santa Maria	2967	353	142	67
COLORADO				
Grand Junction	5641	119	46	22
FLORIDA				
Apalachicola	1308	324	129	65
Tallahassee	1485	283	113	57
GEORGIA				
Atlanta	2961	154	59	29
IDAHO				
Boise	5809	108	39	17
ILLINOIS				
Chicago	6155	79	30	14
INDIANA				
Indianapolis	5699	86	32	15
KANSAS				
Dodge City	4986	126	49	24
LOUISIANA				
Lake Charles	1459	244	96	48
Shreveport	2184	179	70	35
MAINE				
Caribou	9767	68	26	12
MARYLAND				
Silver Hill (Wash. D.C.)	4224	111	43	21
MASSACHUSETTS				
Boston	5624	86	33	16
MICHIGAN				
East Lansing	6909	76	28	13
MINNESOTA				
Minneapolis	8879	71	27	13
MISSOURI				
Columbia	5046	102	38	18
MONTANA				
Great Falls	7750	93	35	16

LC Values for Liquid Systems

Location	Degree Days	LC where solar provides 25%, 50%, 75% of heating load		
		25% BTU/DD Ft² collector	50% BTU/DD Ft² collector	75% BTU/DD Ft² collector
NEBRASKA				
Lincoln	5864	104	39	19
North Omaha	6612	89	34	16
NEVADA				
Las Vegas	2709	218	84	42
Reno	6632	125	47	22
NEW JERSEY				
Seabrook	4812	97	37	18
NEW MEXICO				
Albuquerque	4348	161	64	31
Los Alamos	6600	107	41	21
NEW YORK				
Ithaca	6914	68	24	11
New York	4871	88	34	16
NORTH CAROLINA				
Hatteras	2612	204	79	39
Raleigh	3393	133	52	25
NORTH DAKOTA				
Bismarck	8851	78	29	14
OHIO				
Cleveland	6351	71	26	12
OKLAHOMA				
Oklahoma City	3725	134	53	26
OREGON				
Corvallis	4726	120	42	18
Medford	5008	107	38	16
PENNSYLVANIA				
State College	5934	78	29	14
RHODE ISLAND				
Newport	5804	97	37	18
SOUTH CAROLINA				
Charleston	2033	210	82	41
SOUTH DAKOTA				
Rapid City	7345	97	37	18
TENNESSEE				
Nashville	3578	117	44	21
TEXAS				
Brownsville	600	517	218	110
El Paso	2700	228	88	44
Fort Worth	2405	186	73	37
Midland	2591	202	79	39
San Antonio	1546	262	103	52
UTAH				
Salt Lake City	6052	107	40	19

LC Values for Liquid Systems

319

Location	Degree Days	LC where solar provides 25%, 50%, 75% of heating load		
		25% BTU/DD Ft² collector	50% BTU/DD Ft² collector	75% BTU/DD Ft² collector
VERMONT Burlington	8269	63	24	11
VIRGINIA Sterling (Dulles)	4224	111	43	21
WASHINGTON Pullman Seattle Spokane	5542 4785 6655	100 94 90	36 33 31	16 13 14
WISCONSIN Madison	7863	76	28	13
WYOMING Laramie	7381	106	42	21

LC Values for Liquid Systems

Federal Correctional Institution
Bastrop, Texas
Architects: Caudill Rowlett Scott, Inc.

The campus-like organizing plan reveals that this facility is not a maximum security prison. Both the Federal Bureau of Prisons and the architect, CRS, Inc., intended to make the 43-acre complex a solar demonstration project.

The saw-tooth roof design provides mounting for both collectors and north-facing skylights. There are 25,000 square feet of flat-plate collectors, the absorber plates of which have selective surface coating. Water is used for heat transport and a water-to-water heat exchanger. Forty thousand gallons of water storage are provided. Freeze protection is provided by drain back. When back-up is needed, auxiliary energy is provided by a natural gas boiler.

System control incorporates priority distribution of solar-heated water to the demand loads of domestic hot water, space heating, and space cooling, respectively.

The system has been instrumented, with initial monitoring indicating the following solar contributions: 56 percent domestic hot water, 42 percent heating and 1 percent cooling.

Federal Correctional Institution
Bastrop, Texas
Architects: Caudill Rowlett Scott, Inc.

PHOTOVOLTAICS

Introduction

Photovoltaic (PV) systems convert sunlight into direct electrical current. Although the "photovoltaic effect" was demonstrated in 1931, the first PV cell was not produced until 1954. Because of the abundance of cheap fossil fuels, PVs remained a novelty until the 1960s, when they were used to power instrumentation equipment in space satellites and to provide power in remote locations where utility connections and conventional generators were infeasible. Growing concern over energy focused government and industry attention to make PVs competitive with other sources of electricity within 10 to 20 years.

Today the photovoltaic industry can produce systems that generate electricity at $13 per watt installed cost. Forecasters expect this cost to fall to less than $3 within 10 years. A cost of $3 is equivalent to a range of 13 to 32 cents per kilowatt-hour, depending on solar radiation availability.

While the cost of conventional sources of electricity increases, the cost of PV systems is expected to drop, following the historical trend of the semiconductor industry. PV manufacturing plant capacity, which was about 5 megawatts in 1980, is expected to double in five years. The combined annual revenue of photovoltaic manufacturing firms, which were above $1 billion in 1980, is also expected to double.

Given the recent and projected growth of PVs, they may soon rival more conventional solar thermal systems in market penetration. The primary applications of PVs will likely be these:

—roof-mounted residential systems with capacities of 2 to 8 kilowatts

—commercial, industrial and institutional building systems with capacities of about 500 kilowatts

—central station systems integrated into the utility and possibly near major load centers (e.g., small towns) with capacities of 10 to 100 megawatts.

Photovoltaic systems used in most building applications are expected to connect with the utility. These systems will typically consist of the following two elements:

—an array, which converts sunlight into dc electricity with no moving parts

—a power conditioner, which first converts dc electricity from the array into ac electricity, then supplies this power to building loads and the utility.

The economic feasibility of PV systems has been enhanced by purchase agreements under which energy not needed at the site can be sold to the local utility company. The benefits of this can depend on the "sell-back rate" the utility pays for this power, the length of the purchase agreement, the type of metering, and the temporal relationships among peak loads at the site, peak power production by the PV system, and the peak demand on the utility.

This monograph addresses the major components of the PV system. The first section identifies major system elements, or subsystems, and describes typical system operation. The next three sections discuss each subsystem in more detail. The following sections provide background information on design concerns, system comparison, and determination of system feasibility. The final sections discuss institutional concerns and references for additional information.

Systems Definition

There are two types of photovoltaic (PV) systems for building applications. These types are *stand-alone* systems and *utility-interconnected* systems. As their names imply, these system types are distinguished by their interaction with the electric utility. Diagrams of these systems are shown. Since stand-alone systems are not connected with the utility, any electricity that cannot be used by on-site loads must be sorted or dissipated. With utility-interconnected systems, this excess electricity can be fed back through the grid.

☐ The focus of this report is utility-interconnected systems. This type of system typically consists of the following four major subsystems:

—an Array Subsystem
—a Power Conditioning and Control Subsystem
—a Protection Subsystem
—an optional Storage Subsystem.

☐ The Array Subsystem is a mechanically and electrically integrated assembly of photovoltaic modules designed to provide a specified amount of dc electrical power under specified operating conditions. Typical components of an Array Subsystem include the following:

—photovoltaic modules
—module mounting hardware
—positive and negative bus bars or cables
—module electrical interconnects
—surge arrestors
—manual disconnect switches.

☐ The Power Conditioning and Control Subsystem (PCS) operates as a current source, inverting the dc array output to ac, and acts in parallel with the utility to supply power to building loads. Typical components of the Power Conditioning and Control Subsystem include the following:

—dc/ac inverter
—control protection sensors and feedback circuits
—ripple filter
—isolation transformer
—surge arrestors
—manual disconnect switches and circuit breakers.

☐ The Protection Subsystem protects people, system components and the utility's line from damage in case of abnormal system operation. Typical components of the Protection Subsystem include the following:

—frame and system grounding
—ground fault detectors
—surge arrestors, voltage regulators and blocking diodes

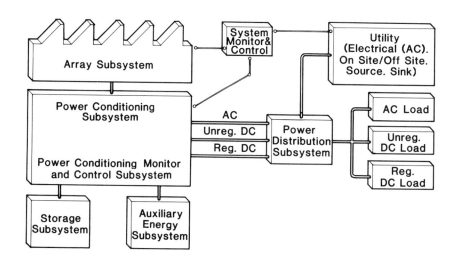

Generalized Photovoltaic Power System

—manual disconnect switches and circuit breakers

—isolation transformers.

☐ If a Storage Subsystem is included in a grid-connected PV system, its use is generally limited to a few hours of capacity for peak shaving or leveling loads. The duty cycle for batteries operating in grid-connected systems is characterized by relatively high maximum charge and discharge rates. In addition, frequent cycling occurs, on a daily basis, although all cycles may not involve a complete discharge or a complete charge. The batteries may also experience rapid shifts between charge and discharge, such as might occur as the result of an abrupt change in load demand.

☐ A typical residential utility-interconnected PV system with a roof-mounted photovoltaic array is shown. The PV array converts solar radiation to dc electricity for input to the power conditioner. The array wiring is shown running through a conduit to a fused outdoor electrical disconnect. Although over-current conditions are not likely to occur from the PV array, fusing may become a code requirement in order to protect the power-conditioning unit from extreme currents in array wiring; e.g., those induced by a close lightning flash.

☐ Also shown in this example is an earth ground wire coming from a metallic frame for the array. This ground wire eliminates the shock hazard potential in static charge buildup or in an electric fault from a solar cell to the frame. The array wiring is protected from lightning induced high voltage by surge arrestors located in the array circuit panel board inside the residence. A second manual disconnect is provided to insure isolation from the PV array when required during power inverter maintenance or repair.

☐ The power conditioner converts the array dc to residence-compatible ac and also contains the system controls. The inverter executes the following functions: automatic start-up (morning), automatic shut-down (evening), and array voltage control. When electrical loads are not satisfied by the PV system, auxiliary power is drawn from the utility grid. When PV system output exceeds electrical loads, that excess power is fed back to the utility. In addition to these normal operations, the control must provide for automatic disconnect from the utility lines in the event of utility power loss—a safety feature to protect those working on downed lines.

☐ Since the generic system allows two-way power flow to the local utility, ratcheted kilowatt-hour meters are provided to record the flow of energy to and from the utility.

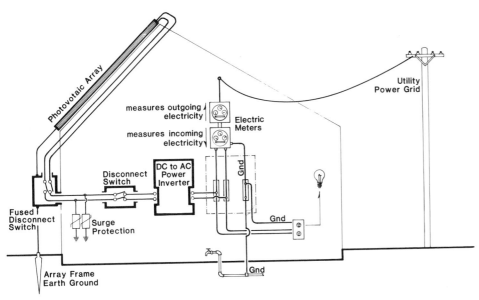

Typical Utility-Interactive PV System

The Carlisle House
Lincoln, Massachusetts
Architects: Solar Design Associates

This house is an all-electric residence, planned as a demonstration of its 7.3-kW PV system. Unlike the prototype systems built and monitored by the U.S. Department of Energy at the MIT Lincoln Laboratory in Concord, Massachusetts and at the New Mexico Solar Energy Institute in Las Cruces, New Mexico, the Carlisle home represents an opportunity to collect data from an inhabited building.

The PV system is utility-interactive and consists of 1000 square feet of roof-mounted PV modules for a 3100 square-foot home. Each of the 126 2 ft. × 4-ft.-modules contains 72 semi-crystalline cells and is rated at 58 Wp. Each source circuit contains 14 modules wired in series to match the input voltage of the self-commutated power inverter. Electric loads include base appliances, auxiliary domestic hot water, heating, cooling and lighting.

Energy-conserving design features are maximized with triple-glazed windows, super-insulated R30 walls, R40 ceilings and rigid foam on the perimeter foundation. Passive solar features include 350 square feet of double-glazed, south-facing windows and clerestories. Also, 100 square feet of solar thermal collectors supplement water heating.

Estimates of PV system performance fall in the range of 60 to 100 percent of the electrical demand. Recent occupancy of the Carlisle home suggests that actual data will soon become available for review.

Photo: Robert C. Lautman

The Carlisle House
Lincoln, Massachusetts
Designers: Solar Design Associates

The Array Subsystem

The two types of array subsystems are *concentrating arrays* and *flat-plate arrays*. Flat-plate array subsystems use no special optics and are usually installed in a fixed position, tilted from the horizontal at an angle calculated to optimize the amount of sunlight received throughout the day. Concentrating arrays generally must track the sun and are further distinguished by their ability to track on one or two axes.

☐ To further understand the operation of array subsystems it is necessary to view both the mechanical and electrical characteristics of their components. Comparisons are shown for both flat-plate and concentrating systems.

☐ Concentrating arrays operate according to a fundamental characteristic of photovoltaic cells whereby the current density (in amperes per square meter) produced by a single cell is proportional to the amount of sunlight (insolation) it receives. There are two types of optical concentrating technologies: point focus concentrators and linear focus concentrators.

☐ As their names imply, point focus concentrators utilize Fresnel lenses to concentrate light onto a single PV cell. Linear focusing systems use parabolic trough mirrors to focus light along PV cells, mounted upon a linear receiver located within the focal point of the trough. These systems reduce the cell area necessary to produce the equivalent amount of power with a flat-plate array.

☐ The basic element of all PV systems is the

Category	Flat Plate	Tracking Concentrator
Cost/WP [1] (1980) (Collector & Cells only)	$6 to $20	One Axis $1 to $4 Two Axis Not available
Diffuse Radiation Collection	Yes	No
Type of Cooling	Passive	Active-Liquid Coolant (some passive)
Power Requirements for Operation[2]	None	a) 1 hp for tracking b) 1/2 hp to 2hp water pump
Total Radiation Collection	Depending on tilt	One Axis—Depending on tilt
Moving Parts	None	a) Collector Structure b) Pumps c) Motors d) Cooling Fluid
Lb/Ft² Aperture Area	3 to 8	4 to 6
Collector Efficiency	8% to 13%	One-Axis 15% to 18% Two-Axis 15% to 20%
Heat Available for Other Uses	Insufficient for Economical collection	30,000 to 50,000 kWh/Yr/Ft² Collector Area
O&M Requirements	Infrequent electrical checking, Module cover cleaning	Machinery checks, Electrical checking, Reflector cleaning
Control Devices Required	None	Tracking Controller (Pre-programmed, Sun following, or combination)
Manufacturers (1980)	15 to 20 companies currently in production	One Axis—Several companies in production Two-Axis—Several companies in testing

[1]Depends upon quantity ordered and efficiency specified
[2]Depends upon size of system and type of collectors

Collector Comparisons

photovoltaic cell, a semi-conductor device that converts sunlight into dc electricity. Although all cells produce about the same amount of voltage (approximately 0.5v), their efficiencies (power output divided by power input) vary considerably, depending on a variety of factors. The most commonly used semiconductor material—practically to the exclusion of all others at this time—is crystalline silicon. Encapsulated silicon cells have a typical electrical conversion efficiency of 11.5 percent at 100 mW/cm^2 insolation, 25° C (77 degrees F), and 1.0 m/sec. windspeed. The photovoltaic module is a portion of the array packaged in a unit that can be shipped, installed and replaced easily. The module provides a means of packaging the PV cell circuit so that it is environmentally sealed.

☐ A concentrating module consists of a number of optical units with mounted PV cells connected in series mechanically and electrically integrated to form a single unit. A flat-plate module is composed of a number of cells connected in series and parallel to obtain the desired voltage and current characteristics. The ratio of cell surface to module surface determines the areal efficiency or packing density of the module. As shown in the accompanying figures, circular cells are not an efficient use of module surface area. This has encouraged development of high-density modules that rely on rectangular or square cells.

☐ Within a typical flat-plate module, the cells are interconnected not only to derive the desired voltage and current, but also to isolate defective cells. Protection from soiling is provided usually by a cover sheet of glass. Rigidity and back support is provided by a layer of Crane glass or a similar material. The cell circuit is encapsulated in a reliable sealant, such as ethylene vinyl acetate (EVA), to protect it from moisture. The current trend in flat-plate technology has been to eliminate module frames, allowing the mounting hardware to provide edge support.

☐ Panels are a mechanical assembly of modules. In concentrator subsystems, panels are usually a single free-standing unit, motorized to provide tracking. The array then consists of a mechanical assembly of PV panels electrically interconnected to produce a specified quantity of dc power.

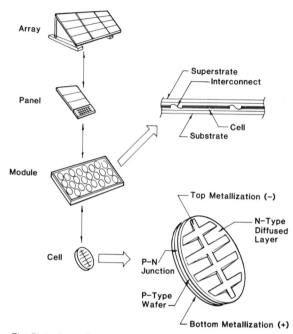

Flat-Plate Array Components

328

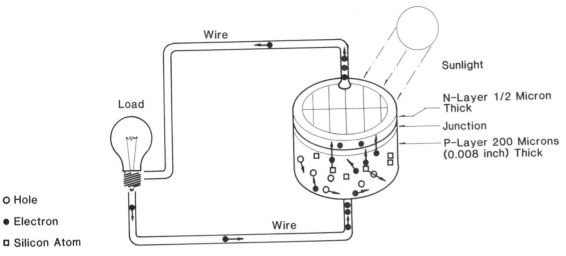

Wire

Load

Sunlight

N–Layer 1/2 Micron Thick

Junction

P–Layer 200 Microns (0.008 inch) Thick

○ Hole
● Electron
□ Silicon Atom

Wire

PV Cell Components

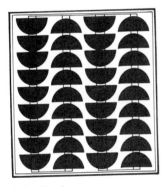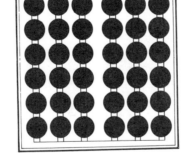

Solar Panels

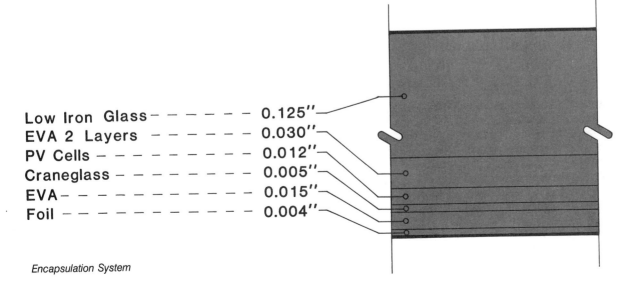

Low Iron Glass — — — — — 0.125″
EVA 2 Layers — — — — — 0.030″
PV Cells — — — — — — 0.012″
Craneglass — — — — — — 0.005″
EVA — — — — — — — — 0.015″
Foil — — — — — — — — 0.004″

Encapsulation System

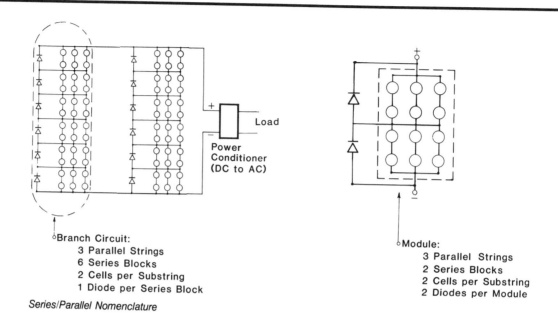

Branch Circuit:
  3 Parallel Strings
  6 Series Blocks
  2 Cells per Substring
  1 Diode per Series Block

Series/Parallel Nomenclature

Module:
  3 Parallel Strings
  2 Series Blocks
  2 Cells per Substring
  2 Diodes per Module

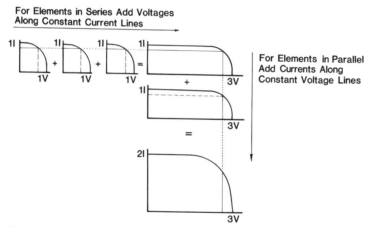

For Elements in Series Add Voltages Along Constant Current Lines

For Elements in Parallel Add Currents Along Constant Voltage Lines

I-V Curve Calculation for Series Parallel Networks

☐ Just as the array subsystem has a mechanical modularity of modules and panels there is also an electrical modularity of modules and source circuits. Module voltage is the sum of the series-connected cell voltages. Module current is that current produced by the paralleled strings of series-connected cells. Characteristics of dc to ac conversion exhibited by modern inverters require the series connection of modules in a source circuit to achieve sufficient operating voltage that minimizes power losses. Source circuit voltage is the sum of the series-wired module voltages, while source circuit current is the current produced by all modules. Several source circuits are connected in parallel to achieve total power output of the array subsystem. Array subsystem voltage is the voltage produced by all source circuits.

The accompanying graphs illustrate the current-voltage (IV) relationships for photovoltaic devices. Single-cell output characteristics are shown in the upper graph. The power output of the cell is equal to the product of the current (I) and voltage (V): watts = I × V. The short circuit current, Isc, and open circuit voltage, Voc, are also shown. The maximum power point is indicated as P_M. Note that power decreases sharply after voltage exceeds about .45 volts.

The middle graph shows the variation of output current and voltage for various solar insolation intensities. For example, the top curve might represent the output characteristics at noon, while the bottom curve might represent sunrise or sunset. This graph shows that while current is proportional to the insolation, voltage is relatively insensitive to it.

The lower graph shows the variation of output current and voltage for various Nominal Operating Cell Temperatures (NOCT). This graph shows that an increase in temperature produces a slight increase in cell current (constant voltage) and a significant decrease in voltage (at constant current).

The general principles for combining the voltage and current of photovoltaic devices are shown. These principles apply to the cell circuit in each module as well as a source circuit in an array. For example, if the three IV curves in the upper left represent three modules in a source circuit, the source circuit IV curve is shown in the upper right. If this source circuit is combined with another one having the same characteristics, the resulting array IV curve is shown in the lower right.

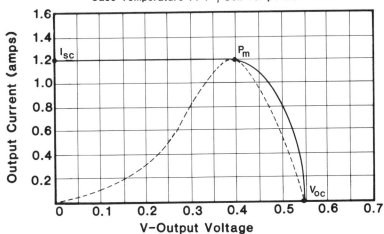

TYPICAL SINGLE CELL CHARACTERISTICS
Nominal 3 inch Diameter, Encapsulated
Case Temperature 77°F , Cell Temperature 88°F

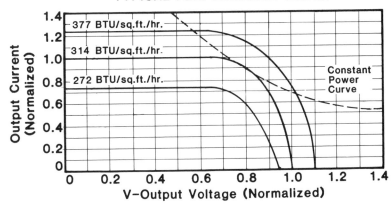

TYPICAL PERFORMANCE CURVE

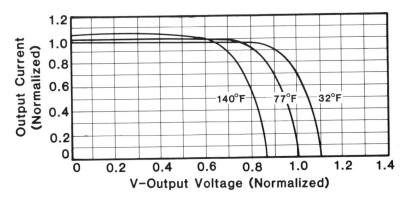

NORMALIZED CURRENT, VOLTAGE CHARACTERISTIC AT SPECIFIED CASE TEMPERATURES

Relationship Between Current and Voltage for Typical PV Cells

331

The Power Conditioning and Control Subsystem

The Power Conditioning and Control Subsystem (PCS) includes all the PV system electrical equipment (power and control) except the solar array, dc wiring from the array, ac wiring to the residence electric service panel and associated components. In addition to its primary function of converting dc energy from the array to ac energy of suitable quality for use in utility interconnected systems, the PCS is responsible for overall PV system operation, control and protection. The PCS discussed in this section is intended for indoor installation and operation.

☐ Power conditioning for the PV system is used to produce utility-compatible ac power from a dc solar array source. It uses an inverter plus ac and dc interface hardware and all necessary control logic and protection. Two types of inverters, line-commutated and self-commutated, are available to convert array dc input into ac output. The line-commutated inverters use the utility's signal to transform, or commute, array dc input into ac output. The self-commutated inverters commute array dc input using an internally driven rotating mechanism. Trade-offs exist in the selection of an inverter type. The dc interface is composed of elements that effectively join the dc from the array to the dc/ac inverter section of the PCS. The ac interface is composed of elements that provide electrical isolation and buffering impedance between the inverter and the ac utility system. This interface includes control and protective devices that make it compatible with both the PV system's and the utility system's operational capabilities and constraints.

☐ Power Conditioning and Control Subsystems used in residential 240 Vac, single-phase applications are nominally rated for an input voltage of about 200 Vdc. They are capable of operating in a voltage window from 160 Vdc to 240 Vdc to interface with as many array types and configurations as practical. Nominally rated input voltages for nonresidential 480 Vac, three-phase applications is about 400 Vdc operating in a voltage window from 320 to 480 Vdc. Since there is only one maximum power point product of array voltage and current, maximum power tracking by the PCS manipulates current and voltage so that the array operates as close to this point as possible. This maximum power tracking manipulation is as frequently specified in system designs as fixed voltage operation. Either fixed voltage operation or automatic tracking of the array maximum power point

Inverter Type	Characteristics
Line Commutated	—Currently more efficient —Less expensive —Utility may require extra equipment to reduce current harmonics —Power factor not as good —Cannot operate when utility is down
Self Commutated	—Less efficient —More expensive —More operation and maintenance may be required due to moving parts, extra equipment, etc. —Power factor better —Current harmonics —Can operate when utility is down

Inverter Characteristics

voltage can be used. However, the selection of a constant voltage level is important since available array energy loss can be predicted as a function of PCS input voltage.

☐ The available array output current varies with insolation and weather conditions. When the array output current increases beyond the operating capability of the PCS (e.g., very cold, sunny day), the unit will either limit the array current by increasing the dc voltage at the array terminals or otherwise protect itself. At low levels of array output current the PCS will shut down. Direct current input power to the PCS is equal to the ac output power divided by the PCS internal- or through-efficiency.

☐ A measure of how efficiently the PCS converts available array energy is its Energy Conversion Performance Factor (ECPF). The ECPF accounts for array energy utilization capability, weighted average conversion efficiency and miscellaneous losses. Although a ripple current is generated by the PCS, this current is usually limited to 5 percent of the nominal or rated dc input current from the array. A conversion ECPF value is typically at least 86 percent. Factors used to determine the ECPF include the following:

—part-load and full-load efficiencies
—standby hours
—operating hours
—no-load losses

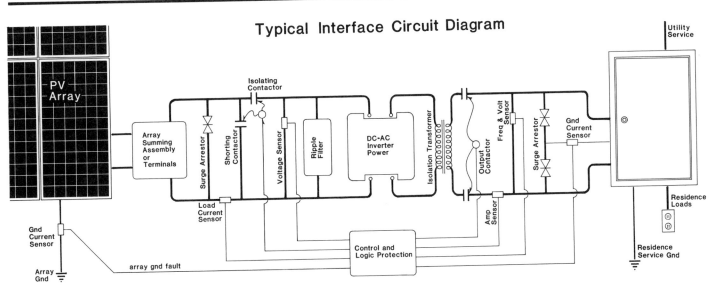

Typical Interface Circuit Diagram

Power-Conditioning, Subsystem Interface Curcuit Diagram

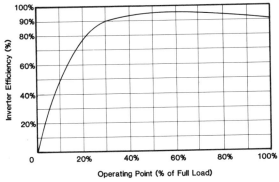

Efficiency of a Solid-State Inverter as a Function of Load

—average array output
—rated array output.

Rated FCS power is delivered at or above the minimum specified efficiency during steady state utility voltage swings within the typical range of 86.7 percent to 105.8 percent Vac of utility voltage. The PCS power rating is based on its ac output power capability at the nominal input (dc) voltage rating at the low end of the required ac voltage operating range (e.g., 86.7 percent of a nominal 240 Vac rated utility service).

☐ Normal (automatic) operation of the PCS consists of the following actions. When the solar radiation incident of the PV array is intense enough to generate an array output power that exceeds the no-load losses of the PCS, the PCS will automatically start, synchronize and connect to the utility line to deliver real power based on power available from the array. The

PCS will simultaneously control volt-ampere-reactive (VAR) flow. When array power falls below the level required to support a positive power output, the PCS will automatically stop converting energy, disconnect from the utility, and shutdown within one to five minutes.

☐ Advanced PCS designs will generally incorporate the features described below:
—*Start up.* The PCS starts automatically for array input voltage within a pre-set range and array input power above the no-load loss for a pre-set duration.
—*Line-Tie.* The PCS incorporates a "walk-in" feature whereby, after synchronization with the utility, the output level is gradually increased over several seconds to the full power available at the time of line-tie.
—*Cycling.* Excessive cycling is prevented during periods of low solar insolation (e.g., late afternoon and during heavy clouds).

☐ PCS operating and storage conditions typically assume any combination of the following external environmental conditions without mechanical or electrical damage or degradation of operating characteristics:
—*Ambient temperature.*
    Operating   −18° C to +45° C*
    *Maximum operating temperature for installation elevations above 1 km is 40° C.
    Non-Operating   −40° C to +60° C
—*Relative humidity.* 0 to 100 percent**
    **95 percent is acceptable if the unit does not require internal air flow for cooling.

☐ The total acoustical noise generated by the PCS, under any condition of operation should be reduced by 75 db measured at a distance of

2 m from any point on the surface of the PCS cabinet. To accommodate the temperature, humidity and acoustical noise conditions the PCS is usually located in an unconditioned, isolated space.

☐ A number of general utility-interconnection parameters affect the selection and specification of PCS. The objectives are to ensure compatibility of the signal produced by the PV system with that from the utility. The primary parameters are listed below. The local utility must be contacted to verify all site-specific requirements.

—*Reactive Current.* The power factor may be limited to 0.95 lagging to 0.95 leading at the output terminals of the PCS while powering from ⅛ to full rated load.

—*Harmonic Distortion.* Total harmonic distortion (THD) in the current waveform may be limited to 5 percent root-mean-squared (rms) at full rated current. The maximum single harmonic current may not exceed 3 percent rms. Total voltage harmonic levels may be limited to 2 percent rms. The maximum single harmonic voltage may not exceed 1 percent rms.

—*Frequency.* The PCS may be required to operate over a frequency range of 58 to 62 Hz, synchronous with the utility.

—*Electrical Isolation.* A dry type isolation transformer may be required at the PCS ac interface and to automatically disconnect when the PCS is in a standby mode.

☐ Electromagnetic interference (EMI) must be minimized in the PCS to prevent the adverse interaction between the PCS and equipment operating at 2 meters or greater distance away, such as telephones, radio, and television.

☐ Since the dc wiring and array can act as an antenna for interference generated within the PCS, EMI radiated from the array must be suppressed. Typically EMI must meet the FCC "Incidental Radiator" classification.

☐ Final acceptance of the PCS can be given after installation and upon successful completion of specified site tests, to be conducted by the system installer. Required field tests and corresponding factory tests are listed.

Name of Test	Factory Tests		Field Tests
	Type	Routine	
Interconnection Cable Check	X	X	X
Load Test	X	X	X
Operational Mode Tests (Start up, Synchronize, Shutdown)	X	X	X
Utility Disconnect Tests	X	X	X
Devices Properly Functioning			X
Ground Connection	X	X	X

☐ The PCS protects the PV system against damage as the result of abnormal conditions detected at its dc and ac interface. Typical protection equipment includes transient overvoltage suppressors, ac and dc undervoltage and overvoltage trip devices, overload current and short circuit protection and ground fault detection.

☐ Examples of abnormal conditions for which protection is required are listed below.

—over or under frequency at ac output terminals (e.g., utility frequency out-of-tolerance for > 2 sec.)

—alternating current fault, overvoltage or undervoltage

—direct current fault or overvoltage

—abnormal current flow in grounding conductor (green wire) (e.g. current in ac ground exceeding 5 milliamps root mean square (ma rms) (ac or dc)

—PCS component malfunction (e.g. internal failure in PCS (no automatic start-up))

—loss and return of utility line voltage (e.g. utility voltage below 87 percent nominal for 2 sec. or above 106 percent nominal for 1 sec.)

—array output overcurrent.

☐ Under several of these conditions, the PCS will disconnect from the utility within 0.5 seconds and shut down. Upon return to normal conditions, the PCS will typically start up automatically and line-tie within one to five minutes. At no time may the PCS inject dc into the utility line under either normal or abnormal conditions including internal component failure. Protection purposes and devices are summarized in the accompanying table.

☐ The accompanying chart indicates the differences among controls built into power-conditioning units, automatic switching using electromechanical controls, and microprocessors. The choice among these depends on several factors:

—how critical the array output is to application
—distance from array to application
—availability of monitoring room and personnel to monitor array
—size of the array field and complexity of wiring
—degree of load management required
—availability of maintenance personnel and frequency of maintenance.

Purpose	Device
System & Worker Protection may be integral part of PCU	—Circuit Breakers —Ground Fault Protection —Surge Arrestor
Utility Protection may be required by Utility	—Harmonic Distortion Monitor —Power Factor Monitor —Isolation Transformer —Alarm & Annunciator
System Protecting for self commutated inverters only	—Intertrip & Autosynchronizing for low or loss of utility voltage
System Protecting for commercial and industrial applications. May be in existing electrical system.	—Phase Over-Current Relays —Over/Under Frequency Relays —Zero Sequence Voltage —Grand Fault Relays (High Voltage)

Typical Protection Devices for Power Conditioning

Category	Inverter Self-Contained	Automatic Switching	Microprocessor
Cost	Included as part of inverter cost	$1000 or $5000 (~20 kW or less)	$10,000 to $50,000 for 24 channels
Complexity	No extra equipment required	Electromechanical Switches	Extra wiring, switches, electrical interfaces required (in addition to microprocessor)
Applications Recommended	Residential and small commercial	Medium to large commercial	Medium to large commercial and all industrial
Disadvantages	No control available for partial system failure or planned shutdown (whole system must be shutdown).	Cannot easily change control sequence once installed	Major cost
Advantages	Simple, no monitoring required	Can control many aspects of system in a limited way. Control may go to main control center if special control panel is provided.	Available to monitor & control any aspect of system: control sequence can be programmed. Control can go to main control center

Control Systems

Mississippi County Community College
Blytheville, Arkansas
Architects: Cromwell, Neyland, Truemper, Levy & Gatchell Inc.

The buildings of the Mississippi County Community College, located on the eastern Arkansas prairie, have forms similar to the groups of farm structures that occasionally dot the local landscape. These particular buildings, however, emphasize the "high tech," innovative nature of the PV system that fills the college's energy needs.

The campus is organized around a central concourse with a glazed barrel-vault roof, which is heated by the sun in the winter and cooled by prevailing southerly breezes and natural convection currents during the summer. A hierarchy of conditioned spaces within the connecting buildings was determined by careful attention to the school's energy consumption and programmatic requirements. Daylighting for task illumination greatly reduces the electricity required by artificial lighting and airconditioning, thereby reducing the size of the PV array.

The energy requirements of the college are met by a concentrating PV system with a design output of 240 kilowatts at 845 W/M² insolation (August Design Day). The system has three primary elements: a concentrating collector array field, a utility-interactive power-conditioning system, and an energy management system.

The PV array field consists of 45 rows of six collectors, each row having an independent sun-tracking system. The parabolic collectors are horizontally mounted in a north-south orientation. Each collector contains approximately 60 cells on either side of a 10-foot receiver. Each solar cell is 12-mil-thick, single-crystalline silicon with an active area of 12.5 square centimeters. Each cell string produces approximately 360 volts at 20 amps, or 7.2 kilowatts. The cells are hydraulically cooled for the most efficient operation, with the dissipated heat used to provide all of the space heating for the buildings, even during periods of low insolation.

The system's dc output is converted to ac power by a line-commutated inverter system. The power-conditioning equipment adjusts the array operating voltage to gain maximum power at all times. Under an agreement with the utility company, excess array power is purchased by the utility grid at the same rate at which it is sold.

Energy management is accomplished by an in-house computer that maintains constant surveillance over system operation and takes corrective action as required to modify system performance and protect personnel and equipment. All operational systems within the college are cycled according to preprogrammed instructions and linked to a comprehensive data-acquisition system to facilitate load shedding when a predefined demand is approached.

Mississippi County Community College
Blytheville, Arkansas
Architects: Cromwell, Neyland, Truemper,
Levy & Gatchell Inc.

Photo: Robert C. Lautman

Mississippi County Community College
Blytheville, Arkansas
Architects: Cromwell, Neyland, Truemper,
Levy & Gatchell Inc.

The Storage Subsystem

Unlike the power-conditioning and PV array subsystems, an electrical storage subsystem is entirely an option for a utility-connected photovoltaic power system. Its principle uses include:

—reduction of peak electrical demand or usage during periods of higher electricity cost
—service as a backup energy supply during utility outages
—increased displacement of on-site loads by PV output.

☐ Since the first two uses of storage are independent of the use of photovoltaic power systems, they may be considered independent advantages in deciding whether storage would be a cost-effective alternative to sellback. From the standpoint of designing utility connected PV systems, the overriding factor in choosing a storage system is economics.

☐ The desirable characteristics of a battery storage system for PV applications include:
—accepts deep discharge without failure
—accepts a large number of charge-discharge cycles without failure
—requires little or no maintenance
—does not generate significant quantitites of dangerous gases
—is cost-effective.

☐ If batteries are included in grid-connected PV systems, they are generally limited to a few hours of capacity for peak shaving or leveling loads. The duty cycle for batteries operating in these types of systems is characterized by relatively high maximum charge and discharge rates. In addition, frequent cycling occurs on a daily basis, although all cycles may not involve a complete discharge or a complete charge. The

batteries may also shift rapidly between charge and discharge, as the result of a transient cloud on an otherwise sunny day or an abrupt change in load demand.

☐ Two types of batteries suitable for PV systems are currently commercially available: Lead-Acid (Pb H_2SO_4) and Nickel-Cadmium (NiCd). A comparison is shown for these battery types in terms of their important characteristics. The comparison also indicates other possible concerns regarding use of currently available storage systems, such as increased maintenance and possible by-product hazards.

☐ The use of a battery storage system generally also requires additional power conditioning equipment to regulate voltages during charging and discharging cycles. A typical arrangement is shown for interfacing batteries with the PV system. The voltage regulator controls battery charge and discharge voltage levels and rates in response to the state of charge.

☐ Several factors in addition to basic design decisions may affect battery sizing, such as the amount of storage capacity required with respect to the load magnitude and the desired safety factor. These factors include the amount of capacity necessary to accommodate self-discharge and parasitic energy losses for ventilation and other auxiliary equipment.

☐ Another important consideration in battery sizing is the fact that many types of batteries do not fail catastrophically, but experience a gradual decline in available capacity as they approach the end of their useful life. For example, it is common practice among lead-acid battery manufacturers to specify end of life as the point at which available capacity falls below 80 percent of rated capacity. In such a

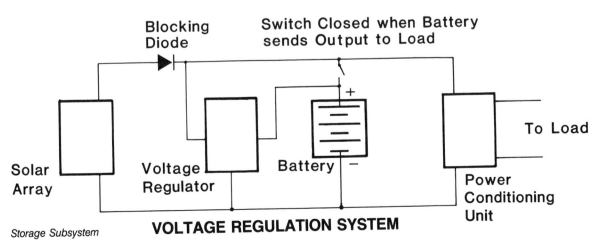

Storage Subsystem

VOLTAGE REGULATION SYSTEM

Factors Favoring A Storage Subsystem	Factors Reducing Desirability Of Storage
Low cost/kWh	High cost/kWh
Utility sell-back rate is a small percentage of normal rate	Utility sell-back rate is a large percentage of normal rate
Utility requires extensive PC equipment to remove harmonics and improve power factor	Utility requires only an isolation transformer
Utility charges by peak load in addition to net kWh (commercial & industrial)	Utility charges by net kWh only (residential)
Some dc loads exist or may be introduced (water heater coil, etc.)	All loads are ac
There is adequate area or existing architecture in which to put the batteries	A new building or wing will have to be built to house batteries
Use	**Approximate Storage Size**
Reduce sell-back to utility	Difference between: array typical day output and typical day fraction of array output which goes directly to the load
Peak shaving	Amount of energy used above the typical peak kW level for which the application is charged
dc Loads	Typical day dc load energy requirements
Nighttime ac loads	Storage is not a good application for grid-connected systems for nighttime ac loads

Factors Determining Desirability of Storage

case it would be necessary to specify an initial capacity equal to 125 percent of the capacity desired, in order for the available capacity to be adequate throughout the battery life. In addition, battery degradation strongly depends on cycling frequency and depth of discharge. Thus, an economic trade-off exists between selection of the design point depth of discharge, the cost of installing sufficient rated capacity to meet the system requirements, and the cost of battery replacement over the life of the system.

☐ Care should be taken to distinguish between battery energy capacity and the manufacturer's rated battery capacity. The energy capacity is of primary interest to the designer and is defined as the total energy (kWh) that can be withdrawn from a fully charged battery. The energy capacity of a given battery varies with temperature, rate of discharge, age of the battery, and the allowable depth of discharge (usually determined by some minimum cutoff voltage). The manufacturer's rated capacity is generally specified as the total number of ampere-hours (current multiplied by hours) that can be withdrawn from a new battery at a specified discharge rate, temperature and recommended cutoff voltage. The specified dis-

charge rate is often stated in terms of the number of hours over which full discharge occurs (e.g., 10 amp-hours at the 10-hour discharge rate).

☐ Battery terminal voltage can be affected by many parameters, including details of cell construction, charge or discharge rate, state of charge, battery age, operating temperature, and, for lead-acid batteries, specific gravity of the electrolyte. Fluctuations in battery terminal voltage during operation can affect the performance of the photovoltaic power system, particularly with regard to array efficiency if dc voltage regulators are not employed. In addition, the battery's operating voltage range can affect the design requirements of inverters, regulators, or other types of power-conditioning equipment. Therefore, it is important that all parameters affecting terminal voltage be identified for the type of cell being considered, and that these factors be accounted for in the system design.

☐ Proper charging conditions are very important to ensure efficient battery operations as well as maximum battery life. In most non-solar battery applications, however, energy dispatching requirements and variations in inso-

Battery Characteristics	Design Considerations
Equalization	Lack of equalization may result in reduced lifetimes, particularly for extended discharge periods.
Charge/Discharge Rate	High charge/discharge rates can increase temperature, decrease efficiency, and shorten battery life.
Self-Discharge Rate	Self-discharge causes battery energy losses.
Parasitic Power Needs	Auxiliary equipment may require continuous power sources (e.g., ventilation).
Extended Operation at Partial State-of-Charge	Partial state-of-charge can decrease charge acceptance (e.g., via sulfation in lead-acid) and reduce capacity.
Corrosion	Chemical degradation may limit battery lifetimes independent of the number of discharge cycles.
Rated Cycle Life	Cycle life divided by cycle frequency is an upper bound on battery life.
Duty Cycle	Cyclic operation, partial charge operation, and periods of deep discharge can adversely affect battery life.
Current-Voltage Characteristics	I–V characteristics affect system operation, voltage levels, battery charge/discharge.
Auxiliary Systems	Ventilation and/or air-lift stratification systems may be required. Flowing electrolyte batteries (REDOX, zinc-chlorine) require pumps, valves, control systems.
Capacity Degradation Over Time	Capacity will degrade over time, especially for deep discharge duty cycles.
Maintenance Requirements	Maintenance is a key tradeoff of battery performance, lifetime, and life-cycle costs.
Ambient Conditions	Battery characteristics are strongly affected by ambient conditions, especially temperature; low temperatures reduce available capacity, high temperatures reduce lifetime (lead-acid).
Safety Requirements	Controlled access, over-current protection, circuit isolation, fire protection, procedures to avoid shorting battery terminals, ventilation, and other safety features may be required.

Battery Characteristics and Design Considerations

lation may result in significantly less control over charging conditions. Battery efficiency decreases at higher charge/discharge rates.

☐ The ambient conditions under which a battery operates can affect its performance characteristics and life. For example, available capacity and voltage of lead-acid cells are a function of operating temperature. Drastic reductions of available capacity occur at very low temperatures, and permanent damage can result if the electrolyte freezes. Also, operation at elevated temperatures will reduce battery life.

☐ Other battery characteristics such as operating voltage range (which can affect power conditioner designs), efficiency, and self-discharge rate are also temperature-dependent. In addition, humidity, wind, rain, snow, ice, airborne pollutants and other ambient conditions may affect the performance of batteries and auxiliary equipment.

☐ Many types of batteries contain or produce potentially hazardous or corrosive materials at some point in the charge/discharge cycle. These may include flammable and/or toxic gases, liquids, and solids. Also, auxiliary systems may contain moving or high temperature parts from which personnel must be protected.

☐ Overcurrent protection, circuit insulation,

and other electrical safety features may be required. The need to protect personnel from electrical shock hazards must also be considered. Care in design and operational procedures should be taken to preclude short-circuiting of battery terminals with tools. Showers or eyewash stations may be required if personnel are exposed to the risk of contact with acid from lead-acid batteries.

☐ Design features necessary to ameliorate safety and environmental concerns will depend on the specific nature of the battery, as well as the type and location of the installation. For example, an application to which the general public could have access may require more stringent safety provisions than one in which physical access to components is restricted to skilled workers. In addition, all applications will be required to conform to local or national safety codes and specifications.

☐ Depending on the type of battery used and the specific nature of the application, various auxiliary devices and equipment may be required for proper operation. For example, lead-acid battery installations may require ventilat-

ing systems to maintain hydrogen concentrations below dangerous levels. Airlift systems to prevent stratification of the electrolyte may also be required in some instances. Similarly, the flowing electrolyte battery designs (for example, zinc-chlorine) require pumps, valves, and associated control systems, while the advanced high temperature batteries require auxiliary heating and cooling equipment.

☐ The photovoltaic system designer may also be responsible for supplying racks or other support structures in addition to intercell bus connectors, cabling, disconnect switches, fuses, or circuit breakers. Protective housings or special rooms may be required to protect or isolate the battery.

☐ Certain physical or operating characteristics of the battery may impose special requirements on the design of the battery enclosure and support systems.

☐ For example, lead-acid batteries may rest directly on the floor or may be placed in tiered racks and stacked three or four layers high. This latter arrangement creates a significant concentrated floor loading condition and can

Category	Lead-Acid (Deep Cycle)	Nickel-Cadmium
Weight/Capacity	100 to 145 Lb/kWh	66 to 100 Lb./kWh
Life in Cycles	1500 to 2000	2000 to 3000
Hazards	Hydrogen gas evolution acid electroyte spills/leaks	
Self Discharge	Possible problem after a few weeks	A problem only after long time intervals (month or greater)
Overcharging Tolerance	Will be damaged by overcharging	Will accept 5% to 10% capacity overcharge for extended periods
Failure Mechanisms	—A battery rated at 75°(F.) will lose half its lifetime if it operates at 110°(F.) —Freezing problem: at near or full discharge, freezes at 32°(F.) —Water loss	—Can operate up to 115°(F.) with no loss of capacity or lifetime —Can operate down to −40°(F.) without failure, although operation at this extreme should be avoided due to efficiency loss —Internal short circuits towards end of life —Water loss towards end of life
Required Maintenance	Water replacement	—Water replacement (none for sealed)
Recommended Temperature Range (Typical)	75° ± 10°(F.)	75° ± 40°(F.)
Typical Energy Efficiency	70 to 80%	80 to 85%
Battery Voltage	Varies with state of charge	Fairly constant with state of charge

Characteristics of Batteries

affect building design requirements. Similarly, flowing electrolyte batteries may require special damping measures to ameliorate vibration induced by electrolyte pumping systems, while the high temperature batteries may present thermal stress problems.

☐ If the batteries contain acid or alkaline solutions, corrosion-resistant coatings may be required on the walls, floor, and other structures in the battery room. Corrosion-resistant floor drains and plumbing should also be provided. The floor drain sump must be of adequate size to contain the total volume of any potential spill, including water used for cell washing, or by fire extinguishing systems.

☐ Many types of battery systems require periodic maintenance to ensure safe and efficient operation as well as to provide maximum lifetime. Maintenance may include periodic visual inspection, checking of electrical connections, and replacement of air filters or other service to auxiliary equipment. Aqueous batteries, such as the lead-acid type, may also require periodic measurement of electrolyte specific gravity and addition of water.

☐ In many applications, selection of the optimum battery type can be significantly affected by both first and life-cycle costs. For example, if maintenance or replacement costs are likely to be high, it may be advantageous to select a battery with low maintenance requirements and long life, even though this may result in a high first cost. Economic evaluation should therefore be on a life-cycle dollars per kilowatt-hour basis, rather than simply first cost dollars per kilowatt or kilowatt-hour. The actual cost of the battery energy storage subsystem over the life of the photovoltaic power system is determined by:

—first cost (dependent on battery type)
—impact on design requirements of other system components, such as the required voltage range of the power-conditioning equipment (dependent on battery type, ambient conditions, and system configuration)
—maintenance costs (dependent on battery type, duty cycle, ambient conditions, system location and economic factors such as inflation)
—salvage value (dependent on battery type and system location)
—energy efficiency (dependent on battery type, duty cycle and ambient conditions)
—auxiliary equipment requirements (dependent on battery type).

Type	General Characteristics	Typical Applications
Automotive (SLI) and Diesel Starting	High discharge rate, relatively low cost, poor cycle life	Automobile starting, lighting and ignition; tractors, snowmobiles and other small engine starting; large diesel engine starting
Motive Power (Traction)	Moderate discharge rate, good cycle life	Fork lifts; mine vehicles; golf carts, submarines; other electric vehicles
Stationary (Float)	Medium discharge rate, good life (years), some types have low self-discharge rates, poor cycle life	Telephone power supplies; uninterruptible power supplies (UPS); other standby and emergency power supply applications
Sealed	No maintenance, moderate rate, poor cycle life	Lanterns, portable tools, portable electronic equipment, also sealed SLI
Low Rate Photovoltaic	Low maintenance, low self-discharge, special designs for high and low ambient temperatures, poor deep cycle life	Remote, daily shallow discharge, large reserve (stand-alone) photovoltaic power systems
Medium Rate Photovoltaic	Moderate discharge rate, good cycle life, low maintenance	Photovoltaic power systems with on-site backup or utility interface, requiring frequent deep cycle operation

Lead-Acid Battery Types

System Design Concerns and Comparison

Several design concerns result from detailed design issues and subsystem interfaces within the PV system. Issues discussed in this section address array sizing, roof constraints, array mounting, array wiring, module interconnection, power conversion sizing, power conversion operation, battery location and fire safety. These concerns are currently the focus of detailed field studies.

☐ There is concern about roof-mounted array sizing when too many site-specific variables exist to provide any natural limits other than available roof area or source circuit size. Usually the system is expected to deliver energy to the building load at the minimum life-cycle cost, including the cost of back-up utility energy. Study results have shown that when sell-back rates of excess electricity to the utility are at least 50 percent of those charged to customers, the largest possible array size produces the least life-cycle cost. Otherwise the array subsystem is limited by site specific series and parallel circuit layout, module mounting details, roof weather protection, and esthetic integration.

☐ The choice of array mounting technique has significant effects on overall system costs. However it is not apparent from the distinct array roof mounting approaches—integral, direct, or standoff—which is the most cost effective. Each approach has offsetting advantages and disadvantages. Module layout, array operating voltage, wiring methods, weather seals, and replacement or maintenance access are affected by mounting technique selection.

☐ Temperature and humidity cycling stresses can cause cell and interconnection failures as well as the delamination of a module's encapsulant system. Other potential degradation agents include ultraviolet irradiation and corrosion. Candidate modules should be carefully selected on the basis of material characteristics to withstand anticipated environmental and mechanical stress conditions.

☐ The primary structural requirement for each module is to limit breakage of cover material, cells and interconnects due to wind, snow, hail and seismic loads. Selection of load combinations should reflect a balance between values that have a low probability of being exceeded,

Mounting Types	Features	Liabilities
Rack	—More options in array placement (ground or roof) —More tilt angle control —Maintenance and installation access —Good for flat roofs	—Structural, material, and labor costs —Roof availability —Land availability —Zoning —Vandalism protection (Ground mounts) —Esthetics —Wind uplift
Stand-off	—Back venting of array —Retrofit applicability —Need not be waterproofed —Lower-profile, more esthetic	—Access more difficult —Roof penetration waterproofing required
Direct	—Structural materials minimized —Array acts as waterproofed membrane —Roofing materials minimized	—Must withstand same loading as code requires for roof —Minimal array cooling, thus higher operating temperatures —Must access electrical connections from top —Access for maintenance difficult —Achieving watertight seal
Integral	—Minimizes roofing materials —Minimizes structural materials —Provides back access through attic for maintenance	—Watertightness critical —Special truss system may be required —Not especially suited to retrofit work —Must withstand same loading as code requires for roof

Comparison of Features and Liabilities of Mounting Types

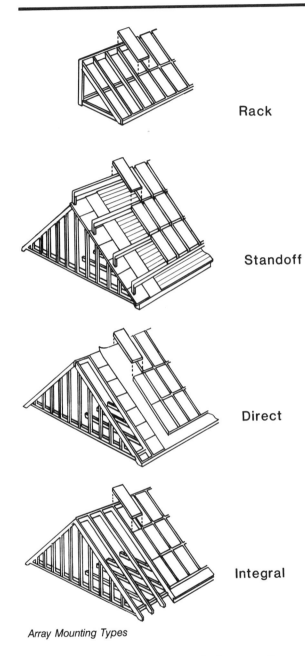

Rack

Standoff

Direct

Integral

Array Mounting Types

and values that do not result in a costly overdesign of the module mounting.

☐ The choice of array wiring methods and system layout has an important effect on overall system costs. While dry location wiring appears least costly, it is not apparent which distinct layout approach is the most cost effective. For example, many roof-mounted designs locate the negative bus along the eave, with the positive bus along the ridge. A wired connection to the earth ground for the negative bus may be provided as an additional safety pre-

caution in case of accidental contact. This connection requires an isolation transformer in the power conversion subsystem. However, the transformer adds economic penalties to initial cost and reduces net power output over the life of the system. If the array bus ground can be safely eliminated, then a lower overall cost results.

☐ Modules with accessible conductive parts are limited by safety standards to produce no more than 30 Vdc at 0° C, to provide protection from electrical shock hazard. Trade-offs between low voltage (<30 Vdc) and advanced module designs that allow higher voltages by elimination of exposed conductive parts should be examined for circuit or layout flexibility. Since PV modules cannot be switched off easily during hours of sunlight, and the current-limiting character of PV cells makes the use of circuit breakers and fuses infeasible, careful consideration of installation and maintenance procedures must be made.

☐ An array subsystem incorporates a variety of features to ensure safety from the low voltage (<30 Vdc) end of a branch circuit to its high voltage (~200 Vdc) end. Appropriate safety features can include the following:
—system, enclosure and equipment grounding, accompanied if necessary by ground fault sensors to short the array or open the array circuit-to-ground connector
—adequate conductor ampacity for the highest expected (i.e. short-circuit) current and operating temperature at that location in the circuit
—adequate insulation for the highest expected (i.e. open-circuit) voltage at that location in the circuit
—redundant safety measures for fail-safe operation
—minimizing potential effects of voltage arcs between an open-circuit cell and adjacent components
—surge protection for circuit elements.

☐ Module interconnection methods must satisfy the National Electrical Code. The key design concern is whether the application can be classified as a wet or dry location. Since low-cost wet location methods do not presently exist, wiring weather protection is critical. In addition, the location and method of splice connections must be carefully considered from a standpoint of both code compliance and cost savings. The number of splice connections as well as length of wiring runs depend on such things as module layout, series and parallel

343

circuit layout, module mounting details and outdoor disconnect location.

☐ Two primary design concerns exist in the area of power conversion. These concerns affect the relationship between power conversion design and operation.

☐ Power-conditioner sizing attempts to achieve two sometimes conflicting objectives. Optimal sizing may require a compromise between the following approaches:

—PCS sized to handle expected peak array output

—PCS sized to maximize periods during which it operates at higher efficiencies.

☐ Present solutions to this problem have first considered the effects of location and temperature on peak array power. The most economical system has been found to be one in which the array subsystem is slightly oversized in relation to the input PCS rating. Example ratios are listed below:

Site	Array kWp/PCS kWp
Albuquerque	0.98
Boston	1.13
Phoenix	1.09
Seattle	1.17

☐ Another set of tradeoffs result in the use of maximum power tracking or constant voltage power conversion. From a design standpoint, there is perhaps a 5 percent life-cycle cost difference.

☐ Field experience has indicated problems in start-up and maximum power tracking. The designer must be aware of the high open circuit voltage that can exist during start-up conditions when there is a low total power output. The specifications of the unit must accommodate these initial conditions.

☐ It is easy to specify a Power Conversion Subsystem operation with ranges within a few percent of the maximum power point; however, test data on maximum power tracking options has indicated difficulty in achieving these specifications. Though not yet perfected, alternative schemes are under development, including the use of a pilot cell. This approach is an open loop control method and, although relatively simple, may not represent the true array operating point over the lifetime of the system as module performance is degraded due to dirt, electrical problems or shadowing.

☐ Location of batteries within a building presents several concerns. Tradeoffs between an interior and exterior location for the batteries usually result in an interior location based primarily on the requirements for maintaining environmental control and access for maintenance. This location assumes battery placement in an equipment room with the equipment for power conversion, control and monitoring.

☐ Design of the room should consider the following requirements: sufficient ventilation to remove any hydrogen buildup; incorporation of a wet area; accommodation for spillage of active battery ingredients; tool and equipment storage; and minimization of unauthorized access to the equipment. A guaranteed amount of ventilation at all times is required to dissipate the small amounts of hydrogen and chemicals emitted under normal operating conditions to prevent hydrogen buildup within the room. A positive 30 to 60 cfm ventilation is suggested to remove hydrogen during equalization of battery charge. These ventilation requirements may produce a slightly greater infiltration loss. To accommodate any possible spillage, a 5 cm drop in the slab can be designed around the battery racks. The batteries can be located in a metal enclosure to minimize general access. If used, the cabinet should have heavy louvers and a locked door. As electrochemical storage systems become more widespread, standard components may be devleoped to resolve these concerns.

☐ Fire safety is an important design concern that must be specifically addressed for each application. One concern is the likely classification of the roof-mounted installation by local building code officials. Another concern is the installation's fire rating classification. Local fire companies may need to be alerted and instructed regarding the potential danger of the energy producing roof. The location of the dc power line adjacent to the normal utility line and the exterior disconnect switch should alert fire personnel that the building has an additional power supply. However, fire personnel must be informed that a disconnect at the switch still permits the array to operate as an active generator in the daylight and only interrupts power supply to the building.

Oklahoma Center for Science and Arts
Oklahoma City, Oklahoma
Designers: Science Applications Inc.

Science Applications, Inc., designed a roof-mounted PV system to provide power for the Oklahoma Center for Science and Arts. The 200 ft. × 400 ft. flat roof on an east-west axis had been designed specifically to accept such an addition.

The system includes a fixed, flat-plate reflector augmented array, interfaced to the facility bus through a PCU with a 480V, 30 output. The array is mounted on an essentially flat roof. The modules are unique; they are 9 ft. square, and have a 12-series by 6 parallel configuration of 10 × 10 cm. square polycrystalline silicon cells. There is 100 percent parallelism in the cell interconnections to maintain efficiency during the periods when the reflector illumination is not uniform. This feature also greatly reduces the adverse effects of single-cell failures. There are 18 source circuits, each with 84 modules in series. A total of 1512 modules are installed. The reflectors are laminated glass mirrors. The reflector panels extend beyond the module rows to minimize end effects during morning and evening. The PCU is a Windworks inverter with a 420V ac output and a step-up transformer which

also provides dc isolation from the facility 480V ac bus.

The power-conditioning unit, interfaced to the ac bus through a transformer, has two advantages: the array voltage is always less than 600V, even under open circuit conditions allowing the use of low voltage wiring; any dc components are completely isolated from the ac line.

The supporting structures are steel, prefabricated into assemblies that hold eight modules and eight reflectors. The base column has a telescoping feature which permits precise alignment of the array without regard to irregularities in the roof plane. The telescoping sections were welded in place after alignment. The structure design offers economy in both fabrication and installation.

The 160,000-square-foot facility is operated every day of the year except Christmas on an average 9 A.M. to 9 P.M. schedule. Loads include exhibits, lighting, a space heater, heating and cooling equipment, elevators, other machinery and electric trucks. The resultant load profiles are relatively smooth and symmetric about a 3 P.M. axis, whereas insolation and PV array output centers about the noon axis.

System installation was completed in January and it is now undergoing test and checkout. It appears that all objectives will be met.

Photo: Robert C. Lautman

Oklahoma Center for Science and Arts
Oklahoma City, Oklahoma
Designers: Science Applications Inc.

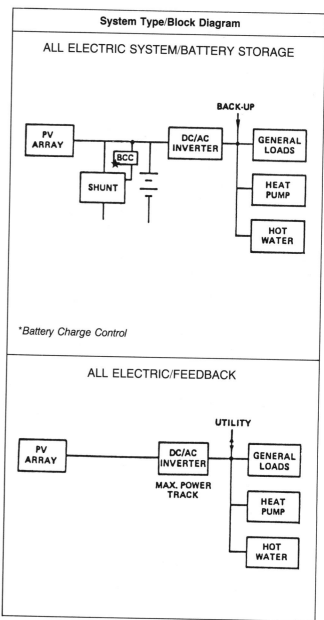

System Type/Block Diagram

ALL ELECTRIC SYSTEM/BATTERY STORAGE

*Battery Charge Control

ALL ELECTRIC/FEEDBACK

System Comparisons

Description	Advantages	Disadvantages	Conclusions
1. ALL-ELECTRIC SYS-TEM/BATTERY STOR-AGE This system involves all-electric loads with space heating and cooling provided by a heat pump. The PV system includes batteries connected directly across the solar array bus, with the solar array operating point established by the voltage of the battery. Battery charge accomplished by limiting the battery charge voltage to a prescribed level. Control is exerted by partial shunting of discrete sections of the solar array current to limit battery charge voltage.	—No max power tracker —Does not require feedback to utility	—Initial cost and maintenance of batteries —Energy dissipated through shunt when PV system output exceeds what load and battery will accept —Energy losses through battery heat dissipation —Digital shunt and battery charge control devices required —Somewhat lower annual energy displacement than with no-battery system —Battery-generated hydrogen gas explosive hazard. Cost of safety features to meet local codes	This PV-only system is less economical and displaces less energy than a system without battery storage utilizing a maximum power tracker and utility feedback. Major factors contributing to disadvantage of this system include cost of battery storage and the losses associated with the charge/discharge cycles.
2. ALL-ELECTRIC/FEED-BACK This system involves all-electric loads, with space heating and cooling provided by a heat pump. The PV system includes a maximum power tracking inverter and permits feedback of excess PV energy to the utility grid connected in parallel with the photovoltaic system.	—Simplest system —Utility essentially acts as electrical storage medium for all excess energy generated by PV array	—Acceptance of feedback by utility —Low buyback rate makes system less attractive	This system is the least complex to implement, assuming utility acceptance of excess PV array output. Large scale sellback of power to the utility from many residences can pose a serious problem to the utility. Of the PV-only systems investigated, the feedback system provided the highest energy displacement for an all-electric residence.

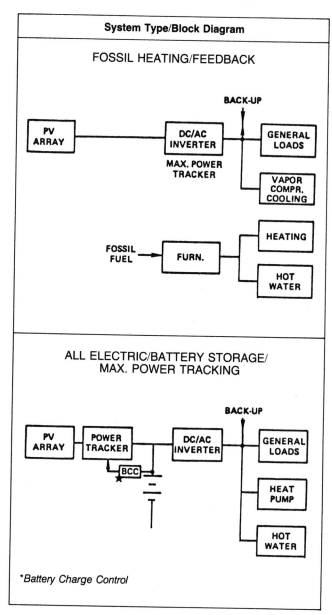

Systems Comparisons

Description	Advantages	Disadvantages	Conclusions
3. FOSSIL HEATING/ FEEDBACK This system involves the general household electrical loads and an electrically driven vapor compression space cooling unit. Domestic hot water and space heating are provided by a fossil fuel fired furnace.	—Utility essentially acts as electrical storage medium —Simple system	—Acceptance of feedback by utility —Economic viability dependent on buy-back rate —PV cannot be used directly for heating	This system proved only slightly less economical than the PV-only feedback system (2.) Thus, either backup energy form—electrical or fossil—can effectively be accommodated by the PV-only systems.
4. ALL-ELECTRIC/BATTERY STORAGE/MAX. POWER TRACKING This system involves an all-electric load, with space heating and cooling provided by a heat pump. The PV system includes a pulse width modulated (PWN) down converted/ maximum power tracker in series with the inverter, and battery storage under control of a battery charge controller. The PV system operates at maximum power, unless the output exceeds the load and battery requirements.	—Potentially higher system output with power tracker for battery storage systems —Does not require feedback to utility	—Increased control complexity —Cost of additional equipment —Higher losses	These systems with battery storage and maximum power tracking, have higher cost configurations and displace less energy than either the battery/ shunt system (2.) or maximum power tracking/feedback system (2.). Therefore, they provide no significant improvement or advantage over these other PV-only systems.

Design Feasibility

Preliminary estimates of cost effectiveness and area requirements are an important first step in deciding whether or not to utilize a photovoltaic power system. This section provides simple nomographs which give quick, rough estimates of PV system economics and PV collector area.

☐ Solar energy is an inherently diffuse power source and large areas are required to collect it. A flat-plate PV system, for example, requires about 10 m² (100 square feet) of collector area to generate a peak output of 1kW at noon on sunny days (assuming 10 percent overall system efficiency). The array size is a key parameter in PV system design because it determines the peak output of the system and also many of the requirements for other PV subsystems. The purpose of this section is to provide a preliminary estimate of PV collector area.

☐ Collector sizing for utility-connected systems is essentially an economic tradeoff analysis. An array size too small will produce too little energy relative to the initial fixed costs of installing the system (many of these initial costs are independent of the array size). On the other hand, an array size too large will provide a large amount of energy, but much of the output will be in excess of the on-site loads, and hence would be less valuable. Because the utility is always present to provide backup power, the availability of PV power at all times is not a factor. Thus, it is not cost-effective to size the array so large (with storage) as to meet *all* of the electric demands, including cloudy days, because then the array energy is not being fully used (significant excess would occur on sunny days). The proper size is a balance which depends on the type of collector, the location, the electric loads, PV system costs, utility electricity costs and many other design variables.

☐ PV systems are likely to be cost-effective for a range of array sizes. This is important because it means that there is some flexibility in the design and that the array area itself need not be critically dependent on particular assumptions about future electricity costs, sellback rates, inflation, etc. (Economic feasibility remains very sensitive to these factors, however.) In the future standard size package systems may be developed for specific building types or applications. For now, however, the designer should go through a sizing analysis, but should not be too concerned with using the exact "optimum" array area.

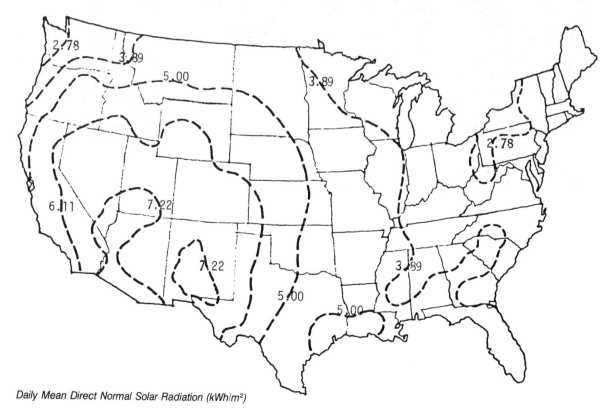

Daily Mean Direct Normal Solar Radiation (kWh/m²)

To a large extent the array size may be dictated by the available area, especially for roof-mounted systems. In estimating the available area for horizontal mounting surfaces, the designer must also account for the spacing between PV modules to prevent shading. Typical cover ratios (ratio of array area to total ground or roof area required) are given for estimating purposes. These cover ratios minimize shading effects to a few percent and may be increased if area is limited. The designer should also consider esthetic aspects such as visual interest or structural appearance in estimating area availability.

Estimating PV Collector Area

Feasibility analysis for PV array size involves the following steps:

1. Estimate the Direct Fraction.

—Estimate Utilization Factor. The utilization factor characterizes how efficiently the energy output of the PV array is utilized for on-site loads. A utilization factor of 0.8 is generally a suitable value for feasibility analysis. In general, the utilization factor is defined as:

$$UF = DF + [(1\text{-}DF) \times SBR]$$

Where:

UF = the utilization factor

DF = the direct fraction of the PV energy—the percent of the PV output that is supplied directly to the building load

(1-DF) = the excess of sell-back fraction

SBR = the sell-back ratio; ratio of sell-back rate to purchased electricity rate.

—Estimate Sell-back Electricity Price Ratio (SBR). The sell-back ratio is the ratio of the selling price of excess electricity sent back to the utility divided by the cost of electricity from the utility. The sellback ratio will generally be less than one, since utilities are not able to use the excess energy (a varying, time-dependent power source) as effectively as their own generation. On the other hand, the sell-back ratio should

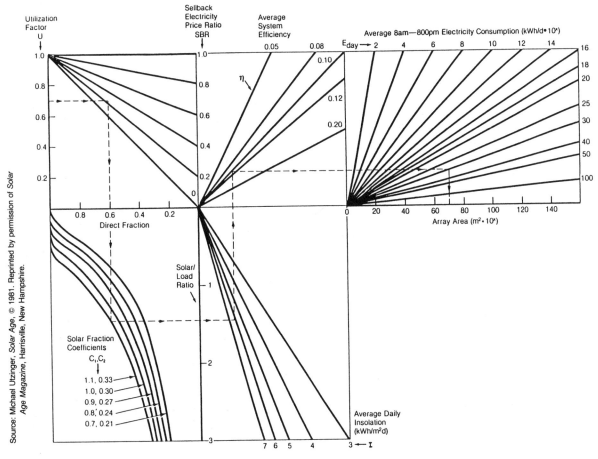

Array Area Nomograph

Source: Michael Utzinger, *Solar Age*, © 1981. Reprinted by permission of *Solar Age Magazine*, Harrisville, New Hampshire.

Collector Type	Cover Ratio*
Flat Plate	
Horizontal Ground or Roof	1.0
Tilted Ground or Roof	
—single row	1.0
—multiple rows	.3
Parabolic Trough	
One-Axis Tracking	.3
Two-Axis Tracking	.25

* *Ratio of collector area to total ground or roof area required (not including area for access, maintenance, or design aesthetics).*

Typical Cover Ratios to Reduce Shading

Load Shape	Annual Clearness Index	Coefficients	
		C_1	C_2
Residential	>0.5	1.1	0.33
	≤0.5	1.0	0.31
Commercial	>0.5	1.1	0.32
	≤0.5	1.0	0.30

Typical Solar Fraction Coefficients

be larger than 0; it is likely that utilities will pay something for the excess generation. Currently, utilities are required to pay for on-site generation at their avoided cost.
—Determine the Direct Fraction. The direct fraction is defined as that fraction of PV system output which directly displaces on-site loads.
2. *Estimate the Solar/Load Ratio.*
—Estimate Solar Fraction Coefficients. The solar fraction coefficients measure the match between load shape and PV output profile and depend on solar radiation, the season, collector type and load characteristics. For this preliminary feasibility analysis, typical values can be estimated as shown.
—Determine the Solar/Load Ratio. The solar/load ratio is the ratio of daytime electric energy consumption to PV system output.
3. *Calculate Array Area.*
—Estimate Average Daily Insolation (kWh/m²d). The solar radiation map in this section can be used to estimate daily insolation for a particular location.
—Estimate Average System Efficiency. The PV system efficiency is defined as the fraction of available insolation energy which is converted to ac electrical output energy, and should include the effects of shading losses (0 to 15 percent for flat-plate collectors, depending on obstructions and row spacing), PV module conversion efficiency (currently about 12 percent for good flat-plate modules with circular cells, 14 percent with closely-packed rectangular cells), electrical wiring losses (2 to 3 percent), and power-conditioning losses (10 percent). A reasonable value suitable for feasibility analysis is 10 percent overall efficiency.

—Estimate Electricity Consumption (kWh/d). The daytime (8 A.M. to 5 P.M. solar time) electricity consumption for the building should be estimated.
—Determine the Collector Array Area (m²).
It should be emphasized that the array area calculated is not necessarily the economically optimum array area. Rather, it is an economically feasible array area consistent with the utilization factor chosen previously. Optimization of the array area requires a more careful analysis of fixed costs (system costs which do not vary with size) and proportional costs (system costs which do vary with size), and should be based on seasonal performance estimates.

Economic Feasibility
□ Economic analysis for PV systems involves the following steps:
1. *Estimate PV System Performance.*
—Estimate Average Daily Insolation (kWh/m²d). The adjoining map can be used to estimate daily mean direct normal solar radiation for a particular location.
—Estimate Average System Efficiency. The PV system efficiency is usually taken to be about 10 percent, based on nominal estimates for typical equipment.
—Determine System Output (kWh/m²d).
—Estimate Utilization Factor. The utilization factor depends on the match between load and PV output, but can be estimated as 0.8 assuming "good" design.
2. *Estimate PV System Cost.*
—Estimate Alternate Electricity Cost ($/kWh). An electric energy cost should be estimated based on average daytime $/kWh energy charges, but not fixed on demand charges which the PV system does not offset.
—Determine Annual Fuel Savings ($/m²y).
—Estimate Installed System Costs ($/m²). The installed PV system cost should be adjusted for available tax credits. For example, federal tax

credits alone can be as much as 40 percent of installed cost for homeowners and 25 percent for businesses. Depreciation should also be included.

3. *Estimate Rate of Return on Investment.*
—Determine Simple Payback (years).
—Estimate Time Horizon (years). The useful life of the PV system is usually 20 to 30 years.
—Estimate Energy Escalation Rate (%/y). It is important to estimate an annual electricity escalation rate, since electricity costs will probably increase over time.
—Determine Rate of Return on Investment.

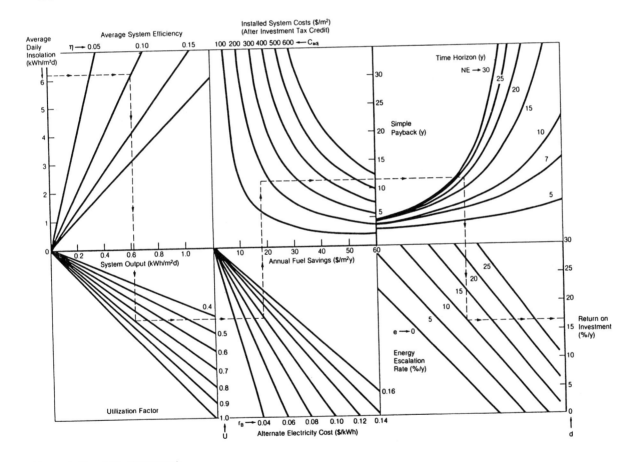

Economic Feasibility Nomograph

Source: Science Applications Inc., *Design Handbook for Photovoltaic Power Systems*, 1981. Prepared by Sandia National Laboratories

Institutional Issues

Institutional issues of potential significance to the widespread use of photovoltaic systems include:
—ordinances, codes and standards
—insurance and liability
—finance and taxation incentives.

The primary zoning ordinance issues are whether PV systems can be installed within the provisions of the ordinances and whether arrays can be properly sited to obtain sufficient sunlight permanently. Within the Model Zoning Ordinance of the American Society of Planning Officials (and potentially any local ordinance) regulations that affect PV systems include:
—**Height restrictions:** roof-mounted array might project above allowable height.
—**Setback restrictions:** array on ground might be placed too close to lot boundaries.
—**Density of site coverage restrictions:** area of array on ground plus buildings might exceed the legal building-to-lot-area ratio.
—**Accessory use limitation:** out-structures might be prohibited or their placement limited.
—**Esthetic or architectural controls:** design, style, materials, or color may be perceived as unallowable when such restrictions exist.

☐ Building codes are sets of regulations designed to ensure that the public health, safety and welfare are protected during the construction and occupancy of a building. Examination of these codes and the National Electrical Code shows that none currently incorporates specific provisions for PV systems. Without such references, the local building official has responsibility to interpret whether or not such systems are in compliance. Regulations in the model building codes and National Electric Code with which PV installation should be checked include the following:

Uniform Building Code
—*Special Hazards* (e.g., battery storage)
—*Building Fire Resistance* (e.g., residential roof arrays)
—*Standby Power and Light* (e.g., integration with utility)
—*Penthouse and Roof Structures* (e.g., roof structures shall not exceed 33.3 percent of the roof area.)
Standard Building Code
—*Penthouse and Roof Structures* (existing building cannot be increased in height unless entire building is altered to meet the code.)

Basic Building Code
—*Explosion Relief* (e.g., battery storage room design)
—*Roof Structures* (e.g., official may interpret glass-covered arrays to be similar to skylights, which require wire glass.)
National Electric Code
—*Guarding of Live Parts* (e.g., lack of criteria for safety)
—*Wiring Methods for 600V or less* (e.g., may be considered service entrance conductor requiring rigid conduit)
—*Lighting Fixtures (vs. General Wiring)* (e.g., interpretation of wire size conflicts for conductors)
—*Generators and Location* (e.g., interpretation of whether PV panels are generators.)

☐ Committees of the Institute of Electrical and Electronics Engineers (IEEE) and the American Society for Testing and Materials (ASTM) are preparing initial drafts of consensus standards. The Jet Propulsion Laboratory issued an *Interim Standard for Safety: Flat-Plate Photovoltaic Modules and Panels*, developed by Underwriters Laboratories to address module construction and performance requirements. The National Electric Code is expected to include specific provisions for photovoltaic systems in its 1984 edition.

☐ Insurance and liability concerns include product liability and liability insurance, manufacturers' warranties, owner and operator liability, and the availability of insurance to owner. Hazards and perils include:
—array damage by environmental conditions or vandalism
—personal injury during installation or use, such as electric shock, components dislodged by wind, or eye damage from reflective concentrators
—property damage, such as to the roof or other parts of a building
—fire caused by the system or additional hazards from some PV materials affected by fire
—chemical damage for systems with battery storage
—communications interference with radio, TV or radar.

☐ As with other products, the PV industry is required to use reasonable care in the design, manufacture, testing, and distribution of its products, to incorporate available safety devices and to furnish adequate warnings for installation and use.

☐ Tax incentives have been enacted on federal and state levels to encourage the application of solar energy technologies by decreasing the initial and/or life-cycle cost of the product to the consumer.

☐ The economics of PV systems is affected significantly by utility buy-back rates, backup power rates, and rate structures (e.g., time-of-day rates). The National Energy Act of 1978 regulates power production facilities up to 80 MW and governs their interconnection with utilities.

☐ The final concerns considered in this discussion are the candidate metering assemblies necessary for the PV systems to operate in parallel with the utility. The figures depict typical schematic representations of net materials and separate metering options. The energy system represents the complete PV system, including array, PCS and ancillary components. Time-of-day and reactive metering are not presented due to the fact that they may be state- and site-specific. Items such as output ac contactors, isolation transformers, etc., if used, are located within the PV subsystem.

☐ The net metering assembly is permanently connected to the service drop with two reversed series-connected revenue meters—each meter (1) measuring total energy flow in one direction and (2) ratcheted to prevent recording in the other direction. With this system, real power flow in either direction is metered.

☐ The separate metering assembly is permanently connected to the service drop with two revenue meters—one recording the total energy output of the PV system and the other recording the total energy consumption of the residential loads. With this system, real power flow in either direction is metered.

☐ Ultimately, selection of the metering assembly is a matter to be determined by the host utility and the pertinent public utility commission. It is assumed here that this choice does not affect the design or operation of the PV system hardware, although it may have some impact on the operating economics.

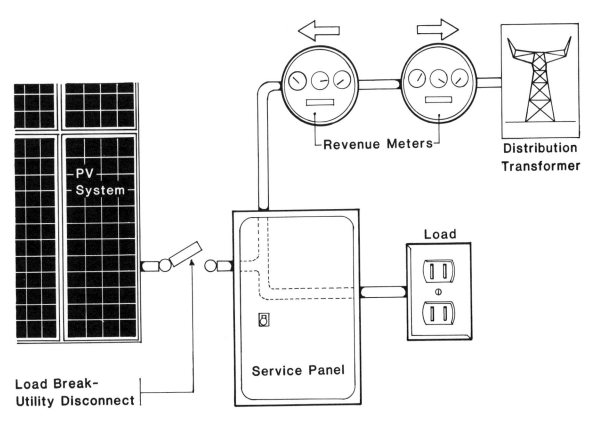

Utility Connected Systems—Parallel with Net Metering

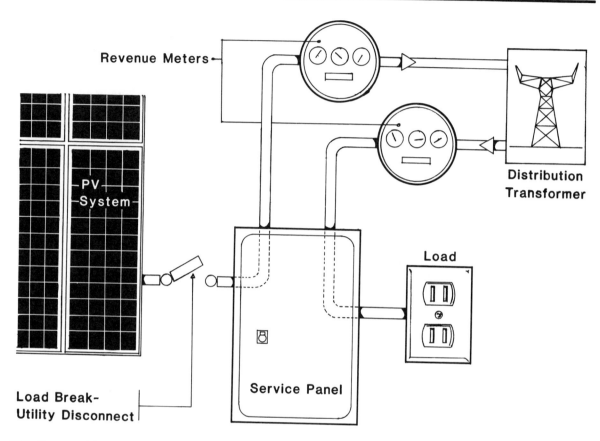

Revenue Meters

Distribution
Transformer

PV
System

Load

Load Break-
Utility Disconnect

Service Panel

Utility Connected Systems—Parallel with Separate Metering

PART TWO: ANALYSIS

THERMAL TRANSFER THROUGH THE ENVELOPE

Introduction

The design of the basic building envelope can have a significant impact on the amount of energy the building consumes. The basic form, selection of wall/roof systems, and selection and placement of insulation are decisions made early in the design process that contribute greatly to this impact. They are discussed in the initial sections of this monograph.

The design of the building envelope can significantly affect the amount of energy a building consumes. The basic building form, for example, determines the building's surface-area-to-volume ration, which in turn affects the amount of solar gain on the envelope and the potential amount of heat transfer into and out of the building through the envelope. Building form can thus be used to minimize heat gain or loss as well as to optimize daylighting, natural ventilation and self-shading as needed.

Beyond the basic building form, thermal transfer through the envelope is determined by the heat conductance of envelope materials. Although an envelope's overall conductance can be calculated, this figure is in fact a summation of the conductance of each individual envelope component. Conductance is affected by both the indoor-outdoor temperature difference and the thermal resistance provided by the material and construction of each envelope component. This monograph provides a table of the thermal resistance characteristics of a range of envelope materials to enable designers to compare the conductance of different envelope materials early in design.

Thermal transfer through the envelope is not instantaneous. Many envelope designs delay thermal transfer by using heavy-mass materials, notably masonry and concrete, to store heat passing through the envelope for a number of hours. This can be used to delay the transfer into the interior of a portion of the solar heat gain received during the day until after the sun sets. As discussed in the "Passive Heating and Cooling" monograph in this handbook, such materials can be manipulated to provide comfortable conditions into the night during the heating season or to delay cooling loads until after the end of the business day in the cooling season.

After the envelope form and materials have been selected, the designer can use the method contained in this monograph to perform a quick hand-calculation analysis of the building envelope. The procedure is based on the Portland Cement Association's *Simplified Thermal Design of Building Envelopes,* which was developed to determine compliance with the American National Standards Institute/American Society of Heating, Refrigeration and Air-Conditioning Engineers, Inc./Illuminating Engineering Society (ANSI/ASHRAE/IES) Standard 90A-80, "Energy Conservation in New Building Design," commonly called "ASHRAE 90A-80." The procedure contains charts and nomographs with which basic decisions affecting form, such as opaque-wall-to-glass ratios, can be quickly evaluated in terms of energy use.

Energy Transfer

The building envelope serves as a selective pathway for environmental forces, both internal and external, to the building. One of these environmental forces is heat flow. To a greater or lesser extent, depending on its thermal properties, (i.e., capacity to store heat, ability to conduct heat, etc.) the building envelope retards the flow of heat. If a material's conductivity is high and/or heat-storage capacity low, heat will flow readily through the material.

As the exterior temperature of the building fluctuates, the exterior surface of the envelope will be bombarded with wavelike patterns of increasing and decreasing temperatures. Depending upon the thermal properties and thickness of the envelope material, this will set up wavelike fluctuations in interior temperature.

Generally, the greater the thickness and heat capacity of the building envelope, and the lower the thermal conductivity, the smaller will be the building interior fluctuations and the greater the time lag between external and internal extremes. The ability of a material to conduct heat is referred to as the material's conductivity (k).

Radiant Energy Transfer

☐ All materials radiate thermal energy in all directions at all times. This thermal radiation consists of long-wave radiation emitted at low temperatures, whereas solar radiation is short-wave radiation emitted at very high temperatures.

☐ Unlike most other materials, polished shiny metal surfaces are generally poor emitters of thermal radiation. The measure of the ability of a material to give off radiant heat is referred to as the material's emittance (e).

☐ Not all materials absorb thermal radiation. The ability of a material to absorb thermal radiation depends upon its surface density and composition as well as the angle of thermal radiation. The more polished or shiny the surface of a material, the more it will reflect thermal radiation. The closer the incident angle is to being parallel to the surface of a material, the more thermal radiation will be reflected.

☐ Glass absorbs almost all thermal radiation. This explains the "greenhouse effect" in which shortwave solar radiation passes through glass, strikes interior objects, and is converted to long-wave infrared (thermal) radiation. The infrared radiation is absorbed by the glass and does not reradiate back to the atmosphere. Thus the area behind the glass captures long-wave radiation.

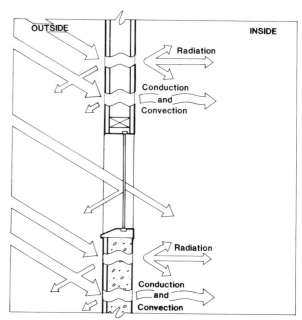

Emittance Values

Surfaces	Normal Emittance (Thermal Radiation)	Absorptance (Solar Radiation)
Black Nonmetallic	.90–.98	.85–.98
Red Brick, Concrete, etc.	.85–.95	.65–.80
Buff Brick, Stone, etc.	.85–.95	.50–.70
White Brick, Tile, etc.	.85–.95	.30–.50
Glass	.90	.04–.40
Dull Metallic	.20–.30	.40–.65
Polished Metallic	.02–.05	.30–.50
Highly Polished Metallic	.02–.04	.10–.40

Energy Transfer

Convective Energy Transfer

☐ Convection is the process by which heat is transferred by the movement of a warm fluid (either a gas or a liquid). Convection occurs when a fluid is warmed, either by radiation or conduction, and rises because it is less dense than cooler fluid. Thus, in a building, the warmer air rises to the top.

☐ Air movement that will transfer heat in and out of a building can also be due to pressure differences between the inside and outside of the building. These pressure differences can be caused by the wind blowing against one side of the building, creating a negative pressure on the opposite side. As a result of the pressure difference, air-leaks infiltrate through the building to the area of negative pressure.

☐ Pressure differences can also occur as a result of temperature differentials between the inside and outside of a building. This phenomenon is called the stack effect. In tall buildings it is particularly pronounced. In the winter, warm air in the building expands and rises, causing a relatively low pressure on the ground levels. Cold air infiltrates here. In the summer, the phenomenon is reversed as cooler air in the building sinks, leaving low pressure at the top where warm air infiltrates. In very tall buildings, of 35 stories or more, a tight horizontal separation at the midpoint of the building can be used to reduce heat loss and gain due to the stack effect. This can be accomplished by using vestibule air locks in stair shafts at the building midpoint or at elevator transfer floors.

Conductive Energy Transfer

☐ Conduction is the process by which heat travels within one substance or from one substance to another by direct molecular interaction. Molecules are continually in motion. As they become hotter, they vibrate more rapidly. Heat travels from warm to cold, i.e., from relatively rapidly vibrating molecules to slowly vibrating molecules as they come in contact with each other.

☐ Thermal mass in the building envelope can help protect the interior environment from climatic fluctuations or from internal fluctuations. Thermal mass in the building envelope will cause a time lag in the impact of heat gains through the envelope, since it will absorb thermal energy from environmental sources that have a higher temperature. In addition, thermal mass will modify the temperature maxima and minima to which the mass is exposed by absorbing heat from the surrounding environment (cooling) or releasing it back to the surrounding environment (heating).

☐ The rate at which heat flows through the building envelope can be calculated, once the resistance to heat flow and the total area of envelope material are known. This rate is generally given in the number of BTUs per hour that flow through a square foot of building envelope per degree-difference between outside and inside temperatures.

☐ To calculate this rate for a given wall section, it is necessary to calculate its overall resistance to heat flow.

☐ Resistance or R-values of various materials are listed in tables of numerous handbooks.

☐ The overall resistance for a particular construction is equal to the sum of the resistances of the separate components.

☐ The overall coefficient of heat transmission is used to calculate the rate of heat flow through the building envelope. This coefficient, called U-value, is the reciprocal of the overall resistance (R).

$$U = \frac{1}{R}$$

To find the rate of conduction of heat flow through the building envelope, the following formula can be used:

$$q = UA \times \Delta t$$

where q = rate of heat transfer in BTU/hr.
Δt = total temperature difference between inside and outside in degrees F.
$U = \frac{1}{R}$ = coefficient of transmission in BTU/ hrs/sq. ft./° F.
R = sum of individual thermal resistances in BTU/sq. ft./° F.
A = cross sectional wall area, in sq ft measured perpendicularly to direction of heat flow.

☐ Besides increasing or decreasing the U-value, there are several other ways of increasing or decreasing the conductive flow of heat through the building envelope. By using thermal mass in the building envelope, the impact of solar radiation on the envelope can be delayed so that its impact as thermal radiation is felt inside the building at a later time. The envelope stores heat as it absorbs it from the environment. This heat is later released to the interior of the building at a time when solar radiation is no longer striking the envelope. In addition, as each successive layer in the building envelope is heated, some heat is absorbed and some is passed on to the next interior layer. The temperature decreases as heat is slowly absorbed by each successive layer of the building envelope. By the time it reaches the interior, its magnitude has decreased compared to what it was outside. The larger the thermal mass, the slower the temperature change and the greater the time lag.

☐ If the temperature outside becomes cooler than the inside, heat flow will be redirected toward the outside. In this case the characteristics of the building envelope can be such that heat never reaches the interior environment of the building.

363

☐ When using reflective materials to impede or increase the conductive flow of thermal energy through the envelope, reflectivity to both solar and thermal radiation as well as emissivity must be considered. Envelope materials that have both high reflectivity as well as high emissivity will be cooler under direct solar radiation than will materials with only high reflectivity. However, if a building envelope is exposed to reflected thermal radiation from the ground, a more reflective material must be used, since a material with high emissivity cannot lose thermal radiation to a surface that is also emitting thermal radiation.

☐ Insulation slows the conductive flow of heat through the building envelope. Certain insulating materials are more efficient than others. Because dead air is a good insulator, constructions that trap it become excellent insulators.

☐ Vapor condenses on a surface whenever the temperature of that surface is lower than the "dew point" of the surrounding air. If vapor condenses on insulation in the wall or roof, the resistance of that insulation will drop to a level much below that of dry insulation. To prevent this, it is necessary to use a vapor barrier on the warm side of the building envelope. In this way, latent heat will be prevented from escaping the building during cold weather, thus helping to reduce heating loads. Similarly, latent heat from outside the building will be prevented from increasing cooling loads.

The Building Form

Both the heating and cooling loads of a building result from combinations of internal and external heat gains and losses. Each load, however, is generated by completely different sources, and is affected by different parameters. In establishing design priorities, it is important to understand the relative significance of these load sources and the variables on which they depend.

☐ External heat gains or losses are those created by the exterior environment (temperature, solar radiation) and can be reduced by using shading and increased thermal resistance. Internal heat gains (lights, people, equipment) are more difficult to reduce and impossible to prevent as they are by definition generated within the building's climate enclosure.

☐ The absolute amount of internal heat gain is a function of the building's use. Minimum internal heat gains are found in residential building types. Maximum heat gains are found in commercial and industrial buildings.

☐ For a given use, the relative amount of internal heat gain versus the external heat gain or loss is primarily a function of building form (area, shape or length-to-width ratio)—because the configuration determines the ratio of floor-area-to-exterior-wall-surface-area which in turn determines the amount of building volume exposed to external climate conditions.

☐ Building form will determine in large part the amount of energy the building will use, if a significant portion of heating and cooling load is due to heat flow through the envelope. Variations in building shape greatly affect the amount of exterior surface area for a given volume enclosed. A tall, narrow building has a relatively high surface-area-to-volume ratio. It has a small roof area and is affected less by solar gain on this surface during the summer months. On the other hand, tall buildings are generally subjected to higher wind velocities, and thus have greater infiltration rates and heat loss. Conversely, low buildings have a greater roof area in proportion to wall area, so special attention must be given to the roof's thermal characteristics. A compactly shaped building will have the smallest amount of exterior surface area for a given volume. Differing building forms provide a large variation of building surface-area-to-volume ratios.

☐ Within the concept of a compact building shape, many building forms can be utilized, depending on the particular requirements. Buildings whose forms shade themselves should also be considered. Horizontally and vertically sloping walls can be used to control the impact of solar radiation. East and west walls that are serrated in plan provide summer sun shading, while permitting low-angle winter sun into the

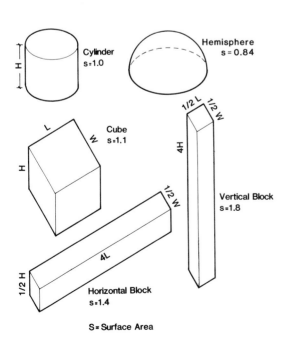

Volume and Surface Area Relationships

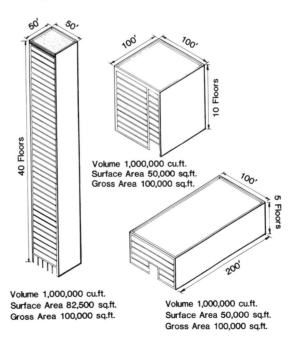

Variations in Building Surface Areas with Differing Building Forms

building through the windows with southern exposures. Indentations in this way also provide windbreaks which help to prevent air infiltration.

☐ In buildings with particularly large enclosed volume for the amount of perimeter surface area, indentations can provide natural light and views for floor areas which would not normally have them.

Obviously, the form of the building assumes less importance in an internally dominated building, and more importance for an externally dominated building.

☐ Victor Olgyay's study of surface-area-to-volume for externally dominated buildings, presented in *Design With Climate*, indicates that the cube is *not* the optimal form of any of the four major climatic regions. Other conclusions Olgyay drew from his study are:

—All shapes elongated on the north-south axis work both in winter and summer with even less efficiency than the cube.

—The optimal shape in all climates is a form elongated along the east-west direction.

—In most commercial buildings, in most climates, the principal penalty of a north-south axis is increased operating costs due to higher peak cooling loads. However, these penalties can be reduced by using a sawtoothed, east-west envelope.

—Although buildings elongated along the east-west axis are the most efficient, the amount of elongation depends on the climate. In cool (Minneapolis) and hot-dry (Phoenix) climates, a compact building form, exposing minimal surface area to a harsh environment, is desirable. In temperate (New York City) climates, there are more options for building shape without severe drawbacks (excessive heat gain or loss).

—In hot-humid (Miami) climates, buildings should be elongated liberally in the east-west direction. In these climates, because of intense summer solar radiation on the east and west

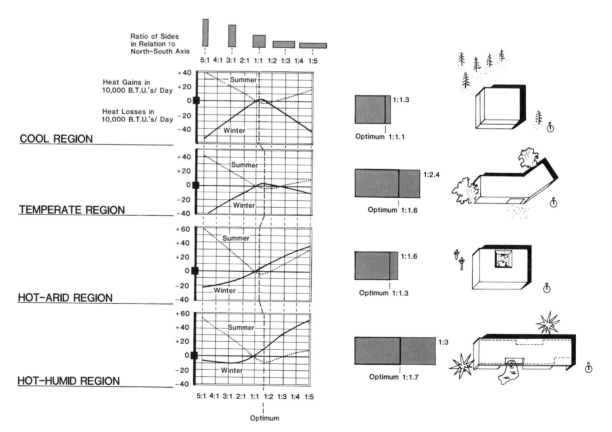

Basic Building Shapes in Different Regions

Source: Victor Olgyay, *Design with Climate*, © 1963. Reprinted by Princeton University Press, Princeton, New Jersey.

sides, buildings shaped along the north-south axis pay a severe penalty in energy for cooling. In all climates, attached units such as row houses, with east and west common walls, are most efficient, since only the end units are exposed.

☐ It is obvious that the variables that affect a building's energy performance are interrelated. Optimization of one variable (such as daylighting) may compromise another (solar gains) to such an extent that the overall performance of the building suffers. Since design can be viewed as a sequential decision-making process, it is important to understand these variable effects on the overall energy performance of the building.

Argonne National Laboratories
Argonne, Illinois
Architects: Murphy/Jahn

The building form and configuration of the Argonne Program Support Facility designed by Murphy/Jahn is a product of several energy-conscious strategies.

The circle encloses a maximum amount of area with minimal enclosure. A segment of the circle is removed to provide southern orientation for the location of the future solar collectors.

These collectors will step back to provide exterior shading for the glazed area. The circular portion faces west, north and east and minimizes the amount of western exposure, which is critical in determining peak airconditioning loads. The round shape is completed by a retention pond which will also provide increased reflectivity for the future collectors and daylight entering the building.

The interior concept is based on open office planning and maximum use of daylight to increase user comfort and conserve energy. Up to 65 percent of the building can be naturally lit through intensified lighting around the perimeter using a light reflective surface at the exterior wall, skylights in the interior zones of the top floor and a three-story atrium which facilitates orientation and spatial comprehension and provides daylight in the interior zones of the lower floors.

Artificial lighting is with a task-ambient system, which is coordinated with natural lighting and air distribution and uses only .5 or 1.5 W/SF according to varying conditions.

The consequent and systematic realization of this concept led to a coordinated and responsive development of structure, enclosure, skylights, ceiling and environmental systems. These technical systems are an integral part of the building's form.

The overall energy consumption of the building is approximately 33,000 BTU/SF/YEAR. This reduces first-and life-cycle costs and is achieved through optimizing passive and active energy strategies.

Argonne National Laboratories
Chicago, Illinois
Architects: Murphy/Jahn

The Building Envelope

The building envelope is a major control mechanism for solar light and heat (radiant) transfer as well as for conductive and convective thermal transfer between space inside and outside the building.

☐ Envelope heat gain and loss are the result of the conduction of heat through the exterior envelope due to a difference between inside and outside temperatures. As the two temperatures seek equilibrium, heat flows into or out of an enclosed space. The envelope gain or loss depends on three variables:
—temperature differences
—exposed area
—transmission.

☐ Given these variables, the designer is rather limited in the number of choices that will modify envelope gain and loss:
—A wider range of allowable interior temperatures will reduce the potential for differences between interior and exterior temperatures.
—The amount of exposed area can be altered by changing geometry, etc.
—Transmission can be altered by changing materials and construction making up the envelope.

☐ Note that it is generally difficult to alter these variables to fit more than one particular time of day or season. Care must be taken, when modifying envelope assumptions to solve one problem, that the solution does not create new problems in the opposite season or time of day.

Temperature Difference (Δt)

☐ Temperature difference is defined as the difference between exterior dry-bulb temperature and interior dry-bulb temperature. When exterior temperature rises above the maximum allowable interior temperature or falls below the minimum allowable temperature, a difference in temperature (Δt) is created.

☐ It is important to determine whether the interior temperature is a minimum, a maximum, or is tracking exterior temperature somewhere in between. In order to compute temperature difference, it is first necessary to find interior temperature (T_i) for the time period under study.

☐ Having a given interior temperature (T_i), it is easy to compute temperature difference (Δt). Simply subtract interior temperature (T_i) from exterior temperature (T_o) and record the results, being careful to record positive and negative results:

—$T_o - T_i = \Delta t$
—If $T_i < T_o$, then Δt is positive (+), which suggests there will be heat flow *into* the building, causing a heat gain.
—If $T_i > T_o$, then Δt is negative (−), which suggests a heat flow *out of* the building and a resulting heat loss. Generally increasing the temperature differences increases thermal transmission.

Exposed Area (A)

☐ Exposed area refers to the number of square feet of surface exposed to the temperature difference. As with solar computations, exposed area is a function of geometry and can be manipulated in the same way. Increasing the exposed area will generally increase thermal transmission.

Transmission (U)

☐ The materials and construction of the exterior envelope of a space impede the flow of heat between interior and exterior temperature differences. Thermal transmission is usually measured in terms of U-values. At times, these calculations can become complex, especially where a number of different materials are used in a wall or roof section.

☐ The following factors can be used in calculations for heat flow calculation.
—"K-factor" indicates thermal conductivity between two surfaces, and equals BTUs per hour transmitted through 1 square foot of homogenous material which is 1 inch thick, adjusted by the difference between outdoor and indoor temperature.

K-factor = BTU/hr./sq.ft./inch/° F

—"C-factor" indicates thermal conductance, and equals BTUs per hour transmitted through 1 square foot of homogenous material or a combination of materials at a thickness *other* than 1 inch, adjusted by the indoor-outdoor temperature difference.

C-factor = BTU/hr./sq.ft./° F

—U-value is the overall coefficient of heat transmission, and is used to describe a structure composed of more than one material. U-factor equals BTUs transmitted per hour per square foot from the air on one side of the entire structure to the air on the other side, adjusted by the indoor-outdoor temperature difference.

U-factor = BTU/hr./sq.ft./° F
—"R-factor" indicates thermal resistance, and is the reciprocal of any of the above factors. R-factors can be added arithmetically, unlike U-factors, allowing the heat conductance of any envelope component to be easily determined.
—"f-factor" indicates the heat conductance of the air film on either side of the structure, and is included in some conductance calculations.

☐ The translation factors allow the designer to take whatever data are available for a particular envelope construction and convert them to a usable format for establishing thermal conductance. Most simple hand-calculation methods use U-factors in their procedures, and rely on the basic formula for conductance:

q = U A Δt,

Where:

q	=	rate of heat transfer in BTU/hr.
U	=	$\dfrac{1}{R}$ = coefficient of transmission in BTU/hr./sq.ft./° F (R = sum of individual thermal resistances in BTU/sq.ft./° F)
A	=	cross sectional wall area, in square feet.
Δt	=	temperature difference between inside and outside, in degrees (F.).

Moisture Control

☐ A number of terms are used when dealing with moisture in the building envelope. Moisture control, moisture tolerance, vapor control, vapor tolerance and condensation are a few. Traditionally, the term "vapor retarder" has been used as it relates to built-up roofing, and "vapor barrier" has been used as it relates to walls and floors. Since no material is an absolute barrier to moisture, the term vapor retarder was selected instead of vapor barrier. The term vapor retarder describes the device or construction element which is intended to reduce the flow of water vapor into or through the structure.

☐ However, there are several important points concerning moisture control which should be emphasized:
—Necessary vapor retarder resistance depends on several factors. When the moisture vapor flow occurs in annual cycles, as it does in heated buildings, the requirement is not as demanding as it would be for a cold storage room which has no chance for drying any moisture accumulation. In a heated structure with an outside covering of materials highly resistant to moisture vapor, moisture may accumulate during the winter season in the cold outer elements of the building envelope. The safe moisture holding capacity—of these elements is an important factor in selecting the retarder requirement. A building with only a metal sheet outside the insulation needs a very high resistance retarder on the warm side. Plastic-faced sidings, aluminum siding, decorative metal panels and other such materials can present condensation problems directly behind the cold side finish. Interior vapor pressure and the length and severity of the winter are also important.
—Heat transmission is increased through building materials when moist.
—The movement of moisture is usually toward the cooler side of the building envelope.
—Insulation actually increases the chance of condensation in the building envelope if a vapor retarder is not used, because insulation reduces heat flow, and thereby results in a lower temperature within the structure. Unless moisture is prevented from entering the structure, condensation may occur at cold surfaces.
—A vapor retarder is the primary moisture control device, but ventilation of the interior space and of certain sections of its building envelope is also an important factor.
—A vapor retarder should be installed as close to the warm side of the building envelope as possible and should be continuous.

☐ Vapor retarders may be classified as structural, membrane or coating retarders. Structural retarders include rigid sheets, such as reinforced plastics, aluminum, stainless steel, and some rigid insulation types which are relatively impervious to moisture vapor flow due to their physical structure and composition. These retarders usually are fastened in place by mechanical means and have provision for vapor sealing at joints.

☐ Membrane retarders include metal foils, laminated foil and treated papers, coated felts and papers and plastic films or sheets. Such retarders are flexible and supplied in roll form or as an integral part of a building material (e.g., insulation). Accessory materials are required for sealing joints.

☐ Coating retarders may be semifluid, mastic type; the fluid paint type (arbitrarily called surface coatings), or the hot melt type. Their basic composition can be asphaltic, resinous, or polymeric.

U-values

R-values represent the heat flow resistance of a material or assembly and U-values represent the heat flow transmittance of a total assembly where U = 1/R. Since energy codes are typically stated in terms of U-values, these are displayed in the tables.

☐ When computing R- and U-Values:

1. Define all materials to be used in the wall/roof under consideration.
2. Determine R-values for each material, air film, and air space defined above. R-values for building materials can be obtained from a variety of sources including *ASHRAE Fundamentals*, manufacturer's data, or from the provided list.
3. The sum of R-values for each appropriate thickness of material, including insulation, gives the resistance of the wall/roof to heat transmission.
4. The U-value or coefficient of heat transmission is calculated simply by taking the reciprocal of the R-value sum (U = 1/R).

Note: U-values are not additive; R-values are.

☐ When selecting/designing a wall/roof to meet U-value requirements of codes and standards:

1. Enter Table 1 for wall/roof system under consideration.
2. Find U-value for system.
3. Enter Table 2 for insulation U-value.
4. Add R-values for system and insulation.
5. The reciprocal of the R-value sum gives the U-value of the total system.

Material	Description	Thickness	R-Value
Poured Concrete	Foundation & Roof 140 pcf Sand & Gravel or Stone Agg. (Not Oven Dried)	6″ 8″ 12″	.48 .64 .96
Lightweight Concrete	Lightweight Agg. Incl. Expanded Shale, Slag Vermiculite & Cinders 120 pcf	6″ 8″ 12″	1.14 1.52 2.28
Very Lightweight Concrete	60 pcf	10″	5.90
Concrete Hollow Core Deck	85 pcf	8″	2.70
Concrete Block (Uninsulated)	3-Hole Load Bearing 100 pcf	4″ 8″ 12″	1.40 1.75 2.14
Concrete Block (Insulated)	3-Hole Load Bearing 100 pcf, With Loose Fill Vermiculite	4″ 8″ 12″	2.33 4.85 6.80
Lightweight Concrete Block (Uninsulated)	3-Hole Non-Load Bearing 60 pcf	4″ 8″ 12″	2.07 2.30 3.29
Lightweight Concrete Block (Insulated)	3-Hole Non-Load Bearing 60 pcf, With Loose Fill Vermiculite	4″ 8″ 12″	3.36 7.46 10.98
Face Brick	Standard Face Brick 130 pcf	4″	.44
Stone Panel	Marble Granite Sandstone Limestone	1″	.08

R-Values of Selected Materials

Design Guide For Insulated Buildings, © 1981. Used with the permission of Owens-Corning Fiberglas Corporation, Toledo, Ohio.

Material	Description	Thickness	R-Value
Gypsum Wallboard	Drywall	3/8" 1/2" 5/8"	.32 .45 .56
Gypsum Roof Deck	Gypsum Fiber Concrete 87.5% Gypsum, 12.5% Wd. Chips 51 pcf	1"	.60
Plywood	Douglas Fir, 34 pcf	1/4" 1/2" 3/4"	.31 .62 .93
Fiberboard Sheathing	18 pcf	1/2"	1.32
Wood Decking	Fir, Pine, Softwoods	1-1/2" 2-1/2" 3-1/2"	1.89 3.12 4.35

Wood Siding	Plywood
	Wood Bevel 1/2" × 8"
	  Lapped
	Wood Shingles (16 in., 7.5
	  Exposure)
		3/8"
		
		1/2"
			.59
			.81
			
			.87

Prefab Sheet Metal Roof Deck	Uninsulated Panel No Backing	26 ga.	NEGL.

Vapor Retarder	Plastic Membrane
	2-Ply Kraft Paper
	  With Asphaltic
	  Adhesive
		.006	NEGL.
			.06

Air Space	Non-Reflective,
	  50°F. Mean
	  10°F. Temperature
	  Difference
		3/4"-4"	.96 45° Slope
			.93 Horizontal
			1.01 Vertical

Air Film	Exterior Wall
	  (15 m.p.h. Wind)
	Interior Wall
	  (Still Air)
	Exterior Roof
	  (15 m.p.h. Wind)
	Interior Roof—45°
	  (Still Air)
	Interior Roof—Level
	  (Still Air)
			.17
			
			.68
			
			.17
			
			.62
			
			.61

Shingles	Asphalt, 70 pcf Slate	1/2"	.44 .05
Built-up Roof	3-Ply, 70 pcf	3/8"	.33

R-Values of Selected Materials

Design Guide For Insulated Buildings, © 1981. Used with the permission of Owens-Corning Fiberglas Corporation, Toledo, Ohio.

Wall Class	Facing	Backup	R-Value	U-Value
Masonry	1. Brick on	Concrete Block Wall	4.05	.247
	2. Brick on	Sheathed Stud Wall	4.44	.225
	3. Brick on	Steel Grid/Frame Wall	2.75	.364
	4. Stone Panel on	Concrete Block Wall	3.77	.265
	5. Stone Panel on	Steel Grid/Frame Wall	2.47	.405
	6. Concrete Block Wall	None	2.60	.385
Metal	7. Metal Siding on	Concrete Block Wall	3.61	.277
	8. Metal Siding on	Steel Girt Wall	.85	1.176
Precast Concrete	9. Precast Concrete Panel Wall	None	1.99	.503
Concrete	10. Concrete Wall	None	1.49	.671
Glass Fiber Reinforced Concrete	11. Glass Fiber Reinforced Concrete Panel Wall	None	2.31	.433
Stucco	12. Stucco on	Sheathed Stud Wall	2.91	.344
	13. Stucco on	Concrete Block Wall	2.75	.364
Miscellaneous Sheet	14. Wood Siding on	Sheathed Stud Wall	4.62	.216
	15. Wood Siding on	Concrete Block Wall	4.54	.220
Curtainwall	16. Spandrel Panel Curtainwall	None	2.31	.433
	17. Spandrel Panel on	Concrete Block Wall	3.61	.277

Roofing Class	Roofing	Deck	R-Value	U-Value
Shingle	18. Shingle or Slate on	Wood Deck	5.04	.198
	19. Shingle or Slate on	Sheathed Rafter	3.32	.301
Membrane	20. Built-up or Single-Ply on	Metal Deck	3.89	.257
	21. Built-up or Single-Ply on	Poured Concrete Slab	1.43	.699
	22. Built-up or Single-Ply on	Precast Concrete Slab	3.81	.262
	23. Built-up or Single-Ply on	Wood Deck	4.86	.206
	24. Built-up or Single-Ply on	Gypsum Deck	6.48	.154
Metal	25. Sheet Metal on	Sheathed Rafter	2.88	.347
	26. Sheet Metal on	Wood Deck	4.60	.217
	27. Metal Panel on	Purlin	.78	1.282

NOTE:

Effects of through-metal conduction losses have not been included. Once a design is selected from the tables, a detailed evaluation of through-metal effects may be necessary when thermal envelope penetrations are excessive.

U-Values of Uninsulated Wall/Roof Systems (Table 1)

Design Guide For Insulated Buildings, © 1981. Used with the permission of Owens-Corning Fiberglas Corporation, Toledo, Ohio.

Material	Description	Thickness	R-Value
Foamboard Insulation	Isocyanurate	½″	3.6
		⅝″	4.5
		¾″	5.4
		⅞″	6.3
		1″	7.2
		1¼″	9.0
		1½″	10.8
		1¾″	12.6
		2″	14.4
		2¼″	16.2
Blown Insulation	Glass Fiber @ 2 pcf	2½″	10.0
		3½″	14.0
		4″	16.0
		6″	24.0
	Glass Fiber @ 6 pcf	5½″	12.1
		7″	15.4
		9″	19.8
		11″	24.2
Formboard Insulation		1″	4.17
		1½″	6.25
		2″	8.33
Batt Insulation		¾″	3.0
		2½″	8.0
		3½″	11.0
		3⅝″	13.0
		6″	19.0

R-Values of Insulation Types (Table 2)

Material	Description	Thickness	R-Value
Semi-Rigid Insulation	Low Density	1½″	6.2
		2″	8.3
		3″	12.4
		4″	16.6
	High Density	1″	4.3
		1½″	6.5
		2″	8.7
		2½″	10.9
		3″	13.0
Blanket Insulation		3½″	11.0
		6″	19.0
		9″	30.0
		12″	38.0
Glass Fiber Roof Insulation		¾″	2.78
		15/16″	3.70
		1⅝″	6.67
		2¼″	9.09
		2⁷/₁₆″	10.0
Composite Insulation		1⁹/₁₆″	8.33
		2″	11.11
		2½″	14.28
		3⁷/₁₆″	20.0
Wood Fiberboard		½″	1.39
		1″	2.78

Design Guide For Insulated Buildings, © 1981. Used with the permission of Owens-Corning Fiberglas Corporation, Toledo, Ohio.

□ The following tables on the following pages are detailed descriptions of the uninsulated wall and roof systems shown in Table 1.

1. Brick on Concrete Block Wall

Materials	R	U
Exterior Air Film	.17	
4″ Face Brick	.44	
Air Space	1.01	
8″ Concrete Block (100 pcf)	1.75	
Interior Air Film (Still Air)	.68	
Basic Wall	4.05	.247
Optional Air Space	1.01	
Optional ½″ Gypsum Wallboard Finish	.45	

2. Brick on Sheathed Stud Wall

Materials	R	U
Exterior Air Film	.17	
4″ Face Brick	.44	
Air Space	1.01	
Building Paper	.06	
½″ Plywood Sheathing	.62	
Air Space	1.01	
½″ Gypsum Wallboard Finish	.45	
Interior Air Film (Still Air)	.68	
Basic Wall	4.44	.225

3. Brick on Steel Grid/Frame Wall

Materials	R	U
Exterior Air Film	.17	
4″ Face Brick	.44	
Air Space	1.01	
½″ Gypsum Wallboard Finish	.45	
Interior Air Film (Still Air)	.68	
Basic Wall	**2.75**	**.364**

4. Stone Panel on Concrete Block Wall

Materials	R	U
Exterior Air Film	.17	
2″ Stone Panel	.16	
Air Space	1.01	
8″ Concrete Block (100 pcf)	1.75	
Interior Air Film (Still Air)	.68	
Basic Wall	**3.77**	**.265**
Optional Air Space "C"	1.01	
Optional ½″ Gypsum Wallboard Finish	.45	

5. Stone Panel on Steel Grid/Frame Wall

Materials	R	U
Exterior Air Film	.17	
2″ Stone Panel	.16	
Air Space	1.01	
½″ Gypsum Wallboard Finish	.45	
Interior Air Film (Still Air)	.68	
Basic Wall	**2.47**	**.405**

6. Concrete Block Wall

Materials	R	U
Exterior Air Film	.17	
8″ Concrete Block (100 pcf)	1.75	
Interior Air Film (Still Air)	.68	
Basic Wall	**2.60**	**.385**
Optional Air Space	1.01	
Optional ½″ Gypsum Wallboard Finish	.45	

7. Metal Siding on Concrete Block Wall

Materials	R	U
Exterior Air Film	.17	
Metal Siding	NEGL.	
Air Space	1.01	
8″ Concrete Block (100 pcf)	1.75	
Interior Air Film (Still Air)	.68	
Basic Wall	**3.61**	**.277**
Optional Air Space	1.01	
Optional ½″ Gypsum Wallboard Finish	.45	

8. Metal Siding on Steel Girt Wall

Materials	R	U
Exterior Air Film	.17	
Metal Siding	NEGL.	
Interior Air Film (Still Air)	.68	
Basic Wall	**.85**	**1.176**
Optional Air Space	1.01	
Optional ½″ Gypsum Wallboard Finish	.45	

9. Precast Concrete Panel Wall

Materials	R	U
Exterior Air Film	.17	
6″ Lightweight Concrete (120 pcf)	1.14	
Interior Air Film (Still Air)	.68	
Basic Wall	**1.99**	**.503**
Optional Air Space	1.01	
Optional ½″ Gypsum Wallboard Finish	.45	

10. Concrete Wall

Materials	R	U
Exterior Air Film	.17	
8″ Concrete (140 pcf)	.64	
Interior Air Film (Still Air)	.68	
Basic Wall	**1.49**	**.671**
Optional Air Space	1.01	
Optional ½″ Gypsum Wallboard Finish	.45	

11. Glass Fiber Reinforced Concrete Panel Wall

Materials	R	U
Exterior Air Film	.17	
⅜″ G.F.R.C. Panel (125 pcf)	NEGL.	
Air Space	1.01	
½″ Gypsum Wallboard Finish	.45	
Interior Air Film (Still Air)	.68	
Basic Wall	2.31	.433

12. Stucco on Sheathed Stud Wall

Materials	R	U
Exterior Air Film	.17	
¾″ Stucco	.15	
½″ Gypsum Board Sheathing	.45	
Air Space	1.01	
½″ Gypsum Wallboard Finish	.45	
Interior Air Film (Still Air)	.68	
Basic Wall	2.91	.344

13. Stucco on Concrete Block Wall

Materials	R	U
Exterior Air Film	.17	
¾″ Stucco	.15	
8″ Concrete Block (100 pcf)	1.75	
Interior Air Film (Still Air)	.68	
Basic Wall	2.75	.364
Optional Air Space	1.01	
Optional ½″ Gypsum Wallboard Finish	.45	

14. Wood Siding on Sheathed Stud Wall

Materials	R	U
Exterior Air Film	.17	
¾″ Plywood Siding	.93	
Building Paper	.06	
½″ Fiberboard Sheathing	1.32	
Air Space	1.01	
½″ Gypsum Wallboard Finish	.45	
Interior Air Film (Still Air)	.68	
Basic Wall	4.62	.216

15. Wood Siding on Concrete Block Wall

Materials	R	U
Exterior Air Film	.17	
¾″ Plywood Siding	.93	
Air Space	1.01	
8″ Concrete Block (100 pcf)	1.75	
Interior Air Film (Still Air)	.68	
Basic Wall	4.54	.220
Optional Air Space	1.01	
Optional ½″ Gypsum Wallboard Finish	.45	

16. Spandrel Panel Curtainwall

Materials	R	U
Exterior Air Film	.17	
¼″ Spandrel Glass	NEGL.	
Air Space	1.01	
½″ Gypsum Wallboard Finish	.45	
Interior Air Film (Still Air)	.68	
Basic Wall	2.31	.433

17. Spandrel Panel on Concrete Block Wall

Materials	R	U
Exterior Air Film	.17	
¼″ Spandrel Glass	NEGL.	
Air Space	1.01	
8″ Concrete Block (100 pcf)	1.75	
Interior Air Film (Still Air)	.68	
Basic Wall	3.61	.277
Optional Air Space "C"	1.01	
Optional ½″ Gypsum Wallboard Finish	.45	

Descriptions of Wall Systems

Design Guide For Insulated Buildings, © 1981. Used with the permission of Owens-Corning Fiberglas Corporation, Toledo, Ohio.

18. Shingle or Slate on Wood Deck

Materials	R	U
Exterior Air Film	.17	
Asphalt Shingles	.44	
Building Paper	.06	
3" Wood Deck	3.75	
Interior Air Film		
(Still Air)	.62	
Basic Roof	**5.04**	**.198**
Retrofit Option:		
Asphalt Shingles,		
Building Paper,		
½" Plywood		
Sheathing	1.12	
Insulation Option:		
½" Plywood		
Sheathing	.62	
Optional ½" Gypsum		
Wallboard Finish	.45	

19. Shingle or Slate on Sheathed Rafter

Materials	R	U
Exterior Air Film	.17	
Asphalt Shingles	.44	
Building Paper	.06	
½" Plywood Sheathing	.62	
Air Space	.96	
½" Gypsum		
Wallboard Finish	.45	
Interior Air Film		
(Still Air)	.62	
Basic Roof	**3.32**	**.301**

20. Built-up or Single-Ply on Metal Deck

Materials	R	U
Exterior Air Film	.17	
Stone	NEGL.	
3-ply Built-Up		
Roof	.33	
¾" Glass Fiber	2.78	
Metal Deck	NEGL.	
Interior Air Film		
(Still Air)	.61	
Basic Roof	**3.89**	**.257**
Optional ½" Gypsum		
Wallboard Ceiling	.45	

21. Built-up or Single-Ply on Poured Concrete Slab

Materials	R	U
Exterior Air Film	.17	
Stone	NEGL.	
3-ply Built-Up		
Roof	.33	
4" Concrete Slab		
(140 pcf)	.32	
Interior Air Film		
(Still Air)	.61	
Basic Roof	**1.43**	**.699**
Optional ½" Gypsum		
Wallboard Ceiling	.45	

22. Built-up or Single-Ply on Precast Concrete Slab

Materials	R	U
Exterior Air Film	.17	
Stone	NEGL.	
3-ply Built-Up		
Roof	.33	
8" Hollow Core Slab		
(85 pcf)	2.70	
Interior Air Film		
(Still Air)	.61	
Basic Roof	**3.81**	**.262**
Optional ½" Gypsum		
Wallboard Ceiling	.45	

23. Built-up or Single-Ply on Wood Deck

Materials	R	U
Exterior Air Film	.17	
Stone	NEGL.	
3-ply Built-Up		
Roof	.33	
3″ Wood Deck	3.75	
Interior Air Film		
(Still Air)	.61	
Basic Roof	4.86	.206
Optional ½″ Gypsum		
Wallboard Ceiling	.45	

24. Built-up or Single-Ply on Gypsum Deck

Materials	R	U
Exterior Air Film	.17	
Stone	NEGL.	
3-ply Built-Up		
Roof	.33	
2″ Gypsum Deck		
(51 pcf)	1.20	
1″ Formboard	4.17	
Interior Air Film		
(Still Air)	.61	
Basic Roof	6.48	.154

25. Metal Panel on Sheathed Rafter

Materials	R	U
Exterior Air Film	.17	
Sheet Metal Roofing	NEGL.	
Building Paper	.06	
½″ Plywood		
Sheathing	.62	
Air Space	.96	
½″ Gypsum		
Wallboard Finish	.45	
Interior Air Film		
(Still Air)	.62	
Basic Roof	2.88	.347

26. Sheet Metal on Wood Deck

Materials	R	U
Exterior Air Film	.17	
Sheet Metal Roofing	NEGL.	
Building Paper	.06	
3″ Wood Deck	3.75	
Interior Air Film		
(Still Air)	.62	
Basic Roof	4.60	.217
Retrofit Option:		
Metal, Building		
Paper, ½″ Plywood		
Sheathing	.68	
Insulation Option:		
½″ Plywood		
Sheathing "B"	.62	
Optional ½″ Gypsum		
Wallboard Finish	.45	

27. Sheet Metal on Purlin

Materials	R	U
Exterior Air Film	.17	
Metal Roof Panel	NEGL.	
Interior Air Film		
(Still Air)	.61	
Basic Roof	.78	1.282
Optional ½″ Gypsum		
Wallboard Ceiling	.45	

Descriptions of Roof Systems

Design Guide For Insulated Buildings, © 1981. Used with the permission of Owens-Corning Fiberglas Corporation, Toledo, Ohio.

Thermal Analysis of the Envelope: A Method

The American National Standards Institute, the American Society of Heating, Refrigerating and Air-Conditioning, Inc., and the Illuminating Engineering Society have developed ANSI/ASHRAE/IES Standard 90A-80, "Energy Conservation in New Building Design." Commonly known as ASHRAE 90A-80, this standard is largely performance-based, allowing a large amount of design freedom because an *overall* energy budget for the building envelope is established, rather than prescriptive design requirements for the various building elements. The designer is therefore free to manipulate the building form, proportion, orientation and materials of building walls, roofs, floors and glazed areas to comply with the energy budget.

☐ The standard is designed to cover new buildings that provide facilities or shelter for public assembly, including educational, business, mercantile, institutional, warehouse and residential occupancies; the heated space of factory and industrial buildings primarily used for human occupancy, such as office space; mobile homes and predesigned, prefabricated buildings. Many state, local and model codes have adopted the standard, with modifications to suit local conditions. The standard does not optimize energy-conserving practices, although its use will eliminate some of the major energy-wasting envelope design practices of today.

The Envelope Heat Budget

☐ The accompanying chart provides the building envelope heat budget of losses (in BTUs) allowed per hour. Usually, a maximum hourly heat budget for thermal design of the building envelope can be found by:

Energy Budget = $\Delta t \times UA$

BTU/h/sq.ft. = $°F \times (BTU/hr./sq.ft./°F) \times sq.ft.$

Where:

Δt = the temperature differential between outside design temperatures (see the accompanying chart) and indoor design temperature.

U = U-values (overall coefficient of heat transmission) for envelope components

A = gross area (in square feet) for envelope components.

☐ The budget figures presented reflect only the maximum heat transmission allowed through the envelope each hour, and do not take into account infiltration, ventilation or other loads that affect the energy use of the building.

☐ To verify a building's compliance with the standard's envelope heat budget, the Portland Cement Association has developed a quick, hand-calculation method, which uses a one-page worksheet, as shown. Explanations of how it can be used to analyze a building for heating and cooling and examples of its use appear later in this monograph.

☐ The worksheet has been divided into four parts to simplify explanation. The procedure's main points include:

—The envelope is divided into three major components: walls, roofs and floors.

—The procedure examines the effects of the *overall* envelope energy budget of the U-values and areas of walls, roofs and floors.

—The heating load determines the energy budget; for buildings over three stories, a cooling load check for compliance is performed.

—The formulas presented on the worksheet are for the base case; special exceptions are noted in the text.

—The base formulas can be used for calculations of buildings already designed. In addition, nomographs in each section allow for easy comparison between design alternatives.

City	Losses allowed per hour (BTU)		
	Entire building	Per Sq Ft	Per Cu Ft
Single-family residence (W30', L70' and H8'4")			
Los Angeles	17,500	8.33	1.000
Tampa	22,605	10.76	1.292
Seattle	19,064	9.08	1.090
Atlanta	28,175	13.41	1.610
Washington, D.C.	27,295	13.00	1.561
Boston	28,669	13.65	1.639
Kansas City	31,411	14.95	1.795
Cleveland	28,347	13.50	1.621
Denver	30,926	14.72	1.767
Chicago	30,104	14.33	1.720
Minneapolis	30,283	14.42	1.731
Three-story apartment, motel, or hotel (W40', L200' and H25')			
Los Angeles	128,800	5.36	0.644
Tampa	163,680	6.82	0.819
Seattle	155,200	6.46	0.776
Atlanta	216,580	9.03	1.084
Washington, D.C.	218,360	9.10	1.091
Boston	236,840	9.87	1.184
Kansas City	256,000	10.66	1.280
Cleveland	236,600	9.86	1.184
Denver	253,444	10.56	1.267
Chicago	248,500	10.40	1.240
Minneapolis	252,560	10.53	1.263

City	Losses allowed per hour (BTU)		
	Entire building	Per Sq Ft	Per Cu Ft

Four-story apartment, motel, or hotel (W40′, L200′ and H33′6″)

City	Entire building	Per Sq Ft	Per Cu Ft
Los Angeles	201,936	6.31	0.754
Tampa	255,018	7.97	0.952
Seattle	232,600	7.27	0.868
Atlanta	335,326	10.48	1.251
Washington, D.C.	335,013	10.46	1.250
Boston	349,928	10.93	1.302
Kansas City	383,130	11.97	1.420
Cleveland	344,045	10.75	1.284
Denver	374,805	11.71	1.399
Chicago	369,998	11.56	1.380
Minneapolis	377,774	11.81	1.409

One-story building, nonresidential (W70′, L200′, and H25′)

City	Entire building	Per Sq Ft	Per Cu Ft
Los Angeles	171,500	12.26	0.490
Tampa	215,490	15.39	0.615
Seattle	202,520	14.46	0.579
Atlanta	286,895	20.50	0.819
Washington, D.C.	288,585	20.62	0.824
Boston	307,148	21.94	0.877
Kansas City	335,360	23.96	0.958
Cleveland	302,445	21.60	0.864
Denver	325,926	23.28	0.930
Chicago	324,577	23.18	0.927
Minneapolis	323,490	23.10	0.925

Building three stories and under, nonresidential (W70′, L200′ and H25′)

City	Entire building	Per Sq Ft	Per Cu Ft
Los Angeles	271,460	9.69	0.775
Tampa	354,090	12.66	1.011
Seattle	247,320	8.83	0.706
Atlanta	410,375	14.66	1.173
Washington, D.C.	362,785	12.96	1.036
Boston	376,588	13.45	1.075
Kansas City	407,040	14.53	1.163
Cleveland	375,245	13.40	1.072
Denver	403,909	14.42	1.154
Chicago	404,096	14.43	1.155
Minneapolis	415,330	14.83	1.187

Building over three stories, all types (W60′, L150′ and H200′)

City	Entire building	Per Sq Ft	Per Cu Ft
Los Angeles	1,048,320	5.83	0.583
Tampa	1,332,540	7.40	0.740
Seattle	1,205,520	6.69	0.669
Atlanta	1,731,666	9.62	0.962
Washington, D.C.	1,734,696	9.63	0.963
Boston	1,814,802	10.08	1.008
Kansas City	1,984,320	11.02	1.102
Cleveland	1,789,320	9.94	0.994
Denver	1,947,201	10.82	1.082
Chicago	1,924,029	10.69	1.070
Minneapolis	1,972,920	10.96	1.096

Building Envelope Heat Budgets.

□ The following table demonstrates the calculation of the envelope loss for the buildings in Chicago.

Chicago—6600 degree days $t_o = 1°$, $t_1 = 72°$, $\Delta_t = 71°$

Single-family residence (W30′, L70′ and H8′4″)
$$\begin{aligned} \text{Envelope loss} &= \Delta t[\text{roof loss} + \text{wall loss}] \\ &= 71[(0.04 \times 2100) + (0.170 \times 2000)] \\ &= 30{,}104 \text{ BTU/hr} \\ &\quad 14.33 \text{ BTU/ft}^2 \\ &\quad 1.72 \text{ BTU/ft}^3 \end{aligned}$$

Three-story apartment, motel, or hotel (W40′, L200′ and H25′)
$$\begin{aligned} \text{Envelope loss} &= \Delta t[\text{roof loss} + \text{wall loss}] \\ &= 71[(0.04 \times 8000) + (0.265 \times 12{,}000)] \\ &= 248{,}500 \text{ BTU/hr} \\ &\quad 10.4 \text{ BTU/ft}^2 \\ &\quad 1.24 \text{ BTU/ft}^3 \end{aligned}$$

Four-story apartment, motel, or hotel (W40′, L200′ and H33′6″)
$$\begin{aligned} \text{Envelope loss} &= \Delta t[\text{roof loss} + \text{wall loss}] \\ &= 71[(0.071 \times 8000) + (0.315 \times 14{,}740)] \\ &= 369{,}998 \text{ BTU/hr} \\ &\quad 11.56 \text{ BTU/ft}^2 \\ &\quad 1.38 \text{ BTU/ft}^3 \end{aligned}$$

One-story building, nonresidential (W70′, L200′ and H25′)
$$\begin{aligned} \text{Envelope loss} &= \Delta t[\text{roof loss} + \text{wall loss}] \\ &= 71[(0.071 \times 14{,}000) + (0.265 \times 13{,}500)] \\ &= 324{,}577 \text{ BTU/hr} \\ &\quad 23.18 \text{ BTU/ft}^2 \\ &\quad 0.927 \text{ BTU/ft}^3 \end{aligned}$$

Building three stories and under, nonresidential (W70′, L200′ and H25′)
$$\begin{aligned} \text{Envelope loss} &= \Delta t[\text{roof loss} + \text{wall loss} + \text{floor loss}] \\ &= 71[(0.071 \times 14{,}000) + (0.265 \times 13{,}500) + (0.08 \times 14{,}000)] \\ &= 404{,}096 \text{ BTU/hr} \\ &\quad 14.43 \text{ BTU/ft}^2 \\ &\quad 1.155 \text{ BTU/ft}^3 \end{aligned}$$

Building over three stories, all types (W60′, L150′ and H200′)
$$\begin{aligned} \text{Envelope loss} &= \Delta t[\text{roof loss} + \text{wall loss}] \\ &= 71[(0.071 \times 9000) + (0.315 \times 84{,}000)] \\ &= 1{,}924{,}029 \text{ BTU/hr} \\ &\quad 10.69 \text{ BTU/ft}^2 \\ &\quad 1.07 \text{ BTU/ft}^3 \end{aligned}$$

Example: Building Envelope Heat Budget for Chicago area.

Simplified Thermal Design of Building Envelopes, © 1981. Used with the permission of Portland Cement Association, Skokie, Illinois.

City	Latitude		Winter temperatures, °F			Winter degree days (65°F. base)	Summer (design dry-bulb) temperatures, °F			Mean air temperature, °F
			Med. of annual extremes	99%	97½%		1%	2½%	5%	
UNITED STATES										
Albuquerque, N.M.	35	0	6	14	17	4400	96	94	92	56
Anchorage, Alaska	61	1	−29	−25	−20	10,800	73	70	67	32
Atlanta, Ga.	33	4	14	18	23	3000	95	92	90	62
Baltimore, Md.	39	2	12	16	20	4600	94	92	89	55
Birmingham, Ala.	33	3	14	19	22	2600	97	94	93	64
Boise, Ida.	43	3	0	4	10	5800	96	93	91	51
Boston, Mass.	42	2	− 1	6	10	5600	91	88	85	50
Charleston, W. Va.	38	2	1	9	14	4400	92	90	88	57
Charlotte, N.C.	35	1	13	18	22	3200	96	94	92	61
Chicago, Ill.	41	5	− 5	− 3	1	6600	94	91	88	50
Cincinnati, Ohio	39	1	2	8	12	4400	94	92	90	54
Cleveland, Ohio	41	2	− 2	2	7	6400	91	89	86	50
Dallas, Texas	32	5	14	19	24	2400	101	99	97	66
Denver, Colo.	39	5	− 9	− 2	3	6200	92	90	89	50
Des Moines, Iowa	41	3	−13	− 7	− 3	6600	95	92	89	50
Detroit, Mich.	42	2	0	4	8	6200	92	88	85	48
Fairbanks, Alaska	64	5	−59	−53	−50	14,280	82	78	75	26
Hartford, Conn.	41	5	− 4	1	5	6200	90	88	85	50
Houston, Texas	29	5	24	29	33	1400	96	94	92	70
Indianapolis, Ind.	39	4	− 5	0	4	5600	93	91	88	53
Jackson, Miss.	32	2	17	21	24	2200	98	96	94	66
Kansas City, Mo.	39	1	− 2	4	8	4800	100	97	94	56
Las Vegas, Nev.	36	1	18	23	26	2800	108	106	104	66
Lexington, Ky.	38	0	0	6	10	4600	94	92	90	55
Little Rock, Ark.	34	4	13	19	23	3200	99	96	94	62
Los Angeles, Calif.	34	0	38	42	44	2000	94	90	87	63
Memphis, Tenn.	35	0	11	17	21	3200	98	96	94	62
Miami, Fla.	25	5	39	44	47	200	92	90	89	75
Milwaukee, Wis.	43	0	−11	− 6	− 2	7600	90	87	84	47
Minneapolis, Minn.	44	5	−19	−14	−10	8400	92	89	86	45
New Orleans, La.	30	0	29	32	35	1400	93	91	90	69
New York, N.Y.	40	5	6	11	15	5000	94	91	88	54
Norfolk, Va.	36	5	18	20	23	3400	94	91	89	60
Oklahoma City, Okla.	35	2	4	11	15	3200	100	97	95	61
Omaha, Neb.	41	2	−12	− 5	− 1	6600	97	94	91	51
Philadelphia, Pa.	39	5	7	11	15	4400	93	90	87	55
Phoenix, Ariz.	33	3	25	31	34	1800	108	106	104	66
Pittsburgh, Pa.	40	3	1	7	11	6000	90	88	85	53
Portland, Maine	43	4	−14	− 5	0	7600	88	85	81	46
Portland, Ore.	45	4	17	21	24	4600	89	85	81	52
Providence, R.I.	41	4	0	6	10	6000	89	86	83	50
Rochester, N.Y.	43	1	− 5	2	5	6800	91	88	85	48
Salt Lake City, Utah	40	5	− 2	5	9	6000	97	94	92	52
San Francisco, Calif.	37	5	38	42	44	3000	80	77	83	57
Seattle, Wash.	47	4	22	28	32	5200	81	79	76	51
St. Louis, Mo.	38	4	1	7	11	5000	96	94	92	56
Tampa, Fla.	28	0	32	36	39	680	92	91	90	72
Washington, D.C.	38	5	12	16	19	4200	94	92	90	57
Wichita, Kan.	37	4	− 1	5	9	4600	102	99	96	57

Note: The Standard recommends 97½ percentile for heavy construction; 99 for others in heating calculations. For cooling, the 2½% is normally used.

Weather Data and Design Conditions

Simplified Thermal Design of Building Envelopes, © 1981. Used with the permission of Portland Cement Association, Skokie, Illinois.

	WORKSHEET BUILDING ENVELOPE THERMAL TRANSMISSION STUDIES	Example Page _____ of _____

WORKSHEET
BUILDING ENVELOPE THERMAL TRANSMISSION STUDIES

References
Notes
Comments

Project:_____

Location:_____ Lat._____

Heating, outdoor design temp._____, degree days_____

    temp. of heated space_____, unheated space_____

    temp. difference Δt_____, temp. difference Δt_____

Cooling, design temp. outdoor_____, indoor_____

temp. difference Δt_____

Description of Project: Stories_____

    size_____ × _____ × _____

    floor_____

    walls_____. Wt._____psf

                          M factor_____

    roof_____. Wt._____psf

                          M factor_____

Areas

floor	_____	×	_____	= _____sq. ft.
walls	_____	×	_____	= _____sq. ft.
	_____	×	_____	= _____sq. ft.
roof	_____	×	_____	= _____sq. ft.
other	_____	×	_____	= _____sq. ft.

PROJECT DESIGN CRITERIA

HEATING
$BTU/ft^2 \times h \times F$

floor — U_{off}_____

walls — U_{ow}_____

roof — U_{or}_____

COOLING

$OTTV_w$_____ $BTU/ft^2 \times h$

SF_____ $BTU/ft^2 \times h$

TD_{eqw}_____ °F

$OTTV_f$ 8.5_____ $BTU/ft^2 \times h$

SF_{sk} 138_____ $BTU/ft^2 \times h$

TD_{eqr}_____ °F

ENVELOPE BUDGET (BTU/Hr.)

Component	A	×	U_o	×	Δt	Total
floor	_____		_____		_____	_____
wall	_____		_____		_____	_____
roof	_____		_____		_____	_____
Total						

Simplified Thermal Design of Building Envelopes, © 1981. Used with the
permission of Portland Cement Association, Skokie, Illinois.

Worksheet

□ The accompanying chart presents the notations used throughout the procedure.

A = area (all areas are ft²)
A_d = door area
A_f = area of fenestration
A_{f1} = area of fenestration, wall 1
A_{f2} = area of fenestration, wall 2
A_i = area of common walls
A_{fl} = opaque area of floor
A_{flo} = area of openings in floor
A_o = overall area
A_{ofl} = gross area of floor
A_{or} = gross area of roof/ceiling assembly
A_{ow} = gross area of exterior walls (above and below grade for heating design, above grade only for cooling design)
A_p = amplitude, °F
A_r = opaque roof/ceiling area
A_{sk} = area of skylights
A_{ur} = gross area of exposed roof of unheated space
A_{uw} = gross area of exposed walls of unheated space
A_w = opaque wall area
A_{w1} = opaque area of wall 1
A_{w2} = opaque area of wall 2
°F = degree Fahrenheit
M = factor to modify U for thermal mass
$OTTV_r$ = overall thermal transfer value, roof, BTU/ft² × h
$OTTV_w$ = overall thermal transfer value, walls, BTU/ft² × h
R = thermal resistance, 1/(BTU/ft² × h × °F)
SC_f = shading coefficient of fenestration
SC_{sk} = shading coefficient of skylights
SF_f = solar factor for fenestration, BTU/ft² × h
SF_{sk} = solar factor for skylights, BTU/ft² × h
t_i = temperature of heated space, °F
t_m = mean air temperature, °F
t_o = outdoor design temperature, °F
t_u = temperature of unheated space, °F
TC = thermal capacitance
TD_{eq} = temperature differential equivalent, °F, cooling design
TD_{eqr} = temperature differential equivalent, roof, °F, cooling design
TD_{eqw} = temperature differential equivalent, walls, °F, cooling design
TDR = temperature difference ratio, below-grade design
T_{gs} = ground surface temperature, °F
U = thermal transmittance (all thermal and gross thermal transmittance values are BTU/ft² × h × °F)

U_d = thermal transmittance of door area
U_e = equivalent U-value, below-grade design
U_f = thermal transmittance of fenestration area
U_{f1} = thermal transmittance of fenestration area, wall 1
U_{f2} = thermal transmittance of fenestration area, wall 2
U_{fl} = thermal transmittance of opaque floor area
U_{flo} = thermal transmittance of floor openings
U_i = thermal transmittance of common wall area
U_o = average thermal transmittance
U_{ofl} = average thermal transmittance of floor area
U_{or} = average thermal transmittance of roof/ceiling area
U_{ow} = average thermal transmittance of gross wall area
U_r = thermal transmittance of opaque roof/ceiling area
U_{sk} = thermal transmittance of skylight in roof/ceiling area
U_{ur} = average thermal transmittance for exposed roof of unheated space
U_{uw} = average thermal transmittance for exposed walls of unheated space
U_w = thermal transmittance of opaque wall area
U_{w1} = thermal transmittance of opaque area, wall 1
U_{w2} = thermal transmittance of opaque area, wall 2
V_o = volume of air change, ft³/min
Δt = temperature difference, indoor-outdoor, °F, heating calculations
ΔT = temperature difference, indoor-outdoor, °F, cooling calculations
ΔT_f = temperature difference between exterior and interior design conditions, fenestration, °F
ΔT_{gs} = temperature difference, below-grade design, °F
ΔT_{sk} = temperature difference between exterior and interior design conditions, skylights, °F

Notations

Simplified Thermal Design of Building Envelopes, © 1981. Used with the permission of Portland Cement Association, Skokie, Illinois.

382

Thermal Analysis of the Envelope: Heating

Part One of the worksheet describes calculations for determining the difference between outside design temperature and indoor temperatures (specified by the standard at 72 degrees (F.) for heating and 78 degrees (F.) for cooling).

□ The inputs needed for Part One are:

1. Project location and latitude
2. From weather data:
—outdoor design temperature (heating and cooling)
—degree days
3. From the standard or design program:
—temperature of heated space
—temperature of cooled space
4. The temperature difference, Δt, for heating can be calculated:
—heating: Δt = temperature of heated space minus outdoor design temperature (winter)

$$t = t_{indoor} - t_{outdoor}$$

—cooling: Δt = outdoor design temperature (summer) minus temperature of cooled space

□ For walls below grade, a special modifier for Δt is necessary to account for ground surface temperatures. Change in temperature (Δt) calculated for walls above grade can be multiplied by a precalculated temperature difference ratio (TDR) found in Figure 1.

□ *Part Two* of the worksheet requires areas (in square feet) of the following envelope components:
—floors
—walls
—roofs
—any other major components.

□ The designer also needs to record the weight, in pounds per square foot, of the walls and roof.

□ In addition, the designer can determine the "M-factor" for walls and roof on the basis of degree days and weight (psf) of the components. The M-factor is a recently developed adjustment factor to account for the thermal inertia provided by heavy mass construction.

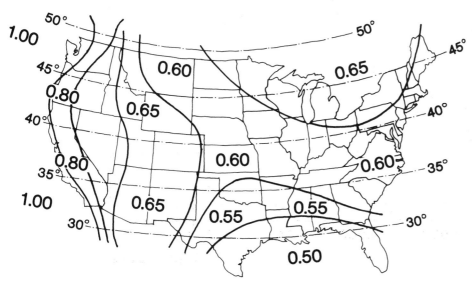

TDR, Temperature, Difference Ratios
Figure 1

Simplified Thermal Design of Building Envelopes, © 1981. Used with the permission of Portland Cement Association, Skokie, Illinois.

383

The M-factor can be obtained from Figure 2. At the present time, there is inadequate data available for a definitive statement on the exact effect of wall weight on building energy consumption. Professional judgement should be exercised when using the M-factor in analysis.

☐ *Part Three* of the worksheet involves calculation of an overall U-value for floors, roof and walls for the heating season. Cooling is done as a check for buildings over three stories.

**Influence of Wall Weight on
U Value Correction for Heating Design**

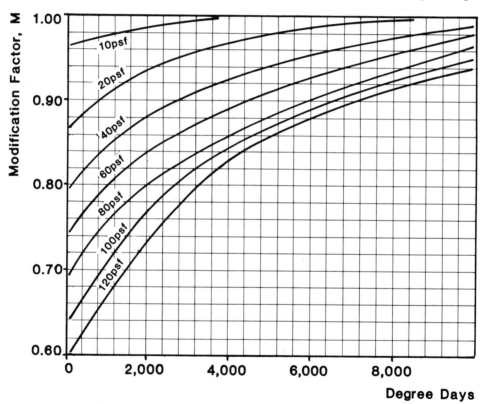

Walls

□ The gross U_{ow} (U-value for walls) is determined by the equation:

$$U_{ow} = \frac{U_wA_w + U_fA_f + U_dA_d}{A_{ow}}$$

Where:

U_{ow} = average thermal transmittance of gross wall area, BTU/sq.ft. × h × °F

A_{ow} = gross area of external walls

U_w = thermal transmittance of opaque wall area, BTU/sq.ft. × h × °F

A_w = opaque wall area, sq.ft.

U_f = thermal transmittance of fenestration

A_f = area of fenestration, sq.ft.

U_d = thermal transmittance of door area, BTU/sq.ft. × h × °F

A_d = door area, sq.ft.

Figure 3 shows heating and cooling criteria for building types, based on degree days per location.

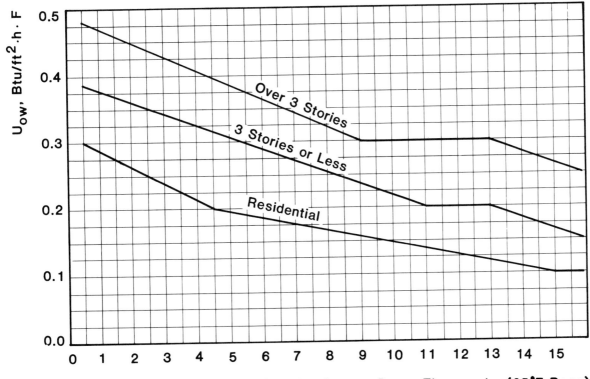

U_{ow}, Walls Heating and Cooling Criteria
Figure 3

More Than One U-Value for Wall Areas

It is important to note that U_{ow} and A_{ow} can be a combination of two or more opaque wall areas, such as U_{w1}, U_{w2}, etc., and A_{w1}, A_{w2}, etc., which will yield:

$$U_{ow} = \frac{U_{w1}A_{w1} + U_{w2}A_{w2}, \text{ etc.}}{A_{ow}}$$

Figures 4 and 5 allow for quick calculation of U-values for buildings that have two different wall U-values, such as basement walls below grade combined with walls above grade.

Figure 4 uses a fenestration U-value of .65 for double glazing; Figure 5 uses a fenestration U-value of 1.13 for single glazing.

Assume U_{ow} = 0.38 for all walls enclosing heated space. Determine: U_{w2}, above grade.

Given: A_{w1} = 30% U_{w1} = 0.10 (transmission
 A_{w2} = 50%   *below grade*)
 U_f = 1.13
 A_f = 20%

Find U_{w2}.

Solution: Plot point ① at U_{ow} = 0.38.
 Draw Line 1 through A_f = 20% and point ①; plot point ②.
 Draw Line 2 through A_{w1} = 30% and U_{w1} = 0.10; plot point ③.
 Draw Line 3; plot point int ④.
 Draw line 4 through A_{w2} = 50%, plot point ⑤.

Answer: U_{w2} = 0.25

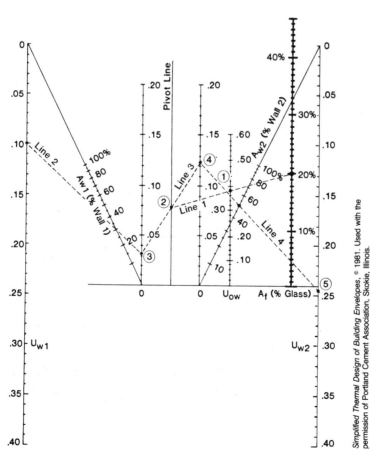

U_{w1} and U_{w2} for Two Opaque Walls (U_f = 1.13)
Example

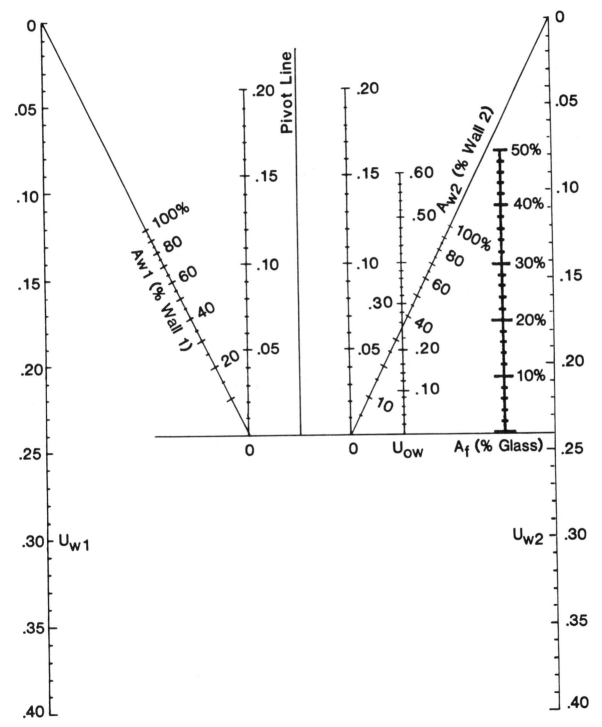

*U*_{w1} *and U*_{w2} *for Two Opaque Walls (U*_f = .65)
Figure 4

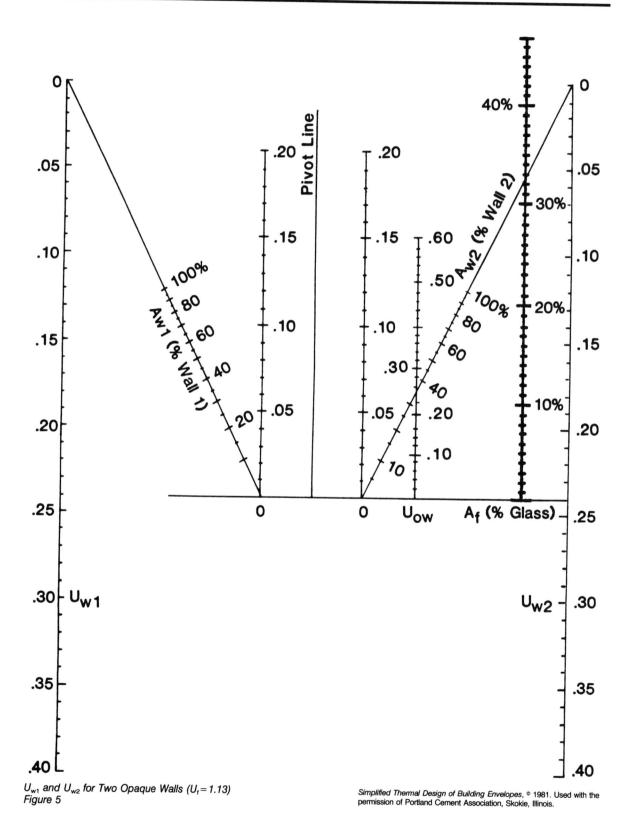

U_{w1} and U_{w2} for Two Opaque Walls (U_f = 1.13)
Figure 5

Design Aid: Opaque Walls/Glass Ratios

☐ Once the value for the overall U-value for the walls (U_{ow}) is known, Figures 6 and 7 can be used to determine the glass-to-wall ratio that will yield a value equal to or lower than the required U_{ow}. (Figure 6 uses a fenestration U-value of 1.13 for single glazing; Figure 7 uses 0.65 for double glazing.)

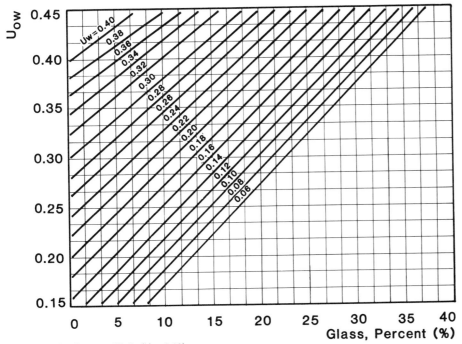

U_w Values for Opaque Walls ($U_f = 1.13$)
Figure 6

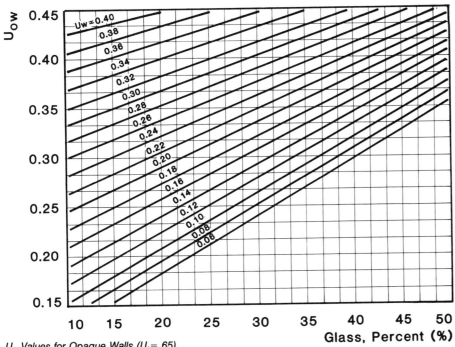

U_w Values for Opaque Walls ($U_f = .65$)
Figure 7

Simplified Thermal Design of Building Envelopes, © 1981. Used with the permission of Portland Cement Association, Skokie, Illinois.

Unheated Spaces

☐ Standard 90A-80 defines heated space as space within a building that is provided with a positive heat supply to maintain an air temperature of 50 degrees (F.) or higher. This provision is significant since it means that, when applying the heating criteria of the standard, the temperature difference of heated spaces can be as much as 22 degrees (F.), i.e., 72 to 50 degrees (F.), yet no temperature difference on either side of the building components need be assumed. For example, no calculations of heat loss through floors are necessary when the space on the cool side of the floor, such as an enclosed basement, crawl space or auto storage, is provided with a positive heat supply to maintain the temperature at 50 degrees (F.) or higher.

☐ The temperature, t_u, of adjacent unheated enclosed rooms can be calculated using an equation recommended in the ASHRAE 1977 *Fundamentals Handbook*:

$$t_u = \frac{t_i(A_iU_i) + t_o(A_{uw}U_{uw}A_{ur}U_{ur} + 2.16 V_o)}{(A_iU_i) + (A_{uw}U_{uw} + A_{ur}U_{ur} + 2.16 V_o)}$$

Where: t_i = temperature of heated space, usually 72 degrees (F.)

t_o = outdoor design temperature (use Tgs for walls below grade)

A_i = area of common walls

U_i = thermal transmittance of common wall area

A_{uw} = gross area of exposed walls of unheated space

U_{uw} = average thermal transmittance for exposed walls of unheated space

A_{ur} = gross area of exposed roof of unheated space

U_{ur} = average thermal transmittance for exposed roof of unheated space

V_o = volume of air change, cubic feet per minute

EXAMPLE: Assume U_i = 0.17; U_{uw} = 0.60; U_{ur} = 0.30; t_o = 10 degrees (F.); t_i = 72 degrees (F.) Calculate t_u (temperature of unheated space). Omit air change.

$$A_i = 100 \times 20 = 2,000 \text{ sq. ft.}$$
$$A_{uw} = 440 \times 20 = 8,800 \text{ sq. ft.}$$
$$A_{ur} = 100 \times 170 = 17,000 \text{ sq. ft.}$$

Using Equation

$$t_u = \frac{72(2000 \times 0.17) + 10(8800 \times 0.60)}{(2000 \times 0.17) + (8800 \times 0.60)}$$
$$+ 17,000 \times 0.30)$$
$$+ (17,000 \times 0.30)$$
$$= 11.97 \text{ degrees (F.) (use 12 degrees (F.)}$$

Therefore, the temperature difference between the heated space and unheated space is 72 − 12 = 60 degrees (F.) = Δt.

The temperature of unheated enclosed spaces located below a heated space can be calculated by a procedure similar to that for unheated rooms above grade. The effects of the slab-on-grade of the unheated space may be omitted from the calculations.

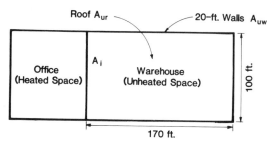

Plan

EXAMPLE: Assume U_w = 0.60; U_n = 0.10; t_u = 10°F; t_i = 72°F. Calculate t_u. Omit air change.

$$t_u = \frac{72(17,000 \times 0.10) + 10(4860 \times 0.60)}{(17,000 \times 0.10) + (4860 \times 0.60)}$$
$$= 32.8 \text{ degrees (F.)}$$

Therefore, the temperature difference between the heated space above the basement and the unheated basement is 72 − 33 = 39 degrees (F.) = Δt.

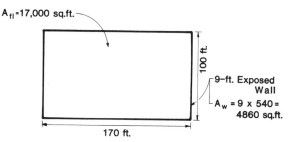

Plan of Unheated Space Beneath Heated Space

Doors

☐ Where doors must be considered, their area can be combined with the area of windows as follows:

1. Solid wood doors can be combined with single-glazed windows by assuming their area to be one-half the actual area. Reason: solid wood doors generally have U-values about one-half the U-value of single glass.

2. The entire area of solid wood doors can be combined with the area of double-glazed windows. Reason: solid wood doors generally have U-values about the same as double-glazed windows.

3. The area of a door protected with a storm door, both of which are 25 percent or more glass, or double-glazed doors, can be combined with double-glazed windows.

Roof

☐ The gross U-value (U_{or}) for a heated roof is determined by the equation:

$$U_{or} = U_r A_r + U_{sk} A_{sk,}$$

Where: U_r and A_r refer to the opaque areas of the roof, and U_{sk} and A_{sk} refer to the skylight areas of the roof.

Figure 8 determines the U_{or} for different building types based on degree days for the specific location.

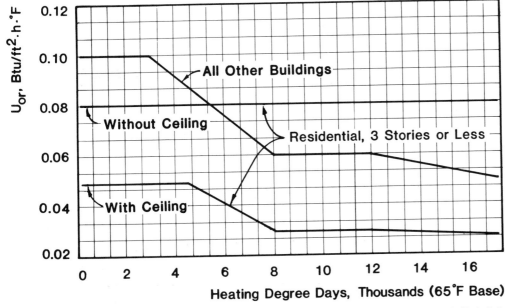

U_{or}, Roofs and Ceilings Heating Criteria
Figure 8

Floors

□ The gross U-value for floors (U_{ofl}), is determined by the equation:

$$U_{ofl} = \frac{U_{fl}A_{fl} + U_{flo}A_{flo}}{A_{ofl}}$$

Where: U_{fl} and A_{fl} refer to opaque areas of the floor, and U_{flo} and A_{flo} refer to, any openings in the floor, and A_{ofl} is the overall area of the floor.

□ *Part Four* of the worksheet simply multiplies the area times the overall U-value times Δt for floor, roof and wall to obtain an energy use estimate that can be compared to the required energy budget.

□ It should be noted that although this method is a quick design tool, it does not attain the same level of accuracy possible with more sophisticated analysis methods.

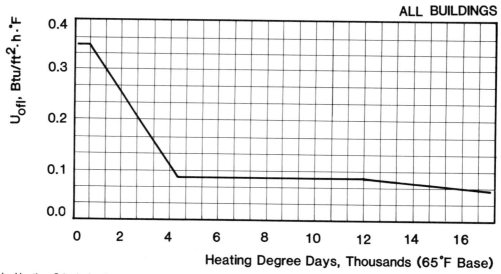

U_{fl}, *Heating Criteria for Floors Over Unheated Spaces*
Figure 9

Thermal Analysis of the Envelope: Cooling

Cooling design criteria for all non-residential buildings of all heights and all residential buildings over three stories are calculated in terms of two equations, one for walls and one for roofs.

Walls

☐ The overall transfer value for walls (OTTV$_w$), shown in Figure 10, is defined in terms of BTU/sq.ft./hr., and is determined by the equation:

$$OTTV_w$$
$$\frac{(U_w \times A_w \times TD_{egw}) + (A_f \times SF_f \times SC_f) + (U_f \times A_f \times T_f)}{A_{ow}}$$

Where:

U_w = thermal transmittance of opaque wall area (BTU/ft.^{2} × h × °F), from Part 3 of the worksheet.

A_w = opaque wall area, sq.ft., from Part 2.

U_f = thermal transmission of fenestration area (BTU/ft.^{2} × h × °F); use 1.13 for single glazing; 0.65 for double glazing.

A_f = area of fenestration (from design).

TD_{eqw} = temperature differential equivalent for walls (determined by wall weight, see Figure 11).

SC_f = shading coefficient of fenestration; see Figure 12.

T_f = temperature difference between exterior design conditions and interior design.

SF_f = solar factor for fenestration; see Figure 13.

A_{ow} = overall area of exterior walls above grade, sq.ft., from Part 3.

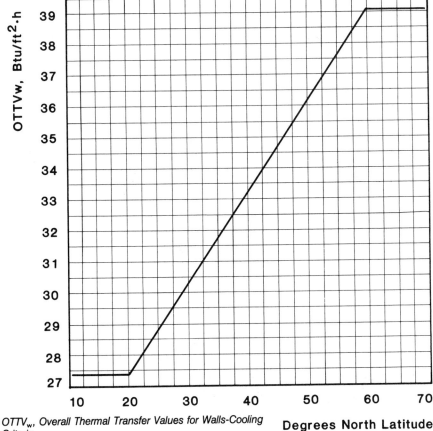

OTTV$_w$, Overall Thermal Transfer Values for Walls-Cooling Criteria
Figure 10

Simplified Thermal Design of Building Envelopes, © 1981. Used with the permission of Portland Cement Association, Skokie, Illinois.

Roofs

☐ For this technique the overall transfer value for roofs (OTTV$_r$) is 8.5 BTU/hr. for all latitudes. This limit is calculated as follows:

$$8.5 = OTTV_r$$
$$= \frac{(U_r \times A_r \times TD_{eqr}) + (A_{sk} \times SF_{sk} \times SC_{sk}) + (U_{sk} \times A_{sk} \times T_{sk})}{A_{or}}$$

Where:

U_r = thermal transmittance of opaque roof/ceiling area, BTU/ft.^{2} · hr. · °F, from Part 3.

A_r = opaque roof/ceiling area, sq.ft., from Part 2

U_{sk} = thermal transmittance of skylights in roof/celing area, BTU/ft.^{2} · hr. · °F; use 1.13 for single glazing; 0.60 for double glazing.

TD_{eqr} = temperature differential equivalent, roof; see Figure 14.

SC_{sk} = shading coefficient of skylights; see Figure 12.

T_{sk} = temperature difference between exterior and interior conditions; same as for wall calcualtions.

SF_{sk} = solar factor for skylights; same as for wall calculations. (See Figure 13).

A_{or} = gross area of roof/ceiling assembly, sq.ft.

☐ The sum of OTTV$_w$ and OTTV$_r$ should be a value equal to or less than the figure indicated in the *Building Envelope Heat Budgets* presented in this monograph.

Type of Glass	Visible Trans-mission	Total Solar Trans-mission	Shading Co-efficient
1/4" clear single	88%	77%	0.93
1/4" gray reflective single	34%	36%	0.60
1" clear insulating	77%	59%	0.79
1" gray reflec. insulating	30%	29%	0.47

Shading Coefficients
Figure 12

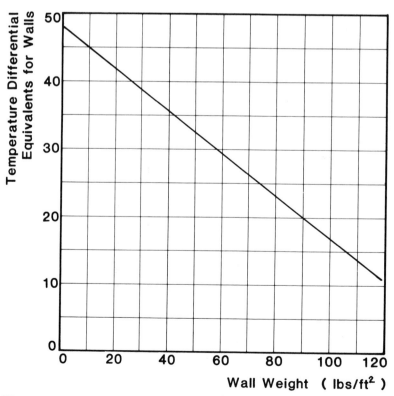

TD$_{eqw}$, Temperature Differential Equivalent for Walls
Figure 11

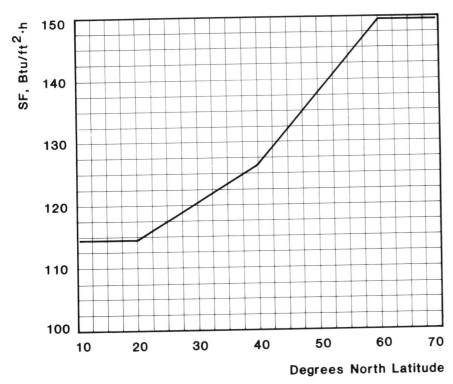

SF, Solar Factor Values for Vertical Glass
Figure 13

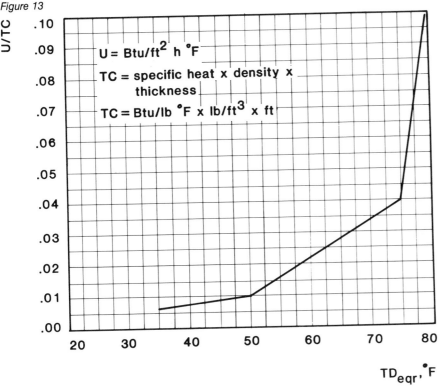

$U = Btu/ft^2 \ h \ °F$

$TC = specific \ heat \times density \times thickness$

$TC = Btu/lb \ °F \times lb/ft^3 \times ft$

TD_{eqr}, Temperature Differential Equivalents for Roof
Figure 14

Design Aid: Percent Glazed Openings

☐ The nomographs presented in Figure 15 allow the designer to quickly determine the maximum percentage of glazed openings that will meet the cooling criteria established by the energy budget. The monographs have set values for:

—TD_{eg} (temperature differential for cooling)
—Latitude
—$OTTV_w$ (overall thermal transfer for walls)
—SF (solar factor for fenestration)

☐ Once these factors are known, the designer can choose the nomograph that best fits the building.

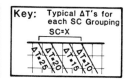

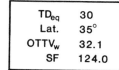
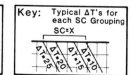

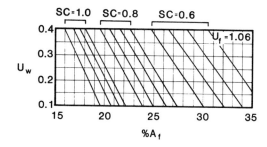

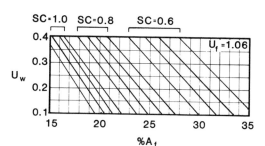

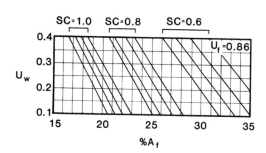

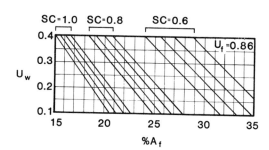

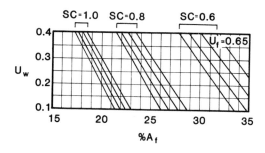

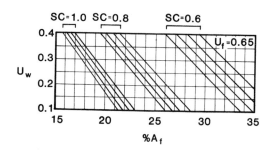

Percent Glazed Openings-Cooling Criteria
Figure 15

Simplified Thermal Design of Building Envelopes, © 1981. Used with the permission of Portland Cement Association, Skokie, Illinois.

□ To use the nomographs, the designer needs to know,

—U-value of opaque wall (U_w)

—Δt (temperature differential)

—SC (shading coefficient of glass)

□ To use the nomograph:

1. Determine the diagonal line that has the appropriate combination of Δt and SC.

2. Choose the correct U_w and draw a horizontal line to the chosen diagonal line.

3. From the point where the two lines intersect, drop a horizontal line. This line will indicate the maximum percentage of glazed area to meet the cooling budget.

□ Conversely, the chart can be used to determine shading coefficients if glass area is known.

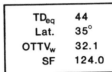

TD_eq	37
Lat.	35°
OTTV_w	32.1
SF	124.0

Key: Typical ΔT's for each SC Grouping SC=X

TD_eq	44
Lat.	35°
OTTV_w	32.1
SF	124.0

Key: Typical ΔT's for each SC Grouping SC=X

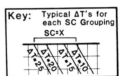

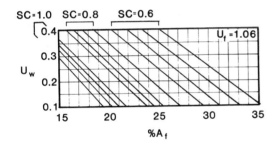

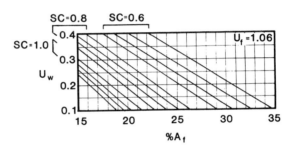

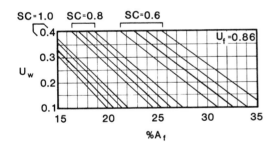

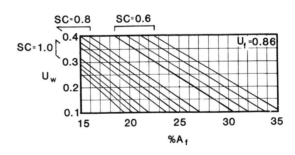

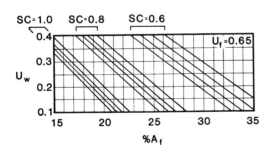

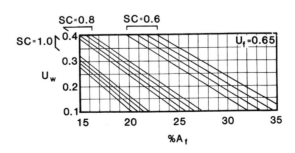

Percent Glazed Openings-Cooling Criteria
Figure 15

Simplified Thermal Design of Building Envelopes, © 1981. Used with the permission of Portland Cement Association, Skokie, Illinois.

TD$_{eq}$	23	
Lat.	40°	
OTTV$_w$	33.5	
SF	127.0	

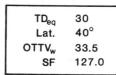

Key: Typical ΔT's for each SC Grouping
SC=X

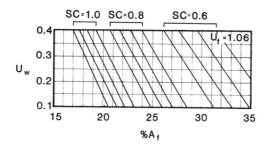

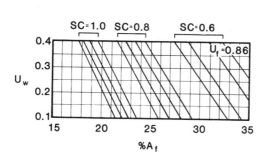

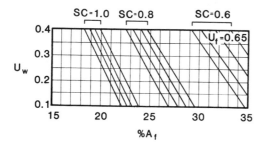

TD$_{eq}$	30	
Lat.	40°	
OTTV$_w$	33.5	
SF	127.0	

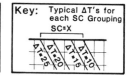

Key: Typical ΔT's for each SC Grouping
SC=X

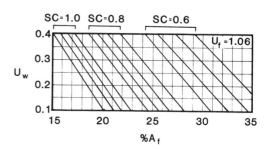

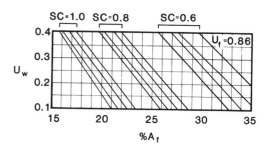

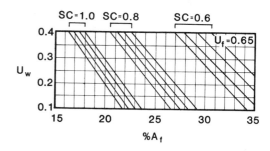

Percent Glazed Openings-Cooling Criteria
Figure 15

TD$_{eq}$	37
Lat.	40°
OTTV$_w$	33.5
SF	127.0

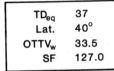

Key: Typical ΔT's for each SC Grouping SC=X

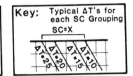

TD$_{eq}$	44
Lat.	40°
OTTV$_w$	33.5
SF	127.0

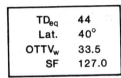

Key: Typical ΔT's for each SC Grouping SC=X

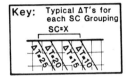

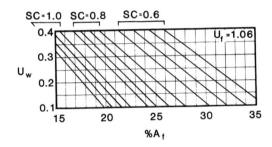

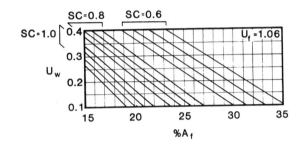

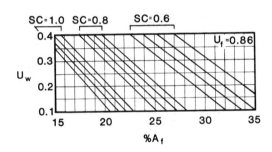

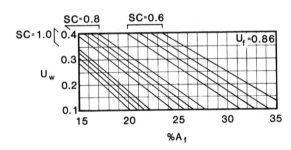

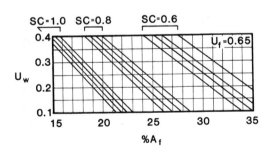

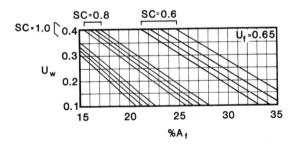

Percent Glazed Openings-Cooling Criteria
Figure 15

Simplified Thermal Design of Building Envelopes, © 1981. Used with the permission of Portland Cement Association, Skokie, Illinois.

TD$_{eq}$	23
Lat.	45°
OTTV$_w$	34.9
SF	133.0

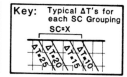

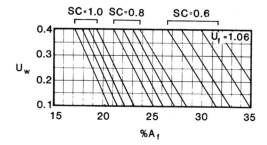

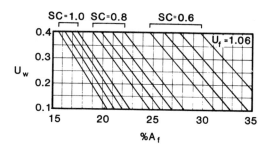

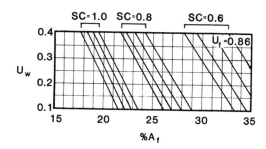

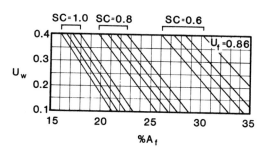

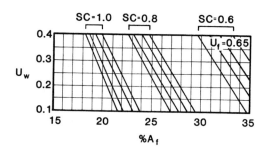

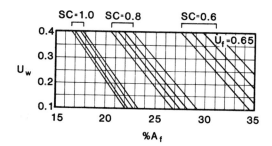

TD$_{eq}$	30
Lat.	45°
OTTV$_w$	34.9
SF	133.0

Percent Glazed Openings-Cooling Criteria
Figure 15

Simplified Thermal Design of Building Envelopes, © 1981. Used with the permission of Portland Cement Association, Skokie, Illinois.

TD_{eq}	37
Lat.	45°
$OTTV_w$	34.9
SF	133.0

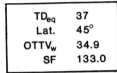

Key: Typical ΔT's for each SC Grouping
SC=X

TD_{eq}	44
Lat.	45°
$OTTV_w$	34.9
SF	133.0

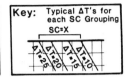

Key: Typical ΔT's for each SC Grouping
SC=X

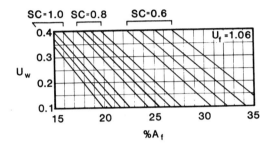

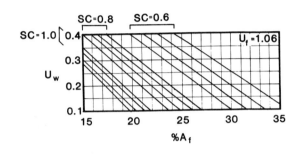

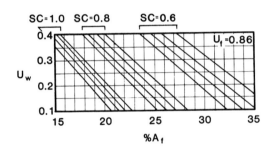

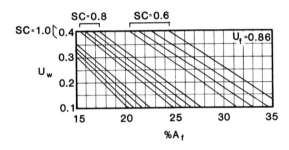

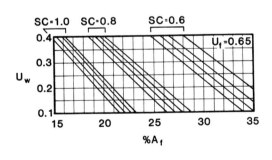

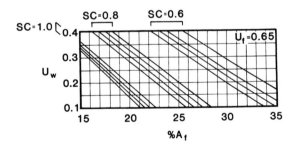

Percent Glazed Openings-Cooling Criteria
Figure 15

Thermal Analysis of the Envelope: Sample Problems

The examples shown here demonstrate the use of the Portland Cement Association's method for thermal analysis. The first example is an office building with parking below, and demonstrates heating and cooling design aids and the procedure for floor-wall tradeoffs.

The second example is a five-story building, and uses the nomographs to select two wall U-values (U_w).

☐ The following example problems demonstrate recommended design procedures for the application of the criteria of the Standard. The procedures (which feature the use of design aids) employ the tradeoff concept in order to show the Standard's flexibility in the proportioning of and orientation of the components and of elements within the components. All of the problems begin with a building envelope budget that conforms to the limitations set by the criteria of the Standard.

☐ The example problems are presented on worksheets similar to the one shown with references added in the right-hand margin to clarify the design procedure.

After arriving at the design U values for the building components, combinations of insulation and other materials can be selected to complete the thermal design of the components.

WORKSHEET
BUILDING ENVELOPE THERMAL TRANSMISSION STUDIES

Example
Page _____ of _____

References
Notes
Comments

Project: _____
Location: _____ Lat _____
Heating, outdoor design temp. _____, degree days _____
    temp. of heated space _____, unheated space _____
    temp. difference Δt _____, temp. difference Δt _____
Cooling, design temp. outdoor _____, indoor _____
    temp. difference _____ Δt _____

Weather Data
Figure 1

Description of Project: _____ Stories _____
    Size _____ × _____ × _____
    floor _____
    walls _____ Wt. _____ psf
        M factor _____
    roof _____ Wt. _____ psf
        M factor _____
        TC _____

Figure 2

Figure 14

Areas
    floor _____ × _____ = _____ sq. ft.
    walls _____ × _____ = _____ sq. ft.
          _____ × _____ = _____ sq. ft.
    roof _____ × _____ = _____ sq. ft.
    other _____ × _____ = _____ sq. ft.

PROJECT DESIGN CRITERIA

HEATING
Btu/ft² × h × F
    floor — U_{of} _____ Figure 9
    walls — U_{ow} _____ Figure 3
    roof — U_{or} _____ Figure 8

COOLING
    $OTTV_w$ _____ Btu/ft² × h
    SF _____ Btu/ft² × h
    TD_{eqw} _____ °F
    $OTTV_r$ _8.5_ Btu/ft² × h
    SF_{ch} _138_ Btu/ft² × h
    TD_{eqr} _____ °F

Figure 10
Figure 13
Figure 11
Constant
Constant
Figure 14

ENVELOPE BUDGET (Btu/h)

Component	A	×	U_o	×	Δt	Total
floor						
wall						
roof						
Total						

WORKSHEET
BUILDING ENVELOPE THERMAL TRANSMISSION STUDIES

Example 6
Page 1 of 3

References
Notes
Comments

Project: OFFICE BUILDING (Heating and Cooling), Parking Below
Location: MINNEAPOLIS, MINN. Lat. 44°-5'
Heating, outdoor design temp. -10, degree days 8400
temp. of heated space 72, unheated space 39 (from page 2) ← assumes 0.5 air changes/hr.
temp. difference Δt 82, temp. difference Δt 33
Cooling, design temp. outdoor 89, indoor 78
temp. difference Δt 11

Description of Project: Stories 2 heated, 1 unheated
size 100' × 200' × 26'
floor 8" Concrete over Parking
walls Precast and Concrete Masonry. Wt. 75 psf
M factor 0.94
roof 8" Concrete, lightweight. Wt. 75 psf
M factor 0.94
TC ____

Areas

floor	100' × 200'	= 20,000 sq. ft.		
walls	600' × 26'	= 15,600 sq. ft.		
	600' × 8'	= 4,800 sq. ft.	← enclosed-unheated space	
roof	100' × 200'	= 20,000 sq. ft.		
other	____ × ____	= ____ sq. ft.		

PROJECT DESIGN CRITERIA

HEATING
BTU/ft² × h × F

floor — U_{ofl} 0.08
walls — U_{ow} 0.28
roof — U_{or} 0.06

COOLING

$OTTV_w$ 34.6 BTU/ft² × h
SF 131.5 BTU/ft² × h
TD_{eqw} 23 °F
$OTTV_r$ 8.5 BTU/ft² × h
SF_{sk} 138 BTU/ft² × h
TD_{eqr} 35 °F

ENVELOPE BUDGET (BTU/Hr.)

Component	A	×	U_o	×	Δt	Total
floor	20,000		0.08		33	52,800
wall	15,600		0.28		82	358,176
roof	20,000		0.06		82	98,400
Total						509,376

Sample Problem 1

Example 6
Page 2 of 3

References
Notes
Comments

OTHER DESIGN CONSIDERATIONS

Because $U_{ofl} = 0.08$ is impractical to attain, try $U_{ofl} = 0.17$ (R4 insulation below slab). Absorb difference in Wall 2. Retain $U_{or} = 0.06$ for the roof.

THE PROBLEM

Determine U_{w2} and % Glass for Heating, then check Cooling

THE SOLUTION

1. Calculate ΔT between heated space and garage, based on 0.5 air changes/hr. in the garage.

Vol. of Air $= 0.5 \times 8' \times 100' \times 200'/60 = 1167$ cfm

$$t_u = \frac{72(20,000 \times 0.17) + 20(4800 \times 0.16) + 70(2.16 \times 1167)}{(20,000 \times 0.17) + (4800 \times 0.16) + (2.16 \times 1167)}$$

$t_u = 39°F$, then $\Delta T = 72 - 39 = 33°F$

2. Increase loss through floor.
$(33 \times 0.17 \times 20,000) - 52,800 = 59,400$ Btu/hr.

3. Revise loss allowed through Wall 2.
$(358,176 - 59,400) = 298,776$ Btu/hr. ← The trade-off

4. Calculate new U_{ow2}
$298,776 / (82 \times 15,600) = 0.234$ Btu/ft².·hr.·°F

5. Determine U_{ow2}, % Glass, and Glass Type

% Glass	$U_f = 1.13$	$U_f = 0.65$	$U_f = 0.89$
10	0.13	0.19	0.16
15	0.07	0.16	0.12
20	—	0.13	0.07
25	—	0.09	

Notes (right margin):
$t_i = 72$, $t_o = -10$
$t_{gs} = 20$, (Ref. 13)
$U_{ofl} = 0.17$,
$A_{fl} = 20,000$
$A_{ow} = 4,800$
$U_{ow} = 0.16$ (Ref. 3)

$U_f = 0.89$ is 50% single + 50% double

CONCLUSION (Heating)

Use 20% double glazing with $U_{ow2} = 0.13$, and $U_f = 0.65$

Sample Problem 1

Example 6
Page 3 of 3

CHECK HEATING

1. Floor - 20,000 × 0.17 × 33 =   112,200
2. Wall2 - 15,600 × 0.13 × 0.80 × 82 =   130,037
3. Glass - 15,600 × 0.65 × 0.20 × 82 =   166,296
4. Roof - 20,000 × 0.06 × 82 =   98,400
                                            506,933 Btu/hr.

Budget - 509,376 Btu/hr. (Design O.K.)

MODIFY U of Wall 2 & ROOF

From page 1,   M factor = 0.94
U_{w2} modified = 0.13 ÷ 0.94 = 0.14
U_r modified = 0.06 ÷ 0.94 = 0.065

CHECK COOLING

Walls - Refer to DA5-13 having constants
For U_w = 0.13, 20% Glass, and ΔT = 11, there is
no problem with excessive heat gain.

Roof - Use equation 5, Chapter 3.
$$OTTV_r = U_r \times A_r \times T Deq.$$
$$\times A_{or}$$
Since there are no skylights, $A_r = A_{or}$
then $OTTV_r = 0.064 \times 35 = 2.24$ Btu/hr.

Budget - 8.5 Btu/hr. (Design OK.)

U_f = 0.61
$T Deq$ = 23
Lat. = 45°
OTTV = 34.9
SF = 133

Sample Problem 1

405

WORSHEET			
WORKSHEET BUILDING ENVELOPE THERMAL TRANSMISSION STUDIES		Example *7* Page *1* of *3*	

WORKSHEET BUILDING ENVELOPE THERMAL TRANSMISSION STUDIES	Example *7* Page *1* of *3*
Project: *Five Story Building (Nomograph Solution)* Location: *Near Washington D.C.* Lat. *38°* Heating, outdoor design temp. *19*, degree days *4000* temp. of heated space *72*, unheated space *None* temp. difference Δt *53*, temp. difference Δt *(32 Below Grade)* Cooling, design temp. outdoor ___, indoor ___ temp. difference Δt ___	References Notes Comments *Basement Temp* *Also 72°* *Where TDR=0.60*
Description of Project: Stories *5* size *100'* × *200'* × *50'* floor *Not applicable – Basement heated* walls *6" - concrete*. Wt. *75* psf *M* factor *0.90* roof *7" - concrete*. Wt. *90* psf *M* factor *0.86* TC *19.9* Areas floor ___ × ___ = ___ sq. ft. walls 1) *5* × *600* = *3,000* sq. ft. 2) *45* × *600* = *27,000* sq. ft. roof *100* × *200* = *20,000* sq. ft. other ___ × ___ = ___ sq. ft.	
PROJECT DESIGN CRITERIA	
HEATING BTU/ft² × h × F floor — U_{ofl} ___ walls — U_{ow} *0.38* roof — U_{or} *0.092* COOLING $OTTV_w$ *33* BTU/ft² × h SF *126* BTU/ft² × h TD_{eqw} *8.5* °F $OTTV_f$ *8.5* BTU/ft² × h SF_{sk} *138* BTU/ft² × h TD_{eqr} *35* °F	
ENVELOPE BUDGET (BTU/Hr.)	*Where U/TC=0.005*

Component	A	×	U_o	×	Δt	Total
floor	*3000*		*0.38*		*32*	*36,480*
wall	*27,000*		*0.38*		*53*	*543,780*
roof	*20,000*		*0.092*		*53*	*97,520*
Total						*677,780*

Sample Problem 2

Example 7
Page 2 of 3

OTHER DESIGN CONSIDERATION

Assume Window area $A_f = 20\%$, all in Wall 2
       Wall 1 area $A_{w1} = 10\%$, from page 1
       Wall 2 area $A_{w2} = 70\%$

THE PROBLEM

A. Determine U_{w2} if $U_{w1} = 0.125$, $U_f = 1.13$ ⟵

B. Alternate – $U_f = 0.65$, $A_f = 30\%$, $A_{w1} = 10\%$; $A_{w2} = 60\%$

⟵ $U_{w1} = 0.125$ is for uninsulated conc. wall below grade. (Ref. 3)

SOLUTION A

Use nomograph for single glass, $U_f = 1.13$
Plot point ① at $U_{ow} = 0.38$
Draw Line 1 through $A_f = 20$ and ①. Plot point ②.
Draw Line 2 through $U_{w1} = 0.125$ and $A_{w1} = 10\%$. Plot point ③.
Draw Line 3 through ② and ③. Plot point ④.
Draw Line 4 through ④ and $A_{w2} = 70\%$ Plot point ⑤.

Answer: $U_{w2} = 0.20$
        U_{w2} modified $= 0.20 \div 0.90 = 0.22$ ⟵ M factor $= 0.90$

Sample Problem 2

SOLUTION B

Example 7
Page 3 of 3

References
Notes
Comments

Use nomograph for double glass, $U_f = 0.65$
Plot point ① at $U_{ow} = 0.38$
Draw Line 1 through $A_f = 20$ and ①. Plot point ②.
Draw Line 2 through $U_{wl} = 0.125$ and $A_{wl} = 10$. Plot point ③.
Draw Line 3 through ② and ③. Plot point ④.
Draw Line 4 through ④ and $A_{w2} = 60$. Plot point ⑤.
Answer: $U_{w2} = 0.28$
$\qquad U_{w2}$ modified $= 0.28 \div 0.90 = 0.31$ ◄── M factor $= 0.90$

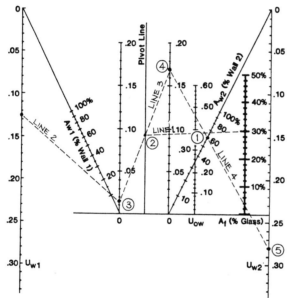

CONCLUSION

With nomographs, two different wall designs can readily be considered and combined with different kinds and percentages of glass.

CHECK SOLUTION A

Wall 1	30,000	× 0.10	× 0.125	× 53 =	19,875
Wall 2	30,000	× 0.70	× 0.17	× 53 =	189,210
Glass	30,000	× 0.20	× 1.13	× 53 =	359,340
Roof	20,000	× 0.092		× 53 =	97,520
					665,945 Btu/hr.

Budget: 677,780 Btu/hr. (Design O.K.)

Solution B also works

ENERGY ANALYSIS

Introduction

This monograph discusses the factors and calculations involved in analyzing a building's energy consumption. Most of the other monographs in this handbook touch on energy analysis in relation to their specific topics but do not attempt the comprehensiveness sought here. This monograph, in turn, does not discuss design directives and strategies to reduce energy use. Such discussions, as well as much of the climate data, building material thermal resistance values and other data needed to analyze a specific building appear in other monographs.

The monograph addresses the internal and external factors that contribute to both building heat gain and heat loss, including internal heat gains, solar gain, infiltration and envelope heat transmission. It also describes the energy use associated with the operating loads from lighting, equipment and domestic hot water. The monograph concludes with a section on the various methods for analytically integrating all these factors.

The publications of the American Society of Heating, Refrigerating and Air-Conditioning Engineers Inc. (ASHRAE) are the source of many of the tables, data and calculation procedures needed for detailed energy analysis. In particular, *ASHRAE Handbook: 1981 Fundamentals* offers valuable guidance for designers interested in energy analysis.

Preliminary Analysis

Traditionally, the design process has been divided into a sequence of three phases: schematic design, design development and construction documents.

Each phase in the design process becomes increasingly detailed, as major decisions made in early design phases are carried out in detail in later phases. Although earlier steps in the sequence can be reviewed, it is usually considered impractical to go back and change design decisions made during earlier phases.

☐ Issues of energy use and energy conservation have been typically addressed during design development.

☐ However, basic building decisions made during the schematic design phase such as siting, configuration, locations of functions, fenestration and facade design can substantially affect energy requirements. They cannot wait to be considered as part of design development when it will be difficult, if not impossible, to change major decisions about building design. Studies show that savings in energy costs can far outweigh the amount spent on such predesign energy analysis.

☐ The first step in preparing the energy analysis is to collect information about both the building program and the environment of the site. Analysis at this stage does not require a detailed building program or site information.

☐ The building program makes it possible to define functional use groups based on activities and required adjacencies. Once functional use groups have been identified, their basic energy-related characteristics can be determined:
—temperature variations allowed within the building spaces (and any daily or seasonal variations)
—ventilation requirements of the building spaces (and any variations)
—internal heat likely to be produced by people, equipment and illumination
—schedules of use.

☐ It would be possible to do an energy analysis on each of the functional use groups as defined from the building program. However, effort can be saved by combining functional groups that have similar energy-related characteristics into energy use groups. The sorting process to establish energy use groups uses three measures of similarity or "screens": similar schedules, similar range of allowed temperature and similar amounts of heat generation.

☐ This sorting process is exemplified in the accompanying figure. Sorting for schedule differences produced three groups. Had cooking not already been in its own group because of allowable temperatures, sorting for internal heat generations would have rendered it separate. Finally, a close look at the difference among the store, office and production areas indicated that the three were not dissimilar enough to merit two separate groups, so they were combined.

☐ Once distinct energy use groups have been sorted out, information about functional requirements can be combined in one composite definition for each energy use group. Note that the functional space with the most limited range of allowed temperatures determines the allowed temperature range for the energy use group in which it is included.

☐ As a result of this sorting process, the energy analysis effort is cut in half—from six functional groups to three energy use groups. The three energy use groups can now be loosely defined as shown.

☐ This analysis of a building's energy use groups can then be combined with basic site information on outdoor temperatures, available insolation, etc., in the process of making preliminary design assumptions about siting, geometric configuration, facade design and fenestration, envelope thermal properties and adjacencies of functions. Without such predesign energy analysis potential energy design strategies will more likely be overlooked until late in the design process, when these early decisions are difficult to modify.

Space/Function	Store	Office	Equipment	Cooking	Production	Storage
Area:	500 Sq. Ft.	500 Sq. Ft.	1000 Sq. Ft.	1000 Sq. Ft.	2000 Sq. Ft.	5000 Sq. Ft.
Temp:	65°–80°F On Shift 50°–90°F Off Shift	65°–80°F On Shift 50°–90°F Off Shift	50°–90°F Always	50°–90°F Always	65°–80°F On Shift 50°–90°F Off Shift	50°–90°F Always
Hours:	24 Hours	8AM–4PM	24 Hours	8AM–4PM, With Seasonal Shifts	8AM–4PM, With Seasonal Shift	24 Hours
Vent:	100–700 CFM	100–700 CFM	700–1300 CFM	100–2300 CFM	200–6000 CFM	700–13,000 CFM
Heat Generated:	4000 BTUh. On Shift 0 BTUh. Off Shift	4000 BTUh. On Shift 0 BTUh. Off Shift	7000 BTUh. On Shift 4000 BTUh. Off Shift	130,000 BTUh. On Shift 2,000 BTUh. Off Shift	23,000 BTUh. On Shift 2,000 BTUh. Off Shift	13,000 BTUh. On Shift 2,000 BTUh. Off Shift

Energy Characteristics of Functional Use Groups

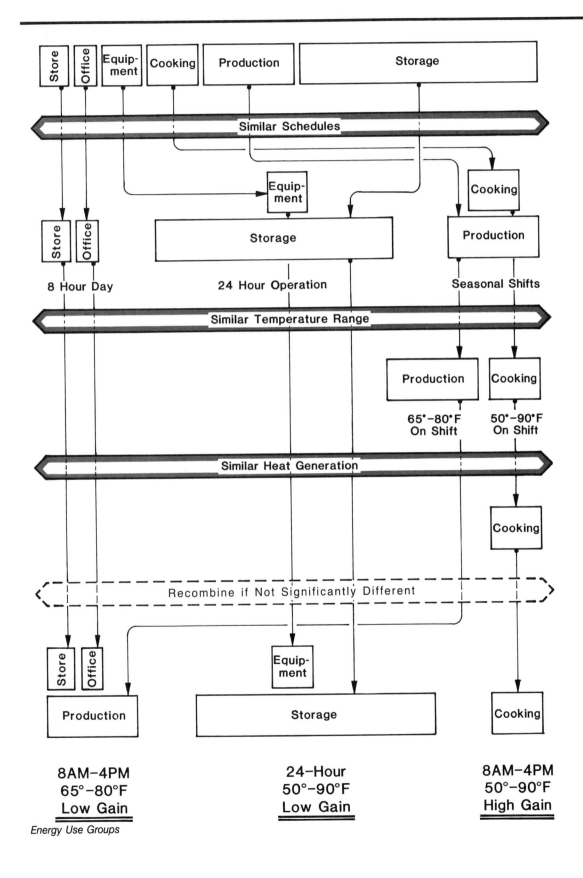

Store
Office
Equip-ment
Cooking
Production
Storage

Similar Schedules

Equip-ment

Cooking

Store
Office

Storage

Production

8 Hour Day   24 Hour Operation   Seasonal Shifts

Similar Temperature Range

Production

Cooking

65°–80°F
On Shift

50°–90°F
On Shift

Similar Heat Generation

Cooking

Recombine if Not Significantly Different

Store
Office

Equip-ment

Cooking

Production

Storage

Cooking

8AM–4PM
65°–80°F
Low Gain

24–Hour
50°–90°F
Low Gain

8AM–4PM
50°–90°F
High Gain

Energy Use Groups

Heat Gain and Heat Loss

In most buildings, controlling heat gains and losses accounts for most energy use. The four basic components of heat gains and losses are:
—internal heat gain
—solar heat gain through glazing
—envelope heat gain and loss
—ventilation/infiltration heat gain and loss.

☐ Internal heat gain is heat generated within a building space, and has three sources: occupants, lights and equipment. Internal heat gains are very regular and tend to follow occupancy patterns.

☐ Solar heat gain through glazing is determined principally by the available insolation (both direct and diffuse sunlight), the exposed glazing area in each orientation and transmission through the glazed area of the envelope into the space.

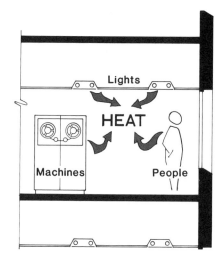

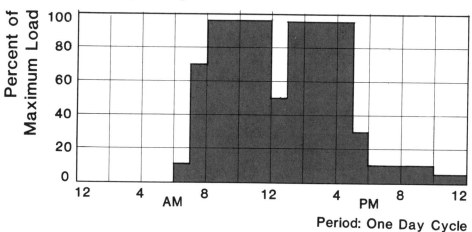

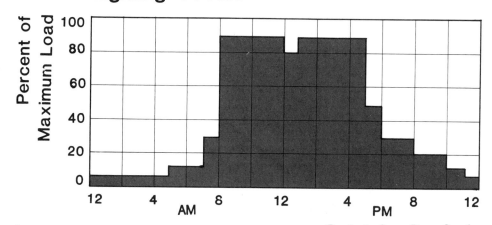

Occupancy and Lighting Profiles

414

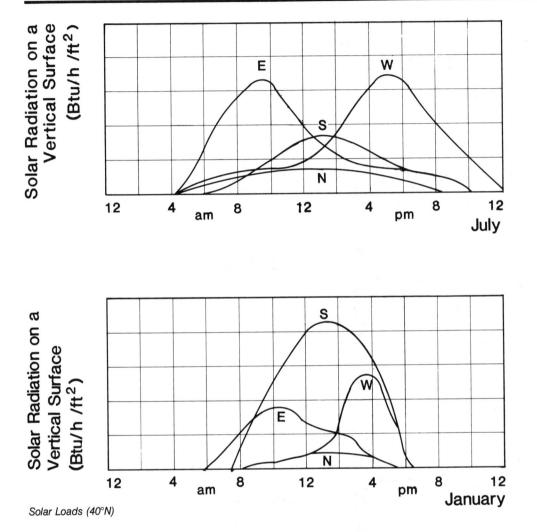

Solar Loads (40°N)

☐ Envelope heat gain and loss is the transmission of heat through the exterior envelope of a space. The principal factors determining the rate and direction of heat flow are the temperature difference between the interior and exterior, the exposed envelope area (walls and roofs) and the heat transmission properties of the envelope.

☐ Mechanical ventilation of a space also creates an opportunity for both heat gains and losses. The principal factors in ventilation heat gain and loss are the temperature difference between the interior and exterior and the ventilation rate.

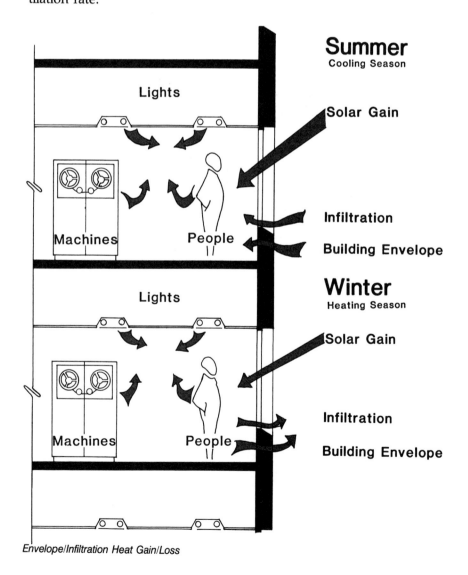

Envelope/Infiltration Heat Gain/Loss

Heat Gains and Losses

☐ Infiltration heat gains and losses are dependent on the construction quality of the building. The rate of infiltration is associated with wind effects on the building, and therefore tends to be high during winter months when winds are high. It is usually assumed that summer winds are sufficiently light that the slight positive pressure provided by mechanical ventilation air is enough to eliminate infiltration.

☐ The *cooling load* is the rate at which heat must be removed from the space to maintain design conditions. This load *generally differs from the instantaneous heat gain,* because heat is stored in building materials for a period and then released gradually.

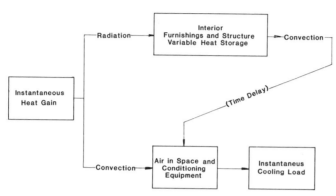

Instantaneous Heat Gain and Cooling Load

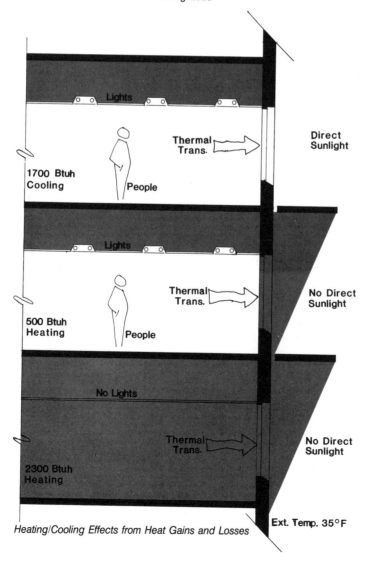

Heating/Cooling Effects from Heat Gains and Losses

Internal Heat Gain

Internal heat gains are produced by heat given off within a building by occupants, lights, and equipment. In many buildings, internal heat gains are the major source of heat gain.

Occupant heat gain is a source of internal heat gain due to the heat given off by people in a space. The human body releases heat and moisture (sensible and latent heat) produced by metabolic processes, with the amount released varying for different activities. The accompanying table indicates typical occupant heat gains.

☐ The latent heat gain caused by occupants can be disregarded when calculating heating loads but should be considered an instantaneous load for cooling calculations. The sensible heat gain is not all converted directly to cooling load. The radiant portion is first absorbed by the surroundings, then transferred to the room air by convection at some later time, depending on the thermal characteristics of the room.

☐ The first step in determining the internal heat gain from occupants is to identify the type of building and the number of occupants. If the number of occupants is unknown, the accompanying tables can be used as a guide.

☐ The second step is to develop profiles of occupancy over a 24-hour period. This should be done for a typical work day, a typical non-work day, and for any special conditions.

☐ Occupancy schedules are also useful in analyzing other loads. The occupancy of a specific space or zone varies in 24-hour, weekly

Building Type	Typical Sq. Ft./Person
Office	200–300
Educational.	
Classrooms	50–100
Dormitories	100–150
Hospital	100–150
Assembly	30–45
Restaurant	25
Mercantile	100–150
Highrise Apartments	300–400

Number of Occupants for Building Types

Building Type	Sensible BTU/Hr.	Latent BTU/Hr.
Office	250	200
Educational:		
Elementary	250	204
Secondary	250	204
College	250	204
Hospital	250	175
Clinic	250	200
Assembly:		
Theater	230	120
Arena	250	250
Restaurant	275	275
Mercantile	250	250
Warehouse	340	450
Residential:		
Hotel	250	200
Nursing	250	175
Highrise Apartment	250	200

Heat Gain per Occupant for Building Types

Degree of Activity	Typical Application	Total Heat (BTU/Hr.)	Sensible Heat (BTU/Hr.)	Latent Heat (BTU/Hr.)
Seated at rest	Theater, movie	350	210	140
Seated, very light work, writing	Offices, hotels, apts.	420	230	190
Seated, eating	Restaurant	580	255	325
Seated, light work, typing	Offices, hotels, apts.	510	255	255
Standing, light work or walking slowly	Retail store, bank	640	315	325
Light bench work	Factory	780	345	435
Walking, 3 mph, light machine work	Factory	1040	345	695
Bowling	Bowling Alley	960	345	615
Moderate dancing	Dance hall	1280	405	875
Heavy work, heavy machine work, lifting	Factory	1600	565	1035
Heavy work, athletics	Gymnasium	1800	635	1165

Rates of Occupant Heat Gains

and annual cycles. The required space conditioning (HVAC) and domestic hot water usage are determined by building occupancy schedules. Internal heat gains due to lights and machines are also proportional to occupancy.

☐ The third step is to calculate the sensible and latent gain from the occupants. The following formula can be used: Annual occupant heat gain (BTU/hr.) = number of occupants × heat gain per person (BTU/hr.)

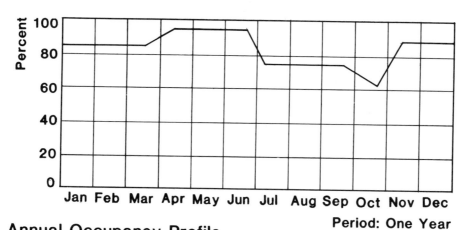

Annual Occupancy Profile

Period: One Year

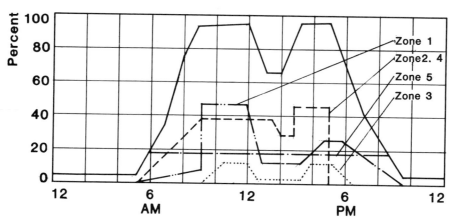

Daily Occupancy Profile

Period: One Day Cycle

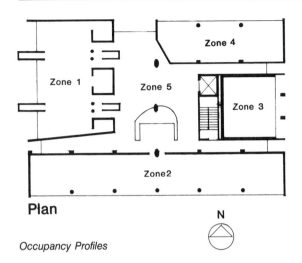

Plan

N

Occupancy Profiles

Determine the cooling load in an office at noon and at 4 P.M. caused by four people seated at light work from 9 A.M. to 5 P.M. The occupant-heat-gain table shows 250 BTU/hr. of sensible heat and 200 BTU/hr. of latent heat per person. The people occupy the space for 8 hours, and noon and 4 P.M. are 3 and 7 hours, respectively, after the people enter, so the cooling load factors are 0.67 and 0.82, respectively. The instantaneous latent loads are 800 BTU/hr. (200 × 4 people) at both times. The sensible loads are 670 BTU/hr. (250 × 4 people × .67) at noon and 820 BTU/hr. (250 × 4 people × .82) at 4 P.M.

The total cooling load for noon and 4 P.M., respectively, are 1470 BTU/hr. and 1620 BTU/hr.

□ ASHRAE developed a set of generalized cooling load factors (CLF), shown in the accompanying table, to be used to adjust sensible cooling loads for the time people spend in the conditioned space and the time elapsed since first entering.

□ The following formula can be used to calculate the cooling load due to occupants:
Occupant cooling load (BTU/hr.) = number of occupants × heat gain per person × CLF (sensible only).

A health care facility has the following space types and occupancies:
—24 hrs./hospital with 15 people (250 BTU/hr. × 15 people × 24 hrs. = 90 MBTU)
—10 hrs./clinic with 12 people (250 BTU/hr. × 12 people × 10 hrs. = 30 MBUT)
—24 hrs./nursing home with 30 people (250 BTU/hr. × 30 people × 24 hrs. = 180 MBTU)
—8 hrs./office with 5 people. (250 BTU/hr. × 5 people × 8 hrs. = 10 MBTU)

It will experience an occupant sensible heat gain of 310 MBTUs per day.

Lighting Heat Gain
□ In the interior zones of most commercial buildings, lighting is by far the most important source of room sensible heat. In the perimeter areas, if not the most important, it is second only to solar heat gain.

□ The following equation can be used to compute an estimate of the sensible heat gain from lights:
Lighting heat gain (BTU/hr.) = total watts × utilization factor (percent) × 3.41 BTU/watt × special allowance factor.

□ Utilization is the ratio of wattage in use to the total installed wattage (in commercial buildings this ratio is usually one).

□ The special allowance factor is used to adjust for power consumer by fixtures using a ballast. It can vary, for instance, from a low of 1.18 for two rapid-start, 40-w lamps on 277 v to a high of 1.30 for one lamp on 118 v. Typically 1.20 is used for most fluorescent fixtures, and 1.0 for incandescent.

Total Hours in Space	Hours after Each Entry into Space																							
	1	2	3	4	5	6	7	8	9	10	11	12	13	14	15	16	17	18	19	20	21	22	23	24
2	0.49	0.58	0.17	0.13	0.10	0.08	0.07	0.06	0.05	0.04	0.04	0.03	0.03	0.02	0.02	0.02	0.02	0.01	0.01	0.01	0.01	0.01	0.01	0.01
4	0.49	0.59	0.66	0.71	0.27	0.21	0.16	0.14	0.11	0.10	0.08	0.07	0.06	0.06	0.05	0.04	0.04	0.03	0.03	0.03	0.02	0.02	0.02	0.01
6	0.50	0.60	0.67	0.72	0.76	0.79	0.34	0.26	0.21	0.18	.015	0.13	0.11	0.10	0.08	0.07	0.06	0.06	0.05	0.04	0.04	0.03	0.03	0.03
8	0.51	0.61	0.67	0.72	0.76	0.80	0.82	0.84	0.38	0.30	0.25	0.21	0.18	0.15	0.13	0.12	0.10	0.09	0.08	0.07	0.06	0.05	0.05	0.04
10	0.53	0.62	0.69	0.74	0.77	0.80	0.83	0.85	0.87	0.89	0.42	0.34	0.28	0.23	0.20	0.17	0.15	0.13	0.11	0.10	0.09	0.08	0.07	0.06
12	0.55	0.64	0.70	0.75	0.79	0.81	0.84	0.86	0.88	0.89	0.91	0.92	0.45	0.36	0.30	0.25	0.21	0.19	0.16	0.14	0.12	0.11	0.09	0.08
14	0.58	0.66	0.72	0.77	0.80	0.83	0.85	0.87	0.89	0.90	0.91	0.92	0.93	0.94	0.47	0.38	0.31	0.26	0.23	0.20	0.17	0.15	0.13	0.11
16	0.62	0.70	0.75	0.79	0.82	0.85	0.87	0.88	0.90	0.91	0.92	0.93	0.94	0.95	0.95	0.96	0.49	0.39	0.33	0.28	0.24	0.20	0.18	0.16
18	0.66	0.74	0.79	0.82	0.85	0.87	0.89	0.90	0.92	0.93	0.94	0.94	0.95	0.96	0.96	0.97	0.97	0.97	0.50	0.40	0.33	0.28	0.24	0.21

Sensible Heat Cooling Load Factors (CLF) for Occupants

Source: American Society of Heating, Refrigerating and Air-Conditioning Engineers, *ASHRAE Handbook: 1981 Fundamentals* ©1981. Reprinted by permission of ASHRAE.

☐ At any time, the space cooling load due to light is the lighting heat gain multiplied by a cooling load factor (CLF),or:

Lighting Cooling Load (BTU/hr.) = total watts × utilization factor (percent)× 3.41 BTU/watt × special allowance factor × CLF.

☐ Calculation of this factor is not completely straightforward, however. As discussed earlier in the section on heat gain from people, some of the energy emanating from lights is in the form of radiation, which is absorbed by room furnishings and does not warm the air until after a time lag. The time lag effect should be taken into account in calculating the cooling load, since the actual load is lower than the instantaneous heat gain, and the peak load may be significantly affected.

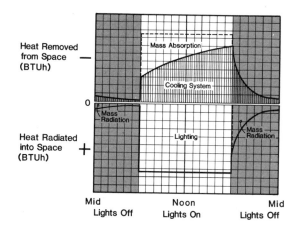

Thermal Storage Effect from Lights

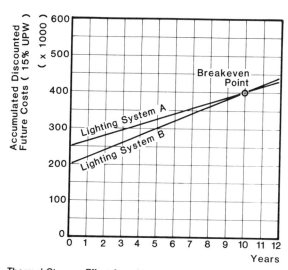

☐ This delayed heat gain from lights requires the use of the cooling load factor (CLF), tables for which are shown here, as are tables for coefficients (a and b) which take into account the effects of furnishings, mechanical system and construction to establish the CLF.

a	Furnishings	Air Supply and Return	Type of Light Fixture
0.45	Heavyweight, simple furnishings, no carpet	Low rate; supply and return below ceiling ($V \le 0.5$ cfm/ft.²)	Recessed, not vented
0.55	Ordinary furniture, no carpet	Medium to high ventilation rate; supply and return below ceiling or through ceiling grill and space ($V \ge 0.5$ cfm/ft.²)	Recessed, not vented
0.65	Ordinary furniture, with or without carpet	Medium to high ventilation rate or fan coil or induction type air-conditioning terminal unit; supply through ceiling or wall diffuser; return around light fixtures and through ceiling space. ($V \ge 0.5$ cfm/ft.²)	Vented
0.75 or greater	Any type of furniture	Ducted returns through light fixtures	Vented or free-hanging in air stream with ducted returns

Table of a Coefficients

Source: American Society of Heating, Refrigerating and Air-Conditioning Engineers, ASHRAE Handbook: 1981 Fundamentals ©1981. Reprinted by permission of ASHRAE.

□ The CLF tables assume (1) the conditioned space temperature is maintained at a constant value and (2) the cooling load and power input to the lights eventually become equal if lights are on long enough. If the cooling system operates either only during the occupied hours or 24 hours a day, the CLF can be considered 1.0. Where some lights are on one schedule and others are on another, each group should be treated separately.

Room Envelope Construction* (mass of floor area, lb/ft.²)	Room Air Circulation and Type of Supply and Return			
	Low	Medium	High	Very High
2-in. Wood Floor (10)	B	A	A	A
3-in Concrete Floor (40)	B	B	B	A
6-in Concrete Floor (75)	C	C	C	B
8-in Concrete Floor (120)	D	D	C	C
12-in Concrete Floor (160)	D	D	D	D

*Floor covered with carpet and rubber pad; for a floor covered only with floor tile take next classification to the right in the same row.

Table of b Classification Values

Source: American Society of Heating, Refrigerating and Air-Conditioning Engineers, *ASHRAE Handbook: 1981 Fundamentals* ©1981. Reprinted by permission of ASHRAE.

		Lights Are On For 8 Hours																							
"a" Coef-ficients	"b" Class-ification	Number of hours after lights are turned on																							
		0	1	2	3	4	5	6	7	8	9	10	11	12	13	14	15	16	17	18	19	20	21	22	23
0.45	A	0.02	0.46	0.57	0.65	0.72	0.77	0.82	0.85	0.88	0.46	0.37	0.30	0.24	0.19	0.15	0.12	0.10	0.08	0.06	0.05	0.04	0.03	0.03	0.02
	B	0.07	0.51	0.56	0.61	0.65	0.68	0.71	0.74	0.77	0.34	0.31	0.28	0.25	0.22	0.20	0.18	0.16	0.15	0.13	0.12	0.11	0.10	0.09	0.08
	C	0.11	0.55	0.58	0.60	0.63	0.65	0.67	0.69	0.71	0.28	0.26	0.25	0.23	0.22	0.20	0.19	0.18	0.17	0.16	0.15	0.14	0.13	0.12	0.12
	D	0.14	0.58	0.60	0.61	0.62	0.63	0.64	0.65	0.66	0.22	0.22	0.21	0.20	0.20	0.19	0.19	0.18	0.18	0.17	0.16	0.16	0.16	0.15	0.15
0.55	A	0.01	0.56	0.65	0.72	0.77	0.82	0.85	0.88	0.90	0.37	0.30	0.24	0.19	0.16	0.13	0.10	0.08	0.07	0.05	0.04	0.03	0.03	0.02	0.02
	B	0.06	0.60	0.64	0.68	0.71	0.74	0.76	0.79	0.81	0.28	0.25	0.23	0.20	0.18	0.16	0.15	0.13	0.12	0.11	0.10	0.09	0.08	0.07	0.06
	C	0.09	0.63	0.66	0.68	0.70	0.71	0.73	0.75	0.76	0.23	0.21	0.20	0.19	0.18	0.17	0.16	0.15	0.14	0.13	0.12	0.11	0.11	0.10	0.10
	D	0.11	0.66	0.67	0.68	0.69	0.70	0.71	0.72	0.72	0.18	0.18	0.17	0.17	0.16	0.16	0.15	0.15	0.14	0.14	0.13	0.13	0.13	0.12	0.12
0.65	A	0.01	0.66	0.73	0.78	0.82	0.86	0.88	0.91	0.93	0.29	0.23	0.19	0.15	0.12	0.10	0.08	0.06	0.05	0.04	0.03	0.03	0.02	0.02	0.01
	B	0.04	0.69	0.72	0.75	0.77	0.80	0.82	0.84	0.85	0.22	0.19	0.18	0.16	0.14	0.13	0.12	0.10	0.09	0.08	0.08	0.07	0.06	0.06	0.05
	C	0.07	0.72	0.73	0.75	0.76	0.78	0.79	0.80	0.82	0.18	0.17	0.16	0.15	0.14	0.13	0.12	0.11	0.11	0.10	0.10	0.09	0.08	0.08	0.07
	D	0.09	0.73	0.74	0.75	0.76	0.77	0.77	0.78	0.79	0.14	0.14	0.13	0.13	0.13	0.12	0.12	0.11	0.11	0.11	0.10	0.10	0.10	0.10	0.09
0.75	A	0.01	0.76	0.80	0.84	0.87	0.90	0.92	0.93	0.95	0.21	0.17	0.13	0.11	0.09	0.07	0.06	0.05	0.04	0.03	0.02	0.02	0.02	0.01	0.01
	B	0.03	0.78	0.80	0.82	0.84	0.85	0.87	0.88	0.89	0.15	0.14	0.13	0.11	0.10	0.09	0.08	0.07	0.07	0.06	0.05	0.05	0.04	0.04	0.04
	C	0.05	0.80	0.81	0.82	0.83	0.84	0.85	0.86	0.87	0.13	0.12	0.11	0.10	0.10	0.09	0.09	0.08	0.08	0.07	0.07	0.06	0.06	0.06	0.05
	D	0.06	0.81	0.82	0.82	0.83	0.83	0.84	0.84	0.85	0.10	0.10	0.10	0.09	0.09	0.09	0.08	0.08	0.08	0.08	0.08	0.07	0.07	0.07	0.07

Cooling Load Factors

Lights Are On For 12 Hours

"a" Coefficients	"b" Classification	Number of hours after lights are turned on																							
		0	1	2	3	4	5	6	7	8	9	10	11	12	13	14	15	16	17	18	19	20	21	22	23
0.45	A	0.05	0.49	0.59	0.67	0.73	0.78	0.83	0.86	0.89	0.91	0.93	0.94	0.95	0.51	0.41	0.33	0.27	0.22	0.17	0.14	0.11	0.09	0.07	0.06
	B	0.13	0.57	0.61	0.65	0.69	0.72	0.75	0.77	0.79	0.82	0.83	0.85	0.87	0.43	0.39	0.35	0.31	0.28	0.25	0.23	0.21	0.18	0.17	0.15
	C	0.19	0.63	0.65	0.67	0.69	0.71	0.73	0.74	0.76	0.77	0.79	0.80	0.81	0.37	0.35	0.33	0.31	0.29	0.27	0.26	0.24	0.23	0.21	0.20
	D	0.22	0.66	0.67	0.68	0.69	0.70	0.71	0.72	0.73	0.74	0.74	0.75	0.76	0.32	0.31	0.30	0.29	0.28	0.27	0.26	0.26	0.25	0.24	0.23
0.55	A	0.04	0.58	0.66	0.73	0.78	0.82	0.86	0.89	0.91	0.93	0.94	0.95	0.96	0.42	0.34	0.27	0.22	0.18	0.14	0.11	0.09	0.07	0.06	0.05
	B	0.11	0.65	0.68	0.72	0.74	0.77	0.79	0.81	0.83	0.85	0.86	0.88	0.89	0.35	0.32	0.28	0.26	0.23	0.21	0.19	0.17	0.15	0.14	0.12
	C	0.15	0.69	0.71	0.73	0.75	0.76	0.78	0.79	0.80	0.81	0.83	0.84	0.85	0.30	0.29	0.27	0.25	0.24	0.22	0.21	0.20	0.19	0.17	0.16
	D	0.18	0.72	0.73	0.74	0.75	0.76	0.76	0.77	0.78	0.78	0.79	0.80	0.80	0.26	0.25	0.24	0.24	0.23	0.22	0.22	0.21	0.20	0.20	0.19
0.65	A	0.03	0.67	0.74	0.79	0.83	0.86	0.89	0.91	0.93	0.94	0.95	0.96	0.97	0.33	0.26	0.21	0.17	0.14	0.11	0.09	0.07	0.06	0.05	0.04
	B	0.09	0.73	0.75	0.78	0.80	0.82	0.84	0.85	0.87	0.88	0.89	0.90	0.91	0.27	0.25	0.22	0.20	0.18	0.16	0.15	0.13	0.12	0.11	0.10
	C	0.12	0.76	0.78	0.79	0.80	0.81	0.83	0.84	0.85	0.86	0.86	0.89	0.88	0.24	0.22	0.21	0.20	0.19	0.17	0.16	0.15	0.14	0.14	0.13
	D	0.14	0.79	0.79	0.80	0.80	0.81	0.82	0.82	0.83	0.83	0.84	0.84	0.85	0.20	0.20	0.19	0.18	0.18	0.17	0.17	0.16	0.16	0.15	0.15
0.75	A	0.02	0.77	0.81	0.85	0.88	0.90	0.92	0.94	0.95	0.96	0.97	0.97	0.98	0.23	0.19	0.15	0.12	0.10	0.08	0.06	0.05	0.04	0.03	0.03
	B	0.06	0.81	0.82	0.84	0.86	0.87	0.88	0.90	0.91	0.92	0.92	0.93	0.94	0.19	0.18	0.16	0.14	0.13	0.12	0.10	0.09	0.08	0.08	0.07
	C	0.09	0.83	0.84	0.85	0.86	0.87	0.88	0.88	0.89	0.90	0.90	0.91	0.91	0.17	0.16	0.15	0.14	0.13	0.12	0.12	0.11	0.10	0.10	0.19
	D	0.10	0.85	0.85	0.86	0.86	0.86	0.87	0.87	0.88	0.88	0.88	0.89	0.89	0.14	0.14	0.14	0.13	0.13	0.12	0.12	0.12	0.11	0.11	0.11

Lights Are On For 16 Hours

"a" Coefficients	"b" Classification	Number of hours after lights are turned on																							
		0	1	2	3	4	5	6	7	8	9	10	11	12	13	14	15	16	17	18	19	20	21	22	23
0.45	A	0.12	0.54	0.63	0.70	0.76	0.81	0.85	0.88	0.90	0.92	0.94	0.95	0.96	0.97	0.97	0.98	0.98	0.54	0.43	0.35	0.28	0.23	0.18	0.15
	B	0.23	0.66	0.69	0.72	0.75	0.78	0.80	0.82	0.84	0.85	0.87	0.88	0.89	0.90	0.91	0.92	0.93	0.49	0.44	0.39	0.35	0.32	0.29	0.26
	C	0.29	0.72	0.74	0.75	0.77	0.78	0.80	0.81	0.82	0.83	0.84	0.85	0.86	0.87	0.88	0.88	0.89	0.45	0.42	0.39	0.37	0.35	0.33	0.31
	D	0.31	0.75	0.76	0.77	0.77	0.78	0.79	0.79	0.80	0.81	0.81	0.82	0.82	0.83	0.83	0.84	0.84	0.40	0.39	0.37	0.36	0.35	0.34	0.33
0.55	A	0.10	0.63	0.70	0.76	0.81	0.84	0.87	0.90	0.92	0.93	0.95	0.96	0.97	0.97	0.98	0.98	0.99	0.44	0.35	0.28	0.23	0.18	0.15	0.12
	B	0.19	0.72	0.75	0.77	0.80	0.82	0.84	0.85	0.87	0.88	0.89	0.90	0.91	0.92	0.93	0.94	0.94	0.40	0.36	0.32	0.29	0.26	0.24	0.21
	C	0.24	0.77	0.79	0.80	0.81	0.82	0.83	0.84	0.85	0.86	0.87	0.88	0.88	0.89	0.90	0.90	0.91	0.37	0.34	0.32	0.30	0.29	0.27	0.25
	D	0.26	0.80	0.80	0.81	0.82	0.82	0.83	0.83	0.84	0.84	0.85	0.85	0.86	0.86	0.86	0.87	0.87	0.33	0.32	0.31	0.30	0.29	0.28	0.27
0.65	A	0.07	0.71	0.77	0.81	0.85	0.88	0.90	0.92	0.94	0.95	0.96	0.97	0.97	0.98	0.98	0.99	0.99	0.34	0.27	0.22	0.18	0.14	0.12	0.09
	B	0.15	0.78	0.81	0.82	0.84	0.86	0.87	0.88	0.90	0.91	0.92	0.92	0.93	0.94	0.94	0.95	0.96	0.31	0.28	0.25	0.23	0.20	0.18	0.16
	C	0.18	0.82	0.83	0.84	0.85	0.86	0.87	0.88	0.89	0.89	0.90	0.90	0.91	0.92	0.92	0.93	0.93	0.28	0.27	0.25	0.24	0.22	0.21	0.20
	D	0.20	0.84	0.85	0.85	0.86	0.86	0.87	0.87	0.87	0.88	0.88	0.88	0.89	0.89	0.89	0.90	0.90	0.25	0.25	0.24	0.23	0.22	0.22	0.21
0.75	A	0.05	0.79	0.83	0.87	0.89	0.91	0.93	0.94	0.95	0.96	0.97	0.98	0.98	0.98	0.99	0.99	0.99	0.24	0.20	0.16	0.13	0.10	0.08	0.07
	B	0.11	0.85	0.86	0.87	0.89	0.90	0.91	0.92	0.93	0.93	0.94	0.95	0.95	0.96	0.96	0.96	0.97	0.22	0.20	0.18	0.16	0.15	0.13	0.12
	C	0.13	0.87	0.88	0.89	0.89	0.90	0.91	0.91	0.92	0.92	0.93	0.93	0.94	0.94	0.94	0.95	0.95	0.20	0.19	0.18	0.17	0.16	0.15	0.14
	D	0.14	0.89	0.89	0.89	0.90	0.90	0.90	0.91	0.91	0.91	0.91	0.92	0.92	0.92	0.92	0.93	0.93	0.18	0.18	0.17	0.17	0.16	0.16	0.15

Cooling Load Factors

Source: American Society of Heating, Refrigerating and Air-Conditioning
Engineers, *ASHRAE Handbook: 1981 Fundamentals* ©1981. Reprinted
by permission of ASHRAE.

Determine the cooling load in a building at noon, 2 P.M. and 4 P.M. due to recessed fluorescent lights, turned on at 8 A.M. and turned off at 6 P.M. Lamp wattage is 800 W. With a special allowance factor of 1.25, total input to the lights is 1000 W. The room has ordinary office furniture, tile flooring over a 3-inch concrete floor, and a medium air-circulation rate. The cooling system runs for 24 hours.
Solution: a = 0.55. The b classification is B. Heat gain from the lights is 800 × 1.00 × 1.25 × 3.41 = 3,410 BTU/hr. The lights are on for 10 hours; noon, 2 P.M. and 4 P.M. are 4, 6, and 8 hours, respectively, after lights are turned on. The corresponding CLFs are 0.73, 0.78 and 0.82; the 3,410 BTU/hr. is multiplied by these factors to find the adjusted sensible heat gain from the lighting at these times, respectively 2490 BTU/hr., 2600 BTU/hr. and 2800 BTU/hr.

Equipment Heat Gain

☐ The determination of the cooling load for buildings must consider the heat gain from all heat producing equipment, including fans and other motors, office machines and appliances. The accompanying table of heat gain for different building activities can be used to determine a preliminary estimate of heat gain from equipment, given the building area.

Building Activities	Heat Gain BTU/Hr./Sq.Ft.²
General Office	3–4
Purchasing & Acct. Depts.	6–7
Offices w/Computer Display	15
Offices w/Digital Computers	75–175
Offices w/Analog Computers	50–150
Laboratories	15–70
Plant (General Assembly)	20
Plant (e.g., Curing Process)	150

Equipment Heat Gains for Building Activities

☐ With the heat gain characteristics and operating use profile of the building's equipment, the following formula can be used to calculate equipment heat gain:
Equipment heat gain (BTU/hr.) = equipment heat gain (BTU/hr./sq.ft.) × area (sq.ft.)
☐ More refined analysis requires consideration of the actual equipment in a building.

The most common heat-producing appliances found in nonresidential buildings are those used for food preparation in restaurants, hospitals, schools, hotels and in-plant cafeterias. For an extensive list of food preparation appliances and the heat gain from them, refer to ASHRAE's *1981 Fundamentals Handbook* (listed in the references).

☐ In comparison to laboratories and computer areas, heat gains from equipment in offices are generally very small; the only heat-generating equipment are electric typewriters, copiers, calculators, and occasionally—posting machines, checkwriters, telewriters, etc.

☐ The effect of the radiant sensible heat from equipment on the cooling load is delayed in the same manner as the heat gain from occupant and lighting load components, already discussed. The accompanying tables provide the cooling load factors (CLF) for equipment. The sensible portion of the cooling load is obtained by multiplying the sensible heat gain by the appropriate CLF, or:
Equipment cooling load (BTU/hr.) = equipment heat gain (BTU/hr.) × CLF

Determine the cooling load in a building at noon, 2 P.M. and 4 P.M. due to an electric appliance. The appliance operates continuously from 9 A.M. to 3 P.M. and does not have an exhaust hood.
The appliance's sensible heat gain equals 1000 BTU/hr. and the latent heat gain equals 300 BTU/hr. The appliance is on for 6 hours, and noon, 2 P.M. and 4 P.M. are 3, 5 and 7 hours, respectively, after the appliance is turned on. The corresponding CLFs are 0.71, 0.79 and 0.29; the 1,000 BTU/hr. is multiplied by these factors to find the adjusted sensible heat gain from the brewer at these times.

☐ When equipment of any sort is driven within a conditioned space by electric motors, the heat equivalent of this operation must be considered in the heat gain. When both the equipment and the motors are in the space, the general equation for calculating this gain, in BTU/hr., is:
Heat gain (BTU/hr.)
$$= \frac{\text{Horsepower Rating}}{\%\text{Motor Efficiency}/100}$$
$$\times \text{ Load Factor} \times 2545$$

Total Opera- tional Hours	Hooded																							
	Hours after appliances are on																							
	1	2	3	4	5	6	7	8	9	10	11	12	13	14	15	16	17	18	19	20	21	22	23	24
2	0.27	0.40	0.25	0.18	0.14	0.11	0.09	0.08	0.07	0.06	0.05	0.04	0.04	0.03	0.03	0.03	0.02	0.02	0.02	0.02	0.01	0.01	0.01	0.01
4	0.28	0.41	0.51	0.59	0.39	0.30	0.24	0.19	0.16	0.14	0.12	0.10	0.09	0.08	0.07	0.06	0.05	0.05	0.04	0.04	0.03	0.03	0.02	0.02
6	0.29	0.42	0.52	0.59	0.65	0.70	0.48	0.37	0.30	0.25	0.21	0.18	0.16	0.14	0.12	0.11	0.09	0.08	0.07	0.06	0.05	0.05	0.04	0.04
8	0.31	0.44	0.54	0.61	0.66	0.71	0.75	0.78	0.55	0.43	0.35	0.30	0.25	0.22	0.19	0.16	0.14	0.13	0.11	0.10	0.08	0.07	0.06	0.06
10	0.33	0.46	0.55	0.62	0.68	0.72	0.76	0.79	0.81	0.84	0.60	0.48	0.39	0.33	0.28	0.24	0.21	0.18	0.16	0.14	0.12	0.11	0.09	0.08
12	0.36	0.49	0.58	0.64	0.69	0.74	0.77	0.80	0.82	0.85	0.87	0.88	0.64	0.51	0.42	0.36	0.31	0.26	0.23	0.20	0.18	0.15	0.13	0.12
14	0.40	0.52	0.61	0.67	0.72	0.76	0.79	0.82	0.84	0.86	0.88	0.89	0.91	0.92	0.67	0.54	0.45	0.38	0.32	0.28	0.24	0.21	0.19	0.16
16	0.45	0.57	0.65	0.70	0.75	0.78	0.81	0.84	0.86	0.87	0.89	0.90	0.92	0.93	0.94	0.94	0.69	0.56	0.46	0.39	0.34	0.29	0.25	0.22
18	0.52	0.63	0.70	0.75	0.79	0.82	0.84	0.76	0.88	0.89	0.91	0.92	0.93	0.94	0.95	0.95	0.96	0.96	0.71	0.58	0.48	0.41	0.35	0.30

Total Opera- tional Hours	Unhooded																							
	Hours after appliances are on																							
	1	2	3	4	5	6	7	8	9	10	11	12	13	14	15	16	17	18	19	20	21	22	23	24
2	0.56	0.64	0.15	0.11	0.08	0.07	0.06	0.05	0.04	0.04	0.03	0.03	0.02	0.02	0.02	0.02	0.01	0.01	0.01	0.01	0.01	0.01	0.01	0.01
4	0.57	0.65	0.71	0.75	0.23	0.18	0.14	0.12	0.10	0.08	0.07	0.06	0.05	0.05	0.04	0.04	0.03	0.03	0.02	0.02	0.02	0.02	0.01	0.01
6	0.57	0.65	0.71	0.76	0.79	0.82	0.29	0.22	0.18	0.15	0.13	0.11	0.10	0.08	0.07	0.06	0.06	0.05	0.04	0.04	0.03	0.03	0.03	0.02
8	0.58	0.66	0.72	0.76	0.80	0.82	0.85	0.87	0.33	0.26	0.21	0.18	0.15	0.13	0.11	0.10	0.09	0.08	0.07	0.06	0.05	0.04	0.04	0.03
10	0.60	0.68	0.73	0.77	0.81	0.83	0.85	0.87	0.89	0.90	0.36	0.29	0.24	0.20	0.17	0.15	0.13	0.11	0.10	0.08	0.07	0.07	0.06	0.05
12	0.62	0.69	0.75	0.79	0.82	0.84	0.86	0.88	0.89	0.91	0.92	0.93	0.38	0.31	0.25	0.21	0.18	0.16	0.14	0.12	0.11	0.09	0.08	0.07
14	0.64	0.71	0.76	0.80	0.83	0.85	0.87	0.89	0.90	0.92	0.93	0.93	0.94	0.95	0.40	0.32	0.27	0.23	0.19	0.17	0.15	0.13	0.11	0.10
16	0.67	0.74	0.79	0.82	0.85	0.87	0.89	0.90	0.91	0.92	0.93	0.94	0.95	0.96	0.96	0.97	0.42	0.34	0.28	0.24	0.20	0.18	0.15	0.13
18	0.71	0.78	0.82	0.85	0.87	0.89	0.90	0.92	0.93	0.94	0.94	0.95	0.96	0.96	0.97	0.97	0.97	0.98	0.43	0.35	0.29	0.24	0.21	0.18

Sensible Heat Cooling Load Factors for Appliances

Source: American Society of Heating, Refrigerating and Air-Conditioning Engineers, *ASHRAE Handbook: 1981 Fundamentals* ©1981. Reprinted by permission of ASHRAE.

☐ The load factor in this equation is the fraction of the rated load delivered under the conditions of the cooling estimate. The 2545 factor converts horsepower to BTU/hr.

☐ If the motor is *outside* the conditioned space but the driven equipment is *inside*, the appropriate equation is:
Heat Gain (BTU/hr.) = Horsepower Rating × Load Factor × 2545

☐ When the motor is *inside* the conditioned space but the driven machine is *outside*, the appropriate equation is:
Heat Gain (BTU/hr.) = Horsepower Rating × Load Factor × 2545 × (100% Motor Efficiency)/percent Motor Efficiency

☐ For a fan or pump in a conditioned space that exhausts air or pumps fluid to outside that space, the last equation above is applicable.

☐ The three locations of equipment with respect to conditioned space can affect total heat gain significantly, as the accompanying table shows. The table assumes load factors of 1.0. For smaller loads, the heat gain is proportionately less.

☐ As with other cooling load components, the cooling load is obtained by multiplying the heat gain by a cooling load factor. In this case, the CLFs for appliances without hoods from the previous table should be used.

426

HORSEPOWER	FULL LOAD MOTOR EFFICIENCY PERCENT	LOCATION OF EQUIPMENT WITH RESPECT TO CONDITIONED SPACE		
		Motor In- Driven Machine In	Motor Out- Driven Machine In	Motor In- Driven Machine Out
		BTU/Hr.	BTU/Hr.	BTU/Hr.
1/20	40	320	130	190
1/12	49	430	210	220
1/8	55	580	320	260
1/6	60	710	430	280
1/4	64	1,000	640	360
1/3	66	1,290	850	440
1/2	70	1,820	1,280	540
3/4	72	2,680	1,930	750
1	79	3,220	2,540	680
1 1/2	80	4,770	3,820	950
2	80	6,380	5,100	1,280
3	81	9,450	7,650	1,800
5	82	15,600	12,800	2,800
7 1/2	85	22,500	19,100	3,400
10	85	30,000	25,500	4,500
15	86	44,500	38,200	6,300
20	87	58,500	51,000	7,500
25	88	72,400	63,600	8,800
30	89	85,800	76,400	9,400
40	89	115,000	102,000	13,000
50	89	143,000	127,000	16,000
60	89	172,000	153,000	19,000
75	90	212,000	191,000	21,000
100	90	284,000	255,000	29,000
125	90	354,000	318,000	36,000
150	91	420,000	382,000	38,000
200	91	560,000	510,000	50,000
250	91	700,000	636,000	64,000

Equipment Heat Gains by Proximity to Conditioned Space

Operating Loads

Operating loads include the electrical loads for lights and equipment. Equipment includes elevators, computers, typewriters, etc., as well as process loads such as for food service or dry cleaning.

Lighting Operating Loads

☐ Commercial buildings use on the average more than 40 percent of their electricity for lighting. To calculate the energy needed to operate the lighting system, the designer must know the optimal levels of illuminance (illumination) needed for the assorted tasks to be performed. The accompanying chart indicates lighting levels in various spaces.

TYPE OF ACTIVITY	ILLUMINANCE RANGE (FOOTCANDLES)		
	LOW	MEAN	HIGH
GENERAL LIGHTING Public Spaces with Dark Surroundings	2	3	5
Simple Orientation for Temporary Visits	5	7.5	10
Working Spaces Where Visual Tasks Are Only Occasionally Performed	10	15	20
ILLUMINANCE ON TASK Performance of Visual Tasks of High Contrast or Large Size	20	30	50
Performance of Visual Tasks of Medium Contrast or Small Size	50	75	100
Performance of Visual Tasks of Low Contrast or Very Small Size	100	150	200

Illuminance Values

Area/Activity	Illuminance (footcandles)
Auditoriums	
Assembly	10 to 20
Social Activity	5 to 10
Banks	
General	10 to 20
Writing Area	20 to 50
Conference Rooms	20 to 50
Drafting Area	
High Contrast	50 to 100
Low Contrast	100 to 200
Educational Facilities	
General	20 to 50
Science Laboratories	50 to 100
Lecture Rooms	100 to 200
Exhibition Halls	10 to 20
Food Service Facilities	
Dining	5 to 10
Kitchen	50 to 100
Hotels (Motels)	
Rooms	20 to 50
Corridors	10 to 20
Lobby	10 to 20
Front Desk	50 to 100
Libraries	
Reading Areas	20 to 50
Book Stacks (active)	20 to 50
Merchandising Spaces	
Stock Rooms	20 to 50
Packaging	20 to 50
Sales	50 to 100
Municipal Buildings	
Police Records	100 to 200
Police Cells	20 to 50
Fire Station	20 to 50
Museums	
Non-sensitive Displays	20 to 50
Lobbies	10 to 20
Offices	
Lobbies	10 to 20
Offices	20 to 50
Residences	
General	5 to 10
Dining	10 to 20
Grooming	20 to 50
Kitchen	20 to 50
Service Spaces	
Stairways, Corridors	10 to 20
Elevators	10 to 20
Toilets, Wash rooms	10 to 20

Illuminance Values for Building Activities

Note:
The Illuminance Values Listed Above Were Abstracted From the 1981 IES Lighting Handbook.

☐ The designer must also know the specifics of the light sources to be provided in the space, such as: types of fixtures, number of fixtures/type and watts per fixture.

☐ The accompanying chart gives lamp wattages for common light sources.

Fluorescent			
Lamp Watts	Length	No. of Lamps	Total Watts
20	24"	1	25
20	24"	2	51
40	48"	1	53
40	48"	2	92
40	48"	3	145
40	48"	4	184
60/HO	48"	1	95
110/HO	96"	2	264
115/SHO	48"	1	138
215/SHO	96"	2	440
39/Slimline	48"	2	95
75/Slimline	96"	2	172
Metal Halide			
400	—	—	440
1000	—	—	1080
1500	—	—	1620
Mercury Vapor			
	Ballast Loss		
40	10	—	50
50	15	—	65
75	15	—	90
100	35	—	135
175	35	—	210
250	42	—	292
400	65	—	465
700	65	—	765
1000	100	—	1100
High Pressure Sodium			
150	—	—	180
250	—	—	300
400	—	—	480
1000	—	—	1200

For types and sizes of fixtures not listed, see manufacturer's data.
Incandescent lamps have same wattage input as rating on lamp.

Light Source Comparison   Source: Huber Buehrer, AIA
Buehrer & Stough
Architects and Engineers
Toledo, Ohio

☐ The designer can use this information to develop working day and non-working day lighting use profiles similar to the ones developed for occupancy loads. Using these profiles, the annual operating loads for the lighting system can be calculated with the following equation:

Annual lighting operating load (kWh/yr.) = total watts × lighted hours per day × lighted days per year × utilization factor (percent) × .001 (conversion w to kw)

☐ Utilization is the ratio of wattage in use to the total installed wattage. In commercial buildings this ratio is usually one.

Equipment Operating Loads

☐ Operating loads for motors and for process loads are considered part of a building's electrical load. For the purposes of this discussion, process loads are defined as energy needed for uses other than maintaining the interior environment and heating domestic water. Some examples of process loads are:
—food service equipment
—elevators and escalators
—computers, typewriters or word processing equipment
—process (non-HVAC) furnaces and boilers.

☐ The annual electrical operating loads for equipment can be determined using the following equations:

Annual equipment operating load (kWh/yr.) = total horsepower × operating hours per day × operating days per year × .746 kW/horsepower.

Annual equipment operating load (kWh/yr.) = total watts × operating hours per day × operating days per year × .001 kW/W.

☐ Power, the rate of energy use, is expressed in watts or kilowatts (1000 W), and time in hours. One watt-hour (Wh) equals one watt of power in use for one hour, and one kilowatt-hour (kWh) equals one kilowatt in use for one hour.

Interior Lights	% Utilization _____						Exterior Lights	% Utilization _____					
Type fixture	**Quan.**	×	**Watts Per Fix.**	×	**.001**	=	**kW**	**Type Fixture**	**Quan.**	×	**Watts Per Fix.**	×	**.001**	=	**kW**

Project_____ Data Collected by_____ Date_____

Average kW utilized = % Utilization × Total kW   Average kW utilized = % Utilization × Total kW

Lighting Data Collection Profile

□ To calculate operating loads for motors and process loads more precisely, the designer needs to determine:
—number and type of each kind of equipment
—operating voltage (V)
—amperage pulled by the motor (I)
—motor horsepower (hp)
—motor efficiency
—power factor (pf).

□ In determining the energy use of electric motors two additional factors must be considered: losses in the motor itself, as indicated by the motor's efficiency and line losses caused by the motor's power factor.

□ The power factor of a device is an indication of the amount of reactive current that the device requires—the lower the power factor, the larger the reactive current. Reactive current does not draw power and does not

therefore show up on the kilowatt-hour meter or the kilowatt-demand meter. It does, however, cause power losses throughout the distribution system, and it does tie up generating capacity. For this reason ASHRAE specifies that "utilization equipment, rated greater than 100 W and lighting equipment greater than 15 W, with an inductive reactance load component, shall have a power factor of not less than 85 percent under rated load conditions."

□ Some motor manufacturers have recently announced lines of high-power-factor, high-efficiency motors that conserve energy. Also, since the power factor is very sensitive to load in motors, sizing motors close to the load requirement instead of oversizing them can both improve the power factor and conserve energy. The newer high-power-factor machines also have better power-factor-versus-load characteristics, which is particularly helpful in situations where motors must handle variable loads.

□ Motor efficiency and power factor and their variation with load and motor size are shown in the accompanying graphs. The curves represent averages and vary with individual manufacturers. Note particularly the extreme sensitivity of power factor to load, and the relation of both efficiency and pf to motor size. The advantages of the high-efficiency, high-pf motor design, particularly in small motors, is clear.

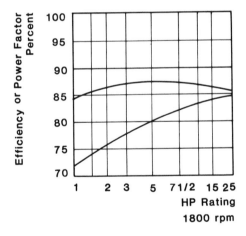

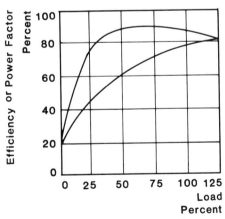

Efficiency and Power Factor vs. Load

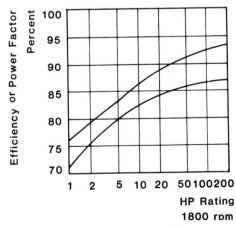

Efficiency and Power Factor vs. hp Rating

431

The nameplate of an AC motor shows the following data: 3 hp, 240 V, 17 amps. Assume an efficiency of 90 percent. Calculate the motor power factor.

Solution:

1 hp	= 746 W

Therefore:

$$3 \text{ hp} = 3 \times 746 = 2238 \text{ W output}$$

$$\text{efficiency} = \frac{\text{output}}{\text{input}}$$

So:

$$\text{Input} = \frac{\text{output}}{\text{efficiency}}$$

$$\text{input} = \frac{2238}{0.9} = 2487 \text{ W}$$

For ac,

$$\text{power (watts)} = \text{volts} \times \text{amperes} \times \text{power factor}$$

So:

$$2487 \text{ W} = 240 \text{ V} \times 17 \text{ amps} \times \text{power factor}$$

So:

$$\text{power factor} = \frac{2487}{240 \times 17} = 0.61$$

The accompanying tables can be useful for tabulating equipment operating loads.

Motor H.P.	R.P.M.	No. Phases and Volts	Full Load Amps	Percent Power Factor	Full Load kW
1/8	1720	1-120	4.0	58	.28
1/4	1725	1-120	5.8	52	.36
1/4	1135	1-120	7.4	51	.45
1/3	3450	1-120	6.0	68	.50
1/3	1730	1-120	6.6	55	.44
1/3	1150	1-120	7.0	55	.46
1/2	3450	1-120	7.4	71	.63
1/2	1730	1-120	9.0	65	.70
1/2	1150	1-120	8.2	60	.59
3/4	3450	1-120	10.2	75	.92
3/4	1730	1-120	10.8	64	.83
3/4	1160	1-120	10.0	68	.82
1	3475	1-120	14.6	69	1.21
1	1730	1-120	13.2	74	1.17
1	1150	1-120	16.0	62	1.19
1 1/2	3440	1-120	18.0	77	1.66
1 1/2	1750	1-120	20.0	67	1.61
1 1/2	1150	1-120	21.0	60	1.51
2	3480	1-120	24.4	75	2.20
2	1760	1-120	24.0	72	2.07
2	1155	1-120	28.0	65	2.18
3	3460	1-120	28.0	88	2.96
3	1750	1-120	36.0	70	3.02
3	1155	1-120	32.0	80	3.07

Motor H.P.	R.P.M.	No. Phases and Volts	Full Load Amps	Percent Power Factor	Full Load kW
1/8	1155	3-460	.6	50	.24
1/4	1730	3-460	.6	66	.32
1/4	1150	3-460	.7	48	.27
1/4	860	3-460	.8	51	.33
1/3	3475	3-460	.7	70	.39
1/3	1730	3-460	.7	65	.36
1/3	1140	3-460	1.0	47	.37
1/3	860	3-460	1.2	49	.47
1/2	1340	3-460	1.1	63	.55
1/2	1730	3-460	1.0	63	.50
1/2	1150	3-460	1.2	58	.55
1/2	865	3-460	1.3	57	.59
3/4	3450	3-460	1.3	80	.83
3/4	1730	3-460	1.5	60	.72
3/4	1130	3-460	1.4	70	.78
3/4	860	3-460	1.8	59	.85
1	3435	3-460	1.8	84	1.20
1	1735	3-460	1.7	74	1.00
1	1150	3-460	1.9	69	1.04
1	860	3-460	2.3	59	1.08
1 1/2	3440	3-460	2.3	80	1.47
1 1/2	1735	3-460	2.4	72	1.37
1 1/2	1125	3-460	2.5	66	1.31
1 1/2	860	3-460	3.3	65	1.71
2	3440	3-460	2.7	75	1.61
2	1730	3-460	3.0	80	1.91
2	1140	3-460	3.4	70	1.90
2	860	3-460	4.0	66	2.10
3	3440	3-460	3.7	87	2.56
3	1730	3-460	4.5	75	2.69
3	1140	3-460	4.8	75	2.87
3	840	3-460	6.0	60	2.87
5	3440	3-460	6.0	94	4.49
5	1730	3-460	7.0	80	4.46
5	1140	3-460	8.0	73	4.65
5	860	3-460	9.4	65	4.87
7 1/2	3480	3-460	9.4	90	6.74
7 1/2	1735	3-460	10.0	82	6.53
7 1/2	1160	3-460	11.0	76	6.66
7 1/2	860	3-460	14.0	62	6.92
10	3450	3-460	12.0	92	8.80
10	1750	3-460	13.0	82	8.49
10	1160	3-460	14.0	77	8.59
10	865	3-460	16.0	67	8.54
15	3440	3-460	18.5	90	13.27
15	1730	3-460	19.0	80	12.11
15	1160	3-460	23.4	68	12.68
15	865	3-460	24.0	68	13.00
20	3455	3-460	25.0	89	17.73
20	1760	3-460	25.0	83	16.53
20	1165	3-460	27.0	79	16.99
20	870	3-460	34.0	67	18.15
25	3480	3-460	31.0	87	21.49
25	1760	3-460	30.0	87	20.56
25	1170	3-460	37.5	70	20.91

Approximate Power Factors and kW

Motor H.P.	R.P.M.	No. Phases and Volts	Full Load Amps	Percent Power Factor	Full Load kW
25	875	3-460	46.0	56	20.52
30	3600	3-460	36.0	90	25.81
30	1760	3-460	36.0	87	24.95
30	1165	3-460	39.0	83	25.79
40	3480	3-460	50.0	90	35.85
40	1755	3-460	50.0	86	34.26
40	1160	3-460	48.0	87	32.89
50	3520	3-460	61.0	91	44.22
50	1760	3-460	60.0	87	41.11
50	1160	3-460	60.0	89	42.54
60	1765	3-460	75.0	83	49.60
100	1760	3-460	112.0	92	82.10

Motor H.P.	R.P.M.	No. Phases and Volts	Full Load Amps	Percent Power Factor	Full Load kW
1/8	1720	1-230	2.0	58	.27
1/4	1725	1-230	2.9	52	.35
1/4	1135	1-230	3.7	51	.43
1/3	3450	1-230	3.0	68	.47
1/3	1730	1-230	3.3	55	.42
1/3	1150	1-230	3.5	55	.44
1/2	3450	1-230	3.7	71	.60
1/2	1730	1-230	4.5	65	.67
1/2	1150	1-230	4.1	60	.57
3/4	3450	1-230	5.1	75	.88
3/4	1730	1-230	5.4	64	.80
3/4	1160	1-230	5.0	68	.78
1	3475	1-230	7.3	69	1.16
1	1730	1-230	6.6	74	1.12
1	1150	1-230	8.0	62	1.14
1 1/2	3440	1-230	9.0	77	1.59
1 1/2	1750	1-230	10.0	67	1.54
1 1/2	1150	1-230	10.5	60	1.45
2	3480	1-230	12.2	75	2.10
2	1760	1-230	12.0	72	1.98
2	1155	1-230	14.0	65	2.09
3	3460	1-230	14.0	88	2.83
3	1750	1-230	18.0	70	2.90
3	1155	1-230	16.0	80	2.94
5	3420	1-230	23.0	88	4.65
5	1745	1-230	25.0	80	4.60
7 1/2	3490	1-230	37.0	82	6.98
7 1/2	1735	1-230	35.0	85	6.84
10	3500	1-230	46.0	86	9.10
10	1740	1-230	42.0	90	8.69

Project _____			Data Collected by _____		Date _____				
No.	Motor Identification	Quantity	Rated H.P.	Volts	Amps	Power Factor	3 Phase only × √3	.001	kW
				×	×		×	=	
								Total kW =	

Motor Data Collection Form

DHW Operating Loads

☐ The amount of energy needed to heat water for domestic use (DHW) varies by building type and level of occupancy. The internal heat gain from hot water systems in most applications constitutes only a small fraction of the internal heat gain in a building, and calculations for DHW heat gain are not considered in this monograph.

☐ The amount of energy needed to heat domestic water depends on:
—the number of occupants
—hot water use per occupant per day
—temperature rise of water (the difference between the desired hot water temperature and the temperature of water entering the heater).

☐ The accompanying chart indicates typical values for occupant use per day

☐ In calculating temperature rise, the average water inlet temperature can often be obtained from the local water company. If not, 55 degrees (F.) is commonly used in calculations. Hot water demand temperature ranges from 90 degrees (F.) to 180 degrees (F.), depending on end use.

☐ A use profile similar to the occupancy profile should be developed for gallons/day. This is especially important for buildings with unusual demand loads for work day and non-work day conditions. From the use profile, the annual energy can be calculated by the following formula:

Annual DHW operating load (kWh/yr.) = total gallons per day × operating days per year × temperature rise × 8.33 lbs./gallons ÷ 3413 BTU/kWh

☐ The accompanying graphs show typical daily DHW use patterns for several types of buildings.

Type of Building	Maximum Hour	Maximum Day	Average Day
Men's Dormitories Women's Dormitories	3.8 gal/student 5.0 gal/student	22.0 gal/student 26.5 gal/student	13.1 gal/student 12.3 gal/student

Motels: No. of Units
   20 or less
   60
   100 or more
	
	6.0 gal/unit
	5.0 gal/unit
	4.0 gal/unit
		
		35.0 gal/unit
		25.0 gal/unit
		15.0 gal/unit
			
			20.0 gal/unit
			14.0 gal/unit
			10.0 gal/unit

Nursing Homes	4.5 gal/bed	30.0 gal/bed	18.4 gal/bed
Office Buildings	0.4 gal/person	2.0 gal/person	1.0 gal/person

Food Service Establishments:
   Type A—Full Meal Restaurants and
     Cafeterias
   Type B—Drive-Ins, Grills, Luncheon-
     ettes, Sandwich and Snack Shops
	
	1.5 gal/max
	meals/hr.
	0.7 gal/max
	meals/hr.
		
		11.0 gal/max
		meals/hr.
		6.0 gal/max
		meals/hr.
			
			2.4 gal/avg.
			meals/day
			0.7 gal/avg.
			meals/day

Apartment Houses: No. of Apartments
   20 or less
   50
   75
   100
   200 or more
	
	12.0 gal/apt.
	10.0 gal/apt.
	8.5 gal/apt.
	7.0 gal/apt.
	5.0 gal/apt.
		
		80.0 gal/apt.
		73.0 gal/apt.
		66.0 gal/apt.
		60.0 gal/apt.
		50.0 gal/apt.
			
			42.0 gal/apt.
			40.0 gal/apt.
			38.0 gal/apt.
			37.0 gal/apt.
			35.0 gal/apt.

Elementary Schools	0.6 gal/student	1.5 gal/student	0.6 gal/student
Junior and Senior High Schools	1.0 gal/student	3.6 gal/student	1.8 gal/student

Domestic Hot Water Demand by Building Type

This is a blank Domestic Hot Water Profile worksheet/chart form, rotated sideways.

Water Heater Schedule

Heater No.	No. of Heaters	Gallons of Storage	Upper Element KW	Lower Element KW	Simultaneous Operation	Interlocking Operation	Maximum KW
1							
2							
3							
4							

Graph of GPH

Heater No. 1—Red
Heater No. 2—Green
Heater No. 3—Yellow

Occupied Days—Red — Unoccupied Nights—Green — Unoccupied Days—Yellow

Week: 4, 8, 12, 16, 20, 24, 28, 32, 36, 40, 44, 48

Month: Jan., Feb., Mar., Apr., May, June, July, Aug., Sept., Oct., Nov., Dec.

Day / Ave. KW

Sun. — R / G / Y

Sat. — R / G / Y

Time of Day: 1, 2, 3, 4, 5, 6, 7, 8, 9, 10, 11, 12, 13, 14, 15, 16, 17, 18, 19, 20, 21, 22, 23

GPH

TIME OF DAY

Domestic Hot Water Profile

436

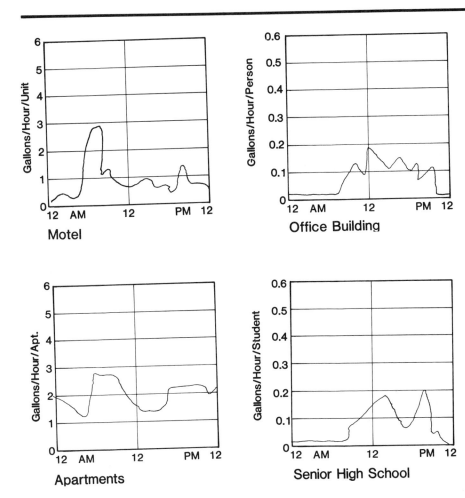

Hot Water Flow Patterns for Building Types

Solar Heat Gain

Three variables determine the amount of solar heat gain through glazing:
—the amount of available insolation (direct, reflected or diffuse sunlight)
—the area of glazing exposed to insolation
—the transmission characteristics of the glazing and any exterior or interior shading device.

☐ Solar heat gain can be the largest single component of space cooling loads, with hourly, daily, and seasonal variations in the intensity of this heat gain. Peak solar heat gains for east exposures occur in the early or midmorning hours in July. West exposures peak from mid- to late afternoon in July. North exposures peak shortly after the maximum outdoor design temperature at 3 P.M. in July. Peak loads for south exposures occur at or shortly after noon, sometime between September and December.

☐ The following formula can be used to compute the maximum solar heat gain for an orientation:
Solar heat gain (BTU/hr.) = insolation (BTU/hr./sq.ft.) × exposed glazing area (sq.ft.) × transmission (percent).

☐ Available insolation is taken directly from weather charts such as the one presented. If data are available, this calculation should be made for all major exposures, and corrected for the tilt of the surface (vertical vs. horizontal).

☐ The third factor, transmission of the incident heat from the exterior to the interior, depends upon qualities of the material the heat is passing through. Solar transmission values are included in the *Shading Coefficients* table in this section.

☐ ASHRAE has developed a method based on cooling load factors to calculate the solar heat gain component of the cooling load using the following formula:

Solar cooling load (BTU/hr.) = glazing area × shading coefficient (SC) × solar heat gain factor (SHGF) × cooling load factor.

☐ The method is based on a reference glazing material of double-strength (0.125-inch) sheet glass. Solar heat gain factor (SHGF) tables represent the solar heat gain factors through this reference material calculated for daylight hours of the twenty-first day of each month for various latitudes.

24 Deg N									
N	NNE/ NNW	NE/ NW	ENE/ WNW	E/ W	ESE/ WSW	SE/ SW	SSE/ SSW	S	HOR
Jan. 27	27	41	128	190	240	253	241	227	214
Feb. 30	30	80	165	220	244	243	213	192	249
Mar. 34	45	124	195	234	237	214	168	137	275
Apr. 37	88	159	209	228	212	169	107	75	283
May 43	117	178	214	218	190	132	67	46	282
June 55	127	184	214	212	179	117	55	43	279
July 45	116	176	210	213	185	129	65	46	278
Aug. 38	87	156	203	220	204	162	103	72	277
Sep. 35	42	119	185	222	225	206	163	134	266
Oct. 31	31	79	159	211	237	235	207	187	244
Nov. 27	27	42	126	187	236	249	237	224	213
Dec. 26	26	29	112	180	234	247	247	237	199

28 Deg N									
N (shade)	NNE/ NNW	NE/ NW	ENE/ WNW	E/ W	ESE/ WSW	SE/ SW	SSE/ SSW	S	HOR
Jan. 25	25	35	117	183	235	251	247	238	196
Feb. 29	29	72	157	213	244	246	224	207	234
Mar. 33	41	116	189	231	237	221	182	157	265
Apr. 36	84	151	205	228	216	178	124	94	278
May 40	115	172	211	219	195	144	83	58	280
June 51	125	178	211	213	184	128	68	49	278
July 41	114	170	208	215	190	140	80	57	276
Aug. 38	83	149	199	220	207	172	120	91	272
Sep. 34	38	111	179	219	226	213	177	154	256
Oct. 30	30	71	151	204	236	238	217	202	229
Nov. 26	26	35	115	181	232	247	243	235	195
Dec. 24	24	24	99	172	227	248	251	246	179

Maximum Solar Heat Gain Factors

Month 1																		
Orientation	**Hourly Solar Radiation BTU/Hr./Sq.Ft.**																	**Daily Total Radiation BTU/Hr./Sq.Ft.**
	4	5	6	7	8	9	10	11	12	13	14	15	16	17	18	19	20	
South	0.	0.	0.	0.	39.	130.	185.	216.	227.	216.	185.	130.	39.	0.	0.	0.	0.	1366
Southwest	0.	0.	0.	0.	5.	20.	71.	124.	169.	198.	203.	172.	63.	0.	0.	0.	0.	1025.
West	0.	0.	0.	0.	5.	14.	22.	27.	29.	79.	116.	122.	53.	0.	0.	0.	0.	467.
Northwest	0.	0.	0.	0.	5.	14.	22.	27.	29.	27.	22.	14.	15.	0.	0.	0.	0.	175.
North	0.	0.	0.	0.	5.	14.	22.	27.	29.	27.	22.	14.	5.	0.	0.	0.	0.	165.
Northeast	0.	0.	0.	0.	15.	14.	22.	27.	29.	27.	22.	14.	5.	0.	0.	0.	0.	175.
East	0.	0.	0.	0.	53.	122.	116.	79.	29.	27.	22.	14.	5.	0.	0.	0.	0.	467.
Southeast	0.	0.	0.	0.	63.	172.	203.	198.	169.	124.	71.	20.	5.	0.	0.	0.	0.	1025.
Horiz.	0.	0.	0.	0.	12.	54.	91.	115.	124.	115.	91.	54.	12.	0.	0.	0.	0.	668.

Solar Radiation Values

32 Deg N									
	N (shade)	NNE/ NNW	NE/ NW	ENE/ WNW	E/ W	ESE/ WSW	SE/ SW	SSE/ SSW	S	HOR
Jan.	24	24	29	105	175	229	249	250	246	176
Feb.	27	27	65	149	205	242	248	232	221	217
Mar.	32	37	107	183	227	237	227	195	176	252
Apr.	36	80	146	200	227	219	187	141	115	271
May	38	111	170	208	220	199	155	99	74	277
June	44	122	176	208	214	189	139	83	60	276
July	40	111	167	204	215	194	150	96	72	273
Aug.	37	79	141	195	219	210	181	136	111	265
Sep.	33	35	103	173	215	227	218	189	171	244
Oct.	28	28	63	143	195	234	239	225	215	213
Nov.	24	24	29	103	173	225	245	246	243	175
Dec.	22	22	22	84	162	218	246	252	252	158

44 Deg N									
	N (shade)	NNE/ NNW	NE/ NW	ENE/ WNW	E/ W	ESE/ WSW	SE/ SW	SSE/ SSW	S	HOR
Jan.	17	17	17	64	138	189	232	248	252	109
Feb.	22	22	43	117	178	227	246	248	247	160
Mar.	27	27	87	162	211	236	238	224	218	206
Apr.	33	66	136	185	221	224	210	183	171	240
May	36	96	162	201	219	211	183	148	132	257
June	47	108	169	205	215	203	171	132	115	261
July	37	96	159	198	215	206	179	144	128	254
Aug.	34	66	132	180	214	215	202	177	165	236
Sep.	28	28	80	152	198	226	227	216	211	199
Oct.	23	23	42	111	171	217	237	240	239	157
Nov.	18	18	18	64	135	186	227	244	248	109
Dec.	15	15	15	49	115	175	217	240	246	89

36 Deg N									
	N (shade)	NNE/ NNW	NE/ NW	ENE/ WNW	E/ W	ESE/ WSW	SE/ SW	SSE/ SSW	S	HOR
Jan.	22	22	24	90	166	219	247	252	252	155
Feb.	26	26	57	139	195	239	248	239	232	199
Mar.	30	33	99	176	223	238	232	206	192	238
Apr.	35	76	144	196	225	221	196	156	135	262
May	38	107	168	204	220	204	165	116	93	272
June	47	118	175	205	215	194	150	99	77	273
July	39	107	165	201	216	199	161	113	90	268
Aug.	36	75	138	190	218	212	189	151	131	257
Sep.	31	31	95	167	210	228	223	200	187	230
Oct.	27	27	56	133	187	230	239	231	225	195
Nov.	22	22	24	87	163	215	243	248	248	154
Dec.	20	20	20	69	151	204	241	253	254	136

48 Deg N									
	N (shade)	NNE/ NNW	NE/ NW	ENE/ WNW	E/ W	ESE/ WSW	SE/ SW	SSE/ SSW	S	HOR
Jan.	15	15	15	53	118	175	216	239	245	85
Feb.	20	20	36	103	168	216	242	249	250	138
Mar.	26	26	80	154	204	234	239	232	228	188
Apr.	31	61	132	180	219	225	215	194	186	226
May	35	97	158	200	218	214	192	163	150	247
June	46	110	165	204	215	206	180	148	134	252
July	37	96	156	196	214	209	187	158	146	244
Aug.	33	61	128	174	211	216	208	188	180	223
Sep.	27	27	72	144	191	223	228	223	220	182
Oct.	21	21	35	96	161	207	233	241	242	136
Nov.	15	15	15	52	115	172	212	234	240	85
Dec.	13	13	13	36	91	156	195	225	233	65

Maximum Solar Heat Gain Factors

Source: American Society of Heating, Refrigerating and Air-Conditioning Engineers, *ASHRAE Handbook: 1981 Fundamentals* ©1981. Reprinted by permission of ASHRAE.

☐ To account for the many different types of glazing and shading devices used, a *shading coefficient* (SC), relating the solar heat gain through a glazing system under a specific set of conditions to that through the reference glazing material is defined:

Shading Coefficient (SC)

$$= \frac{\text{Solar Heat Gain of Glazing}}{\text{Solar Heat Gain of Reference Glazing}}$$

40 Deg N									
	N (shade)	NNE/ NNW	NE/ NW	ENE/ WNW	E/ W	ESE/ WSW	SE/ SW	SSE/ SSW	S	HOR
Jan.	20	20	20	74	154	205	241	252	254	133
Feb.	24	24	50	129	186	234	246	244	241	180
Mar.	29	29	93	169	218	238	236	216	206	223
Apr.	34	71	140	190	224	223	203	170	154	252
May	37	102	165	202	220	208	175	133	113	265
June	48	113	172	205	216	199	161	116	95	267
July	38	102	163	198	216	203	170	129	109	262
Aug.	35	71	135	185	216	214	196	165	149	247
Sep.	30	30	87	160	203	227	226	209	200	215
Oct.	25	25	49	123	180	225	238	236	234	177
Nov.	20	20	20	73	151	201	237	248	250	132
Dec.	18	18	18	60	135	188	232	249	253	113

Type of Glass		Type of Shading					
		Venetian Blinds		Roller Shades			
				Opaque		Trans-lucent	
Type of Glass (Thickness—in.)	Solar Trans-mission Value	Medium	Light	Dark	White	Light	Louvered Sun Screen
Single Glass with Indoor Shading							
Clear (3/32–1/4)	0.87–0.80						
Clear (1/4–1/2)	0.80–0.71						
Clear Pattern (1/8–1/2)	0.87–0.79	0.64	0.55	0.59	0.25	0.39	—
Heat-Absorbing Pattern (1/8)	—						
Tinted (3/16–7/32)	0.74–0.71						
Heat-Absorbing (3/16–1/4)	0.46						
Heat-Absorbing Pattern (3/16–1/4)	—	0.57	0.53	0.45	0.30	0.36	—
Tinted (1/8–7/32)	0.59–0.45						
Heat-Absorbing or Pattern	0.44–0.30						
Heat-Absorbing (3/8)	0.34	0.54	0.52	0.40	0.28	0.32	—
Heat-Absorbing or Pattern	0.29–0.15	0.42	0.40	0.36	0.28	0.31	—
Reflective Coated							
S.C. = 0.30		0.25	0.23				
0.40		0.33	0.29				
0.50		0.42	0.38				
0.60		0.50	0.44				
Insulating Glass with Indoor Shading							
Clear Out (3/32–1/8)	0.87						
Clear In							
Clear Out		0.57	0.51	0.60	0.25	0.37	—
Clear In (1/4)	0.80						
Heat-Absorbing Out (1/4)	0.46						
Clear In	0.80	0.39	0.36	0.40	0.22	0.30	—
Reflective Coated							
S.C. = 0.20		0.19	0.18				
0.30		0.27	0.26				
0.40		0.34	0.33				
Double Glass with Between-Glass Shading							
Clear Out (3/32–1/8)	0.87						
Clear In		0.36	0.33	—	—	—	0.43
Clear Out (1/4)	0.80						0.49
Clear In							
Heat-Absorbing Out	0.46	0.30	0.28	—	—	—	0.37
Clear In (1/4)	0.80						0.41

Shading Coefficients (SC)

□ The accompanying tables provide shading coefficients for a range of typical glazings.

□ The cooling load factor (CLF) tables also shown here consider both the type of construction and the presence or absence of interior shading devices.

Determine the solar heat gain due to glass on the south and west walls of a building at noon in August, located at 32°N. latitude. Assume the room construction material is of medium weight. The south glass is 100 square feet of double insulating glass with no interior shading. The west glass is 100 square feet of single grey-tinted glass with light-colored venetian blinds.

Solution: The data required for the calculations are as follows:

	SC	Maximum SHG	CLF
S. Glass	0.80	111	0.52
W. Glass	0.55	219	0.17

Using the formula,
Solar cooling load (BTU/hr.) = A × SC × SHG CLF
Solar cooling load (south) = 100 × .80 × 111 × .52 = 4618 BTU/hr.
Solar cooling load (west) = 100 × .55 × 219 × .17 = 2048 BTU/hr.
It is important to note that the total load through fenestration is the sum of the load due to solar heat gain *and the load due to conduction heat gain through the fenestration*. Conduction heat gain is discussed in the *Envelope Heat Gain* section of this monograph.

Glass without Interior Shading (includes reflective and heat absorbing glass)

Solar Time, Hr.

N. Latitude Fenes-stration	Room Construction L = Light M = Medium H = Heavy	1	2	3	4	5	6	7	8	9	10	11	12	13	14	15	16	17	18	19	20	21	22	23	24
N	L	0.17	0.14	0.11	0.09	0.08	0.33	0.42	0.48	0.56	0.63	0.71	0.76	0.80	0.82	0.82	0.79	0.80	0.84	0.61	0.48	0.38	0.31	0.25	0.20
	M	0.23	0.20	0.18	0.16	0.14	0.34	0.41	0.46	0.52	0.59	0.65	0.70	0.73	0.75	0.76	0.74	0.75	0.79	0.61	0.50	0.42	0.36	0.31	0.27
	H	0.25	0.23	0.21	0.20	0.19	0.38	0.45	0.50	0.55	0.60	0.65	0.69	0.72	0.73	0.72	0.70	0.70	0.74	0.57	0.46	0.39	0.34	0.31	0.28
NE	L	0.04	0.04	0.03	0.02	0.02	0.23	0.41	0.51	0.51	0.45	0.39	0.36	0.33	0.31	0.28	0.26	0.23	0.19	0.15	0.12	0.10	0.08	0.06	0.05
	M	0.07	0.06	0.06	0.05	0.04	0.21	0.36	0.44	0.45	0.40	0.36	0.33	0.31	0.30	0.28	0.26	0.23	0.21	0.17	0.15	0.13	0.11	0.09	0.08
	H	0.09	0.08	0.08	0.07	0.07	0.23	0.37	0.44	0.44	0.39	0.34	0.31	0.29	0.27	0.26	0.24	0.22	0.20	0.16	0.14	0.13	0.12	0.11	0.10
E	L	0.04	0.04	0.03	0.02	0.02	0.19	0.37	0.51	0.57	0.57	0.51	0.42	0.36	0.32	0.29	0.25	0.22	0.19	0.14	0.12	0.09	0.08	0.06	0.05
	M	0.07	0.06	0.06	0.05	0.04	0.18	0.33	0.44	0.50	0.51	0.45	0.39	0.35	0.32	0.29	0.26	0.23	0.21	0.17	0.15	0.13	0.11	0.10	0.08
	H	0.09	0.09	0.08	0.08	0.07	0.21	0.34	0.45	0.50	0.49	0.43	0.36	0.32	0.29	0.26	0.24	0.22	0.19	0.17	0.15	0.13	0.12	0.11	0.10
SE	L	0.05	0.04	0.03	0.03	0.02	0.13	0.28	0.43	0.55	0.62	0.63	0.57	0.48	0.42	0.37	0.33	0.28	0.24	0.19	0.15	0.12	0.10	0.08	0.07
	M	0.09	0.08	0.07	0.06	0.05	0.14	0.26	0.38	0.48	0.54	0.55	0.51	0.45	0.40	0.36	0.33	0.29	0.25	0.21	0.18	0.16	0.14	0.12	0.10
	H	0.11	0.10	0.10	0.09	0.08	0.17	0.28	0.40	0.49	0.53	0.53	0.48	0.41	0.36	0.33	0.30	0.27	0.24	0.20	0.18	0.16	0.14	0.13	0.12
S	L	0.08	0.07	0.05	0.04	0.04	0.06	0.09	0.14	0.22	0.34	0.48	0.59	0.65	0.65	0.59	0.50	0.43	0.36	0.28	0.22	0.18	0.15	0.12	0.10
	M	0.12	0.11	0.09	0.08	0.07	0.08	0.11	0.14	0.21	0.31	0.42	0.52	0.57	0.58	0.53	0.47	0.41	0.36	0.29	0.25	0.21	0.18	0.16	0.14
	H	0.13	0.12	0.12	0.11	0.10	0.12	0.14	0.17	0.24	0.33	0.43	0.51	0.56	0.55	0.50	0.43	0.38	0.32	0.26	0.22	0.20	0.18	0.16	0.15
SW	L	0.12	0.10	0.08	0.06	0.05	0.06	0.08	0.10	0.12	0.14	0.16	0.24	0.36	0.49	0.60	0.66	0.66	0.58	0.43	0.33	0.27	0.22	0.18	0.14
	M	0.15	0.13	0.12	0.10	0.09	0.09	0.10	0.12	0.13	0.15	0.17	0.23	0.33	0.44	0.53	0.58	0.59	0.53	0.41	0.33	0.28	0.24	0.21	0.18
	H	0.15	0.14	0.13	0.12	0.11	0.12	0.13	0.14	0.16	0.17	0.19	0.25	0.34	0.44	0.52	0.56	0.56	0.49	0.37	0.30	0.25	0.21	0.19	0.17
W	L	0.12	0.10	0.08	0.07	0.05	0.06	0.07	0.08	0.10	0.11	0.13	0.14	0.20	0.32	0.45	0.57	0.64	0.61	0.44	0.34	0.27	0.22	0.18	0.14
	M	0.15	0.13	0.11	0.10	0.09	0.09	0.09	0.10	0.11	0.12	0.13	0.14	0.19	0.29	0.40	0.50	0.56	0.55	0.41	0.33	0.27	0.23	0.20	0.17
	H	0.14	0.13	0.12	0.11	0.10	0.11	0.12	0.13	0.13	0.14	0.15	0.16	0.21	0.30	0.40	0.49	0.54	0.52	0.38	0.30	0.24	0.21	0.18	0.16
NW	L	0.11	0.09	0.07	0.06	0.05	0.06	0.08	0.10	0.12	0.14	0.16	0.17	0.19	0.23	0.33	0.47	0.59	0.60	0.43	0.33	0.26	0.21	0.17	0.14
	M	0.14	0.12	0.11	0.09	0.08	0.09	0.10	0.11	0.13	0.14	0.16	0.17	0.18	0.21	0.30	0.42	0.51	0.53	0.39	0.32	0.26	0.22	0.19	0.16
	H	0.14	0.12	0.11	0.11	0.10	0.11	0.12	0.13	0.15	0.16	0.18	0.19	0.19	0.22	0.30	0.41	0.50	0.51	0.36	0.29	0.23	0.20	0.17	0.15
HOR	L	0.11	0.09	0.07	0.06	0.05	0.07	0.14	0.24	0.36	0.48	0.58	0.66	0.72	0.74	0.73	0.67	0.59	0.47	0.37	0.30	0.24	0.19	0.16	0.13
	M	0.16	0.14	0.12	0.11	0.09	0.11	0.16	0.24	0.33	0.43	0.52	0.59	0.64	0.67	0.66	0.62	0.55	0.47	0.38	0.32	0.28	0.24	0.21	0.18
	H	0.17	0.16	0.15	0.14	0.13	0.15	0.20	0.27	0.36	0.45	0.52	0.59	0.62	0.64	0.62	0.58	0.51	0.42	0.35	0.29	0.26	0.23	0.21	0.19

Glass with Interior Shading (includes reflective and heat absorbing glass)

Cooling Load Factors (CLF)

N. Latitude Fenestration	Room Construction (L=Light, M=Medium, H=Heavy)	Solar Time, Hr.																							
		1	2	3	4	5	6	7	8	9	10	11	12	13	14	15	16	17	18	19	20	21	22	23	24
N	L	0.07	0.05	0.04	0.04	0.05	0.70	0.65	0.65	0.74	0.81	0.87	0.91	0.91	0.88	0.84	0.77	0.80	0.92	0.27	0.19	0.15	0.12	0.10	0.08
	M	0.08	0.07	0.06	0.06	0.07	0.73	0.66	0.65	0.73	0.80	0.86	0.89	0.89	0.86	0.82	0.75	0.78	0.91	0.24	0.18	0.15	0.13	0.11	0.09
	H	0.09	0.09	0.08	0.07	0.09	0.75	0.67	0.66	0.74	0.80	0.86	0.89	0.88	0.85	0.80	0.73	0.76	0.88	0.23	0.17	0.14	0.13	0.11	0.10
NE	L	0.02	0.01	0.01	0.01	0.02	0.55	0.76	0.75	0.60	0.39	0.31	0.28	0.27	0.25	0.23	0.20	0.16	0.12	0.06	0.05	0.04	0.03	0.02	0.02
	M	0.03	0.02	0.02	0.02	0.02	0.56	0.76	0.74	0.58	0.37	0.29	0.27	0.26	0.24	0.22	0.20	0.16	0.12	0.06	0.05	0.04	0.04	0.03	0.03
	H	0.03	0.03	0.03	0.03	0.04	0.57	0.77	0.74	0.58	0.36	0.28	0.26	0.25	0.23	0.21	0.19	0.16	0.11	0.06	0.05	0.05	0.05	0.04	0.04
E	L	0.02	0.01	0.01	0.01	0.01	0.45	0.71	0.80	0.77	0.64	0.43	0.29	0.25	0.23	0.20	0.17	0.14	0.10	0.06	0.04	0.05	0.04	0.02	0.02
	M	0.03	0.02	0.02	0.02	0.02	0.47	0.72	0.80	0.76	0.62	0.41	0.27	0.24	0.22	0.20	0.17	0.14	0.11	0.06	0.05	0.04	0.04	0.03	0.03
	H	0.04	0.03	0.03	0.03	0.03	0.48	0.72	0.80	0.75	0.61	0.40	0.25	0.22	0.21	0.19	0.16	0.14	0.10	0.06	0.05	0.05	0.04	0.04	0.04
SE	L	0.02	0.02	0.01	0.01	0.01	0.29	0.56	0.74	0.82	0.81	0.70	0.52	0.35	0.30	0.26	0.22	0.18	0.13	0.08	0.06	0.05	0.04	0.03	0.03
	M	0.03	0.03	0.02	0.02	0.02	0.30	0.56	0.74	0.81	0.79	0.68	0.49	0.33	0.28	0.25	0.22	0.18	0.13	0.08	0.07	0.06	0.05	0.04	0.04
	H	0.04	0.04	0.04	0.03	0.04	0.31	0.57	0.74	0.81	0.79	0.67	0.48	0.31	0.27	0.23	0.22	0.17	0.13	0.07	0.07	0.06	0.05	0.05	0.05
S	L	0.03	0.03	0.02	0.02	0.02	0.08	0.15	0.22	0.37	0.58	0.75	0.84	0.82	0.71	0.53	0.37	0.29	0.20	0.11	0.09	0.07	0.06	0.05	0.04
	M	0.04	0.04	0.03	0.03	0.03	0.09	0.16	0.22	0.38	0.58	0.75	0.83	0.80	0.68	0.50	0.35	0.27	0.19	0.11	0.09	0.08	0.07	0.06	0.05
	H	0.05	0.05	0.04	0.04	0.04	0.11	0.17	0.24	0.39	0.59	0.75	0.82	0.79	0.67	0.49	0.33	0.26	0.18	0.10	0.08	0.07	0.06	0.06	0.05
SW	L	0.05	0.04	0.03	0.02	0.02	0.06	0.08	0.13	0.16	0.18	0.22	0.38	0.59	0.76	0.84	0.83	0.72	0.48	0.18	0.13	0.11	0.08	0.07	0.06
	M	0.06	0.05	0.04	0.04	0.03	0.07	0.09	0.14	0.16	0.19	0.22	0.38	0.59	0.75	0.83	0.81	0.69	0.45	0.15	0.12	0.10	0.08	0.07	0.06
	H	0.06	0.05	0.05	0.04	0.04	0.08	0.10	0.15	0.18	0.20	0.23	0.39	0.59	0.75	0.82	0.80	0.68	0.43	0.14	0.11	0.09	0.08	0.07	0.06
W	L	0.05	0.04	0.03	0.02	0.02	0.05	0.08	0.11	0.13	0.14	0.15	0.17	0.30	0.53	0.72	0.83	0.83	0.63	0.19	0.14	0.11	0.08	0.07	0.06
	M	0.05	0.05	0.04	0.04	0.03	0.06	0.09	0.11	0.13	0.15	0.16	0.17	0.31	0.53	0.72	0.82	0.81	0.61	0.16	0.12	0.10	0.08	0.07	0.06
	H	0.05	0.05	0.04	0.04	0.04	0.07	0.10	0.12	0.14	0.16	0.17	0.18	0.31	0.54	0.71	0.81	0.80	0.59	0.15	0.11	0.09	0.07	0.06	0.06
NW	L	0.04	0.04	0.03	0.02	0.02	0.06	0.10	0.13	0.16	0.19	0.20	0.21	0.22	0.30	0.52	0.73	0.83	0.71	0.19	0.13	0.10	0.08	0.07	0.05
	M	0.05	0.04	0.04	0.03	0.03	0.07	0.11	0.14	0.17	0.19	0.20	0.21	0.22	0.30	0.52	0.73	0.82	0.69	0.16	0.12	0.09	0.08	0.07	0.06
	H	0.05	0.04	0.04	0.04	0.04	0.08	0.12	0.15	0.18	0.20	0.21	0.22	0.23	0.30	0.52	0.73	0.81	0.67	0.15	0.11	0.08	0.07	0.06	0.05
HOR	L	0.04	0.03	0.03	0.02	0.02	0.10	0.26	0.43	0.59	0.72	0.81	0.87	0.87	0.83	0.74	0.60	0.44	0.27	0.15	0.12	0.09	0.08	0.06	0.05
	M	0.06	0.05	0.04	0.04	0.03	0.12	0.27	0.44	0.59	0.72	0.81	0.85	0.85	0.81	0.71	0.58	0.42	0.25	0.14	0.12	0.10	0.08	0.07	0.06
	H	0.06	0.06	0.06	0.05	0.05	0.13	0.29	0.45	0.60	0.72	0.81	0.85	0.84	0.79	0.70	0.56	0.40	0.23	0.13	0.11	0.09	0.07	0.08	0.07

Source: American Society of Heating, Refrigerating and Air-Conditioning Engineers. ASHRAE Handbook: 1981 Fundamentals ©1981. Reprinted by permission of ASHRAE.

Ventilation/Infiltration Heat Gain

Ventilation can be described as the introduction of outside air to spaces within a building. Infiltration is the uncontrolled introduction of outside air. Ventilation's and infiltration's effects can be calculated together because the air from both sources is the same.

☐ Infiltration varies with the tightness of the building and, to the extent that it is caused by wind, is uncontrollable. Infiltration is balanced by an equal amount of exfiltration, which limits the effects of infiltration to one-half of the total openings at one time. Infiltration is generally a more serious problem in the heating season than during the cooling season.

☐ Most of the time outside air is not at the desired temperature or humidity levels, making it necessary to either add or remove both heat and water vapor. The next two sections examine what is involved in calculating the heat losses or gains associated with ventilation and infiltration.

☐ For purposes here, sensible and latent heat gain must be distinguished so that the available portion of total energy removal capabilities in the cooling apparatus will be sufficient for removing heat and condensing moisture, respectively. When heat is added to the space by ventilation and infiltration air, the space cooling load equals the heat gain (both sensible and latent), since the gain is immediately registered by the space air.

☐ The sensible heat gain in BTU/hr. as a result of a difference in temperature between the incoming and outgoing air is approximated by:

Sensible heat gain(BTU/hr.) = 1.10 × ventilation rate (cfm) × difference in temperature (Δt)

☐ The 1.10 (constant) in this formula is derived from: 60 × 0.075 × (024 + 0.45 W)
Where:

60	=	minutes per hour
0.075	=	pounds of dry air per cubic foot
0.24	=	specific heat of dry air, BTU per pound per degree (F.)
0.45	=	specific heat of water vapor, BTU per pound per degree (F.)
W	=	humidity ratio, pounds of water per pound of dry air. A humidity ratio (W) of 0.01 is used here as a common design condition. Actual values of W can be read from the psychrometric chart.

☐ The latent heat gain in BTU/hr. as a result of a difference in humidity ratio (ΔW) between the incoming and outgoing air can be found with:

Latent heat gain (BTU/hr.) = 4840 × ventilation rate (cfm) × ΔW

☐ The 4840 in this formula is derived from: 60 × 0.75 × 1076
Where:

60	=	minutes per hour
0.075	=	pounds of dry air per cubic foot
1076	=	approximate energy content of 50 percent relative humidity vapor at 75 degrees (F.) less the energy content of water at 50 degrees (F.). The 50 percent relative humidity at 75 degrees (F.) is a common design condition, and the 50 degrees (F.) is normal condensation temperature from cooling and dehumidifying coils.

☐ At many locations during certain periods of the year, the moisture content of outside air will become the predominant factor contributing to ventilation heat gains. In situations where interior humidity loads will rise above acceptable limits, a slightly different calculation for ventilation heat gain can be used, based on two variables:
—Ventilation rate (cfm);
—Average heat content per pound of outside air for a given site (Δh).

☐ Note that ventilation rate is the same as that used in the previous equation, while temperature difference (Δt) has been replaced by the average heat content of air per pound. Although this can be computed, sample figures for a number of cities throughout the U.S. are listed.

Location	BTU per Pound
Albany, N.Y.	5.1
Albuquerque, N.M.	0
Atlanta, Ga.	7.5
Bismarck, N.D.	.8
Boise, Idaho	.8
Boston, Mass.	4.3
Billings, Mont.	.4
Buffalo, N.Y.	5.3
Charleston, S.C.	9.1
Chicago, Ill.	5.7
Corpus Christi, Tex.	13.0
Dallas, Tex.	8.2
Denver, Colo.	0
Detroit, Mich.	5.0
Ellsworth, S.D.	.9
Fairchild, Wash.	.1
Greensboro, N.C.	6.0
Helena, Mont.	0
Kansas City, Mo.	6.4
Kodiak, Alaska	.5
Las Vegas, Nev.	2.1
Los Angeles, Calif.	2.4
Louisville, Ky.	7.8
Lubbock, Tex.	2.2
Memphis, Tenn.	9.6
Miami, Fla.	12.5
Minneapolis, Minn.	4.7
New Orleans, La.	12.1
Omaha, Neb.	5.7
Pearl Harbor, Hawaii	10.3
Phoenix, Ariz.	3.9
Pittsburgh, Pa.	5.0
Portland, Me.	3.5
Portland, Ore.	1.6
Roosevelt Rds, Puerto Rico	15.1
Sacramento, Calif.	1.8
Salt Lake City, Utah	0
San Diego, Calif.	2.7
San Francisco, Calif.	6.7
Traverse City, Mich.	4.7
Tulsa, Okla.	7.1
Washington, D.C.	6.4

Average Heat Content of Air (Ah)

☐ For the hours when humidity is a problem, ventilation heat gain is calculated as follows:

Ventilation heat gain (BTU/hr.) = 4.5 × ventilation rate × Δh

The 4.5 in this formula is derived from: 60 × 0.75

Where:

60 = minutes per hour

0.075 = pounds of dry air per cubic foot

☐ These equations are valid for calculating the cooling load due to infiltration of outside air as well as for the cooling load due to the positive introduction of air for ventilation, provided it is introduced directly into the space.

Ventilation/Infiltration Heat Loss

As discussed with ventilation/infiltration heat gain, heat loss due to ventilation/infiltration of outside air can be divided into *sensible* and *latent*. The energy quantity associated with having to raise the temperature of outdoor air up to indoor air temperature is the *sensible* component. The energy quantity associated with net loss of moisture from the space is the *latent* component.

☐ The energy required to warm outdoor air entering the building is given by:

Sensible heat loss (BTU/hr.) = $0.018 \times V \, (t_i - t_o)$

Where:

V = volume of outdoor air entering building, cubic feet per hour
t_i = indoor air temperature
t_o = outdoor air temperature
0.018 = constant derived from: 0.24×0.075

Where:

0.24 = specific heat of air, BTU per pound per degree (F.)
0.075 = density of air, pounds per cubic feet

☐ When moisture must be added to the indoor air to maintain winter comfort conditions, it is necessary to determine the energy needed to evaporate an amount of water equivalent to what is lost by exfiltration (latent component of infiltration heat loss). This energy can be calculated by:

Latent heat loss (BTU/hr.) = $79.5 \, V \, (W_i - W_o)$

Where:

V = volume of outdoor air entering building, cubic feet per hour
W_i = indoor air humidity ratio
W_o = outdoor air humidity ratio
79.5 = constant dervied from: 1060×0.075

Where:

1060 = latent heat of vapor, BTU per pound
0.075 = density of air, pounds per cubic feet

☐ These calculations of heat loss due to infiltration depend on determination of the volume (V). Two primary methods are used to determine this quantity, the crack method and the air change method.

Crack Method

☐ The crack method calculates the flow produced by the pressure difference acting on each leakage path or building component by foot of length. The accompanying figures provide rough estimates of infiltration rates for different doors and windows. Note that for double-hung windows the length of crack is three times the width plus twice the height, while, for other window types, the crack length is the total perimeter of the movable or ventilating sections.

☐ In calculating window infiltration for an entire structure, it is not necessary to consider the total crack length on all sides of the building, since the wind does not act simultaneously on all sides. In no case, however, should less than half the total crack length be figured. Knowledge of the prevailing wind direction will aid judgment in these computations.

Construction	Infiltration Airflow Volume (in cfh per ft of crack)			
	10 MPH	20 MPH	30 MPH	
Double-hung wood frame window: Non-weatherstripped Weatherstripped	21 13	59 36	104 63	
Double-hung metal frame window: Non-weatherstripped Weatherstripped	47 19	104 46	170 76	
Rolled steel frame glazed window or door (non-weatherstripped) Industrial, pivoted (or awning)	108	244	372	
Rolled steel frame glazed window or door (non-weatherstripped): Residential, casement (or hinged)	18	47	74	
Wood or metal door: Non-weatherstripped Weatherstripped	69 19	154 51	249 92	

Note: Reduce values above by ⅛ (i.e., multiply by ⅞) when storm window (or door) is added to weatherstripped construction, by ½ when added to non-weatherstripped construction.

Door and Window Infiltration

☐ When calculating infiltration/ventilation losses by the crack method V in the previous equations can be substituted as follows:

V = air leakage (ft³/hr. per ft. of crack) × length of crack (ft.)

Air Change Method

☐ Since a certain amount of judgment is required regarding construction quality, weather conditions, room use, and other factors in estimating infiltration by any method, infiltration is sometimes calculated on the basis of an estimated number of air changes, rather than the length of window cracks. This air change method is based on past experience with air leakage. When calculating infiltration/ventilation losses by the air change method V in the previous equations can be substituted as follows:

V = number of air changes × volume of room (ft³).

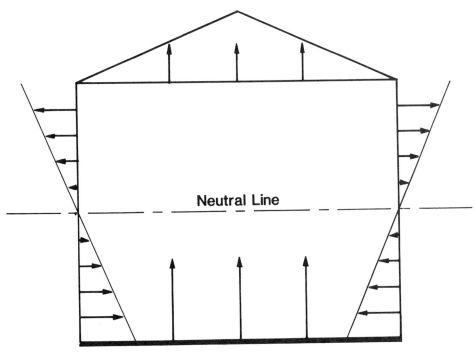

NOTE:
Condition shown assumes no wind pressure. Arrows point from higher to lower pressure and indicate direction of air flow.

Pressure Differences Caused by Stack Effect for a Typical Structure

Envelope Heat Loss

Envelope heat losses involve the transmission of heat through the skin of the building, that is, through the confining walls, glass, ceiling, floor or other surfaces. The rate of heat transmission is a function of two factors, the difference between the outdoor and indoor air temperature and the resistance of building materials to heat flow. The coefficient of heat flow is called the U-value and is expressed in BTU/hr./sq. ft. of building area per degree (F.).

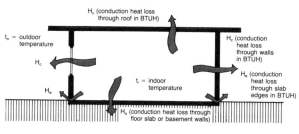

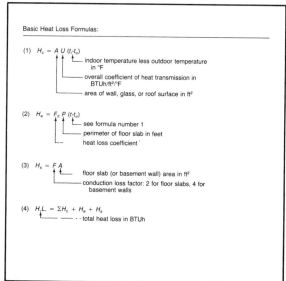

Basic Heat Loss Formulas:

(1) $H_c = A\,U\,(t_i\text{-}t_o)$
— indoor temperature less outdoor temperature in °F
— overall coefficient of heat transmission in BTUh/ft²/°F
— area of wall, glass, or roof surface in ft²

(2) $H_e = F_2\,P\,(t_i\text{-}t_o)$
— see formula number 1
— perimeter of floor slab in feet
— heat loss coefficient

(3) $H_s = F\,A$
— floor slab (or basement wall) area in ft²
— conduction loss factor: 2 for floor slabs, 4 for basement walls

(4) $H_tL. = \Sigma H_c + H_e + H_s$
— total heat loss in BTUh

Envelope Heat Loss

Source: Egan, M. David, *Concepts in Thermal Comfort*, © 1975. Reprinted by permission of Prentice-Hall, Inc., Englewood Cliffs, New Jersey.

☐ U-values of various envelope materials appear in the "Envelope" monograph in this handbook. Tables of outdoor design temperatures appear in the "HVAC Systems" monograph. The basic equation for calculating the heat loss through envelope surfaces is the following:

Envelope heat loss (BTU/hr.) = U × A × (t_i-t_o)

Where:

U = U-value, or thermal resistance, of envelope material, BTU/hr: per square feet per degree (F.)
A = area, square feet
t_O = outdoor temperature, degrees (F.)
t_i = indoor temperature, degrees (F.)

Calculate the transmission loss through an 8-inch brick wall having an area of 150 square feet, if the indoor temperature t_i is 70 degrees (F.), and the outdoor temperature t_o is −10 degrees (F.).
Solution: the overall heat transfer coefficient U of a plain 8-inch brick wall is 0.41 BTU/hr./sq.ft./degrees (F.).
The area is 150 square feet. Substituting in the equation:
Envelope heat loss = 0.41 × 150 × [70 −(−10)] = 4920 BTU/hr.

☐ This calculation process is quite simple. Calculation of the total envelope heat loss is an additive process of accumulating the heat loss through all envelope components.

☐ An envelope's overall thermal conductance (U_O) provides a measure of combined thermal conductance of the respective areas of gross exterior wall, roof/ceiling, and floor assembles.

☐ The equation for U_O is as follows:

$$U_O = \frac{U\text{ wall} \times A\text{ wall} + \text{window} \times A\text{ window} + U\text{ door} \times A\text{ door}}{A_O}$$

Where:
A_O = the gross area of envelope
U = U-value of envelope components
A = area of envelope components

Basements

☐ Outside design temperatures and heat loss calculations for basements or below-grade buildings are more complex. The heat flow

448

across underground walls is not uniform with respect to the depth of the wall, because each heat flow path contains a different thermal resistance based on the length of earth through which it must pass. The accompanying diagrams show the patterns for uniformly insulated and partially insulated walls.

☐ Ground surface temperature fluctuates about a mean value by an amplitude A, which will vary with geographic location and surface cover. Thus, suitable outside (external) design temperatures can be obtained by subtracting the A for the location from the mean annual air temperature, which can be obtained from meteorological records; A can be estimated from the accompanying map.

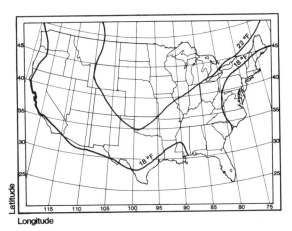

Lines of Constant Amplitude

Consider a basement 28′ × 30′ placed 6 feet below grade, with R = 8.34 insulation applied to the top 2 feet of wall below grade. Assume an internal air temperature of 70 degrees (F.) and an external design temperature (t$_a$ − A) of 20 degrees (F.). The solution will require the use of the accompanying tables for heat loss through basement walls and floors.

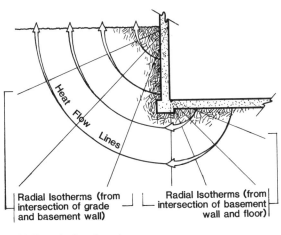

Radial Isotherms (from intersection of grade and basement wall)

Radial Isotherms (from intersection of basement wall and floor)

Uniformly Insulated

Depth	Path Length through Soil Ft.	Heat Loss, BTU/Hr.°F·Ft.²			
		Uninsulated	R = 4.17	R = 8.34	R = 12.51
0-1	0.68	0.410	0.152	0.093	0.067
1-2	2.27	0.222	0.116	0.079	0.059
2-3	3.88	0.155	0.094	0.068	0.053
3-4	5.52	0.119	0.079	0.060	0.048
4-5	7.05	0.096	0.069	0.053	0.044
5-6	8.65	0.079	0.060	0.048	0.040
6-7	10.28	0.069	0.054	0.044	0.037

Heat Loss through Basement Walls

Source: American Society of Heating, Refrigerating and Air-Conditioning Engineers, *ASHRAE Handbook: 1981 Fundamentals* ©1981. Reprinted by permission of ASHRAE.

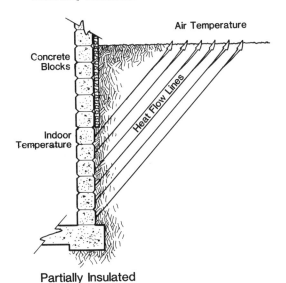

Air Temperature

Concrete Blocks

Indoor Temperature

Heat Flow Lines

Partially Insulated

Heat Flow from Basements

Depth of Foundation Wall below Grade Ft.	Heat Loss, BTU/Hr.F.°F·Ft.²			
	Width of Building Ft.			
	20	24	28	32
5	0.032	0.029	0.026	0.023
6	0.030	0.027	0.025	0.022
7	0.029	0.026	0.023	0.021

Heat Loss through Basement Floors

Source: American Society of Heating, Refrigerating and Air-Conditioning Engineers, *ASHRAE Handbook: 1981 Fundamentals* ©1981. Reprinted by permission of ASHRAE.

The solution is as follows:

Wall	
1st ft. below grade	0.093 BTU/hr.·ft.°F
2nd ft. below grade	0.079 "
3rd ft. below grade	0.155 "
4th ft. below grade	0.119 "
5th ft. below grade	0.096 "
6th ft. below grade	0.079 "
Total per ft. length of wall	0.621 BTU/hr.·ft.°F
Basement perimeter	= 2(28 + 30) = 116 ft.
Total wall heat loss	= 0.62 × 116 = 71.92 BTU/hr.°F
	~72 BTU/hr.°F
Floor	
Average heat loss per ft.²	= 0.025 BTU/hr.°F
Floor area 28 × 30	= 840 ft.²
Total floor heat loss	= 0.025 × 840 = 21 BTU/hr.°F
Total	
Total basement heat loss below grade	= 72 + 21 = 93 BTU/hr.°F
Design temperature difference	= 70 − 20 = 50 °F
Maximum rate of heat loss from below grade basement	= 93 × 50 = 4650 BTU/hr.

Basement Heat Loss Example

Slab On Grade

□ Experimental evidence indicates that heat loss from an unheated concrete slab floor is mostly through the perimeter rather than through the floor and into the ground. The total heat loss is more nearly proportional to the length of the perimeter than to the area of the floor, and can be estimated by the following equation for both unheated and heated slab floors:

Slab heat loss = F_2P

Where:

F_2 = heat loss coefficient, BTU/hr. × degrees (F.)/ft. of perimeter

P = perimeter or exposed edge of floor (ft.)

□ The accompanying table presents heat loss coefficients (F_2) for four wall constructions in three climate areas with and without insulation.

Construction	Insulated	Heat Loss BTU/Hr.° F per Ft.		
		Degree Days (65 °F Base)		
		7433	5350	2950
8-in. block wall, brick facing	Uninsulated	0.62	0.68	0.72
	R = 5.4 from edge to footer	0.48	0.50	0.56
4-in. block wall, brick facing	Uninsulated	0.80	0.84	0.93
	R = 5.4 from edge to footer	0.47	0.49	0.54
Metal stud wall, stucco	Uninsulated	1.15	1.20	1.34
	R = 5.4 from edge to footer	0.51	0.53	0.58
Poured concrete wall, with duct near perimeter	Uninsulated	1.84	2.12	2.73
	R = 5.4 from edge to footer, 3 ft. under floor	0.64	0.72	0.90

Heat Loss through Slab Floor

Source: American Society of Heating, Refrigerating and Air-Conditioning Engineers, *ASHRAE Handbook: 1981 Fundamentals* ©1981. Reprinted by permission of ASHRAE.

Envelope Heat Gain

Heat gain through exterior construction (walls, roof, and glazing) is normally calculated at the time of greatest heat flow. The rate of heat gain depends on the amount of solar radiation absorbed at the exterior surface and the difference between the outdoor and indoor air temperatures.

☐ Cooling loads due to envelope heat gain are affected not only by the amount of radiation absorbed by the envelope, but also by the time lag between the absorption of solar radiation and the transfer of this heat to the interior.

☐ This process can be visualized by picturing a 12-inch brick wall sliced into 12 1-inch sections. Assume that temperatures in each slice are equal at the beginning, and that the indoor and outdoor temperatures remain constant. When the sun shines on this wall, most of the solar heat is absorbed in the first slice, and its temperature rises above that of the outdoor air and the second slice, causing heat to flow to the outdoor air and also to the second slice. The amount of heat flowing in either direction depends on the resistance to heat flow within the wall through the outdoor air film. The heat flow into the second slice, in turn, raises its temperature, causing heat to flow into the third slice. This process of absorbing heat and passing some on to the next slice continues through the wall to the last slice, where the remaining heat is transferred to the inside by convection and radiation.

☐ For this particular wall, when temperatures are 95 degrees (F.) outside and 70 degrees (F.) inside, it takes approximately 7 hours for solar heat to pass through the wall into the room. Because each slice must absorb some heat before passing it on, the magnitude of heat released to the inside space would be reduced.

☐ This process occurs with any type of wall construction to a greater or lesser degree, de-pending on the resistance to heat flow through the wall and the thermal capacity of the wall. The solar heat absorbed at each time interval throughout the day goes through this same process. A rise in outdoor temperature reduces the amount of absorbed solar heat flowing from the wall to the outdoors and thus more flows inward.

☐ "Sol-air" temperatures have been developed to allow for the determination of heat gain due to absorption of solar radiation by building materials. Sol-air temperatures adjust actual outdoor temperatures upward to account for the solar heat in envelope materials left to be conducted through to indoor spaces after a portion of it has been lost to the outdoors through convection and re-radiation. Sol-air temperature tables can be found in ASHRAE's *1981 Fundamentals* handbook. As shown in the example table of sol-air temperatures, the heat remaining to be transmitted to the interior can be considerable.

☐ The sol-air temperature is substituted for actual outdoor temperature in the basic heat gain equation:

Envelope heat gain (BTU/hr.) = $U \times A \times (t_o - t_i)$

Where:

U = U-value, or thermal resistance, of envelope material, BTU/hr. per square feet per degree (F.)

A = area, square feet

t_o = outdoor temperature, degrees (F.)

t_i = indoor temperature, degrees (F.)

☐ Using Sol-air temperatures as a basis, ASHRAE has computed a set of *Cooling Load Temperature Differences* (CLTD) that account for thermal time lag. Using room transfer functions to calculate the rate at which various constructions release heat, ASHRAE developed CLTDs for seven categories of walls and 13 categories of roofs.

Sol-air Temperatures (F), t_g for July 21, 40°N Latitude

Time	Air Temp, F	N	NE	E	SE	S	SW	W	NW	HOR
1	76	76	76	76	76	76	76	76	76	69
2	76	76	76	76	76	76	76	76	76	69
3	75	75	75	75	75	75	75	75	75	68
4	74	74	74	74	74	74	74	74	74	67
5	74	74	74	74	74	74	74	74	74	67
6	74	82	95	97	86	75	75	75	75	74
7	75	82	103	109	97	78	78	78	78	85
8	77	82	103	114	105	83	81	81	81	96
9	80	85	101	114	110	92	85	85	85	106
10	83	89	96	110	112	100	89	89	89	115
11	87	93	94	104	111	108	96	93	93	123
12	90	96	96	97	107	112	107	97	96	127
13	93	99	99	99	102	114	117	110	100	129
14	94	100	100	100	100	111	123	121	107	126
15	95	100	100	100	100	107	125	129	116	121
16	94	99	98	98	98	100	122	131	120	113
17	93	100	96	96	96	96	115	127	121	103
18	91	99	92	92	92	92	103	114	112	91
19	87	87	87	87	87	87	87	87	87	80
20	85	85	85	85	85	85	85	85	85	78
21	83	83	83	83	83	83	83	83	83	76
22	81	81	81	81	81	81	81	81	81	74
23	79	79	79	79	79	79	79	79	79	72
24	77	77	77	77	77	77	77	77	77	70
Avg.	**83**	**86**	**89**	**91**	**90**	**89**	**90**	**91**	**89**	**91**

Sol-air Temperature Table

Source: American Society of Heating, Refrigerating and Air-Conditioning Engineers, *ASHRAE Handbook: 1981 Fundamentals* ©1981. Reprinted by permission of ASHRAE.

□ As shown in the accompanying notes, corrections to CLTD values can be made to account for the reflectivity of envelope surfaces, differences from the assumed indoor and outdoor design mean temperatures (78 and 85°F), and envelope constructions not considered in ASHRAE's calculations. In addition, the accompanying table gives correction factors for situations other than July 21 and 40 degrees North Latitude, the assumed date and location in the tables.

Roof No.	Description of Construction	1	2	3	4	5	6	7	8	9	10	11	12	13	14	15	16	17	18	19	20	21	22	23	24
														Solar Time, hr.											
											Without Suspended Ceiling														
1	Steel sheet with 1-in. (or 2-in.) insulation	1	−2	−3	−3	−5	−3	6	19	34	49	61	71	78	79	77	70	59	45	30	18	12	8	5	3
2	1-in. wood with 1-in. insulation	6	3	0	−1	−3	−3	−2	4	14	27	39	52	62	70	74	74	70	62	51	38	28	20	14	9
3	4-in. l.w. concrete	9	5	2	0	−2	−3	−3	1	9	20	32	44	55	64	70	73	71	66	57	45	34	25	18	13
4	2-in. h.w. concrete with 1-in. (or 2-in.) insulation	12	8	5	3	0	−1	−1	3	11	20	30	41	51	59	65	66	66	62	54	45	36	29	22	17
5	1-in. wood with 2-in. insulation	3	0	−3	−4	−5	−7	−6	−3	5	16	27	39	49	57	63	64	62	57	48	37	26	18	11	7
6	6-in. l.w. concrete	22	17	13	9	6	3	1	1	3	7	15	23	33	43	51	58	62	64	62	57	50	42	35	28
7	2.5-in. wood with 1-insulation	29	24	20	16	13	10	7	6	6	9	13	20	27	34	42	48	53	55	56	54	49	44	39	34
8	8-in. l.w. concrete	35	30	26	22	18	14	11	9	7	7	9	13	19	25	33	39	46	50	53	54	53	49	45	40
9	4-in. h.w. concrete with 1-in. (or 2-in.) insulation	25	22	18	15	12	9	8	8	10	14	20	26	33	40	46	50	53	53	52	48	43	38	34	30
10	2.5-in. wood with 2-in. insulation	30	26	23	19	16	13	10	9	8	9	13	17	23	29	36	41	46	49	51	50	47	43	39	35
11	Roof terrace system	34	31	28	25	22	19	16	14	13	13	15	18	22	26	31	36	40	44	45	46	45	43	40	37
12	6-in. h.w. concrete with 1-in. (or 2-in.) insulation	31	28	25	22	20	17	15	14	14	16	18	22	26	31	36	40	43	45	45	44	42	40	37	34
13	4-in. wood with 1-in. (or 2-in.) insulation	38	36	33	30	28	25	22	20	18	17	16	17	18	21	24	28	32	36	39	41	43	43	42	40
											With Suspended Ceiling														
1	Steel Sheet with 1-in. (or 2-in.) insulation	2	0	−2	−3	−4	−4	−1	9	23	37	50	62	71	77	78	74	67	56	42	28	18	12	8	5
2	1-in. wood with 1-in. insulation	20	15	11	8	5	3	2	3	7	13	21	30	40	48	55	60	62	61	58	51	44	37	30	25
3	4-in. l.w. concrete	19	14	10	7	4	2	0	0	4	10	19	29	39	48	56	62	65	64	61	54	46	38	30	24
4	2-in. h.w. concrete with 1-in. insulation	28	25	23	20	17	15	13	13	14	16	20	25	30	35	39	43	46	47	46	44	41	38	35	32
5	1-in. wood with 2-in. insulation	25	20	16	13	10	7	5	5	7	12	18	25	33	41	48	53	57	57	56	52	46	40	34	29
6	6-in. l.w. concrete	32	28	23	19	16	13	10	8	7	8	11	16	22	29	36	42	48	52	54	54	51	47	42	37
7	2.5-in. wood with 1-in. insulation	34	31	29	26	23	21	18	16	15	15	16	18	21	25	30	34	38	41	43	44	44	42	40	37
8	8-in. l.w. concrete	39	36	33	29	26	23	20	18	15	14	14	15	17	20	25	29	34	38	42	45	46	45	44	42
9	4-in. h.w. concrete with 1-in. (or 2-in.) insulation	30	29	27	26	24	22	21	20	20	21	22	24	27	29	32	34	36	38	38	38	37	36	34	33
10	2.5-in. wood with 2-in. insulation	35	33	30	28	26	24	22	20	18	18	18	20	22	25	28	32	35	38	40	41	41	40	39	37
11	Roof terrace system	30	29	28	27	26	25	24	23	22	22	22	23	23	25	26	28	29	31	32	33	33	33	33	32
12	6-in. h.w. concrete with 1-in. (or 2-in.) insulation	29	28	27	26	25	24	23	22	21	21	22	23	25	26	28	30	32	33	34	34	34	33	32	31
13	4-in. wood with 1-in. (or 2-in.) insulation	35	34	33	32	31	29	27	26	24	23	22	21	22	22	24	25	27	30	32	34	35	36	37	36

Source: American Society of Heating, Refrigerating and Air-Conditioning Engineers, *ASHRAE Handbook: 1981 Fundamentals* ©1981. Reprinted by permission of ASHRAE.

CLTD Table—Flat Roofs

Direct Application of Roof CLTD table Without Adjustments
Values in table were calculated using the following conditions:
— Dark flat surface roof ("dark" for solar radiation absorption)
— Indoor temperature of 78°F
— Outdoor maximum temperature of 95°F with outdoor mean temperature of 85°F and an outdoor daily range of 21°F
— Solar radiation typical of 40 deg North latitude on July 21
— Outside surface resistance. R_o = 0.333 ft.² · °F · hr./BTU
— Without and with suspended ceiling, but no attic fans or return air ducts in suspended ceiling space
— Inside surface resistance, R_i = 0.685 ft.² · °F · hr./BTU

Adjustments to table values:
The following equation makes adjustments for deviations of design and solar conditions from those listed above.

$$CLTD_{corr} = [(CLTD + LM) \times K + (78 - T_R) + (T_o - 85)] \times f$$

Where CLTD is from table
— LM is latitude-month correction for a horizontal surface.
— K is a color adjustment factor and is applied after first making month-latitude adjustments. Credit should not be taken for a light-colored roof except where permanence of light color is established by experience, as in rural areas or where there is little smoke.
K = 1.0 if dark colored or light in an industrial area
K = 0.5 if permanently light-colored (rural area)
— $(78 - T_R)$ is indoor design temperature correction.
— $(T_o - 85)$ is outdoor design temperature correction, where T_o is the average outside temperature of design day.
— f is a factor for attic fan and or ducts above ceiling and is applied after all other adjustments have been made.
f = 1.0 no attic or ducts
f = 0.75 positive ventilation

CLTD Corrections—Roofs

Group	Description of Construction
	4-in. Face Brick + (*Brick*)
C	Air Space + 4-in. Face Brick
D	4-in. Common Brick
C	1-in. Insulation or Air Space + 4-in. Common Brick
B	2-in. Insulation + 4-in. Common Brick
B	8-in. Common Brick
A	Insulation or Air Space + 8-in. Common brick
	4-in. Face Brick + (*h.w. Concrete*)
C	Air Space + 2-in. Concrete
B	2-in. Insulation + 4-in. Concrete
A	Air Space or Insulation + 8-in. or more Concrete
	4-in. Face Brick + (*l.w. or h.w. Concrete Block*)
E	4-in. Block
D	Air Space or Insulation + 4-in. Block
D	8-in. Block
C	Air Space or 1-in. Insulation + 6-in. or 8-in. Block
B	2-in. Insulation + 8-in. Block
	4-in. Face Brick + (*Clay Tile*)
D	4-in. Tile
D	Air Space + 4-in. Tile
C	Insulation + 4-in. Tile
C	8-in. Tile
B	Air Space or 1-in. Insulation + 8-in. Tile
A	2-in. Insulation + 8-in. Tile

	H.W. Concrete Wall + (*Finish*)
E	4-in. Concrete
D	4-in. Concrete + 1-in. or 2-in. Insulation
C	2-in. Insulation + 4-in. Concrete
C	8-in. Concrete
B	8-in. Concrete + 1-in. or 2-in. Insulation
A	2-in. Insulation + 8-in. Concrete
B	12-in. Concrete
A	12-in. Concrete + Insulation
	L.W. and H.W. Concrete Block + (*Finish*)
F	4-in. Block + Air Space/Insulation
E	2-in. Insulation + 4-in. Block
E	8-in. Block
D	8-in. Block + Air Space/Insulation
	Clay Tile + (*Finish*)
F	4-in. Tile
F	4-in. Tile + Air Space
E	4-in. Tile + 1-in. Insulation
D	2-in. Insulation + 4-in. Tile
D	8-in. Tile
C	8-in. Tile + Air Space 1-in. Insulation
B	2-in. Insulation + 8-in. Tile
	Metal Curtain Wall
B	With/without air Space + 1-in./2-in. 3-in. Insulation
	Frame Wall
G	1-in. to 3-in. Insulation

Group Categories for Wall Construction

Source: American Society of Heating, Refrigerating and Air-Conditioning Engineers, *ASHRAE Handbook: 1981 Fundamentals* ©1981. Reprinted by permission of ASHRAE.

North Latitude Wall Facing	1	2	3	4	5	6	7	8	9	10	11	12	13	14	15	16	17	18	19	20	21	22	23	24
Group A Walls																								
N	14	14	14	13	13	13	12	12	11	11	10	10	10	10	10	10	11	11	12	12	13	13	14	14
NE	19	19	19	18	17	17	16	15	15	15	15	15	16	16	17	18	18	18	19	19	20	20	20	20
E	24	24	23	23	22	21	20	19	19	18	19	19	18	18	19	20	21	22	23	23	24	24	24	24
SE	24	23	23	22	21	20	20	19	18	18	18	18	18	19	20	21	22	23	23	24	24	24	24	24
S	20	20	19	19	18	18	17	16	16	15	14	14	14	14	14	15	16	17	18	19	19	20	20	20
SW	25	25	25	24	24	23	22	21	20	19	19	18	17	17	17	17	18	19	20	22	23	24	25	25
W	27	27	26	26	25	24	24	23	22	21	20	19	19	18	18	18	18	19	20	22	23	25	26	26
NW	21	21	21	20	20	19	19	18	17	16	16	15	15	14	14	14	15	15	16	17	18	19	20	21
Group B Walls																								
N	15	14	14	13	12	11	11	10	9	9	9	8	9	9	9	10	11	12	13	14	14	15	15	15
NE	19	18	17	16	15	14	13	12	12	13	14	15	16	17	18	19	19	20	20	21	21	21	20	20
E	23	22	21	20	18	17	16	15	15	15	17	19	21	22	24	25	26	26	27	27	26	26	25	24
SE	23	22	21	20	18	17	15	14	14	15	16	16	18	20	21	23	24	25	26	26	26	26	25	24
S	21	20	19	18	17	15	14	13	12	11	11	11	11	12	14	15	17	19	20	21	22	22	22	21
SW	27	26	25	24	22	21	19	18	16	15	14	14	13	13	14	15	17	20	22	25	27	28	28	28
W	29	28	27	26	24	23	21	19	18	17	16	15	14	14	14	15	17	19	22	25	27	29	29	30
NW	23	22	21	20	19	18	17	15	14	13	12	12	12	11	12	12	13	15	17	19	21	22	23	23
Group C Walls																								
N	15	14	13	12	11	10	9	8	8	7	7	8	8	9	10	12	13	14	15	16	17	17	17	16
NE	19	17	16	14	13	11	10	10	11	13	15	17	19	20	21	22	22	23	23	23	23	22	21	20
E	22	21	19	17	15	14	12	12	14	16	19	22	25	27	29	29	30	30	30	29	28	27	26	24
SE	22	21	19	17	15	14	12	12	12	13	16	19	22	24	26	28	29	29	29	29	28	27	26	24
S	21	19	18	16	15	13	12	10	9	9	9	10	11	14	17	20	22	24	25	26	25	25	24	22
SW	29	27	25	22	20	18	16	15	13	12	11	11	11	13	15	18	22	26	29	32	33	33	32	31
W	31	29	27	25	22	20	18	16	14	13	12	12	10	10	11	13	15	18	22	29	32	35	35	33
NW	25	23	21	20	18	16	14	13	11	10	10	10	10	11	12	13	15	18	22	25	27	27	27	26
Group D Walls																								
N	15	13	12	10	9	7	6	6	6	6	6	7	8	10	12	13	15	17	18	19	19	19	18	16
NE	17	15	13	11	10	8	7	8	10	14	17	20	22	23	23	24	24	25	25	24	23	22	20	18
E	19	17	15	13	11	9	8	9	12	17	22	27	30	32	33	33	32	32	31	30	28	26	24	22
SE	20	17	15	13	11	10	8	8	10	13	17	22	26	29	31	32	32	32	31	30	28	26	24	22
S	19	17	15	13	11	9	8	7	6	6	7	9	12	16	20	24	27	29	29	29	27	26	24	22
SW	28	25	22	19	16	14	12	10	9	8	8	8	10	12	16	21	27	32	36	38	38	37	34	31
W	31	27	24	21	18	15	13	11	10	9	9	9	10	11	14	18	24	30	36	40	41	40	38	34
NW	25	22	19	17	14	12	10	9	8	7	7	8	9	10	12	14	18	22	27	31	32	32	30	27
Group E Walls																								
N	12	10	8	7	5	4	3	4	5	6	7	9	11	13	15	17	19	20	21	23	20	18	16	14
NE	13	11	5	9	7	6	4	9	15	20	24	25	25	26	26	26	26	26	25	24	22	19	17	15
E	14	12	10	8	6	5	6	11	18	26	33	36	38	37	36	34	33	32	30	28	25	22	20	17
SE	15	12	10	8	7	5	5	8	12	19	25	31	35	37	37	36	34	33	31	28	26	23	20	17
S	15	12	10	8	7	5	4	3	4	5	9	13	19	24	29	32	34	33	31	29	26	23	20	17
SW	22	18	15	12	10	8	6	5	5	6	7	9	12	18	24	32	38	43	45	44	40	35	30	26
W	25	21	17	14	11	9	7	6	6	6	7	9	11	14	20	27	36	43	49	49	45	40	34	29
NW	20	17	14	11	9	7	6	5	5	5	6	8	10	13	16	20	26	32	37	38	36	32	28	24
Group F Walls																								
N	8	6	5	3	2	1	2	4	6	7	9	11	14	17	19	21	22	23	24	23	20	16	13	11
NE	9	7	5	3	2	1	5	14	23	28	30	29	28	27	27	27	27	26	24	22	19	16	13	11
E	10	7	6	4	3	2	6	17	28	38	44	45	43	39	36	34	32	30	27	24	21	17	15	12
SE	10	7	6	4	3	2	4	10	19	28	36	41	43	42	39	36	34	31	28	25	21	18	15	12
S	10	8	6	4	3	2	1	1	3	7	13	20	27	34	38	39	38	35	31	26	22	18	15	12
SW	15	11	9	6	5	3	2	2	4	5	8	11	17	26	35	44	50	53	52	45	37	28	23	18
W	17	13	10	7	5	4	3	3	4	6	8	11	14	20	28	39	49	57	60	54	43	34	27	21
NW	14	10	8	6	4	3	2	2	3	5	8	10	13	15	21	27	35	42	46	43	35	28	22	18
Group G Walls																								
N	3	2	1	0	−1	2	7	8	9	12	15	18	21	23	24	24	25	26	22	15	11	9	7	5
NE	3	2	1	0	−1	9	27	36	39	35	30	26	26	27	27	26	25	22	18	14	11	9	7	5
E	4	2	1	0	−1	11	31	47	54	55	50	40	33	31	30	29	27	24	19	15	12	10	8	6
SE	4	2	1	0	−1	5	18	32	42	49	51	48	42	36	32	30	27	24	19	15	12	10	8	6
S	4	2	1	0	−1	0	1	5	12	22	31	39	45	46	43	37	31	25	20	15	12	10	8	5
SW	5	4	3	1	0	0	2	5	8	12	16	26	38	50	59	63	61	52	37	24	17	13	10	8
W	6	5	3	2	1	1	2	5	8	11	15	19	27	41	56	67	72	67	48	29	20	15	11	8
NW	5	3	2	1	0	0	2	5	8	11	15	18	21	27	37	47	55	55	41	25	17	13	10	7

CLTD Table—Walls

Source: American Society of Heating, Refrigerating and Air-Conditioning Engineers, *ASHRAE Handbook: 1981 Fundamentals* ©1981. Reprinted by permission of ASHRAE.

Direct Application of the Wall CLTD Table Without Adjustments:

Values in the table were calculated using the same conditions for walls as outlined for the roof CLTD table. These values can be used for all normal airconditioning estimates usually without correction when the load is calculated for the hottest weather.

For totally shaded walls use the north orientation values.

Adjustments to Table Values:

The following equation makes adjustments for conditions other than those listed in Note (1).

$$CLTD_{corr} = (CLTD + LM) \times K + (78 - T_R) + (T_o - 85)$$

— LM is the latitude-month correction.

— K is a color adjustment factor and is applied after first making month-latitude adjustment

$K = 1.0$ if dark colored or light in an industrial area

$K = 0.83$ if permanently medium-colored (rural area)

$K = 0.65$ if permanently light-colored (rural area)

Credit should not be taken for wall color other than dark except where permanence of color is established by experience, as in rural areas or where there is little smoke.

Colors: Light — Cream

Medium — Medium blue, medium green, bright red, light brown, unpainted wood, and natural color concrete

Dark — Dark blue, red, brown and green

— $(78 - T_R)$ is indoor design temperature correction

— $(T_o - 85)$ is outdoor design temperature correction, where T_o is the average outside temperature on design day.

Additional Insulation:

For each 7 increase in R-value due to insulation added to the wall structures, use the CLTD for the wall group with the next higher letter in the alphabet. When the insulation is added to the exterior of the construction rather to than the interior, use the CLTD for the wall group two letters higher. If this is not possible, due to having already selected a wall on Group A, use an effective CLTD in the load calculation as given in the following table.

CLTD, Uncorrected, When Vertical Wall Structure is "Thermally" Heavier than Group A due to Added Insulation

N	NE	E	SE	S	SW	W	NW
11	17	22	21	17	21	22	17

CLTD Corrections—Walls

☐ The corrected CLTD is used to compute the cooling load caused by envelope heat gain in the following formula:
Envelope cooling load (BTU/hr.) = U × A × CLTD

Determine the cooling load temperature difference for a Group D wall facing south, at 2 P.M. solar time on October 21 at 32 degrees North Latitude. The wall is dark, the indoor temperature is 78°F, the outdoor maximum temperature is 95 degrees (F.), and the outdoor daily range is 21 degrees (F.).
Solution: From the CLTD wall table, the CLTD at 2 P.M. solar time is 16 degrees (F.). However, the value must be corrected for latitude and time of year; from the correction factor table, for a south wall at 32 degrees North Lat. for October 21, the CLTD correction is 11 degrees (F.). Therefore, the corrected CLTD is: 16 + 11 = 27 degrees (F.).
A building 30′ × 100′ × 10′ is located at 32 degrees North Latitude in an area with a design outside dry-bulb temperature of 90 degrees (F.). and a daily range of 20 degrees (F.). The inside design dry-bulb temperature is 78 degrees (F.). Determine the cooling load as a result of heat gain through the roof and south walls at solar noon for July 21. The south wall measures 100′ × 10′.

Constructions are:
—Roof: Built-up roof, 2-inch heavyweight concrete, 2-inch insulation (R = 6.7), and a suspended ceiling of acoustic tile. Assume f = 1.0.
—South Wall: 8-inch heavyweight concrete with 2-inch insulation (R = 6.7) and interior flush.
Solution: The U-values (from U-value tables) and respective areas are shown below.

	Roof (No. 4)	S. Wall (Group B)
U-value	0.091	0.115
Area	3000	1000

☐ The correction factors to be applied to the tabulated CLTDs are:
—Correction for outside conditions: average temperature = 80 degrees (F.). Correction = 80 − 85 = −5 degrees (F.)
—Correction for 78°F inside design dry-bulb temperature: No correction
—Latitude-month correction: No correction
—Color correction: No correction

—Total correction:

Roof, $CLTD_{corr} = [(CLTD+0) \times 1.0 + (0) + (-5)$
$\times 1.0 = CLTD - 5$

S. Wall, $CLTD_{corr}$
$= (CLTD + 0) \times 1.0$
$+ (0) + (-5) = CLTD - 5$

Time	CLTD	CLTD$_{corr}$	UA × CLTD (BTU/hr.)
		Roof	
Noon	25	25 − 5 = 20	.091 × 3000 × 20 = 5460
		South Wall	
Noon	12	12 − 5 = 7	.115 × 1000 × 7 = 805

Lat.	Month	N	NNE NNW	NE NW	ENE WNW	E W	ESE WSW	SE SW	SSE SSW	S	HOR
24	Dec	−5	−7	−9	−10	−7	−3	3	9	13	−13
	Jan/Nov	−4	−6	−8	−9	−6	−3	3	9	13	−11
	Feb/Oct	−4	−5	−6	−6	−3	−1	3	7	10	−7
	Mar/Sept	−3	−4	−3	−3	−1	−1	1	2	4	−3
	April/Aug	−2	−1	0	−1	−1	−2	−1	−2	−3	0
	May/July	1	2	2	0	0	−3	−3	−5	−6	1
	June	3	3	3	1	0	−3	−4	−6	−6	1
32	Dec	−5	−7	−10	−11	−8	−5	2	9	12	−17
	Jan/Nov	−5	−7	−9	−11	−8	−4	2	9	12	−15
	Feb/Oct	−4	−6	−7	−8	−4	−2	4	8	11	−10
	Mar/Sept	−3	−4	−4	−4	−2	−1	3	5	7	−5
	April/Aug	−2	−2	−1	−2	0	−1	0	1	1	−1
	May/July	1	1	1	0	0	−1	−1	−3	−3	1
	June	1	2	2	1	0	−2	−2	−4	−4	2
40	Dec	−6	−8	−10	−13	−10	−7	0	7	10	−21
	Jan/Nov	−5	−7	−10	−12	−9	−6	1	8	11	−19
	Feb/Oct	−5	−7	−8	−9	−6	−3	3	8	12	−14
	Mar/Sept	−4	−5	−5	−6	−3	−1	4	7	10	−8
	April/Aug	−2	−3	−2	−2	0	0	2	3	4	−3
	May/July	0	0	0	0	0	0	0	0	1	1
	June	1	1	1	0	1	0	0	−1	−1	2
48	Dec	−6	−8	−11	−14	−13	−10	−3	2	6	−25
	Jan/Nov	−6	−8	−11	−13	−11	−8	−1	5	8	−24
	Feb/Oct	−5	−7	−10	−11	−8	−5	1	8	11	−18
	Mar/Sept	−4	−6	−6	−7	−4	−1	4	8	11	−11
	April/Aug	−3	−3	−3	−3	−1	0	4	6	7	−5
	May/July	0	−1	0	0	1	1	3	3	4	0
	June	1	1	2	1	2	1	2	2	3	2

CLTD Latitude Month Corrections—Roofs and Walls

Source: American Society of Heating, Refrigerating and Air-Conditioning Engineers, *ASHRAE Handbook: 1981 Fundamentals* ©1981. Reprinted by permission of ASHRAE.

Glazing

☐ Heat gain from solar radiation through glazing was discussed in an earlier section. Whether or not sunlight is present, heat also flows through glazing by thermal conduction, as expressed by the following formula:

Glazing heat gain (BTU/hr.) = $U \times A \times (t_O - t_i)$

Where:

U = overall coefficient of heat transfer for the glazing, BTU/hr. × square feet × degrees (F.)

A = glazing area, square feet

t_O = outside air temperature, degrees (F.)

t_i = inside air temperature, degrees (F.).

☐ The accompanying table of cooling load temperature differences for glazing is used the same for walls as for roofs:

Glazing cooling load (BTU/hr.) = $U \times A \times$ CLTD

Solar Time, Hr. CLTD	1	2	3	4	5	6	7	8	9	10	11	12	13	14	15	16	17	18	19	20	21	22	23	24
F	1	0	−1	−2	−2	−2	−2	0	2	4	7	9	12	13	14	14	13	12	10	8	6	4	3	2

Corrections: The values in the table were calculated for an inside temperature of 78°F and for an outdoor maximum temperature of 95°F with an outdoor daily range of 21°F. The table remains approximately correct for other outdoor maximums 93-102°F and for other outdoor daily ranges 16-34 F, provided the outdoor daily average temperature remains approximately 85°F. If the room air temperature is different from 78 F and/or the outdoor daily average temperature is different from 85 F, the following rules apply: (a) For room air temperature less than 78°F, add the difference between 78°F and the room air temperature; if greater than 78°F, subtract the difference. (b) For outdoor daily average temperature less than 85°F, subtract the difference betwen 85°F and the daily average temperature; if greater than 85°F, add the difference.

CLTD Table—Glass

Source: American Society of Heating, Refrigerating and Air-Conditioning Engineers, *ASHRAE Handbook: 1981 Fundamentals* ©1981. Reprinted by permission of ASHRAE.

Thermal Balance

Thermal balance analysis adds up simultaneously occurring heat gains and heat losses to determine whether there is an overall loss or gain. Thermal balance calculations can be performed for rooms, zones, orientations, or entire buildings. They can also be performed for different times of day or year. The calculation compares the heat gain from lights, occupants, equipment, and solar to the losses and gains from envelope transmission and ventilation, including infiltration.

☐ The balance point is the theoretical condition where building gross heat gains equal gross heat losses. It has nothing to do with the action of an airconditioning or heating system on building loads. It is affected by occupancy schedules, solar gain, and other factors that have time lag effects.

☐ In the balance point model depicted in the accompanying figure, heat gains equal heat losses whenever the outdoor air temperature is above 52 degrees (F.) without sunshine, and 41 degrees (F.) with sunshine. Theoretically, this means that at these temperatures the building needs no heat addition or reduction. This analysis also shows the magnitude of the heat loss and gain components and their interrelations. This can provide an indication of potential tradeoffs among them.

☐ The first figure shown here represents a load analysis of an office building in a relatively cold area, where the effect of weather is noticeable. This is a large building with a relatively low envelope heat loss compared to internal heat gains. This relationship shifts the energy balance point to a lower temperature than it would be otherwise.

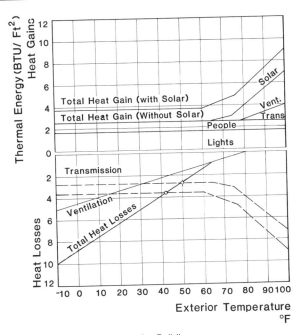

Thermal Balance Analysis of a Building

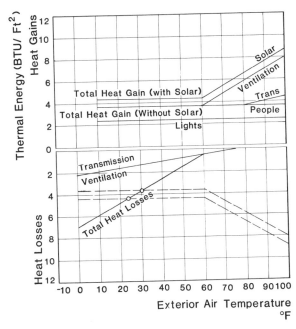

Thermal Balance Analysis of an Office Building (Cold Climate)

459

☐ The second figure represents load analysis of a school, where heat gains due to occupants are large, as are lighting loads. Large heat losses and very small heat gains are attributable to the ventilation air, because the school is in an area where the summer average temperature is only 64 degrees (F.).

☐ The third figure represents the large loads typical in a hospital located in a warm climate. Reduction of large ventilation loads may provide significant opportunities for energy savings.

☐ The graphs discussed thus far plot thermal balance over a year. Graphics of daily thermal balance can give a different view. The figure shown here indicates the wide variations that can occur during a single day.

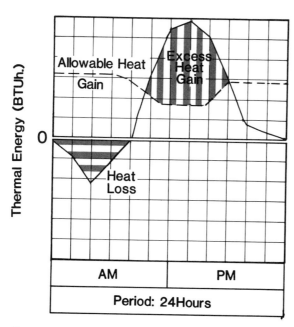

Thermal Balance Analysis (Daily)

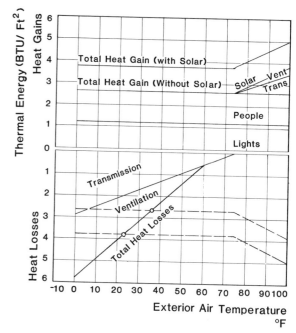

Thermal Balance Analysis of a School (Temperate Climate)

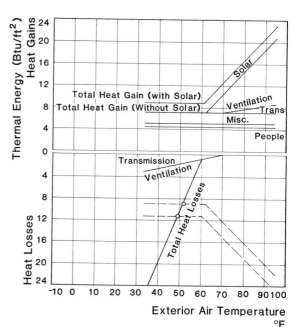

Thermal Balance Analysis of a Hospital (Warm Climate)

460

□ The accompanying figure shows how heat gain/loss components can be analyzed graphically over a year.

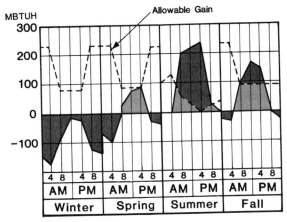

Composite Graph of Energy Performance

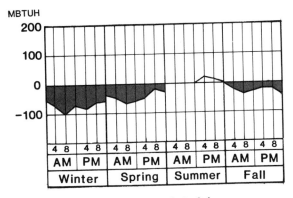

Envelope Heat Gain & Loss

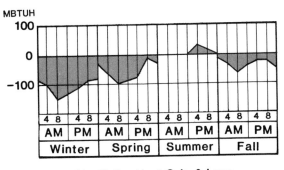

Ventilation Heat Gain & Loss

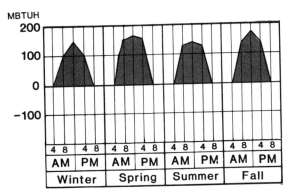

Solar Heat Gain

Composites of Thermal Balance Analysis

Source: Booz-Allen & Hamilton, Inc. *Energy Graphics* (for U.S. Department of Energy). Washington, D.C.: 1980.

Increase Internal Heat Gain	Decrease Internal Heat Gain
Concentrate Density of Heat Gains —Centralize spatial location of heat gain sources —Modify occupancy schedule —Use available heat sources	**Reduce Lighting Use by Employing Daylighting** —Increase window size —Locate windows high in the wall —Control glare with drapes, shutters —Eliminate direct sunlight, reflect into spaces —Slope walls to self-shade windows and reflect light —Use clear glazing —Use light colors on interior walls —Use automatic dimming controls on electric lighting Increase Exposure of High Heat Gain Areas —Increase local volumetric and/or ventilation loss —Isolate heat gain sources —Locate heat gain source in proximity to areas needing heat gain Capture Heat and Store or Transfer to Heat Loss Areas —Heat of light recovery —Heat recovery from condenser water —Water as equipment cooling medium Modify Occupancy Schedule to Shift or Disperse Internal Heat Gains Throughout Period —Shift heat gain operation to time when gain can be accommodated —Stagger operation of equipment to allow heat gain to dissipate —Use heat sinks if available.

Design Strategies for Thermal Balance

Increase Solar Gain	Decrease Solar Gain
Increase Exposure to Direct Solar Radiation —Provide reflectors to concentrate insolation —Avoid shading —Increase surface area to enclosed volume ratio —Slope roof toward south —Use clear glazing Reduce Reflectance —Use dark colors on walls/roof —Texture surfaces Consider Active Solar Heating —Hot water system —Hot air system	**Decrease Surfaces Exposed to Radiation** —Reduce surface area to enclosed volume ratio —Utilize site elements for shading —Orient building to minimize insolation —Configure building edge to provide self-shading —Provide shading devices Increase Reflectance —Use smooth surfaces —Use light colors —Use solar film on glazing Increase Thermal Transmission Resistance —Decrease U Increase Heat Capacity —Increase thermal mass Consider Solar Cooling —Absorption cooling for active systems —Long wave radiation for passive systems

Design Strategies for Thermal Balance

462

Envelope

Decrease Internal Heat Loss: (Winter)*

Decrease U, Increasing Thermal Resistance
—Increase insulation
—Use double roof with ventilation space in between
—Texture surface to increase film coefficient
—Protect insulation from moisture
—Use multiple-layer glazing
—Use operable thermal shutters
—Eliminate thermal bridges
—Use both horizontal and vertical insulation for slab on grade
—Use movable insulation

Decrease Exposure to cold outside air
—Reduce surface area to enclosed volume ratio
—Consider below grade location for part(s) of the building
—Consider compact configuration (low length/width aspect ratio)
—Reduce floor-to-floor dimension
—Avoid elevated buildings, large overhangs, parking garages or intermediate levels

Decrease Infiltration
—Minimize wind effects by orienting major axis into the wind
—Site near existing windbreaks
—Provide vestibules for entrances
—Locate entrances on downwind side of building
—Reduce building height
—Use impermeable exterior surface materials
—Seal all vertical shafts
—Vertically offset or stagger stairwells, elevator shafts, mechanical shafts to avoid chimney effect
—Articulate surface with fins, recesses

Decrease the Temperature Differential
—Consider below grade location
—Employ highly textured surface
—Plant deciduous trees adjacent to building to moderate surface temperatures

Envelope

Increase Internal Heat Loss: (Winter)*

Increase U, Decreasing Thermal Resistance
—Increase openings
—Provide thermal bridges
—Use single glazing
—Decrease film coefficient by using smooth surfaces
—Decrease movable insulation

Increase Exposure
—Increase surface area to enclosed volume ratio
—Elevate building, provide intermediate open spaces
—Consider loose (large amount of edge) configuration

Increase Temperature Differential Through Site Manipulation
—Shade during cold periods
—Absorb cold in mass around building

Decrease External Heat Gain: (Summer)*

Decrease U, Increasing Thermal Resistance
—Increase insulation
—Use double roof with exhausted air space in between
—Texture surface to increase film coefficient
—Protect insulation from moisture
—Use multiple-layer glazing
—Use operable thermal shutters
—Eliminate thermal bridges
—Use both horizontal and vertical insulation for slab on grade
—Use movable insulation

Decrease Exposure
—Reduce surface area to enclosed volume ratio
—Consider below-grade location for part(s) of the building
—Consider compact configuration (low length/width aspect ratio)
—Reduce floor-to-floor dimension
—Avoid elevated buildings, large overhangs, parking garages or intermediate levels

Decrease Infiltration
—Minimize wind effects by orienting major axis into the wind
—Site near existing windbreaks
—Provide vestibules
—Locate entrances on downwind side of building
—Reduce building height
—Use impermeable exterior surface materials
—Seal all vertical shafts
—Vertically offset or stagger stairwells, elevator shafts, mechanical shafts to avoid chimney effect
—Articulate surface with fins, recesses

Decrease the Temperature Differential
—Consider below-grade location
—Use water, fountains to decrease heat buildup
—Employ highly textured surface
—Reduce paved areas in vicinity of building
—Plant deciduous trees adjacent to building to moderate surface temperatures

Design Strategies for Thermal Balance

Ventilation	Ventilation

Ventilation

Decrease Internal Heat Loss: (Winter)*
Decrease Rate, N
—Cascade ventilation
—Use recycled air and minimum fresh air for large requirements
—Filter contaminated air for recycling
—Periodically shut down the system for a short time if allowable
—Credit infiltration toward general ventilation requirement
—Place operable windows on adjacent walls to reduce through-ventilation

Decrease the Temperature Differential
—Increase solar radiation at air intakes during cold periods
—Transfer energy from exhaust air to incoming air

Increase External Gain: (Summer)*

Increase Rate, N
—Increase ventilation rate subject to maximum tolerable level (limited by noise, air movement)
—Orient operable windows to windward and leeward sides of the building

Increase Temperature Differential
—Reduce shade on intake during hot periods
—Reduce evaporative cooling effects

Ventilation

Increase Internal Heat Loss: (Winter)*
Increase Rate, N
—Use economizer cycle (check humidity level)
—Increase ventilation rate subject to maximum tolerable level (limited by noise, air movement)
—Orient operable windows to windward and leeward sides of the building

Increase Temperature Differential
—Shade intake during cold periods
—Consider evaporative cooling

Decrease External Gain: (Summer)*

Decrease Rate, N
—Cascade ventilation
—Use recycled air and minimum fresh air for large requirements
—Filter contaminated air for recycling
—Periodically shut down the system for a short time if allowable
—Credit infiltration toward general ventilation requirement
—Place operable windows on adjacent walls to reduce through-ventilation

Decrease the Temperature Differential
—Shade air intakes during hot periods
—Consider evaporative cooling

Design Strategies for Thermal Balance.

Storage

Use Heat from Storage
Actively:
—Use hot water systems
—Use hot air system with rock storage
—Use eutectic salt storage system

Passively:
—Use Thermal Mass

Storage

Store Heat for Later Use
Actively:
—Use hot water systems
—Use hot air system with rock storage
—Use eutectic salt storage system

Passively:
—Use thermal mass to store heat

Store Cold for Later Use

Actively:
—Use chilled water tanks (run chillers at coolest diurnal temperature)

Passively:
—Use thermal mass to store nighttime cold by use of night flushing

Design Strategies for Thermal Balance

*Notes:
Winter—Condition where inside is kept warmer than outside.
Summer—Condition where inside is kept cooler than outside.
In many climates summer and winter conditions can occur during various times of the year. In some climates winter and summer conditions can occur in the same day.

464

Estimating Energy Use

Although the procedures used for estimating energy use vary considerably by methodology and sophistication, they have three common elements—the calculation of:

—space loads
—operating loads for lighting, DHW and equipment
—HVAC system loads.

☐ Space loads, or heating and cooling loads, determine the amounts of energy which must be added to or extracted from a space to maintain thermal comfort. They are determined by the following heat gains and losses of the building:

—occupant heat gains
—lighting heat gains
—equipment heat gains
—solar heat gains
—ventilation/infiltration heat gains or losses
—envelope heat gains or losses.

☐ Operating loads determine the amounts of energy required to operate the lighting, DHW, conveyance systems and other equipment in the building to perform functions or activities.

☐ The HVAC system loads refer to the amount of energy required to convert fuel or electric energy to heating or cooling effect to meet the space loads. HVAC system loads give consideration to system efficiencies and part-load characteristics.

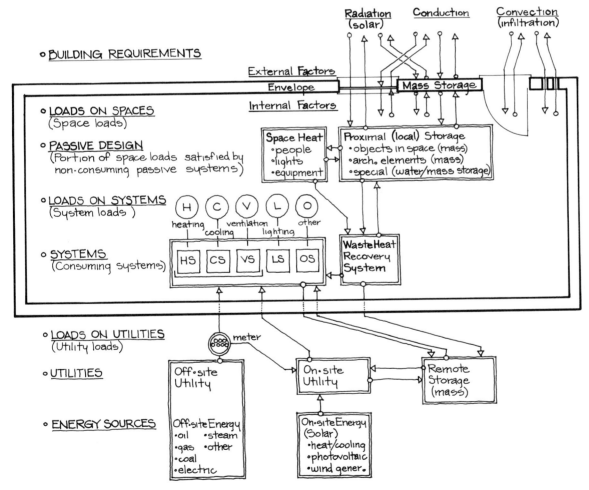

Energy Flow Diagram

465

☐ Four common estimating methods are discussed in this section:
—degree day method
—bin method
—modified bin method
—hour-by-hour simulation.

☐ Prior to the availability of hourly calculation techniques, designers used a great variety of methods for predicting system operating conditions and calculating energy consumption in commercial and industrial buildings. Virtually all these techniques were based on an assumed or measured set of average conditions taken from a relatively small sampling of buildings. However, the diverse architectural and operational characteristics of today's commercial and industrial buildings have greatly limited the applicability of the estimating techniques based on averages. Today, it is not common to find that in a given location, buildings have an annual energy consumption on the order of 50 percent more or less than the average.

Percent Building Load

Energy Use by Building Types (1976)

Degree-Day Method

☐ The *degree-day method* is an average-based technique once common in energy analyses, chiefly for heating season estimates.

☐ Degree days are a temperature statistic for predicting the energy loss of buildings because of the differential of inside-to-outside temperatures. Assuming that energy transfer over time is linearly related to the inside-to-outside temperature difference, the accumulation of inside-to-outside temperature differences over time will give the energy loads on the building over that time.

The degree-day procedure recognizes that although the energy transferred out of a building is proportional to the difference between interior temperature and the outside temperature, the furnace needs to meet only the part that is not met by internal heat sources such as lights, equipment, occupants, and solar gain. In other words, the energy requirements are met by these sources down to the *balance point temperature*, below which the energy requirements of the furnace are proportional to the difference between the balance point temperature and the outside temperature.

At the balance point temperature, heat losses by conduction and ventilation equal the internal gains.

☐ The degree-day method establishes a base temperature, effectively an assumed balance point, usually 65 degrees (F.), below which the building begins to require heating.

☐ A degree day is defined as a 24-hour-period during which the average temperature is one degree below the base. For example if the average temperature for March 15 is 64 degrees (F.), this represents one degree day.

☐ For any one day, there are as many degree days as there are degrees difference in temperature between the mean temperature for the day and 65 degrees (F.). If the average temperature on January 17 is 25 degrees (F.), that day would represent 40 degree days $(65 - 25 = 40)$.

☐ Heating load calculations can be subdivided into degree day increments. This is accomplished by dividing the total heating load by the difference between the base temperature and the outside heating design temperature. For example, if the outside design temperature is 15 degrees (F.) then one fiftieth $(65 - 15 = 50)$ of the calculated heating load is required to satisfy one degree day.

466

☐ This value can be multiplied by the annual degree days and divided by furnace efficiency to estimate annual energy use for heating.

☐ The traditional use of 65 degrees (F.) as a base for degree days is founded on correlations between energy and degree days made in the 1930's. Since then, heat gains from internal sources have gone up severalfold and conductances have decreased with the increased use of insulation. Calculations made with 65 degree-based degree days accordingly overestimate energy loads on most modern buildings.

☐ Recognizing this, the National Climatic Center, Ashville, North Carolina has published degree days to a wide range of base temperatures.

☐ Any load calculation procedure using only mean temperatures as a climate describer will not account for the daily temperature swings. This omission can cause significant underestimation of loads in mild climates. For example, a building might require heat during parts of a day whose proper degree day total is zero.

☐ Degree-day methods for estimating cooling energy are less well established than those for heating. This is because the indoor-outdoor temperature difference under cooling conditions is typically smaller than under heating conditions. As a result, cooling loads depend more strongly on such factors as solar gain and internal loads than do heating loads. Since these loads are highly variable, attempts to correlate cooling energy requirements against a single climate parameter have not been highly successful.

Bin Method

☐ The *temperature frequency occurrence or bin method* is an estimating technique that has become more frequently used in recent years.

☐ The bin method consists of performing a series of instantaneous energy calculations rather than a single calculation in the degree day method. The bin method can take into account varying parameters and characteristics of modern commercial buildings.

State	City	Temperature (F.)	Degree Days
Alabama	Birmingham	10	2,551
Alaska	Fairbanks	−60	14,279
Arizona	Flagstaff	−5	7,152
	Phoenix	35	1,765
Arkansas	Little Rock	10	3,219
California	Los Angeles	40	2,061
	San Diego	45	1,458
	San Francisco	35	3,015
Colorado	Denver	−10	6,283
Connecticut	Hartford	0	6,235
Delaware	Wilmington	5	4,930
District of Columbia	Washington	10	4,224
Florida	Miami	45	214
	Tallahassee	25	1,485
Georgia	Atlanta	10	2,961
	Savannah	25	1,819
Hawaii	Honolulu	60	0
Idaho	Boise	−10	5,809
Illinois	Chicago	−10	6,639
Indiana	Indianapolis	−10	5,699
Iowa	Des Moines	−15	6,588
Kansas	Wichita	−5	4,620
Kentucky	Louisville	0	4,660
Louisiana	Baton Rouge	20	1,560
	New Orleans	25	1,385
Maine	Portland	−10	7,511
Maryland	Baltimore	10	4,654
Massachusetts	Boston	0	5,634

Recommended Outside Design Temperatures and Heating Degree Days

Source: Egan, M. David, *Concepts in Thermal Comfort*, © 1975. Reprinted by permission of Prentice-Hall, Inc., Englewood Cliffs, New Jersey.

State	City	Temperature (F.)	Degree Days
Michigan	Detroit	−5	6,293
Minnesota	Minneapolis	−25	8,382
Mississippi	Jackson	15	2,239
Missouri	St. Louis	−5	5,484
Montana	Billings	−30	7,049
Nebraska	Lincoln	−15	5,864
Nevada	Las Vegas	10	2,709
New Hampshire	Manchester	−10	7,383
New Jersey	Atlantic City	10	4,812
	Newark	0	4,589
	Trenton	0	4,980
New Mexico	Albuquerque	10	4,348
New York	Albany	−10	6,875
	New York	5	5,219
North Carolina	Greensboro	10	3,805
North Dakota	Bismarck	−30	8,851
Ohio	Cincinnati	−5	4,410
Oklahoma	Tulsa	0	3,860
Oregon	Portland	10	4,635
Pennsylvania	Philadelphia	5	5,144
	Pittsburgh	−5	5,987
Rhode Island	Providence	0	5,954
South Carolina	Columbia	20	2,484
	Greenville	10	2,980
South Dakota	Rapid City	−20	7,345
Tennessee	Chattanooga	10	3,254
	Knoxville	5	3,494
	Nashville	5	3,578
Texas	Dallas	10	2,363
	Houston	20	1,396
Utah	Salt Lake City	0	6,052
Vermont	Burlington	−15	8,269
Virginia	Charlottesville	10	4,166
	Richmond	10	3,865
Washington	Seattle	15	4,424
West Virginia	Charleston	0	4,476
Wisconsin	Milwaukee	−15	7,635
Wyoming	Cheyenne	−20	7,381

Recommended Outside Design Temperatures and Heating Degree Days

☐ A bin is a group of temperatures into which all temperatures occurring between the two bin points fall. For example:

45–50 degrees (F.) BIN
45–46–47–48–49–50

50–55 degrees (F.) BIN
50–51–52–53–54–55

55–60 degrees (F.) BIN
55–56–57–58–59–60

☐ Since temperature changes frequently by 2 or more degrees within an hour, it is difficult to establish the length of time the temperature was at a precise degree point. Grouping temperatures into small groups or bins enables them to be measured more realistically.

☐ While the basic bin method provides for load calculations at various temperatures, it assumes that internal load and solar radiation load are constant during the operating period covered by the temperature bins. This drawback can be overcome somewhat by establishing temperature bins on 5-degree (F.) and 1-hour increments instead of 10-degree (F.) and 8-hour increments. The accompanying table shows a cooling energy calculation using the bin method for occupied hours.

Temperature Bin (F.)	Load BTUH/Sq. Ft.	×	Annual Occupied Time, Hours	=	Cooling Energy BTU/Sq. Ft.
90–95	37		91		3360
85–90	34		152		5160
80–85	32		225		7200
75–80	29		270		7810
70–75	26		303		7870
			Total		

Cooling Estimation: Bin Method

☐ In addition to the energy used by the building while occupied, additional energy is consumed during periods when the building is unoccupied with the airconditioning system operating, and during shut-down periods. Each of these can be treated in the same manner as the occupied periods.

☐ Weather data for use with the bin method are available in Air Force Manual 88-29, *Engineering Weather Data*, Government Printing Office, Washington, D.C. 26402.

Modified Bin Method

☐ The modified bin method has the advantage of allowing calculations by use of varying load values, rather than peak load values to establish the load as a function of outdoor dry-bulb temperature. Furthermore, the modified bin method allows the incorporation of HVAC system effects into the energy calculation.

☐ In the modified bin method, average solar gain profiles and average equipment- and lighting-use profiles are used to characterize the time-dependent varying loads. Time dependencies resulting from scheduling are averaged over a selected period, or multiple calculation periods are established. The duration of a calculation period determines the number of bin hours included in it. Normally, two calculation periods representing occupied and unoccupied hours are sufficient.

☐ Loads resulting from solar gains through glazings are calculated by determining a weighted-average solar load for a summer and a winter day, and then establishing a linear relationship of this solar load as a function of outdoor ambient temperature.

☐ Once a total load profile is determined as a function of outdoor ambient temperature for the occupied and unoccupied periods, the performance of the HVAC system is calculated. Then the annual energy consumption is determined using bin-hour weather data.

Hour-By-Hour Method

☐ The greatest flexibility and accuracy in the prediction of energy requirements is achieved by procedures that consider the various energy-related factors with an *hour-by-hour* method. The factors that such calculation techniques should be capable of handling with at least some level of detail are:

—solar load as a function of building construction, location, orientation, time of day and year, internal and external shading devices and patterns, and cloud cover

—hourly variations in building occupancy and the operation of lights and other internal heat sources for different types of days during the year

—infiltration

—night time setback or system shut-off during unoccupied periods

—the effects of lag and heat storage in determining instantaneous heat gain and carryover loads.

☐ These features enable calculation procedures to predict yearly room loads and energy consumption with a degree of precision.

☐ A single hourly calculation can be performed manually, with calculators, micro-computers or large computers.

☐ More sophisticated programs consider more factors or elements of building energy use, but in doing so require much more precise information about the building. In early design stages, when this information is often unavailable, it can be better to use a simpler method

469

with built-in reasonable assumptions about unknown quantities. Manual methods are also preferable for design situations not covered by existing computer programs.

☐ Hour-by-hour methods compute the instantaneous building load, residual stored loads, and resulting HVAC system performance separately for each of a year's 8760 hours. These are then added to obtain monthly and yearly consumption. Maximum demand (rate of energy use) is found by identifying the hour with the highest use. Building heat storage and temperature swing can also be simulated.

☐ A less extensive hour-by-hour analysis can be done for only one or more typical days of each month. The results for each day are multiplied by the number of days in the month to obtain monthly energy consumption. This averaging, however, reduces the accuracy of the estimate by eliminating extremes of weather conditions and solar and internal loads.

☐ Detailed hour-by-hour energy simulation can be very complex. The "DOE-2" program prepared for the U.S. Department of Energy is written in such a way that a user can construct a unique simulator to analyze a specific building. The DOE-2 program also has weather data for 78 U.S. cities. Called TRY (Test Reference Year), this is the actual weather for the year closest to the average of recorded weather. The National Oceanic and Atmospheric Administration (NDAA) is developing another set of city weather data called TMY (Test Meterological Year), which is a statistically generated weather year that averages all recorded data. The two accompanying figures depict the simplified and complex versions, respectively, of what the annual energy simulation programs actually accomplish.

☐ A note of caution is required concerning energy analysis methods in general and computer methods in particular. First, they vary widely in their ability to provide accurate results, giving an adequate solution for one situation and an inadequate one for a different type of building or HVAC system. Their inherent accuracy depends on:

—method of analysis, with more accuracy from sophisticated hour-by-hour methods

—accuracy of load estimating—many of the existing load-estimating methods were developed to conservatively predict maxamim design-load conditions, and as a result estimate part-load conditions inaccurately

—other hidden data and logic assumptions—which can result in misapplications not intended by the methods' authors

—accuracy of system response to building equipment performance—many methods are weak and inflexible in this area. There are at least a dozen types of variable-air-volume HVAC systems available, yet most computer programs are unable to distinguish one from another.

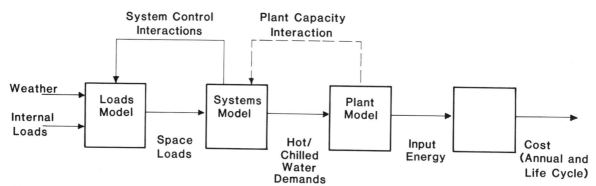

Simulation Method for Energy Estimation (Simplified)

Source: American Society of Heating, Refrigerating and Air-Conditioning Engineers, *ASHRAE Handbook: 1981 Fundamentals* ©1981. Reprinted by permission of ASHRAE.

ECONOMIC ANALYSIS

Introduction

Fuel shortages and rising fuel costs have necessitated the use of design strategies to conserve energy in buildings. While there are many energy-conservation options, only the most cost-effective energy conservation strategies over the building life will be seriously considered by building owners. The most economical alternatives can be determined through life-cycle cost/benefit analysis. This is a quantitative analysis of the costs incurred and benefits received over the life of the building.

The greatest opportunities for saving costs over the life of a building occur at the beginning of the design process. Therefore it is necessary even at this stage of design to use life-cycle cost/benefit analysis to make reasonably cost-effective decisions that will extend throughout the life of the building. Opportunities for saving dollars diminish as the design is refined, so accordingly, decisions made late in the design process have less effect on life-cycle benefits.

This monograph examines techniques for determining the life-cycle costs/benefits of any single design, as well as for determining which of two or more design alternatives is most eco-

nomical. Ways of calculating the rate of return on investment for any particular design strategy are also included, as are several other techniques for assessing the economic advantage of one design alternative compared to another. The foundation of all these techniques is the use of "equivalent dollars," a practice which enables designers to compare future costs and benefits with present ones, while taking into account the time value of money. Equivalent dollars are as powerful, analytically, as they are easy to use, and constitute an important tool for day-to-day design decisions.

Other topics presented include techniques for analyzing the effects of prices that escalate more rapidly than general inflation, the effects of first costs, maintenance, alterations, functional-use costs and taxes on life-cycle costs. Finally, because a life-cycle cost/benefit analysis must project costs into the future it requires a degree of prediction. The monograph also discusses sensitivity analysis, a method for determining the extent to which uncertainties concerning future conditions can affect the results of a life-cycle analysis.

Initial Project Development Costs

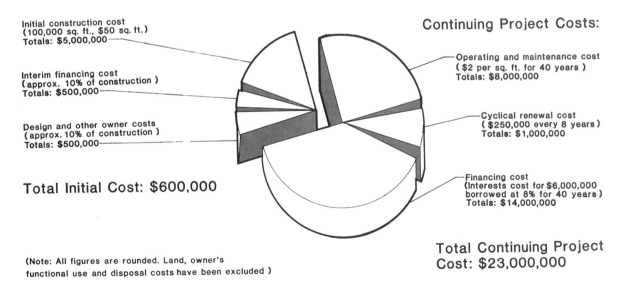

Initial construction cost
(100,000 sq. ft., $50 sq. ft.)
Totals: $5,000,000

Interim financing cost
(approx. 10% of construction)
Totals: $500,000

Design and other owner costs
(approx. 10% of construction)
Totals: $500,000

Total Initial Cost: $600,000

Continuing Project Costs:

Operating and maintenance cost
($2 per sq. ft. for 40 years)
Totals: $8,000,000

Cyclical renewal cost
($250,000 every 8 years)
Totals: $1,000,000

Financing cost
(Interests cost for $6,000,000
borrowed at 8% for 40 years)
Totals: $14,000,000

Total Continuing Project Cost: $23,000,000

(Note: All figures are rounded. Land, owner's functional use and disposal costs have been excluded)

Total Project Development and 40-Year Facility Operating Costs for a Hypothetical Office Building

Fundamentals Terminology

Life-cycle cost/benefit analysis provides an economic assessment of competing design alternatives over the economic life of each alternative. Several characteristics differentiate life-cycle cost/benefit analysis from other analytical techniques. First, life-cycle cost/benefit analysis is neither a decision-making process nor a set of economic guidelines. Rather, it is an analytical technique that can be used in the context of a decision-making process to generate economic guidelines.

Second, life-cycle cost/benefit analysis can be used to assess the consequences of a given decision or to choose among alternatives. That is, it can determine the effects of a decision, or it can play an integral part in the process of making the decision in the first place.

Next, life-cycle cost/benefit analysis deals only with factors that can be measured in dollars or some other equivalent measure. Because this limitation rules out some important consequences of planning and design decisions, life-cycle cost/benefit analysis constitutes only part of the larger assessment and decision-making context.

Next, the life-cycle cost/benefit analysis explicitly measures benefits as well as costs. Thus, while this monograph uses the common acronym (LCC) for life-cycle cost/benefit analysis, it considers economic benefits—fuel savings, for example—as well as costs; non-economic benefits are not measured.

Finally, life-cycle cost/benefit analysis examines these consequences over time, permitting consideration of all relevant costs and benefits within a selected period of time, and providing a straightforward methodology for relating them to each other.

Depreciation Period

☐ The depreciation period is an accounting device that distributes the monetary value (less salvage value) of a tangible asset over the estimated years of productive or useful life. It is a process of allocation, not valuation.

Amortization Period

☐ The amortization period is the number of months or years over which payments of principal and interest are made on a loan.

Residual or Salvage Value

☐ The residual or salvage value of a tangible asset is its expected value (less the cost to remove it) at the end of the life-cycle period under consideration. Residual value can be negative if the costs of removing or otherwise disposing of an asset are greater than its worth (e.g., its scrap value).

Constant Dollars

☐ LCC analysis uses constant dollars, which are usually in present dollars, and which reflect the general purchasing power of the dollar at the time a decision is made.

☐ The basic equations for determining constant dollars appear in the discussion of interest formulas, later in this monograph.

Interest

☐ Interest is the money paid for the use of borrowed money. Interest can also be thought of as the return obtainable by the productive investment of capital.

Interest Rate

☐ The rate of interest is the ratio between the amount payable at the end of a period of time and the money owed at the beginning of that period. Thus if $6 of interest is payable annually on a debt of $100, the interest rate is $6/$100 = 0.06 per annum. This is customarily described as an interest rate of 6 percent, with the "per annum" assumed unless some other period of time is stated.

Equivalence

☐ Payments that differ in total magnitude but are made at different dates can be equivalent to one another. Given an interest rate, any payment or series of payments that will repay a present sum of money with interest at that rate is equivalent to that present sum. Therefore, all future payments or series of payments that would repay the present sum with interest at the stated rate are equivalent to each other.

Escalation

☐ Cost escalation or de-escalation is the change in cost in an item above or below that of the general inflation rate. Labor and fuel are often subject to escalation. The accompanying figure shows estimated future costs for fuel in relation to overall prices.

Opportunity and Discount Rates

☐ The opportunity rate (i) is the best available rate of return that money could earn if placed in the best (in dollar terms) investment available. The exception to this definition is money that is available only on the condition that it be spent for a specific time such as an earmarked loan. In that case, the particular interest rate paid for that money can be defined

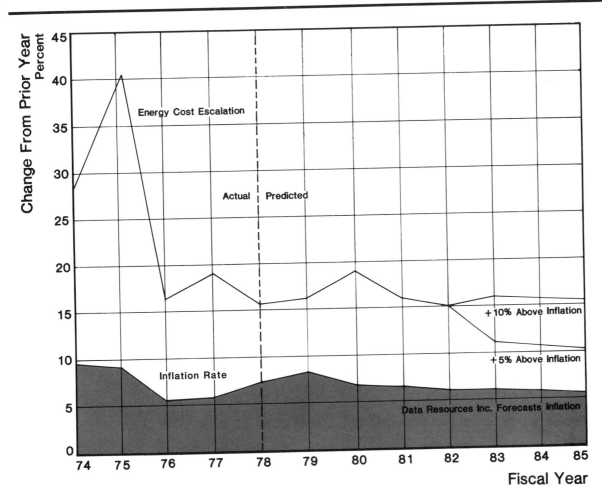

Energy Cost Escalation and Inflation

as the opportunity rate in developing the life-cycle cost.

☐ The opportunity rate is also called the discount rate. Much of the actual calculation involved in doing LCC analysis involves moving sums of value (dollars) backward or forward in time. If future-invested dollars are brought back to the present they are discounted by the interest rate.

☐ The rate of interest at which a client feels adequately compensated for trading money now for money in the future is the appropriate rate to use for converting present sums to future equivalent sums and future sums to present equivalent sums, i.e., the rate for discounting cash flows for that particular investor.

☐ If a client is unsure of the potential return on an alternative investment, the cost of borrowing can be used as the discount rate. However, the earning rate available on alternative investments should take precedence over the borrowing rate as an indicator of the appropriate discount rate and should be taken into account regardless of whether the money is borrowed or not. In selecting the appropriate discount rate, the client might be asked for the after-tax rate of return on other investments, a factor which can vary considerably. If the evaluation is being made for a governmental client, legislative requirements often exist.

☐ Clients sometimes request that high risk projects be evaluated with higher discount rates than those with low risk. Risk can also be treated in other ways, such as basing benefit and cost estimates on probabilities of occurrence, incorporating contingency estimates of cash flow into the calculations, or by using sensitivity analysis to assess the effect of different time horizons or of different amounts of energy savings on the profitability of the investment.

☐ Discount rates can be expressed in either "nominal" or "real" terms. Nominal rates reflect the effects of inflation and the real earning power of money invested over time. Real rates reflect only the real earning power of money, and therefore are lower than a nominal rate, given the same conditions.

☐ Dollar estimates of benefits and costs and discount values must be made compatible with each other by either including or excluding inflation from all values. A real discount rate is appropriate if inflation is removed from the cash flow prior to discounting. A nominal rate is appropriate if cash flows are inflated.

☐ More than any other variable *the discount rate can affect the net benefits of energy conservation investments*. The rate selected determines whether a project appears to be economical or uneconomical. For example, a project that has positive net savings when evaluated using a 6 percent discount rate might yield negative net savings when evaluated at 7 percent.

☐ As the discount rate is increased, the present value of any given future stream of costs or benefits becomes smaller. High discount rates tend to favor projects with quick payoffs over projects with deferred benefits.

Time Frame

☐ LCC analysis rarely examines costs more than 25 to 40 years into the future. LCC time frames are limited to such periods because of the uncertainties associated with forecasting too far into the future and because this is considered the effective life of many buildings. Furthermore, about 80 percent of equivalent-cost dollars are spent in the first 25 years of most projects.

☐ It is also often useful to examine life-cycle costs for each of a building's components, e.g., HVAC systems. A component's life can usually be determined from manufacturers' data, although this information can be affected by a variety of factors, including maintenance practices and technological obsolescence. Improvements in the state of the art can make it more economical to replace a component before it wears out.

☐ The establishment of the time horizon is a function of the owner's operational and/or economic objectives:

—Functionally, the owner may see the building, or various elements within the building, against a limited time horizon. An assembly plant, for example, may be seen against a 20-year time horizon because the owner does not want to project functional changes in the assembly process beyond that point. The design of an operating suite in a hospital may be seen against a shorter time period due to expected technological changes.

—Economically, owners have a wide variety of goals, and often these goals have reasonably definite time horizons associated with them. An owner may plan to stay in business (and in the facility that houses it) until a specific date, or until it is expected that the community can no longer support it. Similarly, owners may tie their economic goals to the length of leases or to the payback of borrowed money.

☐ These owner objectives tend to limit the horizons for life-cycle cost analyses to 10, 15, 20 or 25 years.

☐ Through periodic renewal of a building's elements, it is possible to prolong their physical lives for centuries. Individual building elements, however, can have specific useful or economic lives, and very often an LCC analysis is concerned with the replacement or renewal of building elements at the end of their useful or economic lives. These individual lives do not always conform easily to the overall life cycle being used in the analysis.

☐ Establishing the anticipated lives of building elements is complicated by the wide range of products available and the general lack of documented experience by building owners. In general, the best guide is provided by available owner experience in combination with manufacturers' data.

Equivalence

"Equivalent dollars" provide a means of adjusting present dollars and future dollars to reflect the time value of money, since a dollar received or expended today does not have the same value it would have if it were received or expended in the future. One reason for this discrepancy is that the earning potential of liquid capital is different today, when a dollar received can be put to use to generate additional income from what it would be at a later date, since a dollar to be received in the future offers no earning potential in the interim. Similarly, an expense that must be paid now draws resources from the client that cannot be used for other productive purposes.

□ Equivalent dollars are an integral part of LCC analysis. They are also extremely easy to compute and use: precomputed factors (presented in the Interest Factors Table) are multiplied by any dollar amount to calculate equivalent dollars. These factors are listed by year (into the future) and by interest rate (or discount rate) and can be chosen to incorporate the adjustment for expected inflation or deflation in the discounting procedure.

□ For example, $20,000 received 10 years from now, assuming an interest rate of 10 percent, is worth $7,710 in today's dollars. The Single Present Worth (SPW) factor from the Interest Factors Table for 10-percent interest after 10 years is 0.3855; $20,000 X 0.3855 = $7,710. The Single Compound Amount (SCA) factor performs the reverse: $7,710 invested today at a 10-percent interest rate = $2,710 X 2.594 = $20,000 in 10 years.

□ Equivalent dollars are determined by one of two methods: the present-worth method and the equivalent-annual-cost method.

Present-Worth Method

□ The present-worth method converts all present and future receipts and expenditures to today's cost. Initial costs and benefits are already expressed in present worth. Future amounts are multiplied by the appropriate factor, allowing all dollar amounts to be compared, regardless of when they are spent or received.

□ The present-worth model has a disadvantage if the alternatives under comparison have different estimated lives. It would be incorrect to compare the total present worth of one alternative, having an estimated life of 15 years, with the total cost of another alternative having an estimated life of 20 years. To reduce these two alternatives to equivalency it is necessary to study the total cost of each alternative over an equal number of years.

□ One method of adjusting alternatives with different lives is to choose a time period for study that is a common multiple of the lives of the alternatives.

□ Another method of comparing two alternatives with different lives is to compute the annual cost of each alternative and to then determine the present worth of a given number of years of service.

Equivalent-Annual-Cost Method

□ The equivalent-annual-cost method converts all amounts, regardless of when they are spent or received, to a uniform annual amount. This allows, for example, a combination of capital expenditures in one year, varying maintenance costs in later years and resale value at the end of a given period to be expressed in terms of a constant amount, in equivalent dollars, for each year in the life cycle.

Interest Formulas

□ Interest formulas are used to move values forward or back in time so that they can be compared on an equivalent basis with other values. There are two formulas which apply to single payments of money. The single compound amount formula (SCA) is used to determine the future worth F of a present worth P, y years in the future:

$$F = P\left[(1 + i)^y\right]$$

□ This equation sums up the principal P and the interest paid on the principal and any accrued interest each year for a given number of years. If $1,000 today were invested at i interest, the sum of money owed at the end of the first year would be $1,000 (1 + i); at the end of the second year it would be $1,000 (1 + i) (1 + i); and at the end of the third year it would be worth $1,000 (1 + i) (1 + i) (1 + i). And at the end of y years it would be equal to $1,000 (1 + i)^y.

□ This single compound amount formula is used to find the future worth, F, when there is a single present worth, P, and a given interest rate, i, and numbers of years, y, in the future. For any one interest rate and for any number of years, the factor (1 + i)^y is a constant. Consequently, a table of single compound amount factors can be developed.

☐ The single present worth (SPW) formula is used to determine the present worth, P, of a future sum of money, F, for a given number of years and a given interest rate:

$$P = F \left[\frac{1}{(1 + i)^y} \right]$$

☐ To determine the present worth of a single future value F, multiply it by the single payment present worth factor (SPW), which is $1/(1 + i)^y$. Again, for any one value of i and any one value of y, the SPW factor is a constant.

☐ The following equations allow one to adjust values (dollars) to present, future and annual increments. Tables derived from these formulas (see Interest Factors Table) provide a fast, accurate tool for practical application of LCC analysis:

$$F = P \left[(1 + i)^y \right]$$

— Single Compound Amount (SCA) adjusts a single value from present to future (P to F).

$$P = F \left[\frac{1}{(1 + i)^y} \right]$$

— Single Present Worth (SPW) adjusts a single sum from the future to the present (F to P).

$$F = A \left[\frac{(1 + i)^y - 1}{i} \right]$$

— Uniform Compound Amount (UCA) adjusts a set of equal annual increments to a single future value (A to F).

$$A = F \left[\frac{i}{(1 + i)^y - 1} \right]$$

— Uniform Sinking Fund (USF) adjusts a single sum from the future to equal annual increments (F to A).

$$A = P \left[\frac{i(1 + i)^y}{(1 + i)^y - 1} \right]$$

— Uniform Capital Recovery (UCR) adjusts a single sum from the present to a set of equal annual increments (P to A).

$$P = A \left[\frac{(1 + i)^y - 1}{i(1 + i)^y} \right]$$

— Uniform Present Worth (UPW) adjusts equal annual increments to a single present value (A to P).

where:
P = Present Value
F = Future Value
A = Equivalent Annual Cost
i = Interest Rate (opportunity or discount rate)
y = Study Period (years)

Factor						Use
Single Compound Amount Formula (SCA)	P	→	F?			To find F when P is known
Single Present Worth Formula (SPW)	P?	←	F			To find P when F is known
Uniform Sinking Fund Formula (USF)	A?	+	A? ... A?	→	F	To find A when F is known
Uniform Capital Recovery Formula (UCR)	P	→	A? + A? ... A?			To find A when P is known
Uniform Compound Amount Formula (UCA)	A	+	A ... A	→	F?	To find F when A is known
Uniform Present Worth Formula (UPW)	P?	←	A + A .... A			To find P when A is known

Where:
P = a present sum of money
F = a future sum of money
A = an end-of-period payment (or receipt) in a uniform series of payments (or receipts) over N periods at i interest or discount rate
F? = indicates a future value to be found; P? = a present value to be found; an A? = An annual value to be found.

Discount Factors

☐ In the manipulation of these formulas, some important aspects of the trade-offs between "present" and "future" dollars emerge.

☐ First, the higher the discount rate, the less important future costs are relative to initial costs, and the less worthwhile it becomes to try to avoid future expenditures by increasing initial costs.

☐ Second, as the life cycle used becomes longer and longer, the annual savings needed to justify an extra initial expenditure flattens out; this saving approaches the discount rate itself. This suggests that:
—analyses with very short life cycles and high discount rates require the greatest accuracy
—analyses with very long life cycles tend to be less valuable than those with shorter life cycles
—the significant trade-offs between "today" and "tomorrow" dollars are best seen when life cycles are in the 10- to 30-year range.

Consider an HVAC system expected to cost $50,000 to install initially; a one-time replacement expected to cost $20,000 after 15 years; annual operating and maintenance (O & M) of $5,000 and a salvage value of $10,000 after 30 years. What is the total present worth of this system over a life cycle of 30 years, using a 10-percent discount rate?

PW of initial cost:	$ 50,000
PW of the one-time replacement cost: P = F × (SPW for 15 years, at 10%) P = $20,000 × .2394	4,788
PW of the O & M costs: P = A × (UPW for 30 years, at 10%) P = $5,000 × 9.427	47,135
PW of the salvage value: P = F × (SPW for 30 years, at 10%) P = $10,000 × .0573	(573)
PW of the entire system	$ 101,350

Consider the same situation using the equivalent-annual-cost method:

EAC for initial cost A = P × (UCR for 30 years, at 10%) A = $50,000 × .1061	$ 5,305
EAC of the one-time replacement cost PW of this cost is $4,788 A = P × (UCR for 30 years, at 10%) A = $4,788 × .1061	508
EAC of the O & M costs	5,000
EAC of the salvage value A = F × (USF for 30 years, at 10%) A = $10,000 × .0061	(61)
EAC of the entire system	$ 10,750

			Nonrecurring Costs			Recurring Costs	
Alternative Number: _____							
Discount Rate: _____%							
Life Cycle: _____ Years							
	Year	Amount	Total Present Worth × SPW = PW	Equiv. Uniform Annual Cost × (*) = EUAC	Years	Uniform Annual Cost	Total Present Worth × UPW = PW
Initial Costs:							
Financing Costs:							
O&M Costs:							
Alterations/ Repairs/ Replacements:							
Alterations/ Improvements:							
Functional Use costs:							
Salvage Costs/Values:							
Total Present Worth		$____ ◄				◄	
Equivalent Uniform Annual Cost		$____		◄		◄	

(*) To determine Equivalent Uniform Cost for costs in the baseline year, use the appropriate UCR factor.
To determine Equivalent Uniform Annual Cost for costs in future years, use the appropriate USF factor.

Life-Cycle Cost Analysis Form

Nonrecurring Costs (Baseline year) These are already stated in present worth terms and can be used directly.
Nonrecurring Costs (Future years) These should be brought to their present worth in the baseline year by using the appropriate SPW factor.
Recurring Costs Uniform recurring costs which begin in the first year of the analysis life cycle should be brought to their present worth in the baseline year by using the appropriate UPW factor. Uniform recurring costs which begin in some future year should first be brought to their present worth in the year in which they begin (by using the appropriate UPW factor), and then this number should be brought to its present worth in the baseline year (by using the appropriate SPW factor).

Life-Cycle Cost: Present-Worth Method

Nonrecurring Costs (Baseline year) These should be converted to a uniform annual equivalent by using the appropriate UCR factor.
Nonrecurring Costs (Future years) Costs occurring at the end of the analysis life cycle can be converted to a uniform annual equivalent by using the appropriate USF factor. Costs occurring during the life cycle should first be brought to their present worth in the baseline year and then converted to a uniform annual equivalent by using the appropriate UCR factor.
Recurring Costs Uniform recurring costs over all years in the analysis life cycle are already stated in EUAC terms and can be used directly. If these costs are nonuniform, or if they occur in some but not all years in the analysis life cycle, they should first be brought to their present worth in the baseline year and then converted to a uniform annual equivalent by using the appropriate UCR factor.

Life-Cycle Cost: Equivalent-Annual-Cost Method

A format for completing the life-cycle cost analysis is shown. This format can be used for either the Present-Worth Method or the Equivalent-Annual-Cost Method. The following steps can be used to fill out the form:

1. Fill out an analysis form for each decision or alternative to be analyzed.

2. Enter the DISCOUNT RATE to be used in the analysis.

3. Enter the LIFE CYCLE time frame to be used in the analysis.

4. Enter the NONRECURRING COSTS associated with the decision or alternative, and enter the specific analysis YEAR in which each of these costs is to be incurred. (Initial costs in the baseline year should be entered as year "O"; a one-time replacement cost to be incurred after 15 years is year "15", etc.)

5. Enter the RECURRING COSTS associated with the decision or alternative, and enter the analysis YEARS in which these will be incurred. (Recurring costs occurring in all 25 years of a 25-year analysis life cycle, for example, should be entered on years "1–25"; costs occurring only in the first ten years as "1–10", etc.)

6. If the objective of the analysis is the assessment of a given decision, enter all relevant nonrecurring and recurring costs; if the objective is choice among alternatives, it is necessary to enter only the differential costs among alternatives.

7. If the TOTAL PRESENT WORTH method is to be used for calculating life-cycle cost, bring all nonrecurring and recurring costs listed to their present worth in the baseline year. Note that there is a place on the form in which to enter the appropriate SPW and UPW factors (for future reference). Total all present worth figures to determine a Total Present Worth for the decision or alternative.

8. If the EQUIVALENT ANNUAL COST method is to be used, convert all costs listed to their uniform annual equivalents. Note that there is a place on the form in which to enter the appropriate UCR and USF factors (for future reference). Total all annual cost figures to determine the Equivalent Uniform Annual Cost for the decision or alternative.

Life-Cycle Cost/Benefit Analysis

LCC analysis expresses the consequences of a choice, as far as practical, in terms of monetary value at stated times in the future. An explicitly defined primary criterion should be applied to such monetary figures. In dealing with certain types of proposals, it can also be desirable to have one or more secondary criteria.

LCC Criteria

☐ The primary criterion to be applied in a choice among proposed alternative options should be selected with the objective of making the best use of limited resources, such as land, labor, capital, materials. But, because the market provides money valuations on most resources, it is usually appropriate to express the overall limitation in terms of money.

☐ In evaluating proposed design options, the important issue is whether the option will be productive enough, that is, will it yield a sufficient rate of return as compared with one or more stated alternatives, all things considered? The minimum acceptable rate of return is often the primary criterion used for investment decisions, although other criteria may be as important.

☐ Even the most careful estimates of the monetary consequences of choosing different alternatives will almost certainly turn out to be incorrect. It is often helpful to a decision-maker to make use of secondary criteria—cash flow differences among alternatives, for example—that argue for or against the necessarily uncertain results of applying the primary criterion.

☐ Often, seemingly minor economic side effects are disregarded when individual decisions are made. If the side effects of a particular decision are sufficiently trivial, a study of them would presumably not change the decision. However, a study of interrelationships among a group of decisions may be needed to provide a basis for judgment on whether the side effects are trivial or important.

LCC and the Design Process

☐ In many cases LCC is applied to single building components, leading to restrictive design solutions. A multi-systems approach to optimization of the building as a whole produces more desirable results.

☐ If LCC analysis is used early in the design process it can help identify major determinants of a project's cost and lead to early design decisions to minimize these costs. If the costs associated with major design decisions—open plan office space, use of daylighting and other solar strategies, multi-story vs. single-story construction and related land costs—are not considered until late in the design process, the design can be so locked in that economic decisions cannot be made practically (see accompanying figure). In the extreme, LCC analysis early in a project may indicate that the client's funds would be more effectively used renovating an existing facility instead of designing a new one, or used for another type of investment entirely.

LCC Methodology

☐ The following passages present a general overview of the basic steps in the LCC analysis technique.

1. Clarify the objective of the analysis. Is it to assess the consequences of a given decision, or is it to choose among alternatives on the basis of their economic consequences?
In the first objective, comprehensive cost information will be required for the analysis; in the second objective, only differential cost information, costs that are different from alternative to alternative, need be considered.

2. Identify the alternative(s) to be analyzed. First, concentrate on those planning and design decisions that might have the greatest economic consequences—both initially and over the facility's use period. For example:
—The decision must be made either to build or not to build.
—While the costs of construction are significant, the operational costs of the facility are even more significant. These costs can sometimes be traded off—the costs of a night shift, for example, may turn out to be less than the costs of constructing and operating a new manufacturing facility.
—A determination should be made of building configuration and orientation, with their resulting cost effects on heating, cooling, maintenance, vertical circulation and other continuing cost items.
—While some of these cost effects are felt as initial costs (e.g., the cost of elevators for a highrise alternative), many have continuing influence as well (e.g., the cost of operating, maintaining and replacing the same elevators).
—The choice of mechanical systems is also quite significant, given the importance of fuel, utilities, operating, maintenance and replacement costs for these systems.
—The design of natural and artificial illumination systems provides another opportunity for useful LCC analysis.

—Within any of these major decisions are numerous individual options that can also warrant LCC analysis.

Second, it makes sense to focus on those decisions that rely heavily on what are expected to be expensive continuing cost items. In recent years, fuel and utility costs have risen so sharply that they are in this category. Labor cost—for operating and maintaining a facility and, less directly, as occupants of facilities—are always expensive, and it can be useful to look for situations in which the expenditure of extra present construction dollars can save more future operational dollars.

The selection of alternatives for effective LCC analysis is, in part, a matter of experience. For example, all selected alternatives must meet the performance standards expected of them. Analyzing the economic performance alternatives that must be clearly rejected on other grounds is useless.

3. Establish a time frame for the analysis. Key decisions include the point when the period of analysis starts (its baseline date), how long it runs (its life cycle) and what useful lives of individual building elements may be involved.

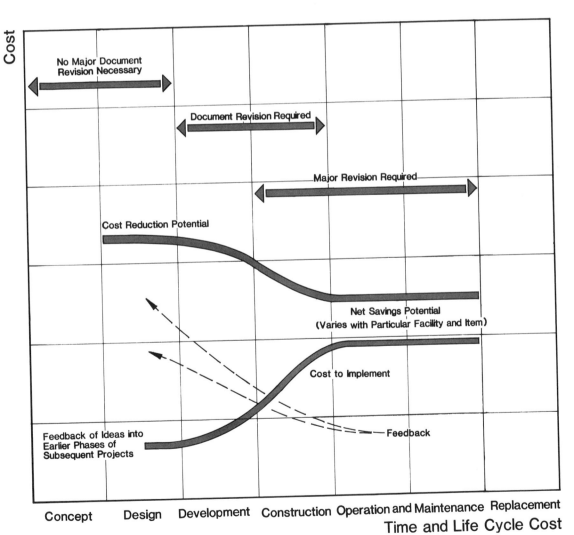

Opportunity for Reducing Costs Over Time

Source: Dell'Isola, Alphonse and Kirk, Stephen J., Life Cycle Costing for Design Professionals, ©1981. Reprinted by permission of McGraw-Hill, Inc., New York.

Cost Category	Costs Potentially Included	Use in the Analysis	Sources of Cost Data
INITIAL CAPITAL IN-VESTMENT COSTS. Costs associated with the initial planning, design, and construction of the facility.	Land costs, including costs of acquisition, options, surveys and appraisals, demolition and relocation, legal and filing fees. Design costs, including cost of consultants and/or in-house staff, as well as required special studies or tests (e.g., test borings). Construction costs, including costs of labor, material, equipment, general conditions (job overhead), contractors' main office overhead, and profit. Other owner costs, including cost of owner project administration, construction insurance, permits, fees and other expenses not included above.	These are usually non-recurring costs, and unless the project development period is a lengthy one, they are usually recorded as occurring in the baseline year. If project development is extended, or if project scheduling alternatives are being considered, it may be desirable to break these costs down year-by-year.	Land and other owner costs usually can be supplied only by the owner. Construction costs can be developed from standard estimating sources and/or from owner, architect, construction consultant, construction manager or cost consultant experience.
FINANCING COSTS. Costs associated with financing capital investment.	Loan fees and one-time finance charges associated with borrowing for the project—both for initial project development as well as major capital improvements. Interest costs for short-term (interim) financing. Note: Interest costs for long-term (permanent) financing usually are considered in establishing the discount rate for the life-cycle cost analysis, and are not included as costs in the analysis proper.	Loan fees and one-time charges are nonrecurring costs and should be recorded in the appropriate year(s). Interest costs which are to be specifically included in the analysis are recurring costs and should be recorded for each of the years in which they are to occur.	From the owner, or the owner's lender or financial adviser.
FACILITY OPERATION AND MAINTENANCE (O&M) Costs. Costs associated with the ongoing operation and maintenance of the facility.	Personnel costs for routine maintenance, cleaning, grounds care, trash removal, space reconfiguration, security, building operation, property management, etc. Costs of fuel, utilities, supplies, equipment and contract services associated with these activities should also be included.	These are usually recurring costs incurred after occupancy of the facility. Some may be incurred during the project development period and should be considered accordingly.	Some O&M costs may be available from the owner, owners associations, and publications. Some manufacturers include O&M data in product literature, but this should be carefully reviewed by owner representatives and other users. Energy efficiency studies can be conducted by designers to predict fuel and utility costs.

484

Cost Category	Costs Potentially Included	Use in Analysis	Sources of Cost Data
FACILITY REPAIR AND REPLACEMENT COSTS. Costs associated with restoring the facility to its original performance.	Costs of major repairs to building elements during the analysis timeframe. Costs of planned replacements of building elements during the analysis timeframe. Includes costs of planning, design, demolition and disposal and other owner costs, as well as costs for labor, materials, equipment, overhead and profit of any outside contractors.	These are usually nonrecurring costs associated with, and recorded in, the specific years in which they occur.	Obsolescence information is often provided by manufacturers, industry associations and sometimes from owner experience.
FACILITY ALTERATION AND IMPROVEMENT COSTS. Costs associated with planned additions, alterations, major reconfigurations and other improvements to the facility.	Costs of all planned capital improvements during the analysis timeframe. Includes costs of land, planning, design, demolition, relocation, disposal and other owner costs, as well as costs of labor, materials, equipment, overhead and profit of any outside contractors.	These are usually nonrecurring costs associated with, and recorded in, the specific years in which they occur.	Information is based on planned functional or economic obsolescence of the facility, and on planned expansion or contraction of the program, as determined by the owner.
FUNCTIONAL-USE COSTS. Costs associated with performing intended functions within the facility.	Salaries and benefits of personnel working in the facility, as well as supplies and services required for the program housed in the facility. Income and real property taxes. Denial-of-use and lost revenue costs associated with delayed or inappropriate scheduling of occupancy, or with using the facility inefficiently; includes continuing rent, unexpired leases, operating in obsolete facilities, etc.	These are usually recurring costs incurred after occupancy. Some (e.g., property insurance and taxes) may also occur during the project development period, and these should be recorded in the appropriate years.	Usually can be supplied by the owner.
SALVAGE COSTS. Costs (or values) of building elements or facilities salvaged during the analysis life cycle.	Costs of salvage operations, including demolition and disposal, if not included above. Salvage values of building elements or facilities recovered as part of replacement, alteration or improvement activities.	Cost of salvage operations are usually nonrecurring and should be recorded in the appropriate year. Value of salvaged facilities or building elements should be entered in the appropriate year as negative numbers (with minus signs).	Information may be available from standard estimating sources, manufacturers, industry associations or owner experience.

The baseline date is the present, when costs need not be discounted, and because it is the starting point, the general assumption is that any costs already incurred on the project are met and cannot be recovered.

In line with the convention of recording costs at the end of the year in which they are incurred is the practice of viewing the baseline date as a baseline year. If the project's development period is a reasonably short one, including time for its planning, design and construction activities requiring capital investment, the period is usually considered as occurring wholly within the baseline year. This allows all initial capital investment costs to be considered in present dollars without further adjustment.

For larger or more complex projects requiring a longer project development time, initial capital investment costs can be considered either as occurring in the baseline year or in the future.

The latter approach can be useful for a project with a long development time if the designer wishes to experiment with different project scheduling approaches. One scheduling approach includes spending extra dollars to overlap design and construction in order to bring the occupancy date closer; with a long project development period, some of these costs are present costs and some are future costs. LCC analysis can be used to assess the economic implications of these scheduling approaches.

4. Select the cost factors to be considered in the analysis. A long list of cost categories can be considered in LCC analysis. This depends on the objectives of the analysis, the costs the owner considers relevant to decisions and the life cycle selected. These include initial capital investment costs, facility operation and maintenance costs, repair and replacement costs, alteration and improvement costs, functional use costs and salvage costs. The accompanying chart indicates the nature of these costs, their uses in LCC analysis and where information about them can be obtained.

5. Determine the life-cycle cost "measure" to be used. Decisions can be assessed or alternatives compared in terms of either of two related cost methods: Total Present Worth Cost or Equivalent Uniform Annual Cost.

6. Perform the analysis. Once all of the above is established, the LCC analysis itself is relatively straightforward. The LCC team isolates the significant costs associated with each alter-native. These costs are then grouped by year over the number of years equal to the economic life of the facility or, if more appropriate, grouped by time spans equal to the mode of operation. In either case, replacement and alteration costs should be considered. A salvage value, if relevant, is also added for the end of the life-cycle period.

All costs are converted to constant dollars by one of the methods referred to in step 5.

Finally, the team adds up the costs and identifies the lowest-cost alternative. It may be necessary to make a sensitivity analysis of each of the assumptions to see if a reasonable change in any of the cost assumptions would change the conclusions.

7. Analyze the results. LCC analyses ultimately produce a series of numbers. What do these mean? How do they relate to the initial assumptions used? Is the lowest-cost alternative always the optimal solution for the owner?

☐ Normally, final design decisions must take into account non-economic considerations such as politics, esthetics, safety and functional convenience. Therefore, after the economically oriented exercise, non-economic criteria are evaluated, with decisions made on the basis of both sets of factors.

☐ The accompanying diagram shows the overall LCC analysis technique.

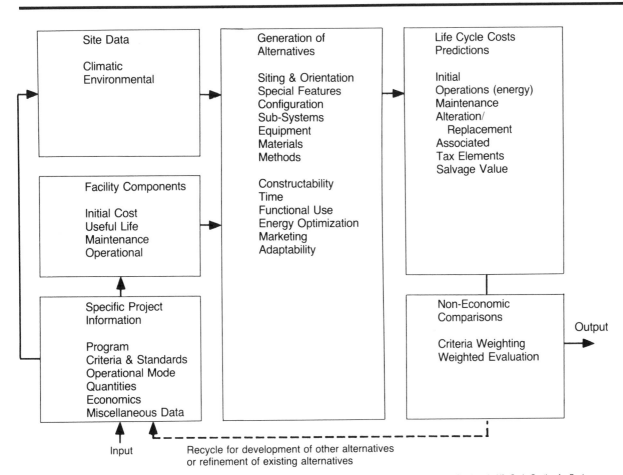

| Site Data

Climatic
Environmental | Generation of
Alternatives

Siting & Orientation
Special Features
Configuration
Sub-Systems
Equipment
Materials
Methods

Constructability
Time
Functional Use
Energy Optimization
Marketing
Adaptability | Life Cycle Costs
Predictions

Initial
Operations (energy)
Maintenance
Alteration/
   Replacement
Associated
Tax Elements
Salvage Value |

Facility Components

Initial Cost
Useful Life
Maintenance
Operational

Specific Project
Information

Program
Criteria & Standards
Operational Mode
Quantities
Economics
Miscellaneous Data

Non-Economic
Comparisons

Criteria Weighting
Weighted Evaluation

Output

Input

Recycle for development of other alternatives
or refinement of existing alternatives

LCC Analysis Flowchart

Source: Dell'Isola, Alphonse and Kirk, Stephen J., Life Cycle Costing for Design Professionals, ©1981. Reprinted by permission of McGraw-Hill, Inc., New York.

The following example evaluates a number of configuration alternatives for a public office building.

As indicated, nine of the alternatives were variations on basic cubic design while the remaining four alternatives experimented with various atrium designs favored by the architect. Basic massing, floors above and below grade, percentage of glazing, initial construction cost and ongoing energy and window cleaning costs were considered as variables. To isolate the relevant cost factors among the alternatives,
—a "bare walls" building enclosure was used;
—lighting and plumbing costs were assumed to be equal in all alternatives and were not included;
—with the exception of window cleaning costs, custodial and janitorial costs were assumed to be equal among the alternatives and not included;
—a penthouse mechanical room was assumed necessary but equal for all alternatives, and was not included.

A summary of the initial and continuing cost parameters used in the study is presented.

Total Present Worth Cost curves were developed for life cycles ranging from 5 to 50 years. These can be seen in the presentation of the results of the analysis.

A 6 percent escalation rate (for all future costs) and interest rates to yield appropriate "real" rates of interest for a public owner were used.

To accommodate so many different variables (13 alternatives, life cycles from 5 to 50 years, several interest/escalation rate combinations), an in-house computer program was used. The results of the life cycle cost analysis are shown.

In considering the curves for the nine basic cube alternatives it can be seen that the "C" alternatives are most economical, both to construct and to operate. Looking at all the curves, the four-story buildings (A2, B2, C2) generally present the lowest life-cycle costs, at least for the first 30 years. This generally confirms the view that buildings with some basement space and nearly cubic configuration are more energy-efficient at the scale of this project.

Configurations	Option	Floors Below Grade	Floors Above Grade	Gross Area (SF)	% of Surface Glazed
	A1	0	3	55,142	25.00
	A2	0	4	55,080	25.00
	A3	0	5	55,350	25.00
	BI	½	2½	55,142	25.00
	B2	½	3½	55,080	25.00
	B3	½	4½	55,350	25.00
	C1	1	2	55,142	25.00
	C2	1	3	55,080	25.00
	C3	1	4	55,350	25.00
	D2	1	3	56,942	15.28
	E2	1	3	56,942	16.47
	F2	1	3	56,942	19.15
	G2	1	3	56,942	17.56

Physical Characteristics of Configuration Alternatives

Initial Costs	
Foundations	$6.00 Sq. Ft. plan
Basement wall	$5.50 Sq. Ft. wall
Lowest floor	$4.00 Sq. Ft. plan
Upper floors	$4.50 Sq. Ft. floor
Exterior walls	$9.00 Sq. Ft. wall ($12.00 for sloping walls in D2, G2)
Roof	$4.75 Sq. Ft. plan
Interior partitions	$16.00 Lin. Ft. partitioning
Glazing	$11.00 Sq. Ft. glazing
Heating and cooling	$0.22 kWh-yr load requirement for heating, cooling
Elevator	$35,000 + $5,000/stop

Operating Costs		
Heating energy	Heating requirement contribution rates of elements, as listed below, totalled on an annual basis and multiplied by 1.6¢/kWh-yr:	
	Roof	3.0940 kWh-yr/Sq. Ft. plan
	Lowest floor	1.4060 kWh-yr/Sq. Ft. plan
	Basement wall	2.4750 kWh-yr/Sq. Ft. plan
	Exterior wall	3.0904 kWh-yr/Sq. Ft. plan
	Glazing	30.94 kWh-Yr/Sq. Ft. glazing
Cooling energy	Cooling requirement contribution rates of elements, as listed below, totalled on an annual basis and multiplied by 1.6¢/kWh-yr:	
	Roof	0.0550 kWh-yr/Sq. Ft. plan
	SE exterior wall	0.0513 kWh-yr/Sq. Ft. wall
	SW exterior wall	0.0245 kWh-yr/Sq. Ft. wall
	NW exterior wall	0.0164 kWh-yr/Sq. Ft. wall
	NE exterior wall	0.0205 kWh-yr/Sq. Ft. wall
	SE glass solar gain	0.5220 kWh-yr/Sq. Ft. glazing
	SW glass solar gain	5.0100 kWh-yr/Sq. Ft. glazing
	NW glass solar gain	0.3680 kWh-yr/Sq. Ft.
	NE glass solar gain	0.3680 kWh-yr/Sq. Ft. glazing
	Glass thermal transmission	0.3074 kWh-yr/Sq. Ft. glazing
	Lights and people	0.4583 kWh-yr/Sq. Ft. glazing
Window cleaning	7.5¢ per year per Sq. Ft. glazing	

Cost Factors for Analysis

The results of the cubic configurations are also shown as a single band, with the four atrium alternatives added. Generally the atrium designs are most costly initially (due to increased gross floor area under cover) but do present energy efficiencies in the future. The sloped walls in alternatives D2 and G2, however, add to both initial and continuing costs, and the additional "glazing box" in D2 adds further to the costs of that alternative. The study does not take the environmental and esthetic considerations of the atrium space into consideration, only the economics.

After reviewing the results of the analysis, and after digesting the results of subsurface investigations which further increased the cost of atrium alternatives, the owner and architects selected one of the basic cubic configurations (C2) for futher development in design.

Atrium Configuration Alternatives

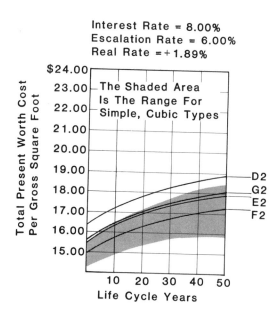

Interest Rate = 6.00%
Escalation Rate = 6.00%
Real Rate = 0.00%

The Shaded Area
Is The Range For
Simple, Cubic Types

Total Present Worth Cost Per Gross Square Foot

D2
G2
E2
F2

Life Cycle Years

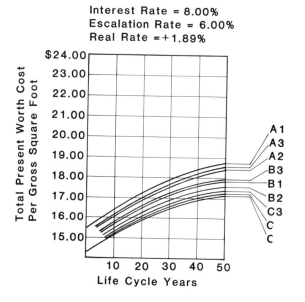

Interest Rate = 8.00%
Escalation Rate = 6.00%
Real Rate = +1.89%

The Shaded Area
Is The Range For
Simple, Cubic Types

Total Present Worth Cost Per Gross Square Foot

D2
G2
E2
F2

Life Cycle Years

Cubic Configuration Alternatives

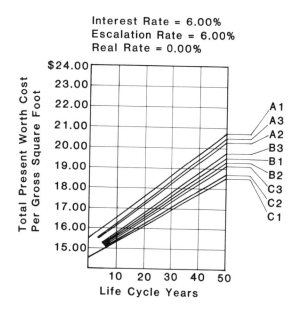

Interest Rate = 6.00%
Escalation Rate = 6.00%
Real Rate = 0.00%

Total Present Worth Cost Per Gross Square Foot

A1
A3
A2
B3
B1
B2
C3
C2
C1

Life Cycle Years

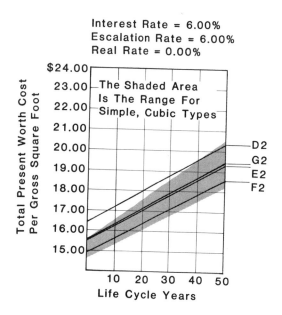

Interest Rate = 8.00%
Escalation Rate = 6.00%
Real Rate = +1.89%

Total Present Worth Cost Per Gross Square Foot

A1
A3
A2
B3
B1
B2
C3
C
C

Life Cycle Years

Life-Cycle Cost Analysis

490

Payback and Break-Even Analysis

Payback

□ Payback analysis is used to determine the number of years in which the initial extra expenditures for different alternatives are paid back. The simple payback can be calculated by the following:

$$\text{Simple payback period} = \frac{\text{initial cost}}{\text{annual savings}}$$

□ Simple payback analysis is easily misunderstood. The time value of money and future benefits are ignored in this payback formula, which can produce misleading results.

□ For clients who seek a rapid turnover of funds, this alternative increases in desirability as the payback period decreases. However *a shorter payback period does not necessarily indicate the most economically efficient investment.* An alternative with a longer payback period may prove more profitable than an alternative with a shorter payback period if it continues to yield savings for a longer period of time.

The following example illustrates why simple payback can be misleading. For instance, if a building owner makes an investment of $150,000, energy costs of $50,000 per year can be saved. For another alternative, the owner invests $200,000 and saves $50,000 a year in energy costs. With simple payback analysis, the first alternative would be the better choice since it pays back in three years as opposed to four years for the second alternative. If however, the life expectancy of the first alternative were three years and that of the second alternative, 20 years, then clearly the second alternative would be better since it would return $50,000 a year for 20 years resulting in a much larger total return than the first alternative.

Break-Even Analysis

□ By altering the value of one of the variables of an alternative and keeping all the other variables between two alternatives constant, a value for the variable that makes the two alternatives equally economical can be found. This value is described as the break-even point.

□ Where all costs are known and the discount rate has been established for two alternatives, time can be used as the variable, to solve for the time when one alternative becomes more attractive than another.

Lighting system A has an initial cost of $150,000 and an annual cost of $25,000, and lighting system B has an initial cost of $200,000 with an annual cost of $15,000. Using a discount rate of 15 percent, break even analysis can be used to find

out when more expensive system B becomes economically more attractive than system A. The total present worths of the two lighting systems can be determined, set equal to each other, and solved for the discount factors that make them equal. In this case it occurs when the present worths equal each other.

Total present worth P of system A:

$P_A = \$150,000 + (\$25,000 \times \text{UPW})$

Total present worth of system B:

$P_B = \$200,000 + (\$15,000 \times \text{UPW})$

Thus:

$\$150,000 + (\$25,000 \times \text{UPW}) = \$200,000 + (\$15,000 \times \text{UPW})$

$(\$10,000 \times \text{UPW}) = \$50,000$

$\text{UPW} = 5.000$

From the Interest Factors Table the UPW for 15 percent and 9 years is 4.772 and the UPW for 10 years is 5.019. The break-even point, then, is just under 10 years, after which lighting system B becomes more economical. Ten years can also be considered the payback period for the extra $50,000 initial-cost investment associated with system B.

This solution can be presented to decision-makers graphically as in the accompanying figure. Given the initial costs and the break-even point, it is a simple matter to draw the two intersecting lines to produce an easily understandable graphic.

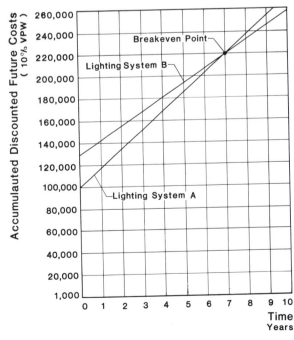

Break-Even Analysis for Lighting Systems

Source: Dell'Isola, Alphonse and Kirk, Stephen J., *Life Cycle Costing for Design Professionals*, ©1981. Reprinted by permission of McGraw-Hill, Inc., New York.

Rate Of Return On Investment

Many clients look at life-cycle costs in terms of the rate of return on the investment. The rate of return is the interest rate that indicates the return from an investment. A client may determine that the rate of return from investing money in a building is less than the return from using that money for an alternative investment.

☐ To determine the rate of return on any investment all costs and benefits must be forecast. This technique enables the decision maker to compare the investment with any alternative investments rather than just the alternatives to satisfy a specific need.

☐ To solve for the expected rate of return a model representing both costs and benefits is developed. The costs are set equal to the benefits, and the unknown in the model is the interest factor that makes the two equal. At some interest rate the conversion factor will make these two equal, and that interest rate is the rate of return on the investment.

☐ A cash flow chart is most valuable in checking to see if all costs and values have been included. Each value must either be spread out into uniform annual costs over the entire cost study, or they must all be brought back to a Present Worth value to evaluate the rate of return. Either Present Worth models or Annual Cost models can be used in determining rates of return. It is sometimes desirable to calculate the rate of return by both methods to be sure that an error has not been made in calculation. It is not likely that the same error will be made in an Annual Cost model and a Present Worth model of the same situation, unless it is an error in interpreting input data.

A simple case of rate of return is shown in the following example. In this problem a sum of money is invested for a given period of time and the original investment must be recovered with interest in obtaining the rate of return.

It is forecast that an investment of $10,000 today will produce a savings of $2,000 a year for the next 15 years. If the investment is made, what rate of return is expected?

$$\$10,000 = \$2,000 \ (UPW; \ 15;?)$$
$$UPW = \frac{\$10,000}{\$2,000} = 5.0$$
$$UPW = 5.847 \ at \ 15\%$$
$$UPW = 4.675 \ at \ 20\%$$

By interpolation:

$$i = .15 + (.05) \left[\frac{5.847 - 5.0}{5.847 - 4.675} \right]$$
$$= .15 + (.05) \left(\frac{.847}{1.172} \right)$$
$$= .15 + .036$$
$$= .186 \ or \ approximately \ 18.6\%$$

To solve for the expected rate of return in this problem a model representing both costs and benefits is developed. The costs are set equal to the benefits, and the unknown in the model is the interest level that makes the two equal. At some interest rate the Uniform Present Worth (UPW) factor will make these two equal, and that interest rate is the rate of return on the $10,000 investment over 15 years (UPW; 15;?). Because the benefit stream is uniform, the UPW is obtained by dividing the investment by the savings to get 5. The value 5 is bracketed by the UPW factors for 15 percent and

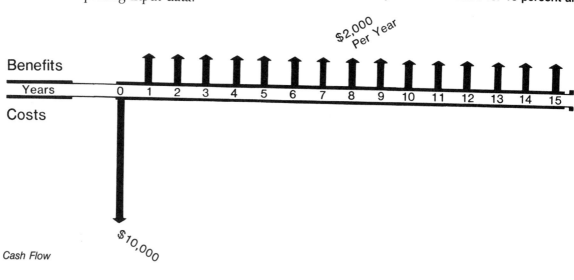

Cash Flow

492

20 percent in the interest tables (Interest Factors Table). By straight-line interpolation the interest rate on this investment is determined to be approximately 18.6 percent.

Every time an extra factor is placed in a model, it creates a new possibility for error. By keeping the model as simple as possible this likelihood is reduced, and the chance for considerable savings in calculation time is enhanced. This is illustrated in the following example.

An alternative has a first cost of $100,000, annual costs of $20,000 a year for the first 6 years, annual costs of $10,000 a year for the next 4 years, and a salvage value of $75,000 at the end of 10 years. It has expected benefits of $25,000 a year for the first 5 years, $30,000 a year for the next 5 years, and $5,000 a year for the final 5 years.

Costs = Benefits

$100,000 + $20,000 (UPW;6;?) + $10,000 (UPW;4;?) (SPW;6;?) = $25,000 (UPW;5;?) + $30,000 (UPW;5;?) (SPW;5;?) + $75,000 (SPW;10;?) + $5,000 (UPW;:5;?) (SPW;10;?)

The model has six different interest factors. The problem can be simplified by combining annual costs and benefits as shown:

$100,000 = $5,000 (UPW;15;?) + [$5,000 + $15,000 (UPW;3;?)] (SPW;6;?) + $60,000 (SPW;10;?)

UPW at 4% = $5,000 (11.12) + [$5,000 + $15,000 (2.775)] (.7903) + $60,000 (.6756)
= $55,600 + $36,848 + $40,536
= $132,984

UPW at 6% = $5,000 (9.712) + [$5,000 + $15,000 (2.673)] (.7050) + $60,000 (.5584)
= $48,560 + $31,792 + $33,504
= $113,856

UPW at 8% = $5,000 (8.559) + [$5,000 + $15,000 (2.577)] (.6302) + $60,000 (.4632)
= $42,795 + $27,511 + $27,792
= $98,098

By interpolation:

$$i = .06 + .02 \left(\frac{\$113,856 - \$100,000}{\$113,856 - \$98,098} \right)$$

$$= .06 + .02 \left(\frac{13,856}{15,758} \right)$$

$$= .06 + .017$$

$$= .077 \text{ or approximately } 7.7\%$$

In the analysis the number of interest factors has been reduced to four. To get an initial interest rate to insert in the mathematical model, the analyst might conclude the interest rate would be between 4 and 6 percent, on the basis that the total returns are $85,000 more than the $100,000 original investment and, if this $85,000 were uniformly returned, it would produce a little more than 5 percent return on the original investment ($85,000 ÷ 15 = 5666.6 $\frac{5666.6}{100,000}$ = .056 × 100 = 5.6%).

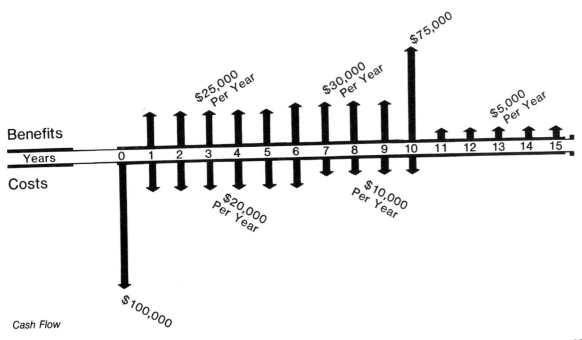

Benefits

$25,000 Per Year $30,000 Per Year $75,000 $5,000 Per Year

Years   0 1 2 3 4 5 6 7 8 9 10 11 12 13 14 15

Costs

$20,000 Per Year $10,000 Per Year $100,000

Cash Flow

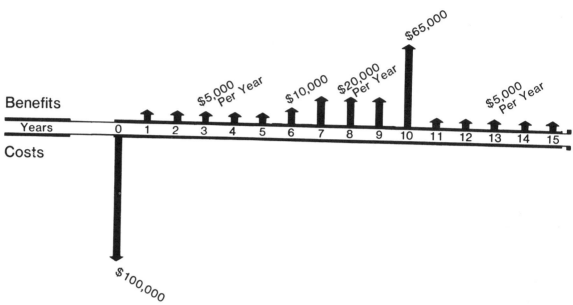

Cash Flow

In substituting the values for the UPW factors at 4 and 6 percent it is seen that the present worth of $100,000 is not bracketed. However, the $100,000 present worth is closer to the 6-percent factor. A still higher interest rate of 8 percent is then used to evaluate the model. Because the present worth at 8 percent is approximately $98,000, the $100,000 is bracketed by the 6 and 8 percent factors. By straight-line interpolation the rate of return is determined to be approximately 7.7 percent.

Rate of Return on Extra Investment

☐ A variation of the rate of return on the investment can be used to compare alternatives, where the decision has been made to use one alternative out of a group, regardless of the rate of return on the investment. Where this decision has been made, the rate of return of the extra investment of one alternative over another can be compared without determining the actual rate of return on either. By determining the rate of return on the extra investment, the decision-maker can then decide whether this extra investment is worthwhile.

☐ If two alternatives will satisfy a given situation, the rate of return on the extra investment can be determined by developing either Present Worth models or Annual Cost models of each alternative and equating like-cost models. The interest rate that makes the two cost models equal is the rate of return on the extra investment.

☐ Rate of return on *extra* investment looks only at the additional costs and benefits associated with one alternative or another. This can greatly simplify analysis, because all costs and benefits that are identical in competing alternatives can be ignored.

Consider two alternatives, each providing satisfactory accomplishments. Alternative A has a first cost of $8,000. Annual costs for the first 5 years are estimated to be $2,000 a year. The annual costs for the next 5 years are expected to be $1,000 a year. The life expectancy of this alternative is 10 years, and a $2,500 salvage value is forecast.

Alternative B has a first cost of $12,000. Its annual costs are estimated to be $1,200 per year. The life expectancy of this alternative is 15 years, and a salvage value of $4,000 is forecast.

Alternative A =

($8,000–$2,500) (UCR;10;?) + $2,500 (i) + ($1,000) (UPW;5;?) (UCR;10;?) + $1,000 =

Alternative B:

($12,000–$4,000) (UCR;15;?) + $4,000 (i) + $1,200

Or Simplifying to:

[($1,000) (UPW;5;?) + $5,500] (UCR;10;?) + $2,500(i) = $8,000 (UCR;15;?) + $4,000 (i) + $200

At i = 12%

[$1,000(3.605) + $5,500](.1770) + $2,500(.12) ≠
$8,000(.1469) + $4,000(.12) + $200;

($9,105)(.1770) + $300 ≠ $1,175 + $480 + $200;

$1,912 ≠ $1,855

At i = 15%

[$1,000(3.352) + $5,500](.1993) + $2,500(.15) ≠
$8,000(.1710) + $4,000(.15) + $200;

$1,764 + $375 ≠ $1,368 + $600 + $200;

$2,139 ≠ $2,168

Interpolating:

$$i = .12 + .03 \left[\frac{1912 - 1885}{(1912 - 1855) + (2168 - 2141)} \right]$$

$$= .12 + .03 \left(\frac{57}{84} \right) = .12 + .03 (.68)$$

$$= .12 + .0204 = .1404 \text{ or approximately } 14\%$$

The extra investment in alternative B is $4,000. The approximate rate of return on this extra investment is 14 percent. If a 14-percent return is a satisfactory use of capital, B can be taken over A. If not, then A would be the better alternative.

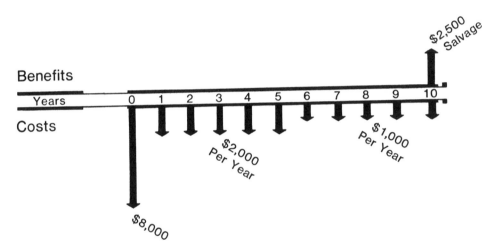

Cash Flow (Alternative A)

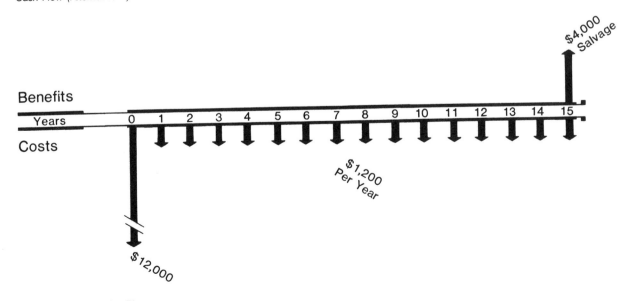

Cash Flow (Alternative B)

Sensitivity Analysis

Sensitivity analysis examines the relative effects of changes in the costs of one or more elements of an LCC analysis. Thus, if the cost of one particular element can be varied over a wide range of values without affecting the decision, the decision under consideration is said not to be sensitive to uncertainties regarding that particular element. On the other hand, if a small change in the estimate of one element alters the decision, the decision is said to be very sensitive to changes in the estimates of that element.

☐ LCC analysis requires estimates of such cost elements as fuel, labor, taxes, repairs, maintenance, insurance, revenue, salvage value, life and other economic factors affecting the particular proposal. Since all estimates are subject to some amount of uncertainty, the sensitivity approach can be very helpful in analyzing a proposal or set of proposals.

☐ Consider, for example, the uncertainties inherent in present estimates of future fossil fuel costs. If two alternatives use the same amount of fuel, the choice between them is not sensitive to fuel cost variations, and will depend on other factors. One alternative, however, may use less fuel but may also have larger maintenance costs. If the designer assumes a relatively high escalation rate for future fuel costs, an LCC analysis might show that even with the increased future maintenance costs of fuel-saving alternative is more cost-effective. If, on the other hand, fuel costs are assumed to escalate at a lower value, LCC analysis might show that expected fuel savings are outweighed by increased maintenance costs.

☐ The designer in this case can prepare similar analyses using different fuel costs in combination with different maintenance costs, salvage values, etc. The value of this to clients is that it provides them explicit knowledge of both the assumptions behind an LCC analysis and the effects that different assumptions would have on the economic implications of alternatives.

A company is planning the construction of service and repair shops of a standardized design at a number of different locations. The following estimates are made for three types of electric lighting systems, any of which will provide the desired level of illumination.

The investment in wiring is determined by other considerations and in this case will be independent of the type of fixture selected. The unit costs of labor for each lamp replacement is

Description	Incandescent	Fluorescent Type I	Fluorescent Type II
First cost installed (including lamps)	$175	$1,050	$1,390
Number of fixtures required	25	40	15
Number of lamps per fixture	1	2	4
Cost per lamp	$2.25	$2.50	$4.25
Rated life of lamps in hours	1,000	4,000	5,000
Watts per fixture	500	90	200

Lighting System Costs

estimated at 72 cents, regardless of the type. Electric energy is estimated to cost 3.4 cents per kWh. There is a 10-year life on the project with a desired minimum rate of return before income taxes of 30 percent. Insurance and property taxes are estimated at 3.5 percent of the first cost.

Differences in the climatic conditions of the several locations indicate that lighting needs will vary considerably in daylight hours, and that the volume of business will also vary with the locations. Some locations consistently require two- or three-shift operation while some require only one shift. The length of time the lighting system is on will obviously affect the annual cost of providing the required illumination.

The accompanying table compares the equivalent annual cost of the three systems at 1,000 and at 4,000 hours per year. The annual investment costs are independent of the amount of use of the lighting. These costs are fixed by the decision to select one of the systems. On the other hand, both the lamp replacement costs and the power costs vary directly with the amount of use.

Description	1,000 Hours per year			4,000 Hours per Year		
	Incand.	Fluor. Type I	Fluor. Type II	Incand.	Flour. Type I	Fluor. Type II
Annual investment charges	$ 62.73	$376.38	$498.26	$ 62.73	$ 376.38	$ 498.26
Lamp replacement	74.25	64.40	59.64	297.00	257.60	238.56
Annual power cost	425.00	122.40	102.00	1,700.00	489.60	408.00
Equivalent annual cost	$561.98	$563.18	$659.90	$2,059.73	$1,128.53	$1,144.82

Comparison of Annual Costs for Lighting Systems

The accompanying graph compares the equivalent annual costs of the three systems as the number of hours of use increases. The cost lines for the incandescent and the Type 1 flourescent systems intersect at approximately 1,000 hours. This is the break-even point between the two systems. If the prospect is that the average use will be more than 1,000 hours per year, one of the two flourescent systems should be chosen over the incandescent systems. The break-even point between the two types of flourescent systems occur at approximately 4,900 hours. Similarly, if the prospect is that the average annual utilization will be greater than 4,900 hours, the Type II fluorescent system should be chosen over Type I. It should be noted that the difference in equivalent annual cost of the two flourescent systems is very small, so nonquantifiable issues might easily determine the decision.

Present electric power rates are such that 3.4 cents per kWh is perceived as a fair price to use in deciding which lighting system to select for a standard service and repair shop. However, changes in rate structures and generating fuel surcharges are expected to cause fluctuations in the price of electric energy, moving toward a trend of increased prices. How sensitive is the problem to changes in the cost of energy per kWh? One way to determine the sensitivity is to compute the break-even points between the Type I fluorescent system and the incandescent system at various rates.

The break-even points can be computed directly. Let x equal the number of hours of use per year at which the equivalent annual cost of the incandescent will equal the equivalent annual cost of the fluorescent system. At 3.4 cents per kWh, the equation is:

$$\$175\,[(UCR, 30\%, 10) + 0.35] + \frac{(\$0.034)(500)(25)x}{1{,}000}$$

$$+ \frac{(\$2.97)(25)x}{1{,}000} = \$1{,}050\,[(UCR, 30\%, 10)$$

$$+ 0.035] \frac{(\$0.034)(90)(40)x}{1{,}000} + \frac{(\$3.22)(80)x}{4{,}000}$$

Entering the value of the capital recovery factor in the equation and solving for x, we find that the break-even point is 1,004 hours per year. This corresponds with the value found in the graph. Repeating this operation for a range of prices in the vicinity of 3.4 cents per kWh gives the break-even points shown in the accompanying table. Note that in this case, the decision is not very sensitive to the price of energy.

The comparative figures for the two types of fluorescent fixtures, also shown in this table, indicate that both are sensitive to increases in the price of electric energy. At 4.0 cents/kWh the break-even point reduces to 4,237 hours of utilization per year. Hence the final choice between the two types of fluorescent fixtures may again rest on the consideration of nonquantifiable factors.

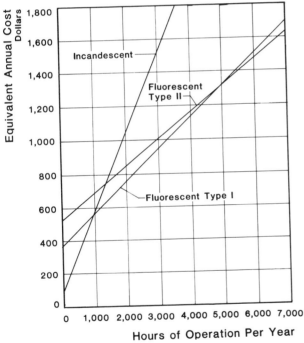

Equivalent Annual Cost Dollars

Incandescent

Fluorescent Type II

Fluorescent Type I

Hours of Operation Per Year

Break-Even Chart for Lighting Systems

	Price of Energy (¢/kWh)					
	3.0	3.2	3.4	3.6	3.8	4.0
Incandescent and Fluorescent Type I	1,175	1,064	1,004	979	927	881
Fluorescent Type II and Type I	5,355	5,087	4,844	4,623	4,422	4,237

Break-Even Points for Lighting Systems at Varying Energy Costs (Hours of Utilization per Year)

First Costs

Of all costs involved in a building, designers are most familiar with first costs. These include the owner's costs for land, design and other professional fees, construction, and all furnishings and equipment (see accompanying figure).

	Costs Potentially Included	Use in the Analysis	Sources of Cost Data
INITIAL CAPITAL INVESTMENT COSTS. Costs associated with the initial planning design and construction of the facility.	Land costs, including costs of acquisition, options, surveys and appraisals, demolition and relocation, legal and filing fees. Design costs, including cost of consultants and/or in-house staff as well as required special studies or tests (e.g., test borings). Construction costs, including costs of labor, material, equipment, general conditions (job overhead), contractors main office overhead, and profit. Other owner costs, including cost of owner project administration, construction insurance, permits, fees and other expenses not included above.	These are usually non-recurring costs and unless the project development period is a lengthy one, they are usually recorded as occurring in the baseline year. If project development is extended, or if project scheduling alternatives are being considered it may be desirable to break these costs down each year.	Land and other owner costs usually can be supplied only by the owner. Construction costs can be developed from standard estimating sources and/or from owner, architect, construction consultant, construction manager or cost consultant experience.

First Costs and Sources of Data

☐ Initial costs for typical office buildings are broken down in the accompanying graph. The following brief examples, however, illustrate possible first-cost alternatives suitable for LCC analysis:

—the use of more expensive HVAC equipment that is more efficient, hence uses less operating energy

—the use of more expensive reflective glazing to reduce heat gain and cooling requirements

—the use of a design which includes the extra first cost usually involved with daylighting, that will reduce future electric costs.

☐ A firm grasp of what first costs will be for various alternative designs facilitates effective initial cost comparisons. Traditional ways of arriving at initial cost estimates include the square-foot method, the material survey method and the building element method.

☐ Cost comparisons by the *square-foot* method are rarely useful, because of potentially wide ranges of quality, regional cost differences and other variations inherent to cost estimations based on a single value. Using different unit costs for different functional areas of the building produces results which are more precise, but still not dependable. Exception can be made for the firm specializing in one building type in a particular region.

☐ The *material survey* method is used on the Information Access System (formerly the *Uniform Construction Index* for analysis, which is derived from the specifications format developed by the Construction Specifications Institute. This cost analysis format follows the 16 subdivisions listed below. Cost elements are broken down into labor and materials for items of work that contractors or construction managers place with subcontractors or execute themselves.

1. General Requirements	9. Finishes
2. Site work	10. Specialties
3. Concrete	11. Equipment
4. Masonry	12. Furnishings
5. Metals	13. Special construction
6. Wood and plastics	14. Conveying systems
7. Thermal and moisture	15. Mechanical
8. Doors and windows	16. Electrical

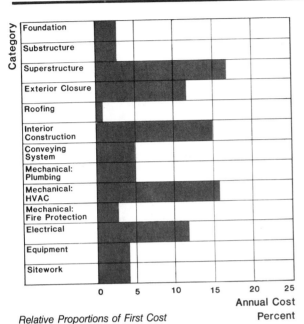

Relative Proportions of First Cost

Source: Dell'Isola, Alphonse and Kirk, Stephen J., *Life Cycle Costing for Design Professionals*, ©1981. Reprinted by permission of McGraw-Hill, Inc., New York.

Building Systems	Uniform Construction Index
Foundations	General requirements
Floors on grade	Site work
Superstructure	Concrete
Roofing	Masonry
Exterior walls	Metals
Partitions	Wood and plastics
Wall finishes	Thermal and moisture protection
Floor finishes	Doors and windows
Ceiling finishes	Finishes
Conveying systems	Specialties
Fixed equipment	Furnishings
HVAC	Special construction
Plumbing	Conveying systems
Electrical	Mechanical
	Electrical

Building Systems from Information Access System

☐ Early in the design process it is generally acceptable to rely on estimates of first costs based on previous projects of a similar nature. As the design becomes more defined it is possible to replace these gross estimates with more realistic costs broken down by building subsystems.

☐ An effective tool for estimating building subsystems is the UNIFORMAT classification developed by the General Services Administration and The American Institute of Architects. The accompanying sample shows how UNIFORMAT can be used to estimate subsystem costs for a computer processing center.

☐ Dodge Building Cost Services of McGraw-Hill Information Systems Company publishes costs of different building systems that can be used to arrive at a relatively quick estimate of building system costs.

☐ Arriving at systems costs is more involved when using the detailed costs of labor and materials in *Dodge Construction Systems Costs*. Data are adjusted for different locations. Labor and material costs of the various elements that make up the building system are combined to form the building element cost.

☐ Note that even the labor and materials costs available from such sources as the Information Access System referred to earlier can be reorganized to provide subsystem costs, as in the accompanying figure. This can be a la-borious process, however. Some cost consultants have developed computer programs that enable them to do this and other types of cost estimations rapidly.

☐ Other sources of published information in this field have been prepared using a variety of data bases, methods of adjusting for different geographic regions, etc. Among them are:
—*Building Construction Cost Data (Means)*
—*Dodge Manual for Building Construction Pricing and Scheduling*
—*Building Cost File*
—*Marshall Valuation Service*
—*Dodge Cost Calculator and Valuation Guide*
—*Boeckh Building Valuation Manual*
—*Building Cost Modifier*

☐ In using these and other cost sources the designer should ascertain their strengths, limitations and appropriate uses.

The following example analyzes four HVAC systems for a 20,000-square-foot office area of a manufacturing facility. The client requires that any initial capital used to obtain future cost savings must bring a return of 20 percent, and must break even in less than 10 years.

The four HVAC Systems identified for analysis are:

A. Absorption and variable volume system. Both oil and waste products are investigated as energy sources, with the latter requiring an estimated additional $12,000 in factory labor for effective

Project Computer Processing Center

Gross Square Footage (GSF—Note 1) 61,819   **Bid Date** 10-79   **Date** 1-79

Element (Levels 2 & 3)	Estimated Cost ($)	Cost Per Gross Sq. Ft. ($)	Percent	Element Quantity	Unit	Cost Per Elem. Qty. ($)
01 Foundation	32,500	0.53	1.2	32,507	SF²	1.00
011 Standard Foundations	32,500	0.53	1.2	32,507	SF²	1.00
012 Special Foundation Cond.					LS	
02 Substructure	41,000	0.66	1.5	32,507	SF²	1.26
021 Slab on Grade	41,000	0.66	1.5	32,507	SF²	1.26
022 Basement Excavation					SF²	
023 Basement Walls					SF³	
03 Superstructure	423,000	6.84	15.4	61,819	SF⁴	6.84
031 Floor Construction	225,000	3.64	8.2	29,312	SF⁵	7.68
032 Roof Construction	182,000	2.94	6.6	32,507	SF⁶	5.60
033 Stair Construction	m4 16,000	0.26	0.6	8	Landing	2,000
Total Structural (01–03)	496,500	8.03	18.1	750,000	CF¹³	0.66
04 Exterior Closure	192,500	311	7.0	14,927	SF⁷	12.90
041 Exterior Walls	173,000	2.80	6.3	14,711	SF⁸	11.76
042 Exterior Doors & Windows	19,500	0.31	0.7	216	SF⁹	90.28
05 Roofing	113,000	1.83	4.1	32,507	SF⁶	3.48
06 Interior Construction	615,000	9.95	22.4	208,000	SF¹⁰	2.96
061 Partitions	102,000	1.65	3.7	30,000	SF¹¹	3.40
062 Interior Finishes	490,000	7.93	17.9	178,000	SF¹²	2.75
063 Specialties	23,000	0.37	0.8	208,000	SF¹⁰	0.11
07 Conveying Systems	102,000	1.65	3.7	6	Landing	17,000
Total Architectural (04-07)	1,022,500	16.54	37.3	750,000	CF¹³	1.36
08 Mechanical	523,000	8.46	19.1	750,000	CF¹³	0.70
081 Plumbing	122,000	1.97	4.4	69	FIXT¹⁴	1,768
082 HVAC	336,00	5.44	12.3	450	TONS¹⁵	746
083 Fire Protection	65,000	1.05	2.4	55,000	SF¹⁶	1.18
084 Special Mechanical Systems					LS	
09 Electrical	226,000	3.66	8.3	300	KVA¹⁷	753
091 Service & Distribution	48,000	0.78	1.8	300	KVA¹⁷	160
092 Lighting & Power	140,000	2.26	5.1	607	FIXT¹⁴	231

UNIFORMAT System for Cost Estimating

Project Computer Processing Center

Gross Square Footage (GSF—Note 1) 61,819   **Bid Date** 10-79   **Date** 1-79

Element (Levels 2 & 3)	Estimated Cost ($)	Cost Per Gross Sq. Ft. ($)	Percent	Element Quantity	Unit	Cost Per Elem. Qty. ($)
093 Special Electrical Systems	38,000	0.62	1.4		LS	
10 General Conditions & Profit	345,000	5.58	12.6			
1001 Mobilization Expenses	10,000	0.16	0.4			
1002 Job Site Overhead	125,000	2.02	4.6			
1003 Demobilization	5,000	0.08	0.2			
1004 Office Expense & Profit	205,000	3.32	7.5			
11 Equipment						
111 Fixed and Movable Equip						
112 Furnishings						
113 Special Construction						
Total Building (01-11)	2,613,000	42.27	45.3	750,000	CF[13]	3.48
12 Site Work	129,500	2,09	4.7	105,000	SF[18]	1.23
12A Overhead & Profit				105,000	SF[18]	
121 Site Preparation	28,500	0.46	1.0	105,000	SF[18]	0.27
122 Site Improvements	49,000	0.79	1.8	105,000	SF[18]	0.47
123 Site Utilities	52,000	0.84	1.9	105,000	SF[18]	0.49
124 Off-Site Work				105,000	SF[18]	
Total Construction (01–12)	2,742,500	44,36	100	750,000	CF	3.66
Contingency @ 10%	274,500	4.44				
Escalation @ 11%	331,842	5.37				
Construction @ Bid Date	3,348,542	54.17				

Notes:
1. Facility gross square footage.
2. Footprint area at grade level.
3. Area of basement walls below grade.
4. Total area suspended floor and roof structure.
5. Area of suspended floors.
6. Area of roof structure.
7. Total exterior area (walls, doors and windows).
8. Area exterior wall (above grade).
9. Area of exterior doors and windows.
10. Total area finished (including partitions).
11. Area of partitions (excluding openings).
12. Total area finished (excluding partitions).
13. Total enclosed facility volume (CF).
14. Total number of fixtures.
15. Combined total of [heating (BTUh/hr) and cooling (BTUh/hr)] ÷ 12,000 BTU/ton.
16. Total area.
17. KVA demand, equivalent to transformer rating.
18. Gross site area.

Source: Dell'Isola, Alphonse and Kirk, Stephen J., *Life Cycle Costing for Design Professionals*, ©1981. Reprinted by permission of McGraw-Hill, Inc., New York.

operation. Operating costs are based on a precise engineering determination of energy required to operate the system for heating, cooling, humidification and auxiliary requirements.

B. Multi-zone Rooftop Units. The system includes a series of multi-zone rooftop heating and cooling units with an average amount of associated ductwork. Operating costs were estimated on the basis of manufacturer-supplied data.

C. Incremental/Unitary System. This system combines incremental units for the perimeter zone of the office area, and unitary units within the interior zone. The unitary system is assumed to be water-cooled and to perform in a manner similar to the perimeter incremental units. Operating costs were calculated on the basis of manufacturer-supplied data.

D. Water-to-Air Heat Pumps. This system consists of a water loop and a series of water-to-air heat pumps concealed in the ceilings of both interior and perimeter zones. Operating cost data were also supplied by the manufacturers of these units. The adjoining table summarizes initial costs as well as annual costs of energy, maintenance and, where required, additional factory labor to operate the system.

Looking at initial installed cost, the incremental/unitary system provides the lowest cost.
The present annual costs value is then summed to provide a "total cost" which includes:
—initial installed cost
—present value of energy costs, over a 40-year period, with energy rates assumed to double over the first five-year period (1973-78) and then to escalate at an annual rate of 5 percent for the next 35 years

—present value of maintenance costs, as proposed by the system suppliers, for the first nine years of operation.

☐ This approach to "total cost" shifts the economical solution from the incremental/unitary system to the water loop heat pump system.
—The energy advantage of the water-to-air heat pump system results from the larger interior cooling load in the office area and the ability of this system to transfer that load to help provide the large perimeter heating requirement. Not only does the system provide significant energy savings, but its extra initial cost, over the incremental/unitary system is small.
—The multi-zone rooftop unit system suffers from the high cost of controls, the need for return ducts and relatively high energy consumption.
—The absorption systems are hindered by very high initial investment costs, and by high operating costs associated with auxiliary equipment. Using the waste material as an energy source is the most energy-efficient but uneconomical of all the alternatives in this case.
—The incremental/unitary system, while the most economical to install, is hindered by the large interior cooling load in relation to the perimeter load, with a resulting increase in energy consumption.

	A₁ Absorption (Oil)	A₂ Absorption (Waste)	B Multi-Zone Rooftop	C Incremental & Unitary	D Heat Pump Water-to-Air
Initial Cost	$178,337	$188,337	$ 95,609	$ 87,831	$ 99,077
Differential	+90,506	+100,504	+7,778	0	+11,246
Annual Costs					
Energy	$ 7,516	$ 3,195	$ 9,375	$ 9,635	$ 6,386
Operating & Maint.					
Years 1 to 3	7,500	8,000	6,000	6,000	6,000
Years 4 to 6	8,500	9,000	7,000	7,000	7,000
Years 7 to 9	9,500	10,000	8,000	8,000	8,000
Additional Factory Labor		12,000			
Total Costs*	$367,540	$416,514	$311,132	$308,243	$258,392
Differential	+109,148	+158,122	+52,740	+49,815	0

*Total costs are calculated in this instance by summing the present values of initial costs, energy costs for 40 years, and maintenance costs for the three 3-year periods and, in the case of Option A2, the additional factory labor required for 40 years.

Initial and Annual Costs for HVAC System Alternatives

☐ While this approach to "total cost" is one way of identifying a least costly system, it still does not answer the owner's question of whether an extra initial investment in a heat pump system will provide a 20-percent return (on the $11,246 needed) and whether the extra investment will break even in less than ten years.

☐ A rate of return on extra investment analysis was performed, comparing Alternatives A, B and D to Alternative C (the one providing the lowest initial cost). The water loop heat pump system presented a 20.95% return on extra investment, breaking even in five years (assuming no discounting of future dollars), in eight years (assuming future dollars discounted at 10 percent annual rate), or in 17 years (assuming future dollars to be discounted at a 20 percent annual rate corresponding to the minimum attractive rate of return target set by the owner).

☐ As a result of the analysis above, the water-to-air heat pump system was recommended. In addition, the technique was used to assist in making a number of structural and other operating decisions relating to the new manufacturing facility.

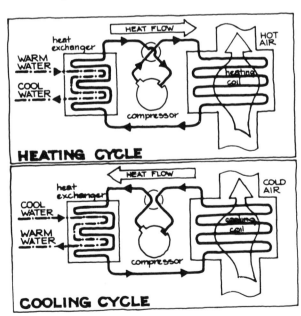

Water-Source Heat Pump Transfer System

Operation and Maintenance Costs

Of the categories of life-cycle costs, energy use has received the most attention during the past several years. From the standpoint of owner costs impact, however, maintenance can be the more significant cost item.

☐ Maintenance costs are high primarily because of the high cost of maintenance staffs' salaries, whether directly, for in-house personnel, or indirectly, through maintenance contracts. Maintenance costs generally are defined to include replacement costs for light bulbs and other items with a cumulative cost less than $5,000 or having a life less than five years.

☐ Easy maintainability requires that an item or a surface can be repaired, adjusted, or cleaned with reasonable effort and cost.

☐ Reasonable effort and cost, in turn, mean that maintenance must not require large amounts of time, unusual worker skills, or expensive equipment that is rarely used (although specialized equipment regularly used can be very economical); that it must not involve a procedure that will prevent the reuse of the item in a short time; and that it must not change the item's original appearance.

☐ The accompanying graph provides an approximate percentage of annual costs for each of the major building systems. As shown, interior construction and mechanical systems can have a significant effect on maintenance costs.

☐ Examples of some of the alternatives with major maintenance implications are:
—the choice between high quality, low maintenance finishes and less expensive finishes that require more periodic maintenance
—the choice between equipment with minimum routine repair and replacement requirements and less expensive elements with higher routine repair and replacement characteristics.

☐ Special care should be taken to ensure that LCC system comparisons are based on comparable levels of maintenance. Estimates of maintenance costs should refer to a uniform, optimum maintenance level.

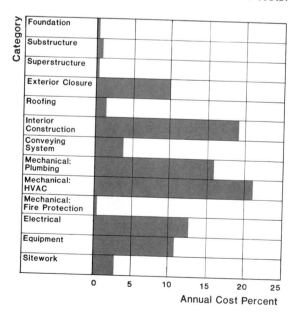

Relative Cost Effects of Maintenance

Energy Costs

The critical need for energy-conserving design stems from the rapid increase in energy costs. A continued scarcity of fuels, increased cost of energy production and delivery, and the mounting demands for energy in an energy-intensive society have combined to render energy a primary economic concern of all those involved in the act of building.

☐ During the last 26 years physical units of energy consumption increased over 134 percent. The unit price per 1,000,000 BTU of energy vacillated, declining during half the years, but overall increased 44 percent. The major portion of this increase, 39 percent, took place during the period 1970 to 76, and the total dollar expenditure for energy increased by $26 billion.

☐ To illustrate the impact of escalating energy costs, present values are tabulated for an annual expenditure of $1 (expressed in present dollars) at different rates of escalation over a 20-year period at 10 percent interest.

Annual Escalation Rate	Present Value
0%	$ 8.51
5%	12.72
10%	20.00
15%	32.95

Energy Costs:
(Percent of Annual Cost)

Uniformat Categories:	5%	10%	15%	20%	25%	30%	35%	40%	45%	50%
01 Foundation	.2%									
02 Substructure	.2%									
03 Superstructure	.1%									
04 Exterior Enclosure			9.5%							
05 Roofing	1.0%									
06 Interior Constr.				14.5%						
07 Conveying System		5.0%								
08 Mechanical: Plumbing		5.0%								
HVAC		5.4%								
Fire Protection	.1%									
09 Electrical Lighting									48%	
Power		8%								
11 Equipment	1.0%									
12 Sitework	2.0%									

Relative Cost Impact of Energy

Source: Dell'Isola, Alphonse and Kirk, Stephen J., *Life Cycle Costing for Design Professionals*, ©1981. Reprinted by permission of McGraw-Hill, Inc., New York.

☐ The present values shown are in effect the additional capital expenditure that would be justified to save $1 at 10 percent interest over a 20-year period; i.e. they represent the amounts one could invest to break even in 20 years. As can be readily appreciated from the figures, capital expenditure for energy savings based on 10 percent annual escalation would be more attractive than, say, capital expenditure for labor savings which may escalate at only 5 percent annually. Energy costs vary depending on the source and geographical location. Actual costs must therefore be based on the specific fuel proposed.

☐ When several possible energy sources are being assessed, it is important that the projected escalation rate of each source be carefully considered, as a differential in escalation may well affect the end result of the analysis.

☐ As a result of both spiralling energy costs and the increasing number of dollars devoted to operating, maintaining, repairing, replacing and altering a building's heating, ventilating and airconditioning systems, the selection of these elements must take both initial and continuing dollars into account.

☐ In the schematic design phase there are at least these opportunities for life-cycle cost analysis:
—selection of basic HVAC system, taking into account *all* differential initial cost factors (examples: differences in building area and volume required for mechanical rooms and distribution networks; impacts on structure, foundation, electrical and other building elements) as well as all differential OMRA costs
—investigation of alternative energy sources, including on-site boiler facility vs. purchased steam; use of solar collection, storage and distribution systems; feasibility of on-site solid waste incineration and heat recovery to provide for HVAC needs
—feasibility of heat recovery from people, lighting, equipment and/or waste warm air to supply part of the energy requirement
—approaches to zoning and controls for heating, ventilating and airconditioning systems
—use of automated energy management systems to optimize energy use, detect off-normal conditions, provide for efficient equipment operation and to limit peak demands
—feasibility of total energy and multiple integrated utility system (MIUS) concepts
—optimum location of mechanical spaces
—feasibility of consolidating activities in the

building which present peculiar heating, cooling or ventilation requirements, or which can be shut down at off hours.

☐ Generally speaking, the design and engineering of the HVAC mechanical elements is such a complex proposition that it will be necessary to use considerable experience and judgment to isolate major competing alternatives as a prelude to any life-cycle cost analysis work.

☐ Power, service and distribution systems are most susceptible to life-cycle cost analysis in the design development phase. During schematics, however, it may be desirable to explore issues such as:

—the feasibility of on-site power generation as an alternative to purchased power

—the issue of aerial vs. underground primary electrical service.

☐ As a major user of energy, and as an important maintenance item, the building's lighting system may require some special attention, even early in design. Questions under study may include:

—trade-offs between natural and artificial illumination (plans for optimizing the amount of window and skylight area for daylighting will also have to consider heat loss and gain through these elements)

—trade-offs between uniform overhead lighting and individual, perhaps flexible, task-oriented lighting

—exploration of heat recovery from lighting elements.

A hospital complex includes 17 different buildings, all sited in close proximity to each other. None of the structures was designed with airconditioning. A study was undertaken to analyze alternative approaches to airconditioning the complex.

Seven schemes were identified. Scheme 1 involves the installation of an air-cooled water chiller adjacent to each building to serve each building. Schemes 2 through 7 require the construction of a central chilled water plant building with new chilled water supply and return lines to the individual structures; these specific alternatives were analyzed:

Scheme 1:	air-cooled water chiller adjacent to each building
Scheme 2:	electrical centrifugal chillers at the central plant
Scheme 3:	electrical centrifugal chillers, but a separate air-cooled chiller at the farthest building
Scheme 4:	single-stage absorption chillers, gas for fuel
Scheme 5:	two-stage absorption chillers, gas for fuel
Scheme 6:	single-stage absorption chillers, oil for fuel
Scheme 7:	two-stage absorption chillers, oil for fuel

Scheme and Initial Cost	EUAC of Initial Cost*	Annual Operating Cost	Total EUAC	Difference Over Scheme 3
1 $7,080,800	$668,430	$177,250	$ 845,680	$ 16,080
2 7,397,200	698,300	132,750	831,050	1,450
3 7,391,600	697,770	131,830	829,600	0
4 7,413,100	699,800	165,050	864,850	35,250
5 7,460,800	704,300	137,200	841,500	11,600
6 7,413,100	699,800	324,320	1,024,120	194,520
7 7,460,800	704,300	242,340	946,640	117,040

*EUAC is Equivalent Uniform Annual Cost. The EUAC of the initial cost is calculated by multiplying Initial Cost by .0944, the Uniform Capital Recovery factor for a 7 percent discount rate and a 20-year life cycle.

Comparison of EUAC for Airconditioning Systems

The interior airconditioning system within each building was composed of fan coil units suspended from the celing, air handling units, exhaust fans and a building chilled water pump.

The initial costs of all schemes were developed. Airconditioning loads were based on square feet served, and the energy consumption for the schemes was calculated using an available computer program. Electric and gas rates were obtained from the regional utility company, and oil rates were based on the hospital's own experience. No abnormal escalation rates were used for energy costs.

The life-cycle cost analysis of the seven alternatives is presented. A 7 percent discount rate and a 20-year life cycle were mandated as part of the owner's fiscal policies.

Reviewing the analysis, Scheme 1 presents the lowest initial cost since it is not necessary to construct the central chiller building and distribution network. The total kW of all the individual chillers, however, is higher than that of the central plant. Also, with the chillers located adjacent to each building, onsite noise levels are higher and there are some questions about the esthetics of these individual units scattered about the site.

Schemes 2 and 3 are alike in concept and close in cost. Scheme 3 was recommended because it reduces the total run of chilled water by some 700 feet—decreasing both first cost and ongoing energy consumption (because of the lower head on the main chilled-water pump).

Taxes

Federal, state and local income and property taxes affect life-cycle costs in a variety of ways. The tax status of building owners varies widely, and tax laws and regulations can be complex and subject to change, requiring that designers consult with owners when analyzing tax effects on life-cycle costs.

□ The primary tax-related factors in LCC analysis are property tax assessments, business-expense and depreciation deductions from income taxes, and energy-conservation income tax credits.

Property Taxes

□ Property taxes are generally based on an assessment of property value. Whenever owners consider additional capital investment, whether present or future, they must be prepared to consider the possibility that property taxes will be proportionally increased. For this reason, it is suggested that property taxes be included in the analysis as a functional-use cost, and that the designer assume that they will be directly related to the amount of capital investment made.

□ One of the difficulties with dealing with property taxes in LCC analysis is that assessment practices are inconsistent from locality to locality and even from time to time within a given locality. *There is no guarantee that a given physical improvement will be assessed at its cost on a dollar-for-dollar basis.* Further, some localities are moving away from assessing improvements on a dollar-for-dollar basis, preferring to place greater emphasis on land value or development potential.

□ Consider two HVAC systems, the initial costs of which are $50,000 and $60,000. If the owner is subject to property tax, if the annual tax rate in the project's locality is $40 per $1,000 of assessed valuation, and if the building is assessed at its full construction cost, then the property taxes attributable to the systems are $2,000 and $2,400, respectively. These costs should be entered in an LCC analysis as annual functional-use costs.

Depreciation Allowances

□ Depreciable fixed assets have a limited life and the initial cost of such assets should be depreciated over that useful life. Depreciation accounts for the reduction in value of property improvements due to physical deterioration or economic obsolescence.

□ To consider depreciation in LCC analysis, two items must be specified: the depreciation period and the method of allocating the depreciation expense for each year of the life of the system. Three of the most commonly used methods are:
—straight line
—declining balance
—sum of the years' digits.

□ Under the straight-line method of depreciation an asset's cost is divided evenly over the allowable depreciation period. A $100,000 asset with a 10-year life is depreciated $10,000 a year for 10 years. If, however, this asset is expected to have a salvage value of $20,000 at the end of 10 years, this is subtracted from its cost, and the asset is depreciated at $8,000 a year for 10 years.

□ The declining-balance and sum-of-the-year's digits depreciation methods accelerate the depreciation in the early years of an asset's useful life on the theory that an asset loses more of its value in the early years. These methods accelerate the timing of depreciation but not the total amount of it.

□ In general, they show a higher present worth for allowable depreciation costs, which is desirable because it gives the greatest tax benefit.

□ The accompanying graph compares the present worths for a $36,000 airconditioning unit using an assumed discount rate of 10 percent for each of the depreciation methods. The method used can depend on an asset's salvage value and useful life.

Energy-Conservation Tax Credits

□ A variety of state and federal tax credits have been enacted to encourage building owners to invest in energy-conserving building elements. Savings due to them should be incorporated in LCC analysis in accordance with the relevant statutory and regulatory provisions.

LCC Analysis

□ Tax-related LCC data are usually categorized as annual functional-use costs or negative costs (benefits). The actual dollar amounts of cost or benefit depend on the owner's tax status and total level of taxable income.

The accompanying table shows the tax effects on the life-cycle costs of two HVAC systems that, without considering taxes, had discounted annual costs of $10,750 and $9,910. Note that the cost-superiority of system B is reversed by tax effects.

508

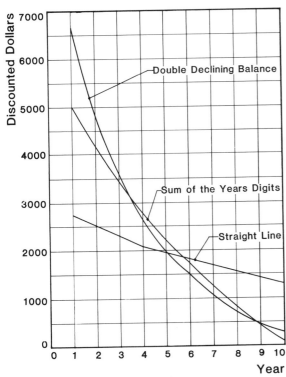

Comparison of Depreciation Methods.

Source: Dell'Isola, Alphonse and Kirk, Stephen J., *Life Cycle Costing for Design Professionals,* ©1981. Reprinted by permission of McGraw-Hill, Inc., New York.

EQUIVALENT UNIFORM ANNUAL COST Without considering property taxes	System A $10,750	System B $9,910
PROPERTY TAXES	$ 2,000	$ 2,400
EQUIVALENT UNIFORM ANNUAL COST Without considering income taxes	$12,750	$12,310

EXPENSES DEDUCTION
  Annual O&M costs
  Property taxes
  Total
	$ 5,000
	2,000
	$ 7,000
		$ 3,000
		2,400
		$ 5,400

DEPRECIATION DEDUCTION
  Depreciable amount (book value minus salvage value)
  Annual deduction (for 30 years)
	$40,000
	$ 1,333
		$45,000
		$ 1,500

TOTAL DEDUCTIONS	$ 8,333	$ 6,900
INCOME TAX BENEFIT FROM THE DEDUCTIONS, 50% tax bracket	$ 4,167	$ 3,450
EQUIVALENT UNIFORM ANNUAL COST Including tax costs and benefits	$ 8,583	$ 8,860

LCC Analysis of Taxes

Other Costs

Alteration Costs

☐ Alteration costs are those incurred when the function of a space is changed or modernized.

☐ Future alteration costs can often be minimized by providing movable partitions, extra wiring conduits, etc. Such measures can increase first costs, so the designer must consult with the owner concerning the desired trade-off between these costs and future flexibility for expected as well as unexpected changes.

☐ Future alteration costs can be quantified by determining the cost of a typical alteration and the frequency with which the alteration might occur. If retail space, for example, has gypsum wallboard partitions, the cost of rearranging them for a new tenant can be estimated. If the space is expected to change hands five times in the 20-year time frame for LCC analysis, this cost is then multiplied by 5 and divided by 20 to arrive at an annual alteration cost.

Replacement Costs

☐ Replacing worn-out building components can be a major cost. LCC analysis in this area considers the trade-offs involved in specifying more expensive but longer-lasting components, the possibility that early replacement would be desirable because of expected technological innovations that will save energy or accomplish other goals and the relationship of replacement cycles to alteration cycles.

☐ The accompanying graph provides an approximate percentage of annual replacement costs building system categories for a typical office building. As shown, replacement costs are most significant for interior construction and HVAC systems.

☐ Functional-use costs are the staff salaries and materials costs incurred in the performance of a building's functions. Although these costs and the effects that design alternatives have on them can be difficult to analyze, they can be such a significant portion of a facility's life-cycle cost that they should not be ignored. The use of closed-circuit video monitoring to minimize the number of guard stations required for security and the practice of providing adjacent locations for interacting functions are common methods of increasing efficiency and reducing functional-use costs. Analysis of a building's program can often reveal other important potential savings in this area.

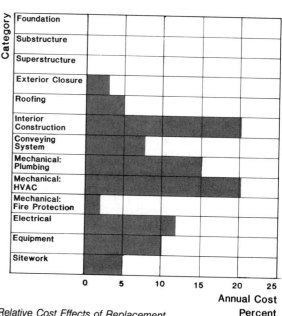

Relative Cost Effects of Replacement

Source: Dell'Isola, Alphonse and Kirk, Stephen J., Life Cycle Costing for Design Professionals, ©1981. Reprinted by permission of McGraw-Hill, Inc., New York.

Denial-of-Use Costs

☐ Denial-of-use costs are the costs attributable to completing a project later rather than sooner. Such costs include extra financing costs, increased construction costs because of inflation, and a delay in the ability of the facility to perform its function, resulting in reduced income for the owner. As with functional use of costs, denial-of-use costs can include costs that are hard to quantify, such as reduced efficiency.

☐ Essentially, however, denial-of-use is not a real cost category, because these costs are generally allocated to other cost categories (financing and construction increases to initial costs, etc.)

☐ Trade-offs to be considered in LCC analysis of denial-of-use costs include the possibility of using fast-track design and construction methods versus the tighter quality control possible with traditional project delivery methods. Depending on the client's needs it might or might not be more efficient to occupy a building in stages as it is completed, rather than all at once.

Salvage Value

☐ For the purpose of evaluating the economic feasibility of an investment, its salvage value is defined broadly here as (1) its residual value, net of the cost of disposal, whenever it is removed or replaced during the study period; or (2) its value at the end of the study period. If an existing investment is being compared with a new alternative, the current salvage or resale value of the existing investment is used to compare against the first cost of the new alternative. The present value of salvage value can generally be expected to decrease, other things being equal, as the discount rate rises, the equipment deteriorates, and the time horizon lengthens.

☐ An example of salvage value is the amount that could be added to the selling price of a building due to its energy-conserving design features. A building buyer might be willing to pay an additional amount for an energy-conserving building only if the extra charge is equal to the capitalized value of fuel savings over the period the buyer owns the building. However, the resale value of the building may well be higher because of the energy-conserving features; that is, the next buyer will also be willing to pay an additional amount in return for expected energy savings. This extra amount is thus a salvage value, although it can be difficult to estimate its dollar value.

Interest Factors

Year Y	SCA P-F	SPW F-P	UCA A-F	USF F-A	UCR P-A	UPW A-P
1	1.020	.9804	1.000	1.000	1.020	0.980
2	1.040	.9612	2.020	.4951	.5151	1.942
3	1.061	.9423	3.060	.3268	.3468	2.884
4	1.082	.9238	4.122	.2426	.2626	3.808
5	1.104	.9057	5.204	.1922	.2122	4.713
6	1.126	.8880	6.308	.1585	.1785	5.601
7	1.149	.8706	7.434	.1345	.1545	6.472
8	1.172	.8535	8.583	.1165	.1365	7.325
9	1.195	.8368	9.755	.1025	.1225	8.162
10	1.219	.8203	10.95	.0913	.1113	8.983
11	1.243	.8043	12.17	.0822	.1022	9.787
12	1.268	.7885	13.41	.0746	.0946	10.58
13	1.294	.7730	14.68	.0681	.0881	11.35
14	1.319	.7579	15.97	.0626	.0826	12.11
15	1.346	.7430	17.29	.0578	.0778	12.85
16	1.373	.7284	18.64	.0537	.0737	13.58
17	1.400	.7142	20.01	.0500	.0700	14.29
18	1.428	.7002	21.41	.0467	.0667	14.99
19	1.457	.6864	22.84	.0438	.0638	15.68
20	1.486	.6730	24.30	.0412	.0612	16.35
21	1.516	.6600	25.78	.0388	.0588	17.01
22	1.546	.6468	27.30	.0366	.0566	17.66
23	1.577	.6342	28.85	.0347	.0547	18.29
24	1.608	.6217	30.42	.0329	.0529	18.91
25	1.641	.6100	32.03	.0312	.0512	19.52
30	1.811	.5521	40.57	.0247	.0447	22.40
35	2.000	.5000	49.99	.0200	.0400	25.00
40	2.208	.4529	60.40	.0166	.0366	27.36
45	2.438	.4102	71.89	.0139	.0339	29.49
50	2.692	.3715	84.58	.0118	.0318	31.42
60	3.281	.3048	114.1	.0088	.0288	34.76
70	4.000	.2500	150.0	.0067	.0267	37.50
80	4.875	.2051	193.8	.0052	.0252	39.75
90	5.943	.1683	247.2	.0041	.0241	41.59
100	7.245	.1380	312.2	.0032	.0232	43.10

2 Percent Interest Factors

☐ The formulas below are used to create the tables that follow. Tables are produced to avoid the necessity to compute each time a formula is used.

$$F = P\left[(1 + i)^y\right]$$

— Single Compound Amount (SCA) adjusts a single value from present to future (P to F).

$$P = F\left[\frac{1}{(1 + i)^y}\right]$$

— Single Present Worth (SPW) adjusts a single sum from the future to the present (F to P).

$$F = A\left[\frac{(1 + i)^y - 1}{i}\right]$$

— Uniform Compound Amount (UCA) adjusts a set of equal annual increments to a single future value (A to F).

$$A = F\left[\frac{i}{(1 + i)^y - 1}\right]$$

$$A = P\left[\frac{i(1 + i)^y}{(1 + i)^y - 1}\right]$$

$$P = A\left[\frac{(1 + i)^y - 1}{i(1 + i)^y}\right]$$

— Uniform Sinking Fund (USF) adjusts a single sum from the future to equal annual increments (F to A).

— Uniform Capital Recovery (UCR) adjusts a single sum from the present to a set of equal annual increments (P to A).

— Uniform Present Worth (UPW) adjusts equal annual increments to a single present value (A to P).

Year Y	SCA P-F	SPW F-P	UCA A-F	USF F-A	UCR P-A	UPW A-P
1	1.060	.9434	1.000	1.000	1.060	0.943
2	1.124	.8900	2.060	.4854	.5454	1.833
3	1.191	.8400	3.184	.3141	.3741	2.673
4	1.262	.7921	4.375	.2286	.2886	3.465
5	1.338	.7473	5.637	.1774	.2374	4.212
6	1.419	.7050	6.975	.1434	.2034	4.917
7	1.504	.6651	8.394	.1191	.1791	5.582
8	1.594	.6274	9.897	.1010	.1610	6.210
9	1.689	.5919	11.49	.0870	.1470	6.802
10	1.791	.5584	13.18	.0759	.1359	7.360
11	1.898	.5268	14.97	.0668	.1268	7.887
12	2.012	.4970	16.87	.0593	.1193	8.384
13	2.133	.4688	18.88	.0530	.1130	8.853
14	2.261	.4423	21.02	.0476	.1076	9.295
15	2.397	.4173	23.28	.0430	.1030	9.712
16	2.540	.3936	25.67	.0390	.0990	10.11
17	2.693	.3714	28.21	.0354	.0954	10.48
18	2.854	.3503	30.91	.0324	.0924	10.83
19	3.026	.3305	33.76	.0296	.0896	11.16
20	3.207	.3118	36.79	.0272	.0872	11.47
21	3.400	.2942	39.99	.0250	.0850	11.76
22	3.604	.2775	43.40	.0231	.0831	12.04
23	3.820	.2618	47.00	.0213	.0813	12.30
24	4.049	.2470	50.82	.0197	.0797	12.55
25	4.292	.2330	54.87	.0182	.0782	12.78
30	5.743	.1741	79.06	.0127	.0727	13.77
35	7.686	.1301	111.4	.0090	.0690	14.50
40	10.29	.0972	154.8	.0065	.0665	15.05
45	13.77	.0727	212.7	.0047	.0647	15.46
50	18.42	.0543	290.3	.0034	.0634	15.76
60	32.99	.0303	533.1	.0019	.0619	16.16
70	59.08	.0169	967.9	.0010	.0610	16.39
80	105.8	.0095	1747.	.0006	.0606	16.51
90	189.5	.0053	3141.	.0003	.0603	16.58
100	339.3	.0029	5638.	.0002	.0602	16.62

6 Percent Interest Factors

Year Y	SCA P-F	SPW F-P	UCA A-F	USF F-A	UCR P-A	UPW A-P
1	1.100	.9091	1.000	1.000	1.100	0.909
2	1.210	.8264	2.100	.4762	.5762	1.736
3	1.331	.7513	3.310	.3021	.4021	2.487
4	1.464	.6830	4.641	.2155	.3155	3.170
5	1.611	.6209	6.105	.1638	.2638	3.791
6	1.772	.5645	7.716	.1296	.2296	4.355
7	1.949	.5132	9.487	.1054	.2054	4.868
8	2.144	.4665	11.44	.0874	.1874	5.335
9	2.358	.4241	13.58	.0736	.1736	5.759
10	2.594	.3855	15.94	.0628	.1628	6.144
11	2.853	.3505	18.53	.0540	.1540	6.500
12	3.138	.3186	21.38	.0468	.1468	6.814
13	3.452	.2897	24.52	.0408	.1408	7.103
14	3.797	.2633	27.98	.0358	.1358	7.367
15	4.177	.2394	31.77	.0315	.1315	7.606
16	4.595	.2176	35.95	.0278	.1278	7.824
17	5.054	.1978	40.54	.0247	.1247	8.022
18	5.560	.1799	45.60	.0219	.1219	8.201
19	6.116	.1635	51.16	.0196	.1196	8.365
20	6.727	.1486	57.28	.0175	.1175	8.514
21	7.400	.1351	64.00	.0156	.1156	8.649
22	8.140	.1228	71.40	.0140	.1140	8.772
23	8.954	.1117	79.54	.0126	.1126	8.863
24	9.850	.1015	88.50	.0113	.1113	8.985
25	10.84	.0923	98.35	.0102	.1102	9.077
30	17.50	.0573	164.5	.0061	.1061	9.427
35	28.10	.0356	271.0	.0037	.1037	9.644
40	45.26	.0221	442.6	.0023	.1023	9.779
45	72.89	.0137	718.9	.0014	.1014	9.863
50	117.4	.0085	1164.	.0009	.1009	9.915
60	304.5	.0033	3035.	.0003	.1003	9.967
70	789.7	.0013	7887.	.0001	.1001	9.987
80	2048.	.0005	20474.	.0001	.1001	9.995
90	5313.	.0002	53120.	.0000	.1000	9.999

10 Percent Interest Factors

Year Y	SCA P-F	SPW F-P	UCA A-F	USF F-A	UCR P-A	UPW A-P
1	1.150	.8696	1.000	1.000	1.150	0.870
2	1.322	.7561	2.150	.4651	.6151	1.626
3	1.521	.6575	3.472	.2880	.4380	2.283
4	1.749	.5718	4.993	.2003	.3503	2.855
5	2.011	.4972	6.742	.1483	.2983	3.352
6	2.313	.4323	8.754	.1142	.2642	3.784
7	2.660	.3759	11.07	.0904	.2404	4.160
8	3.059	.3269	13.73	.0729	.2229	4.487
9	3.518	.2843	16.79	.0596	.2096	4.772
10	4.046	.2472	20.30	.0493	.1993	5.019
11	4.652	.2149	24.35	.0411	.1911	5.234
12	5.350	.1869	29.00	.0345	.1845	5.421
13	6.153	.1625	34.35	.0291	.1791	5.583
14	7.076	.1413	40.51	.0247	.1747	5.724
15	8.137	.1229	47.58	.0210	.1710	5.847
16	9.358	.1069	55.72	.0180	.1680	5.954
17	10.76	.0929	65.08	.0154	.1654	6.047
18	12.38	.0808	75.84	.0132	.1632	6.128
19	14.23	.0703	88.21	.0113	.1613	6.198
20	16.37	.0611	102.4	.0098	.1598	6.259
21	18.82	.0531	118.8	.0084	.1584	6.312
22	21.65	.0462	137.6	.0073	.1573	6.359
23	24.89	.0402	159.3	.0063	.1563	6.399
24	28.63	.0349	184.2	.0054	.1554	6.434
25	32.92	.0304	212.8	.0047	.1547	6.464
30	66.21	.0151	434.7	.0023	.1523	6.566
35	133.2	.0075	881.2	.0011	.1511	6.617
40	267.9	.0037	1779.	.0006	.1506	6.642
45	538.8	.0019	3585.	.0003	.1503	6.654
50	1083.	.0009	7218.	.0001	.1501	6.661
60	4384.	.0002	29219.	.0000	.1500	6.665

15 Percent Interest Factors

Year Y	SCA P-F	SPW F-P	UCA A-F	USF F-A	UCR P-A	UPW A-P
1	1.300	.7692	1.000	1.000	1.300	0.769
2	1.690	.5917	2.300	.4348	.7348	1.361
3	2.197	.4552	3.990	.2506	.5506	1.816
4	2.856	.3501	6.187	.1616	.4616	2.166
5	3.713	.2693	9.043	.1106	.4106	2.436
6	4.827	.2072	12.76	.0784	.3784	2.643
7	6.275	.1594	17.58	.0569	.3569	2.802
8	8.157	.1226	23.86	.0419	.3419	2.925
9	10.60	.0943	32.02	.0312	.3312	3.019
10	13.79	.0725	42.62	.0235	.3235	3.092
11	17.92	.0558	56.41	.0177	.3177	3.147
12	23.30	.0429	74.33	.0135	.3135	3.190
13	30.29	.0330	97.63	.0102	.3102	3.223
14	39.37	.0254	127.9	.0078	.3078	3.249
15	51.19	.0195	167.3	.0060	.3060	3.268
16	66.54	.0150	218.5	.0046	.3046	3.283
17	86.50	.0116	285.0	.0035	.3035	3.295
18	112.5	.0089	371.5	.0027	.3027	3.304
19	146.2	.0068	484.0	.0021	.3021	3.311
20	190.1	.0053	630.2	.0016	.3016	3.316
21	247.1	.0040	820.2	.0012	.3012	3.320
22	321.2	.0031	1067.	.0009	.3009	3.323
23	417.5	.0024	1388.	.0007	.3007	3.325
24	542.8	.0018	1806.	.0006	.3006	3.327
25	705.6	.0014	2349.	.0004	.3004	3.329

30 Percent Interest Factors

Not all the references listed here are currently in print, but out-of-print materials are marked with the AIA Library call number for archival reference purposes. (AIA Library, 1735 New York Avenue, N.W., Washington, DC 20006)

AIA/ASCA Research Council. *Energy Tools: New Products for Architects from the National Energy Laboratories.* Washington, D.C.: AIA/ACSA Research Council, 1992.

AIA Research Corporation. *Passive Solar Design: A Survey of Monitored Buildings.* Washington, D.C.: U.S. Department of Energy, 1978. (AIA Library: NA2542.S6A19)

AIA Research Corporation. *Passive Solar Design: An Extensive Bibliography.* Washington, D.C.: U.S. Department of Energy, 1978. (AIA Library: Z5943.S6A41)

AIA Research Corporation. *Regional Guidelines for Building Passive Energy Conserving Houses.* Washington D.C.: American Institute of Architects, 1978. (AIA Library: NA2542.S6A4)

Allen, Patricia A., ed. *A Bibliography of Reports by Sandia Photovoltaic Projects.* Albuquerque: Sandia National Laboratories, 1981. Available from NTIS, Springfield, VA 21161; order # SAND 81-0135. (AIA Library: Z7914.S5A4 1981)

American Institute of Architects. *Architectural Graphic Standards.* New York: John Wiley & Sons, latest edition.

American Society of Heating, Refrigeration and Air Conditioning Engineers. *ASHRAE Handbook of Fundamentals.* Atlanta: ASHRAE Publications, latest edition.

American Society of Heating, Refrigeration and Air Conditioning Engineers. *ASHRAE Handbook & Product Directory: Applications.* Atlanta: ASHRAE Publications, latest edition.

Brown, G. Z., et al. *Inside Out: Design Procedures for Passive Environmental Technologies.* New York: John Wiley & Sons, 1992.

Burgess, E. L. *Summary of Photovoltaic Application Experiments Designs.* Springfield, Va.: National Technical Information Service, 1981. Order # ALO-71. (AIA Library: TK8322.B86)

Burt Hill Kosar Rittelmann Associates/Min Kantrowitz Associates. *Commerical Building Design: Integrating Climate, Comfort and Cost.* New York: Van Nostrand Reinhold, 1987.

Burt Hill Kosar Rittelmann Associates. *Small Office Building Handbook: Design for Reducing First Costs & Utility Costs.* New York: Van Nostrand Reinhold, 1985.

Dell'Isola, Alphonse, Jr., and Stephen J. Kirk. *Life Cycle Costing for Design Professionals.* New York: McGraw-Hill, 1981.

Egan, M. David. *Concepts in Thermal Comfort.* Englewood Cliffs, N.J.: Prentice-Hall, 1975. (AIA Library: TH6021.E4)

Evans, Benjamin E. *Daylight in Architecture.* New York: McGraw-Hill, 1981. (AIA Library: TH7791.E9)

Givoni, Baruch. *Man, Climate and Architecture.* New York: Elsevier, 1976. (AIA Library: NA2541.G5 1976)

Gupta, Yudi, and Stephen K. Young. *Design Handbook for Photovoltaic Power Systems.* Albuquerque: Sandia National Laboratories, 1981. Available from NTIS, Springfield, VA 22161, order # SAND 80-7147. (AIA Library: TK8322.M34)

Hastings, S. Robert, and Richard W. Crenshaw. *Window Design Strategies to Conserve Energy.* Washington, D.C.: U.S. Government Printing Office, 1977. (AIA Library: TH2275.H3)

Haviland, David S., ed. *Life Cycle Cost Analysis* (two volumes). Washington, D.C.: American Institute of Architects, 1977. (AIA Library: TS168.A4 and TS168.A41)

Illuminating Engineering Society. *IES Lighting Handbook.* New York: IES, latest edition.

Knowles, Ralph L. *Energy and Form: An Ecological Approach to Urban Growth.* Cambridge, Mass.: MIT Press, 1974. (AIA Library: NA2542.3.K56)

Kreider, Jan F., and Frank Krieth. *Solar Energy Handbook.* New York: McGraw-Hill, 1981. (AIA Library: TJ810.S63)

Lam, William M. C. *Sunlighting as Formgiver for Architecture.* New York: Van Nostrand Reinhold, 1986.

Lawrence Berkeley Laboratory and Eley Associates. *Skylight Handbook Design Guidlines.* Palatine, Ill.: American Architectural Manufacturers Association (AAMA), 1988.

Los Alamos National Laboratory and Solar Energy Research Institute. *Engineering Principles and Concepts for Active Solar Systems.* New York: Hemisphere Publishing Corporation, 1988.

Los Alamos National Laboratory and Solar Energy Research Institute. *Passive Solar Design Strategies: Guidelines for Home Builders.* Washington, D.C.: Passive Solar Industries Council, 1990.

Mahone, D. E., et al. *Study of Photovoltaic Residential Retrofits: Executive Summary.* Springfield, Va.: National Technical Information Service, 1982. Available from NTIS, Springfield, VA 21161; order # SAND 81-7019/1. (AIA Library: TK8322.M34)

Marshall, Harold E., and Rosalie T. Ruegg. *Simplified Energy Design Economics.* Washington, D.C.: Center for Building Technology, National Bureau of Standards, 1980. (AIA Library: HD9502.M37)

Mazria, Edward. *The Passive Solar Energy Book,* expanded professional edition. Emmaus, Penn.: Rodale Press, 1979. (AIA Library: NA2542.S6M3)

McGuiness, William J., Benjamin Stein, and John S. Reynolds. *Mechanical and Electrical Equipment for Buildings.* New York: John Wiley & Sons, latest edition.

Moore, Fuller. *Concepts and Practice of Architectural Daylighting.* New York: Van Nostrand Reinhold, 1985.

Moore, Fuller. *Environmental Control Systems: Heating, Cooling, Lighting.* New York: McGraw-Hill, 1993.

Oak Ridge National Laboratory. *Builder's Foundation Handbook.* Springfield, Va.: National Technical Information Service, 1991. Available from NTIS, Springfield, VA 21161; order # ORNL/CON-295.

Olgyay, Victor. *Design with Climate: Bioclimatic Approach to Architectural Regionalism.* Princeton, N.J.: Princeton University Press, 1963. (AIA Library: NA2541.O44)

Olgyay, Victor, and Aladar Olgyay. *Solar Control and Shading Devices.* Princeton, N.J: Princeton University Press, 1957. (AIA Library: NA2541.04)

Owens-Corning Fiberglas Corporation. *Design Guide for Insulated Buildings.* Toledo, Oh.: Owens Corning Corporation, 1981. (AIA Library: TH1715.093)

Pacific Northwest Laboratories. *Architect's and Engineer's Guide to Energy Conservation in Existing Buildings* (two volumes). Springfield, Va.: National Technical Information Service, 1990. Available from NTIS, Springfield, VA 21161; order # DOE/RL/ 01830 P-H4.

Pittman, P. F. *Conceptual Design and Systems Analysis of Photovoltaic Power Systems.* Springfield, Va.: National Technical Information Service. Available from NTIS, Springfield, VA 21161; order #ALO 2744-13. (AIA Library: TK8322.P57)

Portland Cement Association. *Simplified Thermal Design of Building Envelopes for Use with ANSI/ASHRAE/IES Standard 90A-80.* Skokie, Ill.: Portland Cement Association, 1981. (AIA Library: TH1715.P67)

Robinette, Gary O., ed. *Landscape Planning for Energy Conservation.* Reston, Va.: Environmental Design Press, 1977. (AIA Library: NA2542.3.R7)

Sizemore, Michael, Henry O. Clark, and William S. Ostrander. *Energy Planning for Buildings.* Washington, D.C.: American Institute of Architects, 1979. (AIA Library: NA2542.3.S45)

Solar Energy Research Institute (SERI). *Energy Conservation Technical Information Guide* (three volumes). Springfield, Va.: National Technical Information Service, 1987-89.

Stein, Richard. *Architecture and Energy: Conserving Energy Through Rational Design.* New York: Anchor Press, 1977. (AIA Library: NA2542.3.S73)

Swinburne, Herbert. *Design Cost Analysis for Architects and Engineers.* New York: McGraw-Hill, 1980. (AIA Library: TH437.S9)

U.S. Congressional Office of Technology Assessment. *Fueling Development: Energy Technologies for Developing Countries.* Washington, D.C.: U.S. Goverment Printing Office, 1992.

U.S. Department of Commerce, Environmental Science Services Adminstration. *Climatic Atlas of the United States.* Asheville, N.C.: National Climatic Center, latest edition. (AIA Library: QC983.U5)

U.S. Department of Energy. *National Energy Strategy: Powerful Ideas for America.* Washington, D.C.: Government Printing Office, 1991.

U.S. Department of Energy, Office of Conservation and Solar Energy. *Predesign Energy Analysis.* Washington, D.C.: Government Printing Office, 1980. Available from NTIS, Springfield, VA 21161, order # DOE/CS-0171. (AIA Library: NA2542.3.U45)

Vale, Brenda, and Robert Vale. *Green Architecture: Design for an Energy-Conscious Future.* Boston, Mass.: Bulfinch Press, Little Brown, 1991.

Watson, Donald, and Kenneth Labs. *Climatic Design: Energy-Efficient Building Principles and Practices.* New York: McGraw-Hill, 1983 (revised 1993).

Watson, Donald, ed. *Energy Conservation through Building Design.* New York: McGraw-Hill, 1979. (AIA Library: NA2542.3.W3)

Winter Associates. *Passive Solar Construction Handbook.* New York: Steven Winter Associates, 1981. (AIA Library: NA2542.S6W5)

ACKNOWLEDGMENTS

The chapters of the *Energy Design Handbook* were previously published as separate monographs in the *Architect's Handbook of Energy Practice*, prepared by the research staff of the AIA Foundation. The text is formatted for self-study in an approach developed with educational consultants Dr. Dale Alam and Dr. Stuart Rose. The present volume is an edited version of the original monographs, the quality and content of which is much due to the authors and reviewers credited below.

Chapter 1: *Climate and Site* — Stephen C. Diamond, George E. Way, Loren W. Crow, Bruce Harold Schafer

Chapter 2: *The Building Envelope* — Joseph Demkin, James L. Binkley, Peter Kastl, Larry Lord

Chapter 3: *Passive Heating and Cooling* — Harrison Fraker, J. Douglas Balcomb, William Bobenhausen

Chapter 4: *Shading and Sun Control* — William J. Kennish, Drury B. Crawley, Michael G. Bitterice, Thomas Vonier

Chapter 5: *Daylighting* — Benjamin H. Evans, J. W. Griffith, Gary Gillette, Steven Selkowitz

Chapter 6: *HVAC Systems* — Alexander J. Willman, Milton Meckler, Laheri Mehta, P. Richard Rittelmann

Chapter 7: *Active Solar Systems* — John Yellott, Richard L. Crowther, Gordon F. Tully

Chapter 8: *Photovoltaics* — John Oster, Gary J. Jones

Chapter 9: *Thermal Transfer Through the Envelope* — Milton Meckler, Oscar Turner, David M. Schwartz, L. M. Holder III

Chapter 10: *Energy Analysis* — William T. Meyer, Fred S. Dubin, Joseph Denk, J. Delaine Jones

Chapter 11: *Economic Analysis* — Marvin W. Wiley, J. W. Griffith, Rosalie T. Ruegg, Joseph A. Demkin